OPERATIONS AND SUPPLY CHAIN MANAGEMENT

OPERATIONS AND SUPPLY CHAIN MANAGEMENT

Ganesh Vaidyanathan

Rene Ordonez

Kendall Hunt
publishing company

Cover image © Shutterstock, Inc.

Interior illustrations were created by Ganesh Vaidyanathan unless stated otherwise

Kendall Hunt
publishing company

www.kendallhunt.com
Send all inquiries to:
4050 Westmark Drive
Dubuque, IA 52004-1840

Copyright © 2023 by Kendall Hunt Publishing Company

Text ISBN 979-8-7657-1648-9
eBook ISBN 979-8-7657-5681-2
Text with KHP 979-8-7657-9151-6
eBook with KHP 979-8-7657-9152-3

Published in the United States of America

To my daughter Kavya, to her smiles from heaven, and to her memories on earth that keeps my life motivated and inspired.

To Meena, Gautham, my family, and my friends who have made this planet a beautiful place to live.

—Ganesh Vaidyanathan

To my wife Traci and my sons Samuel and Gabriel for their unconditional support and love.

—Rene Ordonez

BRIEF CONTENTS

CONTENTS

PREFACE

The design and execution of the operations and the supply chain as well as how the quality of the goods and the services are managed—all of these are central to the sustainability and the success of a business. Therefore, it is important for a business management student to understand these vital topics. The book covers important topics in the context of operations and supply chain management (OSCM) and presents useful examples of how organizations implement their OSCM strategies. This book is intended for undergraduate-level courses or as an introductory course in operations management.

The book aims to provide vital information that every manager in the field of OSCM should know about, including about processes, techniques, tools, practical insights, and analytical approaches that help organizations to be productive. The motivation for the book's authors is to provide a synergistic and experiential approach to teach business students about the concepts, applications, processes, and practices in the field of OSCM.

Each chapter ends with a detailed case study that synthesizes and reflects the contents and study material presented in the chapter. The case studies are accompanied by a simulation software that can be used by the readers/students to understand the study material presented and expand their knowledge about it in an experiential learning manner. The problems scenarios presented at the end of each chapter are also intended for instructors to use them to measure the knowledge gained by students and positive changes or improvements in their critical thinking and overall learning outcome.

This book covers all the important topics of OSCM in an easy-to-understand manner for business students. The strategies deployed in OSCM plays a pivotal role in effective, optimized, and cost-efficient delivery of goods and services to consumers. Firms need to identify and improve on key performance criteria, including productivity, operational efficiency and cost-effectiveness, to perform well and earn profits. One of the most important and fundamental steps to ensuring the success of OSCM projects is the forecasting of consumer demand. Using this information as the basis, companies can plan their capacity to manufacture goods and deliver services. Sales, operations, and aggregate planning are devised, fine-tuned—and/or continuously improvised—and implemented periodically with necessary updates and revisions to develop a sound and optimal material requirement planning. Procurement of materials and services obtained from outsourcing are implemented using those plans. Inventory is managed to maximize profits. Production and service processes are designed and implemented to enhance efficiency, reduce costs, and maximize profits. The finished goods are delivered through various distribution centers to the end customers in the most cost-effective way using sophisticated logistics software.

A few new topics in the OSCM field, such as data analytics, smart factories, and Industry 4.0, are introduced in this book. Business students need to know the power of data. Data play a key role in all aspects of a business, including in OSCM. Businesses use data to make better decisions. With the insights gained from exploring the data, a business student can gain knowledge about how to improve supply chain performance or enhance operational efficiency and cost-effectiveness. It is important for a business student to understand how data analysis helps an organization to meet its goals. Another benefit of data analysis is it promotes critical thinking—and in this context, of the business student—a highly sought-after skill in the job market.

Data analytics and smart factories play a significant part of the success in modern-day manufacturing and service businesses. The knowledge of technologies used in Industry 4.0 helps a business student to understand how to effectively manage the different aspects of OSCM. Moreover, students need to know that the technologies used in Internet 4.0 provides real-time data and insights that help make better decisions and improve the profitability of businesses. This book will expand a business student's analytical and critical thinking skills. Each example in this book includes a series of steps and a comprehensive analysis to cultivate a student's ability to work through a problem systematically and logically.

Main Features of the Book

- Case studies for deep learning of the material in each chapter 14.
- Simulations of case studies that serve to enhance the learning outcomes of chapter materials chapters 1 through 13.
- Many examples to understand the concepts and practical insights presented in each chapter.
- An introduction to data analytics and how data analytics can be used in OSCM presented in chapter 13.
- Performance metrics and measures for a manager to evaluate the various facets of OSCM strategies presented in Chapter 13.
- The recent advances in OSCM, including the concepts of Industry 4.0., explained in chapter 14 on automation, robotics, and advanced technologies used in OSCM.
- Detailed coverage on how well-known and established and tried-and-tested concepts such as Lean Six Sigma practices are employed in modern-day OSCM with a case study focused on a Kaizen event in chapter 11.
- Detailed coverage of all traditional operations management models from Chapter 1 through Chapter 11.
- Design of distribution centers covered in chapter 12 to enhance supply chain materials
- Extensive use of Microsoft Excel to solve problems in all chapters
- Use of Microsoft Solver to solve capacity management, transportation networks, and prescriptive analytics in chapters 4,12, and 13.

A Note to Instructors

This book focuses on both traditional and contemporary topics in OSCM. The chapters are organized to present to the business students in a logical sequence the flow of goods, services, and information in any business. In general, OSCM often begins with the first step of forecasting market/customer demand.

Based on the demand forecast data, organizations either downscale or ramp up capacity in various operations to meet the demand of goods and services in a cost-rationalized way. Several projects are planned for simultaneously to install the required capacity in manufacturing as well as a host of other important operations, including in supply chain in general and in particular JIT (just-in-time) supplies from outsourced entities—all to meet the demands of customers to their complete satisfaction and with optimum efficiency. In today's world of globalization and outsourcing, JIT especially plays a vital role—for example, in OEM (original equipment manufacturing) entities, to which automobile manufacturers outsource various operations and depend on them for survival. To coordinate marketing and operations, sales and operations planning (S&OP) and aggregate planning are initiated and designed. The information from these plans is used in both materials requirement planning and inventory management. Procurement processes are initiated to bring in materials needed for operations. Operations processes are used in both manufacturing and service industries, as both need resource and material planning. Total Quality Management (TQM), Lean Six Sigma processes, and related tools are deployed to ensure optimum possible quality of goods and services to be delivered. Thus, in today's globalized economy, supply chain management (SCM) plays a vital role in the procurement, production, and delivery planning in any organization, be it for products to be manufactured and sold or for services to be delivered, and through advanced logistics solutions such as JIT promotes operational and cost-effectiveness.

The Chapters 1 to 12 present materials on vital topics in business management and especially supply chain, including the various theories and tools and methodologies used in procurement and production, which are at the core of OSCM in any organization. More particularly, Chapter 4 presents materials that can help the business student improve basic knowledge about OSCM and their ability to analyze and understand the major factors of success in OSCM projects. Chapters 13 and 14 provide the foundations of data analysis and current trends in OSCM, including in digital manufacturing and automation related to smart factories.

Instructors using this book can freely alter the sequence in which they wish to present these chapters to their students, for all chapters covers one major topic each that by itself serves as a standalone course topic and provides discussions specific to that topic. The authors are confident that instructors understand their student population and know what their students need to know and how they can gain from class experience. The case studies are segregated by chapter and follow the material that is discussed in their respective chapters.

Book Contents

The introduction to this book begins with the basics of operations and supply chain management (OSCM). The sustainability strategy, the business processes associated to achieve the OSCM strategy of a firm, and OSCM performance measures, such as total productivity, partial productivity, and multifactor productivity, are discussed.

Time series analysis method is the focus of Chapter 2. Baseline demand, trend, seasonal influence, cyclical influence, and random variations are discussed in this chapter. Other concepts of interest such as simple moving average, weighted moving average, simple exponential smoothing, exponential smoothing with trend adjustment, linear regression analysis, time series decomposition, and causal relationships method are also included. An analysis of forecast errors measured through tools such as root mean squared error (RMSE), standard error estimate (SEE), mean absolute percentage error (MAPE), and mean absolute deviation (MAD) with tracking signal (TS) are included in this chapter.

Chapter 3 focuses on demand management and capacity planning. Examples are presented on of how to measure important criteria such as design capacity, effective capacity, capacity utilization, and capacity efficiency, in order to illustrate to the students and help them understand these criteria and how they are applied in capacity planning and management processes. Excel's Solver is introduced to the students to help them learn how it can be used to solve design capacity problems. The chapter includes the concept of decision tree method to help student learn about the alternatives that can be chosen during capacity planning.

Project management is discussed in Chapter 4. We begin with defining projects and project management and classifying projects. A structural view of how projects are managed is explained. Techniques to estimate project costs and to select projects based on a cost–benefit analysis using net present value (NPV) and payback period are discussed with examples. Methods to schedule a project using a project schedule network diagram (PSND) and earned value analysis (EVA) are included with many examples. The chapter shows how to use learning curves to estimate the implementation of repeated tasks in projects.

Aggregate planning and sales and operations planning (S&OP) are the focus of Chapter 5. All the factors and components of inventory, production, and costs are described vividly to ensure better understanding of various aggregate planning strategies. Strategies to balance inventory and capacity include chase strategy, level strategy, flex strategy, and hybrid strategy with easy-to-understand examples.

Chapter 6 is centered on material resource planning (MRP). Enterprise Resource Planning (ERP) and the advantages of its use in both manufacturing and service businesses are discussed. The time fence zones available to promise inventory are used to determine the master production schedule (MPS). The chapter explains how the bill of materials (BOM) is used to develop MRP and how the BOM and inventory transactions are used in MRP development.

Inventory management is discussed in Chapter 7. Beginning with the push-pull boundary, inventory planning and control and a comparison of the inventory management of goods and services are discussed. ABC classification, Pareto chart analysis, and inventory accuracy are described thoroughly. The various technologies deployed to track inventory, including barcodes, radio frequency Identifier (RFID), and smart labels, are explained. Inventory-ordering models to deal with inventory cycles, including cost-based inventory models, economic order quantity (EOQ), quantity discount inventory models (QDI), and single-period inventory model, are discussed with appropriate examples. Inventory ordering using both the fixed-quantity Q Model and the fixed-time-period P Model is shown with examples.

Procurement, outsourcing, and receiving are covered extensively in Chapter 8. The procurement process, procurement strategy, risk mitigation in procurement, and green procurement are discussed. Techniques to calculate the total cost of ownership and the breakeven analysis of make-versus-buy decisions are shown with examples. A scorecard method to select suppliers is explained. All facets of outsourcing are discussed in some detail. The trends in OSCM, including electronic procurement and electronic data exchange (EDI), are explained. Processes in how a purchase order is processed in organizations and how goods are received and inspected are also discussed.

Chapter 9 focusses on the production process. Customer order decoupling point and how it plays a part in the supply chain are described. Subtractive, additive, net shape, batch, and continuous production processes are explained. The four production system layouts—fixed-position assembly, work center, manufacturing cell, and assembly line—are discussed. Assembly-line balancing to develop an assembly design is explained. Little's Law and how inventory flows through a production process are discussed.

Chapter 10 focuses on the service operations and processes. Labor intensity, consumer interaction, and service customization are discussed. The potential complexity of services and how blueprints are used in industry to understand and analyze the service complexity is explained. The main characteristics of queuing systems, the four basic queuing systems, and how probability distributions help to analyze queuing systems and the analysis of queuing systems are discussed with appropriate examples.

Quality and Lean Six Sigma in Chapter 11 covers quality management principles, Total Quality Management (TQM), and how processes are measured in organizations. The chapter covers Six Sigma process, Lean Six Sigma, and lean manufacturing, fishbone diagrams, just-in-time (JIT) manufacturing, and service and value stream maps. Control charts such as X-bar and R charts, process capability, and process capability index are explained with examples. The case study illustrates a Kaizen event.

Logistics, distribution, and transportation are the focus of Chapter 12. The diverse types of logistics, including the third-party logistics (3PL) and the various functions of logistics management processes, are explained. The chapter discusses how firms distribute their products to their customers, the major functions of its distribution center, and how materials and information flow through the distribution center. A design of a distribution center is discussed along with explanations on how to calculate the capacity of a distribution center. The methods employed by firms to pick and pack goods in distribution centers and how transportation is used in supply chains are explained. The discussions include how Excel's Solver is employed to solve the challenges in transportation networks using the linear programming technique.

Chapter 13 introduces the concept of data analytics and a presents a discussion on the various types of data analytics. How big data and data analytics are used to improve supply chain performance is explained. A discussion on how the three distinct types of data analytics—descriptive analytics, predictive analytics, and prescriptive analytics—can be used with a common software program like Excel is also included in this chapter. The calculations of various performance metrics used in operations and supply chain are included in this chapter.

The automation in OSCM and smart factories are introduced in Chapter 14. The benefits of Industry 4.0 and the smart factory concept along with the components and factors of digital transformation are presented. The chapter discusses and explains in a simple, easy-to-understand manner to students about the use of forefront technologies, smart systems, intelligent automation systems, artificial intelligence, and robots in a smart factory.

To bring more relevance to the discussions in class, students need to be involved in case studies. These case studies reflect "real-world" business situations. Students will benefit from working on these case studies as they bring experiential learning to classrooms. The case studies are an excellent resource for students to understand how operations management plays a vital role in organizations and gain "hands-on" experience that reflects the concepts and tools with which they become familiar by reading the chapter.

Supplemental resources for Students

Audiobook

The eBook can be used as an audiobook. Students can turn on the eReader, which can be accessed online or offline on most devices. Students can use this facility to listen, read, study, and engage with their learning materials. With eReader, students can make notes, highlight material, navigate, and search material easily. Instructors use Bookshelf to discover review materials for course adoption, plan their course, engage with students using shared notes and highlights, and more.

The following online resources are available to students who buy this book at the book website:

Simulations – Interactive Excel Models

The book is accompanied by a set of interactive operations and supply chain management (OSCM) templates built in Excel. These interactive Excel templates bring to life many of the common prescriptive, predictive, and descriptive models used in OSCM decision-making situations and allow students, instructors, and decision-makers to carry out on-the-fly "what-if" analyses by simply changing the parameters of the models. Many of the interactive OSCM models presented in this book are dynamically linked to graphs for visual learning. In introductory OSCM courses where manual calculation of models is part of the instruction and learning process, students can use the interactive models to verify the accuracy of their solutions. In a similar way, instructors can instantaneously generate answer keys to assignment and assessment problems, bypassing the time-consuming manual process.

Videos of Simulations

Solutions to select text exercises and case studies are presented in video demos to augment and enhance the learning process, especially for visual and auditory learners. These video demos include the use of interactive OSCM models.

Data Files

Data for some of the problems and case studies are provided in an Excel workbook.

Supplemental resources for Instructors

The following online resources are available to adopting instructors at the book website:

Test Bank

Test banks that comprise of all the material for this chapter are available on the book website. Using the test banks, you can assign homework, assignments, quizzes, or exams and export them to your favorite Learning Management System.

Electronic Grading tool

The use of the electronic grading tool available in the book website can dramatically reduce the amount of time you spend reviewing homework and grading quizzes.

PowerPoint slides and Image Library

The PowerPoint slides focus on the theoretical aspects of the chapter and can be modified with the image library provided in the book website.

YouTube Videos

Several YouTube videos are provided to aid in teaching the materials in each chapter. The video links can be found on the book website in Instructor Resources.

Chapter Examples

Examples in each chapter can be found in an Excel workbook, on the book website in Instructor Resources.

Case Study

The case study can be used as a tool to evaluate a team of students to learn the book materials. The case reflects a "real-world" business situation and is a "hands-on" experience that integrates the concepts and tools included in this chapter. The students will benefit from working on this case study as it brings the experiential learning in the classrooms. The solutions to case studies can be found in Instructor Resources.

Solution to Chapter Problems

All the quantitative answers to problem solving and critical thinking questions, can be found in an Excel workbook, "Chapter Problem Solving Questions.xlsx", on the book website in Instructor Resources.

Simulations – Interactive Excel Models

The book is accompanied by a set of interactive operations and supply chain management (OSCM) templates built in Excel. These interactive Excel templates bring to life many of the common prescriptive, predictive, and descriptive models used in OSCM decision-making situations and allow students, instructors, and decision-makers to carry out on-the-fly "what-if" analyses by simply changing the parameters of the models. Many of the interactive OSCM models presented in this book are dynamically linked to graphs for visual learning. In introductory OSCM courses where manual calculation of models is part of the instruction and learning process, students can use the interactive models to verify the accuracy of their solutions. In a similar way, instructors can instantaneously generate answer keys to assignment and assessment problems, bypassing the time-consuming manual process.

Videos of Simulations

Solutions to select text exercises and case studies are presented in video demos to augment and enhance the learning process, especially for visual and auditory learners. These video demos include the use of interactive OSCM models.

Data Files

Data for some of the problems and case studies are provided in an Excel workbook in the book website under Instructor Resources.

Instructor Manuals

Detailed Instructor Manuals for each chapter can be downloaded from the book website in Instructor Resources.

ACKNOWLEDGMENTS

We are grateful to many individuals who contributed to the preparation of this book. First, we wish to thank the reviewers for their very detailed comments, suggestions, and insights. We really appreciate their thoughtfulness and intellectual curiosity, which were reflected in their comments. The depth of their knowledge was crucial in revisiting the topics and making this an easier book to handle for the students.

We thank many friends including Asghar Sabbaghi of Roosevelt University for his encouragement and invaluable support during the design of this book. We thank our students and many others who gave us many words of encouragement and confidence.

Finally, Paul Carty, the Director of Publishing Partnerships and Brenda Rolwes, the Senior Publishing Specialist! You are awesome and indeed an immense pleasure to work with! Brenda kept us on track, and made sure all things worked out perfectly. We thank all the associates of Kendall Hunt for their support and guidance throughout this project, including Bailee Bussan (Marketing), Sarah Corey and Paul Meyer-Sales (Sales).

Ganesh Vaidyanathan
Rene Ordonez

ABOUT THE AUTHORS

Ganesh Vaidyanathan

Dr. Vaidyanathan has more than 25 years of industrial experience in automation, advanced manufacturing, strategy, artificial intelligence, e-commerce, and information technology with several high-tech industries in the United States and abroad. He is currently the Professor of Decision Sciences at the Roosevelt University, Chicago. Prior to his academic position, he cofounded eReliable Commerce Inc., where he was the CTO of the B2B financial transactions firm. He has held executive and leadership positions at AlliedSignal (Honeywell), General Dynamics, Click Commerce and Lockheed Martin (NASA). Dr. Vaidyanathan launched products integrated with artificial intelligence decision-making capabilities on the web to be cobranded with customers in the finance vertical business. He has directed various projects for Fortune 100 companies to increase customers' profits by integrating organizational capabilities and stakeholder specifications. He has helped organizations to implement SAP and other enterprise solutions.

Dr. Vaidyanathan has enhanced effective business processes in logistics, procurement, payments, life-cycle costs, decision support systems, and SCM. He has the proven ability in strategic development, managing projects, improving the efficiency of operations, mentoring, and team building. He has consulted with Fortune 100 companies including United Airlines, Mitsubishi, Motorola, and Honeywell in technology, business, and process reengineering. He serves as an advisor and an executive board member to several organizations in the United States and India.

Dr. Vaidyanathan holds a PhD with an emphasis on Robotics and Artificial Intelligence from Tulane University and an MBA from the University of Chicago. Dr. Vaidyanathan currently holds several patents and has authored more than 60 publications and book chapters in operations management, information systems, and project management in journals such as the *Communications of the ACM, Decision Sciences*, and the *Journal of Operations Management*. His textbook "Project Management: Process, Technology, and Practice" is adopted by many universities in the U.S.

Rene Ordonez

René Leo E. Ordoñez is Professor of Business at Southern Oregon University. He holds a Bachelor of Arts degree in Economics from the University of the Philippines, an MBA degree from the University of Akron, and a PhD in Management Science from the Illinois Institute of Technology. He has been a member of the SOU School of Business faculty since 1989 where he served as the Department Chair from

2004 to 2011. Currently, he serves as the Coordinator of the Graduate Programs in Business. He teaches Applied Business Statistics and Operations Management in the undergraduate business program and Strategic Operations Management in the MBA Program. He taught internationally—at Ateneo de Naga University (Philippines), the University of Guanajuato (Mexico), and the Copenhagen School of Business (Denmark).

His research interest is in the use of technology in pedagogy. He has been actively involved in the design, development, and implementation of course curricula that incorporate technology in the classroom as well as in the delivery of course content. Over the past two decades, he created video demo lessons, narrated PowerPoints, and interactive Excel models as teaching supplements for various business statistics and operations management textbooks.

OPERATIONS AND SUPPLY CHAIN MANAGEMENT

Learning Objectives

- Define operations and supply chain management.
- Discuss the operations and supply chain strategies employed by organizations.
- Describe the elements of sustainability.
- Explain how companies can achieve a sustainable future.
- Evaluate the overall performance measures of operations and supply chain management.
- Define efficiency, effectiveness, and value of the supply chain.
- Measure total productivity, partial productivity, and multi-factor productivity.
- Describe the current trends in operations and supply chain management.
- List the potential career opportunities in operations and supply chain management.

McDonalds, the fast-food chain known for French fries and Big Macs, started its franchise operations in the 1950s. Today, McDonalds operates in over 100 countries and serves over 69 billion customers around the world. McDonalds buys over 2 billion eggs annually in the United States alone. The company sells 550 million Big Macs every year and 9 million pounds of French fries every day around the globe. This requires a well-oiled supply chain management system since McDonalds outsources 100% of its supplies[1].

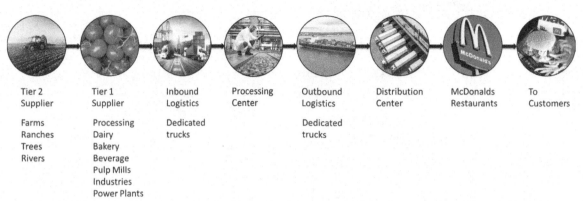

Tier 2 Supplier	Tier 1 Supplier	Inbound Logistics	Processing Center	Outbound Logistics	Distribution Center	McDonalds Restaurants	To Customers
Farms	Processing	Dedicated		Dedicated			
Ranches	Dairy	trucks		trucks			
Trees	Bakery						
Rivers	Beverage						
	Pulp Mills						
	Industries						
	Power Plants						

© Fotokostic/Shutterstock.com; © Ewa Studio/Shutterstock.com; © Daniel Wright98/Shutterstock.com; © Aleksandar Malivuk/Shutterstock.com; © Aleksandr Medvedkov/Shutterstock.com © Aun Photographer/Shutterstock.com; © Vytautas Kielaitis/Shutterstock.com; © Patcharaporn Puttipon4289/Shutterstock.com

The supply chain of McDonalds starts with its Tier 2 suppliers that include the farms delivering potatoes, lettuce, tomatoes, wheat, and other vegetables and the ranches that supply meat products, trees, and water. Tier 1 suppliers use the ingredients and materials from their Tier 2 suppliers to process meat, bakery, dairy, and beverages. For example, beef is supplied by Lopez Foods, potatoes are sent from 100 Circle Farms, chicken furnished by Tyson and Keystone Foods, beverages supplied by Coca Cola, and dairy delivered from Hildebrandt Farms[2]. Tier 2 suppliers also supply the packing materials and the condiments. The processed foods and materials are transported using refrigerated and regular dedicated trucks to various distribution centers. The outbound logistics systems deliver the required products to each McDonalds restaurant. Food is finally prepared in the restaurants and served to customers.

Wait! This is not enough to survive in this modern world! Firms must devise strategies for a sustainable future. McDonalds has a sustainable supply chain that focuses on three E's comprising ethics, environment, and economics. McDonalds endorses the reduction of the use of antibiotics in food animals and enforces a zero-tolerance policy for cruelty to animals. They audit the slaughterhouses of their suppliers to ensure compliance with the industry best practices. McDonalds works with its suppliers to reduce the food and packaging waste. McDonalds works with its suppliers to reduce the impacts on climate including greenhouse gas emissions. McDonalds works with its suppliers to research, share, and scale best practices to increase productivity and efficiency as well as to protect land, livestock, and livelihoods[3].

McDonalds' success is based on its "think global, act local" strategy[4]. Products are adapted for the location yet taste and quality are standardized and maintained throughout the globe. For example, Big Macs are served with vegetable, mutton, or halal patties in India and other countries to be sensitive to various religious beliefs. Guava juice in tropical regions, beer in Germany, chilled yogurt drinks in Turkey, cold pasta in Italy, grilled salmon sandwich in Norway,

Pork burger with sweet sauce in Thailand are other examples of adaptation[5]. Yet the basic structure of their menu remains standardized everywhere—sandwich, French fries, and Coca Cola products. The quality is maintained everywhere using trained staff, tight specifications, and an extensive quality control process. The excellent service is maintained at all locations worldwide. Yet, the service is set to the tastes, value systems, lifestyles, language, and perception of customers to reflect its commitment to customer satisfaction[6]. This combination of quality goods and excellent service is the key to the success of McDonalds.

Goods and Services

We purchase goods from groceries and department stores. We use the services of banks and hospitals. Most products include some kind of services with the purchased goods. For example, if we buy a computer from a store, we buy the computer as well as its related services such as maintenance and warranty extensions. The intent of this goods-services continuum or product-service bundling is to create a value for the customer and lower the customer's total life-cycle cost. The goods-services continuum is shown in Figure 1-1. Pure goods can be either tangible or virtual. For example, books can be bought in paper as well as in digital form. Meanwhile, a law firm offers pure services. In the goods-services continuum, the augmented goods and augmented services offer both products and services. When you buy a new car, you get numerous services such as maintenance offers and warranty. A restaurant offers prepared food, which is a physical good, but also provides services such as the dining experience, the ambiance, the linen, the utensils, the setting and the clearing of the table.

When companies procure or sell products, they too may opt for the bundling of goods and services. Honeywell, Inc. is an example. When they sell their wheels and brake systems to their customers, they get paid on a per-landing

> **Products-services bundling or Goods-services continuum** The spectrum of goods and services offered by industries to create value for their customers.

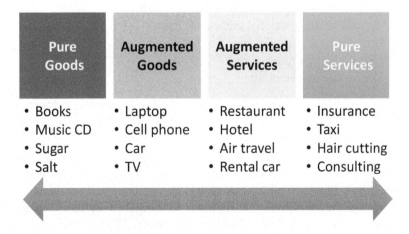

Figure 1-1 Goods-Services Continuum

base, that is, every time an airline lands from its flight, the airline company pays Honeywell, Inc. Companies such as FedEx and UPS offer services such as transportation, logistics, and consulting services along with packaging products.

Firms use systems and business processes to create the goods and the services. A business process is a set of related, structured activities or tasks, where the specific sequence of tasks produces a service or product. For example, purchasing is a business process established in a company. A simple purchasing business process may consist of several activities including filling out a purchase request for an item, getting the purchase request authorized by finance and procurement managers, the purchasing department sending a purchase order to their supplier, the supplier fulfilling the purchase order, and finally, the company paying the supplier for the item.

> **Business process**
> A business process is a set of related, structured activities or tasks, where the specific sequence of tasks produces a service or product.

A system is a collection of interdependent parts that are integrated to accomplish a goal. For example, a computer with a monitor and keyboard is a system. Systems in manufacturing use transformation processes—processes that transform common resources such as labor, machinery, equipment, materials, land, buildings, electricity, gas, and so on into useful goods and services. Systems in service industries use common resources in beneficial services.

Operations and Supply Chain Management (OSCM)

Goods are delivered and services are rendered across the globe regardless of the geographical location. In this interconnected and interdependent world, companies seek goods and services from any part of the globe to:

- Lower operational costs,
- Lower labor costs,
- Focus on their core business processes while delegating mundane time-consuming processes to external agencies,
- Tap and leverage a global knowledge base,
- Gain access to expertise,
- Expand marketing area, and
- Locate that special product.

To access goods and services, companies must use efficient and effective techniques, innovation, and technology. To succeed, companies must use the latest developments in operations and supply chain management.

Supply chain management (SCM) comprises the planning, management, and control of the flow of goods and information between a company and its suppliers and customers. Supply chain management integrates the demand and the supply within and across organizations including the buy, make, and sale of products and services that are valuable to customers. The integration requires extensive coordination and collaboration among suppliers, intermediaries, third-party service providers, wholesalers, customers, and users. The chain of suppliers, operations, logistics and transportation providers, and eventually the customers form a network. Every player in this network is valuable and creates value.

Operations management (OM) involves converting goods and services efficiently and selling the goods and the services to customers to make profits. OM makes use of business practices to create the highest possible efficiency, productivity, and sustainability for an organization. Operations management is focused on achieving the maximum profits by reducing costs and increasing revenues.

To be profitable, firms need to integrate their operations and supply chain management effectively and efficiently. Operations and supply chain management (OSCM) incorporates the design, operations, and continuous improvement of various business processes and systems in a company to satisfy customers with its products. Operations and supply chain management comprises all the businesses involved in creating a product, from raw materials to finished merchandise, and delivering the product to customers.

> **Operations and supply chain management (OSCM)** Operations and supply chain management comprises all the businesses involved in creating a product, from raw materials to finished merchandise, and delivering the product to customers.

Let us look at the operations and supply chain of bottled water in Figure 1-2. To make bottled water, a firm requires water, plastic bottles, plastic caps, and labels. Water from springs and lakes are captured in trucks and brought to the bottled water company. According to Flowater[7], a water purifying company, the retail average cost of a bottle of water is \$1.29. However, the actual cost of water is less than \$0.00001 and the rest is a markup based on water bottle production, packaging, transportation, logistics, marketing, and other functions. There are transportation and logistics costs including truck drivers pay, cost of insurance, and fuel costs. To receive the plastic bottles and caps, similar costs will be incurred along with the cost of producing those bottles and caps. The company also spends money to procure the raw materials.

The focus of the ***operations*** in this company is to purify the purchased water, bottle the water, and pack the bottled water for transportation. Business processes, equipment, electricity, gas, people, materials, and computers are used to fulfill the operations. The company incurs all the costs associated with its operations. Then the bottled water is transported to various distribution centers incurring transportation and logistics costs. Finally, the bottled water is transported to stores and shops to be purchased and consumed by customers.

As seen in Figure 1-2, the raw materials move from the suppliers to the water bottle company and eventually to customers as goods and services.

© Inspiring/Shutterstock.com

Figure 1-2 Operations and Supply Chain Management of Bottled Water

The information and the money collected from the customers flow in the opposite direction so that the manufacturers and the suppliers of raw materials can receive their money. The effective collaboration between all of these companies in the supply chain leads to many benefits including cost-saving, improved revenue, and improvement of all work processes.

Operations and Supply Chain Strategy

To be successful, firms need to employ effective operations and supply chain management strategies. An organization must have a vision in order to be successful. Usually, the vision is followed up with a mission statement and the core values of the organization. The vision looks at the final destination to be reached for the organization and is the big picture of what it wants to achieve. A mission shows the way or acts as a beacon of how to achieve the vision. With the vision and mission, an organization may express its core values which are the fundamental beliefs of the organization. To achieve the vision using the mission and its core values, an organization must develop several strategies. A strategy is a plan of action envisioned to achieve a major goal. Strategy defines how a company would reach from where it is currently to where it wants to be. To implement a strategy, the organization must set goals, objectives, action plans, and tactics. What needs to be accomplished to implement a strategy is a goal and the objectives convey the specific milestones with timelines to achieve a goal. The action plans and the tactics are specific implementation plans of how to achieve an objective. Figure 1-3 shows these components for success as a roadmap.

Figure 1-3 Vision to Action Plans Roadmap for an Organization

FROM PRACTICE: Vision, Mission, and Core Values of Walmart

Walmart, headquartered in Bentonville, Arkansas, is an American multinational retail company and operates a chain of supermarkets, discount department stores, and grocery stores. The subsidiaries of Walmart include Sam's Club, ASDA stores, Flipkart, Bonobos, Jet.com, and Amigo Supermarkets. The table below illustrates the vision, mission, and core values of Walmart.

Vision, Mission, and Core Values of Walmart, Inc.	
Vision	The vision of Walmart, Inc. is focused on saving money for customers. The vision statement reflects the important values for customers including savings and convenience.
Mission	The mission of Walmart, Inc, is to make their customers lives better by saving them money, thus emphasizing what their customers value the most.
Core Values	The core values of Walmart are customer-centric and addresses agility, integrity, and equality.

The primary strategy of the operations and supply chain management is to increase the value of goods and services in the supply chain in terms of improved customer service and quality and lower operational costs. The operations and supply chain management strategy includes the integration of the following strategies:

- Supplier management strategy,
- Customer management strategy,
- Operations strategy,
- Supply chain management strategy, and
- Sustainability strategy.

The integration of these five strategies must be aligned with the business strategy of an organization. For example, if the business strategy of an organization has a sustainability component, then the organization must include such goals as part of the overall OSCM strategy. We will be discussing these strategies in various chapters of this book.

Supplier Management Strategy

Supplier management is a process to engage with the suppliers effectively. The strategy must ensure that both suppliers and the company who seeks the suppliers receive the maximum value. The supplier management strategy focuses on establishing a great relationship with the suppliers, managing the supplier requirements, and communicating clearly with the suppliers. Many firms have reduced the total number of their suppliers to form alliances with a small set of highly competent and trustworthy suppliers in order to improve quality and form meaningful relationships. For example, Ford reduced the number of suppliers by 40% to cut costs in the past. Many companies have involved their suppliers early in their product design efforts in order to develop alternate solutions and develop parts, materials, knowhows, and technologies. Supplier relationships are crucial to just-in-time (JIT) activities, future partnership ventures, and performance measures.

Customer Management Strategy

Customer management strategy focuses on creating a long-term value for the customer. The strategy involves a company's interactions with its current and future customers. Firms integrate their supply chain logistics functions using their transportation and logistics provider partners to deliver products. This integration speeds up the delivery process and improves customer satisfaction. Firms also customize their goods and services to improve customer satisfaction.

Customer relationship management (CRM) is a major part of the customer management strategy. CRM focuses on building and maintaining a profitable long-term customer relationship by providing products to customer satisfaction. A well-managed CRM system consists of the needs and demands of customers. CRM is an integrated approach of managing and coordinating customer interactions across multiple channels such as email, search, social media, telephone, and direct mail. Firms like Amazon and Starbucks take advantage of the wealth of data that they have collected using such integrated systems. They can track the preferences of their customers and their buying patterns to see which products are in demand at any time. Using that information, they can send rewards and sales promotions directly to their loyal customers. The insights from such collected data can be valuable to guide their supply chain decisions[8].

Operations Strategy

The operations strategy concentrates on managing an organization's resources that are essential to produce goods and services and support its long-term competitiveness. The strategy focuses on worker skills, required talents and expertise, use of technology, superior processes, specialized equipment, quality controls, and efficient use of its locations, size, and available facilities. To make good decisions and increase the supply chain flexibility, SCM must integrate information exchange, purchasing, demand management, logistics, transportation, quality management, production planning, and materials management throughout the supply chain using the latest communications, information, and technology systems.

Besides developing new product offerings that include new goods and new services, firms have integrated and optimized their operations with their supply chain systems. Firms have also established strategies to improve the productivity of their employees by training them and by using effective feedback mechanisms. Many companies have developed good career path planning for their employees to reduce the high turnover and the costs of hiring new employees. Efficient fulfillment of customer orders, efficient use of labor, inventory reduction, waste avoidance, and cost savings are the focus of operations strategy in many profitable firms. Firms are using cloud-based information systems to increase flexibility, improve productivity, manage labor efficiently, and reduce IT operational spending. Companies must include continuous process improvement, better system improvements, efficient capacity management, improved workflow, and better demand prediction capabilities in their strategic intent.

Supply Chain Management Strategy

The supply chain for a company includes their suppliers and customers. Apart from managing the suppliers and the customers, firms must manage several aspects of the supply chain as well. A key to a successful supply chain strategy is to have efficient logistics and transportation functions. To accomplish this strategy, firms must reduce inventory along the supply chain while simultaneously maintaining or improving customer service. Firms need to redistribute and replenish their inventory efficiently within their supply chain in smaller lot sizes. A supply chain can accomplish this task by efficiently restocking inventory within the supply chain when and where it is needed and in smaller lot sizes. Companies must also integrate logistics, transportation, distribution, and delivery functions efficiently so that they can control the movement of goods from original suppliers to customers. The short-term goal of supply chain management is to increase quality and productivity while reducing inventory and cycle time. Its long-term strategy is to increase customer satisfaction, market share, and profits[9].

Sustainability Strategy

According to the World Commission on Environment and Development, sustainability is the capability to meet present resource needs without compromising the ability of future generations to meet their own needs[10].

To sustain for the sake of future generations, firms must incorporate sustainability or corporate social responsibility (CSR) in their business strategies. Companies must include a comprehensive sustainability strategy in their OSCM strategy. Sustainability in modern firms has focused on three dimensions including economic success, environmental impact, and corporate social responsibility. This is also called as the **"triple bottom line"** as shown in Figure 1-4.

The triple bottom line is a sustainability framework that assesses the social, environmental, and economic impact of a company on its stakeholders[11]. Stakeholders are individuals, organizations, and other entities who are directly or indirectly influenced by the actions of a company. The triple bottom line framework is based on the principle that the success or failure of sustainability goals cannot be measured only in terms of profit and loss but must also be

Corporate social responsibility (CSR) or Corporate citizenship
A business model practiced by companies to have a good impact on all aspects of society, including economic, social, and environmental.

Triple bottom line
A sustainability framework that assesses the social, environmental, and economic impact of a company.

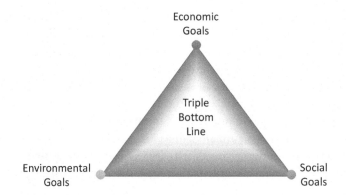

Figure 1-4 Triple Bottom Line Framework

determined in terms of the welfare of the people of our planet. Many companies have used the triple bottom line framework to incorporate the three dimensions into their business and OSCM strategies. As part of the triple bottom line strategy in OSCM, companies can improve their carbon footprint, energy usage, and recycling efforts. Firms can optimize their transportation routes to reduce fuel consumption and carbon emissions across the supply chain.

Economic Goals

Firms must develop and engage in long-term growth strategies to be of value to their shareholders. To accomplish that growth, firms must provide lasting economic benefits to society by preserving the environment and being socially responsible. Firms must align with the interests of their shareholders as well as their communities, suppliers, and customers. They could introduce innovative technologies and practices that provide multiple benefits to their communities and the environment. They could make every effort to develop waste-free processes. They could include ecosystem services in their cost-benefit analysis.

McDonalds and Walmart have set their profitability goals along with many initiatives to protect the environment and be socially responsible. Walmart, while trying to achieve their shareholders goals, have initiated their efforts to achieve zero waste in their operations in the Unite States and Canada by 2025. They plan to reach 100% recyclable, reusable, or industrially compostable private-brand packaging by 2025[12].

Environmental Goals

While achieving economic growth and being responsible socially, the protection, sustenance, and restoration of the health of critical natural habitats and ecosystems becomes the focus of attention. Several steps can be taken to protect our environment. Chemical products and processes could be designed to eliminate toxic hazards, to be recycled, and to reduce total lifecycle costs.

The air that global habitants breathe can be of excellent quality standards with reduced risks from toxics and pollutants by reducing greenhouse gas emissions. The water that all the lifeforms drink must be free of contaminants. We must minimize waste generation to prevent the accidental release of toxins.

Walmart has zero emissions as a target in their own operations by 2040 and they have started working with suppliers to avoid 1 gigaton of greenhouse gas emissions from the global value chain by 2030[13]. McDonalds has changed its food packaging from Styrofoam containers to paper products since foam packaging is hard to recycle. McDonalds claims that they recycle the cardboard boxes used in more than 89% of their restaurants and more than 85% of their packaging is made from renewable resources[14].

FROM PRACTICE: Tesla's Sustainability Efforts

Climate change is reaching alarming levels due to the emissions from burnt fossil fuels for transportation and electricity generation. In 2016, carbon dioxide (CO_2) concentration levels permanently exceeded the 400 parts per million threshold, a level that many climate scientists believe will have a catastrophic impact on the environment. Moreover, global CO_2 emissions are increasing at an alarming rate. The annual CO_2 emissions have doubled over the past 50 years to over 35 gigatons per year. Our earth is on her way to unsustainability!

© JL IMAGES/Shutterstock.com

Tesla's mission is to accelerate the world's transition to sustainable energy. Tesla's ecosystem including solar, batteries, and vehicles aims to reduce the environmental impacts of transportation, electricity production, and energy use by people, homes, and businesses. The materials in a Tesla lithium-ion battery are recoverable and recyclable. Battery materials are refined and put into a cell. At the end of their life, they can be recycled to recover the valuable materials for reuse. Prolonging the life of a battery pack is a better option to recycling for both environmental and business reasons and Tesla does everything it can to extend the useful life of each battery pack. None of the scrapped lithium-ion batteries go to landfills, and 100% are recycled.

Social Goals

Being socially responsible affirms that a company practices business by treating its employees fairly and by being a good neighbor to its community members both locally and globally. A sustainable business must have the support of its employees, its community, and its stakeholders in general. Business could practice the fair means of retention and employment standards with responsible benefits including maternity and paternity benefits, flexible scheduling, and learning and development opportunities. They can give back to their community by offering funds for social causes, sponsorships, scholarships to students, and investment in local public projects. Firms could censure child labor practices and provide a safe working environment.

As part of its corporate social responsibility strategy, McDonalds is planning to commit to the Clinton Global Initiative in collaboration with the Alliance for a Healthier Generation to make nutritious choices and nutrition education a bigger part of the McDonalds' experience[15]. Walmart launched an internal "food waste and damage reduction campaign" and set a goal to reduce the food waste in emerging-market stores and clubs by 15% and in other markets by 10%. Walmart has a goal to make responsible recruitment and promoting human dignity a standard business practice[16].

FROM PRACTICE: Goldman Sachs' Sustainability Efforts

© peampath2812/Shutterstock.com

In 2020, Goldman Sachs, the American multinational investment bank and financial services company, committed $750 billion in financing, investing, and advisory activities in nine areas that are focused on climate transition and inclusive growth by 2030. In 2021, the company reached a target of $156 billion including $93 billion dedicated to climate transition alone. The company created a new team, the Sustainable Finance Group, to coordinate their sustainability efforts across the firm. They launched dedicated sustainability councils within all of their businesses, each led by a senior leader within the firm to integrate the sustainable solutions into their work with clients. To assist their clients to make progress toward their emissions goals, they developed new financing tools that are linked to their progress, like bonds linked to key performance indicators. They have also incorporated a low-carbon tilt into all of their active quantitative equity funds to help clients manage exposure to climate transition risk. Goldman Sachs built one of the largest commercial and industrial solar businesses through their Renewable Power Group, which owns over 2 gigawatts of renewable-energy capacity in the United States and invested in ReNew Power, one of the largest renewable energy developers and operators in India with over 5 gigawatts of operational capacity and 5 additional gigawatts under development. They have funded over $1.6 billion in equity financing to support the construction of a lithium-ion battery factory by the Swedish manufacturer Northvolt AB. They have been highly active in advocating for the United States to rejoin the Paris Agreement. Goldman Sachs was the first U.S. bank to disclose under the Sustainability Accounting Standards Board (SASB) standards. They have expanded their operational carbon commitment to include in their supply chain, targeting net zero carbon emissions by 2030[17].

Operations and Supply Chain Management Process

Firms focus their efforts to achieve their strategy using business processes[18]. The business processes that are associated with achieving the operations and supply chain strategy of a firm include planning, sourcing, making, delivery, return, and enabling as shown in Figure 1-5. Each of these processes is described below.

Planning Process

The planning process includes the processes that are essential to managing the operations and supply chain in firms. Planning is applicable to all the activities in the supply chain such as procuring or sourcing, making of goods, receiving goods, delivery of goods and services, and returns of goods and services.

The main elements of the planning process consist of the following:

- Determine the available resources for the operations and supply chain of an organization,
- Balance those resources with the requirements to manage the supply chain,
- Establish supply chain plans and ensure they align with business goals,

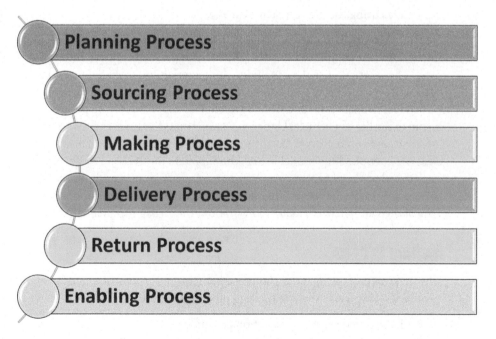

Figure 1-5 Operations and Supply Chain Processes

- Communicate the supply chain plans with suppliers and customers, and
- Institute metrics for efficiency, quality, and potential value to customers in order to monitor and control the operations and supply chains of an organization.

For example, a requirement for raw materials could be the anticipated demand and the balancing act would be the plan to meet that demand with the available resources. An organization can establish several metrics to monitor and control the efficiency of how it meets the demands. They can communicate their supply chain plans with their suppliers and customers and receive information from them to make the supply chain more efficient.

Sourcing Process

Procurement is the process of acquiring the goods and services for the operations of an organization. Sourcing, on the other hand, is more holistic. Sourcing is the process that includes the following:

- Creating a procurement strategy,
- Identifying metrics and selecting suppliers who meet the metrics,
- Negotiating and obtaining goods and services required to make the products of a firm,
- Scheduling material deliveries from suppliers,
- Receiving materials after inspection,
- Transferring materials to production facilities,
- Payment for those materials to the suppliers, and
- Executing the procurement strategy.

General Motors launched a unique parts-buying program that includes inspecting their suppliers' factories and analyzing their suppliers' internal cost data. The internal cost data includes the material costs, the labor costs, the costs of scrap, and other costs. Instead of seeking bids from their vendors, this "One Cost Model" awards contracts to eligible suppliers for the periods ranging up to the life of a vehicle. Under this program, GM analyzes the cost-related information from their suppliers to see whether they can cut costs by more efficient production. This model brings the suppliers into GM's vehicle program earlier so that they can cut costs by optimizing the design and production of parts and jointly identify waste and continuous improvement opportunities. One of their suppliers is Takata Corporation, the airbag supplier[19].

Making Process

The making process includes the processes required to produce goods and/or to offer services. Typically, the making processes include:

- Design and initiate production planning,
- Schedule production activities,

- Coordinate all resources to support production of goods or delivery of services,
- Furnish required materials for production,
- Make finished products ready to meet actual demand,
- Test and package products for sale,
- Execute pricing, delivery, and payment methods, and
- Monitor established metrics such as productivity and quality.

Tesla, the electronics vehicle maker, has one of the world's most advanced automotive plants. Their 10 million square feet of manufacturing and office space on 370 acres of land has created thousands of new jobs. To create a modern workspace, Tesla added skylights to provide the workers with natural light, painted the floors with white epoxy to create a clean work environment, added an employee training center, a modern cafeteria, a gym, a 24/7 in-house medical center, and many outdoor patios. Tesla trains its employees with the advanced skills that are unique to their production processes and seriously takes a proactive approach to their safety. The manufacturing process uses many specialized robots. Tesla designs and performs engineering work on most of the electronics of their vehicles, which gives more control over costs and sourcing of the parts[20].

Delivery Process

The delivery process includes the logistics and transportation process. The process involves delivering finished goods and services to meet the demand and includes:

- Receiving orders,
- Validating orders,
- Reserving inventory,
- Setting delivery dates,
- Consolidating orders,
- Selecting carriers,
- Determining loads,
- Routing shipments,
- Generating shipping documents,
- Picking, packing, and loading shipments,
- Shipping products,
- Moving to warehouses and distribution centers,
- Receiving and verifying products at stores,
- Picking products and stocking shelves,
- Filling shopping carts,
- Delivering order,
- Invoicing customers, and
- Moving information through the supply chain.

Companies have increasingly embraced one-stop global logistics services using service providers called **third-party logistics (3PL)** providers to improve customer service and reduce costs. About 60% of the Fortune 500 companies have at least one logistics provider contract. Information Technology (IT) is a critical factor for 3PL performance since a logistics provider must integrate systems with its clients. IT links the members of a supply chain, such as manufacturers, distributors, transportation firms, and retailers. IT automates some of the logistics workload elements such as order processing, order status inquiries, inventory management, or shipment tracking[21].

Return Process

Return is the process for a customer to bring previously purchased merchandise back to the retailer and in turn receive a refund in the original form of payment, exchange for another product, or receive a store credit. Returns are often due to customers receiving defective products. The return process includes:

- Identify defective or excess product condition,
- Authorize defective or excess product return,
- Initiate return receipt,
- Schedule returns,
- Return product, and
- Give back money or store credit or exchange product.

Amazon has a sound product return policy. Customers can return any item that was purchased on Amazon.com. However, there are different return options depending on the seller, the item, or the reason for the return. Customers can simply visit Amazon's Online Returns Center, start the process, follow the on-screen instructions to get a return mailing label, and choose a return option. Depending on the individual item's eligibility that is determined by Amazon, customers can choose either to return or to exchange or to replace their purchased item. Customers can print the shipping label, ship the item back to Amazon or use any shipping outlet authorized by Amazon, and receive credit for their returned item.

Enabling Process

The enabling process is related to business rules, facilities performance, data resources, contracts, compliance, and risk management. The enabling process includes the following:

- Managing supply chain business rules,
- Managing supply chain performance,
- Managing supply chain data,
- Managing supply chain resources and assets,
- Managing supply chain contracts and compliance,
- Managing supply chain network,
- Managing supply chain risks,

- Managing supply chain procurement, and
- Managing supply chain technology.

Toyota did not have any opportunity to do any advance planning for the devasting event that took place in United States on September 11, 2001. An immediate impact to the supply chain was the heightened security measures at all ports and border crossings between the United States, Canada, and Mexico. The increased security measures created an uncertainty both in the delivery times for parts shipments coming into the United States and the recession that followed the event. Toyota took immediate action to temporarily stop production at its North American plants[22].

OSCM Performance Measures

Operations and supply chain management has been a major factor in the competitive strategy of many organizations. It is quite common for organizations to form alliances with both their suppliers and customers as part of their competitive strategy. Such alliances have been created to:

- Increase financial gains of all members of the supply chain,
- Increase operational performance of all members of the supply chain,
- Reduce total cost,
- Reduce inventories,
- Increase sharing of information,
- Improve service,
- Reduce uncertainty in the supply chain, and
- Enhance control of supply and distribution channels.

Overall Performance of OSCM

The alliances with their suppliers and customers have led many organizations to perform well. The organizations have embraced the following four performance measures to gain competitive and strategic objectives[23]:

- Cost,
- Quality,
- Time, and
- Flexibility.

Cost is the most important measure of performance for many organizations. Organizations should make every effort to minimize cost and increase profits. They can track the costs they incur to see where the money is being spent and minimize unnecessary spending. Typical costs include the fixed and the variable costs incurred to produce goods and implement services. The inventory-related costs, the warehouse costs, the logistics and transportation costs, and the information processing costs are some examples of costs.

Quality is another key measure of supply chain performance. If a product satisfies the customer expectations of price, safety, usability, availability, reliability, and serviceability, then it is considered as a quality product. Quality products generate better revenue. The examples of quality include the perceived value of a product, the number of shipment errors, and the reliability of a product.

Time is an important performance measure of OSCM. Every task in the supply chain consumes time and the optimal total time is always of importance to a customer. The lead time, the product development cycle time, and the shipment delivery time are examples.

Flexibility is the ability to adapt to current and future changes. The flexibility of a company may be determined by how well the company responds to a sudden increase in demand for a product, if a machine breaks down, or if their employees go on strike. It is the ability and the speed at which a company responds to changes in their customer requirements. Capacity utilization, delivery flexibility, and production volume flexibility are some examples of flexibility.

We will be discussing the overall performance measures including cost, quality, time, and flexibility in various parts of this text. However, let us focus on some of the key measures employed by most companies in this chapter.

Efficiency, Effectiveness, and Value

To be successful, companies must maximize the potential of their operations and supply chain. They must develop several performance measures and metrics that are essential to fully integrate their operations and supply chain in order to maximize effectiveness and efficiency[24]. They must provide value to all the members of the supply chain. So, what is efficiency and effectiveness? What is value?

Efficiency is defined as the ability to accomplish something at the lowest possible cost and with the least amount of wasted time, effort, or competency. Effectiveness is defined as the degree to which something is accomplished to produce a desired result. Effectiveness refers to doing the right things and efficiency refers to doing the right things the best way. It is possible to be effective without being efficient and vice versa. For example, suppose Tom, the manager at a local company, hires a person by reducing the time taken for the approval process. This is efficient. However, If Tom hires the right person at the right time for a much-needed vacancy, it is effective.

Value is a measure of the benefit provided by a good or service. Tap water is free. But, if a consumer buys a bottle of water for a price, then the bottled water is perceived to be of a higher value to that customer. Suppliers add value to manufacturers by providing valuable raw materials who in turn provide value to their customers with valuable goods and services. This is the value chain. The value chain is a process in which a company adds value to its raw materials to produce products that are eventually sold to consumers. The value chain gives companies a competitive advantage in the industry.

Value chain The value chain is a process in which a company adds value to its raw materials to produce products eventually sold to consumers for its competitive advantage in the industry.

Efficiency The ability to accomplish something at the lowest possible cost and with the least amount of wasted time, effort, or competency in performance. Efficiency refers to doing the right things the best way.

Value A measure of the benefit provided by a good or service.

Effectiveness The degree to which something is accomplished to produce a desired result. Effectiveness refers to doing the right things.

Productivity

According to the U.S. Bureau of Labor Statistics, productivity increases have enabled the businesses in the United States to produce nine times more goods and services since 1947 with a slight increase in the number of hours worked[25]. Productivity is the efficiency with which companies produce goods or services. It is a measure of how well a company uses its resources. When we use software like Microsoft Word to type an essay instead of writing on a paper, our productivity increases because we can make corrections as we author the essay using the software.

Productivity is a crucial factor to measure the performance of firms. Increasing productivity helps businesses to be more profitable. A productivity growth or an increase in productivity offers an organization the opportunity to increase their output without increasing the inputs such as labor and material costs. Productivity is measured as:

$$Productivity = \frac{Output}{Input} \qquad \text{Eq. 1-1}$$

> **Productivity**
> Productivity is the efficiency with which companies produce goods or services.

where output is the quantity of goods or services produced. The output can be in terms of dollars as well. The input can be the labor, materials, capital, energy, equipment, or other expenses. For example, Mary built a small doghouse for her pet. The doghouse, in terms of dollar value or the cost to make the doghouse, is the output. The time spent by Mary to build the doghouse in terms of dollar value is the labor input. The cost of the wood and the nails she used to build the doghouse is the material input. The cost of the power saw and the power drill are the equipment input, and the electricity used to power the saw and the drill is the energy input. Therefore, the total input equals the cost of wood, nails, power saw, power drill, and electricity. We have three different measures of productivity including:

- Total productivity,
- Partial productivity, and
- Multifactor productivity.

If we add up all the different components of the inputs, we can call that total input. We can use individual input such as labor, material, equipment, or energy to find the partial productivity. For the multifactor productivity, we can add labor and materials or materials, labor, energy, and so on.

Example 1-1

Pampered Pets, Inc., builds small to large residences for pets. Their production data for the month of March is given below. What is the total productivity, partial productivity of labor and material, and multifactor productivity of labor + material and material + energy?

Finished goods	$ 2,500,000
Work-In-Progress (WIP)	$ 3,150,000
Labor costs	$ 300,000
Material costs	$ 123,000
Energy costs	$ 30,000
Other costs	$ 25,000

Let us first identify the outputs and inputs. We see that the finished goods and WIP are outputs and all the costs are inputs.

Using Eq. 1-1, Total Productivity $= \dfrac{(2,500,000+3,150,000)}{(300,000+123,000+30,000+25,000)} = 11.82$

Partial productivity measures:

Using Eq. 1-1, Labor Productivity $= \dfrac{(2,500,000+3,150,000)}{300,000} = 18.83$

Using Eq. 1-1, Material Productivity $= \dfrac{(2,500,000+3,150,000)}{123,000} = 45.93$

Multifactor productivity measures:

Using Eq. 1-1, Labor & Material Productivity $= \dfrac{(2,500,000+3,150,000)}{(300,000+123,000)} = 13.36$

Using Eq. 1-1, Material & Energy Productivity $= \dfrac{(2,500,000+3,150,000)}{(123,000+30,000)} = 36.93$

Analysis: To check whether these productivity measures are good or bad, we need to compare them with prior months. If there was an increase in productivity, it is good for the company and is due to a technology innovation. If there was a decrease in productivity, it is due to the increase in costs and the company has to monitor and rectify the problems in the future. For example, if the total productivity for February was 11.28, then March was more productive for Pampered Pets than February. The reason may be the workers were more trained in March than in February or even more cheerful now that spring is in the air!

Example 1-2

The East Corner Bakery has furnished the following data. Compare the total productivity and the partial productivities of labor and materials for the past two months.

	June	July
Total Sales	$ 12,460	$ 16,000
Labor costs	$ 6,400	$ 6,800
Material costs	$ 2,200	$ 3,000

Let us first identify the outputs and inputs. We see that the total sales is the output and all the costs are inputs.

For the month of June,

Using Eq. 1-1, Total Productivity $= \dfrac{12460}{(6400+2200)} = 1.45$

Using Eq. 1-1, Labor Productivity $= \dfrac{12460}{6400} = 1.95$

Using Eq. 1-1, Material Productivity $= \dfrac{12460}{2200} = 5.66$

For the month of July,

Using Eq. 1-1, Total Productivity $= \dfrac{16000}{(6800+3000)} = 1.63$

Using Eq. 1-1, Labor Productivity $= \dfrac{16000}{6800} = 2.35$

Using Eq. 1-1, Material Productivity $= \dfrac{16000}{3000} = 5.33$

Analysis: July has better productivity than June. While the labor productivity was better in July, the material productivity of July seems to be less than that of June. This may be because while the sales were higher in July, there was a 36% increase in material costs and the labor costs increased by only about 6%.

Major Trends in Operations and Supply Chain Management

Operations and supply chain management has continuously undergone positive changes over the years. The field is undergoing a drastic change with the integration of more and more new technologies. The current trends in OSCM include digital manufacturing, Blockchain technology, and Industry 4.0.

Digital Manufacturing

Digital manufacturing is solving complex operations problems and improving supply chains using computer technologies. Real-time information can be collected by computer technologies and used to respond effectively to the disruptions in operations and supply chain processes. Digital manufacturing increases the ability to collaborate with suppliers because of real-time information at hand. Digital manufacturing provides companies with many benefits including increased profits, reduced risks, and faster speed to bring products to the market. It is an integrated approach for all facets of manufacturing — planning, scheduling, inventory control, cost control, quality management, and shop floor operations. This integrated view leads to better communication between various functions of a business. Enterprise resource planning (ERP), computer-integrated manufacturing (CIM), flexible manufacturing, lean manufacturing, and design for manufacturability (DFM) are some of the important examples of digital manufacturing.

Blockchain Technology

The Blockchain is an incorruptible digital *ledger* of transactions programmed to record every supply chain transaction. The name Blockchain was coined for the way the technology stores transaction data—in blocks that are linked together to form a chain. The blocks record and confirm the time and sequence of transactions that are logged within a discrete network governed by rules agreed *a priori* by the network participants. Each block contains a hash and a digital fingerprint. The hash of the previous block is linked to the next and this arrangement prevents any block from being altered and is immutable. In summary, the Blockchain serves as a database for recording transactions. Three attributes of supply chain management have been used with Blockchain technology including supply chain contracts, trust in supply chains, and reverse logistics[26].

Industry 4.0 and Smart Factories

The first industrial revolution started in late 18th century in England, which transformed production from human/animal power to machine power. The second industrial revolution introduced assembly lines with the use of oil, gas, and electric power. Advancement in communication such as telephones and telegraphs helped make mass production and transportation possible. The third industrial revolution began in the middle of the 20th century through the addition of computers and advanced telecommunications to enhance manufacturing and service processes. The fourth industrial revolution, otherwise known as Industry 4.0, is revolutionizing the way companies manufacture and distribute their products by integrating various innovative technologies into their operations and supply chains. We will discuss this trend further in Chapter 14.

Careers in OM and SCM

The three-sector economics model includes primary, secondary , and tertiary sectors. The primary sector consists of the extraction of raw materials such as farming, logging, hunting, fishing, and mining. The secondary sector consists of the manufacturing industries that produce finished and usable products and construction companies that build cities, facilities, and roads. The tertiary sector consists of the service industries to facilitate the transport, distribution and sale of goods and services. According to the three-sector economics model, goods and services flow from the primary sector to the tertiary sector through the secondary sector.

Since all organizations have processes, suppliers, and customers, there are plenty of career opportunities for operations and supply chain professionals in all three sectors of the economy. Services firms such as healthcare, information technology, sports, arts, hotels, and restaurants and all manufacturing companies must plan, schedule, coordinate, and manage their operations and supply chains. Several opportunities are also available in local/state/national governments, non-profit organizations, and consulting companies. The following are some of the job areas in operations and supply chain management.

Logistics

Logisticians, the professionals who collect and analyze data to coordinate the logistics of a company, may have titles such as Logistician, Logistics Manager, Operations Manager, Production Manager, Production Planner, Program Manager, Supply Management Specialist, or Supply Chain Manager. Logistics analysts analyze the data obtained from various supply chain processes and use that data to make decisions to improve their logistics processes. Roles in logistics are projected to grow between 5% to 9% from 2016 to 2029[27].

Transportation

Transportation managers, the professionals who work in operations management, fleet management, freight management, or traffic management, plan and oversee transportation operations. Roles in transportation are projected to grow at a 5% to 9% rate through 2029[27].

Purchasing

Purchasing professionals oversee the activities of an organization's purchasing of materials, products, and services as well as developing relationships with suppliers and negotiating contracts. Roles in purchasing are projected to grow at a 5% to 9% rate through 2029[27].

Operations Planning and Control

These professionals coordinate and expedite the flow of work and materials within or between departments of an organization. Typical job titles include Master Scheduler, Material Coordinator, Materials Planner, Planner, Production Assistant, Production Clerk, Production Controller, Operational Excellence Manager, Production Planner, Production Scheduler, Scheduler. Roles in operations planning are projected to grow at a 3% to 4% rate through 2029[27].

Quality

Professionals who work in quality, six sigma, and lean six sigma, plan, direct, or coordinate quality assurance programs, formulate quality control policies, and control the quality of goods and services. Typical job titles include Director of Quality, Quality Assurance Manager, Quality Control Manager, Quality Control Supervisor, Quality Manager, Six Sigma Consultant, and Continuous Improvement Specialist. Roles in operations planning are projected to grow at a 1% to 2% rate through 2029[27].

General Operations

These professionals plan, direct, or coordinate the operations of organizations, oversee multiple departments or locations, formulate policies, manage daily operations, and plan the use of materials and human resources. Typical job titles include Business Manager, General Manager (GM), Operations Director, Operations Manager, Plant Superintendent, and Store Manager. Roles in operations planning are projected to grow at a 5% to 7% rate through 2029[27].

FROM PRACTICE: OSCM Professional Organizations

Being a member of the organizations shown below helps professionals in operations and supply chain management to meet people for networking, compare their business to similar businesses, know the trends in the industry, and keep an eye on their competition.

American Production and Inventory Control Society	https://www.ascm.org/
The Council of Supply Chain Management Professionals	https://cscmp.org/
International Warehouse Logistics Association	https://www.iwla.com/
Material Handling Association of America	https://www.mhi.org/
Project Management Institute	https://www.pmi.org/

Formulae from this Chapter

Productivity	$Productivity = \dfrac{Output}{Input}$	Eq. 1-1

Case Study: Strategy and Productivity Challenges at Inglewood Construction

Rob Inglewood, the owner of the Inglewood Construction Company, has been thinking about the productivity of his company for quite some time. He believes that if he can keep up the productivity, cut costs, and provide high-quality products and service, his company will do better. Rob was also contemplating about the role his company should play in the future. He had heard of sustainability strategies from his business school days and he wanted to connect with his community in a meaningful way. He knew that the operational strategies would need to be revised. He wanted to reinvent the overall operations strategy and align the new operations strategy with his sustainability initiatives.

Inglewood Construction has provided the highest quality remodeling services for home renovations, additions, and restorations in the area. The company has prided themselves with their quality craftsmanship and stunning designs that enhance the beauty, function, and value of the homes of their customers. The company's experience has been valued by many of their customers. Inglewood has completed many projects in the community. The company's extensive portfolio of projects includes restoration of historical homes, remodeling complete homes and basements, remodeling kitchens and bathrooms, room, floor, and garage additions. The company has expertise in repair and maintenance of both interior fixtures as well as exterior fixtures. The company also performs may other in-home maintenance tasks as well. The revenues of Inglewood construction for the last year are as follows:

Jan	Feb	Mar	Apr	May	Jun
$ 286,000	$ 213,000	$ 547,000	$ 634,000	$ 536,000	$ 540,000
Jul	Aug	Sep	Oct	Nov	Dec
$ 529,000	$ 635,000	$ 456,000	$ 348,000	$ 246,000	$ 235,000

© Sergey Nivens/Shutterstock.com

To complete projects for their customers, the company's workforce works 8 hours a day for 6 days a week. The number of working days for each month of the past year is given below:

Jan	Feb	Mar	Apr	May	Jun	Jul	Aug	Sep	Oct	Nov	Dec
22	21	24	22	23	23	22	24	23	22	23	23

Currently, the company markets its services to the community members by radio ads. They also send out coupons with the region's newspaper on Sundays. After hitting the $5 million revenue mark, the company is planning to market its services to the regional members by TV. Rob meets potential customers personally for big projects and sends his two sons to meet with customers for smaller and maintenance projects. They gather the requirements of a project and make a deal for that project with the potential customer. Rob, his two sons, and his project manager schedule each project and implement the project. They have made a nice deal with a local lumber yard and hardware store for all the materials for their projects. Once a project is completed, a quality inspector checks the worksite to make sure that the work has been done as per the customer's expectation. Then, only upon satisfaction, the customer pays the amount owed for the project.

One of the main problems that Rob faced was the constant mobility of his workforce. Since he had multiple projects at the same time, he had to split his workforce in the best way possible to meet his customers' expectations. The workforce had some issues with illness and tardiness in the past. Currently, he feels that he has hired better and more dependable workers who would get projects completed in time. However, he thinks that the mobility of his workforce from one place to another place to implement projects is costing his company the productivity improvements that he is seeking. He knows that his current project manager is doing all he can to accomplish the projects on schedule and under budget. Rob feels that the company can do better.

However, before he hires a good project manager to manage all his projects, he wants to analyze his current conditions first. The number of workers for each month is shown below:

	Jan	Feb	Mar	Apr	May	Jun	Jul	Aug	Sep	Oct	Nov	Dec
No of Full-time workers	14	16	20	22	24	24	24	24	24	24	20	16
No of Part-time workers	3	5	5	5	8	8	8	8	8	8	5	2

The full-time workers get paid $25 per hour on an average and the part-time workers get $15 per hour.

© Ground Picture/Shutterstock.com

Case Questions

A. Where would you place this company—as products or services in the goods-service continuum?

B. Write a vision statement for the company.

C. Based on your vision, write the mission and core values for the company.

D. What is the operations and supply chain management strategy of the company?

E. What should the company do in Rob's quest for a sustainability strategy?

F. What are the current operations and supply chain strategy for the company?

G. Explain the operations process of the company.

H. Describe the six OSCM processes of the company.

I. What is the average total productivity of the company for the year?

J. What is the monthly labor productivity of the company?

K. Which month has the best labor productivity? Why?

L. Which month has the worst labor productivity? Why?

M. Plot the monthly labor productivity with the average labor productivity and show the best and the worst months.

Summary

- Goods are items that are useful, satisfy human wants, and provide utility. Services are rendered by organizations as transactions with no physical goods being transferred from the seller to the buyer. Goods are physical, tangible articles, while services are nonphysical and intangible.

- Products-services bundling or the goods-services continuum is a spectrum of goods and services offered by industries to create value for their customers. The goods-services continuum consists of pure goods, augmented goods, augmented services, and pure services. The intent of this goods-services continuum or product-service bundling is to create value for the customer's use of the goods and lowering the customer's total lifecycle cost.

- Firms use systems and business processes to create such goods and services. A business process is a set of related, structured activities or tasks, where a specific sequence produces a service or product.

- Operations and supply chain management (OSCM) incorporates the design, operations, and continuous improvement of various business processes and systems in a company's supply chain system in order to satisfy customers with its products and services. OM and SCM effectively and efficiently operate as OSCM.

- Supply chain management (SCM) comprises all the planning, management, and control of the flow of goods and information between a company and its suppliers and customers.

- Operations management (OM) consists of the use of business practices to create the highest possible efficiency, productivity, and sustainability in an organization.

- A strategy is a plan of action envisioned to achieve a major goal. Strategy defines how a company would get from where it is currently to where it wants to be.

- The primary strategy of operations and supply chain management is to increase the value of goods and services to customers in the supply chain with regard to improved customer service and quality, and lower operational costs.

- Operations and supply chain management strategy includes integration of supplier management strategy, customer management strategy, operations strategy, supply chain management strategy, and sustainability strategy.

- To sustain for the sake of future generations, firms must incorporate sustainability or corporate social responsibility (CSR) in their business strategies. Corporate Social Responsibility (CSR) or Corporate Citizenship is a business model practiced by companies to have a good impact on all aspects of society, including economic, social, and environmental.

- A triple bottom line is a sustainability framework that assesses the social, environmental, and economic impact of a company.

- The processes that are associated with achieving the operations and supply chain strategy of a firm include planning, sourcing, making, delivery, return, and enabling processes.

- To assess their performance, organizations have embraced cost, quality, time, and flexibility as performance measures to gain competitive and strategic objectives.
- To be successful companies must maximize the potential of their supply chain. They must develop performance measures and metrics that are essential to fully integrate their supply chain to maximize effectiveness and efficiency, and must provide value to all the members of the supply chain.
- Effectiveness is the degree to which something is accomplished to produce a desired result. Efficiency is the ability to accomplish something at the lowest possible cost and with the least amount of wasted time, effort, or competency in performance. Value is a measure of the benefit provided by a good or service.
- Productivity is the efficiency with which companies produce goods or services. It is a measure of how well a company uses its resources. We have three different measures of productivity including total productivity, partial productivity, and multifactor productivity.

Review Questions

1. What is a goods-services continuum?
2. What is products-services bundling?
3. Why do organizations consider a goods-services continuum?
4. What is a business process?
5. How are business processes important to organizations?
6. Define operations and supply chain management.
7. What is SCM and OM?
8. What is a vision and what is a strategy? How are they related to each other?
9. What business model should companies follow to make sure that they are around for future generations?
10. What processes are associated with achieving the operations and supply chain strategy of a firm?
11. Describe each of the six OSCM processes with an example.
12. What is a triple bottom line strategy?
13. What are the four broad factors used to assess the performance of organizations?
14. Explain effectiveness, efficiency, and value.
15. What is productivity? How do companies measure productivity?
16. What are the trends in OSCM?
17. How is digital manufacturing used in OSCM?
18. OSCM has potentially a lot of career choices. Explain.

Critical Thinking Questions

1. Using the Internet, investigate the goods-services continuum of Whirlpool Corporation, the home appliance company. What goods and services do they offer? What is their SCM strategy? Describe their operations and supply chain activities. Compare their efficiency ratios to the industry standards.

2. Choose an industry. Using the Internet, investigate how one of the prominent members of that industry has maintained its sustainability. Offer your recommendations for that company to improve their sustainability.

3. How can companies maximize the potential of their supply chain? Why should they maximize that potential? Explain with appropriate examples.

4. Pick your favorite company. Find out its vision, mission, and core values. Describe how any one of their strategies aligns with their vision and core values.

5. Which of the five OSCM strategies discussed in this chapter is of most importance to a company? Why?

6. Research using the Internet to find a company that has excelled in the triple bottom line strategy.

7. Identify each of the following costs as fixed costs, variable costs, inventory-related costs, warehouse costs, logistics costs, or information processing costs:
   a. Rent
   b. Electricity
   c. No. of hours worked on an activity
   d. Consulting fees
   e. Holding costs of finished goods
   f. Obsolescence costs of products
   g. Product delivery costs
   h. Product ordering costs
   i. Software maintenance costs

8. Pick a company of your choice. Research using the Internet and describe their operations and supply chain strategy.

9. Pick a disruption that happened recently in the global supply chain. How did that disruption impact U.S. manufacturing and service sectors? What processes, strategies, and trends would have helped to alleviate the impact?

10. Choose one of the three trends in OSCM. Using the Internet, find out which U.S. company has adopted which trend. Describe how that adoption has benefitted that company.

11. Pick an industry in which you would like to start your career. Find out the productivity of a few companies in that industry using the Internet.

Problem Solving Questions

1. Waco Furnishers produce ornamental, decorative home furniture. Duffy Waco, the CEO of the company, is concerned with his facilities department. He obtained some data for 2021 from his IT group on the facilities department that showed that they worked on 46 projects with an average cost of a project being $48,000. All the facilities staff were involved in those projects and their wages and benefits totaled $1,497,600. The cost of material used for those projects was $1,300,000, the electricity charge was $10,400, cost of equipment and tools was $45,000, and other costs came to $100,000.
   a. What is the productivity of the facilities department?
   b. What is the labor productivity of employees of the facilities department?
   c. What is the labor and material productivity?
   d. Duffy called his friend who ran a similar enterprise who said that the productivity of his company's facilities department is about 0.95. What do you think of the facilities department of Waco Furnishers? What should Duffy Waco do?

2. Plastic Pro, Inc., a manufacturer of plastic items, had two recent contracts for TV covers, one from MikeDance, Inc. and the other from BonneyM, LLC. The MikeDance contract produced 5,000 covers and took 15 workers 2 weeks (40 hours per worker per week) to complete. They also hired 5 temporary workers for the same 2 weeks and time to help their workers. The BonneyM contract produced 4,000 covers by 30 workers in 3 weeks (40 hours per worker per week). The BonneyM contract workers worked a total of 60 hours overtime in order to complete the project.
   a. On which contract were the workers more productive?
   b. If each unit of MikeDance can be sold for $25 and BonneyM can be sold at $41 per unit and the labor was paid $2,000 for each MikeDance worker and $3,000 for each BonneyM worker, on which contract were the workers more productive?
   c. Explain the difference in productivity.

3. McDonalds on Main Street delivered 240,000 hamburgers last year with eight full-time and part-time employees. This year they have delivered 250,000 hamburgers with ten full-time and part-time employees. What is the percentage change in productivity over the past year?

4. Tin Cups Inc. has the following data for the first 6 months of the year.

	Jan	Feb	Mar	April	May	June
Units produced	1200	1100	1240	1360	1280	1250
No of workers	40	38	45	42	40	45
No of working days	21	20	23	21	22	22
No of hours per day	8	8	8	8	8	8

Compare the average productivities of those months and explain the difference in productivity.

5. Top Hats, a hat manufacturer from the Midwest United States, produced two similar hats, one for a university in Michigan and the other for a university in Indiana that year. They managed to sell 160,000 Michigan hats at a price of $20 per hat and 180,000 Indiana hats at a price of $19.50 per hat. Since these two hats were produced as two different batches there was a difference in labor costs as well. The first batch of Michigan hats was produced in 40 hours at a rate of $18 per hour while the Indiana hats were produced in 48 hours at the same rate.
   a. What is the labor productivity for each line of hats in terms of units per hour?
   b. What is the labor productivity for each line of hats in terms of dollars?
   c. Explain the difference in productivity.

6. A project manager of an operation project at a company is examining two in-house projects. Project 1 was completed by 10 engineers in 3 weeks and Project 2 was completed by 12 engineers in 17 days. A week is 5 days and the engineers work for 8 hours a day. Project 1 produced 3,200 modules while Project 2 produced 4,800 modules. On which project were the engineers more productive? Explain the difference.

7. Lakewood Pantry had sales of $60,000 in March and $58,000 in April. The store employs three full-time workers who work for 40 hours in a week. In March, the grocery store hired an extra worker who worked for 10 hours a day for 5 days. April had 4 weeks and March had 5 weeks. In April, the store hired a part-time worker who worked for 40 hours.
   a. What is the productivity for March and April?
   b. What is the percentage change in productivity from March to April?

8. The Do-it-Yourself store around the corner of the Main Road in Elmwood, NV, has the following data. The last year's revenue was $1.2 million. The employee labor costs were $180,000, the inventory cost was $520,000, and the utilities cost was $25,000. Find the various partial productivity and the total productivity of the store. If the owner wants to increase the total productivity to be greater than 2.0, how much sales should he expect while keeping all the costs the same?

References

1. Boxaroundtheword.com. (2019). *McDonald's Supply Chain Management Is The Secret to Their Success!* Retrieved June 10, 2021, from https://box-aroundtheworld.com/mcdonalds-supply-chain-management/

2. McDonalds. (2021). *McDonald's Food Suppliers*. Retrieved June 10, 2021, from https://www.mcdonalds.com/us/en-us/about-our-food/meet-our-suppliers.html.

3. Khandelwal, R. (2020). *McDonald's Supply Chain: A Must-Know for Investors*. Retrieved June 10, 2021, from https://marketrealist.com/2019/11/must-know-mcdonalds-supply-chain-2/

4. Vignali, C. (2001). McDonald's: "think global, act local"–the marketing mix. *British Food Journal, 103*(2), 97–111.

5. Ibid.

6. Hilly, N. R., Singh, S., & Tariyal, M. (2015). Service quality of McDonald's. *Global Journal of Enterprise Information System, 7*(3), 71–79.

7. Flowater. (2021). *The Real Cost of Bottled Water*. Retrieved June 10, 2021, from https://www.drinkflowater.com/blog/the-real-cost-of-bottled-water-2/.

8. Davenport, T. H., & Harris, J. G. (2007). *Competing on analytics: The new science of winning*. Harvard Business Press.

9. Wisner, J. D. (2003). A structural equation model of supply chain management strategies and firm performance. *Journal of Business Logistics, 24*(1), 1–26.

10. WCED. (1987). *Our common future*. Oxford University Press.

11. Elkington, J. (2018, June 25). 25 Years ago, I coined the phrase "Triple Bottom Line." Here's why it's time to rethink It. *Harvard Business Review,*

12. Walmart. (2021). *Sustainability: Using our strengths to help people live better and preserve the planet*. Retrieved June 15, 2021, from https://corporate.walmart.com/global-responsibility/sustainability/.

13. Ibid.

14. McDonalds. (2021). *Your right to know*. Retrieved June 12, 2021, from https://www.mcdonalds.com/gb/en-gb/help/faq/19263-what-is-mcdonalds-corporate-social-responsibility-csr-policy.html.; McDonalds. (2014). *McDonald's Announces 2020 Corporate Social Responsibility and Sustainability Plans*. Retrieved June 12, 2021, from https://www.csrwire.com/press_releases/36995-mcdonald-s-announces-2020-corporate-social-responsibility-and-sustainability-plans.

15. Ibid.

16. Makower, J. (2015). *Walmart sustainability at 10: An assessment*. Retrieved June 15, 2021, from https://www.greenbiz.com/article/walmart-sustainability-10-assessment.

17. Goldman Sachs. (2021). David Soloman, *Chairman & CEO: Goldman Sachs Update on Our 2030 Sustainable Finance Commitment*. Retrieved June 28, 2021, from https://www.goldmansachs.com/media-relations/press-releases/2021/announcement-04-mar-2021.html.

18. APICS.org. (2007). *SCOR: Supply Chain Operations Reference Model*. Retrieved June 15, 2021, from http://www.apics.org/docs/default-source/

scor-p-toolkits/apics-scc-scor-quick-reference-guide.pdf; White, S. K. (2018, October 10). What is SCOR? A model for improving supply chain management. *CIO Magazine*.

19. Sedgwick, D. (2015, may 11). GM shifts buying strategy for suppliers. *Automotive News*. Retrieved June 15, 2020, from https://www.plasticsnews.com/article/20150511/NEWS/150519997/gm-shifts-buying-strategy-for-suppliers.

20. White, G. (2020). *How the Tesla Model S is made*. Retrieved June 15, 2021, from https://manufacturingglobal.com/technology/how-tesla-model-s-made.

21. Vaidyanathan, G. (2005). A framework for evaluating third-party logistics. *Communications of the ACM, 48*(1), 89–94.

22. Iyer, A., Seshadri, S., & Vasher, R. (2009). *Toyota supply chain management*. McGraw-Hill.

23. Slack, N., Chambers, S., Harland, C., Harrison, A., & Johnston, R. (1995). *Operations management*. Pitman Publishing; De Toni, A., & Tonchia, S. (2001). Performance measurement systems: Models, characteristics, and measures. *International Journal of Operations & Production Management 21*(1/2), 46–70; Elrod, C., Murray, S., & Bande, S. (2013). A review of performance metrics for supply chain management. *Engineering Management Journal, 25*(3), 39–50.

24. Gunasekaran, A., Patel, C., & Tirtiroglu, E. (2001). Performance measure and metrics in a supply chain environment. *International Journal of Production Economics, 21*(1/2), 71–87.

25. USBLS. (2022). *Productivity 101: Why is productivity important?* Retrieved June 20, 2021, from https://www.bls.gov/k12/productivity-101/content/why-is-productivity-important/home.htm

26. Breese, J. L., Park, S. J., & Vaidyanathan, G. (2019). Blockchain technology adoption in supply chain management: Two theoretical perspectives. *Issues in Information Systems, 20*(2), 140–150.

27. O*NET. (2021). *O*NET Online*. Retrieved June 20, 2021, from https://www.onetonline.org/ find/ quick?s=supply+chain+management

CHAPTER 2

DEMAND FORECASTING

Learning Objectives

- Define demand.
- Discuss why forecasting is important.
- Forecast demand using quantitative methods.
- Apply quantitative methods to evaluate errors in forecasting.

To know how much to manufacture, firms forecast customer demand for a time horizon, say for next week, next month, next quarter, or next year. An operations and supply chain plan is then developed based on the forecast. Various data for a variety of products as shown in the figure below are extracted and aggregated to forecast demand. Many companies focus on a monthly plan, that is, to match demand with supply for the next 30 days[1]. Once a company estimates the demand for a timeframe, they can check whether they have the capacity to produce the goods and meet that demand. The goods are manufactured based on the plan and then shipped to customers.

But there are problems in this process. Supplier problems, material delivery problems, operations problems, and errors in demand forecast are examples.

Proctor Gamble (P&G), the American multinational consumer goods company, specializes in a wide range of personal health, consumer health, personal care, and personal hygiene products. In 2014, P&G streamlined the company,

dropping and selling off around 100 brands from its product portfolio in order to focus on the remaining 65 brands that generated 95% of the company's profits. In 2020, P&G's revenues reached US$70.95 billion with a net income of US$13.03 billion with 99,000 employees. With operations in 36 countries, the company manufactures popular brands such as Bounty, Crest, Always, Tide, Downy, Gain, Febreze, Dawn, Cascade, Swiffer, Pampers, Luvs, Puffs, Charmin, Gillette, Head & Shoulders, Aussie, Old Spice, Pantene, Oral-B, Scope, Pepto-Bismal, Vicks, Ivory, and Olay.

P&G is known to manage one of the best supply chains in the world. According to the Global Planning Digitization Leader for Supply Chain and Planning Director of North American Product Supply, P&G has embraced continuous demand management planning[1]. P&G executes the demand/supply planning for products like Tide multiple times a day, which means that what is manufactured to be shipped may be adjusted several times a day. This offers flexibility, the flexibility that we discussed in the first chapter as a performance measure, which satisfies their customers, for example, a sudden sales promotion of Tide.

That kind of flexibility in their forecasting helps P&G during random disastrous events. When the big hurricane Irma struck the United States in 2017, P&G used their technology to see what plants, supplier plants, and distribution centers were in the path of the storm. P&G was ready with their disaster recovery and business continuity plans. Right after the storms passed, P&G initiated its business continuity plans and repositioned the inventory to supply consumers with what they needed the most[1].

P&G actively manages the inventory of its customers, which is called vendor managed inventory (VMI). Their customers enjoy the benefits through this process including eliminating the need for purchase orders, having the item on their shelves, and minimizing inventory costs. P&G benefits as well as they receive advance notice of sales and thereby obtain accurate data for the demand for their goods. One of P&G's first collaborations to use VMI was with Walmart, where P&G continuously monitored and automatically replenished Pampers baby diapers at all Walmart stores[2].

Gartner, a prominent global research and advisory firm, named P&G as one of five supply chain 'Masters' for the sixth consecutive year. Other companies to earn that title are Apple, Amazon, McDonalds, and Unilever. Gartner's scoring for the 'Masters' title is based on how companies demonstrate the supply chain leadership in customer-driven partnerships, advanced analytics, and corporate social responsibility[3].

Demand Demand is the quantity of a good and/ or a service that consumers are willing to purchase during a period of time.

Demand

Demand is the quantity of a good and/or a service that consumers are willing to purchase during a period of time. Demand is the total quantity required by all consumers in a market for a good and/or a service. Firms make focused efforts to estimate, plan, and manage the consumer demand for their goods and services. They spend a lot of money to estimate the right amount of demand for each one of their products. They want to make sure that the right amount of demand is as accurate as possible. This is because, underestimated demand would turn away prospective customers without the product while overestimated demand would build inventory and losses.

Many companies and industries have made mistakes in estimating demand. For example, in the early 80s, 67 new types of personal computers were introduced in the U.S. market with an expectation of explosive growth. Only 15 million units were shipped compared to a prediction of 28 million units and as a result, many manufacturers went out of business[4]. During the 2011 Christmas season, Best Buy failed to manage a proper level of inventory to fulfill their customer orders due to poor forecasting. This led to customer distrust and overall negative publicity for Best Buy. The company cancelled orders rather than delaying shipping which implies that they oversold products that they did not have in stock[5].

FROM PRACTICE: Oatly Shortage at Starbucks

Starbucks included Oatly as an option to its menu nationwide in March 2020. Oatly, a plant-based milk option like almond, coconut, and soy, was included in the Iced Brown Sugar Shaken Oatmilk Espresso which combines brown sugar and cinnamon and is then topped off with oat milk. As demand for Oatly's oat milk surged, some customers had a tough time finding the dairy-free milk at their local coffeehouse.

© Bored Photography/Shutterstock.com

Oatly Group AB, a Swedish food company, produces oat milk, ice cream, cold coffee, yoghurt substitutes, cooking cream, spread, and custard. All products are certified kosher and vegan and are non-GMO product verified. Oatly Group AB has planned to open a second plant in Utah to meet the growing demand. However, the plan and the product were delayed due to the COVID-19 pandemic[6].

Forecasting

The forecasts of the future demand in OSCM are important to produce goods in a manufacturing company like General Motors or to procure goods to sell in a retail company like Macy's. For example, Hewlett Packard (HP), the personal computer manufacturer, determines the forecast of the future demand of their personal computers (PC). They use the forecast of the future demand to order the PC components from various suppliers and assemble the PCs to fulfill their customer orders. Intel, one of their suppliers of microprocessors, also must forecast to determine its own production of microprocessors to fulfil HP's demand. Intel not only sells to HP but also to other companies who use their microprocessors in their products. They need to use the forecast information from HP as well as the forecast information from other customers to determine a total forecast of future demand of their microprocessors. The supplier of Intel, SUMCO Corporation from Japan who supplies wafers, has to forecast the future demand of wafers that are needed to produce microprocessors worldwide and can use the information gathered by Intel. Therefore, at each stage of the supply chain, firms need to forecast the future demand of their products.

Is forecasting the demand for the future easy to accomplish? We can say that forecasting some products is easier than others. Products such as milk and paper towels are easier to forecast than fashion goods[7]. Furthermore, forecasting becomes exceedingly difficult when suppliers face unprecedented times or when consumers become irresolute with products or during political instability or in tough economic periods. For example, if you eat bread regularly with all your meals, you may find it easy to forecast and buy the required amount of bread for a week. If you drink milk rarely, forecasting to buy milk for that week is tougher. Moreover, even if you forecast, the forecasting error to buy the bread may likely be less than the forecasting error of your milk supply.

A principal component to a company's financial planning is its budget, which is set based on the forecasts of the future demand. The finance and accounting departments use the forecast for the financial planning and control of the company. The marketing department uses the forecasts to promote sales and plan new products. The operations department that includes the production and the purchasing departments uses forecasts for their operations planning, production planning, determining manufacturing capabilities, facilities layout, procurement plans, inventory management, and distribution capabilities. To plan and decide on what goods to produce, how many units to produce, how much money to allocate, and what is needed for operations over any period of time, whether it is short-term or long-term, companies use two types of forecasts. The two types are strategic forecasts and tactical forecasts.

Strategic Forecasts

Strategic forecasts
Strategic forecasts are used to establish the strategy of how a company will meet the demand of consumers in the next 6 months or next year.

Strategic forecasts, forecasts with a strategic intent, are used to establish how a company can meet the demand for their products. As we discussed in Chapter 1, companies use strategies to achieve their vision. The strategy using forecasts links the operations of companies to their visions. The demand forecast provides the necessary data to evaluate whether they can meet the demand and achieve their operations strategy. Companies can either adjust their strategy to the forecasts or adjust the forecasts to suit their strategy. At the strategic level, firms use the forecasts to decide on the acquisitions of new infrastructure, technology, expertise, or skills.

Tactical Forecasts

Apart from planning for months ahead, companies have to plan their day-to-day operations. Tactical forecasts help companies to make decisions on meeting demands for a brief period of time—daily or weekly or even for a few weeks. Tactical forecasts are used to make decisions on the scheduled weekly production, the replenishment of inventory, and other adjustments in the daily operations. At the tactical level, firms use forecasts to align their available resources to meet customer demands.

> **Tactical forecasts**
> Tactical forecasts are used to align available resources and make decisions to meet customer demands on a daily or weekly basis.

FROM PRACTICE: Strategic and Tactical Forecasting at IKEA

IKEA, the Swedish company that designs and sells ready-to-assemble furniture, kitchen appliances, and home accessories, has been the world's largest furniture retailer since 2008. IKEA is well known for its contemporary and eco-friendly designs, new product innovation, and efficient operations. IKEA operates over 375 stores in 30 countries with about 12,000 products. The demand planning process at IKEA consists of two sub-processes including the sales frame planning, which takes a long-term and top-down perspective, and the tactical forecasting process, which takes a short-term and bottom-up perspective. The sales frame planning using the strategic forecast is performed on a 5-year rolling horizon based on aggregate sales volumes and is updated three times per year. The tactical forecasting is done weekly on an 84-week rolling horizon based on the selling volumes at the store level, that is, the stock-keeping unit (SKU) level. A **stock-keeping unit** (SKU) is a scannable bar code, often seen printed on product labels in a retail store, that allows vendors to automatically track inventory[8].

© Fishman64/Shutterstock.com

Forecasting Methods

Forecasting is complex in nature and to carry out forecasting, many techniques or methods have been developed and are available for use. Each of these methods has its own exclusive use and a manager should be careful in choosing the right method. The selection of a method depends on many factors including the context of the forecast, the availability of historical data, the relevance of available data, the desired degree of accuracy, the time period of forecast, the life-cycle stage of a product, and the cost of forecasting. Managers often select a method using trade-offs between those selection factors. For example, a manger may choose a method for a high degree of accuracy that may cost more to obtain data than an economical one with a slightly lower accuracy. Traditionally there are four methods and currently we have a new method using Artificial Intelligence (AI). In this chapter, we will focus on the **time series analysis method** and briefly show how the **causal relationships method** works. The following are the five different methods used for forecasting demand including:

1. Qualitative method,
2. Simulation method,
3. Artificial intelligence method,
4. Time series analysis method, and
5. Causal relationships method.

Qualitative Method Qualitative methods are used when obtaining data is a problem or when there is a scarcity of data. For example, when a new product is introduced into a market, there is no historical data. Managers bring together unbiased and logical information on the market conditions as qualitative information. They use such qualitative information and demand estimates relying on pure human judgment. Market research, forecasts by experts, expected growth of comparable products in the market, personal insights and judgments, and facts about future scenarios are often used to forecast demand.

Simulation Method A simulation uses computer models to understand the different scenarios of forecasts. A computer model represents the key characteristics or behaviors of forecasting, for example, past demand, consumer choices, lead time of product, planned advertising or marketing efforts, and so on. A simulation model is used to show what might happen if a company takes certain actions. Using the simulation, a company can use forecasting methods to understand the impact of a sales promotion, the impact of competition, the impact of a newer product model, and so on. Simulated environments allow companies to also test innovative ideas before they make a business decision.

Artificial Intelligence Method Business Intelligence Analysis (BIA) can play a pivotal role to forecast demand based on the available data. Machine learning (ML) is a subset of artificial intelligence (AI). Machine learning can predict the future demands of a product. ML uses many different sets of rules in the calculations or the problem-solving operations to discover and learn patterns from the given data. The future demands are predicted using the trends and patterns found in that data.

Time Series Analysis Method

Time series analysis method is the focus of this chapter and this method is based on using the past *actual demand* data to predict the *future demand* or simply the *forecast*. What is in the actual demand data? For example, Home Depot sells garden materials and equipment to maintain the exterior of your house.

The garden materials are not in demand throughout the year in Chicago. Because of the four seasons in the Midwest United States, certain goods are sold only during certain parts of the year. For example, lawn mowers are not sold from November to March. The actual demand that reflects the sales data for an entire year contains the variation in sales due to the seasonal effects. Let us say further that a newly designed outdoor furniture was selling a lot during the past few months. That trend is also reflected in the same sales data.

Time series analysis takes into account all the data points taken over time. The sales data may contain an internal structure of factors, called the **components of demand**. A trend or a seasonal variation in sales are part of the components of demand. The use of time series analysis is to obtain an understanding of those components of demand in the actual demand data, fit a model using that data, and forecast future demand.

FROM PRACTICE: Artificial Intelligence at Starbucks

Firms that are data-driven perform better, have better predictions of demand, and are more profitable. Big data can be used to analyze all the transactions, to understand customer needs, and to plan resources to meet the demand. Big data technology uses artificial intelligence theories and methods.

Starbucks, the Seattle-based coffee company, uses a predictive analytics software to learn about their consumers. Starbucks uses predictive analytics on the data collected from customer loyalty cards, websites, and mobile apps to understand what coffee is consumed, where the coffee was bought, and when the coffee was bought. Using the predictive analytics, they obtain real insights into planning future demand for their beverages[9].

© Wachiwit/Shutterstock.com

Elements of Demand

Demand consists of two elements including a systemic element and a random element. A random element, like an earthquake or flooding, cannot be forecasted. A random element cannot be explained by historical demand patterns either.

A systemic element can be explained by the historical demand patterns and can be forecasted. The systematic element measures the expected value of demand and consists of a **baseline demand**, demand patterns, and variations. The baseline demand is the stationary part of an actual demand. If you have consumed one loaf of bread every week for the past 2 months, you can forecast that you will consume one loaf of bread next week. From your past demand of one loaf per week, you have decided to buy one loaf for the coming week. This is an example of a baseline demand. The baseline demand serves as the starting point against which all future demands can be measured. Let us take a deep look at the demand patterns and the variations.

Components of Demand Patterns and Variations in Forecasting

Let us see what components make up the patterns and the variations in the demand data. The demand patterns and variations can be broken down into four components including:

1. Trend,
2. Seasonal influence,
3. Cyclical influence, and
4. Random variations.

Trend   The trend shows how a demand for a product has changed over time. It is either the rate of growth or the decline in the demand for a given period. There are many types of trends. In Figure 2-1, the sales data that indicates the actual demand is shown as points and the solid line shows the trend line. A **linear trend** is the easiest to comprehend and analyze. If the trend continues, the future demand will grow at the same pace. An **exponential trend** suggests that the sales have been increasing at an increasing rate and if the trend continues, the future demand will increase at an increasing rate. An **S-curve** or the **Sigmoidal curve trend** shows that the sales were slowly growing up to

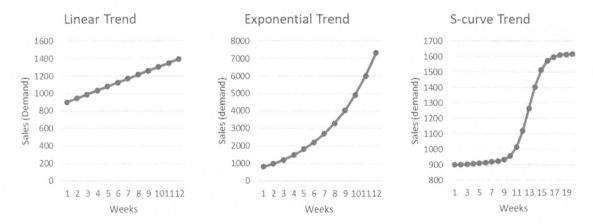

Figure 2-1 Common Types of Trend in Demand

a point and then rapidly increasing and then slowing down after a few weeks. A new product can have the S-curve trend. As this product gains traction in the market, the sales begin to grow. At first, the growth is slow, and then it develops more rapidly, as consumers begin to warm up to the product. The growth continues for some time. Eventually, due to various internal and external factors, the growth rate declines, and then gradually, the sales taper off. Internal supply chain problems or external competition can affect the sales growth. In this type of trend, the tapering or the inflection point is important. The future demand depends on how the company takes the right steps to resolve those internal and external factors to make the product sales grow again.

FROM PRACTICE: Trend analysis at Hershey

The Hershey Company, one of the largest chocolate manufacturers in the world from Hershey, Pennsylvania, manufactures chocolates, cookies, cakes, and milkshakes. The insights from the sales help Hershey to spot opportunities and understand how consumers feel about their products and purchase their products during various holidays. The company analyzes the information received from their retail sales to learn how different demographic groups are embracing the holiday seasons. For example, insights from the trend analysis have shown for years that baking around the winter holidays is a growing trend among younger consumers. On the arrival of winter, Hershey responds by showing photographs of how baked goods look in their packaging, merchandising, and advertising[10].

© Nikola Bilic/Shutterstock.com

Seasonal Influence A seasonal pattern occurs for a brief period of time, that is, on a daily or weekly basis and is repetitive. For example, lawn movers are used during spring, summer, and fall while not used in winter in many parts of the United States. Hence, there is a low demand for lawn mowers during winter. But detergents are used during the entire year and do not have such seasonality effects in their demand. Restaurants around office buildings are busier at lunch than at dinner time and there is more demand for theaters on weekends. The demand shows the seasonal fluctuations or variations or patterns. The seasonal influence in demand for products shows regular or systematic variation.

The automotive industry is influenced by seasonality with peak demands occurring in the spring and fall. The lowest auto sales are in January, February, and into the beginning of March. In the United States, car dealers often encounter problems selling inventory during the winter months as consumers are less motivated in the wintry weather to purchase a car. Also, tax refunds in spring combined with the nice weather encourage consumers to venture outdoors and purchase cars. To compensate for these adverse effects on car demand, many automakers bring out newer models and sales promotions to spark the interests of consumers and ignite sales.

FROM PRACTICE: Seasonal Influence at Hershey

Holidays like Halloween, Easter, and the winter holiday season drive roughly one-quarter of Hershey's business! But in order for the seasonal candy sales to deliver the growth for the company, their strategies support their business in a sustainable way. By applying data and trend-line information to their strategies in seasonal merchandising, packaging, and media buying, they help their retailers meet their needs year-round. For example, the knowledge of stronger sales of Reese's eggs and Cadbury eggs that sell in different geographic areas of the United States allows them to create stronger merchandising units. Since some seasons are longer than others, insights into consumer sentiment and demand allow them to place the right products on the shelves at the right time when shoppers actually want them. For example, consumers are sensitive about seeing winter-holiday items before Halloween but in the winter, they see the signal of spring when they see Easter eggs[10].

© Brent Hofacker/Shutterstock.com

Cyclical Influence Cyclical influence occurs over a longer period than the seasonal element but is harder to predict. One of the reasons for the shifts in the business cycle include the changes in the general economy. For example, during an economic expansion, consumer spending increases leading to a higher demand for certain goods such as cars. Car manufacturers respond by increasing production and hiring new staff. The other scenario is during economic contraction when car manufacturers might reduce the number of production shifts. Such cyclical influences on demand may occur during political elections or due to sociological pressures.

Random Variation Random variations exhibit no pattern. These are unusual variations or variations caused by an event that is unpredictable. For example, a local flood might cause a temporary increase in flooring materials demand, or an information security breech might lead the demand to drop for a period of time.

FROM PRACTICE: Cyclical Influence in Demand for Ford Motors

Ford Motor Company, the American multinational automaker, manufactures automobiles and commercial vehicles. Ford is the second-largest U.S.-based automaker behind General Motors and the fifth largest in the world behind Toyota, Volkswagen, Hyundai-Kia, and General Motors. The economy influences

© Art Konovalov/Shutterstock.com

The industry in a cyclic fashion as the economy goes through a business cycle that includes alternating periods of growth, decline, recession, and expansion. The operational planning of Ford Motors recognizes the impact of the business cycle on the spending habits of consumers and hence the demand. Consumer spending increases during growth and expansion and diminishes during downturns and recessions. So, Ford scales its operational plans to match the changing economic times. For example, during the 2008–2009 economic recession, Ford laid off employees and shut down unprofitable plants. They started manufacturing fewer pickup trucks and sport utility vehicles and increased the production of small-engine cars as a result of rising gas prices[11].

FROM PRACTICE: Random Variational Influence of Semiconductor Supply at Toyota

Toyota, the Japanese multinational automotive manufacturer, operates worldwide with more than 360,000 employees and is one of the ten largest companies in the world by revenue. Toyota is a global market leader in the sales of hybrid electric vehicles and a market leader in the hydrogen fuel-cell vehicles area. Toyota pioneered the just-in-time (JIT) manufacturing strategy.

© Toanorh/Shutterstock.com

One of the key components of cars is the computer chips. After the Fukushima disaster in 2011, Toyota experienced major disruptions in its supply chain. Since then, Toyota has decided to stockpile the computer chips as the lead time of computer chips was too long. Toyota also required their suppliers to stockpile anywhere from 2 to 6 months' worth of computer chips. This action by Toyota has served the company well during the global shortage of semiconductors during the pandemic of 2021. All automakers experienced semiconductor shortages except Toyota. Toyota surprised their rivals and the investors when it announced that its output would not be disrupted significantly by chip shortages even as Volkswagen, General Motors, Ford, and Honda have been forced to slow or suspend some production[12].

Time series analysis results in predicting the future demand based on past sales data. For example, in a **naïve approach**, if you have consumed one gallon of milk every week for the past 2 months, you can forecast that you will consume one gallon of milk next week. From your past or actual demand of one gallon of milk per week, you have decided to buy one gallon of milk for the coming week. We can use the naïve approach for forecasts if we do not anticipate any fluctuations in the actual demand.

But this is not the best way to forecast for businesses since fluctuations in the actual demand of their products happen all the time. Firms may decide to use the sales data of the past months to predict the future demand for the next month. Weekly, monthly, quarterly, and yearly data may be used to forecast the future demand. Now, that sales data, regardless of whether it is weekly, monthly, quarterly, or yearly, may contain one or two or three or all four components of demand that we just discussed. There are several forecast methods used in time series analysis. In this section, we will focus on how to forecast from the past data or actual demand. In particular, we will focus on the following methods:

1. Simple moving average,
2. Weighted moving average,
3. Simple exponential smoothing,
4. Exponential smoothing with trend adjustment, and
5. Linear regression analysis.

Firms use different methods for strategic or tactical forecasting. Different methods are used for different forecast time periods as well. The future demand is forecasted for one of the three time periods: short-term, medium-term, or long-term.

Short-Term Forecast Short-term forecasts include the immediate future and are concerned with daily demand requirements. A short-term forecast rarely extends beyond 2 or 3 months into the future. This is used to make short-term decisions such as replenishing inventory.

Medium-Term Forecast Medium-term forecasts involve anywhere from 1 or 2 months to 1 year. A medium-term forecast is useful to develop a strategy for securing additional resources for the upcoming year.

Long-Term Forecast Long-term forecasts are implemented for a period longer than 1 year. Long-term forecasts help firms to plan new products, build new facilities, or secure long-term financing.

In some firms, a medium-term forecast could be a couple of years, while in some other firms a long-term forecast could be in terms of quarters. Table 2-1 shows when to select the most appropriate forecasting method using time series analysis. In general, forecasting becomes more difficult with greater loss in accuracy as firms attempt to forecast further into the future.

Table 2-1 Selection of Forecasting Method

| Method | Accuracy | | | When to Use |
	Short-term	Medium-term	Long-term	
Simple Moving Average	Can be used for poor to good forecast	Should not be used as it results in poor forecast	Should not be used as it results in very poor forecast	Used when demand has no observable trend or seasonality but just the baseline
Weighted Moving Average	Can be used for poor to fair forecast	Should not be used as it results in poor forecast	Should not be used as it results in very poor forecast	Used when demand has no observable trend or seasonality but just the baseline
Simple Exponential Smoothing	Can be used for fair to good forecast	Can be used for poor to good forecast	Should not be used as it results in very poor forecast	Used when demand has no observable trend or seasonality but just the baseline
Exponential Smoothing with Trend Adjustment	Can be used for fair to good forecast	Can be used for poor to good forecast	Should not be used as it results in very poor forecast	Used when demand has baseline and observable trend but no seasonality
Time Series Decomposition	Can be used for fair to very good forecast	Can be used for good to very good forecast	Can be used for good to very good forecast	Used when demand has baseline, trend, and seasonality

Moving Averages

When the actual demand does not have any observable trend or seasonality influences, a moving average method is useful in removing random fluctuations in the actual demand to forecast future demand. By calculating the moving average, the impacts of random or extraordinary fluctuations on the actual demand over a specified time period are reduced. The reason for calculating the moving average is to help smooth out the actual demand data over a specified period of time by creating a constantly updated average actual demand.

When calculating moving averages, we will find the average actual demand over the most recent time period. Each time a new forecast is made, the oldest period demand is eliminated and the demand for the newest period is included. For example, if we want to forecast for Thursday using a moving average of three days, we will use the average of Monday, Tuesday, and Wednesday actual demand data. If we want to forecast for Friday using a three-day moving average, we will discard the Monday actual demand data and include the Thursday actual demand data. In this case, we used a 3-day moving average, that is, we used the actual demand data of past 3 days and hence, the time period was 3.

The shorter the time period, the more sensitive the forecast will be to changes in actual demands. The longer the time period, the less sensitive the forecast will be to demand changes but the forecast response will be a lot smoother. There is no one correct time period to select when calculating moving averages. The best way to figure out which time period works the best is to experiment with a number of different time periods until you find the one that fits your strategy. In this section, we will consider two moving averages methods including a simple moving average method and a weighted moving average method.

Simple Moving Average

The simple moving average to forecast for a time period is calculated using the following formula:

$$F_t = \frac{A_{t-1} + A_{t-2} + A_{t-3} + \ldots A_{t-n}}{n}$$ Eq.2-1

where,

F_t = Future demand for time period t

A_{t-1} = Actual demand for the period $t–1$, A_{t-2} = Actual demand for the time period $t–2$, etc.

n = number of time periods considered

Weighted Moving Average

The simple moving average method places equal importance on all actual demand. Sometimes, managers and forecasters might feel that the actual demand for a particular time period was or the actual demands for a few time periods were more important. In this case, we can place a weight on the actual demand for those important time periods. However, the total of all weights must be equal to 1. The weighted moving average to forecast for a time period is calculated using the following formula:

$$F_t = w_{t-1}A_{t-1} + w_{t-2}A_{t-2} + w_{t-3}A_{t-3} + \ldots w_{t-n}A_{t-n}$$ Eq.2-2

where,

F_t = Future demand for time period t

A_{t-1} = Actual demand for the period $t–1$, A_{t-2} = Actual demand for the time period $t-2$, etc.

w_{t-1} = weight of actual demand for the period $t-1$, w_{t-2} = weight of actual demand for the period $t–2$, etc.

$w_{t-1} + w_{t-2} + \ldots + w_{t-n} = 1$

n = number of time periods considered

Usually, the most recent demands, that is, the actual demands of the most recent periods, are more important. As we vary the effects of the past data, the weighted moving average method tends to be more accurate than the simple moving average method. In any case, more data leads to better accuracy.

How to choose weights? An experience with the past actual demand data plays a pivotal role in the selection of weights. Higher weighting is usually placed on the most recent time period but it depends on the company's demand forecasting analyst. Demand forecasting analysts must have experience to allocate weights for the time periods of actual demand. The experience of an analyst combined with experimented trial-and-error methods is the best way to choose weights.

Example 2-1

Forecast the future demand for the 13th week using 3-week, 6-week, and 9-week simple moving averages of the data (in units) provided by Chitown Computer Repair, LLC.

Weeks	Past Actual Demand (units)	Simple Moving Averages		
		3-week	6-week	9-week
1	900			
2	945			
3	990			
4	1,020	945		
5	940	985		
6	1,125	983		
7	1,170	1,028	987	
8	1,000	1,078	1,032	
9	1,100	1,098	1,041	
10	1,005	1,090	1,059	1,021
11	1,020	1,035	1,057	1,033
12	1,300	1,042	1,070	1,041
13		**1,108**	**1,099**	**1,076**

To calculate the 3-week moving average demand forecast for the 13th week, use Eq. 2-1:

$$F_{13} = \frac{1300 + 1020 + 1005}{3} = 1108 \text{ units}$$

To calculate the 6-week moving average demand forecast for the 13th week, use Eq. 2-1:

$$F_{13} = \frac{1300 + 1020 + 1005 + 1100 + 1000 + 1170}{6} = 1099 \text{ units}$$

To calculate the 9-week moving average demand forecast for the 13th week, use Eq. 2-1:

$$F_{13} = \frac{1300 + 1020 + 1005 + 1100 + 1000 + 1170 + 1125 + 940 + 1020}{9} = 1076 \text{ units}$$

Analysis: To find the 3-week moving average for the 4th week, simply use the past three weeks' data: 900, 945, and 990 and find their average value. A rising moving average indicates that the demand is on an upward trend, while a declining moving average indicates a downward trend. The longer-term moving averages are considered to be more reliable trend indicators. However, we cannot say that one moving average is more accurate than the other.

Example 2-2

Chitown Computer Repair, LLC., finds out that during the past 3 weeks sales were significant. The forecasting manager places the importance of sales as weights. She allocates 50% weight on the 11th week sales; 30% weight on the 10th week sales; and 20% weight on the 12th week sales. What is the 13th week sales forecast in this case?

Using the data from Example 2-1, we can see that,

$A_{t-1} = 1300$; $A_{t-2} = 1020$; $A_{t-3} = 1005$.

We are also given the weights as designated in Eq 2-2 as:

$w_1 = 0.20$; $w_2 = 0.50$; $w_3 = 0.30$

Using Eq. 2-2, we get,

$$F_{13} = (0.20 \times 1300) + (0.50 \times 1020) + (0.3 \times 1005) = 1072 \text{ units}$$

Analysis: Compare this to the answer from Example 2-1. We got a forecasted demand of 1,108 units using the simple 3-week moving average and 1,072 units using the weighted moving average. Since the forecaster at Chitown Computer Repair had some knowledge about the past demand data and used weights to represent that knowledge, the forecasted demand of 1,072 units using the weighted moving average is more accurate than the simple moving average for the same period.

Exponential Smoothing

Smoothing is a common statistical process and we use smoothed data in our day-to-day lives. For example, let us consider the winter days in any Midwest U.S. city. If we take the daily temperature highs and lows during the winter months, there are days when the temperature highs and lows are lower than the next day or greater than the next day. This kind of "jumping around" of temperatures makes it difficult to compare two winters. If we remove the "jumping around" of temperatures, we can easily compare two or more winters in that city. This removal of the "jumping around" of temperatures is called smoothing. One of the easiest ways to smooth out the "jumping around" of temperature data is to find the average of highs and lows. This is exactly what we did when we used the moving averages methods.

In demand forecasting, we can use smoothing to remove the random variation from the actual demand. Smoothing helps us to see better patterns. For example, we detect the trends in time series analysis when we smooth demand data. What we are doing by smoothing is to smooth out the irregular roughness in the data to see a clearer view of the data.

Exponential smoothing methods are often used to forecast instead of the weighted moving average method. Forecasts using exponential smoothing methods are weighted averages of the actual demands but with the weights decaying exponentially as the time periods get older. This means that the more recent the time period, the higher the associated weight. This method generates reliable forecasts and for a wide range of time series, which is a great advantage and of major importance to forecasting in the industry. The method is also simple to use but the results are accurate. We will discuss exponential smoothing in two different methods:

1. Simple exponential smoothing, and
2. Exponential smoothing with trend correction.

Simple Exponential Smoothing

The simple exponential smoothing method is used when actual demand has no observable trend or seasonality. Here, we use a **baseline smoothing constant** α (alpha), to accomplish the exponential smoothing in forecasting. The smoothing constant α represents the weight applied to the demand of the most recent time period.

The smoothing constant determines the level at which the actual demands influence the forecast. The value of the smoothing constant used for forecasting is between 0 and 1. Smaller values of α are recommended when there is a lot of "jumping around" of actual demands while larger values of α are recommended where there is very little "jumping around" of actual demands. The simple exponential smoothing to forecast for a time period is calculated using the following formula:

$$F_t = F_{t-1} + \alpha(A_{t-1} - F_{t-1}) \qquad \text{Eq.2-3}$$

where,

α = Baseline smoothing constant
F_t = Exponentially smoothed forecast or future demand for period t
F_{t-1} = Exponentially smoothed forecast for the period $t–1$, i.e., the past period
A_{t-1} = Actual demand for the period $t–1$, i.e., the past period

Example 2-3

Chitown Computer Repair, LLC., decides to use simple exponential smoothing instead. What is the 13th week sales forecast in this case if the forecaster decides to use a smoothing constant of 0.2 and assumes that the demand and the forecast are the same for the 11th week?

To find the forecast for the 13th week using the simple exponential smoothing method, we need three period's data, the smoothing constant, the exponentially smoothed forecast for the 12th week, and the actual demand for the 12th week.

We have the assumed a value of 1020 units for both demand and forecast for the 11th week. We need to find the exponentially smoothed forecast for the 12th week first. Using Eq. 2-3, we get the exponentially smoothed forecast for the 12th week as:

$$F_{12} = F_{11} + \alpha(A_{11} - F_{t11}) = 1020 + 0.2(1020 - 1020) = 1020 \text{ units}$$

Now we can find the exponentially smoothed forecast for the 13th week:

$$F_{13} = F_{12} + \alpha(A_{12} - F_{t12}) = 1020 + 0.2(1300 - 1020) = 1076 \text{ units}$$

Analysis: Compare this to the answers from Examples 2-1 and 2-2. We got a forecasted demand of 1,108 units using the simple 3-week moving average and 1,072 units using the weighted moving average. We have 1,076 units using the simple exponential smoothing method. Since the forecaster at Chitown Computer Repair, LLC. had some knowledge about the past demand data and used the smoothing constant to represent that knowledge, the forecasted demand of 1,076 is even more accurate.

Linear regression

Linear regression uses historical or past data to project future demand by assuming that the relationship is linear, that is, falls on a straight line. This is the kind of relationship that is shown as a linear trend in Figure 2-1 between the actual demands and time periods. Linear regression is used in long-term forecasts. In this book, we will use this technique in trend-adjusted exponential smoothing and static linear regression methods. This technique is also used both in time series and causal relationships methods.

The linear regression line is a straight line of the form **Y = a + bX** where Y is the dependent variable that we are planning to solve, X is the independent variable, a is the Y intercept, and b is the slope of the straight line. In our case, we will find **a** and **b** using the Y, the demand data and X, the time periods. Linear regression is easily implemented using Microsoft Excel as shown in Example 2-4.

Exponential Smoothing With Trend Adjustment

The trend-adjusted exponential smoothing method, also known as the Holt's model, can be used when a trend is observed in the time series but does not have the seasonal influences. If the simple exponential method is used on data where there is an observable trend, the forecast will lag the trend. Lagging the trend means, for example, if actual demand data is increasing for a number of time periods, then the forecasted demand will be too low and if actual demand data is decreasing for a number of time periods, then the forecasted demand will be too high. Therefore, if there is an observable trend in the actual demand data, then an exponential smoothing with trend adjustment must be used. Therefore, in order to adjust the trend, we use another smoothing constant β (Beta) known as the **trend smoothing constant** along with the baseline smoothing constant α (alpha) that was introduced for simple exponential smoothing.

The forecast of the initial time period F_i in a series of demand data consists of two parts, the initial baseline estimate B_i and the initial trend pattern estimate T_i.

Therefore,

$$F_i = B_i + T_i \qquad \text{Eq.2-4}$$

To find F_i, we will assume a linear trend as shown in Figure 2-1 and use a linear regression method with actual demand data. We can then use the B_i and T_i to forecast with trend-adjusted exponential smoothing. As long as we have the actual demand data falling on a straight line, we can comfortably use a method called linear regression for forecasting. In this case, since we have a trend in the demand data and since we do not have any seasonal influences, the relationship between the demand and the time period is linear.

When we deal with the trend-adjusted exponential smoothing method, we will use regression. The initial baseline estimate B_i will equal to **a** and the initial trend estimate T_i will equal to **b** in the linear equation $Y = a + bX$. We can use the B_i and T_i that we found using the linear regression method as B_{t-1} and T_{t-1} respectively for a time period $t-1$ if we do not have the baseline and trend estimates for the time period $t-1$. We can then use Bi and Ti to calculate the initial time period forecast F_i using Eq. 2-4.

The exponentially smoothed forecast F_t, the baseline estimate B_t, and the trend estimate T_t can be calculated using the following formulae:

$$B_t = \alpha A_{t-1} + (1-\alpha)(B_{t-1} + T_{t-1}) \qquad \text{Eq.2-5}$$

$$T_t = \beta(B_t - B_{t-1}) + (1-\beta)(T_{t-1}) \qquad \text{Eq.2-6}$$

$$F_t = B_t + T_t \qquad \text{Eq.2-7}$$

where,

α = Baseline smoothing constant

β = Trend smoothing constant

A_{t-1} = Actual demand for the period $t-1$, i.e., the past period

B_{t-1} = Baseline estimate of demand for the period $t-1$, i.e., the past period

T_{t-1} = Trend estimate of demand for the period $t-1$, i.e., the past period

B_t = Baseline estimate of demand for the period t

T_t = Trend estimate of demand for the period t

F_t = Exponentially smoothed forecast or future demand for period t

Example 2-4

Using the demand data series for Chitown Computer Repair, LLC, as shown in Example 2-1, find the exponential smoothing forecast with trend adjustment for the 13th week assuming $\alpha = 0.1$ and $\beta = 0.2$.

Step 1:   Using linear regression, find the initial baseline estimate and initial trend estimate from all the known past periods. The data that we will use for this example are:

Weeks	1	2	3	4	5	6	7	8	9	10	11	12
Actual Demand (units)	900	945	990	1,020	940	1,125	1,170	1,000	1,100	1,005	1,020	1,300

In Microsoft Excel, click on the regression tool. The regression tool can be found in the tab Data > Data Analysis > Regression as shown below:

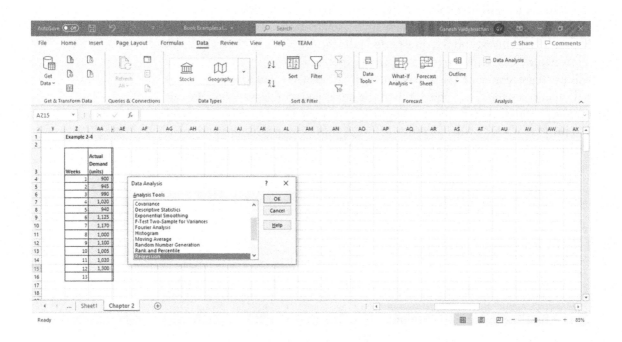

Click ok and select data for both x- range (weekly data) and y-range (actual demand data) for the given 12 weeks. Then, the following window will pop up:

Now, click OK and the result of the linear regression is shown as below:

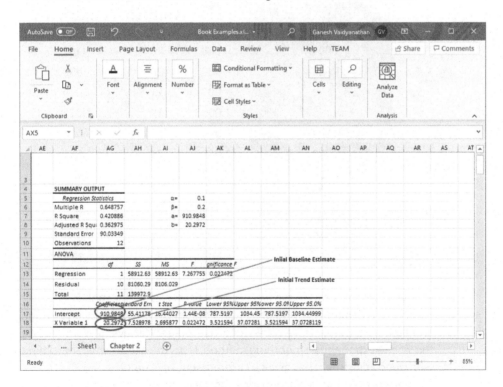

The intercept coefficient 'a' is the initial baseline estimate B_i and the x-variable coefficient 'b' is the slope or the initial trend estimate T_i.

Step 2:   Using the actual demand for a current time period, calculate the trend-adjusted exponential smoothing forecast for the next time period using Eq. 2-5, Eq. 2-6, and Eq. 2-7.

In this case, B_i and T_i are used for the first or initial period.

For Week 1, Baseline estimate $= B_1 = B_i = 960.98$ and Trend estimate $= T_1 = T_i = 20.29$.

Using Eq. 2-7, we get the forecast for week 1 as $910.98 + 20.29 = 931$ units.
Using Eq. 2-5, we get $B_2 = (0.1 \times 900) + ((1 - 0.1) \times (910.98 + 20.29)) = 928$ and
Using Eq. 2-6, we get $T_2 = (0.2 \times (928 - 910.98)) + ((1 - 0.2) \times 20.29) = 20$
Using Eq. 2-5, we get the forecast for week 2 as $928 + 20 = 948$ units.
Continuing similar calculations, we get 1,174 units for week 13.

Therefore, the trend-adjusted exponential smoothing forecast for the 13th week is 1,174 units.

Note: We used Excel to calculate these numbers and these will be different than your hand-held calculator due to round-off errors.

Weeks	Actual Demand (units)	Baseline	Trend	Forecast (Units)
1	900	911	20	931
2	945	928	20	948
3	990	948	20	967
4	1,020	969	20	990
5	940	993	21	1,013
6	1,125	1,006	19	1,025
7	1,170	1,035	21	1,056
8	1,000	1,068	23	1,091
9	1,100	1,082	22	1,104
10	1,005	1,103	22	1,125
11	1,020	1,113	19	1,132
12	1,300	1,121	17	1,138
13		1,154	20	**1,174**

Analysis: Compare this to the answer from Examples 2-1 through 2-3. We got a forecasted demand of 1,108 units using the simple 3-week moving average and 1,072 units using the weighted moving average. We have 1,076 units using the simple exponential smoothing method. Now, the exponential smoothing with trend adjustment has given us a forecast of 1,174 units.

The regression analysis provides the best forecast among all methods that we have discussed so far. Regression analysis gives a detailed look at the data and exploits how one variable affects another. The regression line represents the relationship between the dependent variable and the independent variable.

Time Series Decomposition

Remember that the time series data consisting of the past actual demands usually includes all the components of the demand patterns and the variations including the trend, the seasonal influence, the cyclical influence, and the random variations. Of the four components, we will consider only the **trend** and the seasonal influences called **seasonality** in this book.

When the past actual demand data shows an observable trend and seasonality, we must identify the trend and seasonality, and separate the time series data into the trend and the seasonality components. This process is called **decomposition**. It is easy to identify the trend that is observable in a demand data series if we plot the data. However, we will use the linear regression method that we used in the past section to estimate and show the trend. Once we know the trend, it is then possible to identify the seasonal influence. To calculate the forecast including trend and seasonality, we need to calculate three variables:

1. FT, the forecast that includes the trend,
2. SF, the seasonality factor, and
3. SR, the seasonality ratio.

$$Forecast\ including\ trend\ and\ seasonality = FT \times SF \qquad \text{Eq.2-8}$$

and,

$$SR = \frac{Actual\ Demand\ for\ the\ period}{FT\ for\ the\ period} \qquad \text{Eq.2-9}$$

Since we are assuming that the trend is of linear form, to decompose the demand data we will take the following steps:

Step 1: Perform a linear regression analysis on the actual demand data to establish the trend equation.

Step 2: Use the trend line to calculate FT, the forecast that includes the trend.

Step 3: Calculate the seasonality ratio (SR) from the past demand data.

Step 4: Calculate SF, the seasonality factor using the seasonality ratio.

Step 5: Forecast with the seasonality factor and trend using Eq. 2-8.

Example 2-5 shows how to forecast demands that include trend and seasonality.

Example 2-5

Using the demand data series for ABEXA, Inc. given below, find the forecast that includes the trend and the seasonal influence for Year 3.

Year	Year 1 Qtr 1	Year 1 Qtr 2	Year 1 Qtr 3	Year 1 Qtr 4	Year 2 Qtr 1	Year 2 Qtr 2	Year 2 Qtr 3	Year 2 Qtr 4
Actual Demand (units)	900	945	990	1,080	940	980	1,100	1,300

Let us plot the above data first to see the trend line:

ACTUAL DEMAND (UNITS)

The linear trend can be seen on the above graph as a straight line. The seasonal effects during the last quarter of each year can also be seen and we can derive the seasonal factor from the actual demand as follows.

Step 1: Perform a linear regression to establish the trend equation.

Using Y as the demand and X as the time period, we can run the linear regression in Excel as we did for Example 2-4 to get the trend equation: $Y = 863.04 + 32.8X$.

Step 2: Use the trend line to calculate the forecast that includes the trend.

For each period, calculate the forecast including trend. For example, for Period 1, forecast including trend = $863.04 + (32.8 \times 1) = 895.83$ where $X = 1$

Note: We used Excel to calculate these numbers and will be different than your hand-held calculator due to round-off errors.

Step 3: Calculate the seasonality ratio.

> For each period, calculate the seasonality ratio. For example, for Period 1, seasonality ratio is actual demand divided by forecast including trend = 900/895.04 = 1.00

Step 4: Calculate the seasonality factor using the seasonality ratio.

> For each period, calculate the seasonality factor. Seasonality factor is obtained by taking the average of the seasonality ratios of the same periods (in this case, same quarters). For the 1st week, we will take the average of seasonality ratios of Year 1 Qtr 1 and Year 2 Qtr 1 which is equal to 0.96. The seasonality factor for the Yr 1 Qtr 2 and Year 2 Qtr 2 will be equal to 0.95 and so on. Notice that the seasonality factor will be the same for all 1st quarters and the same for all 2nd quarters, and so on.

Step 5: Forecast using the seasonality factor and trend using Eq. 2-8.

> Now, we can calculate the forecast with trend and seasonality for all quarters of Year 3 by multiplying the seasonality factor by the forecast including trend of the same time period. For example, the forecast with trend and seasonality for 1st Qtr of Yr 3 (period = 9) is: forecast including trend for 1st Qtr of Yr 3 × seasonality factor of 1st Qtr Yr 3 = 1158.21 × 0.96 = 1112 units.

Year	Quarter	Period X	Actual Demand (units) Y	Forecast including Trend FT	Seasonality Ratio SR	Seasonality Factor SI	Forecast including Trend and Seasonality
Yr 1	1	1	900	895.83	1.00	0.96	
Yr 1	2	2	945	928.63	1.02	0.95	
Yr 1	3	3	990	961.43	1.03	0.97	
Yr 1	4	4	1,080	994.23	1.09	1.12	
Yr 2	1	5	940	1027.02	0.92	0.96	
Yr 2	2	6	930	1059.82	0.88	0.95	
Yr 2	3	7	1,000	1092.62	0.92	0.97	
Yr 2	4	8	1,300	1125.42	1.16	1.12	
Yr 3	1	9		1158.21		0.96	**1,112**
Yr 3	2	10		1191.01		0.95	**1,129**
Yr 3	3	11		1223.81		0.97	**1,190**
Yr 3	4	12		1256.61		1.12	**1,408**

> **Analysis:** Since we are using the regression analysis, the forecast is as accurate as possible. The seasonality factor of quarter 4 is more than 1 and therefore, the forecast including the seasonality for that quarter is more than the forecast due to trend. Since the trend line is positively upwards, the forecast for Year 3 is higher than the actual demands of Year 2.

When we discuss the trend and the seasonality and their relationships to the future demand or the forecast, we need to understand a concept called auto-correlation.

Autocorrelation Correlation is a measure of the strength of a linear relationship between two variables. For many students, the more hours they spend on studying, the higher their scores in exams. That is an example of a strong positive correlation. In some cases, the more the late submission of assignments, the less the grades for those students. That is an example of a negative correlation. Just like correlation that measures the linear relationship between the demand and the time periods, autocorrelation measures the linear relationship between lagged values of a time series. Autocorrelation refers to the degree of correlation of the actual demands between two successive time periods. In many cases, the value of a demand at a time period is related to the demand at a previous time period. When regression is performed on time series data, often errors are autocorrelated; that is, each error is correlated with the error immediately before it. Positive autocorrelation of the errors tends to make the estimate of the error variance too small. Negative autocorrelation of the errors tends to make the estimate of the error variance too large. Where there is a high degree of autocorrelation there is a strong relationship between the current and the future demand.

Causal Relationships Method

A causal relationship exists when one variable in a data set has a direct influence on another variable. Time series models assume that the future demand is only related to patterns of its own past demand, for example, patterns of demand in past time periods. Causal relationship methods assume that factors other than the patterns of demand in past time periods can affect the future demand. Causal techniques, such as linear regression methods, usually take into consideration all factors such as surveys, macroeconomics indicators, product features, social chatter, and so on, that can impact the dependent variable. For example, the demand forsnow blowers in Chicago can be related to the snowfall over the past few years. Example 2-6 shows how to forecast two causal relationship factors using the linear regression model.

Example 2-6

Sicard, Inc. makes snow blowers and isconsidering ramping up their sales promotions in Chicago for the year 2022. Their forecasting manager is looking at the past sales data. What does the demand forecasting of sales data for 2022 indicate if the *Farmers' Almanac* predicted a light winter for the year 2022 equal to 34.1 inches?

One factor that has a causal relationship to snow blower sales is the amount of snowfall. The weather website, https://www.weather.gov/, shows the snowfall for the past 100 years. The data is available on the student book website. Using the data, we can find the causal relationship between snowfall and demand of snow blowers. The given data can be plotted as shown below:

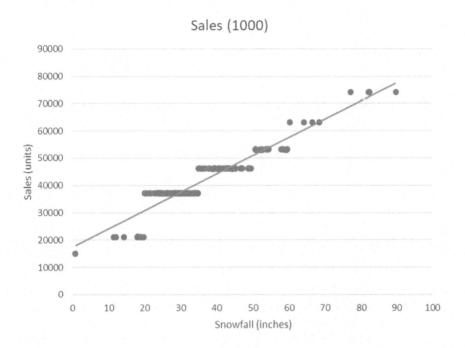

Sales (1000)

We can see that there is a linear relationship between snowfall and sales from the past 100 years. Using the linear regression model that we discussed in Example 2-4, we see that the linear regression model equation is:

Demand for 2022 = 17473.95 + (667.43 × snowfall for 2022), If snowfall for 2002 equals 34.1, then the demand for 2022 can be forecasted to be 40,233 units using the above equation.

> **Analysis:** The demand for 2022 is less than the past year and the company should consider this prediction when planning for production and sales promotions.

Forecast Accuracy

Forecasts are not perfect. There are errors in most forecasts and in this section, we will discuss those errors and how to estimate the errors. Forecast errors are the difference between the actual demand and the forecast or the future demand. There are two types of errors including *Bias errors* and *Random errors*.

Random Error Random error is due to random variations or noise and cannot be explained by the forecast model being used. For example, a normal person's body temperature may vary every time a measurement is made using a thermometer. This is a random error and can be because of the variations in normal processes in the body or the way that the thermometer works.

Bias Error or Systematic Error corresponds to inaccuracy. Errors occur due to a variety of reasons. One source of error is due to the linear regression line that we have been using to forecast demand. If we used a trend line that closely relates to the variations in demand rather than a linear trend, then the error can be reduced but then the analysis gets more complicated. The other sources of errors are from the selection of the variables and using the wrong seasonal data points. For example, the thermometer measurements may have a systematic error because it may be defective and it always indicates either a higher or lower temperature.

Forecast Error Measurement

Forecast error can be measured as root mean squared error (RMSE), standard error estimate (SEE), mean absolute percent error (MAPE), and mean absolute deviation (MAD) with tracking signal (TS). Let us discuss these terms and see how to calculate these different errors.

Root Mean Squared Error RMSE is defined as the standard deviation of the prediction errors. Prediction errors, also called residuals, are a measure of how far the data points are or how spread out these residuals are from the regression line. The lower the RSME, the better the fit of the regression model.

Also called Standard Deviation of Residuals, Example 2-7 shows how to calculate RMSE. RMSE is calculated using the following formula:

$$RSME = \sqrt{\frac{\sum_{t=1}^{n}(A_t - F_t)^2}{n-1}} \qquad \text{Eq.2-10}$$

where,

A_t = Actual demand for the period t

F_t = Forecasted future demand for period t

n = Number of time periods and $n-1$ is used here to represent the sample standard deviation.

Standard Error Estimate SEE, also called standard error, is another error that is calculated to include the degrees of freedom. In linear regression, two parameters including mean and slope are computed. The residual error is created by using these two parameters and therefore, it has two degrees of freedom. Hence, n–2 degrees of freedom used in the calculation of variation. The square root of the variation gives the deviation. The difference between the forecasted demand and the actual demand is called a residual. Example 2-7 shows how to calculate SEE. SEE is calculated using the following formula:

$$SEE = \sqrt{\frac{\sum_{t=1}^{n}(A_t - F_t)^2}{n-2}} \qquad \text{Eq.2-11}$$

Example 2-7

For the data shown in Example 2-4, find the Root Mean Squared Error and Standard Error Estimate.

Step 1: Do a regression of the actual demand "Y", and time period "X" to find the intercept "a" and slope "b" for the linear regression line equation in the form of $Y = a + bX$.

  As we got in Example 2-4, the linear regression equation is: $Y = 910.98 + 20.3\,X$

Step 2: Find the forecasted demand using the linear regression function.
  For example, for the Period 1, $F_t = 910.28 + (20.3 \times 1) = 931$ units

Step 3: Calculate the Forecast Error which is the actual demand minus the forecasted demand for each period
  For Period 1, Forecast Error $= A_t - F_t = 900 - 921 = -31$

Step 4: Calculate the Forecast Error Squared which is the square of the actual demand minus the forecasted demand for each period.
  For Period 1, Forecast Error Squared $= (A_t - F_t)^2 = (931 - 900)^2 = (-31)^2 = 979$

Step 5: Calculate RSME using Eq. 2-10.

  Using the forecast error squared for all 12 periods,

$$RSME = \sqrt{\frac{\sum_{t=1}^{12}\left(A_t - F_t\right)^2}{12 - 1}} = 85.84$$

Step 6: Calculate SEE using Eq. 2-11.

$$SEE = \sqrt{\frac{\sum_{t=1}^{12}\left(A_t - F_t\right)^2}{12 - 2}} = 90.03$$

Analysis: RSME tells us how spread out the residuals are from the regression line. You can see from the regression result that the standard error is 90.03. We can calculate MAPE by taking the sum of absolute values of the actual demand deviation changes of all time periods and dividing the result by n, the number of time periods. We use $n-1$ in calculating RSME since we are using a sample of demand data, that is, for a few weeks in Example 2-5. If we use the entire demand data, or the entire population, in our analysis, we can use n instead of $n-1$ in Eq. 2-10.

Mean Absolute Percent Error MAPE is derived as a percentage of the deviation of actual and forecasted demands. The absolute value of the percentage deviation is summed for every forecasted point in time and divided by the time periods as shown below:

$$MAPE = \frac{100}{n}\sum_{t=1}^{n}\left|\frac{A_t - F_t}{A_t}\right| \qquad\qquad \text{Eq.2-12}$$

Mean Absolute Deviation With Tracking Signal MAD is the average of the deviations of forecast from actual demand for a time period. MAD shows how "spread out" the forecast values are from the actual demand in a data set. MAD is different than standard deviation. While the standard deviation is the square of the difference between actual and forecast, MAD is just the absolute difference as shown below:

$$MAD = \frac{\sum_{t=1}^{n}|A_t - F_t|}{n}$$ Eq.2-13

Tracking Signal   Tracking signal is a measure used to evaluate the forecast errors. It warns if there are unexpected changes in demands from the forecasts or if there is a persistent tendency for actual demands to be higher or lower in a systematic fashion. If the forecast is consistently lower than the actual demand, then the tracking signal will be positive. Example 2-8 shows how to calculate MAD and TS. TS is calculated using the following formula:

$$TS = \frac{\sum(A_t - F_t)}{MAD} = \frac{CFE}{MAD}$$ Eq.2-14

where,
    CFE = Cumulative Forecast Error equal to $\sum(A_t - F_t)$
    MAD = Mean Absolute Deviation

Example 2-8

As shown in the following table, consider the actual demands and the forecasts for computers for 12 weeks at a local store. What is the MAD and the TS?

Weeks	Actual Demand (units)	Forecast (Units)	Forecast Error (Actual-Forecast)	Absolute Forecast Error	Absolute Cumulative Forecast Error	MAD	Cumulative Forecast Error (RSFE)	Tracking Signal (TS)
1	900	910	−10	10	10	10	−10	−1.00
2	945	910	35	35	45	23	25	1.11
3	990	910	80	80	125	42	105	2.52
4	1,020	910	110	110	235	59	215	3.66
5	940	1,000	−60	60	295	59	155	2.63
6	1,125	1,000	125	125	420	70	280	4.00
7	1,170	1,000	170	170	590	84	450	5.34
8	1,000	1,000	0	0	590	74	450	6.10
9	1,100	1,100	0	0	590	66	450	6.86
10	1,005	1,100	−95	95	685	69	355	5.18
11	1,020	1,100	−80	80	765	70	275	3.95
12	1,300	1,100	200	200	965	80	475	5.91
					Overall MAD =	**80.42**	Overall TS =	**5.91**

Step 1: Calculate the Forecast Error which is the actual demand minus the forecasted demand for all periods.

For Period 1, Forecast Error $= A_t - F_t = 900 - 910 = -10$

Step 2: Calculate the absolute forecast error for all periods. This is the absolute value of the forecast error.

For Period 1, Absolute Forecast Error $= |A_t - F_t| = |-10| = 10$

Step 3: Calculate the Absolute cumulative forecast error for all periods. This is the absolute forecast error for that period plus the absolute forecast error the past period.

For Period 1: Absolute cumulative forecast error $= 10 + 0 = 10$, Since there was no period 0, we use 0

For Period 2: Absolute cumulative forecast error $= 35 + 10 = 45$

Step 4: Calculate MAD for each period using Eq. 2-13. It is equal to the absolute cumulative forecast error for that period divided by that period.

For Period 1: $10/1 = 10$

For Period 2: $45/2 = 23$

Step 5: Calculate overall MAD. The overall MAD is calculated using Eq. 2-13, which is the sum of the absolute forecast error for all periods divided by the number of periods.

$$\text{Overall MAD} = \frac{\sum_{t=1}^{12} |A_t - F_t|}{12} = 80.42$$

Step 6: Calculate the cumulative forecast error for each period. This is the forecast error for that period plus the forecast error the past period.

For Period 1: $-10 + 0 = -10$, Since there was no period 0, we use 0.

For Period 2: $35 + (-10) = 25$

Step 7: Calculate TS for each period using Eq. 2-14. It is equal to the Cumulative Forecast Error divided by MAD for that period.

For Period 1: $-10/10 = -1$

Step 8: Calculate overall TS. The overall TS is calculated using Eq. 2-14, which is the cumulative forecast error for all periods divided by overall MAD.

$$\text{Overall TS} = \frac{\sum (A_t - F_t)}{MAD} = \frac{475}{80.42} = 5.91$$

Analysis: MAD shows how "spread out" the forecast values are from the actual demand in a data set. If forecast is consistently lower than the actual demand, then the tracking signal will be positive. In our data set, we can see that the forecast is almost always lower than the actual demand and hence the positive tracking signals.

A positive tracking signal indicates that the demand is higher than the forecast and a negative tracking signal shows that the demand is lower than the forecast. As a general rule of thumb, TS equal to 3.75 is an approximation to check the value of TS using the relationship between a normally distributed forecast error and the MAD. If TS > 3.75 there is persistent under forecasting. On the other hand, if this is less than −3.75 then, there is persistent over forecasting. As long as the tracking signal is between −3.75 and +3.75, we can assume that the forecast model is working correctly.

In our case with a TS of 5.91 in Example 2-7, we see that the forecast model underestimated actual demands and we need to reconsider our forecasting model as our forecasting model is not working well. Suppose in Example 2-8, if we had forecasted 1,350 units—a correction overestimating the demand, instead of 1,100 units for the 12th time period, we would have a TS of 3.31, meaning our forecast model is working correctly.

Differences in Forecast Error Methods

Let us compare the different error calculation methods that we have discussed so far. In the last section, we discussed four methods including the root mean squared error (RMSE), the standard error estimate (SEE), the mean absolute percent error (MAPE), and the mean absolute deviation (MAD) with tracking signal (TS). All these can be employed to see whether the forecasting methods are working well or not. Table 2-2 shows the main differences between these different error calculation methods.

Table 2-2 Error Calculations Methods

Error Calculation Methods	Differences
Root Mean Square Error (RMSE)	Easy to use;
	It is always positive, and a lower value indicates better forecast model;
	If the data has outliers and should not be ignored this is a better option;
	Disadvantages include it does account for positive or negative value.
Standard Error Estimate (SEE)	The measure of variability with respect to the regression line;
	Smaller values are better because it indicates that the observations are closer to the fitted line;
	Easy to obtain from Excel's regression analysis output.
	When the sample is large, the standard error of estimate is acceptable.
Mean Absolute Percent Error (MAPE)	The smaller the MAPE the better the forecast;
	Quite simple to calculate;
	Used since many managers understand percentages well;
	Drawbacks include placing a heavier penalty on negative errors than on positive errors[13] and producing infinite or undefined values for zero or close-to-zero actual values[14].
Mean Absolute Deviation (MAD) with Tracking Signal (TS).	Good to use with Tracking Signal;
	Is less biased for higher forecast errors;
	Does not necessarily penalize large errors;
	If the data has outliers and should be ignored this is a better option;
	Used to check whether the forecast model is working correctly or not.

FROM PRACTICE: P&G Distancing From Forecasting

For Procter & Gamble, the business strategy to meet their customer demands has shifted toward the consumer-driven supply network (CDSN). P&G uses the term supply network instead of supply chain as the information flows in many directions, not just along a chain of suppliers and customers.

© Simon Kadula/Shutterstock.com

The strategy is to use the real demand, not what is forecasted, so that the company can concentrate on producing what is actually selling in the market. CDSN focuses on the data from their customers like Walmart and when P&G's products are purchased by consumers. P&G uses the scanner data at the point of sale (POS) for their daily production schedule.

Keith Harrison, the global product supply officer for P&G said that they are running some of their plants on a six- to eight-hour response time based on the aggregated sales data. The company is using the demand data in their replenishment plan for certain products with a few large retail customers. Harrison added that they aggregated the data from the systems such as handling ordering, shipping, and billing into usable numbers to become the demand field for the plant systems. That demand field drives the replenishment plans, which are displayed in P&G's supplier portal where they find their way back into suppliers' systems. The company has some suppliers who can see their production plan, and those suppliers run their operations with that live data within a few hours.

Harrison pointed out that ultimately P&G would like to have all of its 140 plants in 80 countries and many of its 100,000 suppliers work off of real data, not forecasts[14]. However, that is a long way!

Formulae from this Chapter

Simple Moving Average	$F_t = \dfrac{A_{t-1} + A_{t-2} + A_{t-3} + \ldots A_{t-n}}{n}$	Eq. 2-1
Weighted Moving Average	$F_t = w_{t-1}A_{t-1} + w_{t-2}A_{t-2} + w_{t-3}A_{t-3} + \ldots w_{t-n}A_{t-n}$	Eq. 2-2
Simple Exponential Smoothing	$F_t = F_{t-1} + \alpha\left(A_{t-1} - F_{t-1}\right)$	Eq. 2-3
Exponential Smoothing with Trend Adjustment	$F_i = B_i + T_i$	Eq. 2-4
	$B_t = \alpha A_{t-1} + \left(1 - \alpha\right)\left(B_{t-1} + T_{t-1}\right)$	Eq. 2-5
	$T_t = \beta(B_t - B_{t-1}) + \left(1 - \beta\right)\left(T_{t-1}\right)$	Eq. 2-6
	$F_t = B_t + T_t$	Eq. 2-7
Time Series Decomposition	*Forecast including trend and seasonal influence* $= FT \times SF$	Eq. 2-8

(continued)

Seasonality Ratio	$SR = \dfrac{Actual\,Demand\,for\,the\,period}{Forecast\,including\,Trend\,for\,the\,Period}$	Eq. 2-9
Root Mean Squared Error	$RSME = \sqrt{\dfrac{\sum_{t=1}^{n}\left(A_t - F_t\right)^2}{n-1}}$	Eq. 2-10
Standard Error Estimate	$SEE = \sqrt{\dfrac{\sum_{t=1}^{n}\left(A_t - F_t\right)^2}{n-2}}$	Eq. 2-11
Mean Absolute Percent Error	$MAPE = \dfrac{100}{n}\sum_{t=1}^{n}\left|\dfrac{A_t - F_t}{A_t}\right|$	Eq. 2-12
Mean Absolute Deviation	$MAD = \dfrac{\sum_{t=1}^{n}\left|A_t - F_t\right|}{n}$	Eq. 2-13
Tracking Signal	$TS = \dfrac{\sum\left(A_t - F_t\right)}{MAD} = \dfrac{CFE}{MAD}$	Eq. 2-14

Case Study: Demand Forecasting at Hemmer Shelves, Inc.

Hemmer Shelves was founded by Henry Hemmer, a second-generation crafts-man in 1994. Hemmer focused his attention on the Northwest Indiana area operating from Goshen, Indiana and his business flourished. Hemmer's prod-uct showroom is open to retail shop owners and the general public. His show-

pieces demonstrated skilled woodwork. The showroom was well lit, enhancing his intricate work and displaying elegance and a bright lifestyle. The company had a broad selection of shelving ideas and many great choices for all types of customers. The retail store was well stocked with all associated fixtures and fasteners. Hemmer offered an excellent selection of shelving supplies at the best possible prices.

Hemmer Shelves manufactures a variety of shelves including fixed, adjustable, corner, floating, and pull-out shelves. Hemmer makes fixed shelves of the same material as the structural components of the closet. Their ninety-degree angle, curved corner cut, angular corner cut, rotat-ing shelf, adjustable shelves attach to the closet panels or supports. The pull-out shelf made by Hemmer is installed using side mount drawer slides so that the shelves slide like a drawer. Hemmer's floating shelves show off a contemporary look.

© Ground Picture/ Shutterstock.com

At the outset, the home improvement industry had been facing various challenges over the past few years. Shortage of labor and subcontracting costs had increased the cost of home improvement projects[15].

While the overall home improvement industry enjoyed year-round sales, certain projects were seasonal. Spring was the best time for improvement projects such as deck, pool, HVAC upgrades, and gutter repairs. Summer was really good for projects such as furnace repair and fireplace repair. Fall usually is best suited for winterizing projects, caulking, weather stripping, and installation of doors and windows. That time of the year is also great for outdoor painting, lawn care, and exterior house projects. Late winter projects include indoor painting, kitchen and bathroom remodeling because of availability of subcontractors.

Hemmer has noticed that winter, spring, and late fall—January, February, March, April, September, October, November, December—have been the best time for sales of shelving. To begin with, home organization has gained a lot of traction, especially during the COVID-19 lockdown in 2020. An interesting statistic is that in 2021, the home organizing industry was approximately $11.4 billion and it is expected to grow over the next few years[16]. Moreover, storage strategies and especially pullout shelves have been at the forefront of trends for 2022 and beyond[17]. According to Revenue the Persistence Market Research Report[18], retail shelving is predicted to have a year-over-year growth of 8.1%.

With the seasonal and trend of shelving in his outlook, Henry wanted to forecast the demands for the next year. Henry uses the lowest of the averages as the actual demand for the periods in the future. He wanted to try all available options at his disposal to forecast the demand. His historical forecasted data for the past 3 years are shown below:

2019											
Jan	Feb	Mar	Apr	May	Jun	Jul	Aug	Sep	Oct	Nov	Dec
1400	1300	1400	1500	1400	1200	1100	1150	1250	1420	1400	1420

2020											
Jan	Feb	Mar	Apr	May	Jun	Jul	Aug	Sep	Oct	Nov	Dec
1480	1420	1560	1580	1500	1430	1410	1405	1470	1500	1520	1480

2021											
Jan	Feb	Mar	Apr	May	Jun	Jul	Aug	Sep	Oct	Nov	Dec
1530	1520	1575	1620	1540	1520	1470	1475	1520	1580	1590	1570

Hemmer's historical actual demand is given in the following table:

Actual Demand											
2019											
Jan	Feb	Mar	Apr	May	Jun	Jul	Aug	Sep	Oct	Nov	Dec
1380	1320	1420	1510	1410	1180	1080	1130	1300	1430	1430	1425
2020											
Jan	Feb	Mar	Apr	May	Jun	Jul	Aug	Sep	Oct	Nov	Dec
1510	1500	1590	1520	1420	1390	1350	1400	1480	1510	1530	1490
2021											
Jan	Feb	Mar	Apr	May	Jun	Jul	Aug	Sep	Oct	Nov	Dec
1560	1510	1580	1640	1550	1530	1490	1480	1530	1600	1620	1610

Case Questions

A. Forecast the demand for shelves for all months of 2022 using a 3-month moving average method.
B. Forecast the demand for shelves for all months of 2022 using a 6-month moving average method.
C. Forecast the demand for shelves for all months of 2022 using a 9-month moving average method.
D. Henry feels that the weights for any recent 3 months can be estimated as 45%, 30%, 25%. Calculate the weighted moving average for all months of 2022.
E. What will be the forecast for all months of 2022 if Henry applies a smoothing constant of 0.2?
F. Calculate MAD for the 2021 and 2022 forecasts.
G. Plot the data and explain whether there is a trend or not.
H. Is there a possibility of seasonal influence by looking at the plot?
I. Forecast including trend and seasonal influence for all the months of next year.
J. What is the change in forecast including trend and seasonal influence over forecast with just trend?
K. Which quarter in 2022 shows the maximum seasonal influence in forecast?

Summary

- Demand is the quantity of a good and/or a service that consumers are willing to purchase during a period of time.
- Firms make focused efforts to estimate, plan, and manage consumer demand for their goods and services. They want to make sure that the right amount of demand is as accurate as possible.

- Forecasts of future demand in OSCM are important to offer goods and services.
- The two types are strategic forecasts and tactical forecasts. Strategic forecasts are used to establish the strategy of how a company will meet the demand of consumers in the next 6 months or next year. Tactical forecasts help companies to make decisions on meeting for a relatively short period of time—daily or weekly or even for a few months.
- There are five different methods used for forecasting demand including qualitative method, simulation method, artificial intelligence method, time series analysis method, and causal relationships method.
- Demand consists of two elements including a systemic element and a random element.
- Systematic element measures the expected value of demand and consists of a baseline demand and various demand patterns and variations in forecasting.
- Components that make up the patterns and variations in demand data include trend, seasonal influence, cyclical influence, and random variations.
- Time series analysis method is the focus of this chapter and this method is based on using past actual demand data to predict future demand.
- Time series analysis results in predicting future demand based on past sales data.
- Several forecast methods are used in time series analysis including simple moving average, weighted moving average, simple exponential smoothing, exponential smoothing with trend adjustment, and linear regression analysis.
- Simple moving average is a forecast method based on averaging past actual demands.
- Weighted moving average is a forecast method using weighted averages of past actual demands.
- Simple exponential smoothing is a forecast method that uses a smoothing constant α to represent the weight applied to the most recent time period's demand.
- Exponential smoothing with trend adjustment is a linear regression forecast method that uses a smoothing constant α to represent the weight applied to the most recent time period's demand and another smoothing constant β to adjust the trend.
- Time series decomposition is the process of separating time series data into its components such as trend and seasonal influence that can be used to calculate a forecast that includes trend and seasonal influences.
- Causal relationship methods assume that factors other than the patterns of demand in past time periods can affect demand forecast.

- Forecast errors are the difference between actual demand and the forecasted demand. There are two types of errors including bias errors and random errors.
- Forecast error can be measured as root mean squared error (RMSE), standard error estimate (SEE), mean absolute percent error (MAPE), and mean absolute deviation (MAD) with tracking signal (TS).
- Root Mean Squared Error (RMSE) is defined as the standard deviation of the prediction errors.
- Standard Error Estimate (SEE), also called standard error, is an error that is calculated to include the degrees of freedom.
- Mean Absolute Percent Error (MAPE) is derived as a percentage of the deviation of actual and forecasted demands.
- Mean Absolute Deviation (MAD) is the average of the deviations of forecast from actual demand for a time period.
- Tracking signal (TS) is a measure used to evaluate the forecast errors.

Review Questions

1. What is demand? How do companies use past demand for their goods and services?
2. Why do companies spend a lot of time, money, and effort to understand their past actual demands for their goods and services?
3. What is forecasting?
4. Is forecasting easy to accomplish?
5. How is forecasting important for a manufacturing company?
6. How is forecasting important for a service company?
7. How does forecasting help functions of a company?
8. What is strategic forecasting?
9. What is tactical forecasting?
10. What are the five different forecasting methods discussed in this chapter?
11. What is time series method?
12. What is baseline demand?
13. What are the components of demand patterns and variations in forecasting?
14. What is trend in forecasting?
15. What is seasonal influence in forecasting?
16. What method can you use if demand data has no trend or seasonality influences?
17. What is exponential smoothing with trend adjustment?
18. What is autocorrelation?
19. What is forecast accuracy?
20. Define bias error.
21. Define all the errors that are discussed in this chapter.

Critical Thinking Questions

1. What is the difference between strategic forecasting and tactical forecasting? Discuss with appropriate examples.
2. Explain the main differences among the five forecasting methods discussed in this chapter.
3. Why is the time series analysis method used more frequently than the other four methods discussed in this chapter?
4. What is the basic difference between trend and baseline estimates in forecasting?
5. What is the basic difference between trend and seasonal influence n forecasting?
6. Why is linear trend easier to use in forecasting than exponential or S-curve trend?
7. What is the main difference between simple and weighted moving averages?
8. When do you use the causal relationship method?
9. What is the difference between bias error and random error?
10. What are the differences between RMSE and SEE?
11. Would you use MAD without TS? Why? Why not?

Problem Solving and Critical Thinking Questions

1. Picaso Stores in Palatine, IL sells various art supplies. Their sales of aluminum panels, which are used for mounting fine art and photographs, for 2021 are shown below:

Month	Jan	Feb	Mar	Apr	May	Jun	Jul	Aug	Sep	Oct	Nov	Dec
Demand	250	275	320	312	340	260	400	420	380	375	290	220

   a. Forecast the demand for aluminum panels for Jan 2021 using a 3-month moving average method.
   b. Forecast the demand for aluminum panels for Jan 2021 using a 6-month moving average method.
   c. Forecast the demand for aluminum panels for Jan 2021 using a 9-month moving average method.
2. Using the data available from Picaso Stores, forecast the demand for aluminum panels for the 1st Quarter of 2022 using a three-quarter moving average method.

3. Fred Focaster, the Chief Planner at Flowcast, Inc., has the following demand data from the past.

Month	Jan	Feb	Mar	Apr	May	Jun	Jul	Aug	Sep	Oct	Nov	Dec
Demand	2500	2750	3200	3120	3400	2600	4000	4200	3800	3750	3000	3600

    a. If Fred decides that the most recent month of that data was more important than its past month by 60%, what is the forecast of next month?

    b. If Fred changes his mind and weighs the recent three months as 45%, 30%, 25%, what is the forecast for the next month?

4. Thayut Thaibhojanwat started a nice Thai restaurant recently. His count on number of customers is given below:

Day	1	2	3	4	5	6	7	8	9	10
Customer	12	9	10	12	8	14	15	17	18	20

    a. How many customers can Thayut expect on the 11th day of his new restaurant if he decides to forecast using a 3-day, 5-day, and 9-day moving average?

    b. What would be his best forecast if he placed ads in the local newspaper only on the 7th day?

5. Yachtsman, Inc. manufactures yachts in the Lake Placid area. Their actual sales for 2021 is tabulated below.

Month	Jan	Feb	Mar	Apr	May	Jun	Jul	Aug	Sep	Oct	Nov	Dec
Actual	2345	2856	2759	2978	2899	2940	2931	2999	3028	2765	3190	3178

If the forecast for January 2021 was 2200 yachts,

    a. Calculate forecasts for February through December of that year as well as the forecast for January 2022 assuming a 0.25 smoothing constant.

    b. Calculate MAD for the 2021 forecasts.

6. If the actual demand for August 2021 is 3,000 units and the forecast for September 2021 is 4,000 units and assuming a smoothing constant of 0.25, what is the forecasted value for August 2021?

7. Seko, Inc. sells spare parts for small engines. Their past demands are as follows:

Months	Jan	Feb	Mar	Apr	May	Jun	Jul	Aug	Sep	Oct	Nov
Actual Demand	2465	2976	2879	3098	3019	3060	3051	3119	3148	2885	3310

    a. What is the forecast for December using α of 0.3 and β of 0.25?

    b. What are the December month's baseline and trend estimates?

    c. What is the percentage change in December's forecast from its past month?

8. The actual demand for June is 48,540 units and the forecast for June is 42,500 units that consists of a 6% trend with no seasonal influence. If α is 0.2 and β is 0.3, what is the forecast for July?

9. Kim Kray, the forecaster at Krayon, Inc., wants a simple way to forecast the demand for Crayons. He has data of actual demand in cases of Crayons sold for the past years from his marketing department.

Year	2012	2013	2014	2015	2016	2017	2018	2019
Demand	2465	2976	2879	3098	3019	3060	3051	3119

    a. His weightage for the last three years of demand starting at 2019 are 50%, 30%, and 20%. Calculate the weighted moving average and a 3-year simple moving average for 2019.

    b. Using the best forecast from the above question, what will be the forecast for 2010 if Kim applies a smoothing constant of 0.2?

10. Kim Kray from the past question realizes that there might be some trend in the demand data and he wants to adjust forecast for the trend in his forecast with a trend smoothing constant of 0.3.

    a. What is his forecast after adjusting the trend for 2010?

    b. How does this new forecast help Krayon, Inc.?

11. Dhal Star, Inc., an ethnic store in Chicago, sells lentils in kilograms. Their actual sales for some of the months in 2021 are shown below:

Month	Apr '21	May '21	Jun '21	Jul '21	Aug '21	Sep '21	Oct '21	Nov '21	Dec '21
Actual	7147.20	6957.60	7056.00	7034.40	7197.60	7267.20	6636.00	7656.00	7627.20

    a. Using linear regression, find the trend line.

    b. Using the linear trend line, find the forecasts for all the months in 2021.

    c. What is the forecast of lentil sales for January 2022?

    d. What is the standard error estimate for the months in 2021? Explain what this error represents in the forecast.

    e. Plot the actual and forecast of sales of lentils for the entire period showing the trend line with appropriate chart title and axis titles.

12. Trackstar Industries, manufacturer of tractor parts, has the following data.

Month	Jan	Feb	Mar	Apr	May	Jun	Jul	Aug	Sep	Oct	Nov	Dec
Actual	810	851	891	918	846	1013	1053	900	990	905	918	1170
Forecast	910	910	910	910	1000	1000	1000	1000	1100	1100	1100	1100

    a. What is the forecast error for each month?

    b. Which month shows the maximum forecast error? Plot using appropriate data to show the maximum forecast error.

    c. Which month shows the maximum change in forecast error?

13. Trackstar Industries, manufacturer of tractor parts, has the following data.

Month	Jan	Feb	Mar	Apr	May	Jun	Jul	Aug	Sep	Oct	Nov	Dec
Actual	810	851	891	918	846	1013	1053	900	990	905	918	1170
Forecast	910	910	910	910	1000	1000	1000	1000	1100	1100	1100	1100

a. Is the forecast model working correctly? Explain your answer.
b. Did the forecast model work correctly at any time? Explain your answer.

14. Tommy Talbot predicted the following data with the actual demands using a sophisticated forecasting method. Is the method he used giving him acceptable answers? Show your analysis using an appropriate graph.

Month	Jan	Feb	Mar	Apr	May	Jun
Actual	265	275	340	430	350	420
Forecast	250	325	400	350	375	450

15. Rex Reynolds of Rexford Rehearsals asked his forecaster to check the seasonal influence of certain dress items that they make in Rexford, Rhode Island. His forecaster Ray Redmond got the following data from their IT department.

Year	2018 Q1	2018 Q2	2018 Q3	2018 Q4	2019 Q1	2019 Q2	2019 Q3	2019 Q4	2020 Q1	2020 Q2	2020 Q3	2020 Q4
Actual Demand	4800	3500	4300	3000	3500	2700	3500	2400	3200	2100	2700	1700

a. Forecast including trend and seasonal influence for all quarters of 2021.
b. Plot to show actual demand, trend line, and seasonal forecast.

16. Pamery Properties LLC owns almost 120,000 apartments around Chicago and its suburbs. The apartments are rented throughout the year. Pat Pamery, the sole proprietor of the LLC is looking at his past rental demand as shown below and trying to forecast for the next year.

Year	2019 Q1	2019 Q2	2019 Q3	2019 Q4	2020 Q1	2020 Q2	2020 Q3	2020 Q4
Actual Demand	2000	2250	2300	2350	2400	2450	2500	2550

a. Plot the data and explain whether there is a trend or not.
b. Is there a possibility of seasonal influence by looking at the plot?
c. Depending upon your answer for the past question, forecast including trend and/or seasonal influence.

17. Red's Repairs, a local company in the city of Detroit, repairs and overhauls garden and farm equipment. Their repairs and overhauls for the past two years are shown below:

Year	2018 Q1	2018 Q2	2018 Q3	2018 Q4	2019 Q1	2019 Q2	2019 Q3	2019 Q4
Actual Demand	4800	3500	3670	3700	4970	3700	3600	3700

Red Buttons, the owner, wants to know the forecast for repairs and overhauls equipment for the next year.

a. Forecast including trend and seasonal influence for all the quarters of next year.
b. What is the change in forecast including trend and seasonal influence over forecast with just trend?
c. Which quarter shows the maximum seasonal influence in forecast?

18. Consider the following demand data from Bob's Bicycles Company.

Month	Jan	Feb	Mar	Apr	May	Jun
Actual Demand	2650	2750	3400	4300	3500	4200
Forecast	2500	3250	4000	3500	3750	4500

a. Calculate RMSE, SEE, MAPE, MAD, and TS.
b. Explain how Bob's Bicycles owner can interpret each one of those errors.
c. Which one of these errors can the owner of Bob's Bicycles use with confidence?

19. Ray Rainer, the owner of Rainstop Industries who makes umbrellas, has the following data for the past years. He knows that there is a causal relationship between average rainfall and the sale of umbrellas.

Year	2000	2001	2002	2003	2004	2005	2006	2007	2008	2009	2010
Sales (1000)	53127	53163	46051	37097	37104	37116	37142	37089	37157	46060	46135

Year	2011	2012	2013	2014	2015	2016	2017	2018	2019	2020
Sales (1000)	53155	46112	46119	21123	46127	46180	21172	37087	53157	37130

He was advised to use 34" of rainfall for 2022.

a. Visit https://www.statista.com/statistics/504400/volume-of-precipitation-in-the-us/ to get average precipitation in the United States and using that data, forecast the sales of umbrellas in the United States for 2022. The data file is also available on the student and instructor website.
b. What is the standard error estimate of the forecast? How should Ray interpret the error?
c. Plot the demand for umbrellas versus year.

References

1. Banker, S. (2019, November 5). Procter & Gamble embraces continuous planning and execution. *Forbes*. Retrieved July 5, 2021, from https://www.forbes.com/sites/stevebanker/2019/11/05/procter--gamble-embraces-continuous-planning-and-execution/?sh=51479f283ed1

2. Martin. J. (2021). *What Is Vendor Managed Inventory?* Retrieved July 5, 2021, from https://quickbooks.intuit.com/global/resources/inventory-mgmt/what-is-vendor-managed-inventory/

3. Gartner (2010). *P&G Supply Chain Ranked Among the Top Five "Supply Chain Masters."* Retrieved July 5, 2021, from https://us.pg.com/blogs/pg-supply-chain-ranked-among-supply-chain-masters-by-gartner/

4. Barnett, W. (1988, July). Four steps to forecast total market demand. *Harvard Business Review*. Retrieved July 5, 2021, from https://hbr.org/1988/07/four-steps-to-forecast-total-market-demand

5. Taylor, D. P. (2020). *7 Reasons Supply and Demand Matters to Your Business*. Retrieved July 10, 2021, from https://www.fool.com/the-blueprint/supply-and-demand-business/; Tao, R. (2014). *Inventory Management Stockouts-Case Studies*. Retrieved July 19, 2021, from https://www.tradegecko.com/blog/inventory-management/out-of-stock-problems-and-solutions-walmart-nike-bestbuy-case-studies.

6. Starostinetskaya, A. (2021). *Starbucks Is Facing an Oatly Shortage "Due to High Demand."* Retrieved July 6, 2021, from https://vegnews.com/2021/4/starbucks-oatly-shortage

7. Chopra, S., & Meindl, P. (2004). *Supply chain management: Strategy, planning, and operation*. Prentice Hall.

8. Jonsson, P., Rudberg, M., & Holmberg, S. (2013), Centralised supply chain planning at IKEA, *Supply Chain Management: An International Journal, 18*(3), 337–350.

9. Wilson, E. (2018). *How Starbucks Uses Predictive Analytics and Your Loyalty Card*. Retrieved July 11, 2021, from https://demand-planning.com/2018/05/29/how-starbucks-uses-predictive-analytics-and-your-loyalty-card-data/

10. Hershey (2000). *The Insighter: In Candy, Seasonal Momentum Helps Retailers Win All Year*. Retrieved July 15.2021, from https://www.thehersheycompany.com/en_us/blog/in-candy-seasonal-momentum-helps-retailers-win-all-year.html

11. Cole-Ingait, P. (217). *Factors That Influence Ford Motors Operational Planning*. Retrieved July 15, 2021, from https://bizfluent.com/info-7757855-factors-ford-motors-operational-planning.html.

12. Reuters. (2021). *Why Toyota Had a Big Pile of Chips When Semiconductor Shortage Dealt Others a Bad Hand*. Retrieved July 16, 2021, from https://www.autoblog.com/2021/03/09/toyota-how-it-avoided-semiconductor-shortage/.

13. Makridakis, S. (1993). Accuracy measures: Theoretical and practical concerns. *International Journal of Forecasting, 9*(4), 527–529; Kim, S., & Kim, H. (2016). A new metric of absolute percentage error for intermittent demand forecasts. *International Journal of Forecasting 32*(3), 669–679.

14. SuplyChainBrain. (2006). *Procter & Gamble Uses Consumer Demand Info to Drive Supply Network*. Retrieved July 31, 2021, from https://www.supplychainbrain.com/articles/575-procter-gamble-uses-consumer-demand-info-to-drive-supply-network

15. Douglas-Gabriel, D. (2018, March 28). Planning your home improvement projects by the seasons. *The Washington Post*.

16. Peysakhovich, R. (2022). 51 home organizing industry statistics & trends for 2022. *Onedesk*. Retrieved June 23, 2022, from https://www.getonedesk.com/home-organizing-statistics.

17. Parker, M. (2022). *40 Home Design Trends That Will Shape 2022*. Retrieved June 23, 2022, from https://www.houzz.com/magazine/40-home-design-trends-that-will-shape-2022-stsetivw-vs-144187632

18. Persistence Market Research. (2022). Retail Shelving System Market. Retrieved June 23, 2022, from https://www.persistencemarketresearch.com/market-research/retail-shelving-system-market.asp#:~:text=Newly%20released%20retail%20shelving%20system,8.1%25%20to%2010.5%20Mn%20units

CAPACITY AND DEMAND MANAGEMENT

Learning Objectives

- Define demand management.
- Define capacity.
- Compute design capacity and effective capacity.
- Calculate capacity utilization and capacity efficiency.
- Describe the capacity management strategy.
- Explain capacity planning.
- Estimate the capacity requirements.
- Evaluate the capacity alternatives to meet requirements.

To know whether they can meet the forecasted future demand, firms need to make sure they have the necessary capacity in their plants, warehouses, distributors, and sales channels. The output level of a company depends on the efficient use of its resources. Capacity is the maximum output level a company should maintain to produce its products or deliver its services. That is one of the reasons that companies plan their capacity management to ensure that they have adequate resources to maximize their potential production and sales operations.

Ford, the American multinational automobile manufacturer, was founded by Henry Ford in 1903. Ford manufactures a variety of commercial vehicles, performance vehicles, sport utility vehicles (SUVs), crossovers, trucks, vans, future electric vehicles under the Ford brand and luxury cars under its Lincoln brand. In 2021, Ford's revenue was $134.6 billion with 199,000 employees[1]. Headquartered in Dearborn, Michigan, Ford is the 2nd largest US-based automaker and the 5th largest in the world. Typically, a Ford car consists of over 7,000 separate parts bought from 2,400 suppliers. Ford sold roughly 539,000 cars during the fourth quarter of 2020[2]. Raw materials pass through six to ten suppliers before reaching Ford as parts for a manufacturing capacity of over 6 million cars and trucks per year.

To remain competitive, Ford wants the most cost-effective and efficient supply chain, the least inventory, and the maximum sale of its products. Moreover, the whole automotive business is globally interconnected and the operations managers must envision a global picture in whatever they do. For Ford, doors and hinges come from Canada, suspension stabilizer linkages are imported from Japan, sliding sunroofs are exported by Germany, and axle assemblies are supplied from Oregon[3].

Ford employs capacity planning concepts to decide on their total design capacity. In an interview, David G. Thomas, Director, Global Capacity Planning, Ford Motor Co., explained how Ford combined the data from entirely separate plants, suppliers, and customer bases for its global capacity management planning[4]. To be operationally successful, the supply chain activities and the resource planning have to be planned and managed very well. The demand side and the supply side must work together in an efficient fashion to manage the production planning. Ford's managers work with cross-functional groups to organize and manage capacity planning to support what the customers want.

Demand Management

If products are unavailable for customers due to being out of stock, firms will lose revenue as the customers will look for substitutes or go to other suppliers over time. On the other hand, if products are not selling and simply piled up as unused inventory, firms are wasting money. Therefore, the goal of demand management is to maintain sufficient inventory levels to meet the customer demands without having a surplus. Demand management involves forecasting the requirements of consumers. Using the forecast, firms can plan to meet the demand for the goods and services without major disruptions.

> **Demand management**
> Demand management is the process of predicting and planning to meet the demand for goods and services.

The main objective of demand management is to meet customer demand. The demand management process consists of the following activities:

- Forecasting the demand of consumers;
- Coordinating the forecasts with procurement, operations, and distribution capabilities;
- Collaborating with marketing for potential business opportunities;
- Executing contingency plans when there are interruptions to the operational plans; and
- Meeting unanticipated demands.

To meet consumer demands, companies must be prepared with a good operations and supply chain (OSCM) plan. The plan must take into account both the anticipated and the unanticipated demand. A customer changing the order to buy blue shirts instead of the red shirts they ordered in the first place is an example of an unanticipated demand. Companies rely on forecasting in order to be proactive to the demands of consumers. Forecasting will help firms to plan and be prepared to coordinate their operations activities efficiently and effectively. It gives them the ability to either partially or fully meet unanticipated demand. Firms may face unanticipated ebbs or upswings in demand due to unprecedented times and events.

Companies should have enough production capacity to meet both the anticipated and the unanticipated demands. Only then can businesses make sure they can produce enough products to meet the forecast or future demands. Let us discuss what capacity is and how capacity management can help firms to be reactive and flexible to meet future demands.

FROM PRACTICE: OSCM Strategy at Pfizer

The pharmaceutical industry operates in a highly competitive environment. The rising pressures on drug prices, patents expiring, generic drugs capturing the market, and the increasing regulatory demands are creating a challenge in operations and supply chain activities for pharmaceutical industries such as Pfizer. Pfizer is committed to high-quality, competitive pharmaceutical products. To rise to the challenge and its commitment, Pfizer has envisioned a framework to improve the performance of its supply network by aligning its supply operations with the volatility of market demand.

Pfizer worked with the Boston Consulting Group (BCG) to develop and implement a new OSCM strategy at its manufacturing site in Freiburg, Germany. The production strategy involved a highly flexible pull system leveraging different supply chain and inventory strategies for different Pfizer products based on their demand and volatility patterns. This approach was expected to reduce the inventory levels and meet the demand. Pfizer Freiburg produces more than 4.9 billion capsules and tablets and 190 million packs per year. Pfizer Freiburg received an industry first KAIZEN Continuity Award 5S Best in Class 2009 until 2011 from the KAIZEN Institute[5].

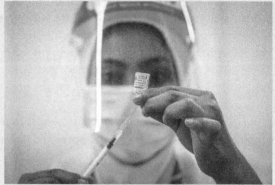

© Afif Abd. Halim/Shutterstock.com

Capacity

From the operations viewpoint, demand management is a process[6]. The process focuses on planning and managing capacity, and how to reduce the variability in demand by introducing flexibility. In this section, we will discuss capacity planning and management.

> **Capacity** Capacity is defined as the ability to produce the required output using available resources within a specific time period.

Capacity is defined as the ability to produce the required output of products using the available resources within a specific time period. Capacity is the maximum number of products that can be produced or the maximum number of services rendered in a period of time. For example, in a restaurant, capacity is the number of customers who can be accommodated during a particular time—for instance during lunch hours—using the available tables, chairs, operating staff, menu items, stored items, and so on. In an automobile manufacturing plant, capacity can be described as the number of vehicles manufactured or assembled in a day or a shift. The maximum room capacity determines which class can be held in a classroom.

For a firm, capacity means investments. The capacity involving a larger, complex technology costs more. Capacity also involves a long-term commitment of resources and cannot be increased or decreased without additional costs. For example, buying an over-capacity furnace in anticipation of a greater demand is great but if the increased demand does not happen, then the firm is stuck with the over-capacity furnace.

Capacity goes hand in hand with demand as the capacity of a firm is decided on the basis of a continuing demand for its products and services. But often the capacity is either in excess or less than the demand as the demand depends on the trend, the seasonal, the cyclical, or the random variations. Both excess capacity and under capacity poses a problem for firms. A lack of capacity or under capacity leads to a firm falling short of its customer demand, resulting in a loss of revenue. Excess capacity occurs when demand for a product is less than the amount of product that a business could potentially produce. Excess capacity is also caused by overinvestment in resources and external shocks such as natural disasters and financial crises. Excess capacity results in nonproductivity or inefficiency in using existing resources such as idle workers in a production plant or empty tables in a restaurant. However, on a positive note, excess capacity also means that a firm is ready for more production and to be competitive when the demand arises. The question is when does the demand increase? Often, it is tough to answer!

FROM PRACTICE: Excess Capacity in German Auto Industry

In the years 2020–2021, due to the Corona virus pandemic, international automotive industry sales plummeted by about 18% from 2019. The vehicle sales were down in all the major economies in the world. Many car companies had to decrease or even stop production.

The auto industry is the key sector of the German economy and it employs over 830,000 people. Professor Dr. Ferdinand Dudenhöffer of the University of Duisburg-Essen and the founder of Center Automotive Research stated that a structured reduction of excess capacity in Germany and Europe was essential and a boost in the demand for automobiles was warranted. The automotive industry proclaimed that the vehicle sales have almost completely come to a standstill. BMW and Volkswagen proposed "innovation bonuses" to boost car sales, especially for the purchase of low-emission vehicles[7].

Design Capacity

Design capacity Design capacity is the maximum output rate designed to produce with the available resources in a given period.

Design capacity is defined as the maximum output rate designed to produce with the available resources in a given period. It is the originally designed capacity to produce the maximum output under ideal conditions using resources such as labor, materials, power, and facilities. Design capacity can be calculated based on a single type of product or a mix of products. Operations managers take into account the time taken to produce products as an input and the design capacity as an output. For example, a car parts manufacturer can use 5,000 hours available in a month to make 2,000 Product A or a mix of 1,200 Product A and 1,000 Product B. The number of products, either the 2,000 Product A or the 3,200 Product A and Product B mix, is the design capacity.

Available machine time Available machine time is the total number of hours of all machines that are operated to produce products in a given timeframe.

The available machine time is the total number of hours of the machines that are operated to produce products in a given timeframe, for example in a day or a month or a quarter or a year. The available machine time in hours is calculated using the following formula:

$$Available\ machine\ time = No\ of\ machines \times No\ of\ hours \qquad \text{Eq. 3-1}$$

For a single product, design capacity of a product can be calculated using the following formula:

$$Design\ capacity = \frac{Available\ machine\ time}{Time\ taken\ to\ produce\ one\ unit} \qquad \text{Eq. 3-2}$$

Equation 3-2 can be rewritten as:

$$Available\ machine\ time = Design\ capacity \times \\ Time\ it\ takes\ to\ produce\ one\ unit \qquad \text{Eq. 3-3}$$

For a mix of products, design capacity can be calculated by solving for the number of variables equal to the number of products. For example, if the same machines in a factory can produce a maximum of two or more products, that is, Product A, Product B, . . . Product N, in a given time period,

$$Available\ machine\ time \\ = (Design\ capacity\ of\ A \times Time\ it\ takes\ to\ produce\ one\ unit\ of\ A) \\ + (Design\ capacity\ of\ B \times Time\ it\ takes\ to\ produce\ one\ unit\ of\ B) \\ + ... + (Design\ capacity\ of\ N \times Time\ it\ takes\ to\ produce \\ one\ unit\ of\ N) \qquad \text{Eq. 3-4}$$

Examples 3-1 and 3-2 show how to the calculate design capacity for a single product. Examples 3-3, 3-4, and 3-5 demonstrate how to the calculate design capacity for a mix of products.

Example 3-1

Pedal Fast, Inc. has 50 machines and the machines are used to manufacture bicycle wheels from 6 a.m. until 10 p.m. If it takes 30 minutes to make one bicycle wheel, what is the daily design capacity?

Using Eq. 3-1, Available machine time = 50 machines × 16 hours = 800 machine hours

It takes 30 minutes to make one bicycle wheel which is equivalent to 30/60 or 0.5 hours

Using Eq. 3-2, the daily design capacity is calculated as:

$$Design\ capacity\ of\ bicycle\ wheels = \frac{800}{0.5} = 1,600\ wheels$$

Analysis: The daily design capacity is 1,600 wheels. This is the maximum capacity of the bicycle manufacturing plant for a day with respect to machine time of 16 hours. To increase the capacity, the company can increase the available machine time, increase the number of machines, or decrease time taken to make one bicycle wheel.

Example 3-2

Pedal Fast, Inc. has 50 machines and the machines are used to manufacture bicycle wheels 16 hours a day. If it takes 30 minutes to make one bicycle wheel, what is the design capacity for a 25 working days per month?

Using Eq. 3-1, Available machine time = 50 machines × 16 hours × 25 = 20,000 machine hours

Using Eq. 3-2, design capacity for that month is calculated as:

$$Design\ capacity\ of\ bicycle\ wheels = \frac{20,000}{0.5} = 40,000\ wheels$$

Analysis: The monthly design capacity is 40,000 wheels. This is the maximum capacity of the bicycle manufacturing plant for a month with respect to machine time of 16 hours. To increase the capacity, the company can increase the available machine time, increase the number of working days, increase the number of machines, or decrease the time taken to make one bicycle wheel.

Solver

Microsoft's Excel's Solver is an add-in program that can be used for "what-if" analysis. Solver is typically used to find an optimal value. An optimal value may be either the maximum or the minimum value. For example, if you want to find the *maximum* number of chairs to buy around a table in your home, the optimal value may be 2 or 4 or 6 depending on the size of the table and the available space. The optimal value for a formula cell in an Excel cell, called the *objective cell*, can be subject to *constraints* or limits, on the values of other formula cells on a worksheet. Solver works with a group of cells, called *decision variable cells*, which are used in computing the formulas in the objective and the cells containing the constraints. Solver adjusts the values in the decision variable cells to satisfy the constraints on the constraint cells and shows the result in the objective cell. For example, you can maximize the profit or minimize the cost based on a set of constraints and an objective function.

To add solver to your Excel, you have to add Solver as an add-on software. Go to File > Options > Add-ins and choose Solver Add-in. In Microsoft Excel, Solver can be found in the tab Data.

Constraint
Constraint is a logical condition or real-world limit that must be satisfied when solving an optimization problem. Examples are limits on production capacity, market demand, available funds, and so on.

Example 3-3

Pedal Fast, Inc. has 50 machines and the machines are used to manufacture bicycle wheels and chainrings from 6 a.m. until 10 p.m. If it takes 30 minutes to make one bicycle wheel and 15 minutes to make a chainring, what are the daily design capacities of wheels and chainrings?

Step 1:   Set up the problem.

Using Eq. 3-1, Available machine time = 50 machines × 16 hours = 800 machine hours

Let us assume: X = Design capacity of wheels and
Y = Design capacity of chainrings

Using Eq. 3-3, we get, 800 = (0.5X + 0.25Y). This is the objective function used to solve the problem.

We will use Excel's Solver feature to find X and Y as follows.

Step 2:   In an Excel sheet, set up the problem as follows. You need to enter the equations since Solver expects equations to solve the problem:

	A	B	C
1	No of machines	50	
2	No of hours/day	16	hours
3	Time to make 1 wheel	0.5	hours/unit
4	Time to make 1 chainring	0.25	hours/unit
5			
6	Available machine time	=B1×B2	hours
7	Objective function	=(B3×B8) + (B4×B9)	units
8	Design capacity of wheels (X)	0	units
9	Design capacity of chainrings (Y)	0	units

Cell B7 is the objective cell and cells B8 and B9 are the decision variable cells.

Step 3: Enter data in Solver

Go to Data and click on Solver and enter the data as shown:

Set the objective equal to a value of 800 as shown in the Solver parameters window and the design capacity of the two products as changing variable cells and type the constraints that are essential to solve the problems.

Here, we have two variables which need to be positive and integer and therefore we can set the constraints as:

1. Design capacity of wheels must be an integer, i.e., a whole number;
2. Design capacity of chainrings must be an integer, i.e., a whole number.

We can, of course, set more constraints if we have any. At this time, we have only these two constraints. Constraints are logical conditions that a solution to an optimization problem must satisfy. Examples 3-4 and 3-5 illustrate problems with multiple constraints. The solving method used in this problem is set to the default method which is the Generalized Reduced Gradient Nonlinear method. This methods looks at the slope of the objective function as it changes the design capacity of wheels and chainrings to determine the most optimum solution based on the input value. This method is highly dependent on the input values.

Step 4:   Click on the solve button and click on OK. You will see the following
           results:

	A	B	C
1	No of machines	50	
2	No of hours/day	16	hours
3	Time to make 1 wheel	0.5	Hours/unit
4	Time to make 1 chainring	0.25	Hours/unit
5			
6	Available machine time =	800	800 hours
7	Objective function	800	0.5 X + 0.25 Y
8	**Design capacity of wheels (X)**	**1,280**	**units**
9	**Design capacity of chainrings (Y)**	**640**	**units**

Therefore, the daily design capacity of wheels is 1,280 units and design
capacity of chainrings is 640 units.

Analysis: We had to use the Solver since we did not know X and Y values and
we had to satisfy the maximum available time of 800 hours. Solver found the
optimal value of 1,290 and 840 units as design capacities of wheels and chainrings. The solving method used in this problem is set to the default method
which is the Generalized Reduced Gradient Nonlinear method. This methods
looks at the slope of the objective function as it changes the design capacity
of wheels and chainrings to determine the most optimum solution based on
the input value. This method is highly dependent on the input values.

Example 3-4

Suppose the operations manager at Pedal Fast, Inc. from Example 3-2 wants
to produce more of Product B than Product A the next day. What are the daily
design capacities of wheels and chainrings?

Step 1:   Set up the problem.

           Using Eq. 3-1, Available machine time = 50 machines $\times$ 16 hours = 800
           machine hours

           Let us assume: X = Design capacity of wheels and
                             Y = Design capacity of chainrings

           Using Eq. 3-3, we get, 800 = (0.5X $\times$ 0.25Y). This is the objective function
           used to solve the problem.

           We will use Excel's Solver feature to find X and Y as follows.

Step 2:   In an Excel sheet, set up the problem as follows. You need to enter the
           equations since Solver expects equations to solve the problem:

	A	B	C
1	No of machines	50	
2	No of hours/day	16	hours
3	Time to make 1 wheel	0.5	hours/unit
4	Time to make 1 chainring	0.25	hours/unit
5			
6	Available machine time	=B1×B2	hours
7	Objective function	=(B3×B8)+(C4×C9)	units
8	Design capacity of wheels (X)	0	units
9	Design capacity of chainrings (Y)	0	units

Cell B7 is the objective cell and cells B8 and B9 are the decision variable cells.

Step 3:   Enter data in Solver.

Set the objective equal to a value of 800 as shown in the Solver parameters window and the design capacity of the two products as changing variable cells and type the constraints that are essential to solve the problems. In this case, we have three constraints. The additional constraint is that Product B should be greater than Product A:

1. Design capacity of wheels must be an integer, i.e., a whole number;
2. Design capacity of chainrings must be an integer, i.e., a whole number;
3. Design capacity of chainrings > Design capacity of wheels.

Go to Data and click on Solver and enter the data as shown:

Step 4: Click on the solve button and click on OK. You will see the following results:

	A	B	C
1	No of machines	50	
2	No of hours/day	16	hours
3	Time to make 1 wheel	0.5	Hours/unit
4	Time to make 1 chainring	0.25	Hours/unit
5			
6	Available machine time =	800	800 hours
7	Objective function	800	0.5 X + 0.25 Y
8	**Design capacity of wheels (X)**	**961**	**units**
9	**Design capacity of chainrings (Y)**	**1,278**	**units**

Therefore, the daily design capacity of wheels is 961 units and design capacity of chainrings is 1,278 units.

Analysis: We had to use the Solver since we did not know X and Y values and we had to satisfy the maximum available time of 800 hours. Solver found the optimal value of 961 and 1,278 units as design capacities of wheels and chainrings. The solving method used in this problem is set to the default method which is the Generalized Reduced Gradient Nonlinear method. This methods looks at the slope of the objective function as it changes the design capacity of wheels and chainrings to determine the most optimum solution based on the input value. This method is highly dependent on the input values.

Example 3-5

Philloton, Inc. from Philadelphia assembles two exercise bicycles. Recumbent 268 Model is more popular than Upright 961. The company sells each Upright 961 for $2,400 and each Recumbent 268 for $2,555. It costs Philloton $1,800 to assemble an Upright 961 unit and $1,855 to assemble a Recumbent 268 unit including parts cost. The company has only $58,000 to assemble both models and only 160 hours to assemble. Using the resources available as constraints, determine how many units of each model can be assembled by the company for maximum profits.

Step 1: Set up the problem

Let us assume: X = Design capacity of Upright 961, and
Y = Design capacity of Recumbent 268 Model

In this case, we need to maximize profits, which will be the objective function:

Profits = ($2400–$1800)X + ($2555–$1855)Y

We will use Excel's Solver feature to find X and Y as follows.

Step 2: In an Excel sheet, set up the problem as follows. You need to enter the equations since Solver expects equations to solve the problem:

	A	B	C	D	E	F
1	**Single unit information**					
2	Model	**Upright 961**	**Recumbent 268**			
3	Item retail price	2400	2555			
4	Item cost	1800	1855			
5	Item profit	=B3–B4	=C3–C4			
6						
7	Assembly time (hours)	4.5	5.5			
8						
9	**Total assembly information**			**Totals**	**Resources**	**Slack**
10	Number of units	1	1			
11	Cost	=B10×B4	=C10×C4	=B11+C11	58000	=E11–D11
12	Profit	=B10×B5	=C10×C5	**=B12+C12**		
13	Assembly time (hours)	=B10×B7	=C10×C7	=B13+C13	160	=E13–D13

Step 3:   Enter data in Solver.

Set the objective equal to cell D12 as shown in the Solver parameters window and the design capacity of the two products as changing variable cells and type the constraints that are essential to solve the problems. In this case, we have three constraints. The additional constraint is that Product B should be greater than Product A:

1. Design capacity of wheels must be an integer, i.e., a whole number;
2. Design capacity of chainrings must be an integer, i.e., a whole number;
3. Design capacity of chainrings > Design capacity of wheels.

Go to Data and click on Solver and enter the data as shown:

We have to maximize profits, cell D12 by changing cells B10 and C10. The constraints are as follows:

- Units of both Models >=1;
- Units of both Models = Integer;
- Units of Recumbent > Units of Upright;
- Total cost <= Resources Cost;
- Total time <= Resources time.

Enter all these constraints in the Solver Parameters pop-up window.

Step 4:   Click on the solve button and click on OK. You will see the following results:

Total assembly information			Totals	Resources	Slack
Number of units	12	19			
Cost	$21,600	$35,245	56,845.00	$58,000	1,155.00
Profit	$7,200	$13,300	**$20,500**		
Assembly time (hours)	54.0	104.5	158.50	160.0	1.50

Therefore, the daily design capacity is 12 Upright 961 and 19 Recumbent 268 for a maximum profit of $20,500.

Analysis: As desired, the company can make more Recumbent 268 models than Upright 961 models. There is a slack of $58,000 - $56,845 = $1,155 and 160 − 158.50 = 1.5 hours. The slack, which is the leftover resources, is minimum for both assembly time and cost, which means the company is using all its resources of money and time effectively. The solving method used in this problem is set to the default method which is the Generalized Reduced Gradient Nonlinear method. This method looks at the slope of the objective function as it changes the design capacity of the exercise bicycle models, Upright 961 and Recumbent 268 to determine the most optimum solution based on the input value. This method is highly dependent on the input values.

Actual Output and Capacity Utilization

Actual output
Actual output is the number of products that is actually produced during a period of time.

Capacity utilization
The ratio of actual output to the maximum possible output or design capacity.

Actual output is the number of products that is actually produced during a period of time. For example, the design capacity of a company may be to produce 1,600 bicycle wheels per Example 3-1. While the company is designed to produce 1,600 bicycle wheels in a day, they may end up producing only 1,400 wheels because of a sudden breakdown of a machine or a smaller number of machine operators due to absenteeism or a quality problem that was identified that day. Other problems may include power cuts or material supply problems. Such problems may be beyond the control of the operations team in that organization.

Actual capacity can be used to measure capacity utilization. Capacity utilization is the measure of how a firm has utilized its resources compared to the designed use of its resources. It is the ratio of the actual output to the maximum designed output or the design capacity. Capacity utilization is calculated using the following formula:

$$Capacity\ Utilization = \frac{Actual\ Output}{Maximum\ designed\ Output} = \frac{Actual\ Output}{Design\ Capacity} \times 100\%$$

Eq. 3-5

Capacity utilization provides an insight into how a firm is utilizing its resources and how a company can increase its output without increasing the costs associated with the production. The higher the capacity utilization, the lower the cost per unit. Attaining the design capacity may not be possible all the time but firms can increase their capacity utilization by:

- Managing quality problems before they arise,
- Training employees to do multiple roles,
- Maintaining machines and equipment well and in good condition,
- Managing with an effective OSCM plan,
- Subcontracting some of the manufacturing activities without increasing cost of products,
- Eliminating waste, and
- Managing well-designed disaster recovery plans.

Effective Capacity and Efficiency

Design capacity is the capacity that was designed originally and that can be achieved under ideal conditions with the available resources. But, in reality, there are constraints in firms to fully use the design capacity. Some of the constraints are the routine maintenance work on machines, employee lunch and coffee breaks, product mix changes, scheduling snags, and other delays. These constraints pose a hinderance to achieving the design capacity in organizations. The end result is the effective capacity which is defined as the maximum amount of work that is attainable in a given period due to the constraints.

> **Effective capacity** Effective capacity is the maximum amount of work that is attainable in a given period due to constraints.

Effective capacity can be used to calculate the efficiency of the operational capacity system of the organization. Efficiency is calculated using the following formula:

$$Efficiency = \frac{Actual\ Output}{Maximum\ attainable\ Output} = \frac{Actual\ Output}{Effective\ Capacity} \times 100\%$$

Eq. 3-6

> **Efficiency** The ratio of actual output to the maximum attainable output or the effective capacity.

As an example, the design capacity of a company may be to produce 1,600 bicycle wheels. But in reality, the firm may be set up to produce only 1,500 bicycle wheels because of constraints such as routine maintenance work on a machine that lasts half a day and employee lunch and coffee breaks that amount to 1 hour daily. Now the company is set up to have maximum attainable capacity of only 1,500 bicycle wheels, which is the effective capacity. While the company is capable of producing 1,600 bicycle wheels on a particular day, their maximum attainable capacity is only 1,500 bicycle wheels. But, in the end, they may end up producing only 1,400 that day as actual output because of problems that are beyond the control of the operations team in that organization. Therefore, the effective capacity is less than design capacity and the actual output is less than effective capacity. Example 3-6 illustrates how to calculate the capacity utilization.

Effective capacity can be increased. Several measures can be taken to improve effective capacity in a firm including:

- Spending optimal time on the maintenance of machines and equipment,
- Managing with an effective OSCM plan,
- Subcontracting some of the manufacturing activities without increasing cost of products, and
- Improving processes continually.

Example 3-6

Pedal Fast, Inc. has 50 machines and the machines are used to manufacture bicycle wheels 16 hours a day. It takes 30 minutes to make one bicycle wheel. On an average, the effective capacity has been measured as 1,500 wheels. On a particular day due to some unforeseen problems, the firm was able to produce 1,400 wheels. What is the capacity efficiency and capacity utilization?

Actual Output = 1,400 wheels for that day

Effective capacity = 1,500 wheels on that day

Using Eq. 3-1, Available machine time = 50 machines × 16 hours = 800 machine hours

Using Eq. 3-2,

$$Design\ capacity\ of\ bicycle\ wheels = \frac{800}{0.5} = 1,600\ wheels$$

Using Eq. 3-6,

$$Efficiency = \frac{1,400}{1,500} \times 100 = 93.33\%$$

Using Eq. 3-5,

$$Capacity\ Utilization = \frac{1,400}{1,600} \times 100 = 87.50\%$$

Analysis: The actual output is less than the effective capacity and the effective capacity is less than the design capacity. Although the efficiency of manufacturing is 93.3%, Pedal Fast can utilize only 87.5% of the design capacity. There is a lot of room for improvement. For instance, the company can maintain machines and equipment better. See earlier pages for ways to improve capacity utilization.

Capacity Management Strategy

A capacity management strategy ensures that a business maximizes its output of products and services under all conditions to meet the demand. Companies that execute a capacity management strategy well may enjoy an increase in revenues due to fulfilled orders, attract more customers, and experience a growth in market share.

Firms determine what resources are needed to meet the demand for their products or services. Firms have to maintain the balance of excess capacity to under capacity. This involves the capacity management factors such as how much raw materials, equipment, labor, and investment in facilities should be acquired over a period of time to meet the future demand for products and services. The capacity management in a firm may involve the workers working overtime, outsourcing a part of their business operations, or purchasing additional equipment. A good capacity management strategy will help a firm to:

> **Capacity management strategy** A strategy to maximize a company's output of products and services under all conditions to meet demand.

- Plan production cycles ahead of time to maximize production efficiency,
- Reduce the overall costs of doing business,
- Manage inventory better and deal with problems in the supply chain,
- Allow better allocation of human and material resources for maximum efficiency, and
- Understand current operations and changing needs well.

Capacity management of a firm is strategic in nature. The goal of strategic capacity management is to achieve a level where there is a balance between the production capabilities and the demand. Capacity management is accomplished by removing all the bottlenecks in the production process and utilizing the available resources effectively. Almost all companies employ capacity management strategy to decide their design capacity. To manage capacity, firms employ one of the following four types of strategies:

1. Lead strategy,
2. Lag strategy,
3. Match strategy, and
4. Dynamic strategy.

Lead Strategy

The lead strategy involves an upfront investment in the anticipated capacity. In this strategy, firms plan to increase their capacity in advance even before the actual demand increases. Organizations use this strategy well ahead of time when they anticipate that their competitors may face inventory shortages due to a sudden increase in future demand. This strategy is risky if the anticipated future demand does not materialize as it will lead to an increase in inventory storage costs. This strategy is often used when a company expands or where the demand for products and services increases suddenly. Small firms usually avoid this kind of strategy.

Lag Strategy

The lag strategy is more conservative than the lead strategy. Firms wait to add more capacity until the current capacity is stretched to its limits. Firms avoid the risks of excess inventory but might face under capacity of their products and services if the demand increases suddenly, which may lead to losing customers to competition.

Match Strategy

The match strategy is neither conservative nor aggressive and is a risk-averse strategy. This strategy uses smaller incremental changes to a firm's capacity based on demand fluctuations. Whenever a firm knows that the demand for its products or services will increase, the company boosts its production or service in small amounts. If the demand goes up rapidly, the firm may not lose sales entirely as they can respond a bit. However, using this strategy, a firm can never capitalize on a significant spike in demand. On the other hand, the firm will not lose when there is a sudden downward spike in demand.

Dynamic Strategy

The dynamic strategy is a forecast-driven strategy. This strategy involves adding capacity before it is required, based on actual demand and sales forecast figures. It decreases the risk of shortage or wastage of inventory. However, this type of strategy depends on accurate forecasts.

FROM PRACTICE: Capacity Management Strategy at Amazon Web Services

Cloud computing supports dynamic resource usage and is highly flexible in nature. Firms use as many or as few resources as and when needed. Amazon Web Services (AWS) automatically allocates the resources for the cloud users based on their workload need. AWS implements a cloud capacity management strategy to ensure that the workloads of their customers have the required resources. A good capacity management strategy ensures that the AWS servers operate with enough CPU, memory, and storage to support the applications.

The AWS capacity management strategy is to determine how many servers should be included to host an application and maintain sufficient backup systems in place to make sure that the application is available if some servers crash. An effective capacity management strategy can help determine which workloads to move to the cloud so that the resource allocations can be easily scaled up and down[8].

© Yu Chun Christopher Wong/Shutterstock.com

Capacity Planning

Capacity planning determines the production capacity required to meet the manufacturing demand or the service capacity required to meet the service demand. Since capacity requirements involve significant amount of money and other resources, it is necessary to plan in advance. For example, a company with a new, innovative product that is expected to be sold in the markets in a year or two has to plan far ahead to have the necessary capacity to produce the product. For a store to sell new product lines, the store owner has to plan capacity expansion far ahead of actually procuring those new product lines. Capacity planning is the process through which firms affirm their output of goods and services with their resources and constraints.

> **Capacity planning**
> Capacity planning is the process of determining the design capacity needed by an organization to meet changing demands for its products.

Capacity planning is the first step when an organization decides to produce products or promote services. Capacity planning must be designed and implemented for the current operational activities as well as for the future growth and expansions. Capacity planning is linked to supply chain planning, inventory management, maintenance, scheduling, and to every other aspect of the operation in a company. Capacity planning is a necessity in operations and supply chain activities because organizations need to:

- Have capacity to meet the customers' demand,
- Reduce supply chain costs to stay competitive in the market,
- Coordinate resources to perform a variety of operational activities,
- Improve the cost efficiency of operations, and
- Invest to meet current and future capacity requirements.

Capacity Planning Types and Process

Capacity planning is the starting point for sales and operations planning, supply chain planning, maintenance planning, scheduling, and other operational activities. Companies should follow their own capacity planning process to ensure there is enough capacity for the current and the future demand for their goods and services. Companies execute capacity planning in three common types based on capacity requirements:

1. Capital-intensive capacity planning,
2. Operations capacity planning, and
3. Short-term capacity planning.

Capital-Intensive Capacity Planning If the capacity requirement involves long-term, capital-intensive resources such as plants, buildings, and equipment, then long-term capacity planning is required. Typically, acquisition or disposal of such resources takes longer than 6 months. We will consider this type of capacity planning in this chapter.

Operational Capacity Planning If the capacity requirement involves operational activities such as employee hiring and layoffs, subcontracting, and minor equipment purchases, then medium-term capacity planning is envisioned and executed as aggregate planning. The aggregate planning and the sales and operations planning are typically planned for the next few months or few quarters and is discussed in detail in Chapter 5.

Short-Term Capacity Planning If the capacity requirement involves staff overtime, human resources issues, or making adjustments to fluctuations in demand, short-term capacity planning is implemented. This planning done daily or weekly in organizations. This type of planning is discussed in later chapters.

The capacity planning process involves understanding the current capacity as well as the future needs to add or reduce current capacity. The capacity planning process is shown in Figure 3-1. The four-step capacity planning consists of estimating both the current and future capacity requirements. Once capacity requirements are known, companies evaluate various options using financial models to decide on the most desired option to meet the capacity requirements. The best option is included in the capital-intensive capacity planning and operations capacity planning and implemented. The result of the implementation is monitored continuously. Improvements and adjustments are made on a daily or weekly basis as short-term capacity planning. Let us discuss each one of the steps of this process next.

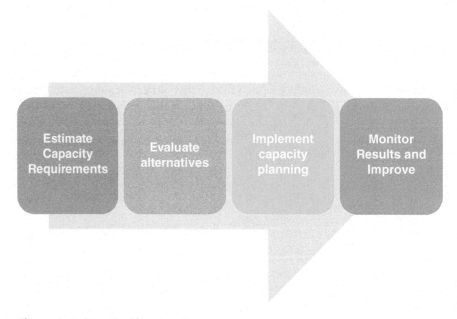

Figure 3-1 Capacity Planning Process

Estimate Capacity Requirements

What kind of capacity is needed for a company? It depends on the goods and services that the company wants to provide to its customers. For example, the capacity planning calculations consider the number of machines, the number of employees needed to operate those machines, the hours or shifts available, and the mix of goods to be produced. These factors are included to know whether a manufacturing operation has the required capacity to meet the forecasted demand. With the right and accurate capacity plan, operation managers can proactively add or subtract resources to meet the forecasted commitments. The capacity requirements are calculated as shown in Example 3-7.

Example 3-7

Burpee Soda makes two types of carbonated drinks, Burpee Club Soda, and Burpee Seltzer. Bob Burpee, the owner wants to determine machine, equipment, and labor requirements for the next 4 years. His marketing manager has forecasted a 4-year demand for these two products, which is shown in the following table. The plant is equipped with three machines each capable of filling and packaging 80,000 cans of Burpee Club Soda and 100,000 cans of the Seltzer in a year. Each machine requires two operators and dedicated light-duty equipment. What are the machine, operators, and equipment requirements for all the 4 years?

Demand	Year 1	Year 2	Year 3	Year 4
Soda	140,000	160,000	240,000	260,000
Seltzer	250,000	280,000	340,000	400,000

Since the same machines are used to fill and pack both types of carbonated drinks, we can combine the demand in cans/year from the above table as:

	Year 1	Year 2	Year 3	Year 4
Demand for Soda	140,000	160,000	240,000	260,000
Demand for Seltzer	250,000	280,000	340,000	400,000
Total Demand (soda + seltzer)	390,000	440,000	580,000	660,000

Since all machines are used to fill and pack both the carbonated drinks, we can also calculate the design capacity as:

$$3 \text{ machines} \times (80{,}000 + 100{,}000) = 540{,}000 \text{ cans/year}$$

Let us take a look at the calculations for Year 1. The actual output is equal to the demand since a firm does not want to produce more than the demand. Therefore, the actual output is equal to 390,000 cans for Year 1 and the design capacity is 540,000 cans for the same year.

Using Eq. 3-6, the capacity utilization for Year 1 $= \dfrac{390,000}{540,000} \times 100 = 72.22\%$

In Year 1, the company is using 72.22% of the design capacity and therefore, the machine requirement = capacity utilization × number of machines = 0.7222 × 3 = 2.17 machines. We can also calculate number of machines as:

= total demand/ a machine's capacity = 390,000/180,000 = 2.17 machines

Similarly, the operator requirement = 0.7222 × 2 = 1.44 operators, and the equipment requirement = 0.7222 × 1 = 0.72 equipment.

We can continue to calculate for the remaining periods and the result is:

	Year 1	Year 2	Year 3	Year 4
Design Capacity=	540,000	540,000	540,000	540,000
Actual Output=	390,000	440,000	580,000	660,000
Capacity Utilization=	72.22%	81.48%	107.41%	122.22%
Machine Requirement =	2.17	2.44	3.22	3.67
Operators Requirement=	1.44	1.63	2.15	2.44
Equipment Requirement=	0.72	0.81	1.07	1.22

Analysis: For Year 1, the firm is using 72.22% of the available capacity. Both the design capacity and actual output was calculated using 3 machines and therefore, the capacity utilization is calculated as a percentage only. Therefore, we multiply 3 machines to calculate machine requirement. The same logic is used to calculate operator and equipment requirements.

For Year 1, the company is under utilizing its machines, operators, and equipment. They were able to cope with the demand to produce more in Year 2.

But for Years 3 and 4, the company must expand to match the design capacity. Actual output cannot be more than the design capacity. The company has to buy one more machine and hire another operator as you can see that the machine requirement is greater than 3 and the operator requirement is greater than 2. This means that the company must start both the capital-intensive capacity planning and the operational capacity to meet the demands of the third and fourth year. Instead, they can outsource the extra demand to another company.

Capacity buffer
Capacity buffer is the amount of capacity designed specifically to be in excess of expected demand.

When a company under-utilizes their machines, operators, and equipment, there is a capacity buffer. A buffer gives the operations managers a leeway or flexibility when unforeseen events occur. This buffer in capacity helps to meet sudden, unanticipated demands. Usually, companies design their capacity to be more than the expected demand.

FROM PRACTICE: Capacity Planning Using Microsoft's Cloud Services

AccuWeather, Amtrak, BMW, Bosch, British Petroleum, Caesars Entertainment, Coca-Cola, GEICO, Honeywell Inc., HP, Miami Heat, NBC Universal, Seattle Seahawks, Uber, Verizon, and Walgreens have something in common. They all use Microsoft's Azure Cloud Services. Azure's "As A Service" model removes the need for businesses to invest in expensive company owned and managed IT infrastructure. Azure offers many options to minimize cost and to meet capacity requirements.

© Burdun Iliya/Shutterstock.com

Companies who use cloud services must plan the required capacity at Azure using their operational capacity plan. For example, they must plan to scale up by adding machines or service instances based on increased demand and scale down to remove the resources when not needed. They have to know in advance whether they will have spikes in the traffic such as during the Superbowl or the holiday seasons. Microsoft advises their customers to monitor the performance of their applications over time and use the results of the monitoring to adjust capacity requirements as and when necessary[9].

Evaluate Alternatives Using a Decision Tree Method

As the capacity planning is being executed, a company might want to evaluate different options that are available to them and decide on the best alternative that meets their demands. This frequently happens when considering capital-intensive capacity planning. For example, a company may want to check out the possibility of whether to expand their current factory or to build a new factory or rent an existing building to meet the future demand. One method to solve such a problem is to use a decision tree.

Decision Tree Method

A decision tree is a common method used to make decisions. It is simple and can be generated based on the description of a situation containing alternatives, probabilities, costs, and revenues. It is a visual tool and has a tree-like structure in which the decision nodes are typically represented by squares. Each decision node is a point of decision making, for example, whether to buy a sofa or rent one. There are branches from each decision point showing the available choices or options. On those branches, there may be one or more chance nodes. A chance node is represented by a circle. The chance node is a point of evaluating the chances or probabilities of outcomes, for example, when buying a sofa, what is the probability of it being sold in a "good" condition or in a "usable" condition. The branches terminate as an end node usually represented by a triangle. The end node shows the net payoff for that branch of the tree.

To reach a decision, we start with the net payoffs of all the options. The net payoff is the profit or loss from the sale of an item or a service after deducting all the associated costs.

$$Payoff = Revenue - Costs \qquad \text{Eq. 3-7}$$

For a decision to go with the most profitable option, we will consider the maximum expected value at each decision point. The results are based on expected values calculated using the following formula.

The expected value (EV) for an alternative is calculated by multiplying each possible payoff (PO) of the alternative by its probability (P) and summing the results. Therefore, the EV for n payoffs of an alternative is:

$$EV = \sum_{1}^{n} PO_n \times P_n \qquad \text{Eq. 3-8}$$

We simply multiply the payoff PO with probability P for each alternative and add them to get the EV. For example, let us have an alternative or option with two situations:

1. payoff PO_1 with a probability P_1 for the first situation such as strong economic growth, and
2. payoff PO_2 with a probability P_2 for the second situation such as weak economic growth.

Then Eq. 3-8 can be written as:

$$EV = (PO_1 \times P_1) + (PO_2 \times P_2) \qquad \text{Eq. 3-9}$$

The expected value decision criterion selects the alternative that offers the best expected value, that is, the highest value when considering payoffs and the lowest value when considering costs. Let us explore the decision tree in Example 3-8.

Example 3-8

Aaron Capstan, the owner and CEO of Sports Caps, has to make a decision on the future of his store. The sales had been great over the past two years and he sees growth for the next year with the addition of sports memorabilia. He is running out of space and the demand for sports-related products has spurred a need to expand. He started out with these options on his mind—expand his store by buying the next store, rent an old building in the same neighborhood and refurbish it, or build a new store in the best part of the town. He collected the following data.

The expansion will bring in $220,000 as revenue for the next year with strong sales and the revenue will be $180,000 with weak sales. The cost of expansion is estimated at $100,000. Strong sales at this neighborhood have a probability of 65%. The rent of the old building will be $2,500 per month, closing the current store and moving will cost $3,000 and the expected refurbishment cost will be $40,000. The expected revenue is $280,000 under strong sales and $200,000 under weak sales. Building a new store at a new location will cost $380,000 including relocation. The new neighborhood is close to a huge park with several softball diamonds, tennis courts, and soccer fields. The revenue in this case is estimated to be $450,000 under strong growth and $400,000 with weak growth. Another option is to leave the current store open in addition to the new location only in the case of strong sales. The cost of closing the current store is $2,000. A strong growth in this neighborhood has a probability of 90%. If he does nothing, Aaron will have revenue of $190,000 from the current store with strong sales and a revenue of $150,000 with weak sales. What should Aaron decide?

Step 1: Calculate the payoffs of all alternatives.

Identify the alternatives. There are four alternatives in this problem: expansion, rent, build, and do nothing. The alternative build has two options by itself, one with keeping the current store open and the other with the current store closed. Expected Values for each payoff can be calculated using Equation 3-9 as we have two situations in each case, namely strong sales and weak sales.

Payoff for expansion = Revenues – cost of expansion

Payoff for rent = Revenues – Yearly rent – Close and Move expense - refurbishment cost

Payoff for Build with open current store = Revenue from new building + Revenue from current store – building cost with relocation

Payoff for Build with closed current store = Revenue from new building + building cost with relocation – current store closing cost

Payoff for Do Nothing = Revenues

Step 2: Draw the decision tree.

The payoffs for each alternative are shown below as end nodes of each branch, to the right of the blue triangle. Draw the chance nodes as shown as orange circles. Every chance node has two chances or probabilities, strong and weak. The decision tree is shown in the figure below:

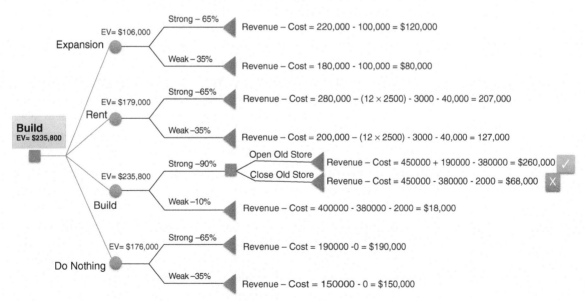

Step 3:   Calculate the EV.

In the case of new building with strong sales, we choose the option with the highest payoff, that is, move to the new building with the old store open as well. Then, we calculate the expected values for all alternatives using Eq. 3-9.

For Expansion, EV = ($120,000 × 65%) + ($80,000 × 35%) = $78,000 + $28,000 = $106,000

Step 4:   Choose the best option

The highest expected value with a value of $285,800 is chosen as the best alternative.

> **Analysis:** The best option is to build a new store with the current store open. The current store gives Aaron $190,000 while he is building the new store. Note that the expansion of the store is the least preferred alternative. If Aaron does nothing, he is going to lose money.

Implement Capacity Planning

Once the capacity requirements are determined and alternatives evaluated, the next step is implementation of the capacity plans. Firms must decide whether to produce a good or provide a service themselves. An alternative is to out-source parts of the operations of producing goods and services.

If an organization has the available capacity, they themselves would produce the goods and services. If an organization wants to increase capacity rapidly, then they usually consider outsourcing. Outsourcing is also preferred if a firm lacks certain expertise to increase the capacity or if a flexibility to handle the excess capacity is required. In addition to outsourcing, companies must understand the issues regarding how to meet the future demand. The main issues are capacity balance and capacity expansion frequency.

Capacity Balance When firms decide to increase or reduce capacity, they must consider tackling the issues with capacity balance. A capacity balance is a requirement, when the output of one subprocess should match the input of the next subprocess in production. In many operations, there will be capacity imbalances as it is tough to synchronize the operations in such a way that all outputs of a subprocess meet the inputs of the subsequent subprocess. There are a number of reasons for this imbalance. One reason is that the design capacity of each subprocess differs. The other reason is that each subprocess may encounter problems such as labor shortage, supply chains, process variance, quality, or unexpected maintenance. These imbalances cause bottlenecks in the manufacturing process.

Bottlenecks Bottlenecks happen when one or more subprocesses produce more products than the other subprocesses. As a result, the capacity of a system is reduced to the bottleneck capacity of the operations. Now, the imbalances can be dealt by adding capacity or reducing capacity before the bottleneck.

Most production processes have subprocesses. A subprocess is a set of activities with a logical sequence that are involved in a single process. For example, consider the assembly of a ball-point pen as illustrated in Figure 3-2. The assembly of ball-point pens involves the following subprocesses:

Subprocess A subprocess is a set of activities with a logical sequence that are involved in a single process.

Capacity balance A capacity balance is a requirement where the output of one subprocess should match the input of the next subprocess in production.

Bottlenecks Bottlenecks are points of congestion in manufacturing operations caused by constraints or limits in one or more subprocesses.

A. Ink making,
B. Construction of point and body of the pen,
C. Metal components cut to required dimensions,
D. Ball inserted into point,
E. Construction of plastic components of the pen,
F. Ink filling,
G. Assembly of pens, and
H. Final assembly, packaging, and shipping.

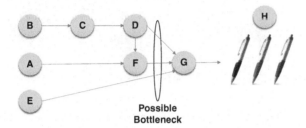

Figure 3-2 Subprocesses in Manufacture of a Pen
Source: Ganesh Vaidyanathan/© Barghest/Shutterstock.com

The process starts with three subprocesses A, B, and E. Each of those activities is followed by other subprocesses during the production of ball-point pens. Capacity balances must be followed, for example, input to subprocess F must be balanced with outputs of subprocesses A and D. It is subprocess G that we are concerned with more than other subprocesses. Since there are outputs from three different subprocesses that feed the subprocess G, there are high chances for an assembly bottleneck at G.

Capacity Expansion Frequency When the demand is expected to increase, capacity expansion—the addition of capacity—is an important strategy in manufacturing and service industries. Expanding the manufacturing facilities or the service centers is often considered as a capacity expansion. For example, in a software company, capacity expansion is in terms of more programmers. In a warehouse, capacity expansion is by adding storage space. Capacity expansion can be accomplished in one of three ways to meet the demand:

1. Frequent small additions or reductions,
2. Infrequent large additions or reductions, or
3. A combination of small but frequent and large but infrequent additions or reductions.

The costs of expanding capacity include the removal of old machines or equipment or facilities, the addition of a new machine or equipment, the lost time during changeover, and any purchasing costs. If expansion of capacity is done frequently, these costs add up and can become very expensive. Infrequent large additions may bring such costs down, but they may add to the cost related to excess capacity. When the demand decreases for a product, the removal or scaling down of the capacity is often required. In some these cases, firms may have to resort to drastic measures such as selling their facilities.

FROM PRACTICE: NFL Coping With Capacity Reduction During COVID-19

In consultation with public-health authorities as a part of capacity planning, the National Football League (NFL) capped Super Bowl LV spectator capacity at 22,000. A football game at Raymond James Stadium, which has a capacity of around 65,000 expandable to more than 70,000, did not have even 22,000 spectators. COVID-19 made a significant impact on the sports and the entertainment industries as events were restricted in capacity for safety. The pandemic significantly affected the NFL revenues, with estimates in the hundreds of millions of dollars per team and $3 billion to $4 billion for the league as a whole. Despite the financial impact, the games continued on schedule. Several Super Bowl advertising regulars like Anheuser-Busch, Coca-Cola, and PepsiCo opted out of the Super Bowl LV ads. Super Bowls typically bring millions of dollars in economic impact into host cities. But the reduced capacity in the stadium, the absence of Super Bowl week parties, fans, and celebrities created an impact of lesser degree on the host city[10].

© Eder/Shutterstock.com

FROM PRACTICE: Disney Theme Park Employs Apps for Capacity Management

Even before the COVID-19 pandemic began in the year 2020, Walt Disney World was establishing new approaches to address their capacity management. The strategy was to improve the experiences of visitors to the theme park. Disney introduced a free planning tool called the Disney Genie. The Disney Genie app allows the guests to spend less time planning and waiting and more time doing the things they love to do. One of its highly touted features is the ability to create custom itineraries for guests. Guests can tell the Disney Genie app what they want to do and it will do the planning for them. Guests can also use Disney Genie to join virtual queues, see current and forecasted attraction wait times, mobile order food, make reservations at restaurants, and more. There is even a virtual assistant to help guests at any time. This online-only reservation system for tickets proved to be a great way to manage capacity. The mobile order and pay options decrease the contact points between the employees and the guests. Moreover, they help Disney staff to redistribute traffic to less crowded locations[11].

© George Sheldon/Shutterstock.com

Monitor Results and Improve

Capacity requirements must be monitored on an ongoing basis. Firms must develop a comprehensive method to monitor all available resources to ensure that such resources are available to all operational activities. Organizations should prioritize and assign capacity resources effectively with continuous planning and monitoring. They should avoid overestimating or underestimating resource utilization requirements by generating accurate future demand. Based on monitoring capacity, firms must improve their capacity utilization rate and efficiency continuously.

FROM PRACTICE: Capacity Planning and Supply Chain at Qualcomm

© Remus Rigo/Shutterstock.com

During 2020, the COVID-19 pandemic slowed the global supply chain as manufacturers suspended work until safety precautions were enacted. The global trade continued at a reduced capacity well into 2021. By mid-2021, major American ports lacked the necessary staff to process the inbound cargo, leading to container ships being stalled outside ports for days or weeks. The trucking industry was short on drivers as well, resulting in a huge problem in the supply chain networks. Christiano Amon, CEO of Qualcomm, said in an interview that Qualcomm acted very fast in the beginning of this crisis. Qualcomm was in a unique position because of their foresight with their suppliers to secure their capacity for future volumes. They leveraged that capacity to redesign their products across multiple plants and use every possible capacity effectively. This has led Qualcomm to enjoy significant capacity improvements and supply improvements as well as to a much more balanced supply-demand situation[12].

Formulae from this Chapter

Available machine time	$\text{Available machine time} = \text{No of machines} \times \text{No of hours.}$	Eq. 3-1
Design Capacity	$\text{Design capacity} = \dfrac{\text{Available machine time}}{\text{Time taken to produce one unit}}$	Eq. 3-2
Available machine time for one product calculation of design capacity	$\text{Available machine time} = \text{Design capacity} \times \text{Time it takes to produce one unit}$	Eq. 3-3

(continued)

Available machine time for multiple products calculation of design capacity	Available machine time = (Design capacity of A × Time it takes to produce one unit of A) + (Design capacity of B × Time it takes to produce one unit of B) + … + (Design capacity of N × Time it takes -to produce one unit of N)	Eq. 3-4
Capacity Utilization	$Capacity\ Utilization = \dfrac{Actual\ Output}{Design\ Capacity} \times 100\%$	Eq. 3-5
Efficiency	$Efficiency = \dfrac{Actual\ Output}{Effective\ Capacity} \times 100\%$	Eq. 3-6
Net Payoff	$Payoff = Revenue - Costs$	Eq. 3-7
Expected Value	$EV = \sum_{1}^{n} PO_n \times P_n$	Eq. 3-8
Expected Value	$EV = (PO_1 \times P_1) + (PO_2 \times P_2) + … + (PO_n \times P_n)$	Eq. 3-9

Case Study: Capacity and Demand Management at Flowers Lawncare

According to the IBIS World Landscaping Services Industry Report, the landscape services industry has a market size of $105.1 billion in 2021 and employs more than 1 million people. The market size of the industry in the United States has been growing at 2.5% on average between 2016 and 2021. The National Gardening Survey reports the 35- to 44-year-old age bracket had the highest mean of spending of all age groups in 2019 at $609.

Flora Flowers, a young entrepreneur from Schaumburg, Illinois wants to start a new lawncare company. The company will provide lawncare for single-family homes in the area including mowing lawns, trimming edges, and blowing away excess grass and leaves. She is very confident that she can get 260 homeowners as her customers. Flora's employees would be visiting their yards 4 times a month for 8 months in a year. For the lawncare purposes, Flora has divided the houses in that area as 60 small, 80 medium, and 120 large houses, based on their yard sizes. She estimates that it will take half an hour to mow the lawn, trim edges, and blow extra grass and leaves for a small house.

© ilove/Shutterstock.com

A medium house will take 45 minutes and a large house will take an hour to do similar work. She plans to hire employees who can work 40 hours a week each with 5 hours of lunch break per week. Flora wants to establish multiple teams each consisting of a few employees to work on multiple streets at a time to maximize efficiency. She can equip each team with two riding lawn mowers, a push lawn mower, an edge trimmer, a leaf blower, and a truck with a trailer to carry the equipment. She is planning to add a 10% buffer to the weekly total hours for equipment maintenance, employee fatigue, and for any mishaps that can happen during work. She also plans another 15% buffer for equipment setup, that is, unloading equipment from the trailer, adding gas to the equipment, prepping up the worksite, loading the equipment back on the trailer. She can divide the work teams to take care of an entire street at a time so that the setup times are also efficient.

Flora's overall strategy is to provide a low-cost, quality service. Flora plans to charge $40 for a weekly visit to the small house that consists of mowing, edging, and blowing. She also plans to charge $50 for the medium house and $60 for the large house. She thinks she could maintain those charges due to the yearly contracts signed by the homeowners. She can buy a John Deere 42 in. Twin Bagger Tractor for $2,800, a Craftsman Deluxe High-Wheel 21 in. Gas Lawn Mower for $350, a RYOBI 25cc Gas Jet Fan Blower for $240, a DEWALT 2-Cycle Gas Edger with Attachment Capability for $200. She expects to spend $2,000 per week for gas to operate the equipment and about $1,000 per week for gas for the pickup trucks. She plans to buy used pickup trucks with trailers at $15,000 each. The labor is estimated to cost $750 per worker per week. Maintenance for equipment and trucks will cost $10,000 per year.

Flora also wants to estimate future needs of the company. The market survey also shows that there will be roughly 5% increase each year for the next 2 years and an 8% increase each year for the following 2 years in home sales. She is planning to assume to use the same growth figures as revenues for lawncare as well. If she increases the number of employees, she wants to figure out the costs as she did for the current year using her original team strategy. She is assuming a 2% increase in price, gas, and maintenance of equipment.

As Flora was planning the capacity, she was thinking of an alternative plan as well. In the same area, a lawncare company was on sale complete with workers and all equipment for $300,000. The revenue for that company has been estimated at $400,000 per year for the current and next 4 years in the case of a strong economy and 20% less every year for a weak economy. Comparatively, Flora had estimated revenues as 20% less per year and same costs as the first year for all the years for both alternatives in the case of weak economy. The market survey shows that there is a 55% probability for a strong growth for the current year.

Case Questions

A. Estimate the capacity requirements of employees. What is the capacity utilization and efficiency? How many teams should Flora establish? What are capacity requirements of all equipment?

B. What should Flora do to increase the capacity utilization and efficiency?

C. What is the profit or net payoff for the first year?

D. What are the net profits or payoff for the five years? What are the net payoffs or profits if Flora considers, due to the 5-year timeframe, the time value of the revenue and cost streams by assuming a 10% discount rate? Use appropriate Excel Math functions such as Round, Ceiling, and Floor for round-off numbers. *Note:* Time value of money is covered in Chapter 4 if the students are not exposed to it in their finance classes.

E. What should Flora Flowers decide based on the current year revenues and costs: buying and running an existing company that is for sale or buying equipment and hiring labor and starting a company on her own?

F. What should Flora Flowers decide based on the five years discounted payoffs and costs: buying and running an existing company that is for sale or buy equipment and hire labor and start a company on her own?

G. Recommend a capacity planning action plan for Flora Flowers.

Summary

- The goal of demand management is to maintain sufficient inventory levels to meet customer demands without having a surplus. Demand management involves forecasting the requirements of consumers.
- Demand management is the process of predicting and planning to meet the demand for goods and services.
- To meet consumer demands, companies need to be prepared with a good operations and supply chain (OSCM) plan. The plan must take into account both anticipated and unanticipated demand.
- Capacity is defined as the ability to produce output using available resources within the specific time period. It is the maximum number of products that can be produced or maximum number of services rendered in a period of time.
- A lack of capacity or under capacity leads to a firm falling short of its customers' demands, resulting in a loss of revenue.
- Excess capacity results in nonproductivity or inefficiency in using existing resources such as idle workers in a production plant or empty tables in restaurants.

- Design capacity is defined as the maximum output rate designed to produce with the available resources in a given period. It is the capacity that was designed originally and that can be achieved under ideal conditions with resources such as labor, materials, power, facilities, technology, and services.
- Available machine time is the total number of hours of all machines that are operated to produce products in a given timeframe.
- A constraint is a logical condition or real-world limit that must be satisfied when solving an optimization problem. Examples are limits on production capacity, market demand, available funds, and so on.
- Actual output is the number of products that are actually produced during a period of time. It is the observed or actual output of a product in an organization during a timeframe.
- Capacity utilization is the ratio of actual output to the maximum possible output or design capacity.
- Effective capacity is the maximum amount of work that is attainable in a given period due to constraints.
- Efficiency is the ratio of actual output to the maximum attainable output or effective capacity.
- Capacity management strategy is to maximize a company's output of products and services under all conditions to meet demand.
- To manage capacity, firms employ one of the following four types of strategies including lead strategy, lag strategy, match strategy, and dynamic strategy.
- Capacity planning is the process of determining the design capacity needed by an organization to meet changing demands for its products.
- Companies execute capacity planning in three common types based on capacity requirements including capital-intensive capacity planning, operations capacity planning, and short-term capacity planning.
- The capacity planning process involves understanding current capacity as well as future needs to add or reduce current capacity.
- Four-step capacity planning consists of estimating both current and future capacity requirements.
- Capacity buffer is the amount of capacity designed specifically to be in excess of expected demand.
- As the capacity planning is being executed by a company, they may want to evaluate different options and decide on the best alternative to meet their demands available to them using a decision tree.
- Net payoff is the profit or loss from the sale of an item or service after deducting all associated costs.
- The expected value for an alternative is calculated by multiplying each possible payoff of the alternative by its probability and summing the results.

- Once capacity requirements are determined and alternatives evaluated, the next step is to implement capacity. If an organization wants to increase capacity rapidly, then they usually consider outsourcing.
- A capacity balance is a requirement when the output of one subprocess should match the input of the next subprocess in production.
- Capacity imbalances are also caused by bottlenecks in the manufacturing process. Bottlenecks happen when one or more subprocesses produce more products than the other subprocesses. As a result, the capacity of a system is reduced to the bottleneck capacity of operations.
- Capacity expansion can be accomplished in one of three ways to meet demand including frequent small additions or reductions, infrequent large additions or reductions, or a combination of small but frequent and large but infrequent additions or reductions.

Review Questions

1. Define demand management.
2. What is the goal of demand management?
3. Why do organizations need a good operations and supply chain (OSCM) plan?
4. Define capacity.
5. What happens if an organization has under capacity or excess capacity?
6. What is design capacity?
7. What is available machine time?
8. What is a constraint? Give an example of a constraint with respect to capacity management.
9. What is actual output?
10. Define capacity utilization.
11. What is effective capacity?
12. Define efficiency.
13. Why is capacity management strategy important to firms?
14. What are the four types of strategies?
15. Why is capacity planning useful to organizations?
16. What are the steps in the capacity planning process?
17. Define capacity buffer with an example.
18. What is the most common tool used to evaluate different alternatives to meet the available demands?
19. What is net payoff?
20. What is expected value?
21. Define capacity balance.
22. Define bottleneck.
23. How is capacity expansion accomplished in an organization?

Critical Thinking Questions

1. How does increased demand affect capacity?
2. How does capacity management help firms to meet demand?
3. What should companies do once they have forecasts of their demand?
4. If a demand forecast of a good is known for the next 12 months, which month's forecast should be used in a capacity management strategy?
5. Is effective capacity always less than design capacity? If so, why? If not, why not?
6. How can you improve the efficiency in an organization? Discuss with an example.
7. How can you improve capacity utilization? Discuss with an example.
8. Why should firms maintain capacity buffers? Explain with an example.
9. Why should companies fill their labor and machine requirements to meet design capacity instead of meeting effective capacity or actual output?
10. Why do we add strong and weak sales or economy components to determine expected value in a decision tree method?
11. Zeb Pens, LLC is looking at an increased market share for its products. Moreover, the company has been informed that there are inventory shortages. Which capacity management strategies should Zeb Pens consider? Show the advantages and disadvantages of those choices.
12. Deb Industries is planning to increase their capacity next year. Though the demand for their products is increasing, there seems to be a cautious consumer spending forecast. What strategy should the company employ?
13. Bob Bean is planning to start a gourmet coffee and pastry shop on the Magnificent Mile in Chicago. What capacity problems would Bob face?
14. What causes capacity imbalance in a manufacturing system?
15. What causes a bottleneck in a manufacturing system?
16. How do bottlenecks reduce design capacity?

Problem Solving Questions

1. Trent Transmissions has a factory in Detroit that produces transmissions. The factory has 2 shifts with 6 machines, 8 hours a shift, 6 days a week. It takes an hour to produce a transmission. What is the factory's available time per week?
2. If the capacity utilization is 93% and an efficiency of 98%, what is the design and effective capacity at the Trent Transmissions' Detroit plant?
3. UltraWomen Cosmetics currently produces 21,900 units and is operating at 65% of the firm's capacity. What is its full capacity level?

4. A small lathe shop to make old automotive small parts is designed to operate at an output of 550 units per day. In the past month, the plant averaged 490 units per day. What was their capacity utilization rate last month?

5. A computer service has a design capacity of 120 repairs per day. Its effective capacity, however, is 90 repairs per day, and its actual output is 60 repairs per day. What is the efficiency and utilization capacity? If the owner wants to improve the efficiency of the service, what do you recommend?

6. Sweeps, the local vacuum cleaner repair shop, can repair a daily maximum of 20 vacuum cleaners. On a particular Monday, they were able to repair only 15 vacuums even though the shop can repair 18 vacuum cleaners a day on average a day due to some snag or other. What is the efficiency of vacuum cleaner repairs? If the demand increases to 25 vacuum cleaners, what should the store manager do?

7. Hoffy Beer Corporation has a beer-processing facility located in Hoffman Estates, IL. The beer facility has a system efficiency of 92%, and the utilization is 85%. Three beer lines are operated 5 days a week and three 8-hour shifts per day. What is the weekly effective capacity for the facility if it takes 1 second to produce a six-pack?

8. In a job shop, effective capacity is only 50% of design capacity, and actual output is 60% of effective output. What design capacity would be needed to achieve an actual output of 18 jobs per week? What is its effective capacity?

9. Lofty Leather located in Saginaw, MI, has 10 machines to manufacture leather jackets and French berets 8 hours a day. It takes 30 minutes to make a jacket and 5 minutes to make a beret. Lofty makes more berets than jackets and if the company works for 262 days in 2022, what are the yearly design capacities of the products?

10. Sarah's Cookies in Sarasota, FL, makes two types of cookies — chocolate chip and oatmeal. Chocolate chip cookies have been selling more than oatmeal cookies. A box of chocolate chip cookies costs the company $1.20 and a box oatmeal cookies costs $1.10. The company has budgeted $120,000 a month to manufacture both boxes of cookies. The manufacturing is accomplished with 50 manufacturing department employees who work 8 hours a day, 5 days a week, and for 4 weeks during the month of September. Using the resources available as maximum resources, determine the design capacities or how many units of each type of cookies can be manufactured.

11. Café Noveau, a retro café bar in Paris, France, is planning to ramp up its operations. It takes two minutes to make a freshly brewed coffee for a customer, one additional minute to do the transaction, and two minutes to serve a pastry. For a customer, an employee takes care of all three activities. Both coffee and the pastry-coffee combo are served more than just pastries. Pierre, the owner, has hired three employees

to work from 6am to 6pm for all days of the week. He has allowed each employee to take a 10-minute break every 2 hours during their time at work. What is the demand in terms of customers for the week? Note: Use a local optimizer like GRG Nonlinear method.

12. The Puffy Pillow Company manufactures high-quality pillows at their facility in Frostbite Falls, Minnesota. The process involves three distinct departments: Cutting, Stuffing, and Sewing. Jamie Holse is the Manufacturing Manager for Puffy Pillow. She has developed a monthly production plan for the next half year:

Month	1	2	3	4	5	6
Planned Production (units)	65,000	72,000	74,000	71,000	80,000	82,000

Jamie has also collected some data about each of the production departments:

Department	Time Required Per Pillow (hours)	Total Production Hours Available (monthly)
Cutting	.25	24,000
Stuffing	.45	34,000
Sewing	.85	60,000

Jamie needs to assess the capacity implications that the monthly production plan holds for her facilities.

a. Calculate the projected monthly capacity utilization (as a percentage of production hours available) for each of the three departments.

b. Which department is of greatest concern for Jamie? Why?

13. Flowing Faucets makes faucets. Larry Leaky, the owner has forecasted 5-year demand as shown in the following table. The plant is equipped with four machines each capable of producing 60,000 faucets in a year. Each machine requires two operators and a dedicated laborer.

Demand	Year 1	Year 2	Year 3	Year 4	Year 5
Faucets	180,000	200,000	260,000	220,000	280,000

a. Determine machine and labor requirements for the 5 years.

b. What should Larry Leaky plan for these years to meet capacity requirements?

14. Lucky Pizza is a favorite pizza place in Water City, NY. They deliver high-quality pepperoni, sausage, meatsy, and veggie pizzas. The owner has forecasted pizza delivery for the next 3 months as follows:

Demand	September	October	November	December
Pepperoni	300	350	320	340
Sausage	200	210	190	130
Meatsy	290	300	250	300
Veggie	80	85	80	90

They have two production lines in their facility. Each line equipped with an oven is capable of producing about 500 pizzas. Each line has a dough maker, a pizza maker, and a packer. Determine the capacity requirements for the 4 months.

15. Wakarusa Chocolate Factory is considering the possibility of building an additional facility to add another product line. There are currently two options—buy an existing space or build a brand-new space. Buying an existing space will cost $2 million. If demand is low, the company expects to receive $4 million in discounted revenues (present value). If demand is high, it expects $6 million in discounted revenues. For the second option, the cost is $5 million. For low demand, the company expects $5 million in discounted revenues and if demand is high, the company expects $8 million. The probability of demand being high is 45%. What should Wakarusa Chocolate Factory do?

16. Mumbai Masala, an Indian grocery chain in the West Ridge suburbs of Chicago has been very profitable over the past years. Mahesh Patel, the owner, has located a property in the western suburbs of Chicago. The land has a permit and is currently zoned for homes. He wants to buy the land for $1 million and develop the property. With the current permit, he can build five four-storied buildings each with 12 condos of various sizes on each floor and sell those with a profit of $10 thousand a piece. If he applies for a new permit to rezone and build stores, he has two options. One option is to build a department store with a return of $5 million in a strong economy and $4 million in a weak economy. But the cost of permit, rezoning, and associated costs will amount to $1.5 million. The probability of a strong economy is 70%. The probability of getting the new permit with rezoning is 60%. Another alternative to the department store is a possibility of building a small mall. He can sell the shops in the small mall and make a profit of $4.5 million in a strong economy and $4 million in a weak economy. What should Mahesh do?

References

1. Forbes. (2021). *Ford Motor Co*. Retrieved November 6, 2021, from https://www.forbes.com/ companies/ford-motor/?sh=5d7f2e631dfd

2. Carlier, M. (2021). *Ford Motor Co. - vehicle sales in the United States by segment Q4 2019–Q4 2020*. Retrieved November 6, 2021, from https://www.statista.com/statistics/239967/ford-motors-vehicle-sales-in-the-united-states-by-segment/.

3. Maverick, J. B. (2021). *Who Are Ford's Main Suppliers?* Retrieved November 6, 2021, from https://www.investopedia.com/ask/answers/052715/who-are-fords-f-main-suppliers.asp.

4. Thomas, D. G. (2017). *Creating Global Data Standards*. Retrieved November 6, 2021, from https://www.supplychainbrain.com/articles/25010-creating-global-data-standards.

5. Seller, C., Field, P., Werner, A., Schepers, G., & Lesmeister, F. (2012). Tailoring Production to *Demand at Pfizer*. Pharma Manufacturing.

6. Croxton, K. L., Lambert, D. M., García-Dastugue, S. J., & Rogers, D. S. (2002). The demand management process. *The International Journal of Logistics Management, 13*(2), 51–66.

7. World Today News. (2020). *The double disaster of the German auto industry*. Retrieved November 6, 2021, from https://www.world-today-news.com/auto-industry-slump-in-sales-and-overcapacity-world/.

8. Tozzi, C. (2020, October 9). *The importance of cloud capacity management and how to do it*. Techtarget.

9. Microsoft. (2021). *Plan for capacity*. Retrieved November 16, 2021, from https://docs.microsoft.com/en-us/azure/architecture/framework/scalability/design-capacity.

10. Maske, M. (2021). *NFL caps Super Bowl attendance at 22,000, including 7,500 vaccinated health-care workers*. Retrieved November 9, 2021, from https://www.washingtonpost.com/sports/2021/01/22/super-bowl-attendance-tampa/.

11. Whitten, S. (2021). *Disney launches Genie, an all-in-one app for park visitors to plan trips and skip long lines*. Retrieved November 16, 2021, from https://www.cnbc.com/2021/08/18/disneys-genie-app-is-an-all-in-one-trip-planner-for-its-theme-parks.html.

12. Amon, C. (2021). *Qualcomm CEO talks Apple, cloud computing, car technology, handsets, metaverse, and more*. Retrieved November 18, 2021, from https://finance.yahoo.com/ video/qualcomm-ceo-talks-apple-cloud-154340779.html

PROJECT MANAGEMENT

Learning Objectives

- Define and classify projects.
- Define project management.
- Explain how projects are managed.
- Describe the benefits and success factors of project management.
- Estimate project costs.
- Select OSCM projects based on cost-benefit analysis and payback period.
- Monitor project costs and schedule using earned value management.
- Schedule projects using the project network model.
- Use learning curves to estimate the implementation of repeated tasks in projects.

Organizations implement various projects to ensure the necessary capacity in their plants, to build new processes, or to explore new products. They must use good project management skills and techniques to bring such projects to successful completion. Project management is implementing the activities of projects effectively to accomplish the goals and objectives of projects.

We have witnessed the execution of many projects in awe and admiration. One such project is the James Webb Space Telescope (JWST) project by NASA. The James Webb Space Telescope, NASA's premier space observatory of the next decade, was successfully launched on the Christmas morning of December 25, 2021, atop an Ariane 5 rocket from Europe's Spaceport in French Guiana.

© Jbruiz/Shutterstock.com

The Webb telescope has endured years of delays, including a combination of factors brought on by the pandemic and technical challenges[1]. But the world's most powerful and complex space observatory will answer questions about our solar system, peer into the atmospheres of exoplanets, some of which are potentially habitable, and it could uncover clues in the ongoing search for life outside of Earth.

The telescope is equipped with a mirror that can extend 21 feet and 4 inches (6.5 meters) to collect more light from the objects. It includes 18 hexagonal gold-coated segments each 4.3 feet (1.32 meters) in diameter. A unique project management strategy was devised to fit the large mirror inside a rocket. A NASA team designed the telescope as a series of moving parts that can fold in an origami style and fit inside a 16-foot (5-meter) space for launch[2].

The total cost of the project exceeded $10 billion. Originally, the cost of the telescope was estimated to be only around $3.5 billion[3], and expected launch date was postponed from earlier dates to 2021.

Successful project management and successful projects rely on many factors and one good factor is a project champion. The former senator Barbara Mikulski championed the JWST project. Thousands of scientists, technicians, and engineers from 14 countries have spent 40 million hours to build the telescope, which includes instruments from the Canadian Space Agency and the European Space Agency. It took hundreds of people from the United States and Europe to manage this project to a successful completion and launch into space.

Projects

Operations involves many projects. Deciding on the future location of a store to actually moving to the new location is an operations project. Another type of an operational project is establishing a supply chain where a company's management must coordinate the integration of the entire supply chain from purchasing raw materials to supplying finished goods to customers in a most cost-effective manner. A streamlining process to eliminate waste and implementing that process is an operations project. Another operations project is to devise an inventory management strategy which involves planning and storing optimal supplies, materials, and products on hand. Note that many of the subsequent activities of these projects may not be projects—they might be just routine operational activities. Routine work like manufacturing products are not projects since this is considered part of an operations activity rather than a project.

A project is a unique activity that has a beginning and a definite end. A project has constraints and requirements. A project creates value for its stakeholders.

Types of Projects

Typical operations projects include activities to reduce costs and improve customer satisfaction with goods and services. Organizations often select a number of projects to be implemented. The selected projects form a project portfolio for a particular duration of time. For example, a company may decide on six major projects as part of a project portfolio for the upcoming year. Such a portfolio of projects includes projects of many types. Wheelwright and Clark[4] suggest a framework where projects are categorized into five types including:

- Basic research projects,
- Alliances and partnership projects,
- Breakthrough projects,
- Platform projects, and
- Derivative projects.

Each project in an organizational project portfolio can be identified as one of these five types.

Basic Research Projects Basic research projects include research projects and advanced development projects to implement future commercial products, new systems, and novel services. For example, a process team may implement a new service to benefit the customers of a company. Intel Corporation recently announced a $3.5 billion project to equip its New Mexico operations for the manufacturing of advanced semiconductor packaging technologies.

Alliances and Partnership Projects A strategic alliance is a clearly defined partnership between two organizations with shared goals. These projects involve these organizations pooling resources to strengthen both their brands

> **Project** A project is a unique activity that adds value, expends resources, has beginning and end dates, and has constraints and requirements that include scope, cost, schedule, performance, resources, and value.

and increase market share. For example, the operations project between Starbucks and Barnes & Noble resulted in a successful co-branded Starbucks "B&N Cafes" inside most Barnes & Noble locations.

Breakthrough Projects Successful breakthrough projects generate new products, systems, services, and processes that are different than those of the previous generation. Examples are new applications, 3-D manufacturing, and 5G telecommunications infrastructure. These projects incorporate innovative technologies or materials that require new processes.

Platform Projects Platform projects entail product, system, service, or process changes. Designing and developing a new digital camera is a platform project.

Derivative Projects Derivative projects are cost-reducing, add-ons, or enhancements to existing products, systems, services, or processes. They involve incremental product, system, service, or process changes. A project to design and develop a new lens for a camera is a derivative project.

Project Management in Operations

Now that we know what a project is, let us take a look at how projects are managed. Successful projects need successful project management. Successful project management requires good planning and required resources with a commitment to complete projects, a skilled project manager, good communications and information flows, and an excellent value proposition to stakeholders.

Management is the act of getting people together to accomplish the desired goals and objectives. Management comprises planning, organizing, and controlling an organization or a group of people and other needed resources to accomplish a goal. Resources may consist of people, finance, technology, and natural resources. Project management is the act of collaborating with people and using the required resources such that a project is planned, organized, and controlled effectively to accomplish the project goals and the objectives.

Project management brings great benefits to individuals and organizations. The following are some of the potential benefits of project management[5]:

- Project management will help to deliver projects successfully;
- Project management will make sure that the scope of a project as required by a customer is completely met;
- Project management provides a process that can be followed to successfully complete projects;

> **Project management**
> Project management is the act of collaborating with people and using the required resources such that a project is planned, organized, and controlled effectively to accomplish the project goals and the objectives.

- Success from project management will inspire individuals and organizations to perform efficiently in the future;
- The project management process will help individuals and organizations to map a clear strategy to complete a project successfully;
- Project management will force individuals and organizations to identify and assess all perceived risks and exposures so that they can identify problems before they surface;
- Project management will help to measure goals and objectives; and
- Project management will help individuals and organizations to save time and money.

FROM PRACTICE: Project Management in Operations

Every time a company changes an existing process, creates something new, or implements a one-time job, it is engaging in a project. Work that is not repetitive and operational may be classified as a project. For instance, a product itself is not a project but the process of creating the product is a project. Manufacturing organizations lose an average of 11.8% of the money invested in projects due to poor project performance. Manufacturing companies lose more money in projects than companies in the energy, construction, and healthcare sectors. In summary, only one in two projects is completed within the initial budget. The primary cause of project failure is changes in the project scope. There are many success stories as well!

A global manufacturer of personal care and household products set an ambitious, aggressive timeline of one year from groundbreaking to build an operational 475,000 square foot, $60 million manufacturing facility. Normally it would require 24 months to complete this type of project. The project manager worked with over 20 senior internal leaders from over 25 corporate and site-level operating units in improving communications

among business units and leadership, building awareness among team members on the strategic implications of the program, and managing the schedule to ensure successful completion. He used lean manufacturing principles to translate existing corporate policies to fit a new manufacturing culture. The new manufacturing facility was delivered on time, beginning production one year after breaking ground. The project provided an expected savings in excess of $12 million per year. The company also realized 33% of their projected return 7 months ahead of schedule[6].

Components of Project Management

Although each project is unique, all projects have a common theme with the same set of components as shown in Figure 4-1. For projects to be successful, the foundation is, of course, governance, strategy, leadership, and management. Project performance domains, models, methods, and artifacts of project management help project managers to effectively monitor, control, and manage projects. Scope, time, cost, resources, performance, and value form the six basic pillars of project management. To be successful in project implementation, project teams must tailor various project approaches and processes at their disposal to various activities of their current projects. A typical project comprises these activities:

Figure 4-1 Components of Project Management

Adapted from Vaidyanathan, G. (2022). *Project Management: Process, Technology, and Practice.* Kendall-Hunt Publishing.

- A clear definition of the project, including good rationale and alignment to corporate goals;
- Organizing and developing a project structure with associated channels of communication, accountabilities, responsibilities, and reporting facilities;
- Defining project requirements from customers and establishing a project scope for success;

- Planning the project to include analysis of activities, and defining and developing major tasks with milestones;
- Planning clear and adequate communications;
- Evaluating risks at all stages of a project and planning to mitigate these risks;
- Estimating time, costs, resource requirements and performance measures, and project value;
- Scheduling all activities;
- Continuously monitoring and controlling scope, time, cost, performance factors, and project value;
- Implementing the project;
- Bringing closure to a successful project; and
- Creating and benefiting from project value.

Project Management Success Factors

To understand the benefits provided by good project management practices, we need to understand the factors of project success. Success of projects depends heavily on the success of project management. It requires careful monitoring and control of many factors. Let us explore those success factors.

The scope of a project depends on the requirements of project customers. The requirements are often dynamic in the sense that they change from time to time. For example, a simple requirement like bread for you and your family can change depending on your family's bread consumption since during some weeks, you may consume more bread than usual. Every project must have a pre-defined scope. This pre-defined scope of the project defines a **baseline** for the project performance measurement. The scope of a project has to be accurate and elaborate with no ambiguity. Poor scope definition and underestimation of the complexity of projects and their interdependency with other projects or with existing services or products causes projects to fail. The scope of a project includes the following:

- How much can be achieved in the current project?
- When must the project be completed?
- When and for how long will resources (people, facilities, equipment, and so on) be available?

Proper management of the scope is critical to avoid cost and schedule overruns. The scope actually defines a project plan so that the project manager can stick to the plan. Project scope should be neither too broad nor too narrow. A project scope that is too broad or ambitious can cause severe problems by increasing time and costs. A narrow scope will lead to confusion and uncertainty in the management of a project. Any change to a project's scope must be controlled by the project manager.

The cost and duration of projects are other crucial factor of success. If a project costs more than the expectations of a company or it takes a longer than

> **Project scope** The scope of a project is the work that needs to be accomplished to deliver the results of the project with specified features and functions.

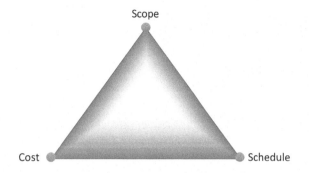

Figure 4-2 Crucial Factors of Project Success

expected time frame, then the company may not be in a position either to initiate the project or proceed with the project. These three factors including scope, cost, and schedule form the crucial success factors of project as shown in Figure 4-2.

There are other factors that influence the success of projects and project management. There are constraints such as project risks, environment, social responsibility factors, and compliance to government regulations and regulatory codes. In summary, the success factors and constraints in a project are[7]:

- Scope: Completion of projects within scope per customer;
- Cost: Completion of project within allocated budget;
- Time: Completion of project within allocated schedule or period of time;
- Resources: Completion of project using allocated resources;
- Quality: Completion of project within established quality and performance standards;
- Value: Completion of project to maximize project value for stakeholders;
- Internal and External Risks: Completion of project by managing internal and external project risks efficiently;
- Environmental factors: Completion of project by managing internal and external environmental factors;
- Social responsibility factors: Completion of project by commitment to social responsibility toward internal and external stakeholders; and
- Regulatory factors: Completion of project by complying with internal and external standards and regulatory codes.

FROM PRACTICE: Project Management at Vodafone

Vodafone Group PLC is a British multinational telecommunications company providing services in Asia, Africa, Europe, and Oceania. One of their strategic customers requested to replace its existing, obsolete network with a highly capable, fully managed Global Local Area Network (GLAN) in 42 different sites across the world. With a contract of 5 years of service, the Vodafone customer program delivery project team planned to complete the project by November 2019.

© DaLiu/Shutterstock.com

The project was identified as highly complex after assessing the risks. One high-severity risk was the possibility of the occurrence of a total network failure during the implementation resulting in a lack of service and losses of millions of euros. To begin with, there was a delay in signing the contract that put huge pressure on the project schedule. However, with all these problems and risks, Vodafone implemented the project successfully with on-time delivery and cost savings. This was because of the skillful execution by the project manager who used the standards of the Project Management Institute (PMI). Using a project management approach based on PMI standards, workshops were conducted with suppliers to agree on the required resources, good communication plans were enforced, and the progress of the project and delivery was controlled efficiently[8].

FROM PRACTICE: Scope Management at New Energy, Inc.

© hrui/Shutterstock.com

New Energy, Inc. is a fast-growing supplier of "green" energy solutions, including wind turbines, solar technology, and so on. One of their projects included a scope to obtain the best package of solutions, procure the package, and install the package. Three different departments wanted three different solutions. The requirement analysis was not conducted thoroughly. The project manager went with one package picked by one department, ignoring the requirements of the other two departments. A team member discovered that the project scope did not include many changes to the systems and coded something quickly that was agreed to by the project manager, but the coding was not tested properly. The package was implemented on schedule, but with several problems. The problem in this case was that the scope was not well defined and there was a lack of formal scope management[9].

FROM PRACTICE: Project Management at INDOT

Several State Departments of Transportation including the Indiana Department of Transportation (INDOT) have a problem with completing projects on time and within budget. Time delays, cost overruns, and changes are generally due to factors such as design errors, unexpected site conditions, changes in project scope, weather conditions, and other project changes. In 2001, INDOT incurred approximately $17,028,000 in cost overruns, representing approximately 9% of the

(continued)

total amount for all contracts in 2001. The results of a survey showed that with respect to cost overruns, INDOT has an average rank compared to other states. 55% of all INDOT contracts experienced cost overruns.

12% of all INDOT contracts experienced time delays and the average delay per contract was 115 days. A study by Purdue University[10] determined that the average cost overrun amount and rate differ by project type as follows: bridge projects by 8.1%; road construction by 5.6%; road resurfacing by 2.6%; traffic projects by 5.6%; and maintenance projects by 7.5%. The study also revealed other influential factors of cost overrun including contract bid amount, difference between the winning bid and second bid, difference between the winning bid and the engineer's estimate, project type, and location by district.

Project management provides relevant approaches, methods, models, artifacts, and tools to manage the project success factors and maximize the project benefits when confronted by obstacles. Every project comprises all the above components. Each of those components consists of many activities. In this chapter, we will focus on a few topics of interest from the operations management perspective. In the following sections, we will concentrate on the following important activities of the crucial project management factors as shown in Figure 4-2:

- Cost estimation and selection of projects using cost-benefit and payback period analysis,
- Scheduling projects using PDND and CPM, and
- Monitoring costs and schedule in projects using EVA.

Cost Estimation and Selection of Projects

Cost is a major factor in the success of a project. Projects that are over budget are often terminated because the stakeholders may run out of money or perceive such projects as failures at any time during the project. It is safe to say that many projects that run out of money do so because of poor estimating, poor budgeting, or poor control. In this section we will discuss project costs, cost estimation and analysis, budgeting, and cost control in projects.

Project Costs

Project costs comprise the following major costs:

- Direct material and labor costs;
- Indirect material and labor costs;
- Fixed costs; and
- Variable costs.

Direct Material and Labor Costs Material and labor costs that are used solely for a project become the direct material and labor costs for that project. The computers and printers employed in an operations project are direct materials. The direct labor is also called touch labor because these workers typically "touch" the project while it is being implemented. The salaries, wages, and fringe benefits of the project team members are part of direct costs as are the cost of equipment procured specifically for the project and materials and supplies used directly for it. Other direct costs include those incurred in travel, consulting, or contracting, or outsourced services.

Indirect Material and Labor Costs Indirect material costs include any material and labor costs that are necessary to complete a project, but do not become an actual part of the final project. Among the indirect materials used in a project are pens, notepads, and other supplementary materials. Costs of electricity and other utilities, telephone, Internet, paper towels, office supplies, and postage are examples of indirect costs.

Fixed Costs Office space and electricity are examples of fixed costs as they are not affected by rises and falls in project activities.

Variable Costs Variable costs vary in direct proportion to changes in the level of project activities. The number of hours worked on an activity in a project by team members is a variable cost.

These four types of costs are important in calculating the total costs of a project. Example 4-1 illustrates the different cost types.

> **Project cost** The sum of all costs to complete a project.

> **Direct material and labor costs** Direct material and labor costs are the costs of materials that are entirely linked to the execution of the project.

> **Indirect material and labor costs** Indirect materials costs include any material and labor costs that are necessary to complete a project, but do not become an actual part of the final project.

> **Fixed costs** Fixed costs remain constant regardless of changes in the level of project activities.

> **Variable costs** Variable costs vary in direct proportion to changes in the level of project activities.

Example 4-1

Rebus Inc., a manufacturer of board games and puzzles, reported their manufacturing labor costs for their full-time employees as $400,000 for the first week of May. Expenses of clerical services was $40,000. The benefits for their employees amounted to $74,000, pension costs were $30,000, indirect salary was $40,000; equipment rental and depreciation was $15,000 and $5,000 respectively; supplies $2,500; utilities $4.500; legal fees $2,000 and accounting fees $2,000. Two consultants got paid $8,000 each during the same period. Calculate the indirect rate based on direct labor and indirect rate based on total direct costs.

We can use Excel to solve the problem as shown below:

	A	B	
1	Direct and Indirect Costs of a Project		
2	**Direct Cost Base**		
3	Direct Labor Costs	$400,000	
4	Consulting Costs	$16,000	
5	Total Direct Costs	$416,000	=sum(b3:b4)
6	**Indirect Cost Pool**		
7	Clerical Services	$40,000	
8	Benefits	$74,000	
10	Pension Costs	$30,000	
11	Indirect Salaries	$40,000	
12	Facility Rental Costs	$15,000	
13	Equipment Depreciation	$5,000	
14	Utilities	$4,500	
15	Supplies	$2,500	
16	Legal Fees	$2,000	
17	Accounting Fees	$2,000	
18	Total Indirect Costs	$215,000	=sum(b7:b17)
19	**Indirect Rates**		
20	Indirect Rate Based on Direct Labor	53.75%	=b18/b3
21	Indirect Rate Based on Total Direct Costs	51.68%	=b18/b5

Analysis: Separate the direct and indirect costs. The total direct costs are more than the total indirect costs. Direct labor is person-hours that are directly attributable to project activity. Indirect labor is used to provide supporting services to the project such as accounting, clerical, and purchasing. An indirect cost rate is the percentage of a project's indirect costs to its direct costs and is a standardized method of charging individual projects for their share of indirect costs. The indirect cost of labor refers to amounts paid for employees who support the manufacture of board games and puzzles but are not directly involved in making them.

Cost Estimation

To begin with, cost is measured as a monetary amount—dollar, pound, yen, euro, rupee, yuan, and so on—that is paid to acquire goods, services, and project expenses. Before a project is started, the anticipated costs of that project should be identified. This is called cost estimation. The level of effort and expertise needed to accomplish cost estimation is high in most projects. Project managers need to create time to gather adequate historical data, select appropriate estimating methods, consider alternatives, or carefully apply the proper method to estimate a project. Cost estimates are completed by totaling the costs of individual project elements. There are three common methods employed in estimating costs at different timeframes during a project:

- Rough order of magnitude estimate (ROME);
- Approximate historical estimate (AHE); and
- Detailed estimate (DE).

We will define the three methods in this section. Project managers use these methods to estimate costs and add an extra amount called a buffer to the estimate in order to give a realistic estimate of a project. Example 4-2 shows the comparison of the first three estimates.

Rough Order of Magnitude Estimate (ROME)   This is a rough estimate of project costs and is calculated before the actual project starts. Senior management looks at this estimate to make decisions on which projects are cost effective and for cost-benefit analysis. The accuracy of ROME is usually between −25% and +75%[7].

Approximate Historical Estimate (AHE)   Sometimes project managers do not have a detailed knowledge of a project. They use a top-down estimate called an approximate historical estimate. As the name suggests, organizations use historical data and knowledge from past projects that were similar in scope to estimate costs. AHEs are also used for budgetary purposes in organizations. The accuracy of AHE is between −10% and +25%[7].

Detailed Estimate (DE)   Many projects are estimated using detailed actual costs. After the requirements are gathered and the scope of the project is established, detailed estimates of the project can be determined. The accuracy of DE is about −5% to +10%[7].

> **Cost estimation**
> Cost estimation is the process of determining the cost of a project.

> **ROME** A rough order of magnitude estimate provides a rough estimate of what a project costs before the actual project has started.

> **AHE** Approximate historical estimates are made without detailed knowledge of a project.

> **DE** A detailed estimate is prepared from well-developed plans and real quotes.

Example 4-2

The IT operations project of Riverside, Inc. was initiated recently. Steve Banks, the IT manager, produced an initial rough estimate of $80 per hour for labor and $80,000 for equipment for the implementation of a new data center. Upon reviewing a similar project, he revised his equipment cost as $85,000 and added $3,000 for Internet services and $40,000 as miscellaneous costs. After receiving the requirements from his stakeholders, he had to revise the equipment costs to be $90,000. He also found out that the Internet costs are $200 and the labor cost to be $5 more than he anticipated. If the project is projected to be implemented in 240 hours and if he includes a 5% buffer for contingency purposes, what are his ROME, AHE, and DE estimates?

The data is shown in the following table. Steve's final estimate is $149,020. The total cost is the sum of Internet services, labor, equipment, and other costs.

	Hours	ROME	AHE	DE
Contingency Cost Factor		5%	5%	5%
Internet Services			$3,000	$3,200
Labor cost per hour		$80	$80	$85
Equipment costs		$80,000	$85,000	$90,000
Labor costs	240	$19,200	$19,200	$20,400
Other costs		$0	$40,000	$35,420
Total cost		$99,200	$147,200	$149,020
Total cost with contingency cost factor		$104,160	$154,560	$156,471

Analysis: The DE is the most accurate of the three estimates. The AHE is more accurate than the ROME method.

Cost-Benefit Analysis Using NPV and Payback Period

> **NPV** The present value of cash flows from the project at a rate of return compared to the initial investment in the project.

After costs are estimated initially for projects, senior management decides on which projects they should fund and implement. The selection of these projects usually involves a cost-benefit analysis. A cost-benefit analysis is the simplest way of comparing projects to determine whether to go ahead with a particular project. The projects that are deemed to be the most beneficial would be selected as projects to be implemented. To do a cost-benefit analysis, we have to introduce the concept of Net Present Value (NPV).

Cash Flows and NPV

Cash flow in a project is the net amount of money being transferred in and out of the project. Benefits from the projects are the inflow and project expenses are outflows.

$$Cash flows = Total Benefits - Total Costs$$

NPV can be calculated in many ways:

1. If there's one cash flow from a project that will be paid one year from now with an initial investment, use Eq. 4-2.
2. To analyze a longer-term project with multiple cash flows, use Eq. 4-3.
3. The NPV calculation can be done in Microsoft Excel as well using the following Microsoft Excel function:

   NPV(discount rate, Years 1 to 4 cashflows) – cashflow for year 0 or initial investment.

Net Present Value (NPV)   NPV is the present value of cash flows from the project at a rate of return compared to the initial investment in the project. A dollar today is worth more than a dollar tomorrow because today's dollar can be invested right now to earn interest immediately. To calculate the present value, we must discount future cash flows at an appropriate rate called the "discount rate." A project should be selected only if the NPV is positive. Example 4-3 illustrates how to calculate NPV.

If C_t is the expected payoff at time period t, and r is the discount rate,

$$Present\ Value\ (PV) = \frac{C_t}{(1+r)^t} \qquad \text{Eq. 4-1}$$

If there is one cash flow from a project that will be paid one year from now with an initial investment, then

$$Net\ Present\ Value\ (NPV) = Present\ Value - Initial\ Investment \qquad \text{Eq. 4-2}$$

For a multi-year project. If t is the number of years or periods and n is the last year of cash flow,

$$NPV = \sum_{t=1}^{n} \frac{C_t}{(1+r)^t} - Initial\ Investment \qquad \text{Eq. 4-3}$$

where the Σ symbol represents addition for each one of the year's NPV from 1 to n.

Example 4-3

You have land worth $1,000,000 and you want to build an office building on the land, which will cost you $500,000. Because the city is expanding, this office building may be sold for $1,750,000 next year. Therefore, you will be investing $1,500,000 and expecting $1,750,000 a year from now. What is the present value and net present value?

The present value of $1,750,000 one year from now must be less than $1,750,000 since a dollar today is worth more than a dollar tomorrow. If the discount rate is 10%, the present value using Eq. 4-1 is:

$$PV = \frac{1,750,000}{(1+0.1)^1} = \$1,590,909$$

Using Eq. 4-2,

$$NPV = \$1,590,909 - \$1,500,000 = \$90,909.$$

| *Analysis:* Since the NPV is positive, this is a good project to implement.

Payback Period

The next financial consideration in project selection is the payback period analysis. This method determines the amount of time a project will take to recuperate its investments. Payback analysis determines how much time will lapse before the benefits overtake the costs. For example, in Example 4-1, it took less than a year to make up the initial investment of $1,500,000. Payback occurs when net costs equal net benefits accumulated over the project years. Now, let us take a look at how cost-benefit analysis is performed in organizations using Example 4-4.

Example 4-4

Biz Baez, Inc. is deciding on whether to restore an existing lab or build a new one. If the discount rate is 13%, compare the two projects to decide on the most beneficial project using cost-benefit analysis using the following cost data:

Project 1	Restoration of a Product Lab				
	Year 0	Year 1	Year 2	Year 3	Year 4
Total Benefits	$500,000	$600,000	$650,000	$700,000	$800,000
Total Costs	$800,000	$540,000	$600,000	$400,000	$350,000
Project 2	New Product Lab				
	Year 0	Year 1	Year 2	Year 3	Year 4
Total Benefits	$0	$1,000,000	$1,200,000	$1,800,000	$2,500,000
Total Costs	$2,000,000	$800,000	$500,000	$400,000	$300,000

For projects 1 and 2, we can calculate the cash flows = Total Benefits – Total Costs and then calculate the NPV using Microsoft Excel using the function:

NPV(discount rate, Years 1 to 4 cashflows) – Initial investment, i.e., cashflow for year 0

	A	B	C	D	E	F
1	Discount rate		13%			
2		Year 0	Year 1	Year 2	Year 3	Year 4
3	**Project 1**	**Restoration of a Product Lab**				
4	**Cash Flows**	**($300,000)**	**$60,000**	**$50,000**	**$300,000**	**$450,000**
5	**NPV**	**$276,163**	=NPV(C1,C4:F4)+B4			
6	**Project 2**	**New Product Lab**				
7	**Cash Flows**	**($2,000,000)**	**$200,000**	**$700,000**	**$1,400,000**	**$2,200,000**
8	**NPV**	**$1,044,765**	=NPV(C1,C7:F7)+B7			

Since the NPV of both projects are positive, the company can choose both projects. However, let us check the payback periods for both projects, which is shown below:

Step 1: Find the discounted costs and benefits for each year using Eq. 4-1.

Step 2: Calculate accumulated discounted benefits and costs. For example, accumulated discounted cost of year 2 = discounted cost of Year 2 + discounted cost of Year 1.

Step 3: Plot the accumulated discounted costs and benefits.

Step 4: The intersection of the accumulated discounted costs and benefits is the payback period.

The cost-benefit analysis and the payback analysis are shown next:

	A	B	C	D	E	F	G	H
1		Discount rate:	13%		Project 1			
2	Year	Discount Factor	Benefits	Discounted Benefits	Accumulated Discounted Benefits	Costs	Discounted Costs	Accumulated Discounted Costs
3	0	1.00	$500,000	$500,000	$500,000	$800,000	$800,000	$800,000
4	1	0.88	$600,000	$530,973	$1,030,973	$540,000	$477,876	$1,277,876
5	2	0.78	$650,000	$509,045	$1,540,019	$600,000	$469,888	$1,747,764
6	3	0.69	$700,000	$485,135	$2,025,154	$400,000	$277,220	$2,024,984
7	4	0.61	$800,000	$490,655	$2,515,809	$350,000	$214,662	$2,239,646
8					Project 2			
9	Year	Discount Factor	Benefits	Discounted Benefits	Accumulated Discounted Benefits	Costs	Discounted Costs	Accumulated Discounted Costs
10	0	1.00	$0	$0	$0	$2,000,000	$2,000,000	$2,000,000
11	1	0.88	$1,000,000	$884,956	$884,956	$800,000	$707,965	$2,707,965
12	2	0.78	$1,200,000	$939,776	$1,824,732	$500,000	$391,573	$3,099,538
13	3	0.69	$1,800,000	$1,247,490	$3,072,222	$400,000	$277,220	$3,376,758
14	4	0.61	$2,500,000	$1,533,297	$4,605,519	$300,000	$183,996	$3,560,754

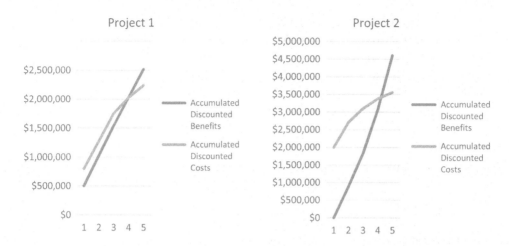

Analysis: The NPV is positive for both projects and therefore both projects are good to be implemented. But, if we need to choose only one of the two projects, then we can do a payback period to see if one of them gives a better payback than the other. As seen in the above charts, the payback periods for both projects are around 3 to 3.5 years. Therefore, the company can accept both projects for implementation. However, since the company wants to select only one project, they should select Project 2 because the NPV of Project 2 is greater than Project 1.

Scheduling Projects

A project schedule is used to deliver the project scope. Scheduling is a plan to implement a project using an ordered sequence of activities with time allotted for each activity. A common method for scheduling is a Project Schedule Network Diagram (PSND). The PSND shows the sequential and logical relationships between tasks in a project. The PSND is used to help project managers plan, schedule, monitor, and control their projects and is useful because it provides the following information:

- Expected project completion time;
- Critical activities that directly affect the completion time; and
- The start and the end times of all activities.

> **Project schedule network diagram (PSND)** A project schedule network diagram shows the sequential and logical relationships between tasks in a project.

A network diagram consists of activities with a start and an end. An activity is a specific task, or set of tasks, which is part of the scope of a project, uses up some of the resources of a project, and requires some finite time to be completed. In Figure 4-5a, "A" and "B" are activities. Activity A is connected to activity B, and, therefore, activity A is the predecessor to activity B. Activity A lasts for 2 weeks, and activity B lasts for 1 week, which are the durations of the activities A and B.

Activity A has to be completed before activity B is begun. A project will have only one start activity and one finish activity. An activity can have predecessors with no successors, can have successors with no predecessors, or can

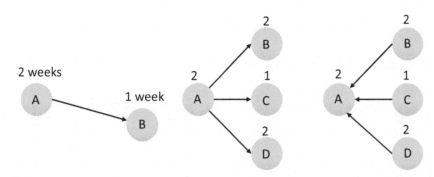

Figure 4-5a Activities   **Figure 4-5b** Burst   **Figure 4-5c** Merge

have both predecessors and successors. In Figure 4-5b, called a "burst," activity A should take place before activities B, C, and D. Here activities B, C, and D are successor activities. In Figure 4-5c, also called a "merge," activity A can be begun only after activities B, C, and D are completed. Here, activities B, C, and D are predecessors. If any activity is delayed, it will delay the completion of the entire project. Scheduling using PSND includes the following four times:

- ES = the earliest time when an activity can start;
- EF = the earliest time when an activity can finish;
- LS = the latest time when an activity can start; and
- LF = the latest time when an activity can finish.

To calculate the earliest starting times, we must make a forward pass through the network from left to right. The earliest start time of a successor activity is the earliest finish date of a predecessor. The earliest finish time is the total of the earliest start time and the activity duration. To calculate the latest times, we must make a backward pass through the network by calculating the latest finish time. Because the activity time is known, the latest start time can be calculated by subtracting the activity time from the latest finish time, which is the earliest start time of the activities. The results of the forward and backward passes will provide you with the slack in the system. Slack can be calculated as either the difference of ES and LS or the difference of EF and LF.

In any project, there are critical activities and the path of those critical activities is called the critical path. The critical path is the longest path of the network and determines the total duration of the project and also the shortest amount of time necessary to accomplish the project. The critical path in a PSND follows the activities whose slack are equal to zero.

Example 4-5 illustrates these steps to determine the critical path of a project. To find the critical path, these are the steps to follow:

1. Draw the network diagram or PSND,
2. Make a forward pass through the network,
3. Make a backward pass through the network,
4. Calculate slack of all activities, and
5. Determine the critical path.

> **Slack** Slack—sometimes referred to as float—is the amount of time that an activity in a project network can be delayed without causing a delay to subsequent activities or project completion. Slack can be calculated as either the difference of ES and LS or the difference of EF and LF.

> **Critical path** The critical path is the longest path of the network.

Example 4-5

Find the critical path and the total slack of a project whose activities to select a 3rd Party Logistics provider are shown below:

Activity	Description	Predecessor	Duration (Weeks)
A	Design RFQ to select a 3rd Party Logistics Provider		2
B	Send RFQs to 10 3PL providers	A	3
C	Receive RFQs and evaluate	B	8
D	Design interviews and analysis criteria	C	3
E	Select top 3 providers	C	6
F	Conduct interviews	D, E	5
G	Analyze interview results	F	4
H	Select 3rd Party Logistics Provider	G	2

Step 1:   Draw the network diagram or PSND.

From the table shown above, Activity A is the start of the project. Activity B can begin when activity A is completed. Once B is completed, activity C can begin. Activities D and E can start once activity C is completed. Activity F can begin once both activities D and E are completed. Activity G can start once activity F is completed and activity H, the end activity of the project, can start once activity G is completed. This is the PSND:

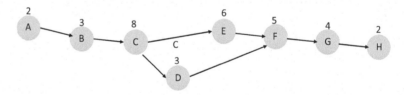

The network diagram or PSND shows each activity with its duration and sequenced according to the project scheduling plan as shown in the table above.

Step 2:   Make a forward pass through the network.

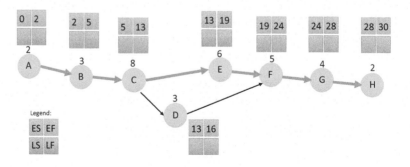

We start with activity A and run the forward pass all the way to activity H as follows:

- Activity A: ES = 0 (we start the project); because duration is 2, EF = 0 + 2 = 2;
- Activity B: ES = 2 (same as EF of activity A); because duration is 3, EF = 2 + 3 = 5;
- Activity C: ES = 5 (same as EF of activity B); because duration is 8, EF = 5 + 8 = 13;
- Activity D: ES = 13 (same as EF of activity C); because duration is 3, EF = 13 + 3 = 16;
- Activity E: ES = 13 (same as EF of activity C); because duration is 6, EF = 13 + 6 = 19;
- Activity F: This activity is a "merge" of two activities—D and E. For a forward pass, we take the maximum of the EF of D and E to get the ES for this activity. Therefore, ES = max{16,19} = 19; because duration is 5, EF = 19 + 5 = 24;
- Activity G: ES = 24; because duration is 4, EF = 24 + 4 = 28;
- Activity H: ES = 28; because duration is 2, EF = 28 + 2 = 30.
  Note: It takes 30 weeks to complete this project.

Step 3:   Make a backward pass through the network.

We start with activity H and run the forward pass all the way to activity A as follows:

- Activity H: LF = 30 (this is the end of the project and therefore the same as EF of activity H); because duration is 2, LS = 30–2 = 28;
- Activity G: LF = 28 (same as LS of activity H); because duration is 4, LS = 28–4 = 24;
- Activity F: LF = 24; because duration is 5, LS = 24–5 = 19;
- Activity E: LF = 19; because duration is 6, LS = 19–6 = 13;
- Activity D: LF = 19; because the duration is 3, LS = 19–3 = 16;
- Activity C: Here there is a "burst" of two activities—D and E. For a backward pass, we take the minimum of the LS of D and E to get the LF of C. Therefore, LF = min{16,13} = 13; because duration is 8, LS = 13–8 = 5;
- Activity B: LF = 5; because duration is 3, LS = 5–3 = 2;
- Activity A: LF = 2; because duration is 2, LS = 2–2 = 0.

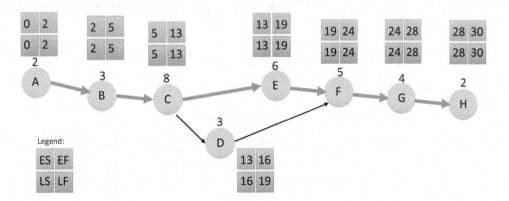

Step 4:   Calculate slack of all activities.

In this step, we use the ES, EF, LS, and LF that we computed for each activity to calculate the slack of each activity. Slack can be calculated as either the difference of ES and LS or the difference of EF and LF.

Activity	Description	ES	EF	LS	LF	Slack
A	Design RFQ to select a 3rd Party Logistics Provider	0	2	0	2	0
B	Send RFQs to 10 3PL providers	2	5	2	5	0
C	Receive RFQs and evaluate	5	13	5	13	0
D	Design interviews and analysis criteria	13	16	16	19	3
E	Select top 3 providers	13	19	13	19	0
F	Conduct interviews	19	24	19	24	0
G	Analyze interview results	24	28	24	28	0
H	Select 3rd Party Logistics Provider	28	30	28	30	0

The slack of each activity is shown in the table above. Note the slacks for activities A, B, C, E, F, G, and H. They are all equal to zero.

- Therefore, the critical path is A-B-C-E-F-G-H.
- The total slack is equal to 3 weeks.
- The total duration of the project is 30 weeks.

The critical path is shown in the following figure:

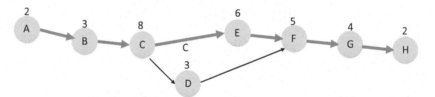

Analysis: The critical path is the path of all activities whose slacks are equal to zero. According to the above figure, it will take 2 + 3 + 8 = 13 days to complete C. Suppose activity D is after activity C, then after the 13 + 3 = 16 days, we will be ready to start to activity E. But activity F can be started only after completing both activities D and E. To complete activity E and be ready to start activity F, it will take 13 + 6 = 19 days. Therefore, we need to wait for 19 − 16 = 3 days in order to complete activity E and start activity F. Those three days are the slack days.

Variance in Scheduling Activities

Project scheduling and PSND can be used in times of uncertainty as well. Instead of the duration for an activity, estimated duration can be found using three estimates of time:

- Optimistic time: The shortest time in which an activity can be completed.
- Most likely time: The completion time having the highest probability.
- Pessimistic time: The longest time that an activity might require.

PSND assumes a beta probability distribution for the time estimates. For a beta distribution, the expected time for each activity can be approximated using the following average:

$$Expected\ Time = \frac{Optimistic\ Time + \left(4 \times Most\ Likely\ Time\right) + Pessimistic\ Time}{6} \qquad \text{Eq. 4-4}$$

This expected time may be used in the network diagram instead of the normal duration period for each activity. To calculate the variance for each activity duration, use the following equation:

$$Variance = \sigma^2 = \left(\frac{Pessimistic\ Time - Optimistic\ Time}{6}\right)^2 \qquad \text{Eq. 4-5}$$

The standard deviation of the critical path cannot be computed by summing the standard deviations (σ) of the activities since standard deviations cannot be added. However, the variance for the critical path can be calculated by summing the activity variances. The standard deviation (σ) is the square root of the variance and hence the total path standard deviation is:

$$\sigma_p = \sqrt{\sum\left(variances\ on\ the\ critical\ path\right)} \qquad \text{Eq. 4-6}$$

The uncertainty related to the time estimates can be measured using the standard deviation. If we assume that the sum of all completion times of all activities on the critical path is distributed normally, the probability of completing the network by any specified due date can be computed. Using the areas of the cumulative standard normal distribution given in Appendix A, we can calculate the probability of completing the project in a specified period of time:

$$Z = \frac{\left(D - E\right)}{\sigma_p} \qquad \text{Eq. 4-7}$$

where,

E is the sum of the expected time of the critical path,
D is the desired due time, and
σ_p is the total path standard deviation.

Example 4-6 uses the variances in activities to calculate the probability of completing the project a week earlier.

Example 4-6

For the problem presented in Example 4-5, what is the probability of completing the project in 29 weeks if each activity has an optimistic, most likely, and pessimistic time?

Activity	Optimistic Time	Most Likely Time	Pessimistic Time
A	2	2	2
B	3	3	3
C	7	8	9
D	3	3	3
E	4	6	8
F	4	5	6
G	3	4	5
H	2	2	2

The steps to calculate the probability of completing a project in a specified period of time:

1. Calculate the variances of each activity using the three estimates of time using Eq. 4-5.
2. Calculate total path standard deviation using Eq. 4-6.
3. Calculate the Z-score using Eq. 4-7.
4. From the table in Appendix A, find the single-tail normal probability distribution for the Z-score.

Step 1:   Calculate the variances of each activity using the three estimates of time.

The following table shows the variances calculated using Eq. 4-5:

Activity	Optimistic Time	Most Likely Time	Pessimistic Time	Estimated Time	Variance
A	2	2	2	2	0.00
B	3	3	3	3	0.00
C	7	8	9	8	0.11
D	3	3	3	3	0.00
E	4	6	8	6	0.44
F	4	5	6	5	0.11
G	3	4	5	4	0.11
H	2	2	2	2	0.00

Step 2:   Calculate total path standard deviation.

Using Eq. 4-6, $\sigma_p = 0.88$

Step 3:   Calculate the Z-score.

The total number of days in the critical path = 30 weeks.

If the project has to be completed in 29 weeks, then $Z = \dfrac{(29 - 30)}{0.88} = -1.1339$

Step 4:   From the tables, find the single-tail normal probability distribution for the Z-score.

From Appendix A, the single probability distribution for the Z-score of 1.1339 is 0.8708. But the area of the probability that we need is $1 - 0.8708 = 0.1292$ or 12.92%. Therefore, the probability of completing the project 1 week short is 12.92%.

Analysis: The probability of completing the project prior to the project schedule is often sought by project leaders. To successfully complete the project on time, the duration of each activity has to be estimated with some accuracy. In the case of reducing the number of project days, the optimistic, most likely, and pessimistic times need to be estimated with accuracy as well. The larger the σ_p, the smaller the Z. The lower the Z-score, the probability of completing the project gets better. In Excel, this probability is obtained by =1-NORM.S.DIST(-1.1339,TRUE).

Learning Curves

Learning from past projects helps project managers to estimate the time taken for certain activities. A learning curves method is one such tool. A learning curve is a graphical representation of the changing rate of learning for a given project activity. For example, a carpenter makes his first chair in four days. The next chair he makes will take less than four days because he has learned how to make a chair. Learning, as it is gained, improves performance on a project. A learning curve provides direct labor required to perform repeated activities. Learning curve theory is based on the following assumptions:

> **Learning curves**
> Learning curves are graphical representations of the changing rate of learning for a given project activity.

- The amount of time required to complete a task will be less each time the task is undertaken;
- The unit time will decrease at a decreasing rate; and
- This reduction of time will follow a predictable pattern.

Table A-1 in Appendix A is used for individual units and Table A-2 is typically used for cumulative units. Example 4-7 illustrates how to use learning curves.

Example 4-7

In a local bank, a manager is deciding on a commercial loan and he needs to estimate the time taken for a project. According to the project schedule, there are five loan applications. The activity is estimated to be performed for the first time in 100 hours by the bank manager. The manager estimates the learning improvement as 80%. What are the estimated performance times for the second, third, fourth, and fifth times?

Using Table A-1 in Appendix A, we see that the learning curve value for the second repetition with an 80 percent learning curve is 0.8. Therefore, estimated performance time for the 2nd time of the same activity is: $100 \times 0.8 = 80$ hours.

For the third repetition, the learning curve is 0.7021. Therefore, the estimated performance time for the 3rd time of the same activity is: $100 \times 0.7021 = 70.21$ hours.

Similarly, the estimated performance time for the 4th time of the same activity is: $100 \times 0.64 = 64$ hours.

The estimated performance time for the 5th time of the same activity is: $100 \times 0.5956 = 59.56$ hours.

> *Analysis:* Learning curves can be used in many activities of operations and supply management. For example, learning curves are useful in estimating the number of hours in which a worker can complete an operation activity.

Monitoring Costs and Schedule in Projects

A project manager continuously monitors scope, cost, and schedule of a project and communicates the progress to all stakeholders of the project. To monitor and manage cost and schedule, project managers use a tool called an Earned Value Analysis (EVA). EVA uses the work in progress to indicate the future of a project. EVA examines actual cost at any period during the progress of a project. This provides project managers greater insight into potential risk areas and allows them to plan ahead to progress their projects. In summary, EVA provides project managers an "early warning" signal and enables them to identify and control problems before they become out of control.

> **EVA** Earned Value Analysis is primarily used to measure and track costs and schedules in a project.

Once the project is selected, organizations have to allocate budgets to carry out various projects. A budget is a financial plan for a defined period for a project. Usually, budgets are allocated at least 1 year before the beginning of the project. In some organizations, the budgets are developed 2 years in advance. EVA uses the budget as a baseline for calculating several factors that show how a project is progressing. In this section, we will detail various EVA factors that are used for monitoring cost and schedule of projects.

1. Budget at completion (BAC): Budget at completion is the baseline budget of a project.
2. Planned Value (PV): PV is the budgeted amount of cost for work scheduled to be accomplished on a given activity for a given period of time.

$$PV = Planned\ completion\ \% \times Budget\ at\ completion \qquad Eq.\ 4\text{-}8$$

3. Earned Value (EV): EV is the amount of cost budgeted for completed work of a given activity for a given period of time.

$$EV = Actual\ completion\ \% \times Budegt\ at\ Completion \qquad \text{Eq. 4-9}$$

4. Actual Cost (AC): AC is the actual amount spent in completing the work accomplished within a given time period.
5. Cost Variance (CV): CV compares deviations of actual cost from the budget and does not take schedule into account. If cost variance is negative, it means that performing the activity costs more than planned or budgeted cost. The negative variance signifies project cost overrun. Positive CV is good; it means that the project is progressing within budget.

$$CV = EV - AC \qquad \text{Eq. 4-10}$$

6. Cost Variance Percentage (CVP): Cost variance can be represented as a percentage.

$$Cost\ Variance\ \%\ (CVP) = \frac{CV}{EV} \qquad \text{Eq. 4-11}$$

7. Schedule Variance (SV): SV compares deviations only from the schedule and does not take cost into account. If schedule variance is negative, it means that it took longer to perform the activity than planned. Positive SV is good; it means that the project is progressing ahead of schedule.

$$SV = EV - PV \qquad \text{Eq.4-12}$$

8. Schedule Variance Percentage (SVP): Schedule variance can be represented as a percentage rather than a cost by using the formula:

$$Schedule\ Variance\ \%\ (SVP) = \frac{SV}{PV} \qquad \text{Eq. 4-13}$$

9. Cost Performance Index (CPI): If CPI is equal to 1, then planned and actual costs are equal meaning the budget was perfect or the costs were exactly budgeted. If CPI is less than 1, then the project is over budget. If CPI is more than 1, then the project is within budget.

$$CPI = \frac{EV}{AC} \qquad \text{Eq. 4-14}$$

10. Schedule Performance Index (SPI): If SPI is equal to 1, then the project is on schedule. If SPI is less than 1, then the project is behind schedule. If SPI is more than 1, then the project is ahead of schedule.

$$SPI = \frac{EV}{PV}$$

Eq. 4-15

FROM PRACTICE: EVA at Monica Park, Brazil

Monica Park, an indoor amusement park in Rio de Janeiro, Brazil has 30 attractions, 10,000 square meters was built in 10 months for $5 million. The park has an area of 10,000 square meters, including areas for fast food, special parties, and a shop with products related to the theme of Monica, a child book character famous in Brazil. The earned value analysis (EVA) had a significant role in the integrated management of scope, time, and cost during the construction of the project.

© Bruno Martins Imagens/ Shutterstock.com

EVA contributed to the cost management of this project as the project completed on time and on budget. EVA allowed scope change management to work with the final budget of the project by providing alternatives so that the project team could decide on what activities to reduce scope so as to fit cost overruns in other activities. The project managers measured the delays and the project progress using the schedule variance. EVA provided more perception about the project costs and the related elements of scope, performance, suppliers, and quality[11].

Example 4-8 shows the monitoring of cost and schedule of a project using EVA.

Example 4-8

EVA, Inc., a local transportation company from Evansville, Indiana, has initiated a small logistics project. The company budgets a week-long activity of the project at $20,000. The project manager finds that at the end of the second day of the 5-day week, 20% of the work is complete and $9,000 has been spent. The planned activity was 30% complete at the end of the second day. How should the project manager report the progress of the project to the stakeholders?

To report the progress of the project, the project manager needs to compute CV, SV, CPI, and SPI of the project.

Using Equations 4-8 through 4-15, the EVA analysis can be done on the project.

BAC = $20,000; this is the budget for the project.
AC = $9,000; this is the actual cost of work performed.

At the end of the second day,

PV = 30% × $20,000 = $6,000
EV = 20% × 20,000 = $4,000
CV = $4,000 – $9,000 = — $5,000. Therefore, we have a cost overrun in the project.
CVP = —5000/4000 = —125%
SV = $4,000 – $6,000 = —$2,000. Therefore, we have a schedule overrun in the project, that is, the project is behind schedule.
SVP = —2000/6000 = —33%
CPI = 4000/9000 = 0.44. Therefore, the project is over budget at the end of second day.
SPI = 4000/6000 = 0.66 and thus the project is behind schedule at the end of second day.

Analysis: Earned Value Analysis is a great tool for project managers. Operational project managers can use EVA for many of their projects where cost and schedule are involved are necessary to control. In this example, you can see that at the end of the second day of the week-long project, the project is over budget and behind schedule. The project manager has enough time to steer the project to a successful completion.

Formulae from this Chapter

Present Value	$Present\ Value\ (PV) = \dfrac{C_t}{(1+r)^t}$.	Eq. 4-1
Net Present Value	$NPV = Present\ Value - Investment$	Eq. 4-2
Net Present Value over multiple time periods	$NPV = \sum\limits_{t=1}^{n} \dfrac{C_t}{(1+r)^t}$	Eq. 4-3
Expected Time	$EV = \dfrac{Optimistic\ Time + (4 \times Most\ Likely\ Time) + Pessimistic\ Time}{6}$	Eq. 4-4
Activity Variance	$\sigma^2 = \left(\dfrac{Pessimistic\ Time - Optimistic\ Time}{6} \right)^2$	Eq. 4-5
Standard Deviation of the critical path	$\sigma_p = \sqrt{\sum (variances\ on\ the\ critical\ path)}$	Eq. 4-6

(continued)

Z-score	$Z = \dfrac{(D - E)}{\sigma_p}$	Eq. 4-7
Planned Value	$PV = Planned\ completion\ \% \times Budget\ at\ completion$	Eq. 4-8
Earned Value	$EV = Actual\ completion\ \% \times Budegt\ at\ Completion$	Eq. 4-9
Cost Variance	$CV = EV - AC$	Eq. 4-10
Cost Variance Percentage	$CVP = \dfrac{CV}{EV}$	Eq. 4-11
Schedule Variance	$SV = EV - PV$	Eq. 4-12
Schedule Variance Percentage	$SVP = \dfrac{SV}{PV}$	Eq. 4-13
Cost Performance Index	$CPI = \dfrac{EV}{AC}$	Eq. 4-14
Schedule Performance Index	$SPI = \dfrac{EV}{PV}$	Eq. 4-15

Case Study: New Testing Facility Project Management at Neubear, Inc.

Tim Tribune, the operations project manager at NeuBear, Inc. was deeply engrossed in the terminal of his office computer that morning. Rod Tester, the VP of Operations and Tim's boss, had sent an email the previous night, asking Tim for an update on the progress of a new project. The tone of the email showed some anxiety on the project and Tim, knowing Rod well, became equally anxious. He wanted to give Rod a thorough picture of the progress of the new testing lab (NTL) project.

© Maxx-Studio/Shutterstock.com

NeuBear, Inc. was established in 1989 in Saginaw, Michigan. The family-owned business is ISO-9001 certified, has 60 employees and enjoys $40 million in revenues. The company manufactures specialized cylindrical roller bearings, spherical roller bearings, tapered roller bearings, and needle bearings for automobile manufacturers. A bearing is a machine element that constrains moving parts to only the desired motion and reduces friction between those moving parts. A roller bearing is a bearing in which a shaft runs on a steel rollers held in a cage. For example, friction is reduced in car wheels using roller bearings. Roller bearings perform very well under shock and impact loading and are therefore used in car wheels.

The company's current lab was an old building with an old HVAC system. Furthermore, the testing equipment was old and desperately needed an upgrade. The company's founders decided to build a new lab on their premises. They selected Tim to be their project manager even though this is a facilities project. Tim is an operations manager and has a good knowledge of project management. The company followed a culture of teamwork and considered teamwork more important than ownership of departmental turfs. Tim selected a team consisting of a facilities engineer, a test engineer, and a senior process engineer. The team met and spent a few days to decide on the many aspects of the project. The initial budget for the project included $500,000 for the new building. They had three testing machines estimated at $240,000, $60,000 allotted for quality control systems, and $250,000 for a computer system to collect and analyze data. One of the founders knew a person who shared this knowledge to do the estimate.

Tim sought a request for quote and received a quote from a reputable construction company to build the test lab. The quote detailed material and labor costs for the building as follows:

Materials		Labor	
Description	Amount	Job	Amount
Foundation	$31,200	Site Preparation	$38,720
Rainwater system	$5,588	Build base & frame	$69,769
Electrical system	$6,224	Install Roof	$32,875
Lumber	$125,000	Install windows	$12,400
Paint	$7,190	Install siding	$58,080
Roof materials	$18,200	Interior woodwork	$51,480
Siding	$21,793	Lighting & HVAC	$45,600
Flooring	$24,251	Interior dry wall	$46,800
Windows	$8,000	Flooring	$15,210
Miscellaneous	$16,000	Painting	$12,340
Transportation	$4,800	Cleanup	$4,000

As the team worked on details of the project, they came across some cost discrepancies from the original estimate. The team came to know that there was a newer and much more sophisticated impact testing machine which was not in the original estimate. They also discovered that there was a new line of ultrasonic testing equipment that would be suitable for the work that is planned to be done in the lab. An upgraded computer system with more sophisticated data collection and analysis was also recommended by the process and testing

engineers. Tim took note of all these requirements. With discussions with other stakeholders including their customers, he found out later that their customers required more stringent quality testing. New equipment for a quality testing system with all the sensor integration was required at a cost of $85,000. The testing equipment cost increased by 18% and the upgraded computer system cost an extra $45,000. The original estimate did not include the team's time on the project as well as the cost to install the equipment. The contractor also quoted $86,000 to help install the equipment including the process piping and electrical systems. Tim estimated a maximum of 2 months to complete the project. He calculated that the time spent by the team toward the project during that period would cost the company $6,000 per month per team member. Benefits for each team member amounted to $2,000 per month. The clerical service for the project is estimated at $800, and utilities are estimated to be $1,900 during the project term. Supplies and miscellaneous costs are estimated to be $1,000. The equipment depreciation will not be a factor in project costs.

The executive team of the company has foreseen a benefit of $800,000 for the second year and then a 15% increase in benefits every year for the next 3 years. The costs of the facility are estimated to be $150,000 per year from the second year onwards.

Tim Tribune, his team members, and the contractor devised a schedule for the project as follows:

Activity	Description	Optimistic Time	Most Likely Time	Pessimistic Time	Predecessor
A	Site Preparation	3	2	3	
B	Foundation	2	2	2	A
C	Build base & frame	3	4	5	B
D	Install Roof	3	3	3	C
E	Install windows	3	3	3	C
F	Install siding	3	2	3	C
G	Lighting & HVAC	3	3	3	D, E, F
H	Interior dry wall	3	3	3	G
I	Painting	3	3	3	H
J	Interior woodwork	3	4	5	I
K	Flooring	3	3	3	I
L	Cleanup	3	3	3	J, K

M	Install Equipment foundations	3	3	3	L
N	Install Equipment	3	4	5	M
O	Install process piping	6	7	8	N
P	Lay out electrical system	3	3	3	N
Q	Configure and connect computer system	3	4	5	N
R	Test all the equipment	3	3	3	O, P, Q
S	Hand over the project to Testing Dept.	2	2	2	R
T	Close the project	1	1	1	S

They rounded up estimated time from the three time estimates to zero decimal places. Tim presented the estimates and schedule to the founders with all relevant information from the stakeholders. The founders of the company accepted all the recommendations and increased the budget to the same amount as the detailed estimation presented by Tim. The project started on January 3 of that year.

On January 28th, Tim saw the email from Rod. He went through the project files in his computer and found the following as of January 27 evening: 52% of the work is complete and $950,000 has been spent. The planned activity was 58% complete on January 27th evening. He reported his findings to Rod. Rod asked him to report the progress of the project on February 4th as the top executives and the company's key customer were to meet on February 5th, 2022, to assess the progress of the project. Tim found out that as of February 4, 75% of the work is complete and $1,100,000 has been spent. The planned activity was 72% complete on January 27th evening.

Case Questions

    A. How would you classify this project?

    B. From the description in the case, what kind of project organizational structure was employed at NeuBear, Inc.?

    C. What is the scope of this project? How well was the scope managed?

    D. What are the direct and indirect costs in this project?

    E. Identify the two estimates in this case and compute both the estimates for this project.

    F. What is the NPV and payback period of this project? Is this project acceptable?

    G. List the activities of this project.

    H. Draw the project schedule network diagram.

    I. What is the critical path of this project?

    J. What is the total duration and slack in this project?

    K. What is the probability of competing this project 2 days ahead of its scheduled delivery date?

    L. What is the probability of completing this project 1 day ahead of its scheduled delivery date?

    M. What was in Tim's reports to Rod on January 28, 2022, and February 4, 2022?

Summary

- A project is a unique activity that adds value, expends resources, has beginning and end dates, and has constraints and requirements that include scope, cost, schedule performance, resources, and value.
- Projects are categorized into five types including basic research projects, alliances and partnership projects, breakthrough projects, platform projects, and derivative projects.
- Project management is the act of collaboration among people and other required resources such that a project is planned, organized, and controlled effectively to accomplish its goals and objectives.
- Project management comprises several activities or components.
- Success of projects depends heavily on the success of project management.
- Scope, cost, and time are the main drivers of successful projects.
- The scope of a project is the work that needs to be accomplished to deliver the results of the project with specified features and functions.
- Proper management of scope is critical to avoid cost and schedule overruns. The scope actually defines a project plan so that the project manager can stick to the plan.
- Cost is a major factor in the success of a project.
- Project cost is the sum of all costs to complete a project.
- Direct material and labor costs are the costs of materials that are entirely linked to the production of the final product.
- Indirect materials costs include any material and labor costs that are necessary to complete a project, but do not become an actual part of the final project.
- Fixed costs remain constant regardless of changes in the level of project activities.

- Variable costs vary in direct proportion to changes in the level of project activities
- There are three common methods employed in estimating costs at different timeframes during a project including rough order of magnitude estimate (ROME), approximate historical estimate (AHE); and detailed estimate (DE).
- Cost estimation is the process of determining the cost of a project.
- Net Present Value (NPV) is the present value of cash flows from the project at a rate of return compared to the initial investment in the project.
- The payback period analysis is an important financial method to determine the amount of time a project will take to recuperate its investments.
- A project schedule is the delivery of a project scope.
- A project schedule network diagram shows the sequential and logical relationship between tasks in a project.
- Slack—sometimes referred to as float—is the amount of time that an activity in a project network can be delayed without causing a delay to subsequent activities or project completion.
- Slack can be calculated as either the difference of ES and LS or the difference of EF and LF.
- The critical path is the longest path of the network.
- Learning from past projects helps project managers to estimate time taken for certain activities. The learning curves method is one such tool. A learning curve is a graphical representation of the changing rate of learning for a given project activity.
- Earned Value Analysis is primarily used to measure and track costs and schedules in a project.

Review Questions

1. Define a project.
2. What are the three characteristics that define a project?
3. What are the differences between projects and non-projects?
4. How can projects be classified? Give an example of each classification.
5. What is project management? What are its benefits?
6. What is the difference between project success and project management success?
7. Explain the components of project management.
8. What are the crucial factors of project success?
9. What is NPV? Why should NPV be considered for project selection?
10. What is payback? Why should payback be considered for project selection?

11. What is project scope, and how is it useful in a project?
12. What is scheduling?
13. What is a critical path?
14. Why are project networks used?
15. What is an activity? How are activities related to merges and bursts in project networks?
16. Why is PSND important to project managers?
17. What is an expected time in a project network?
18. What is the variance used in a project network?
19. Describe forward and backward passes.
20. What is slack? How is this principle useful in project scheduling?
21. Why are monitoring important in projects?
22. What are the different types of costs in projects?
23. What is the difference between direct and indirect costs?
24. What are the common methods in estimating costs in projects?
25. What is the accuracy of those common methods in cost estimation?
26. Why is Earned Value Analysis used in project management?
27. What is variance in EVA?
28. Define PV, EV, CV, and SV. How is each one of these factors useful in project management?
29. Define CPI and SPI. How is each one of these factors useful in project management?
30. What are learning curves? How can they be used in projects?

Critical Thinking Questions

1. Is project management important in small firms? Why? Why not?
2. A company is trying to recruit a testing engineer for the Operations Department. Is this a project? If so, why? What are the four characteristics that define this HR project? If not, why not, and what characteristics of this activity define this as not being a project?
3. In general, how could each of the following situations influence your choice for a project or a non-project? Explain your answers in as much depth as possible.
   a. A complex task.
   b. A task with low complexity that is not unique.
   c. A task with low complexity that is unique in nature.
   d. A task with high complexity but very low uniqueness.
   e. A task with high complexity that is unique.
   f. A unique task.
4. You are planning a new project for your company. Which one of the three estimates would you consider?
5. Out of the three methods of estimating costs, which one is the best method? Why?

6. Can overtime be identified after completing backward and forward passes?

7. East-West Products Corporation, a company that has manufacturing facilities in the United States and India, is working on some projects. How would you classify each of the projects? Explain your rationale.

   a. A new furnace worth $4 million in response to increased sales forecast
   b. Solar heating of process water in one of the facilities in Chennai, India
   c. A new gym/fitness facility in Valley Forge, PA
   d. A 200-bed dormitory facility in India for employees
   e. A new product development in Valley Forge, PA, for a new market
   f. Changes to a product that will cost $40 million due to customer complaints
   g. Disposal of toxic waste from manufacturing in the United States and India
   h. A new promotional campaign for a new product
   i. A new data center facility in India
   j. Wireless Internet service to all manufacturing plants with RFID equipment
   k. SAP project to integrate all facilities
   l. Upgrade to modern facilities in Valley Forge, PA, and Mishawaka, IN
   m. Six Sigma projects in Valley Forge, PA, and Mishawaka, IN

8. Which one of the crucial factors of project success is the most important? Why?

9. A restaurant has a new catering order for a Christmas celebration at a company. Explain the project scope and how cost and schedule may play a role in this project.

10. Silbury, Inc. finds out that their learning curve is 85% in their processes. Pilbury, Inc. has a learning percentage of 80%. Which firm has the faster learning rate?

Problem Solving Questions

1. Redbud Industries of Billings, Montana, is a manufacturer of indoor artificial flowers and plants. The operations crew consists of 20 regular employees and 4 part-time consultants. Regular employees get paid at a rate of $70 per hour and work 40 hours a week during a 4-week month. The consultants are paid $5,000 each for the same month. Employees enjoy benefits that cost the company about 15% of their salary. The clerical expense for the month is $45,000. Utilities and space costs $15,000 for the month. Miscellaneous expenses are $12,000 during the same period. Equipment rental and depreciation

are $20,000 and $10,000 respectively. Six laborers for the operations are paid $15 per hour for the period. Calculate the indirect rate based on direct labor and indirect rate based on total direct costs.

2. Riverside Bank is estimating a project at their premises. The rough estimate for the project was calculated as $1,250,000 and the detailed estimate came to $1,056,252. If those estimates included a contingency factor of 5%, what are the original estimates excluding the contingency factor?

3. Koch Industries is considering two projects that are independent of each other. The initial investment for Project 1 is $271,000 and for Project 2 is $324,300. The firm's discount rate is 14%. The cash flows are as follows:

Year	Project 1	Project 2
1	$ 51,000	$ 75,000
2	$ 51,000	$ 75,000
3	$ 51,000	$ 75,000
4	$ 51,000	$ 75,000
5	$ 51,000	$ 75,000

Which project can be accepted?

4. A project has the following event predecessors and successors:

Activity	Time Estimates (weeks)			Activity predecessor
	Optimistic	Most Likely	Pessimistic	
A	2	2	3	
B	3	3	3	
C	3	3	4	A
D	2	4	5	A
E	5	6	7	B
F	2	2	5	C, D
G	6	6	7	D, E
H	2	2	4	F, G

a. Draw the PSND.
b. Determine the critical path.
c. Calculate the total slack time.
d. What is the probability of completing this project 1 week before the expected time of completion?

5. A new operations project at Prodops, Inc. consists of the following activities:

Activity	Predecessor	Estimated Duration (days)
A		2
B		3
C		3
D	A	3
E	D	3
F	E	2
G	F	3
H	F	5
I	G, H	6
J	G	2
K	H	4
L	I, K	4
M	J	2

a. What is the critical path? What is the total slack?
b. Which activity has the largest slack?

6. A project has the following activities:

Activity ID	Predecessor	Estimated Duration (weeks)
A		0
B	A	10
C	A	20
D	B, C	30
E	B, C	20
F	E	40
G	D, F	20
H	G	0

a. How long will the project last?
b. Which jobs can be delayed without delaying the early start of any subsequent activity?

7. These are the activities of a service framework project in a Midwest company:

Activity ID	Activity	Predecessors	Estimated Duration (weeks)
A	Study feasibility		6
B	Gather information		4
C	Consider alternatives		6
D	Define problem	B	1
E	Find a solution	C	1
F	Prototype	A, D, E	10
G	Initial test	F	5
H	Final test	F	8
I	Measure performance	G, H	5
J	Implement	I	25

    a. Find the critical path.
    b. How long will the project take to complete?

8. Rob, the project manager of Cobler, Inc. has been executing a project with a budget of $10M.

Activity	Completion Date	PV ($M)	EV ($M)	AC ($M)
A	January 31, 2022	8	8	13
B	February 27, 2022	4	3	6
C	March 30, 2022	6	8	4
D	April 30, 2022	15	12	10
E	May 30, 2022	20	20	25
F	June 30, 2022	9	8	4
G	July 30, 2022	20	14	21
H	August 30, 2022	15	0	0
I	September 30, 2022	25	0	0

On July 30, 2022, the project is 60% complete and he needs help with following measurements:
    a. What is the cost variance?
    b. What is the schedule variance?
    c. What is the cost performance index?
    d. What is the schedule performance index?

9. Ray Lenard, the project manager of Leows, Inc., did not control a project where the budget was estimated to be $8 million initially. He researched and came across many other similar projects and decided to add another 25% for direct overhead costs. The customer for the project, Meows, Inc., was ready to pay $10.7 million upon completion. A 10-month delay of the project due to numerous problems with the project start meant the project was completed two and half years after its initiation. As a result of the delay, the customer paid an additional $1 million to cover miscellaneous costs.
   a. Was the project over or under budget?
   b. Was there a cost overrun or not? If so, by how much?

   At 90% of project completion:

   c. What would have been the status of the budget?
   d. Was there a cost overrun or not? If so, by how much?

10. Acro, Inc. is just planning to make a new product. They have completed two units so far. The first unit took 15 hours to complete and the next unit took 13 hours. What would be the learning percentage to make a new product?

11. Beatrice, the manufacturer of high-end personal boats produced their first unit under R&D funding in 2,000 labor hours; the second took 1,900 labor hours. The company is planning to make four more units. How many labor hours should they plan for the four more units?

12. Determine the status of nine projects with the following EVA numbers:
   a. BAC = $5,000; EV = $6,000; AC = $8,000
   b. EV = $10,000; AC = $17,000
   c. EV = $6,000; PV = $8,000
   d. SV = $3,000; PV = $4,000
   e. EV = $5,000; AC = $10,000
   f. EV = $5,000; PV = $8,000
   g. BAC = $12,000; CPI = 0.55
   h. SV = $0

13. A has three activities. The first two activities have been completed and the third activity is 50% complete. The expectation for the third activity was 50% complete on February 12, 2022. The first activity was planned to cost $2,240,000 and it was completed for $1,580,000. The second activity was expected to cost $3,500,000 but was actually done for $2,800,000. The third and final activity was expected to cost $7,500,000. The company has spent $6,000,000 so far. Calculate the schedule variance, schedule performance index, and cost index for the project on February 12, 2022. What is the status of the project?

References

1. GAO. (2021). *James Webb Space Telescope: Project nearing completion but work to resolve challenges continues.* Retrieved December 26, 2021, from https://www.gao.gov/products/gao-21-406

2. CNN. (2021). *Ford Motor Co.* Retrieved December 26, 2021, from https://www.cnn.com/2021/ 12/25/world/james-webb-space-telescope-launch-scn/index.html.

3. Greenfieldboyce, N. (2021). *Why some astronomers once feared NASA's James Webb Space Telescope would never launch.* Retrieved December 26, 2021, from https://www.npr.org/ 2021/12/22/ 1066377182/why-some-astronomers-once-feared-nasas-james-webb-space-telescope-would-never-la.

4. Wheelwright, S. C., & Clark, K. B. (1992). Creating project plans to focus product development. *Harvard Business Review, 70*(2), 70–82.

5. Vaidyanathan, G. (2022). *Project management: Process, technology, and practice.* Kendall-Hunt Publishing.

6. Viter, I. (2021). *Project management trends in manufacturing for 2018.* Epicflow; Cabanis-Brewin, J. (2018, December 14). Project management for manufacturing. *Industry Today.*

7. Vaidyanathan, G. (2022). *Project management: Process, technology, and practice.* Kendall-Hunt Publishing.

8. Kerzner, H. (2008). *Project management: A systems approach to planning, scheduling, and controlling* (9th ed.). John Wiley & Sons.

9. Larson, R., & Larson, E. (2009). Top five causes of scope creep . . . and what to do about them. Paper presented at PMI® Global Congress 2009—North America, Orlando, FL. Newtown Square, PA: Project Management Institute.

10. Bordat, C., McCullouch, B. G., Labi, S., Sinha, K. C. (2014). *An Analysis of Cost Overruns and Time Delays of INDOT Projects.* Joint Transportation Research Program Report, West Lafayette, Indiana: Purdue University.

11. Valle, J. A., & Soares, C. A. P. (2006). The Use of EVA—Earned Value Analysis in the Cost Management of Construction Projects. Paper presented at PMI® Global Congress 2006—EMEA, Madrid, Spain. Newtown Square, PA: Project Management Institute.

AGGREGATE, SALES AND OPERATIONS PLANNING

Learning Objectives

- Define and describe aggregate planning.
- Define and describe sales and operations planning.
- Describe the aggregate planning factors companies use.
- Explain various costs used in the aggregate planning process.
- Develop various aggregate strategies.

The marketing, operations, and finance functions in a company find themselves in a predicament over sales, supply chain, and keeping track of revenues. A business process to alleviate the problems is employed in most companies. Sales and operations planning (S&OP) is focused on solving the problems that arise when companies coordinate marketing, operations, and finance. Aggregate planning is employed to plan the operations in a company to minimize the cost of resources in order to meet customer demands.

Del Monte Foods, Inc., is a $3.6 billion American food production and distribution company[1] headquartered in Walnut Creek, California. Del Monte Foods is one of the country's largest producers and distributors of processed food. With a portfolio that includes popular brands such as Del Monte, S&W, Contadina, College Inn, Fruit Burst, Fruit Naturals, Orchard Select and SunFresh, Del Monte Foods serves the United States, Canada, Mexico, South America, the Middle East, the Philippines, the Indian Subcontinent, Southeast Asia, and Kenya.

(Clockwise from left to right) © Walter Eric Sy/Shutterstock.com; © DenisMArt/Shutterstock.com; © Andriy Blokhin/Shutterstock.com; © DenisMArt/Shutterstock.com; © Billy F Blume Jr/Shutterstock.com

S&OP is typically a consensus process that involves the internal and external stakeholders of an organization. S&OP can help lessen the impact of the demand fluctuations. Del Monte Foods is cited as a model for the successful implementation of S&OP plans. The company makes changes to its demand-planning process leading to improved visibility and forecasting accuracy by using the downstream data as an additional demand signal. For example, Wal-Mart has a tool called Retail Link that provides sales, inventory, and forecast information at the store level. Del Monte Foods brings such data into their system from Walmart, using a tool called One Network to back propagate that demand from the retailer supply network into their supply network so that they can project where that demand is going to hit in their supply chain network. Using this method, Del Monte Foods can determine the entire view of their supply chain. This method is more robust than the usual statistical modeling. Del Monte Foods has been successful as this method has provided them a high 80% accuracy in their forecasts. Their forecasts had been in the 50% to low 60s on average before they started using S&OP[1].

> **Sales and operations planning** Sales and operations planning (S&OP) is a process companies use to balance and manage supply and demand.

Sales and Operations Planning

Sales and operations planning (S&OP) is a process companies use to balance and manage supply and demand. The demand for products changes over time, as we discussed in Chapter 2, due to trend, seasonal influence, cyclical influence, and random variations. Such influences create increases or decreases in sales or revenues of a company's product. Snow blowers and jackets in winter and lawn mowers and hiking supplies in summer are examples. These variations lead to many problems in the supply chain such as excess inventory during periods of low demand and stockouts during periods of high demand.

The goal of S&OP is to manage this variability effectively by managing both the supply and the demand. Typically, S&OP is a coordinated effort of many functional areas in a company. People from sales, marketing, product development, engineering, finance, logistics, distribution, and production meet to identify, decide on, and manage the balance. The cross-functional team must involve the alignment of the operations plan to the business plan in the balance as well. The team determines the most feasible S&OP plan and its limitations. The final output of the meeting is the aggregate plan. From the aggregate plan, the Master Production Schedules (MPS) and the Materials Requirements Plans (MRP) are developed. This process is shown in Figure 5-1. As shown in the figure, there are inputs that are both internal and external to companies. The external inputs include market demand, economic conditions, availability of raw materials, forecasting, competitive activities, availability of subcontracting or outsourcing. The internal inputs include current workforce, inventory on hand, production capacity, internal processes, and forecasting.

Aggregate Planning

Companies must anticipate customer demand and produce goods to meet the demand. To meet the demand, they must determine the capacity levels, the operations levels, the labor requirements, and the outsourcing requirements. They have to decide whether to invest in a plant with a larger capacity to meet the demand and then hold the excess inventory that was produced during the slow periods. Or they have to decide whether to go to a smaller plant to save money and outsource when there is a higher demand. Such decisions require different labor force and production planning. Aggregate planning helps companies to make such decisions.

The aggregate planning defines how a company should best utilize its resources. Consider, for example, a company that has to manage their complex supply chains. Once the products are ready to be launched, the company has to build inventory of the products to meet the expected demand. This involves forecasting the demand for the next few quarters and resolving any backlog problems. In this situation, the company must use aggregate planning to decide its production capacities, labor utilization, inventory, any back-ordering in the case of not being able to satisfy the demand on time, and any subcontracting in the case of low capacity. Aggregate planning applies these

> **Aggregate planning** The aggregate plan determines planned levels of production, capacity, inventory, and labor force to minimize the cost of resources or maximize profits and meet customer demand.

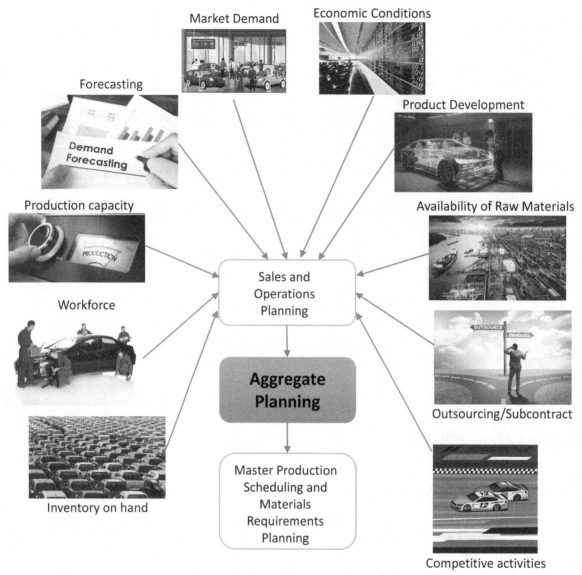

(*Clockwise from bottom left to right*) © Issarawat Tattong/Shutterstock.com; © Photodiem/Shutterstock.com; © Olivier Le Moal/Shutterstock.com; © Vitalii Vodolazskyi/Shutterstock.com; © ClassicVector/Shutterstock.com; © i viewfinder/Shutterstock.com; © Gorodenkoff/Shutterstock.com; © Travel mania/Shutterstock.com; © Elnur/Shutterstock.com; © komangpuja/Shutterstock.com

Figure 5-1 Aggregate, Sales & Operations Planning

kinds of strategic level decisions while determining the operational levels in their plants.

The result of aggregate planning has a significant impact on the performance of the supply chain since it takes the inputs from all the stages of the supply chain. The output of the aggregate planning must be of excellent value to all the partners and the suppliers of a company as well. The outcome of an aggregate plan is to maximize a facility's productivity at the lowest possible cost.

Aggregate Planning Factors and Costs

What are the key factors we need to know to develop S&OP and aggregate plans? What do firms gain by developing S&OP and aggregate plans? We will answer these questions in this section.

Both the S&OP and the aggregate plans are developed using the information gathered by the managers in a company. Using the information and the knowledge gained over many years of planning, the managers develop the S&OP and the aggregate plans. The plans will be used to make decisions and recommendations. As shown in Figure 5-1, the factors or inputs that are used to develop these plans are both internal and external to companies. In general, the following information is required to develop the plans.

Planning Horizon

A planning horizon must be considered to create an aggregate plan. A planning horizon is the time period over which the aggregate plans are prepared. In general, aggregate planning takes place in a continuous fashion. Planning horizons are accomplished for a short term, an intermediate term, or a long term. The short-term aggregate plan is usually for a single day to a few months, while the long-term aggregate plan is for more than a year. Many companies use an intermediate-term planning horizon, which is between 3 to 18 months.

> **Planning horizon, short-term, intermediate-term, and long-term planning horizons**
> - A planning horizon is the time period for which the aggregate plans are prepared.
> - A short-term horizon plan is for a single day to a few months.
> - An intermediate-term horizon plan is for 3 to 18 months.
> - A long-term horizon plan is for more than a year.

Inventory

In manufacturing terms, we use either stock or inventory for goods. Stock refers to the finished goods that are available to sell to customers. Inventory refers to raw materials, work-in-process (WIP) that is used to create goods, and the finished goods. Raw materials inventory are the basic components used to produce the finished goods. Work-in-process inventory refers to the materials and components that are used to make finished goods. Finished goods inventory are items that are available for customers to purchase.

> **Stock** Finished goods that are available to sell to customers.

> **Inventory** Inventory consists of raw materials, work-in-process (WIP) used to create goods, and the finished goods.

Inventory on Hand

Inventory on hand is the number of materials, components, or goods that a company has available for sale or use at a particular time period.

Beginning Inventory

Beginning inventory is the inventory at the start of a time period. The beginning inventory is equal to the inventory on hand at the beginning of a time period. The beginning inventory is equal to the inventory at the end of the immediately preceding period. For example, if a firm has 100 widgets at the end of April, the beginning inventory at the beginning of May is 100 widgets.

Ending Inventory

Ending inventory is the inventory left at the end of a time period. For example, if the beginning inventory at the beginning of May is 100 widgets and the firm sells 60 widgets during May, the ending inventory of May is 100 minus 60 widgets equal to 40 widgets. Now suppose the firm produces 40 widgets during May, then the ending inventory is equal to the 40 widgets plus the 40 widgets that they produced during May, which equals 80 widgets. Ending inventory can be calculated using the following equation:

$$Ending\ Inventory = Beginning\ Inventory + Actual\ Production - Demand\ Forecast$$

Eq. 5-1

Safety Stock

Companies keep an extra number of materials or components for future use. These extra items are the safety stock. The safety stock eliminates the worry of running out of stock. Firms leave the safety stock for the future when they run out of the required inventory. Safety stock is stored for the following reasons:

- Compensate for forecast inaccuracies,
- Prevent an out-of-stock situation,
- Protect against unforeseen spikes in demand,
- Protect against unforeseen supply variations,
- Protect against unforeseen transportation delays, and
- Protect against price fluctuations.

Excess Inventory

Excess inventory is the inventory that has not yet been sold or that has exceeded the projected consumer demand for that product. An excess inventory is usually caused by buying more materials or components than necessary, inaccurate forecasting, cancelled orders, or unpredictable consumer demand. A bad economy or unforeseen weather changes can also cause a company to have excess inventory.

FROM PRACTICE: Excess Inventory and Holding Inventory in U.S. Retail Companies

An excess inventory results in cash flow problems. Therefore, retailers have to get rid of a surplus of inventory. There are many options. One option is placing the excess inventory on sale. It increases revenue but decreases the profit margin. Another option is to donate the excess inventory to improve public relations. Firms often donate perishable products to city missions, soup kitchens, and similar organizations and nonperishable products to charities. Yet another option is to sell them to other companies.

© Sundry Photography/Shutterstock.com

Walmart and Macy's clear out their excess inventories by discounting and offering deeper promotions. Walmart promotes aggressive price rollbacks to boost the sales of some higher-margin goods including apparel. Holding the excess merchandise is expensive because of high warehousing costs. In 2021, Walmart stores and distribution centers had 32% more merchandise, Target had 43% more goods compared to a year earlier, and Best Buy had 9% more merchandise in the first quarter. Macy's inventories rose 17% in 2021[2,3].

Stockout

When a particular item is no longer available, that item is out of stock. Stockout is another term used when firms run out of inventory of a particular item. Stockouts impact the inventory of finished goods and therefore revenues and profits.

FROM PRACTICE: Baby Formula Stockout in the United States

In the week of April 23, 2022, 40% of infant formulas were out of stock across the nation[4]. The shortages were due to a combination of the scarcity of some ingredients in the supply chain that are used to make formula and the worker shortages to get products out of the warehouses and onto the store shelves. Moreover, some parents had stockpiled the available products, which worsened the shortage for others. Moreover, the shutdown of the Abbott Labs was one of the big problems and only a few companies could make baby formula.

© The Toidi/Shutterstock.com

(continued)

Abbott Nutrition had recalled several lots of its Similac, Alimentum, and EleCare formulas after at least four babies became sick with bacterial infections and closed its Michigan plant in February 2022. The Federal Drug Agency (FDA) and Abbott tested the environmental and the product samples at the plant and found five environmental samples containing Cronobacter sakazakii bacteria. However, the product samples tested negative. Meanwhile, Abbott imported millions of cans of infant formulas from its Ireland facility to help with the U.S. shortage. Since then, Abbott has agreed with regulators on the steps needed to resume production at its Sturgis, Michigan, manufacturing plant[5].

Backordering

Firms frequently allow their customers to place orders even if they do not have stock or inventory on hand. This process is called backordering. For example, airlines allow customers to book flights over the flight capacity. Firms allow backordering knowing the sudden increase of their goods and services and that their goods and services are being sold more than they have on hand. There is an advantage for the firms until the demand for the goods and services catches up with the existing capacity. In general, backordering reduces overstocking goods, which in turn reduces inventory holding costs. Many firms allow backordering so that they can spend less on starting inventory and reduce the amount of capital tied up with excess inventory.

Subcontracting

When a manufacturing company requires more goods than they can produce to meet the demand, it is common for the manufacturing company to contract to another company to make those goods. This is called subcontracting. Subcontracting is employing another business to perform a task that cannot be managed internally. Subcontracting or outsourcing is also conducted to reduce costs, avoid capital investment, or acquire talent and expertise that a company does not possess.

Backlog

Inventory backlogs happen when a company has more orders than they can produce or if the company accumulates a buildup of unfulfilled orders.

FROM PRACTICE: Backorders at Boeing

Boeing, the American multinational corporation, designs, manufactures, and sells airplanes, rotorcraft, rockets, satellites, telecommunications equipment, and missiles. In April 2021, Boeing's aircraft orders outpaced cancellations for a third consecutive month. However, deliveries of its bestselling 737 Max planes were in backorder as the company was fixing an electrical issue following two fatal crashes. The company won orders for 25 new planes in March while customers canceled 17, bringing the net gain in orders for the month to 8. Boeing has 4,045 planes on backorder, close to 3,200 of them for Max jets and 433 for Dreamliners as of the end of April[6]. Following a challenging year in

© Andreas Zeitler/Shutterstock .com

2020 due to the COVID-19 pandemic, 2021 and 2022 were expected to be the recovery years for the commercial aircraft manufacturing industry in general. For the year 2021, Boeing delivered 340 aircraft, compared to 157 and 380 in 2020 and 2019, respectively. Boeing delivered 806 jets in 2018. By the end of January 2022, Boeing's backlog (total unfilled orders) was 5,179 aircraft, of which 4,162, or 80%, were 737 NG/MAX narrowbody jets[7].

Production

Production is the process of manufacturing goods from raw materials and/or components. Producing goods is the focal point of many manufacturing companies. As we discussed in Chapter 2, the forecast of future demand is important to produce goods in a manufacturing company.

Production Requirement

Production requirement is the number of goods required to be produced in order to meet the demand forecast during a given time period. To calculate the required production amount for a given time period, we need to take the demand forecast, the beginning inventory, and the safety stock. Production requirement can then be calculated as:

$$Production\ requirement = Demand\ Forecast + Safety\ Stock - Beginning\ Inventory \qquad \text{Eq. 5-2}$$

Demand forecast gives the number of goods that need to be produced to satisfy the needs of customers. A firm must maintain its safety stock and therefore we add the amount of safety stock to the demand forecast. If we have some inventory already, then we do not need to produce that amount. Therefore, we subtract the beginning inventory amount.

If a company has returned stocks that can be sold to customers or if the company has either rebuilt stocks or stock from other sources including subcontracts, those number of goods have to be subtracted from Equation 5-1.

Production Rate

Production rate is the number of goods produced during a given period of time. For example, if a company produces 60 units in an hour, the production rate is 60 units per hour. Then again, the production rate is also the amount of time it takes to produce one unit of a good. For example, if the same company can produce one unit in 1 minute, then the production rate is the same 60 units per hour.

It is natural for companies to increase production rates since doing so will lower the time taken to produce a good or decrease production costs. However, if the output has defects, it will affect the production rate. Limited raw materials can reduce the production rate. Unskilled or poorly trained personnel can cause the production rate to drop as well.

Required Production Time

Required production time is the time taken to produce the production requirement. For example, if the production requirement is 1,000 units and it takes 5 hours to produce a unit, then the required production time is equal to 5,000 hours.

$$Required\ Production\ Time = Production\ requirement \times Time\ to\ produce\ a\ unit$$
$$Eq.\ 5\text{-}3$$

Number of Workdays

This is the number of workdays in a given time period. For example, in the United States, the number of working days in 2022 is calculated by adding up all the weekdays (Monday to Friday) and subtracting the 11 public federal holidays that fall on weekdays. This equals about 260 working days per year. For all our calculations in this book, we will consider a 5-day week of 8 hours of work each day unless otherwise specified.

Production Time in Regular Shift or in Overtime

The production time is equal to the number of working days multiplied by the number of available workers. If a company plans to employ 10 workers for an 8-hour 5-day week, then the available production time for that week is equal to 8 hours per day times 5 days times 10 workers equal to 400 worker-hours.

Production in Regular Time or in Overtime

This is the actual number of units produced.

$$Actual\ Production = \frac{Actual\ Production\ Time}{Production\ rate} \qquad Eq.\ 5\text{-}4$$

Labor

Companies cannot exist without workers who exert their powers of body or mind in a combined effort to produce goods and services. Labor, as the workforce is called, consists of people who are unskilled, semi-skilled, skilled, and professional.

Unskilled labor refers to workers who have no particular skills essential to operate machines or use knowledge to produce goods and services. This type of work usually involves simple duties that do not require making decisions and judgment. In many cases, unskilled labor requires physical strength. Examples include grocery store clerks, fast food restaurant workers, and janitors.

Semi-skilled labor requires more skills than an unskilled labor job. The types of skills necessary are not complex but include the ability to monitor and perform repetitive tasks. Examples are security guards, truck drivers, bartenders, and flight attendants.

Skilled labor refers to workers who possess specialized training or skills. These workers have to make simple decisions and exercise judgment. They must have knowledge of a particular trade or industry in which they work. Examples include law enforcement officers, nurses, plumbers, and electricians.

Professionals possess an even higher degree of skills. They perform activities that require a certain level of education, skill, or training. Examples include accountants, bankers, technicians, teachers, engineers, lawyers, and doctors.

Person-Hour

A person-hour is the amount of work performed by a worker in 1 hour.

Worker Hours

Worker hours is the total time in hours spent by a worker during the number of working days.

$$Worker\ Hours = Number\ of\ workdays \times worktime\ per\ day \qquad Eq.\ 5\text{-}5$$

For example, if the number of working days in a time period is 20 days and a worker works for 8 hours as worktime per day, the worker hours is equal to $20 \times 8 = 160$ person-hours.

Required Workforce

This is the number of workers required to meet production requirements. The required workforce can be calculated as:

$$Required\ workforce = \frac{Required\ production\ time}{Worker\ Hours} \qquad Eq.\ 5\text{-}6$$

Overtime

Overtime refers to hours that exceed normally scheduled working hours. To calculate the overtime amount, multiply the normal pay by a company's overtime rate. For example, if a company's overtime rate is one and a half times the hourly wage and if the hourly wage is $20, the overtime per hour is equal to $20 \times 1.5 = $30 per hour.

Hiring and Layoffs

Hiring is to engage the personal services of a person. Firms employ people and pay them to do a particular job. A layoff is considered a separation from employment due to the lack of available work.

Costs

One of the main reasons for implementing aggregate planning is to minimize operations costs. The costs associated with the aggregate plans include the following:

Straight-Time Cost

This is the cost to produce goods or services per hour during the regular 8-hour period in a working day.

Overtime Cost

This is the cost to produce goods or services per hour in overtime work.

Basic Production Cost

Basic production cost is the cost to produce goods and services. This is calculated as:

$$Basic\ Production\ Cost = Required\ production\ time \times Straight\ time\ cost \quad \text{Eq. 5-7}$$

Inventory Holding Cost

Inventory holding costs are due to the costs that are involved in storing unsold inventory. The inventory holding costs are calculated as the sum of unsold inventory costs. Examples include the costs to store the goods, the cost to insure the goods, the costs due to damaged, spoiled, or obsolescent inventory, the labor costs to transport and move the products to and from storage, and any opportunity costs. Minimizing these costs is a big part of the OS&M strategy.

FROM PRACTICE: Low Inventory Holding Costs at Trader Joe's

Almost 80–90% of products sold at Trader Joe's, the grocery chain, are private inhouse labels, and this allows the company to reduce its costs. The company buys directly from the manufacturers to avoid the supply chain middlemen. The company uses the just in time (JIT) method in order to prevent stockouts from ever happening. The JIT method allows Trader Joe's to maintain its stocks relatively low compared to the other grocery stores

© The Image Party/Shutterstock.com

like Safeway or Krogers. Trader Joe's holds around 2,000 to 4,000 SKUs. Another interesting point is that Trader Joe's offers fewer options or varieties than their major competitors such as Whole Foods or Safeway. Lesser options of Trader Joe's leave their consumers with an easier time purchasing products. This allows Trader Joe's to restock its shelves and warehouse much more easily. The limited variety and lower SKU also reduces the holding costs of inventory[8].

Inventory Ordering Cost

Costs of ordering inventory include the cost incurred to calculate quantities to order, the cost associated with tracking inventory, the cost to maintain inventory, and the cost to prepare purchase orders.

Backordering Cost

Backorder costs are costs incurred by a firm when it is unable to immediately fill an order and promises their customers that they will fill the customer order at a later date. This situation happens when a firm does not have goods readily available for a customer. Customers who need the products may even pay and wait for the product to be shipped at a later date. Firms who allow backorders will notify their customers that the delivery of the order will take longer than the standard time for delivery.

Stockout Cost or Shortage Cost

These costs are associated with stockouts. The stockout cost is a loss of income for a firm that is associated with a shortage of inventory. When inventory is not available, a firm loses a sale. Moreover, the firm may lose their customers permanently as they may reach out to the competition. Stockout costs are also called shortage costs.

Hiring, Training, and Layoff Costs

These are the costs associated with the hiring, training, and layoffs of employees in a company. Many companies hire temporary workers to avoid these costs.

Aggregate Planning Benefits and Activities

The S&OP and aggregate planning is important for a company because those plans help to optimize its production and costs in order to fulfill its goals. While the benefits of these plans are many, some of the key benefits for a company include:

- Specifies what materials and other resources are needed and when they should be procured to minimize cost of operations,
- Maximizes productivity at the lowest possible cost,

- Provides targets for inventory levels, production levels, and sales
- Determines capacity and minimizes the cost by balancing against such capacity,
- Helps to use its production capabilities with maximum efficiency,
- Reduces the need to invest in building goods or stocks for future periods of high demand,
- Increases production rates by anticipating changes in customer demand,
- Lowers operating costs,
- Improves supply chain relationships, and
- Improves customer satisfaction by providing enough supply to meet demand at all times.

To reap the above-mentioned benefits, a company must consider many planning activities. The planning activities of S&OP and aggregation are shown in Figure 5-2.

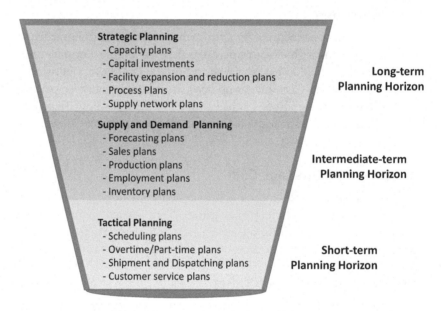

Figure 5-2 Aggregate, Sales & Operations Planning Over Planning Horizons

Aggregate Planning Strategy

The sales, operations, and aggregate planning strategy provides the production requirements for a firm. Based on the demand forecast, organizations develop those plans to obtain the requirements of labor, raw material, working capital, and so on. The objective of aggregate planning is to:

- Minimize inventory investment,
- Maximize production rate, and
- Maximize utilization of available resources.

Firms use the aggregate, sales and operations planning factors and costs that we discussed in the last section. Moreover, organizations have to work with certain constraints. Such constraints include:

- Limits on available capital,
- Limits on stockouts,
- Limits on overtime costs, and
- Limits on hiring and layoff costs.

To accomplish those objectives and be equipped with the knowledge of the factors, costs, and constraints, organizations determine the following through the aggregate, sales and operations plans:

- Production requirement,
- Inventory levels,
- Required workforce, and
- Total cost of operations.

In summary, a company's aggregate plan specifies the resources that are approved for use by its management. These resources include the number of workers, that is, the size of the workforce, the level of inventory to be held for a particular period, any authorized level of overtime, the number of units to be produced in-house, and the number of units or services to be subcontracted. Let us take a look at how to implement an aggregate plan to balance inventory and capacity.

Strategies to Balance Inventory and Capacity

Aggregate planning plays a significant role in the profitability of a firm. If the available inventory and the capacity are unable to meet the demand, a company will lose sales and profits. A bad aggregate plan will result in excess inventory or large stockouts. Firms need to invest in their capacity to lower inventory costs. The lack of required capacity investments may lead to delays in product delivery. Firms must analyze the tradeoffs between the inventory and the capacity costs to develop the S&OP and aggregate plans. Therefore, companies must use the following strategies to balance inventory and capacity costs:

1. Chase strategy,
2. Level strategy,
3. Flex strategy, and
4. Hybrid strategy.

Chase Strategy

In this strategy, firms match production capacity with demand forecast by hiring and laying off workers. This strategy can become expensive as hiring and layoffs are not easy in reality. Furthermore, to hire trained workforce is not possible at all times. Workforce morale is impacted in a negative sense because of frequent hiring and layoffs. This strategy is good to implement when an appropriate trained workforce is readily available in the market, to minimize inventory levels, and when inventory holding costs are high. Example 5-1 shows how a chase strategy is implemented in a company.

Example 5-1

ACEG Industries is planning to develop aggregate plans for a planning horizon consisting of January, February, March, and April. The inventory holding cost is $2 per month; the stockout cost is $5 per month; the subcontracting cost is $10 per hour; the backorder cost is $80 per unit; hiring and training cost is $300 per worker; the layoff cost is $400 per worker; straight-time cost is $5 per hour; and the overtime cost is two times the straight-time cost. It takes 5 hours to produce a unit, the workers work 8 hours a day for 5 days a week, and the material cost is $80 per unit. The subcontractors think it will take 10 hours to product a unit. The company plans to maintain 20% of monthly demand as safety stock and the beginning inventory is 100 units. Overtime is permitted only on approval.

The demand forecast and the number of workdays for ACEG Industries are shown below:

	January	February	March	April	Total
Demand Forecast	4,000	2,000	3,000	3,500	12,500
Working Days per Month	21	22	23	24	90

Develop an aggregate plan for ACEG Industries using a chase strategy.

Choosing a chase strategy (match production capacity with demand forecast by hiring and laying off workers), and using the steps shown, we get:

Step 1: Calculate safety stock as 20% of the monthly demand. For January, it is 20% of 4,000 = 800

Step 2: Using Eq. 5-2, calculate production requirement. For January, it is 4,000 + 800 − 100 = 4,700

Step 3: Using Eq. 5-1, calculate ending inventory; For January, it is 4,700 + 100 − 4,000 = 800

Step 4: It takes 5 hours to produce a unit; it will take 5 × 4,700 = 23,500 hours to meet production requirement

Step 5: Using Eq. 5-5, we can calculate the worker hours to be 21 days × 8 hours/day = 168 hours

Step 6: Using Eq. 5-6, number of workers required is 23,500/168 = 140 workers

Step 7: Repeat steps 1 through 6 for all months, February to April, and identify new hires and layoffs for each month.

Step 8:   Calculate the materials cost using production requirement, straight-time cost using required production time; hiring and layoff costs using the number of hires and layoffs. The total cost using the chase strategy is $1,427,500 for ACEG Industries.

	Units	Formula	January	February	March	April	Total
				Production Plan: Chase Strategy			
Beginning Inventory	units		100	800	400	600	
Demand Forecast	units		4,000	2,000	3,000	3,500	12,500
Safety Stock	units		800	400	600	700	
Production Requirement	units	Eq. 5-2	4,700	1,600	3,200	3,600	13,100
Ending Inventory	units	Eq. 5-1	800	400	600	700	
Required production time	hours	Eq. 5-3	23500	8000	16000	18000	
Working Days per Month	days		21	22	23	24	90
Worker hours	hours	Eq. 5-5	168	176	184	192	720
Required workforce		Eq. 5-6	140	46	87	94	
New Workers Hired				0	41	7	
Laid Off Workers				94	0	0	
Materials Cost			$376,000	$128,000	$256,000	$288,000	$1,048,000.00
Straight Time Cost			$117,500.00	$40,000.00	$80,000.00	$90,000.00	$327,500.00
Hiring Cost			$0.00	$0.00	$12,300.00	$2,100.00	$14,400.00
Layoff Cost			$0.00	$37,600.00	$0.00	$0.00	$37,600.00
Total Cost			$493,500.00	$205,600.00	$348,300.00	$380,100.00	**$1,427,500.00**

Analysis: The chase strategy is to match production capacity with demand forecast by hiring and laying off workers. In this example, the total cost using the chase strategy includes materials cost, straight-time cost, hiring cost, and layoff cost. To lay off 94 workers in February, hire 41 workers for March, and then add another 7 workers for April is a daunting task for this company.

Level Strategy

In this strategy, firms maintain a constant workforce to produce a constant production output. In other words, the strategy is to maintain a steady production rate and a steady employment level. This strategy allows the inventory surplus to absorb the increased demand or the smooth demand requirements over time as backorder. The stable workforce is welcome to the employees of a firm and avoids the problems associated with hiring and layoffs of employees.

The firm can build up inventory at times of lower demand and fulfill orders during periods of peak demand. This is shown in Example 5-2. Since inventory levels vary because of varying demand,

$$Level\ Production\ Output = \frac{Total\ Demand + Total\ Safety\ Stock - Beginning\ Inventory}{Total\ Time\ Period}$$

Eq. 5-8

where, Time Period equals the total time period in months or years considered for the level strategy.

$$Level\ Inventory = Level\ production\ output - Demand\ Forecast \qquad Eq.\ 5-9$$

where, Demand Forecast equals the demand forecast for that time period.
   Ending inventory is calculated as:

$$Level\ Ending\ Inventory = Level\ Inventory + Beginning\ Inventory \\ - Backorder\ for\ the\ Past\ Month \qquad Eq.\ 5-10$$

Average inventory is calculated as:

$$Average\ Inventory = \frac{Beginning\ Inventory + Ending\ Inventory}{2} \qquad Eq.\ 5-11$$

Example 5-2

Using the data from Example 5-1, develop an aggregate plan for ACEG Industries using a level strategy.
   The steps to develop a level strategy are as follows:

Step 1: Using Eq. 5-8, total the demand forecasts and the safety stocks for the months of January to April and divide the total by 4 as 12,500 + 2,500 = 15,000/4 = 3,750 units. 3,750 units is the level inventory for the time period of four months to get level production output.

Step 2: Calculate the required production time by multiplying the local production output by 5 since it takes 5 hours to produce a unit: $3,750 \times 5 = 18,750$ hours.

Step 3: Using Eq. 5-9, find the level inventory for January as 3,750 − 4,000 = −250 units.

Step 4: In our case, we have a beginning inventory of 100 units for January. Using Eq. 5-10, calculate the ending inventory as 100 + (−250) - backorder inventory (which is 0 as there are no backorders for the previous month) = −150 units. Since we cannot have a negative number for ending inventory, we will make the ending inventory 0 and then leave the 150 units as backorder inventory.

Step 5: Using Eq. 5-11, calculate the average inventory for January.
Step 6: Repeat steps 1 through 5 for all months, February to April.

	Units	Formula	**Production Plan: Level Strategy**				
			January	**February**	**March**	**April**	**Total**
Demand Forecast	units		4,000	2,000	3,000	3,500	12,500
Safety Stock	units		800	400	600	700	2,500
Level Production Output	units	Eq. 5-8	3,725	3,725	3,725	3,725	14,900
Required production time	hours		18,625	18,625	18,625	18,625	
Level Inventory	units	Eq. 5-9	−275	1,725	725	225	
Beginning Inventory	units		100	0	1,550	2,275	
Level Ending Inventory	units	Eq. 5-10	0	1,550	2,275	2,500	
Average Inventory	units	Eq. 5-11	50	775	1,913	2,388	
Backorder Inventory	units		175	0	0	0	
Materials Cost			$298,000.00	$298,000.00	$298,000.00	$298,000.00	$1,192,000.00
Straight Time Cost		Eq. 5-5	$93,125.00	$93,125.00	$93,125.00	$93,125.00	$372,500.00
Inventory holding cost			$100.00	$1,550.00	$3,825.00	$4,775.00	$10,250.00
Backorder cost			$14,000.00	$0.00	$0.00	$0.00	$14,000.00
Total Cost			$405,225.00	$392,675.00	$394,950.00	$395,900.00	**$1,588,750.00**

Step 7: Calculate the materials cost using production requirement, straight-time cost using required production time; inventory holding costs using average inventory and the backorder costs.

Analysis: The level strategy is to maintain a constant workforce to produce a constant production output. In this example, the level production output is 3,750 units every month. It takes 5 hours to produce a unit. With 18,750 hours, the company can produce 18,650/5 = 3,750 units per month. In this example, apart from the usual material cost and straight-time cost, we have inventory holding cost and backorder cost due to overproduction and underproduction due to the constant workforce policy of the company. The company has to resort to backorders in January since they do not have enough beginning inventory and workforce to produce the demand of 4,000 units. The total cost using the level strategy is $1,597,600 for ACEG Industries compared to $1,427,500 using the chase strategy.

Flex Strategy

In this strategy, firms maintain a stable workforce. The workforce may be allotted an overtime or provided a flexible work schedule to produce the goods and services. The overtime or varying workhours are directed toward meeting the demand. The employees welcome a stable workforce and the stable workforce policy avoids the problems associated with hiring and layoffs of employees. This strategy helps firms to maintain low levels of inventory. Example 5-3 illustrates the flex strategy. To maintain a stable workforce, we use this equation:

$$Flex\ Required\ Workforce = \frac{Total\ Required\ Production\ Time}{Total\ Available\ Production\ Time} \qquad Eq.\ 5\text{-}12$$

where,

Total Required Production Time = Sum of required production time of all time periods considered in the planning horizon, and

Total Available Production Time = Sum of available production time of all periods considered in the planning horizon.

Example 5-3

Using the data from Example 5-1, develop an aggregate plan for ACEG Industries using a flex strategy using only overtime if needed. Use a constant workforce based on demand and available time.

These are the steps and the results of choosing a flex strategy (constant workforce and overtime if needed).

The steps to develop a flex strategy are as follows:

Step 1:   Here we need to find the constant workforce. We will find the constant workforce needed to meet the demand. Therefore, the production requirement of January is the same as January's demand which is 4,000 units.

Step 2:   Converting production requirement to hours using the 5 hours to a unit, we get 20,000 hours to produce 4,000 units.

Step 3:   Find the total production requirement time for all 4 months, total those hours, and divide that by the available total number of working hours for the 4 months to find the workforce needed; = 62,500/720 = 87 workers (rounded up). We have a constant workforce of 87 workers using Eq. 5-12.

Step 4:   There are 8 hours to a day for a regular shift. Calculate the available production time for a regular shift for January = 21 days × 8 hours/day × 87 workers = 14,616 hours; this can be converted to 14,616/5 = 2,923 units of production during regular time for January.

Step 5:   If we have a beginning inventory of 100 units, can produce 2,923 units during regular time, and with a production requirement to produce 4,000 units, we have to produce 4,000 − 100 − 2,923 = 977 units in overtime.

	Units	Formula	January	February	March	April	Total
Production Plan: Flex Strategy with Overtime							
Demand Forecast	units		4,000	2,000	3,000	3,500	12,500
Production Requirement	units	Eq. 5-2	4,000	2,000	3,000	3,500	12,500
Required production time	hours		20000	10000	15000	17500	62,500
Working Days per Month	days		21	22	23	24	90
Available production time/worker	hours		168	176	184	192	720
Flex Required workforce		Eq. 5-12	87	87	87	87	
Beginning Inventory	units		100	0	1,062	1,264	
Production time regular shift	hours		14,616	15,312	16,008	16,704	
Production regular shift	units		2,923	3,062	3,202	3,341	
Required production in overtime	units		977	0	0	0	
Ending Inventory	units		0	1,062	1,264	1,105	
Safety Stock	units		800	400	600	700	
Excess Stock	units		0	662	664	405	
Overtime	hours		4,885	0	0	0	
Materials Cost			$312,016	$244,992	$256,128	$267,264	$1,080,400.00
Straight Time Cost			$73,080.00	$76,560.00	$80,040.00	$83,520.00	$313,200.00
Overtime Cost			$48,850.00	$0.00	$0.00	$0.00	$48,850.00
Inventory holding cost			$0.00	$1,324.80	$1,328.00	$809.60	$3,462.40
Total Cost			$433,946.00	$322,876.80	$337,496.00	$351,593.60	**$1,445,912.40**

Step 6:   The 977 units in overtime plus the 100 beginning inventory plus the regular shift production of 2,923 meets the demand for January. There is no ending inventory left for January. Let us consider the safety stock now. The company expects a safety stock of 800 units and there is no safety stock left for this month. If the firm wants to produce to meet the safety stock, they can always pay overtime and get the safety stock. Therefore, we will take 0 ending inventory of January as the beginning inventory of February. There is no excess inventory or stock either for January. If there exists an ending inventory, we can subtract the safety stock and use the result as excess inventory. We can use the ending inventory as the beginning inventory for the next month. Overtime

production of 977 units can be converted into hours using 5 hours per unit as: $977 \times 5 = 4{,}885$ hours.

Step 7: Repeat steps 1 through 5 for all months, February to April.

Step 8: Calculate the materials cost using production requirement, straight-time cost using required production time; inventory holding costs using excess inventory, and the overtime costs using overtime hours.

Analysis: The flex strategy is to maintain a constant workforce but the workforce is allotted overtime or provided flexible work schedule to produce goods and services. In this example, apart from the usual material cost and straight-time cost, we have overtime cost. The company also has inventory holding cost because the company has produced excess stock. The total cost using the flex strategy with overtime is $1,445,886.40 compared to the level strategy of $1,597,600 and $1,427,500 using the chase strategy for ACEG Industries.

Hybrid Strategy

Hybrid strategy is a combination of the level, chase, and flex strategies. For example, firms may use a chase strategy for the first quarter and then switch over to either level or flex strategy for the next quarter. Companies pursue this type of mixed strategies to create a balance between production rate, workforce, and inventory levels to meet the demand. Example 5-4 illustrates a hybrid strategy.

Example 5-4

Using the data from Example 5-1, develop an aggregate plan for ACEG Industries using a chase strategy for the first 2 months. Use the workforce from February and develop a flex strategy for the next 2 months using subcontracting if needed. No overtime is allowed.

Following the steps of a chase strategy for January and February, using the workforce from February, and following the steps to develop a flex strategy for March and April and using subcontracting if needed, we get:

	Units	Formula	January	February	March	April	Total
Production Plan: Hybrid Strategy (Jan & Feb: Chase; Marc & Apr: Flex)							
Beginning Inventory	units		100	800			
Demand Forecast	units		4,000	2,000	3,000	3,500	12,500
Safety Stock	units		800	400			
Production Requirement	units	Eq. 5-2	4,700	1,600	3,000	3,500	12,800
Ending Inventory	units	Eq. 5-1	800	400			

	Units	Formula	January	February	March	April	Total
Production Plan: Hybrid Strategy (Jan & Feb: Chase; Marc & Apr: Flex)							
Required production time	hours		23500	8000	15000	17500	
Working Days per Month	days		21	22	23	24	90
Worker hours	hours	Eq. 5-5	168	176	184	192	720
Required workforce		Eq. 5-6	140	46	46	46	
New Workers Hired				0			
Laid Off Workers				94			
Production Requirement	units	Eq. 5-2			3,000	3,500	
Required production time	hours				15,000	17,500	
Beginning Inventory	units				400	0	
Production time regular shift	hours				8,464	8,832	
Production in regular shift	units				1,693	1,766	
Production by subcontract	units				907	1,734	
Ending Inventory	units				0	0	
Safety Stock	units				600	700	
Excess Stock	units				0	0	
Subcontract hours	hours				9,072	17,336	
Materials Cost			$376,000	$128,000	$208,000	$280,000	$992,000.00
Straight Time Cost		Eq. 5-5	$117,500.00	$40,000.00	$75,000.00	$87,500.00	$320,000.00
Hiring Cost			$0.00	$0.00			$0.00
Layoff Cost			$0.00	$37,600.00			$37,600.00
Subcontract Cost					$90,720.00	$173,360.00	$264,080.00
Inventory holding cost					$0.00	$0.00	$0.00
Total Cost			$493,500.00	$205,600.00	$373,720.00	$540,860.00	**$1,613,680.00**

Analysis: The hybrid strategy is to follow a combination of any of the chase, level, and flex strategies. The costs vary depending on the combination of strategies. The total cost using the hybrid strategy is $1,613,680 compared to the flex strategy with overtime of $1,445,886.40, the level strategy of $1,597,600 and $1,427,500 using the chase strategy for ACEG Industries.

The most economical strategy is the chase strategy. The company may opt to go with the flex strategy to avoid the hassle of hiring and firing strategy and because the cost difference ($18,386) is not that much from the chase strategy.

Formulae from this Chapter

Ending Inventory	Ending Inventory $= Beginning\ Inventory + Actual\ Production - Demand\ Forecast$	Eq. 5-1
Production requirement	Production requirement $= Demand\ Forecast + Safety\ Stock - Beginning\ inventory$	Eq. 5-2
Required Production Time	Required Production Time $= Production\ requirement \times Time\ to\ produce\ an\ unit$	Eq. 5-3
Actual Production (units)	$Actual\ Production = \dfrac{Actual\ Production\ Time}{Production\ rate}$	Eq. 5-4
Worker Hours	$Worker\ Hours = Number\ of\ workdays \times worktime\ per\ day$	Eq. 5-5
Required Workforce	$Required\ workforce = \dfrac{Required\ production\ time}{Worker\ Hours}$	Eq. 5-6
Production Cost	Basic Production Cost $= Required\ production\ time \times Stratight\ time\ cost$	Eq. 5-7
Level Production Output	Level Production Output $= \dfrac{Total\ Demand + Total\ Safety\ Stock - Beginning\ Inventory}{Total\ Time\ Period}$	Eq. 5-8
Level Inventory	Level Inventory $= Level\ production\ output - Demand\ Forecast$	Eq. 5-9
Level Ending Inventory	Level Ending Inventory $= Level\ Inventory + Beginning\ Inventory - Backorder\ for\ the\ Past\ Month$	Eq. 5-10
Average Inventory	Average Inventory $= \dfrac{Beginning\ Inventory + Ending\ Inventory}{2}$	Eq. 5-11
Flex Required Workforce	Flex Required Workforce $= \dfrac{Total\ Required\ Production\ Time}{Total\ Available\ Production\ Time}$	Eq. 5-12

Case Study: Aggregate Planning at Rowland Industries

Robert Rowland is the President of Rowland Industries. Rowland Industries manufacturers paddleboats and pedal boats. The company from Columbus, Mississippi, has been doing well in the past years and has established itself as one of the premier small boat manufacturers within its distributor and customer base.

Robert and his team meet every month to develop Sales and Operations (S&OP) plans, and to review and improve the aggregate plans for the next 6months. These meetings last an entire day and are always well attended by various functions including sales, marketing, operations, finance, and the executive team. Prior to a monthly planning session, several information and analyses are prepared by appropriate departments and shared with the executive team including:

- Review of any newly introduced products,
- Demand forecasts,
- Updated inventory levels,
- Updated production capabilities,
- Working capital and other pertinent financials.

The monthly S&OP meeting involves high-level decision-making activities to determine planned levels of production, capacity, inventory, and labor force to minimize the cost of resources and maximize the profits and meet customer demand. Various members of the team provide accurate and current information of demand forecast, production capabilities, inventory levels, and resource availability. Using the available information, the team generates plans.

This aggregate and S&OP process is an important aspect of uniting all key constituents of a firm to meet and accomplish an objective: a single goal. The senior level executives of a firm who are responsible for sales, marketing, procurement, manufacturing, supply chain, and finance meet to discuss the needs and constraints of each of their respective areas as well as the overall company objectives. The meeting is also to establish agreement on an operating plan for the next month, quarter, and year. This process is repeated each month. The team has used the process for their aggregate, sales and operations plans for the past years. The demand forecasting provided by the marketing department has been accurate enough for them to produce good aggregate plans in the past. Though the product line is seasonal in certain parts of the country, the sales have been good

© Rawpixel.com/Shutterstock.com

throughout the year as the company had been targeting the Pacific West, West South, East South, and parts of South Atlantic regions of the United States.

During each meeting, Robert insisted that his team must assess risks to their supply chain. The team paid special attention to quality of products, supply problems, demand spikes and troughs, potential demand disruptions, obsolescence, and market disruptions. Understanding those risks was essential to the firm as they could include contingencies in their aggregate and S&OP plans. Some of the important factors considered by the team during the meeting are as follows[9]:

- Changes since last meeting,
- Company performance against company's goals and key performance indicators
- New risks,
- Decisions to be considered now and in the near future,
- Performance of products,
- Progress of product development efforts,
- Resource constraints,
- Utilization of key resources,
- What went well with the last S&OP plans, and
- Any need to revise long-term plans.

The employees of Rowland Industries work on Monday through Friday. The company maintains two shifts. Each shift runs for 8 hours with half-an-hour break, although the employees get paid $20 per hour for the full 8-hour regular shifts. Overtime is contingent on the aggregate plans and if necessary, employees are paid one and a half times the regular shift wages. The Human Resources Director at Rowland uses Internet to sites such as indeed.com to identify and recruit employees. The new hiring plan includes task-oriented, team-oriented, productivity-related, process-related, and labor-related training. The cost of hiring and training is estimated to

© Nopkamon Tanayakorn/Shutterstock.com

be about $1,500 for a production worker. To lay off a production worker, it costs $1,200 for the company.

The manufacturing department insists on having a safety stock equal to one-tenth of the next month's demand. The inventory holding cost is $400 per boat per month; the stockout cost is $1,250 per boat per month; the subcontracting cost is $800 per hour; the backorder cost is $800 per unit. It takes 7½ hours to make a boat and the material costs to make a boat are $950. The demand forecasts and the number of workdays are shown below:

	January	February	March	April	May	June
Demand Forecast	1,600	1,500	1,200	1,300	1,400	1,600
Working Days per Month	21	20	23	21	22	22

Case Questions

A. Prepare an aggregate plan based on a chase strategy.

B. Prepare an aggregate plan based on a flex strategy with overtime permitted. Use a constant workforce based on demand and available time.

C. Prepare an aggregate plan based on a flex strategy with subcontract if needed. Use a constant workforce using the lowest demand in the planning horizon.

D. Prepare an aggregate plan based on a flex strategy with a constant workforce and subcontract if needed.

E. Prepare an aggregate plan based on a flex strategy with a constant workforce. No subcontract or overtime. Vary inventory and use stockouts and excess stocks.

F. Prepare an aggregate plan based on a hybrid strategy. Rowland was expecting a new contract and was prepared to go with a chase strategy. During the month of March, they discovered that they did not get that contract. Therefore, they kept the number of workers as of March and went with a flex strategy from April using a flex strategy with constant workforce and subcontract if needed.

G. Which of the above strategies is the most cost-effective for Rowland Industries?

H. Of the subcontracting strategies, which is the most cost-effective?

I. If hiring cost equals $ 2,500 and layoff cost equals $ 1,500, which is the best strategy?

J. If subcontract costs went up to $1,300, which is the best strategy?

Summary

- Sales and Operations Planning (S&OP) is a process used by companies to balance and manage supply and demand.

- The goal of S&OP is to handle the variability in sales and revenues effectively by managing both supply and demand.
- S&OP is a coordinated effort of many functional areas in a company including sales, marketing, product development, engineering, finance, logistics, distribution, and production.
- The final output is the aggregate plan.
- From the aggregate plan, Master Production Schedules (MPS) and Materials Requirements Plans (MRP) are developed.
- An aggregate plan determines planned levels of production, capacity, inventory, and labor force to minimize the cost of resources or maximize the profits and meet customer demand.
- The outcome of an aggregate plan is to maximize a facility's productivity at the lowest possible cost.
- Aggregate planning defines how a company should best utilize its facilities.
- Aggregate planning applies strategic level decisions while determining the operational levels in their plants.
- S&OP and aggregate plans are developed using information consisting of many key factors.
- Using the information and the knowledge gained over years of planning, the planners in a firm develop S&OP and aggregate plans.
- A planning horizon is the time period for which the aggregate plans are prepared.
- A short-term horizon plan is for a single day to a few months.
- An intermediate-term horizon plan is for 3 to 18 months.
- The long-term horizon plan is for more than a year.
- Inventory consists of raw materials, work-in-process (WIP) used to create goods, and the finished goods.
- Raw materials inventory are the basic components used to produce the finished goods.
- Work-in-process inventory refers to materials and components that are used to make finished goods. Finished goods inventory are items that are available for customers to purchase.
- Stocks are finished goods that are available to sell to customers.
- Inventory on hand is the number of materials, components, or goods that a company has available for sale or use at a particular time period.
- Beginning inventory is the inventory at the start of a time period.
- Ending inventory is the inventory left at the end of a time period.
- Safety stock eliminates the worry of running out of stock. Firms leave the safety stock for use when needed and when there is no way to get required inventory.
- Excess inventory is inventory that has not yet been sold or that has exceeded the projected consumer demand for that product.
- Stockout is another term used when firms run out of inventory of a particular item. Stockouts impact the inventory of finished goods and therefore revenues and profits.

- Firms frequently allow their customers to place orders even if they do not have stock or inventory on hand, called backordering.
- When a manufacturing company requires more goods than they can produce, it is common for the manufacturing company to contract to another company to make those goods, called subcontracting.
- Inventory backlogs happen when a company has more orders than they can produce or accumulates a buildup of unfulfilled orders.
- Production is the process of manufacturing goods from raw materials and/or components. Producing goods is the focal point of many manufacturing companies.
- Production requirement is the number of goods required to be produced in order to meet demand forecast during a given time period.
- Production rate is the number of goods produced during a given period of time.
- Production rate is also the amount of time it takes to produce one unit of a good.
- Required production time is the time taken to produce the production requirement.
- Available production time is equal to the number of working days multiplied by the number of available workers.
- Labor as the workforce is called consists of skilled, semi-skilled, skilled people, and professionals.
- Unskilled labor refers to workers who have no particular skills essential to operate machines or use knowledge to produce goods and services.
- Semi-skilled labor requires more skills than an unskilled labor job.
- Skilled labor refers to workers who possess specialized training or skills.
- Professionals possess an even higher degree of skills.
- A person-hour is the amount of work performed by the average worker in 1 hour.
- Worker hours is the total time in hours spent by a worker during the number of working days.
- Required workforce is the number of workers required to meet production requirements.
- Overtime refers to hours that exceed normally scheduled working hours.
- Hiring is to engage the personal services of a person.
- A layoff is considered a separation from employment due to a lack of available work.
- Straight-time cost is the cost to produce a good or service per hour during the regular 8-hour period in a working day.
- Overtime cost is the cost to produce a good or service per hour for overtime work in a working day.
- Basic production cost is the cost to produce the goods and services.

- Inventory holding costs are the costs associated with holding inventory that is unsold.
- Backorder costs are costs incurred by a firm when it is unable to immediately fill an order and promises their customers that they will fill the customer order at a later date.
- Stockout cost is a loss of income for a firm that is associated with a shortage of inventory.
- Sales, operations, and aggregate planning strategy provides the production requirements for a firm.
- Aggregate planning plays a significant role in the profitability of a firm.
- The four strategies of aggregate planning include chase, level, flex, and hybrid.
- In a chase strategy, firms match production capacity with demand forecast by hiring and laying off workers.
- In a level strategy, firms maintain a constant workforce to produce a constant production output.
- In a flex strategy, firms maintain a stable workforce.
- Hybrid strategy is a combination of the level, chase, and flex strategies.

Review Questions

1. What is Sales and Operations Planning (S&OP)?
2. What is the goal S&OP?
3. What is the final output of S&OP?
4. What does an aggregate plan determine?
5. What is the outcome of an aggregate plan?
6. Describe a planning horizon with an appropriate example.
7. What is a long-term horizon plan?
8. What are the three types of inventory?
9. What is stock?
10. What is inventory on hand?
11. What is beginning and ending inventory?
12. What is safety stock?
13. What is excess inventory?
14. What is stockout?
15. What is backordering?
16. Why do inventory backlogs happen in a firm?
17. What is production?
18. What is production rate?
19. How is labor classified in a firm?
20. What is inventory holding cost?
21. What is backorder cost?
22. What are the four strategies of aggregate planning?

Critical Thinking Questions

1. Does S&OP or aggregate planning balance and manage supply and demand? How and why or why not?
2. Does aggregate planning need the coordination of several departments in a company?
3. How do companies maximize a facility's productivity at the lowest possible cost using the material from this book chapter?
4. A company is developing an aggregate plan for the next year. What kind of planning horizon is this?
5. Why do companies subcontract?
6. Is subcontracting better than paying overtime to employees?
7. Is there a difference between aggregate planning in a manufacturing company versus a service company? Explain.
8. What is the common planning horizon aimed for by sales and operations planning?
9. A tailoring shop that makes golf apparel in Asia employs temporary workers as required and lays them off during days of low demand. What is this type of aggregate planning called?
10. What are the most common decision factors for aggregate planning in a manufacturing company?
11. What are the most common decision factors for aggregate planning in a service organization?
12. Explain the advantages and disadvantages of the four types of aggregate planning.

Problem Solving Questions

1. Reb Manufacturing, Pvt. Ltd., an Indian company, plans to hold 20% of the forecast demand every month as safety stock. The company takes 5 hours to produce a unit. Employees work for 8 hours a day, 5 days a week, and get paid $12 per hour as straight time and 1½ times as overtime. The inventory holding cost is $8 per unit per month; the stockout cost is $10 per unit per hour; the subcontracting costs is $25 per hour; the hiring and training per worker is $25; the layoff cost is $40 per hour and the backorder cost is $10 per unit. The company has 300 units at the beginning of January and the material cost is $65 per unit. If the demand is as follows, what is the total material cost and the ending inventory at the end of June?

	January	February	March	April	May	June
Demand Forecast	1450	1400	1350	1400	1450	1500

2. Dill Industries wants to maintain their regular production units at 400 units per month and plans to make another 30 units using overtime. Do not consider material costs. It costs $40 per unit in regular time and $60 per unit in overtime time. The inventory holding cost is $10 per unit and the stockout cost is $20. Develop an aggregate plan.

	Jan	Feb	Mar	Apr	May	Jun
Forecast	400	420	420	440	420	420

3. It takes 5 hours to produce a unit at a local manufacturing firm. Employees work for 8 hours a day, 5 days a week, $10 per hour as straight time and 1½ times as overtime. The inventory holding cost is $20 per unit per month; the stockout cost is $10 per unit per hour; the subcontracting cost is $25 per hour; the hiring and training per worker is $120; the layoff cost is $150 per hour and the backorder cost is $20 per unit. The company does not hold any inventory at the beginning of the year while material cost is $15 per unit. Develop an aggregate plan using a chase strategy and the following data:

	January	February	March	April	May	June
Beginning Inventory	0					
Demand Forecast	1700	1500	1100	1000	1200	1600
Safety Stock	350	375	275	225	275	400
Number of Working Days by Month	22	20	21	21	22	20

4. Develop an aggregate plan for Redwood Industries from Flanders, NJ. The executive management wants to keep a constant workforce based on production requirement for the first month of the year. They would like to use stockouts and excess inventory to meet the fluctuations in the following demand:

	Jan	Feb	Mar	Apr	May	Jun	Jul	Aug	Sep	Oct	Nov	Dec
Forecast Demand	3,000	2,800	4,000	3,100	3,000	3,500	3,200	2,850	4,000	4,000	5,000	4,250
No of workdays	21	20	23	21	22	22	21	23	22	21	22	22

The company wants to hold 300 units every month as safety stock. It takes 2 hours to produce a unit. Employees work for 8 hours a day, 5 days a week, and get paid $12 per hour as straight time and 1½ times as overtime. The inventory holding cost is $8 per unit per month; the stockout cost is $10 per unit per hour; the subcontracting cost is $25 per hour; the hiring and training per worker is $25; the layoff cost is $40 per hour and the backorder cost is $10 per unit. The company does not hold any inventory at the beginning of the year while material cost is $15 per unit.

5. Neil Special Pottery, LLC has decided to use a regular output of 800 units per month for this year. They can use overtime up to 80 units per month and use subcontracting for the remaining units to match the demand forecast. They figure out that the overtime cost is 1½ times their regular shift cost of $20 per unit. They have an outsourced supplier who offers their pottery products at $90 per unit. Their accounting department has informed that the average balance inventory cost is $20 and materials cost $40 per unit. Develop an aggregate plan with appropriate costs for the following demands:

	Jan	Feb	Mar	Apr	May	Jun
Forecast Demand	760	800	840	880	860	960

6. Becky Bright, the President of Brighter Products, LLC, is planning to prepare an aggregate plan. The company manufactures desk lamps in a contemporary style. The capacity of the plant is 1,500 lamps per month and it takes 30 minutes to make a lamp. At the beginning of July, they find that they have no lamps in the warehouse. The company pays their workers $20 per hour for regular shift work and $30 for overtime. The materials cost $15 per unit. The inventory carrying cost is $15 per unit. Becky hires only bright talent and does not want to lay off workers as she can assign them to other jobs. Hiring costs are $150 per worker at their plant.
   a. Develop a chase plan to match the forecast demand for the following demand.

	Jul	Aug	Sep	Oct	Nov	Dec	Total
Forecast Demand	1550	1600	1550	1700	1670	1600	9,670

   b. Ms. Bright wants to consider an alternative plan with no overtime but use a subcontractor who can deliver excess products required at $25 per unit. Would this alternative plan cost less for Brighter Products?
7. Regas, Inc. has planned to use the same number of workers as of September for the rest of the year and has set 4,500 hours of maximum overtime. On the first day of August, the company has 120 workers. Workers work for 8 hours per day; there is no inventory on hand for the month of August. A unit can be produced in 15 minutes. If the hiring cost is $60 and lay off costs are $75, inventory holding cost is $10 per unit per month, straight-time labor is $10 per hour, overtime is $15 per hour, backorder is $20 per unit, and the number of working days and demand forecasts are given below, what is the total cost of this aggregate plan?

	Aug	Sep	Oct	Nov
Forecast Demand	60,000	44,000	80,000	20,000
Number of Working Days	23	22	21	22

8. Develop a production plan and calculate the annual cost for NewUnits, Inc. whose demand forecast is provided below. Inventory at the beginning of fall is 500 units. At the beginning of fall the company has 25 workers, they plan to hire temporary workers at the beginning of April and lay them off at the end of May. During any time, except January, the company plans for overtime of its regular workers to prevent stockouts if necessary. The costs are hiring, $150 for each temporary worker; layoff, $200 for each worker laid off; inventory holding, $10 per unit-quarter; backorder, $20 per unit; straight time, $15 per hour; overtime, $18 per hour. Assume that the productivity is 0.75 unit per worker hour on an eight hours per day. Temporary workers get paid the same as regular workers.

	Jan	Feb	Mar	Apr
Forecast Demand	10,000	12,000	8,000	12,000
Number of Working Days	60	60	60	60

9. Reputed Lenses, Inc. makes contact lenses. They hire 4 temporary workers in addition to their 15 full-time employees. Each full-time employee can produce 300 units while the temporary workers can make 250 units per month. Their beginning inventory is 500 units. It costs $35 to produce a lens and the carrying cost is $25 per year. Develop an aggregate plan. The demand for lenses is as follows:

	May	June	July	August
Forecast	3,200	2,800	3,100	3,000

10. Ben Bright's Lamps & Candle, Inc. is expecting the demand of their products as shown below. They believe that they need to keep 10% of the demand as safety stock. They want to maintain a minimum workforce based on the monthly minimum demand for the 6 months. The daily 8-hour production is rate is 0.5 hours per unit. The material cost is $2 per unit produced; the straight-time cost is $2 per unit. The company has planned to subcontract units that cannot be produced for $1.50 per unit. Develop an aggregate plan.

	January	February	March	April	May	June
Demand Forecast	30,000	25,000	32,000	33,000	34,000	33,000
Working Days per Month	21	20	23	21	22	22

References

1. Katz, J. (2010, March 22). Retailers Help Del Monte see the future. *Industry Week*.

2. Cavale, S., & McLymore, A. (2022, May 27). U.S. retailers' ballooning inventories set stage for deep discounts. *Reuters*.

3. Miksen, C. (2022). What do retailers do with surplus inventory? *Chron Newsletter*. Retrieved May 10, 2022, from https://smallbusiness.chron.com/retailers-surplus-inventory-36258.html.

4. Moyer, M. W. (2022, May 11). Some baby formulas are out of stock. *The New York Times*.

5. Reuters. (2022). *Explainer: What happened with Abbott baby formula that worsened a U.S. shortage?* Retrieved May 20, 2022, from https://www.reuters.com/business/healthcare-pharmaceuticals/what-happened-with-abbott-baby-formula-that-worsened-us-shortage-2022-05-16/.

6. Josephs, L. (2021). *Boeing orders outpace cancellations for third consecutive month, but Max deliveries still paused.* Retrieved June 1, 2022, from https://www.cnbc.com/2021/05/11/boeing-logs-more-orders-than-cancellations-but-some-max-jets-still-grounded.html.

7. Forecast International. (2022). *Airbus and Boeing report January 2022 commercial aircraft orders and deliveries.* Retrieved June 1, 2022, from https://dsm.forecastinternational.com/wordpress/2022/02/11/airbus-and-boeing-report-january-2022-commercial-aircraft-orders-and-deliveries/.

8. Ager, D. L., & Roberto, M. A. (2013). Trader Joe's. Harvard Business School Case 714-419.

9. Palmatier, G. E., & Crom, C. (2003). *Enterprise sales and operations planning: Synchronizing demand, supply, and resources for peak performance.* J. Ross Publishing.

MATERIAL REQUIREMENTS PLANNING

Learning Objectives

- Define Enterprise resource planning (ERP).
- Explain the components of enterprise resource planning.
- Describe the advantages of enterprise resource planning.
- Explain the material planning process.
- Describe the master production schedule (MPS).
- Explain the relationship between the aggregate plan and the MPS.
- Describe time fences and time fence zones in the MPS.
- Calculate the available to promise inventory.
- Define material requirements planning (MRP).
- Explain how the bill of materials (BOM) is used to develop MRP.
- Explain how the BOM and inventory transactions are used in MRP development.
- Develop material requirements planning.

Companies use computer applications called material requirements planning (MRP) to estimate quantities and schedule raw materials. MRP is an inventory management system. From the aggregate plans that we developed in the past chapter, MRP is developed to calculate the inventory requirements for components and raw materials. An MRP process minimizes inventory levels, reduces customer lead time, optimizes inventory management, and improves productivity.

The Kraft Heinz Company is the third-largest food and beverage company in North America and the fifth-largest food and beverage company in the world with eight $1 billion+ brands. In addition to Kraft and Heinz, the company's products include Boca Burger, Gevalia, Grey Poupon, Oscar Mayer, Philadelphia Cream Cheese, Primal Kitchen, and Wattie's.

© Joni Hanebutt/
Shutterstock.com

© Jonathan Weiss/
Shutterstock.com

© OleksandrShnuryk/
Shutterstock.com

© Wirestock Creators/
Shutterstock.com

© rblfmr/
Shutterstock.com

In 2015, Kraft Foods voluntarily recalled 242,000 cases of their Kraft Macaroni and Cheese Dinner due to the possibility that some boxes may have contained fragments of metal[1]. Kraft had shipped and distributed the recalled product in the United States, Puerto Rico, and a few Caribbean and South American countries. A comprehensive electronic system could have prevented these kinds of issues before they occurred, tracked the issues, or prevented them from spreading. This event took place before the merger with Heinz. Moreover, the U.S. Food and Drug Administration (FDA) was planning to crack down on food traceability compliance later that year. Food traceability compliance required companies to integrate the packaging labels containing ingredients, shelf-life, packaging contents, and a general assurance of process compliance to the regulatory guidance of the FDA[2] in their manufacturing processes. Since many companies like Kraft were using the Enterprise Resource planning (ERP) software as an integrated solution to their manufacturing, such standards had to be integrated into their ERP system processes.

Partnering with Infosys, an outsourcing company from India, Kraft moved on to SAP, an ERP system, and upgraded all of its SAP systems in 2008. In 2022, Kraft Heinz started to use SAP and Microsoft Azure to eliminate supply chain disruptions. Kraft used Microsoft's machine learning and analytics to drive innovation and efficiencies across their supply chain. These actions were to ensure a quick entry of their products into the market[3].

By joining forces with Microsoft, Kraft Heinz was transforming itself to create a more collaborative supply chain and to anticipate future demand as early as possible[4].

Enterprise Resource Planning

Enterprise resource planning (ERP) is a commercial software system that integrates and manages all the functions and the processes of a company. An ERP system functions as a single system to control and manage all the activities of an organization. The software includes a company's accounting, finance, supply chain, operations, sales, marketing, quality, materials management, plant maintenance, and human resource functions. Typically, ERP systems are built using the unique business processes of a company with a centralized database. The centralized database collects all the enterprise's transactional data in one place to be shared by various functions and employees of that enterprise. The centralized database eliminates data duplication and provides data integrity. There are two types of databases including the master data and the transactional data. Transactional data consists of the day-to-day transactional activities of the organization. For example, sales records, access logs, and planned orders are all examples of transactional data while data on customers, vendors, or materials are examples of master data. Both the transactional and the master data are used for various activities such as financial accounting, production planning, plant maintenance, or project systems.

> **Enterprise resource planning (ERP)** Enterprise resource planning (ERP) is a commercial software system that integrates and manages all the functions and processes of a company.

A functional view of an ERP system is shown in Figure 6-1. Once a sales order is placed in the system by a sales team, the whole company and all its functions can see that sales order instantly. As a result, the whole firm starts to plan and execute—materials management places raw materials orders, production starts their manufacturing planning, the human resource department initiates hiring of workers if necessary, accounting gets ready to update the transactions—all activities go into motion in order to fulfill the sales order. Currently, most firms in the world use an ERP system to manage their businesses.

ERP systems comprise many modules such as financial accounting, production planning, and plant maintenance as shown in Figure 6-1. Let us take a look at these functional modules next.

Sales and Distribution

The sales and distribution module is used to manage sales orders as well as shipping, billing, and invoicing of the goods and services. The module optimizes all the tasks and activities carried out in sales, delivery, and billing. The key elements of this module include pre-sales support, inquiry processing, quotation processing, sales order processing, delivery processing, pricing, goods availability check and credit management, and billing.

Financial Accounting and Control

The financial accounting and control module is used for financial reporting. This module records all the financial transactions. This module with the company-defined chart of accounts has several sub-modules including accounts receivables, accounts payables, asset management, general ledger, and bank accounting. The journal entries are automatically posted.

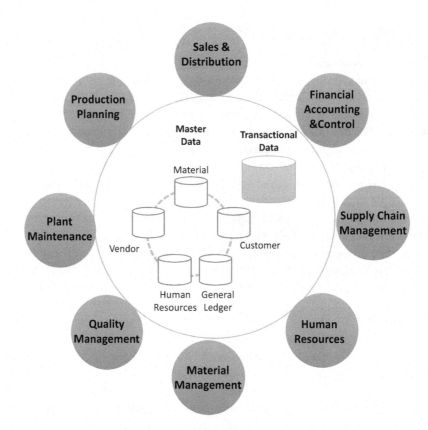

Figure 6-1 Enterprise Resource Planning

Supply Chain Management

The supply chain management module controls the production planning, the business forecasting, and the demand planning functions. The SCM module helps an organization to manage its supply chain process by connecting the suppliers, the customers, the business partners, and the retailers. The sub-modules include warehouse management, advanced planning and optimization, forecasting, and transportation management.

Human Resource Management

The human resource management is a complete integrated module for supporting the planning and control of personnel activities in an organization. This module consists of many features including personnel development, personnel cost planning, event management, time management, time and payroll integration, payroll, recruitment training, and travel management.

Material Management

The material management module deals with managing the materials and the resources of an organization as well as the procurement, vendor evaluation, material valuation, inventory management, invoice verification, and material requirement planning functions. The module supports the day-to-day procurement, inventory management, and reorder point processing.

Quality Management

The quality management module helps companies to implement and manage quality control processes by preventing defects, enabling continuous process improvement, and establishing quality controls. The module includes quality planning, quality inspection, and quality control.

Plant Maintenance

The plant maintenance module supports and maintains equipment and systems in a firm. The module focuses on inspection of systems and equipment in a company. The module is also used in preventive maintenance, repairs, and restoration of systems, equipment, and facilities.

Production Planning

Production planning aligns the demand with the manufacturing capacity. It creates production and procurement schedules for components and finished products. This module is used to plan and control various manufacturing activities such as Bill of Materials (BOM), routings, work centers, aggregate planning, sales and operations planning, master production scheduling, material requirements planning, shop floor control, production orders, and product costing.

Advantages of ERP

The main reason that companies implement ERP is to improve their internal processes and achieve their business goals. Usually, companies have to customize the software to their business practices and therefore, the implementation of an ERP system is expensive and time-consuming. The software is complex and employees have to be trained very well to use the software. However, the advantages are many and exceed the disadvantages. ERP promises many advantages such as:

Improved Productivity

ERP engages and connects the users internally and externally with customers, suppliers, and partners. This creates an efficient, collaborative environment to proactively meet customer requirements.

Enhanced Insight

ERP provides the right information at the right time to users. The real-time information that is available can be used for real-time analysis to address problems and pursue new opportunities.

Better Governance

ERP gives users a comprehensive corporate governance functionality. This enables companies to comply with various standards and regulations including Sarbanes-Oxley, Basel III, global accounting standards, and global human resources regulations.

Reduced Costs

ERP enables companies to manage costs by leveraging their investments. By reducing the time and effort required by the workforce to implement daily activities, ERP reduces or eliminates repetitive manual processes.

Data Visibility

ERP collects data from all departments in the company and makes them accessible and available to employees as and when needed.

Plan and Control Operations and Supply Chain Activities

The production planning module of ERP software encompasses all the activities to plan and control the operations and supply chain management activities of a company. In this chapter, we will focus on some of those activities such as bill of materials (BOM), master production scheduling (MPS), and material requirements planning (MRP).

FROM PRACTICE: ERP Systems

Amazon uses SAP. Starbucks uses Oracle. Toyota uses Microsoft's Dynamics. SAP, Oracle, and Dynamics are all ERP software. The CIO magazine[5] places Oracle as No. 2 in market share with SAP leading the market share. Gartner places Oracle's Fusion Cloud ERP as the leader in its latest Magic Quadrant. SAP, on the other hand, seems to be holding its top position with annual revenue approaching $30 billion. Microsoft is

an ERP powerhouse with its products targeted toward small to midsize businesses. A newcomer to the market is Workday, which has included financial management and enterprise planning to its human capital management solution. Sage, another ERP vendor, is making progress with its cloud platform with accounting and payroll for small businesses. Infor offers an ERP system with industry-specific modules and a cloud platform. Epicor has a solid operational ERP solution for midmarket manufacturing and distribution companies. According to Gartner[6], the ERP software market grew 4% to a market size of $40 billion in total software revenue.

Material Requirements Planning Process

The aggregate planning in a firm is a high-level planning activity. The aggregate plan specifies the production output levels for a company's major product lines. The aggregate plan includes the present and future inventory levels of the company's products.

The quantities of a company's products that are specified in the aggregate plan must be planned for production. Companies use disaggregation to get the specific periods of production time to produce the required number of products. Disaggregation is breaking the aggregate plan into specific product requirements which leads to the Master Production Schedule (MPS). The master production schedule must be translated to the finished product requirements as time-phased requirements for subassemblies, component parts, and raw materials. This translation is known as material requirements planning (MRP). This process is shown in Figure 6-2. Let us discuss how to implement MPS and MRP next.

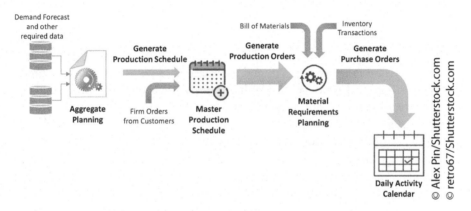

Figure 6-2 Material Requirements Planning Process

FROM PRACTICE: Planning at Coca-Cola

Coca-Cola sells 1.7 billion servings a day. The Coca-Cola production and distribution network comprises of 742 facilities and more than 650 distribution centers. The company sells an entire line of beverages that includes more than 200 brands worldwide. The company synchronizes demand, operations, and inventory planning through their sales and operations planning (S&OP) effort. The way it works is that the demand for their products involves the daily interaction with their marketing and sales numbers. The operations concentrate on the financial implications of optimizing production and distribution. Their inventory planning considers the aggregate planning for the correct inventory levels. Usually, their best accuracy of the demand forecast is 55 to 70% and the company absorbs the remaining demand by building inventory[7].

Master Production Schedule

A master production schedule, also called the **master schedule**, specifies the schedule of planned production quantities of various products in a company. In other words, the master production schedule specifies what needs to be produced, how much needs to be produced, and when it should be produced.

MPS uses aggregate planning, which includes the forecast demands for a company's products and the firm orders from customers. The master production schedule enables the marketing department to make delivery commitments to customers. It enables the production department to evaluate capacity requirements and level schedules. It enables the finance department to minimize inventory. It provides senior management with information to evaluate whether the strategic objectives of the company can be achieved. Master production scheduling helps companies to know when and how much to produce the finished goods. Operations managers typically fine-tune MPS constantly to reap benefits.

Aggregate Plan and MPS

Firms operate to sell their goods and services. Firms sell either a specific product or a family of products. A **product family** is a group of similar goods to meet the diverse needs or tastes of customers. For example, Toyota has Toyota Highlander, Toyota 4Runner, Toyota Sienna, Toyota Highlander Hybrid, and Toyota Sequoia as a Minivan & SUV product family.

The aggregate plan that we discussed in the last chapter does not specify any particular product or product family. But MPS specifies each product of a product family. This distinction between an aggregate plan and an MPS for a sofa manufacturer with three different product lines is shown in Figure 6-3.

Time Fences in MPS

The aggregate planning and the MPS are developed to manage the impacts of increasing or decreasing demand. The MPS must consider the capacity of the facility, the lead times, the production of products, and the development

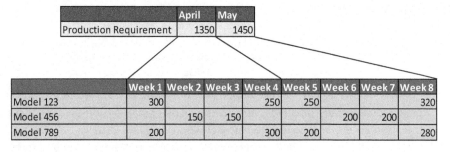

	April	May
Production Requirement	1350	1450

	Week 1	Week 2	Week 3	Week 4	Week 5	Week 6	Week 7	Week 8
Model 123	300			250	250			320
Model 456		150	150			200	200	
Model 789	200			300	200			280

Figure 6-3 Aggregate Planning and MPS for a Product Family

of services. To achieve these as well as to maintain the flexibility of production schedules, the MPS uses what are called **time fences**.

A time fence is a selected period during which it is permitted to make changes to product schedules. The purpose of time fences is to eliminate the expediting of orders and backlogs and to maintain a controlled product flow through the production process. Time fences can be categorized as demand time fence (DTF) and planning time fence (PTF)[8].

Demand Time Fence (DTF)

According to the *APICS Dictionary*, the demand time fence is defined as "that point in time inside of which the forecast is no longer included in total demand and projected available inventory calculations; inside this point, only customer orders are considered."

Planning Time Fence (PTF)

According to the *APICS Dictionary*, the planning time fence (PTF) is defined as "a point in time denoted in the planning horizon of the master scheduling process that marks a boundary inside of which changes to the schedule may adversely affect component schedules, capacity plans, customer deliveries, and cost."

Time fences are divided into three zones including the frozen, the slushy, and the liquid zones[9,10]. The three zones are shown in Figure 6-4. The DTF and PTF are determined based on the remaining capacity necessities in each period.

Time fences are shown for a period of 12 months in Figure 6-4. The DTF falls on the end of the fourth month. The PTF falls on the end of the seventh month. To the left of DTF is the zone called the "frozen" zone comprising periods 0 through 4. The production plans cannot be changed in this zone since

> **Time fences** A time fence is a selected period during which it is permitted to make changes to product schedules. Time fences are a series of time intervals to allow changes in customer orders.

> **Demand time fence** The point in time up to which only customer orders are considered.

> **Planning time fence** The point in time from which changes to product schedules are allowed.

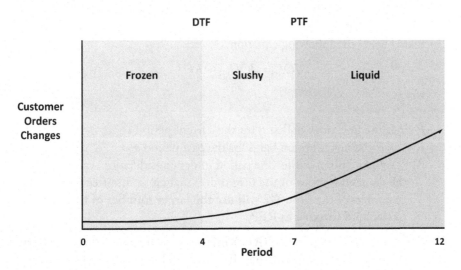

Figure 6-4 Time Fence Zones for Master Production Scheduling

the customer orders placed in this period need to be manufactured without any delay. Management can make any changes after considering all the possible risks and impacts. However, changes in orders can create major disruptions in production.

The zone between the DTF and PTF is called the "slushy" zone comprising periods 5 through 7. The changes to the production plans can be made after careful consideration of the available capacity and the resources essential for the production. Of course, management must approve any changes to the production plans. Changes in orders can create less disruption in production during the slushy zone. Specific parts and components can be added according to available capacity.

The zone to the right of the PTF is called the "liquid" zone comprising periods 8 through 12. The production plans can be changed easily to accommodate additional customer orders or cancel existing orders.

MPS Quantity, Available to Promise, and Inventory On-Hand

> **MPS quantity**
> Planned production in units for a particular time period. MPS quantity can be either the exact amount of the required number of units produced at a particular period or a specific quantity produced in a batch.

The input to the MPS includes the beginning inventory, the demand forecast, and the firm orders comprising new and old committed customer orders. Let us start with the inventory we have on hand. Inventory on-hand (IOH) is the inventory that is physically available at a company's disposal. For example, this is the stock that is available to a retail outlet or an eCommerce website or a manufacturing company, ready to be sold to consumers. If the on-hand inventory is reaching to none at any particular period, then it is an indication to replenish the inventory either by production or by subcontracting as per the aggregate plans. This replenishment is the planned production in units, also called **MPS quantity**. The MPS quantity can be either the exact amount of required number of units produced at a particular period or a specific quantity produced in a batch. The inventory on-hand for a particular period can be calculated using the following equation:

$$IOH_t = IOH_{t-1} - RFP_t \qquad \text{Eq. 6-1}$$

where,

> **Inventory on-hand**
> Stock that is available to a retail outlet or eCommerce website or a manufacturing company, ready to be immediately sold to consumers.

IOH_t is the inventory on hand for the current period t

IOH_{t-1} is the inventory on hand for the past period $t-1$

RFP_t is the requirement for the period under consideration, can be either the demand forecast or the firm orders that are committed to by the customers of the firm. **We will use the larger number of firm orders or demand forecast as RFP$_t$.**

Firms use available to promise (ATP) inventory as uncommitted inventory. This is an important feature of the MPS. The ATP amounts can be used by marketing to promise definite delivery dates to new customers. ATP amounts are the remaining units that are not sold for a particular time period. ATP can be calculated using the following formula:

$$ATP = IOH_t - Firm\ Orders + MPS\ Quantity \qquad \text{Eq. 6-2}$$

> **Firm orders** Orders that are committed to by customers.

FROM PRACTICE: ATP at Costco and Walmart

ATP, available to promise inventory, is very useful to manage inventory. ATP helps companies to avoid overstocking of products or the fear of running out of stock. Furthermore, ATP strikes a wonderful advantage of customer satisfaction as well as profitability. ATP permits companies like Costco and Walmart to store a minimum amount of products. This enables them to avoid overstocking and manage inventory levels effectively and efficiently. Walmart implements an available to promise model to maintain low inventory in their warehouses. The ATP process used at Walmart allows them to effectively use their warehouse space as well as stocking the products for sale in their stores. Costco also uses their available to promise process effectively. Costco stocks an average of 3,700 Stock Keeping Units (SKUs) per warehouse[11].

© Michael Vi/Shutterstock.com

© Jonathan Weiss/Shutterstock.com

The MPS quantity and the ATP are explained further in Example 6-1.

Example 6-1

CompAir, Inc. manufactures tables in Grove, PA. At the start of Week 1, the beginning inventory of Model-123 is 1,000 tables. The demand forecasts and firm orders are given in the table below.

At the beginning of:	Week 1	Week 2	Week 3	Week 4	Week 5	Week 6
Demand Forecast	100	150	100	100	100	100
Firm Orders	150	100	150	250	250	300

Develop a Master Production Schedule to determine planned production units and available to promise units if the company decides to produce 1,250 units as a batch at any time when the IOH becomes negative.

Step 1: Using Eq. 6-1 and the larger number of the demand forecast or the firm orders, calculate the inventory on-hand units. Calculate IOH_t : if Firm Orders > Forecast, IOH_{t-1}-Firm Orders; else, IOH_{t-1}-Forecast. For Week 1, firm orders are greater than demand forecast. Therefore, IOH = 1,000 − 150 = 850.

Step 2: When the inventory on-hand becomes negative for a period, the company produces 1,250 units as the MPS quantity or production to replenish finished goods inventory. For Week 6, the IOH is negative and therefore, the firm produces 1,250 units.

Step 3: For each period, calculate ATP using Eq. 6-3. For example, for Week 1, ATP = 850 − 150 + 0 = 700 units.

At the beginning of:	Week 0	Week 1	Week 2	Week 3	Week 4	Week 5	Week 6
Demand Forecast		100	150	100	100	100	100
Firm Orders		150	100	150	250	250	300
Inventory On-Hand	1000	850	700	550	300	50	−250
MPS Quantity							1,250
Available-to-promise Inventory		**700**	**600**	**400**	**50**	**−200**	**700**

Analysis: With the production of 1,250 Model-123 tables, the company can accommodate the maximum of firm or forecast very easily. The marketing department can use the ATPs for each period in their sales activities. For example, the marketing department can tell prospective customers that they have 700 units available for sale.

Material Requirements Planning

Material requirements planning (MRP) is a system to help manufacturing companies to plan, schedule, and manage their inventory. The two main objectives of MRP are to ensure the availability of raw materials or components when required and maintain optimum levels of materials and components. The advantages of an MRP system are the availability of materials and components when required, minimized inventory levels, reduced customer lead times, increased manufacturing efficiency, and optimized inventory management.

Material requirements planning is a software system that aims to improve productivity in firms. MRP I, the first inventory management software, evolved in the early 1950s. General Electric Corporation and the Rolls Royce Corporation computerized the first MRP system[8]. MRP II , the next generation of MRP, incorporated marketing, finance, accounting, engineering, and human resources aspects into the planning process.

FROM PRACTICE: Artificial Intelligence in SAP Software

SAP is taking advantage of "state-of-the-art" technologies to improve its products and offer more capabilities to users. Machine learning and artificial intelligence (AI) is used in the advanced production planning processes to develop better plans and schedules. Machine learning is also being used to continually monitor conditions and activities in production. Cloud computing offers better security, higher availability, and more reliable and sustainable systems by back-up, fail-over, and disaster recovery. In-memory databases are also used to boost performance and faster response times[12].

© Michael Vi/Shutterstock.com

From the MPS, MRP is developed as the requirements to produce a product in several time periods. But we need to know the details of a product to create such requirements. The detail of a product is established in its Bill of Materials (BOM). Figure 6-2 illustrates the addition of the Bill of Materials and the inventory transactions to MPS in order to develop the MRP. Let us discuss these factors next.

Bill of Materials (BOM)

A bill of materials (BOM) is a complete list of all the parts and components required to build a product. A BOM consists of all the raw materials, assemblies, subassemblies, parts, and components needed to manufacture a product. For example, various components of a simple chair are shown in Figure 6-5.

Figure 6-5 shows the product structure of a chair. From the product structure, we can determine the end items that are required to produce a chair. Note that there are three main components including a seat, a leg assembly, and a back assembly. These three main components can be put together using fastening hardware. The main components can either be produced or subcontracted and a company can assemble those components to produce chairs. The fastening hardware can be supplied by vendors for the final assembly. The product structure can be redrawn to describe the items in a bill of material and in various levels of the product assembly as shown in Figure 6-6.

The Chair at Level 0 is the end item. The end item A is composed of one B, one C one D, two Es, two Fs and four Gs. These compositions are shown as levels in Figure 6-6. The items at each level are components of the next level up. In Figure 6-6, we also show the quantities of each item in parentheses. These quantities of each item refer to the amounts to complete the assembly at the next higher level. The bill of materials for the chair (without the fastening hardware and glue) consists of the quantities of components A, B, C, D, E, F, and G. The procurement of components depends upon their lead times.

> **Bill of materials (BOM)** A bill of materials (BOM) is a complete list of all the parts and components required to build a product.

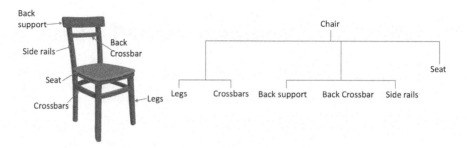

Figure 6-5 Chair Assembly with Components
Source: © Alfmaler/Shutterstock.com and Ganesh Vaidyanathan

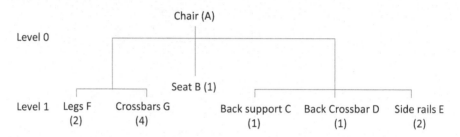

Figure 6-6 Chair Assembly as BOM Items in Levels

Lead Time

Lead time is the time it takes for a supplier to deliver the required goods for production. It measures how long it takes to complete the procurement process from the beginning to the end.

Lead time is important in the MRP development process. It allows the necessary components to arrive so that the production can be continued without any interruption. Factors that can impact the lead time include raw materials supply, logistics and transportation problems, labor shortages, natural disasters, human errors, and other uncontrollable issues. Firms can improve lead times by implementing a just-in-time (JIT) strategy. For critical parts, a company may use a backup supplier. Some companies work only with a supplier who keeps inventory on-hand.

Inventory Transactions

When we develop an MRP, we require certain inventory transactions in addition to the bill of materials. The data that are required to develop an MRP include the following:

- Inventory on-hand,
- Safety stock, and
- Order size.

We have discussed inventory on-hand in this chapter and safety stock in the last chapter. Let us discuss the order size now.

Order Size

The amount of the BOM items in a time period is called the order size or the manufacturing order quantity. In MRP systems, the order size may be one of the following:

- **Computed Order Quantity (COQ) or Batch quantity** that is computed using decision rules and optimizing techniques, or
- **Discrete Order Quantity (DOQ) or Lot-for-lot (L4L)** quantity that is needed at that time period to meet net requirements.

Consider an office supply store that sells an average of 15 laptops a week. To replenish the laptops that were sold in her store, the store manager has a few options. She can order 15 laptops which is DOQ or L4L every week. If the manufacturer of the laptops promises to deliver 60 laptops at a time or if the store manager optimizes her procurement to 60 laptops at a time based on some calculation, then that planned purchase of 60 laptops is COQ or batch quantity.

Material Requirements Planning (MRP) Calculations

The MRP calculations are a result of "exploding" the MPS. The explosion is the process of obtaining information on how many items in a bill of material must be ordered and when those items must be ordered to satisfy the gross requirements or the production plan. We will take the gross requirements from the MPS and then plan to order the BOM components in a time period comprising days or weeks.

The MRP calculations result in the Planned Order Receipts (POR) and the Planned Order Releases (PORL). The calculations are maintained as MRP records. An MRP record consists of the following:

- Gross requirements,
- Scheduled receipts,
- Planned order receipts,
- Projected inventory balance,
- Net requirements, and
- Planned order releases.

Gross Requirements (GR)

Gross requirements are production requirements that are shown in the MPS for a particular time period. This is the total number of products, that is, the end items in the MRP, that must be ready for customer delivery. This is calculated in the master production schedule as requirements from customers.

Scheduled Receipts (SR)

These are components that are supplied by vendors or transferred from other plants and scheduled to arrive at the beginning of a time period. These can be open orders, that is, orders that have been placed already.

Planned Order Receipts (POR)

Planned order receipts are the quantity that is expected to be received at the beginning of the period under consideration. POR depends on the order size. If the company decides to follow the lot-for-lot (L4L) policy, then POR will equal the net requirements. If the company decides to pursue the computed order quantity (COQ) policy, this quantity will be equal to a computed optimized quantity.

Projected Inventory Balance (PIB)

This is the expected amount of inventory that will be available at the beginning of the time period under consideration. The projected inventory balance must be calculated for each time period. The PIB for a time period t can be calculated as:

$$PIB_t = PIB_{t-1} - GR_t + SR_t + POR_t \qquad \text{Eq. 6-3}$$

where,

PIB_t = Projected inventory balance at the beginning of a time period t
PIB_{t-1} = Projected inventory balance at the beginning of the past time period, $t-1$
GR_t = Gross requirements for the time period t
SR_t = Scheduled receipts for the time period t
POR_t = Planned order receipts at the beginning of a time period t

The projected inventory balance at the start of an MRP calculation is:

$$PIB_0 = Inventory\ on-hand - Safety\ stock \qquad \text{Eq. 6-4}$$

where,

PIB_0 is the PIB of the initial time period.

Net Requirements (NR)

Net requirements are the actual amount of a bill of material item that is needed at a time period. Any scheduled receipt for that time period must be included. This is also the required quantity for a time period.

$$NR = GR_t - SR_t - PIB_{t-1} \qquad \text{Eq. 6-5}$$

Planned Order Releases (PORL)

This is the amount that is planned to be ordered for a time period. PORL is offset by the lead time. Example 6-2 shows how to compute MRP for our chair example and Example 6-3 shows how to calculate MRP for a simple product family.

Example 6-2

AmshChair, LLC, a company from Middleton, Indiana, has gross requirements of 1,250 chairs from their master production schedule shown in Example 6-1. They have 100 units as initial inventory for the end item. Assume that lot-for-lot (L4L) lot sizing is used for all Items. They are scheduled to receive 100 units of B in Week 2, 50 units of C in Week 3, and 200 units of E in Week 4. Use the bill of materials of the chair shown in Figure 6-6 to find the necessary planned order releases for all components. The lead time for all components is 1 week. The company does not have any safety stock policy.

We will use the product structure and the bill of materials shown in Figure 6-6.

Step 1: Enter the inputs—LT, IOH, SS, and Order Size for all items A, B, C, D, E, F, and G that we developed for the chair.

Step 2: Enter the 1,250 units of A as GR for Week 6 equal to the MPS quantity calculated in Example 6-1.

Step 3: Since there is no SS but IOH = 100 for the end item A, using Eq. 6-4, the PIB for Week 1 is equal to 100. Since there are no GRs for these weeks, PIB will not change.

Step 4: Calculate the PIBs for Weeks 2 to 5 using Eq. 6-3. For the 6th week, since GR > Week 5 PIB, we need to find the net requirements using Eq. 6-5 which is 1,250 − 1 00 = 1,150. Since there is an L4L order policy for item A, the POR is equal to the net requirements = 1,150.

Step 5: Calculate the PIB for Week 6 using Eq. 6-3 = 100 − 1,250 + 0 + 1,150 = 0.

Step 6: Since the lead time for A Is 1 week, planned order (PORL) will be released in Week 5.

Step 7: MRP for item B (level 1) will be next. Since the BOM quantity of B is 1, the same number of A must be for B equal to 1,150. Since we need additional Bs only when end item A is made, our GR for item B is for Week 5, the week the planned order is released.

Step 8: Follow steps 3 through 6 for item B.

Step 9: Item C and Item D are also level 1 and equal to a quantity of 1 in the BOM. Follow steps 3 through 6 for items C and D.

Step 10: Item E is level 1 but there are 2 Es for each A. Therefore, for Week 5, the GR for item E will be equal to 1,150 × 2 = 2,300. Follow steps 3 through 6 for item E.

Step 11: Item F is level 1. For each item A, we need 2 Fs. The GR for item F is equal to $2 \times$ PORL of A in Week 5 = $1,150 \times 2 = 2,300$.

Step 12: Follow steps 3 through 6 for item F.

Step 13: Item G is level 1. For each item A, we need 4 Gs. The GR for item G is equal to $4 \times$ PORL of A in Week 5 = $1,150 \times 4 = 4,600$.

Step 14: Follow steps 3 through 6 for item G.

A		Week 1	Week 2	Week 3	Week 4	Week 5	Week 6
LT = 1 week	Gross Requirements						1,250
IOH = 100	Scheduled Receipts						
Safety Stock = 0	Projected inventory balance	100	100	100	100	100	0
Order size = L4L	Net Requirements						1,150
	Planned-Order Receipts						1,150
	Planned-Order Releases					1,150	
B							
LT = 1 week	Gross Requirements					1,150	
IOH = 0	Scheduled Receipts		100				
Safety Stock = 0	Projected inventory balance	0	100	100	100	0	0
Order size = L4L	Net Requirements					1,050	
	Planned-Order Receipts					1,050	
	Planned-Order Releases				1,050		
C							
LT = 1 week	Gross Requirements					1,150	
OOH = 0	Scheduled Receipts			50			
Safety Stock = 0	Projected inventory balance	0	0	50	50	0	0
Order size = L4L	Net Requirements					1,100	
	Planned-Order Receipts					1,100	
	Planned-Order Releases				1,100		
D							
LT = 1 week	Gross Requirements					1,150	
IOH = 0	Scheduled Receipts						
Safety Stock = 0	Projected inventory balance	0	0	0	0	0	0
Order size = L4L	Net Requirements					1,150	
	Planned-Order Receipts					1,150	
	Planned-Order Releases				1,150		

		Week 1	Week 2	Week 3	Week 4	Week 5	Week 6
E							
LT = 1 week	Gross Requirements					2,300	
IOH = 0	Scheduled Receipts				200		
Safety Stock = 0	Projected inventory balance	0	0	0	200	0	0
Q = L4L	Net Requirements					2,100	
	Planned-Order Receipts					2,100	
	Planned-Order Releases				**2,100** ◄┘		
F							
LT = 1 week	Gross Requirements					2,300	
IOH = 0	Scheduled Receipts						
Safety Stock = 0	Projected inventory balance	0	0	0	0	0	0
Q = L4L	Net Requirements					2,300	
	Planned-Order Receipts					2,300	
	Planned-Order Releases				**2,300** ◄┘		
G							
LT = 1 week	Gross Requirements					4,600	
IOH = 0	Scheduled Receipts						
Safety Stock = 0	Projected inventory balance	0	0	0	0	0	0
Q = L4L	Net Requirements					4,600	
	Planned-Order Receipts					4,600	
	Planned-Order Releases				**4,600** ◄┘		

Analysis: The company has 100 chairs as inventory on-hand. Using the several receipts that are scheduled to arrive at various times, the company will meet the demand of 1,250 chairs. The company needs to release planned orders of these items:

- 1,050 seats(B) during Week 4
- 1,100 back supports (C) during Week 4
- 1,150 back crossbars (D) during Week 4
- 2,100 side rails (E) during Week 4
- 2,300 legs (F) during Week 4
- 4,600 crossbars (G) during Week 4

The reason all the items are to be released for purchase during Week 4 is that there is one level below in the BOM and all the items have a lead time of 1 week.

Example 6-3

Comp Orleans, a company from Kenner, LA, assembles industrial compressors. The product structure for compressor Model CO123A is as follows: The end item "A" is composed of one item "C" as subassembly and one unit of an item "D". The subassembly C is composed of 1 unit of "E" and 2 units of "D". The end item of the other model CO234B, "B", is a part of the same product family. Item B is composed of a subassembly C which is further composed of 2 Ds and 1 E. For the first week of the month of March, the firm orders are 1,200 Model CO123A compressors and 800 Model CO234B respectively while demand forecast is 400 compressors and 200 compressors, respectively. The inventory on-hand for A, B, C, D, E are 100, 50, 150, 100, and 100 respectively. The company decides to maintain a safety stock of 50 units for each of C, D, and E. The lead time for A, B, and C are 1 week while D and E have 2 weeks of lead time. The company also decides that E and F would have to be in a batch order size of 2,000 while using L4L for the rest of the items. There are three transfer of units from their subcontractors: 200 units of item B in the beginning of the third week of February, 300 units of item D in the beginning of the second week of February, and 300 units of E in the beginning of the third week of February. Develop an MRP plan for all items by finding the planned order releases for each item for the month of February.

First, let us draw the BOM and product structure as a figure shown below:

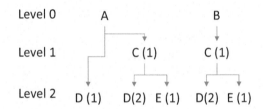

Step 1: Enter the inputs—LT, IOH, SS, and Order Size for all items A, B, C, D, and E.

Step 2: The GR for end item A is $1,200 + 400 = 1,600$ and for item B is $800 + 200 = 1.000$

Step 3: For A, the PIB for Week 1 is 100 (IAH).

Step 4: Calculate the PIBs for Weeks 2 to 4 using Eq. 6-3. For the 6th week, since GR > Week 4 PIB, we need to find the net requirements using Eq. 6-5 which is $1,600 - 100 = 1,500$. Since there is an L4L order policy for item A, the POR is equal to the net requirements $= 1,500$.

Step 5: Calculate the PIB for Week 5 using Eq. 6-3 $= 100 - 1,600 + 0 + 1,500 = 0$.

Step 6: Since the lead time for A is 1 week, PORL $= 1,500$ will be released in Week 4.

Step 7: MRP for item B (level 0) will be next. This is another end item. Follow steps 3 through 6 for item B. The POR and PORL for item B are 750 since we have an SR of 200 and an IOH of 50.

A		Week 1	Week 2	Week 3	Week 4	Week 5
LT = 1 week	Gross Requirements					1600
IOH = 100	Scheduled Receipts					
Safety Stock = 0	Projected inventory balance	100	100	100	100	0
Order size = L4L	Net Requirements					1500
	Planned-Order Receipts					1500
	Planned-Order Releases				1500 ◄——┘	
B						
LT = 1 week	Gross Requirements					1000
IOH = 50	Scheduled Receipts			200		
Safety Stock = 0	Projected inventory balance	50	50	250	250	0
Order size = L4L	Net Requirements					750
	Planned-Order Receipts					750
	Planned-Order Releases				750 ◄——┘	
C						
LT = 1 week	Gross Requirements				2250	
IOH = 150	Scheduled Receipts					
Safety Stock = 50	Projected inventory balance	100	100	100	0	0
Order size = L4L	Net Requirements				2150	
	Planned-Order Receipts				2150	
	Planned-Order Releases			2150 ◄——┘		
D						
LT = 2 weeks	Gross Requirements			4300	1500	
IOH = 100	Scheduled Receipts		300			
Safety Stock = 50	Projected inventory balance	50	350	50	550	550
Order size = 2000	Net Requirements			3950	1450	
	Planned-Order Receipts			┌——— 4000	2000	
	Planned-Order Releases	4000 ◄——┘ 2000 ◄———————————————┘				
E						
LT = 2 weeks	Gross Requirements			2150		
IOH = 100	Scheduled Receipts			300		
Safety Stock = 50	Projected inventory balance	50	50	200	200	200
Order size = 2000	Net Requirements			1800		
	Planned-Order Receipts			2000		
	Planned-Order Releases	2000 ◄——————————————┘				

Step 8: Item C is level 1 and equal to a quantity of 1 in BOM for each item A and B. GR for item C is 1,550 + 750 (add the PORs of A and B). Follow steps 3 through 6 for item C. The POR and PORL for item C are 2,150.

Step 9: Item D is level 2 and for each item C, we need 2 item Ds. Also, we need 1 item D for each item A. So, GR for item D for the Week 4 corresponding to Item A is $1,500 \times 1 = 1,500$. GR for item D for the Week 3 corresponding to item C is $2,150 \times 2 = 4,300$.

Step 10: Using the safety stock of 50 and the SR of 300 and considering the GR of 4,300, net requirements of D at the beginning of Week 3 $= 4,300 - 350 = 3950$. But the order size is 2,000. We can order two of the order sizes to total 4,000 as POR. The PIB for Week 3 is $350 - 4,300 + 0 + 4,000 = 50$. The POR is 4,000 which will be released in Week 1 since LT = 2 weeks. For Week 4, net requirements $= 1,500 - 50 = 1,450$. We can order 2,000 as POR. The PIB for Week 4 is $50 - 1,500 + 0 + 2,000$. The POR is 2,000 which will be released in Week 2 since LT = 2 weeks.

Step 11: For each item C we need one item E. We need 2,150 Cs in Week 3. So, GR for Week 3 for item E is 2,150. With the safety stock of 50 and the SR of 300 during Week 3, using Eq. 6-5, we can calculate net requirements for Week 3 $= 2,150 - 300 - 50 = 1,800$. The PIB for that week is equal to $50 - 2,150 + 300 + 2,000 = 200$. The POR is 2,000 which will be released in Week 1 since LT = 2 weeks.

Analysis: The company has to make 1,600 Model CO123A compressors and 1,000 Model CO234B during Week 5. The company needs to release planned orders of these items:

- 2,150 Part Cs during Week 3
- 4,000 Part Ds during Week 1 and 2,000 Part Ds during Week 2
- 2,000 Part Es during Week 1

Part C is a common part for both the compressor models. Part D is used both in the Level 0 item as well as in the Level 1 items.

FROM PRACTICE: MRP Software

APICS, the Association for Supply Chain Management, led a crusade to promote the benefits of MRP systems to corporations even in the early 1970s[13]. Since then, many companies have invested in MRP systems. Material requirements planning (MRP) is driven by master production schedule (MPS) to ensure that the production plans are consistent with product demand. MRP is integrated with purchase orders, inventory, bill of materials, routings, and work orders in a company. Two major software programs are used in large companies around the globe. NetSuite ERP, a cloud-based software solution, consolidates financial management, inventory management and order fulfillment. Industries that use this solution

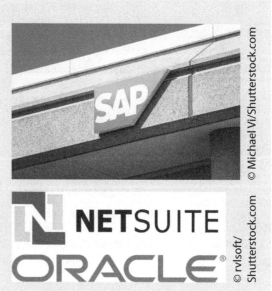

© Michael Vi/Shutterstock.com

© rvlsoft/ Shutterstock.com

include Cisco, Dell, Lexis Nexis, Sony, and some educational and financial services firms. SAP S/4 HANA , the ERP software from SAP, is the other MRP solution that consolidates all the functions in a company. Honeywell, BP, Coca-Cola, 3M, ConAgra, BASF North America, Audi AG, McDonalds, Burger King, Ford, Airbus, Samsung, BMW, and Citrix are some of the prominent users of SAP.

Formulae from this Chapter

Inventory On-Hand	$IOH_t = IOH_{t-1} - RFP_t$	Eq. 6-1
Available to Promise Inventory	$ATP = IOH_t - Firm\ Orders + MPS\ Quantity$	Eq. 6-2
Projected Inventory Balance	$PIB_t = PIB_{t-1} - GR_t + SR_t + POR_t$	Eq. 6-3
Project Inventory Balance (Initial)	$PIB_0 = Inventory\ on\ hand - Safety\ stock$	Eq. 6-4
Net Requirements	$NR = GR_t - SR_t - PIB_{t-1}$	Eq. 6-5

Case Study: MRP at NEOWYNDOW Industries

Walter Wynn of NeoWyndow Industries is trying to keep his cool while planning his next purchase of items for their windows product family. It has been a frustrating experience for him to place orders for the various components and subassemblies for the past 2 years. The problem was partly due to the unpredictable demand for the products, which he personally blamed on global warming! The main problem was that the company had postponed buying software for production planning as they were in a quest to buy a good ERP package at an affordable price. He often mumbled to himself that there is no software package at an affordable price!

© Milta/Shutterstock.com

NeoWyndow Industries manufactures windows of varied sizes. They have been in business for the past 8 years and their sales have been increasing. Walter started the firm from his garage making windows for himself and his family members. Currently, he has successfully expanded the market in his community and is planning to grow outside his community. He has four workers who help him to assemble the products and two others who deliver and install the windows. He is also planning to hire a salesperson who can grow his business beyond his community.

The company's product family consists of three models. Walter thinks he can make up to 400 windows every month that includes all the three models. Walter has estimated the demand forecast for his product lines for the first week of the next 2 months as shown in the table below:

Product Model	Month 1		Month 2	
	Firm Orders	Forecast	Firm Orders	Forecast
Model-NW35-120S	120	80	125	85
Model-NW45-120S	80	20	80	20
Model-NW55-120S	60	30	50	40

Model NW is their first introduced product family and it comes in three sizes. NW35, the simplest of the models, has been extremely popular in the neighborhood and is projected to enjoy a good growth rate. The other two models are beginning to gain popularity. Walter hopes to sell more of NW55 models as his profit margin on those is particularly good.

Walter has done an excellent job of developing the product family such that he can purchase the materials in bulk for some of the components. All models have the same product structure. Each window is composed of one glass pane, an aluminum frame assembly, and a latch assembly. The frame assembly consists of a unit of frame materials, four corner brackets, two seals, and six screws. The latch assembly consists of a latch with four screws.

Walter has a contract with his long-time friend, Adam Baniukiewicz, to provide and deliver the latch assembly. Adam is a subcontractor who makes latches, locks, and other hardware. Adam has offered to send 50 latch assemblies to NeoWyndow on the first day of the second week of every month. For the reminder of the latch assemblies required by the company, Walter assembles them by buying the latches and the screws separately. Walter has to buy the screws in bulk and he has arranged from a local supplier to deliver 1,000 of them on the same day. He buys the latches in batches of 500 each time with 1 week of lead time. The company receives the corner brackets in bulk supply of 500 at a time but with a lead time of 1 week. Walter, with his years of experience, keeps corner brackets as a safety stock. He usually likes to keep 100 corner brackets as safety stock. The same vendor supplies the latches and the

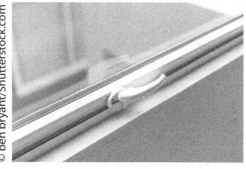

© ben bryant/Shutterstock.com

corner brackets. The glass panes have to be ordered a week in advance of their delivery and are ordered as a lot-for-lot quantity. The seals for the windows are ordered in quantities of 200 with a lead time of 1 week. The aluminum frames are delivered on the first day of the second and third week of every month by a local company, 300 at a time. Walter has a long-term supplier agreement with that local company for the aluminum frames.

When Walter starts the first day of the first week, he has 20 windows as inventory that includes 3 Model NW35,

10 Model NW45, and 7 Model NW55. But Walter is confident that he can sell those 20 windows very soon!

Case Questions

A. Develop a monthly MPS for the customer requirements and calculate ATP for each week.
B. Show the bill of materials as a product structure hierarchical tree.
C. Prepare a weekly MRP plan for the next 2months. Assume 4 weeks for each month.
D. If Walter decides to keep only 50 corner brackets as safety stock, how do the MRP plans change?
E. A local hardware company desperately needs 20 windows in Week 2 of the second month. Develop the MRP plans for Walter.

Summary

- An enterprise resource planning (ERP) system is a commercial software package that integrates and manages all functions and processes of a company.
- ERP enables the integration of transactions-oriented data and business processes throughout an organization.
- ERP includes a company's financials, supply chain, operations, sales, marketing, quality, materials management, plant maintenance, and human resource activities.
- ERP systems are built using the unique business processes of a company with a centralized database. The centralized database collects all the enterprise's transactional data in one place to be shared by various functions of that enterprise. The centralized database eliminates data duplication and provides data integrity.
- The common business processes ensure that all employees of the enterprise use the business processes that are tied together in the same software. ERP systems involve business processes including financials, procurement, inventory, manufacturing, logistics, quality management, human capital management, customer management, plant maintenance, and order fulfillment.
- The main reason that companies implement ERP is to improve their internal processes and consequently to achieve their business goals.
- ERP takes a long time to implement and is expensive.
- The production planning module of an enterprise resource planning software system encompasses all the activities to plan and control various manufacturing activities. In this chapter, we focused on some of those activities such as bill of materials (BOM), master production scheduling (MPS), and material requirements planning (MRP).

- The aggregate plan includes the present and future inventory levels of the company's products.
- Disaggregation is breaking the aggregate plan into specific product requirements, which leads to the master production schedule (MPS).
- The master production schedule must be translated to the finished product requirements as time-phased requirements for subassemblies, component parts, and raw materials called material requirements planning (MRP).
- The master production schedule specifies the quantity of products to be manufactured along with when they should be completed and in what quantities.
- A product family is a group of similar goods to meet the diverse needs or tastes of customers.
- A time fence is a selected period during which it is permitted to make changes to product schedules. Time fences are a series of time intervals to allow changes in customer orders.
- Demand time fence is the point in time up to which only customer orders are considered.
- Planning time fence is the point of time from which changes to product schedules are allowed.
- Time fences are divided into three zones including frozen, slushy, and liquid zones.
- Inventory on-hand (IOH) is the inventory that is physically available at a company's disposal.
- The replenishment of inventory at a correct time is the planned production in units, also called MPS quantity.
- MPS quantity can be either the exact amount of required number of units produced at a particular period or a specific quantity produced in a batch.
- Firms use available to promise (ATP) inventory as uncommitted inventory.
- Firm orders are orders that are committed to by customers.
- Material requirements planning (MRP) is a system to help manufacturing companies to plan, schedule, and manage their inventory.
- The two main objectives of MRP are to ensure the availability of raw materials or components when required and maintain optimum levels of materials and components.
- The advantages of an MRP system are availability of materials and components when required, minimized inventory levels, reduced customer lead times, increased manufacturing efficiency, and optimized inventory management.
- MRP develops MPS into requirements to produce a product in particular time periods.
- A bill of materials (BOM) is a complete list of all the parts and components required to build a product.

- Lead time is the time it takes for a supplier company to deliver goods for production. It measures how long it takes to complete the procurement process from beginning to end.
- Inventory transactions such as inventory on-hand, safety stock, and order size are required to develop an MRP.
- Order size may be either computed using Order Quantity (COQ) or Lot-for-Lot.
- COQ or batch quantity is computed using decision rules and optimizing techniques.
- Lot-for-lot (L4L) or discrete order quantity (DOQ) is the quantity that is needed at a particular time period to satisfy production requirements.
- Gross requirements are production requirements that are shown in MPS for a particular time period.
- Scheduled receipts are components that are supplied by vendors or transferred from other plants scheduled to arrive at the beginning of a time period.
- Planned order receipts are the quantity that is expected to be received at the beginning of the period under consideration.
- Projected inventory balance is the expected amount of inventory that will be available at the beginning of the time period under consideration.
- Net requirements are the actual amount of a bill of material item that is needed at a time period.
- Planned order releases (PORL) are the amount planned to be ordered for a time period.
- PORL is offset by the lead time.
- When a PORL is executed, that amount becomes scheduled receipts for the next period.

Review Questions

1. What is ERP?
2. How does ERP help companies?
3. What do ERP packages include?
4. Explain how ERP functions in a company.
5. What modules are there in an ERP package? Explain each of those modules.
6. What are the advantages of implementing ERP in a company?
7. Which ERP module focuses on MRP?
8. Describe the material requirements planning process.
9. What is disaggregation in production terms?
10. What are the inputs to MPS? What are the outputs?
11. What are the inputs to MRP? What are the outputs?
12. What is a master production schedule?
13. Describe a product family with an example.
14. What are time fences in production?

15. How are time fences classified?
16. How are customer orders classified in time fences?
17. Define MPS quantity.
18. Define available to promise inventory.
19. What is inventory on-hand?
20. How do you calculate requirements for period RFP when calculating ATP?
21. What are the advantages of MRP?
22. Describe BOM with an example.
23. What are levels in product structure with respect to BOM?
24. What is lead time?
25. Describe inventory transactions that are inputs to MRP.
26. What are the types of order size?

Critical Thinking Questions

1. Why is there a centralized database in ERP?
2. How did companies manage without ERP?
3. How does ERP provide right information at the right time for its users?
4. Why is the production planning module important?
5. Does the aggregate plan include the present and future inventory levels of a company's products?
6. How is MPS different from aggregate planning?
7. How is MRP different from MPS?
8. What is the major difference between PTF and DTF?
9. What happens if the time falls exactly between frozen and slushy zones?
10. What is the major difference between available to promise inventory and inventory on-hand?
11. What are the various sources of demand in an MRP system? Are they dependent on each other?
12. How are firm orders different from demand forecast?
13. Is it better to have a correct number for demand forecast or a firm order?
14. How does lead time influence production planning?
15. How do companies view critical parts in terms of MRP?
16. How are scheduled receipts different from gross requirements?
17. How are net requirements different from gross requirements?
18. What is the difference between PORL and POR?
19. What are the disadvantages of L4L?
20. What are the disadvantages of COQ?
21. Why do companies carry safety stock?
22. Do the companies need to carry safety stock for all their product items?

Problem Solving Questions

1. A company from a Mid-Atlantic U.S. state has two different product lines. Models A, B, and E belong to Product Family 1 while Models C and D are part of Product Family 2. The forecast demands as shown for 8 weeks are:

	Month 1				Month 2			
	Week 1	Week 2	Week 3	Week 4	Week 5	Week 6	Week 7	Week 8
Model A	200			250	250			320
Model B		150	150	300	125	200	200	
Model C	300		150	300	150		155	280
Model D	200	300		300		145		280
Model E	150			300	200		160	280

The firm orders during the same period are:

	Month 1				Month 2			
	Week 1	Week 2	Week 3	Week 4	Week 5	Week 6	Week 7	Week 8
Model A	80		30		10			
Model B		100	80	40	10			
Model C	100		70	50	20			
Model D	120	50		20	10			
Model E	50			10	15			

    a. If there are no other sources for the sale of their products, what are the production requirements for the two months?

    b. Determine the MPD quantity.

2. The demand forecast of table lamps for the next 4 weeks is projected as 100 units for a retail store. The starting inventory is 100 lamps. The supplier supplies a batch of 100 lamps once every period. The customer orders for the 4 weeks are 90, 80, 60, and 25. Prepare a master schedule.

3. If the beginning inventory on the first day of the first week of the first month is 100 for product family 1 and 200 for product family 2, and using the data from Problem 1, find the ATPs for the two product families.

4. Corner Solutions in Iowa makes furniture drawer assemblies for home and industrial use. The drawer assembly consists of a front board, side boards, and a bottom assembly. The bottom assembly consists of a bottom board and two siderail assembly. Each siderail assembly consists of a slider, a stationary arm, and four screws. Create a BOM as a product structure.

5. A company's product A is composed of three B components, two C components, and two D components. Component C has two E units and one F unit. Component D has three G units and two H units. Create a BOM as a product structure.

6. A company's product A is composed of one B component, two C components, and three D components. Component C has two E units and two F units. Component D has three G units and three H units. The company has 20 products in their warehouse.
   a. Create a BOM as a product structure.
   b. If the total demand for their compressors is 200 units, calculate the net requirements for all the components.
   c. What is the projected inventory balance of each component?

7. Mechanics Industries from Mechanicsburg, PA, manufacturers custom hinges. The end product A is composed of three item Bs and one item C. Item C is made of four item Ds, while item B is made of three item Cs and two item Ds. At the beginning of Week 6, 120 units are needed. The lead times for the end product and item C is 1 week while for other items lead time is 2 weeks. The inventory on-hand for the items are 20, 40, 40, 30, and 20, respectively. There is a scheduled receipt of 100 units for item B at the beginning of Week 3. Prepare the material requirements plans for all the items based on net requirements.

8. Sudden Brakes, a bicycle shop, sells and services bicycles. Due to the weeklong Ragbrai event that happens in the third week of July of that year, there have been heavy demands for brake assemblies as people start training for the event right from the first week of May. May has 5 weeks; June has 4 weeks. A brake assembly for a bicycle is made of 2 units of A and 4 units of B. B is made of 2 units of D. A is made of 3 units of C and 4 of D. Unit D is made of 2 units of E. All units have a lead time of 1 week except D which takes 2 weeks; Suda, the owner, expects that his demand would be 250 units of brake assemblies every other week starting from the beginning week of May and expects an increase of 50% during the event. He wants to have a safety stock of 125 units of the brake assembly and has 400 units as initial inventory. All components are procured based on net requirements. Show the BOM with levels as a product structure and develop an MRP for Suda.

9. The Acrobath Company assembles and sells a product called an "A." The "A" is made up of 2 units of a subassembly called "E" and 3 units of a material called "D" ("D" is purchased from a supplier), and 2 units of a subassembly called "C." The "E" subassembly is prepared at Acrobath from 1 unit of "F" (purchased from a supplier) and 2 units of a purchased material named "G." Each "C" is assembled in a process that includes 1 unit of "E." As we begin

Week 1 of operations planning at Acrobath, there are no units of "A" available in finished goods inventory. It usually takes 2 weeks to complete assembly of an order for "A," and the units are ordered as needed. There are 400 units of item "C" in inventory as Week 1 begins, and another 150 units are scheduled to arrive during Week 1. It takes the shop floor 2 weeks to complete an order of item "C." Item "C" is also ordered using a "lot-for-lot" policy. There are 400 units of item "D" in inventory at the beginning of Week 1, and a shipment of 450 units is expected to arrive during Week 2. It takes the supplier 2 weeks to deliver an order of item "D." Item "D" is ordered in packages containing 700 units each. There are 235 units of item "E" in inventory at the beginning of Week 1. Unit "E" takes 3 weeks to assemble at Acrobath, and they are produced in batches of 700 units. There are 700 units of item "E" scheduled to arrive from the shop floor at the beginning of Week 1 in the current schedule. There are currently 700 units of item "F" in inventory at Acrobath. It takes 2 weeks for the supplier to deliver an order of "F" to Acrobath, and the supplier permits Acrobath to order on a "lot-for-lot" basis. Although there are no units of "G" in inventory currently, Acrobath is expecting delivery of 1,400 units during Week 1. The lead time for item "G" is 1 week, and the supplier allows Acrobath to order the item on a "lot-for-lot" basis. The Master Production Schedule expresses a need for 120 units of item "A" in weeks 3, 4, 5, and 8 of the current plan.

a. Given this information, complete the Materials Requirements Plan for item "A" and all of its dependent parts.

b. Once you have completed the MRP for the situation at Acrobath, review your result. Explain what decisions must be made immediately in order to enact the plan. What issues must be anticipated for later in the planning horizon? How are these decisions related to the MRP you have created?

c. Assume that the immediate decisions you expressed above in (b) have been enacted. On Wednesday morning of Week 1, you receive a call from the supplier providing "D" to Acrobath. You are informed that the 450 units expected to arrive during Week 2 have been delayed. What is the impact?

10. A company has a product. One unit of A is made of 3 units of B, 1 unit of C, and 2 units of D. B is composed of 2 units of E and 1 unit of D. C is made of 1 unit of B and 2 units of E. E is made of 1 unit of F. Items B, C, E, and F have 1-week lead times; A and D have lead times of 2 weeks. Lot-for-lot (L4L) is used for Items A, B, and F; lots of size 60, 60, and 250 are used for Items C, D, and E, respectively. Items C, E, and F have on hand (beginning) inventories of 20, 50, and 150, respectively; all other items have 0 beginning inventory.

They are scheduled to receive 20 units of A in Week 2, 50 units of E in Week 1, and 50 units of F in Week 1. There are no other scheduled receipts. If 40 units of A are required in Week 8, find the necessary planned order releases for all components.

References

1. Gelski, J. (2015). *Kraft recalls 242,000 cases of Macaroni & Cheese Dinner.* Retrieved June 20, 2022, from https://www.foodbusinessnews.net/articles/5763-kraft-recalls-242-000-cases-of-macaroni-cheese-dinner#:~:text=%E2%80%93%20Kraft%20Foods%20Group%20voluntarily%20is,Used%20By%E2 %80%9D%20dates%20of%20Sept.

2. Staley, J. (2015). *Food ERP Systems and the Kraft Heinz merger.* Retrieved June 20, 2022, from https://blog.datixinc.com/blog/food-erp-systems.

3. Salgado, A. (2022). *Kraft Heinz taps Microsoft to build up supply chain visibility.* Retrieved June 20, 2022, from https://www.supplychaindive .com/news/Kraft-Heinz-Microsoft-partnership-supply-chain-tech-investment/622636/

4. Evatt, M. (2022). Kraft Heinz and Microsoft join forces to accelerate supply chain transformation. *ERP Today.* Retrieved June 20, 2022, from https://erp.today/kraft-heinz-and-microsoft-join-forces-to-accelerate-supply-chain-transformation/.

5. Neal Weinberg, N. (2022). 10 most powerful ERP vendors today. *CIO Magazine.* Retrieved June 21, 2022, from https://www.cio.com/article/304902/10-most-powerful-erp-vendors-today.html.

6. Gartner Research. (2022). *Market Share Analysis: ERP Software, Worldwide, 2020.* Retrieved June 21, 2022, from https://www.gartner.com/en/documents/4000842.

7. Bowman, R. J. (2015). *Demand planning at Coca-Cola: What's the secret formula?* Retrieved June 21, 2022, from https://www.supplychainbrain .com/blogs/1-think-tank/post/20951-demand-planning-at-coca-cola-whats-the-secret-formula.

8. Ross, D. (2016). *Managing the Demand Forecast: Part 3.* Retrieved June 20, 2022, from https://www.apics.org/sites/apics-blog/thinking-supply-chain-topic-search-result/thinking-supply-chain/2016/12/06/managing-the-demand-forecast-part-3.

9. Oden, H. W., Langenwalter, G. A., & Lucier, R. A. (1993). *Handbook of material and capacity requirements* (1st ed.). McGraw-Hill.

10. Amaranti, R., Muhammad, C. R., & Septandri, M. V. (2020). Determining the changes in the Master Production Schedule (MPS) at the company with Make to Stock (MTS) and Make to Order (MTO) strategies. *IOP Conference Series: Materials Science and Engineering, 830,* 4.

11. CFI. (2021). *Material Requirements Planning (MRP)*. Retrieved June 20, 2022, from https://corporatefinanceinstitute.com/resources/knowledge/other/material-requirements-planning-mrp/

12. SAP.com. (2022). *What is MRP (material requirements planning)?* Retrieved June 20, 2022, from https://www.sap.com/insights/what-is-mrp.html

13. Miller, J. G., & Sprague, L. G. (1975, September). Behind the growth in Materials Requirements Planning. *Harvard Business Review*.

7

INVENTORY MANAGEMENT

Learning Objectives

- Define inventory management.
- Explain the push-pull boundary.
- Compare inventory management of goods and services.
- Explain inventory planning and control.
- Explain ABC inventory classification.
- Describe how inventory accuracy can be achieved.
- Identify technologies to track inventory.
- Describe the economic order quantity model and how companies use the model.
- Describe how companies use discount quantities to order inventory.
- Calculate reorder points and order sizes using the fixed quantity model.
- Calculate order size using the fixed time period model.

Firms spend a lot of money to manage their inventory. Companies want to make sure that they have the right amount of stock on hand to sell their goods or provide their services. Inventory management is the process of ordering the raw materials, managing the work in progress, and storing the finished goods.

Walmart, the American multinational retail corporation, operates a chain of hypermarkets in 24 countries. Walmart is the world's largest company by revenue according to the Fortune Global 500 list. Walmart has 210 distribution centers all over the world. Walmart owns Sam's Club to help small business owners save money on merchandise purchased in bulk. There are about 600 Sam's clubs in the United States and

© dizain/Shutterstock.com

more than 200 globally. Walmart stores carry grocery, consumables, pharmacy, technology, apparel, home, and office products. Walmart markets many products under brands such as Equate, Bonobos Fielder, Mainstays, George, Onn, Parent's Choice, Time and Tru, Wonder Nation, and No Boundaries.

Walmart is well known for its "state-of-the-art" techniques in inventory management. One of their early success stories is their implementation of the vendor-managed inventory (VMI) model. Walmart's vendors actually manage the inventory after accessing the sales data from every Walmart store. Walmart has shifted the inventory control activities to its vendors as the vendors decide when and how much to send goods to each and every Walmart store[1].

Walmart initiated the VMI model with Proctor & Gamble (P&G), the American multinational consumer goods corporation. P&G took over the responsibility for managing their own products in Walmart's stores based on the real-time sales data shared by Walmart. This mutually beneficial relationship reduces the probability of stockout as well as optimizes inventory management.

Walmart also uses another method called "just-in-time"(JIT) inventory. At Walmart, the JIT inventory method is employed in the form of cross-docking. Cross-docking facilitates the trucks of suppliers and customers to meet at a chosen place like a company's warehouse. Here, the goods are transferred from the suppliers' trucks directly to Walmart's trucks. The trucks deliver the goods to various Walmart stores all over the country. This leads to a quicker delivery of the goods to the stores and provides a quick response to demand fluctuations.

Both the VMI and the JIT inventory models increase Walmart's operational efficiency.

Inventory Management

Inventory is an asset to an organization. The need to manage inventory is common to all industries. If sold, the inventory becomes revenues. But until it is sold, the inventory ties up cash. Therefore, keeping too much inventory as stock costs money and reduces cash flow in both the manufacturing and the service industries. Organizations must have enough inventory to fulfill their customer orders. They must have a process to warn them of a potential shortage of inventory in the future. Organizations must track the inventory of all the materials and the components at all times to identify what to order at what time. The main aim of inventory management is to save money by knowing how much inventory is procured, stored, used, and sold. By keeping the right amount of stock at various locations such as stores, warehouses, or their premises, organizations can access their inventory to fulfill customer orders. In summary, inventory management is procuring the right amount of goods at the right time and keeping the inventory costs low while fulfilling the orders by customers.

Consider, for example, the restaurant next to your home consumes 10 loaves of bread every day. They know that a loaf of bread is fresh for a maximum of a week. Would the restaurant buy 70 loaves for a week's consumption or 150 loaves to store as inventory for 2 weeks? It depends on how far they have to drive to get the bread or when the bread distributor would deliver the bread. It also depends on the price of gas, available time, the cost of a loaf, changes in demand, and so on. Consider, as another example, that a manufacturer uses 200 bolts a day for their production needs. Should they order 1,400 bolts for a week or 10,000 bolts at a time? It depends on the price of bolts, transportation costs, changes in time, and so on.

There are two types of making goods—building the inventory in anticipation of the demand and building the goods only after an order by a customer. The first type is called "push" and the second type is called "pull." The "pull" environment helps companies to avoid the costly mismatching of supply and demand as well as increase the potential to customize their products. Many firms have shifted to a "pull" environment as it is beneficial for them to react to demand rather than making and storing their products. The point at which a company switches from making or storing the inventory in anticipation of a demand to building or storing the products in order to react to a demand is called the **push-pull boundary**.

> **Inventory management** Inventory management Is procuring the right amount of goods and services at the right time and keeping the inventory costs low while fulfilling the orders by customers.

> **Push-pull boundary** The point at which a company switches from making or storing the inventory in anticipation of a demand to building or storing the products in order to react to a demand.

FROM PRACTICE: Push Type of Inventory Management From Postcards to Smart Vending

Vending machines fall under the category of convenience services. In the late 1800s, coin-operated vending machines sold many products like postcards and chocolate in Europe. In 1888, the Thomas Adams Company's vending machines dispensed Tutti-Frutti gums on New York City train platforms[2]. This push type of inventory management has caught up throughout the world as vending machines dispense snacks, candy, cigarettes, and beverages.

© DeymosHR/Shutterstock.com

Intelligent Dispensing Solutions (IDS), a leading hardware and software provider of inventory management solutions, allows customers to dispense even larger items from their vending machines. Currently, we have smart vending machines. Digital touch display, Internet connectivity, cameras, and various types of sensors, advanced payment systems, and RFID have contributed to the development of smart vending machines.

FROM PRACTICE: Pull Type of Inventory Management

Just-in-time (JIT) is an example of a pull environment in inventory management. Firms order inventory on an "as-needed" basis with JIT inventory management. In this system, raw materials are delivered just when the production is about to begin. In manufacturing companies, the JIT process requires dependable suppliers. The advantages of the JIT inventory model are increased revenue, minimized waste, and reduced inventory costs. In fast food restaurants, a pull system is employed. After the customer places an order, the restaurant workers start making the meal to the taste of their customer.

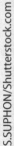

© S.SUPHON/Shutterstock.com

© Bankrx/Shutterstock.com

In a grocery store, the milk shelf is an example of a pull system. As customers purchase milk, less gallons of milk remain on the shelf. When the milk shelf is almost empty, a staff member of the grocery store restocks the shelf with new gallons of milk from the storeroom. Whenever the gallons of milk in the storeroom is low, additional gallons of milk are ordered and brought into the storeroom. The number of gallons of milk on the shelves depends on the current demand for milk.

Inventory Management in Service Industries

Service industry businesses can improve quality, enhance customizations, offer better process, and increase response times by wisely selecting the right kind of inventory[3]. In service industries, the push-pull boundary must be placed before a customer arrives. Therefore, there needs to be an inventory of goods and services that can be bought by a customer. There is not much physical stock in service companies since inventory is mostly intangible. Therefore, the inventory of services involves process and steps to complete a sale.

Service industries use both the push and pull systems of inventory management. For example, an auto repair shop orders only after the inspection of a vehicle and then only the parts it needs. The repair of the vehicle is terminated, the parts are ordered, and the repair work is resumed only when the parts reach the auto shop.

Dell, for example, uses both push and pull systems of inventory management. You find Dell computers ready to be purchased in retail stores such as Best Buy. You can order a Dell computer online using your own specifications.

Amazon is another example of using of both push and pull systems of inventory management. Amazon has placed its warehouses strategically close to many main cities. The company uses a push system by storing many products in those warehouses. On the other hand, it sells products from individual and third-party sellers using a pull strategy.

Inventory Management in Manufacturing Industries

The "push" type of manufacturing has been popular for a long time. A push system depends on forecast demand and production is completed before the customer orders. MRP is used to manage inventory in this type of system. Companies make sure that they have enough inventory to match demand forecast. This type of system is useful for companies involved in mass-production items, seasonal items, or food items. Coca-Cola is an example of a company that uses a push type system.

On the other hand, the pull system depends on customer orders and which are only produced when a customer places an order. This system helps a company to limit inventory for required work and prevent producing excess goods. Many manufacturing companies use the JIT method of inventory management as a means of pull system for inventory management. Firms order inventory on an "as-needed" basis with JIT inventory management. In this system, raw materials are delivered to the manufacturing sites just when the production is about to begin. For example, Toyota, Ford, and all other auto manufacturers follow the JIT method of inventory management.

Inventory Management and Control

Inventory control is a process that is used to maintain optimum inventory levels in a firm. Inventory control is an important part of inventory management. Successful implementation of inventory models involves controlling the inventory accurately and efficiently. Firms create internal policies and procedures for inventory management to control inventory. The managers and the employees of a company follow those policies and procedures to handle the company's inventory. The policies and procedures define how inventory is classified, how inventory flows through the operations and supply chain, who can order inventory, and so on. A good inventory management and control system helps a business to achieve better efficiency and profits. In addition, there are other benefits to inventory management and control including:

- Reduce inventory inaccuracies,
- Know inventory levels in "real time,"
- Identify and predict future inventory requirements,
- Improve workflow,
- Save money by streamlining inventory ordering,
- Make informed decisions, and
- Trust inventory data to fulfill customer orders.

To manage and control inventory, businesses implement the following activities:

1. Classify the inventory to place inventory orders.
2. Achieve accuracy of inventory by counting and tracking inventory.
3. Decide how much inventory to order and when.

We will discuss these key inventory-related activities next.

ABC Classification

ABC classification
Inventory items are classified as A, B, and C to help companies prioritize their inventory in order to make decisions.

Many firms have a vast number of inventory items. It is a huge task to use inventory control models for all those items. To alleviate this problem, firms use inventory classifications. Inventory can be classified as A, B, and C items. These three distinct items help companies to prioritize their inventory in order to make decisions. Inventory items vary in terms of cost, potential for revenue, and costs due to stockouts. To exercise appropriate control over inventory, companies classify inventory as:

A Items

These items are extremely important, they are consumed a lot, and they have a high dollar value. The high dollar value can be because of either low cost and high usage or high cost and low usage. A business must make sure that they do not run out of these items.

B Items

These items are moderately important, they sell not as much as A items, and they are of average dollar value.

C Items

These items are less important, they do not sell as much as items A and B, and they are of lower dollar value. The low dollar value may be because of either low demand or low cost.

The classification of inventory depends on the kind of business and their products. It also depends on whether a company can afford to have an item as stockout or not. Perishability or non-perishability of an item also plays a significant role in the classification scheme. Moreover, classifications change as firms add or drop items from their inventory. The ABC implementation is illustrated in Example 7-1. Example 7-1 shows the three A, B, and C classifications for a home appliance store. The annual value for the items in the store can be shown as a Pareto chart as in Figure 7-1.

Example 7-1

Ashley Appliances, a local store specializing in selling home appliances, has an inventory as shown in the following table. Classify the inventory using ABC analysis in an approximate ratio of 80:15:5.

Items	Refrigerator	Range oven	Washer and Dryer	Dish-washer	Micro-waveoven	Toaster Oven	Fryer Oven	Blender	Hand Vacuum	Iron	Garment Steamer
No of Items sold annually	240	200	160	100	800	400	450	750	800	600	500
Average Cost per unit	$1,500	$1,000	$900	$600	$200	$180	$130	$40	$35	$25	$18

Step 1: Calculate the annual value of each item. Annual value = No of items sold annually × average cost per unit.

Step 2: Sort the items in terms of descending order of their annual value.

Step 3: Calculate the percentage of each item in terms of their annual value to the total annual value.

Step 4: Calculate the cumulative percentage of the items and then split the items into the three A, B, and C categories by setting the cumulative percentages in the ratio of 80:15:5.

The calculations are shown in the table below:

Items	No of Items sold annually	Average Cost per unit	Annual Value	Percentage of Value	Cumulative Percentage	
Refrigerator	240	$1,500	$360,000	32%	32%	
Range oven	200	$1,000	$200,000	18%	49%	
Microwave oven	800	$200	$160,000	14%	63%	**75–80%**
Washer/Dryer	160	$900	$144,000	13%	76%	
Toaster Oven	400	$180	$72,000	6%	82%	
Dishwasher	100	$600	$60,000	5%	88%	
Fryer Oven	450	$130	$58,500	5%	93%	**81–95%**
Blender	750	$40	$30,000	3%	95%	
Hand Vacuum	800	$35	$28,000	2%	98%	
Iron	600	$25	$15,000	1%	99%	**96–100%**
Garment Steamer	500	$18	$9,000	1%	100%	
Total	**5,000**		**$1,136,500**			

Analysis: The high-valued items such as the refrigerator, the oven, and the washer/dryer units are classified as A items. The microwave oven is an A item because of its high number of sales. The inventory of these items must be managed extremely well so that customers do not go anywhere else. The inventory of B items such as the toaster oven, dishwasher, fryer oven, and blenders have to be managed well. As far as the number of items is concerned, there are 4 items classified as "A" out of 11 items in terms of sales value.

Usually, the ABC classification of inventory follows the Pareto Principle, also known as the 80/20 rule. The Pareto Principle states that 20% of the inventory makes up the 80% of sales value. In this example, it is roughly 28%, 1,400 items classified as "A" out of 5,000 total units.

Pareto chart

Microsoft's Excel can be used to show a Pareto chart. A Pareto chart is a sorted histogram chart. It contains columns sorted in descending order and a line representing the cumulative total percentage. This chart highlights the biggest factors in a set of data, which helps us to see the most common issues or values. In Excel, choose the X-axis and Y-axis values, click on Insert, click on Insert Statistic Chart, and then under Histogram, pick Pareto. It is that simple! The X-axis is usually the category and the Y-axis is usually the values of the category.

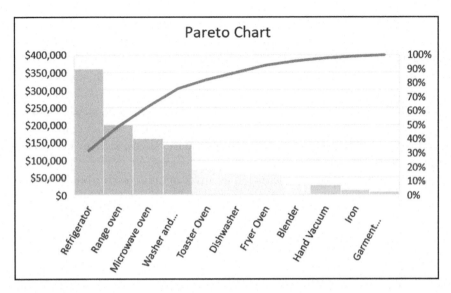

Figure 7-1 Pareto chart for Example 7-1

We can view the ABC categories using a Pareto chart. A Pareto chart is a bar graph arranged with the longest bars on the left and the shortest to the right. This illustrates the most significant on the left and the least significant on the right of the chart as shown in Figure 7-1.

Inventory Accuracy

For a business, the accuracy of its inventory affects forecasting, customer satisfaction, and the overall efficiency of the supply chain. This is true for manufacturing companies as well as retail and other service businesses. It is important for businesses to keep track of their inventory and ensure the accuracy of their inventory. To track their inventory, firms use two types of inventory accounting methods including periodic and perpetual inventory.

Periodic Inventory or Cycle Counting Method

Periodic inventory or cycle counting involves a physical count of the inventory at the premises of a business on a particular day or over a few days. This is a cost-effective method but prone to a margin of error due to possible counting errors. The physical count can be time-consuming for a firm that carries thousands of inventory items. After a company counts its physical inventory, its accounting department adjusts the inventory account to match the cost of the ending inventory. Companies count their inventory monthly, quarterly, or annually.

Perpetual Inventory or Automated Counting Method

Perpetual inventory or automated counting uses software that obtains data from the point-of-sale (POS) systems and the asset management systems.

> **Periodic inventory or cycle counting method** Periodic inventory or cycle counting involves a physical count of the inventory at the premises of a business on a particular day or days.

> **Perpetual inventory or automated counting method** A perpetual inventory or automated counting method uses software that obtains data from the point-of-sale (POS) systems and the asset management systems.

This is costlier to implement than the periodic inventory method but more accurate. The systems continuously update the inventories as and when the materials and the components are received and the products are sold.

However, when companies execute the periodic inventory and the perpetual inventory, they will invariably find out that the inventory records from the perpetual inventory is different from the actual physical count of periodic inventory. To prevent this inaccuracy, companies have a few options including increasing the frequency of periodic inventory, retaining more safety stock, or identifying and eliminating the source of errors[4]. We will discuss the third option next in this section through various exciting innovative technologies to track inventory.

Technologies to Track Inventory

Many businesses have adopted automated identification and data collection (AIDC) technology to track the components, equipment, materials, and parts. AIDC refers to identifying the stock, collecting their data, and capturing that data directly into the computer systems[5]. These technologies can be broadly classified as:

- Barcodes,
- Radio frequency Identifier (RFID), and
- Smart labels.

Barcodes

Barcodes are the most used inventory tracking method. A barcode represents data in a visual, machine-readable form. The linear or one-dimensional barcodes can be scanned by special optical scanners called **barcode readers**. These barcodes are commonly found on all grocery store items. The retail grocery stores in the United States adopted the Universal Product Code (UPC or UPC code) during the 1970s. UPC barcodes, preprinted on most items in any store, are used to track items as well as process items at checkouts. The barcodes are also used to identify the patients in hospitals and to access patient data. Businesses use the barcodes to keep track of rental cars, airline luggage, registered mail, and parcels. It is also used to board passengers on planes and allow spectators to enter sports arenas and theatres. In the manufacturing setting, the barcodes are used to track the inventory and the time spent on a particular workorder.

© Bacho/Shutterstock.com

Person holding a barcode reader

Radio Frequency Identifier (RFID)

Radio frequency identification (RFID) is a wireless form of the automated identification technology. The main component is the transponder or tag, which comprises a chip and an antenna mounted onto an enclosure. The examples of transponders are car keys, tollbooth tags, and smart cards. A chip consists of a processor, memory, and a radio transmitter. The memory will vary, depending on the manufacturer, from just a few characters to kilobytes. The transponders communicate via radio frequency to a reader, which has its own antennas. The readers can interface through a wired or wireless medium to a main computer. The two most common types of RFID technologies are active and passive. The power of an active RFID tag dictates the communication distance and the capacity of the memory. The passive RFID transponder is powered by an electromagnetic signal that is transmitted from a reader. The passive tags do not require an on-board battery and can be detected from a distance ranging from a few inches to a few feet, whereas active tags have an on-board battery, and therefore have a far longer read/write range and memory size.

Person holding a RFID reader

© metamorworks/Shutterstock

Smart Labels

Smart Labels are labels that include a chip, an antenna, and bonding wires. The labels can be made of paper, fabric, or plastics. The smart labels differ from the RFID tags in that they incorporate both RFID and barcode technologies. For tracking the stock within short distances, barcodes are used. RFID can be used for tracking items from a longer distance than the barcodes. Smart labels are applied directly on packages, pallets, or other shipping containers. Smart labels are one of the key technologies for Industry 4.0 smart factory. In an Industry 4.0 smart factory, traditional labels such as barcodes are not appropriate. This is because the smart factories of the future must automate the collection of data and use such data to coordinate with other systems in the company. Moreover, the smart labels can be used for interactions with the manufacturing systems without requiring tablets and smartphones[6].

Person using a Smart Label reader App

© Sophon Nawit/Shutterstock.com

FROM PRACTICE: RFID and Smart Labels at Lululemon, Decathlon, and Walmart

Athletic apparel retailer Lululemon uses RFID tags throughout its network of nearly 500 stores resulting in a 98% inventory accuracy. By using RFID, the company can access any product at any time across their supply chain network[7].

(continued)

Decathlon, the sports equipment retailer with over 1,600 stores in more than 50 countries, uses RFID tags at checkouts resulting in tripling their labor productivity, cutting their stockouts, and raising their revenue by 2.5%. Its scan-and-go solution in Europe allows shoppers to scan and pay for the items with their smartphones, automatically disabling RFID tags and avoiding the checkout lines altogether[7].

Walmart is looking to use RFID smart labels in some of their store products. This decision will certainly accelerate the broad use of RFID smart labels. Many companies use RFID in their manufacturing, warehousing, and transportation processes but not in their products[8].

Inventory Ordering

To produce goods or to sell goods, businesses need to build inventory. To build their inventory, businesses rely on planning, designing, and implementing various inventory policies. An inventory ordering policy consists of rules set by a company on when and how much to order the materials for replenishment.

Let us consider the inventory at a department store, for example, men's shirts. Shirts are ordered based on their demand, which is how many shirts are being sold. A store receives a quantity of shirts and over a period, those shirts are sold. As the inventory of shirts reaches a particular point or at a particular time interval, a new order to buy shirts is issued by the department store. The key point to note is that the shirts are ordered to avoid both excess stock and stockouts. This buying and selling occurs in cycles and is called **inventory cycles** as shown in Figure 7-2.

> **Inventory cycle** The inventory cycle is the process of ordering and receiving inventory over time.

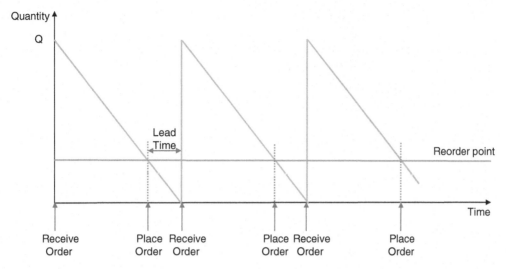

Figure 7-2 Inventory Cycle

In Figure 7-2, the shirts are assumed to be sold at a constant rate and the orders for the shirts are placed based on a constant lead time. If the lead times are different and if the shirt sale rates vary, then the orders have to be placed accordingly. Therefore, both the quantity of shirts to be ordered and the reorder point are critical. If there is sudden surge in the sale of the shirts, there will be a shortage of shirts or if there is slow sale of shirts, there will be unsold shirts left in the store. We will focus on the following inventory ordering models to deal with inventory cycles in this chapter:

- Cost-based Inventory Models–Economic order quantity and Quantity discount inventory models
- Single-period inventory model
- Multi-period inventory model–Fixed Quantity and Fixed Time Period models

> **Inventory policy**
> An inventory ordering policy consists of rules set by a company on when and how much to order the materials for replenishment.

Economic Order Quantity (EOQ) Model

The economic order quantity (EOQ) model is used to determine how much material can be ordered at a time. The EOQ model is used when the demand and the inventory costs are constant over time. This model is used to identify an ideal, fixed order size that minimizes inventory costs such as inventory holding costs and inventory order costs.

The inventory holding costs and the inventory order costs are inversely proportional to each other. For example, let us consider two scenarios in our shirts example: multiple orders with small quantities and one larger quantity of order. If the department store orders multiple small quantities of shirts, inventory holding costs will be lower but the store has to order more frequently,

> **Economic order quantity (EOQ)** An ideal fixed order size that minimizes inventory costs such as inventory holding costs and inventory order costs.

resulting in higher inventory ordering costs. If the store orders one large quantity of shirts, they will be ordering less frequently than in the previous scenario, resulting in lower ordering costs, but the store will end up carrying more inventory, which will lead to higher inventory holding costs.

We can calculate the annual inventory holding costs by taking the average amount of the inventory and multiplying that with the holding cost of one unit as shown in the following equation:

$$Annual\ inventory\ holding\ cost = \frac{Q}{2}H \qquad\qquad \text{Eq. 7-1}$$

where,   Q = order size in units, and
         H = annual holding cost per unit of average inventory per year

The annual ordering cost depends on the annual demand, the order size, and the ordering cost. Larger order sizes lead to a smaller number of orders, resulting in lower ordering costs. For example, if a store orders 500 shirts per order for an annual demand of 2,000 shirts, they order 4 times over the year. If they order 250 shirts each time, then they would order 8 times. Therefore, if **D** is the annual demand, the annual number of orders will be:

$$Annual\ number\ of\ orders = \frac{D}{Q} \qquad\qquad \text{Eq. 7-2}$$

Therefore, if **S** is the ordering cost per order, the annual ordering cost will be:

$$Annual\ inventory\ ordering\ cost = \frac{D}{Q}S \qquad\qquad \text{Eq. 7-3}$$

The total annual inventory cost is the sum of the annual inventory ordering cost, the annual inventory holding cost, and the actual cost of the units. If C is the cost of a unit, the total annual inventory cost, **TC**, will be:

$$TC = \frac{D}{Q}S + \frac{Q}{2}H + DC \qquad\qquad \text{Eq. 7-4}$$

EOQ is the ideal amount of units to be ordered. To find the ideal order size, we need to find the optimum order size. The optimum order size is equal to an order size where the total cost is minimum. The minimum total inventory cost occurs when the slope of the total cost curve reaches 0 and at the point where the holding cost is equal to the ordering cost as shown in Figure 7-3.

If we take the derivative of the total inventory cost with respect to Q and set it equal to 0, we get:

$$\frac{d(TC)}{dQ} = \frac{-D}{Q^2}S + \frac{1}{2}H + 0 = 0$$

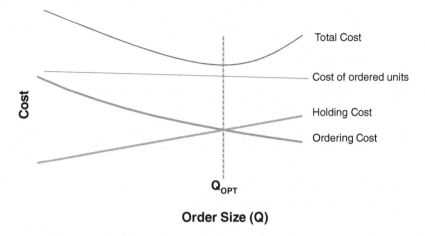

Figure 7-3 EOQ and Total Inventory Cost

Rearranging the above equation will give:

$$-\frac{D}{Q^2}S = -\frac{1}{2}H$$

$$2DS = Q^2H$$

$$Q^2 = -\frac{2DS}{H}$$

$$EOQ = Q_{OPT} = \sqrt{\frac{2DS}{H}} \qquad \text{Eq. 7-5}$$

The inventory policy using the EOQ model is ordering inventory to the order size equal to EOQ and reordering $\frac{D}{Q}$ number of times annually. Let us look at Example 7-2 to understand EOQ calculation.

Example 7-2

Westman Industries is looking forward to selling 1,000 units this year. The annual holding cost is $5 per unit and ordering cost is $65 per order. If the cost of the unit is $10 per unit, what is their inventory policy using the EOQ model? What is the total inventory cost?

D = 1,000 units per year
S = $65 per order
H = $5 per unit
C = $10 per unit

Using Eq. 7-5, $Q_{OPT} = \sqrt{\dfrac{2 \times 1000 \times 65}{5}} = 161$ units

Using Eq. 7-2, No of orders $= \dfrac{1000}{161} = 6.2 \approx 6$

The total inventory cost, using Eq. 7-4 is:

Total Cost of Inventory $= \left(\dfrac{1000}{161} \times 65 \right) + \left(\dfrac{161}{2} \times 5 \right) + \left(1000 \times 10 \right) = \$10,806$

> **Analysis:** The company's inventory policy using EOQ is o order 161 units 6 times in the year. EOQ is used extensively in industries.

> **Quantity discount inventory (QDI) model** When prices vary with order size as discounts, this model is used to find the optimal order size.

Quantity Discount Inventory (QDI) Model

In many instances, businesses offer discounts for larger orders. The sellers often offer an incentive to attract customers to purchase in larger quantities. For example, a manufacturer of coffee mugs may offer two price levels: a price of 75¢ per mug for a purchase of 100 to 500 mugs and a price of 60¢ per mug for purchasing 500 mugs or more. Note that the prices offered by the seller are the costs for the buyer. Therefore, the costs vary with the order size in this model. When the costs vary with the order size as discounts, we must identify the optimal quantity at the lowest cost. There are two scenarios for this model.

Scenario 1: Inventory holding cost is constant.
Calculate the EOQ using Eq. 7-5. This is the common minimum quantity for all the cost levels. If the quantity is corresponding to the lowest cost level, then that quantity is the overall optimum order size. If it is not, then calculate the total inventory cost for this minimum quantity using its cost. Also, calculate for other *minimum* quantities that are provided for each cost level. The quantity corresponding to the lowest total inventory cost is the overall optimum order size. Example 7-3 illustrates this scenario.

Example 7-3

Westman Industries is looking forward to selling 1,000 units this year. The annual holding cost is $5 per unit and ordering cost is $65 per order. The cost of the unit is $20 per unit for a purchase less than 500 units, $15 per unit for purchases less than 1,000 units, and $10 for 1,000 units or more. What is their inventory policy using the QDI model? What is the total inventory cost?

No of units	Cost per unit
1 – 499	$20
500 – 999	$15
1000 or more	$10

D = 1,000 units per year; S = $65 per order; H = $5 per unit

Step 1:   Calculate Q_{OPT} using Eq. 7-5. If Q_{OPT} is 1,000 or more, then this is the optimal quantity with the lowest price. If not, go to step 2.

Here, $Q_{OPT} = \sqrt{\dfrac{2 \times 1000 \times 5}{65}} = 161$ units. The order size of 161 falls in the costliest price level of $20. 161 is not the optimal quantity to purchase. Therefore, go to Step 2.

Step 2:   Calculate TC using Eq. 7-4 for the three cost levels. Use 500 as the minimum quantity for the $15 cost level and 1,000 as the minimum of the $20 cost level as shown below:

	No of units		
	1–499	500–999	1000 or more
Price	$20	$15	$10
EOQ	161		
Lowest Qty to buy		500	1000
TC	$ 20,806.23	$16,380.00	$12,565.00

Analysis: The lowest TC of $12,565 falls in the 1,000 or more range or the $10 cost level. Therefore, the minimum of 1,000 units is the optimal order size. Since the company is planning to sell 1,000 units, their inventory policy must be to buy 1,000 units once this year for a total cost of $12,565. This method is useful when suppliers give discounts.

Scenario 2: Inventory holding cost is a percentage of unit cost.
In this scenario, beginning with the lowest unit price, calculate the EOQ using the following formula:

$$EOQ = Q_{OPT} = \sqrt{\frac{2DS}{pC}} \qquad \text{Eq. 7-6}$$

where, p is the percentage of C, the cost per unit. If this EOQ is within the quantity range of that lowest unit cost, then this EOQ is the order size with the lowest cost. If not, calculate EOQ and the total inventory cost TC for all price levels. The total inventory cost in this case is as follows:

$$TC = \frac{D}{Q}S + \frac{Q}{2}pC + DC \qquad \text{Eq. 7-7}$$

The order size corresponding to the lowest total inventory cost TC, is the optimal order size. As shown in Figure 7-4, the Q_{OPT} for various cost levels falls at the lowest points of their slopes. The actual optimal quantity (Q_{OPT}) can fall anywhere in the Q_{OPT} zone based on inventory holding and inventory ordering costs. Example 7-4 illustrates this scenario.

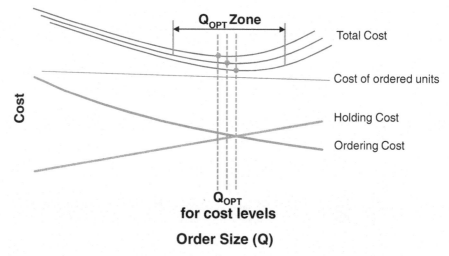

Figure 7-4 EOQ and Total Inventory Costs for QDI Model

Example 7-4

Westman Industries is looking forward to selling 1,000 units this year. The ordering cost is $65 per order. The annual holding costs are 20% of purchase costs. The cost levels are given in the table below. What is their inventory policy using the QDI model? What is the total inventory cost?

No of units	Cost per unit
1 – 499	$20
500 – 999	$15
1000 or more	$10

D = 1,000 units per year; S = $65 per order

Step 1:   Calculate Q_{OPT} using Eq. 7-6 for the lowest cost level. If Q_{OPT} is 1,000 or more, then this is the optimal quantity with the lowest price. If not, go to step 2.

Here, $Q_{OPT} = \sqrt{\dfrac{2 \times 1000 \times 5}{20\% \times \$10}}$ = 255 units. The order size of 255 falls in the costliest price level of $20,255 is not the optimal quantity to purchase. Therefore, go to Step 2.

Step 2:   Calculate TC using Eq. 7-7 for the three cost levels. Use 500 as the minimum quantity for the $15 cost level and 1,000 as the minimum of the $10 cost level as shown below:

	No of units		
	1–499	**500–999**	**1000 or more**
Price	$20	$15	$10
EOQ	180	208	255
Lowest qty to buy		500	1000
Holding cost	$360.56	$750.00	$1000
Ordering cost	$360.56	$130.00	$65.00
Cost of units	$20,000.00	$15,000.00	$10,000.00
Total cost	$20,721.11	$15,880.00	$11,065

Analysis: The lowest total cost of $11,065 falls in the 1,000 or more range or the $10 cost level. Therefore, the minimum of 1,000 units is the optimal order size. Since the company is planning to sell 1,000 units, their inventory policy must be to buy 1,000 units once this year for a total cost of $11,065.

Single-Period Inventory Model

> **Single-period inventory (SPI) model** This model addresses how much to order for items purchased one time, expected to be used once, and not reordered again, with no leftover stocks.

There are many occasions when products and services are purchased one time, expected to be used once, and not reordered again. Consider a flight that has 189 seats. An airline company has only a limited number of seats to offer but there may be more people wishing to board the flight. The airline has to take flight cancellations into consideration as customers tend to cancel their flights for a number of reasons. The cost of underestimating the number of cancellations is revenue lost due to empty seats. The cost of overestimating the cancellations means the company has to offer incentives for passengers who can afford to take the next flight to make way for passengers who insist taking that overbooked flight, which is once again lost revenues. There are many similar examples such as hotel room and rental car reservations. Ordering tickets for concerts and sporting events, selling Christmas trees, newspapers, and magazines are other examples are one-time purchases. These are classic single-period inventory problems. This single-period inventory model is also used to stock perishable items such as produce, flowers, baked items, dairy products, and so on.

Let C_o be the cost per unit of overestimated demand. The expected marginal cost is equal to the cost of the overestimated unit times the probability of an excess unit. If the probability of excess unit is p, then the expected margin cost $= p \times C_o$. Let C_u be the benefit per unit of underestimated demand. The expected marginal benefit is equal to the cost of the underestimated unit times the probability of that unit being sold. If the probability of that unit being sold is $1-p$, then the expected marginal benefit $= (1-p) \times C_u$. The maximum profit occurs when the expected margin cost is equal to the expected margin benefit. Therefore,

$$p \times C_o = (1-p) \times C_u$$

Rearranging,

$$p = \frac{C_u}{C_o + C_u} \qquad\qquad \text{Eq. 7-8}$$

Example 7-5 illustrates this model.

Example 7-5

Steven's motel in Niles, MI, fills up for the local university's games. Steven finds a room in another nearby hotel for $150 for any overbooking and the average rate is $100 a room. If the average cancellation is six with a standard deviation of 2.5, how many rooms should the motel overbook?

Using Eq. 7-8, with $C_u = 100$ and $C_o = 150$, $p = \dfrac{100}{150 + 100} = 0.4$.

Using the Excel function NORM.S.INV, we get a Z-score of -0.253. The negative sign indicates that Steven should overbook.

Steve can overbook by $\bar{X} + z\sigma = 6 + (-0.253 \times 2.5) = 5$ rooms

> **Analysis:** It is common for hotels to overbook during popular events. However, overbooking too many rooms is a problem as the hotel may lose revenues. If $C_u < C_o$, it makes sense to overbook rooms. If $C_o > C_u$, then it makes sense to underbook rooms. Steve can overbook by 5 rooms.

> **Multi-period inventory model**
> The model addresses how much to order as well as when to reordered in each period before the stocks are sold out completely.

Multi-Period Inventory Model

The key difference between the single-period model and the multi-period model is that the multi-period model may involve stock leftovers from previous periods. In the multi-period inventory model, the sales of products are extended from one period to multiple periods and a decision on order quantity in each period is made before the demand is realized[9]. A company ordering nuts and bolts for assembly of their products, a business ordering athletic shoes for their stores, and a restaurant ordering spices periodically are examples where leftover products are sold or used over time and decisions to order the necessary replenishments are made in each period. These products and services are mostly available to customers throughout the year. In some cases, businesses may hold on to some seasonal products like snow blowers and lawn mowers to be sold next time around. In this book, we will consider two types of multi-period inventory models including:

- Fixed quantity Q model, and
- Fixed time period P model.

Fixed Quantity Model (Q Model)

The fixed quantity Q model is an inventory control model where the order size remains fixed and the inventory is reordered upon a decision when the inventory level drops to a specified quantity. The reorders of parts, components, and materials are triggered at any time when the inventory level reaches a predetermined quantity, which may include safety stocks as well. Q models are employed often for high-priced or critically important items. In the fixed quantity model, the order size is equal to Q_{OPT}, the economic order quantity EOQ. To know when to order items, we need to compute the reorder point.

> **Fixed quantity model (Q model)** In the Q model, the order size remains fixed and reorders are based on a decision when the inventory level drops to a specified quantity.

Reorder Point

The reorder point is calculated when the inventory reaches a certain predetermined quantity, at which time the items are reordered. The reorder point depends on the following factors:

- Rate at which an item is being used (demand per time period like per day or per week),
- Lead time to receive the item,
- Variability in demand (we will assume that lead time is constant).

> **Reorder point** The reorder point is the time when inventory is reordered and happens when the inventory of an item reaches a predetermined quantity.

Scenario 1: Average demand and lead time in a time period are constant. Let us look at a scenario when the demand rate and the lead time are constant as shown in Figure 7-5. Suppose the demand forecasted is d for a time period like a day or a week. Then the average demand forecasted for n days or n weeks is:

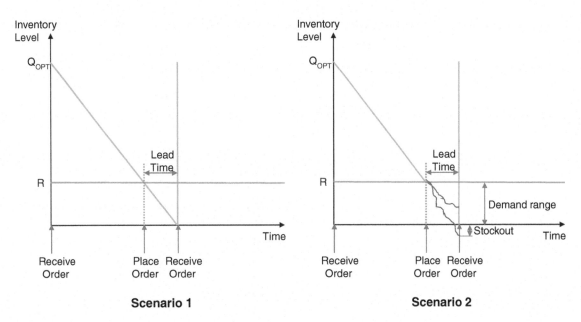

Figure 7-5 Fixed Quantity Model (Q Model)

$$\bar{d} = \frac{\sum_{i=1}^{n} d_i}{n}$$
Eq. 7-9

In this scenario, if both the demand and the lead time are constant, the reorder point R can be calculated using the following formula:

$$R = \bar{d}L$$
Eq. 7-10

where, $\bar{d}$ = average demand in a time period like a day or a week, and
L = lead time expressed in the same time units

The inventory policy if using the Q model with constant demand and lead time is an order size Q_{OPT} reordered when the quantity reaches R, the reorder point. Example 7-6 illustrates this model.

Example 7-6

The annual demand for microwave ovens in a department store is 500 units. The inventory ordering and holding costs are $2.50 per order and $1 per unit annually. If the cost per unit is $8 and the lead time is 5 days, what is the inventory policy for the department store? Assume 365 days in that year.

Using Eq. 7-5, $Q_{OPT} = \sqrt{\dfrac{2 \times 500 \times 2.5}{1}} = 50$

The demand and lead time are constant.

$\bar{d}$ = 500/365 = 1.37, since D = 500 annually. Therefore, R = 1.37 × 5 = 6.85 ≈ 7 units

The inventory policy is to order 50 microwave ovens when the inventory reaches 7 units.

Analysis: The department store should have the policy to order 50 microwave ovens when the inventory reaches 7 units. The 7 units is not a safety stock policy. It is just the reorder point based on the demand and the lead time.

Scenario 2: Variability in demand and lead time is constant.

The other scneario is when there is a variability in the demand as shown in Figure 7-5. Because of the variability in the demand, there exists a possibility that the actual demand can exceed d, the average demand. In this case, the stockout protection is required during the lead time period. This means additional inventory of an item in the form of safety stock must be held by the business to avoid stockouts during the lead time period of the item. The reorder point R can be calculated as:

$$R = \bar{d}L + Safety\ Stock$$
Eq. 7-11

The required amount of safety stock depends on the probability that the inventory on hand is enough to meet the actual demand during the lead time. This probability indicator is called the **order cycle service level**. For example, if the order cycle service level is 95%, then there is 95% probability that the demand for that product would not exceed the actual demand or that 95% of the replenishment cycles will be completed without a stockout. The order cycle service level can be converted to a Z-score. This Z-score is the probabilty of not stocking out.

Order cycle service level The order cycle service level is an indicator of the probability of maintaining enough stock to meet demand.

The product of the order cycle service level Z-score and the standard deviation of demand during the lead time will give us the safety stock quantity. Therefore,

$$Safety\ Stock = z\,\sigma_L \qquad\qquad \text{Eq. 7-12}$$

where z is the z-score and σ_L is the standard deviation of demand during the lead time.

Therefore,
$$R = \bar{d}L + z\,\sigma_L \qquad\qquad \text{Eq. 7-13}$$

The daily or weekly demand is independent since there is a variability in demand. For independent variables, the variance of their sum or difference is the sum of their variances. Therefore, for a lead time of n days or weeks, σ_L can be calculated using σ as the daily or weekly standard deviation of demand:

$$\sigma_L = \sqrt{\sigma_1^2 + \sigma_2^2 + \ldots + \sigma_n^2} = \sqrt{\Sigma_{i=1}^{n}\sigma_i^2} \qquad\qquad \text{Eq. 7-14}$$

where, σ_1, σ_2, . . . , σ_n are the standard deviations of demand on day 1, day 2, . . . day n. Examples 7-7 and 7-8 illustrate the computation of σ_L and R for Scenario 2.

Example 7-7

If the standard deviation in demand is 5 units per day and if the lead time is 6 days, what is the standard deviation of demand during the lead time?

Using Eq. 7-14, we can find the standard deviation to be:

$$\sigma_L = \sqrt{5^2 + 5^2 + 5^2 + 5^2 + 5^2 + 5^2} \text{ or } \sqrt{\Sigma_{i=1}^{n}5_i^2} \text{ or } \sqrt{6 \times 5^2} = 12.25 \approx 12 \text{ units}$$

Analysis: Since the lead time is 6 days, we will use the demand of 5 units for each day. Since the demand of each day is independent of other days, we can find the variances as their sum, or difference is the sum of their variances.

Example 7-8

The annual demand for microwave ovens in a department store is 500 units. The inventory ordering and holding costs are $2.50 per order and $1 per unit annually. The cost per unit is $8 and the lead time is 5 days. The daily demand is normally distributed with a standard deviation of 4.5. The store manager wants to maintain an order cycle service level of 95%. What is the inventory policy for the department store? Assume 365 days in that year.

$$\text{Using Eq. 7-5, } Q_{OPT} = \sqrt{\frac{2 \times 500 \times 2.5}{1}} = 50$$

The demand has a variance and the store manager wants a 95% service level of order cycle. The Z-score for 95% is 1.64 from the **Total Area Standard Normal Distribution table** (See Table A-3 in Appendix) as shown below.

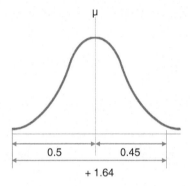

Table: Area of Standard Normal Distribution

Z	0.4
1.6	0.9485

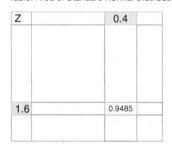

The daily demand, $\bar{d}$ = 500 units/ 365 days = 1.37 units and is normally distributed with a standard deviation of 4.5.

Since each day's demand needs to be taken into account for the lead time of 5 days, we must use Eq. 7-14.

$$\sigma_L = \sqrt{5 \times (4.5)^2} = 10.06 \text{ units}$$

The required safety stock = $1.64 \times 10.06 = 16.49 \approx 17$ units

We can compute the reorder point using Eq. 7-13

$R = (1.37 \times 5) + (1.64 \times 10.06) \approx 24$ units

The inventory policy is to order 50 microwave ovens when the inventory reaches 24 units.

Analysis: Since the daily demand varies and the lead time is constant, we will use the second scenario of the Q Model. In this case, the department store must order 50 microwave ovens whenever the inventory reaches 24 units.

Fixed Time Period (P) Model

> **Fixed time period model (P model)**
> In the P model, inventory is reordered at regular fixed time intervals and the order size varies.

The fixed time period P model is an inventory control model where inventory is reordered at the end of a **predetermined time period** and the order size varies. Here the interval of time between any two subsequent ordering is fixed. The reorders of parts, components, or goods are triggered at the end of a predetermined time period at regular intervals. The inventory levels resulting from this model may tend to be higher than the fixed quantity model. However, many retail businesses use this type of model. This is also due to many suppliers who tend to push their products to be bought at regular intervals as they can transport their products strategically thus saving shipping costs. Since many retailers cannot afford to continuously monitor the inventory levels, they can check the inventory periodically like once a week or once a fortnight and use the fixed time period model. For our analysis, we will assume that the demand varies and the lead time is constant. The Q model orders are triggered by quantity while the time period triggers the orders in P model.

In the fixed time period models, the orders are placed at regular time periods, T. The order size of a product is dependent on the usage of the product which can vary from one period to another. In the case of the Q model, we need the safety stock as a protection during the lead time period. But in the P model, we need the protection from both the lead time and the next order cycle. Hence, there is a higher possibility of stockouts. The order size in a P model is determined using the following equation:

$$Q = \bar{d}\left(T + L\right) + z\,\sigma_{T+L} - I \qquad\qquad \text{Eq. 7-15}$$

where,

T = The time period as shown in Figure 7-6
I = current interval level or the inventory on-hand at reorder time
σ_{T+L} = standard deviation of demand over the time period and lead time

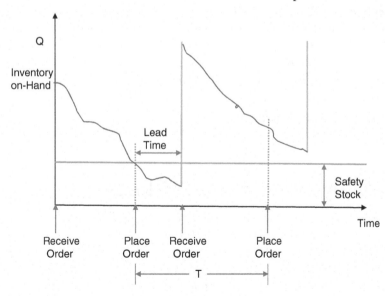

Figure 7-6 Fixed Time Period Model (P Model)

We can calculate σ_{T+L} using the following equation:

$$\sigma_{T+L} = \sqrt{\sigma^2 (T+L)}$$ Eq. 7-16

where, σ is the daily or weekly standard deviation of demand
         L = Lead time

Example 7-9

The annual demand for microwave ovens in a department store is 500 units. The daily demand is normally distributed with a standard deviation of 4.5. The store manager wants to maintain an order cycle service level of 95%. What is the inventory policy for the department store if at the time of ordering inventory is 15 units, lead time is 5 days, and the time period is 20 days? Assume 365 days in that year.

Using Eq. 7-16,

$$\sigma_{T+L} = \sqrt{4.5^2 (20+5)} = 22.5 \text{ units}$$

The demand has a variance and the store manager wants a 95% service level of order cycle. The Z-score for 95% is 1.64 using Table A-3 in Appendix.

The daily demand, $\bar{d} = 500/365 = 1.37$ units

Using Eq. 7-15, we get order size:

$$Q = 1.37 \times (20+5) + (1.64 \times 22.5) - 15 = 56.15 \approx 57 \text{ units.}$$

The inventory policy is to order 57 microwave ovens after 20 days from the previous order.

> **Analysis:** In this mode, we have varying demand and a constant lead time. Using this model, the department store must order 57 microwave ovens after 20 days from the previous order. With a similar order cycle service level of 95% from the Q model we computed in Example 7-8, the department store had to order 50 microwave ovens whenever the inventory reached 24 units. Depending on the actual sales, the department store manager has to choose either the Q or the P model.

FROM PRACTICE: NetSuite's Inventory Control at Philz Coffee

The inventory at a restaurant affects its net profit and restaurants often find it difficult to find the sweet spot. They need to have enough inventory for their customers to buy items but not so much that products' life expires or spoils. Philz Coffee knows that by using software. Philz Coffee is an American coffee company and coffeehouse chain based in San Francisco, California. The company struggled with disparate systems for tracking and replenishing inventory. Then, the company implemented an integrated NetSuite platform from Oracle to help with accounting, inventory, and sales. As it grows and extends business models, NetSuite for restaurants adapts and scales with Philz Coffee. The revenues increased by 400% and now, Philz Coffee has more than a dozen locations in the Bay Area and has expanded to the DC area and Chicago[10].

© flowgraph/Shutterstock.com

Formulae from this Chapter

Annual Inventory Holding Cost	$\frac{Q}{2}H$	Eq. 7-1
Annual No of orders	$\frac{D}{Q}$	Eq. 7-2
Annual Inventory Ordering Cost	$\frac{D}{Q}S$	Eq. 7-3
Total Inventory Cost when Inventory Holding Cost is constant	$TC = \frac{D}{Q}S + \frac{Q}{2}H + DC$	Eq. 7-4
Economic Order Quantity	$EOQ = Q_{OPT} = \sqrt{\frac{2DS}{H}}$	Eq. 7-5
Economic Order Quantity when Inventory Holding Cost is a percentage of Unit Cost	$EOQ = Q_{OPT} = \sqrt{\frac{2DS}{pC}}$	Eq. 7-6
Total Inventory Cost when Inventory Holding Cost is a percentage of Unit Cost	$TC = \frac{D}{Q}S + \frac{Q}{2}pC + DC$	Eq. 7-7
Probability of Excess Unit	$p = \frac{C_u}{C_o + C_u}$	Eq. 7-8
Average demand	$\bar{d} = \frac{\sum_{i=1}^{n}d_i}{n}$	Eq. 7-9

(continued)

Reorder Point for Q model with no demand or lead time variability	$R = \bar{d}L$	Eq. 7-10
Reorder Point for Q model with demand variability	$R = \bar{d}L + Safety\ Stock$	Eq. 7-11
Safety Stock for Q model with demand variability	$Safety\ Stock = z\ \sigma_L$	Eq. 7-12
Reorder Point for Q model with demand variability	$R = \bar{d}L + z\ \sigma_L$	Eq. 7-13
Standard deviation of demand during the lead time	$\sigma_L = \sqrt{\sigma_1^2 + \sigma_2^2 + \ldots + \sigma_n^2} = \sqrt{\Sigma_{i=1}^{n}\sigma_i^2}$	Eq. 7-14
Order size for P model	$Q = \bar{d}(T + L) + z\ \sigma_{T+L} - I$	Eq. 7-15
Standard deviation of demand over the time period and lead time	$\sigma_{T+L} = \sqrt{\sigma^2(T + L)}$	Eq. 7-16

Case Study: Inventory Management at Bombay Boutique

Brinda Bhatt, the owner of Bombay Boutique in Bakersfield, CA, is a famous fashion designer of women's dresses and gold jewelry. Brinda buys dresses and jewelry from a few known suppliers and alters them to fit her clients perfectly. A perfect fit is what her clients are after and her business model is just that! The boutique has become famous throughout the region. It has become known for the carefully created fashion products for the personal celebration of her clients. Her business caters to affluent clients who want fitted dresses and exotic fashion jewelry from all over the world. She displays her inventory in her 4,000 sq. ft. store. The business website displays a fantastic catalog of all her fabulous dresses and exotic jewelry. Her clients have to make appointments and visit her store for the fitting. They can browse through her display or the compendium, choose the merchandise to their liking and give their measurements. When ready, she will ship the dress and/or jewelry to their homes. Her policy included that all orders will be shipped within 5 days. Because of this turnaround policy, she was strict with her suppliers to supply her materials in 5 days' time as well. The supplied materials include both dresses and fashion jewelry.

Brinda started the boutique about 10 years back. She is originally from Mumbai (Bombay) and became a citizen after her marriage with a

© pikselstock/Shutterstock.com

local Bakersfield gentleman. As a California resident of 20 years, Brinda has a strong community presence. Working in her father's business in India, she learned the ropes of her business. She loved to do social work and has a passion for helping others which she incorporates into the boutique. Brinda's store is on the first floor of a three-storied building in an affluent section of Bakersfield. She uses the other floor as a warehouse for her dresses and suits. All the floors are immaculately kept for client visits.

© fipïoto/Shutterstock.com

The boutique's business model of appointments for fitted dresses and jewelry was extremely popular. On the same street, one can access several award-winning restaurants, bustling cafes, a sparkling bar scene, a colorful weekend farmer's market, plentiful parking, and a major train line. Brinda charges 15% of the item cost as fitting charges except Model BB-81-6-01 for which people are willing to pay 20% of the cost of this item. She loses an average of 5% of an item cost each time a potential client misses their appointment as she has to pay the attendant and an opportunity cost of a potential sale. Her inventory includes dresses, jewelry, and accessories. A snapshot of the inventory is shown in the following table:

Items	No of Items sold annually	Average Cost per unit
Model BB-78-4-01	220	$950
Model BB-78-S-02	450	$1,000
Model BB-81-6-01	700	$1,290
Model BB-81-8-02	160	$900
BB-J-Star-1	400	$180
Model BB-81-8-01	100	$600
Model BB-81-6-02	450	$130
BB-J-Lily-2	750	$40
Floral pins	800	$35
Scarfs	600	$25
Leather gloves	500	$18

Model BB-81-6-01 is the best-selling product and Brinda is interested in maintaining this product's inventory well and efficiently. On that sweltering summer Bakersfield afternoon, Brinda started analyzing the fitting appointments for the Model BB-81-6-01. She identified the probabilities of cancellations of appointments for the model as follows for the past month:

No shows	0	1	2	3	4	5	6	7	8	9	10
Probability	0.15	0.08	0.09	0.1	0.15	0.12	0.09	0.07	0.06	0.05	0.04

Her intent was to find out how many overbookings can be made for this model. Depending on whether the number of clients showing up for the appointments is greater than the number of overbookings, Brinda multiplied the difference of number of cancellations and number of overbookings by the cost of cancellations or cost of overbooking. Then she calculated the sumproduct, that is, the sum of the products of corresponding ranges, for each number of overbooking cost by the probability range to get the expected cost of overbooking. Brinda planned to overbook appointments for Model BB-81-6-01 by the number of overbookings that corresponded with minimum expected cost of overbooking. She then checked out this number of overbooking using the SPI model. She also found that there were 3 cancellations on average for the past month with a standard deviation of 2.4.

For the Model BB-81-6-01, the annual holding cost is $2 per unit and ordering cost is $45 per order. The cost of the unit is $25 per unit for a purchase less than 100 units, $20 per unit for purchases up to 499 units, and $15 for 500 units or more. There is variance in demand but not in lead time. The daily demand is normally distributed with a standard deviation of 4.5 and Brinda wants to maintain an order cycle service level of 95%. At the time of ordering, the inventory is 15 units and she is considering a time period of 20 days. Assume 365 days in that year.

Case Questions

A. Classify the boutique's inventory using ABC analysis in an approximate ratio of 80:15:5. Create a Pareto chart to illustrate your results.
B. How can Brinda ensure inventory accuracy? Please explain in detail, including the reasons for her course of action.
C. What should Brinda do to ensure good inventory management practices?
D. Using the probabilities that were identified by Brinda, how many appointments can Brinda overbook for the Model BB-81-6-01?
E. Using the SPI model, how many appointments can Brinda overbook for the Model BB-81-6-01?
F. What is the inventory policy using the EOQ model?
G. What is the inventory policy using the QDI model?
H. What is the inventory policy using the Q model with and without demand variance?
I. What is the inventory policy using the P model?
J. Compare the four models and recommend the best inventory policy for Bombay Boutique.

Summary

- Inventory management is procuring the right amount of goods and services at the right time and keeping inventory costs low while fulfilling customer orders.

- The push type of making or storing goods is building inventory in anticipation of demand.
- The pull type of making or storing goods is building or storing goods only after an order by a customer.
- The point at which a company switches from making or storing inventory in anticipation of a demand to building or storing in order to react to a demand is called the push-pull boundary.
- In service industries, the push-pull boundary must be placed before a customer arrives. The inventory of services involves processes and steps to complete a sale.
- A push system depends on forecast demand and the production is completed before customer orders. This type of system is useful for companies involved in mass-production items, seasonal items, or food items. Coca-Cola is an example of a company that uses a push type system.
- Effective inventory planning and control is an important part of doing business. A good inventory planning and control system helps a business to achieve better efficiency and profits.
- Inventory can be classified as A, B, and C items. These three distinct items help companies to prioritize their inventory in order to make decisions. Inventory items vary in terms of cost, potential for revenue, and costs due to stockouts. To exercise appropriate control over inventory, companies classify inventory as:
- A items are items that are important, consumed a lot, and have a high dollar value. The high dollar value can be because of either low cost and high usage or high cost and low usage.
- B items are items that are important, sell not as much as A items, and have average dollar value.
- C items are items that are least important, do not sell as much as items A and B, and have lower dollar value. The low dollar value may be because of either low demand or low cost.
- The accuracy of inventory affects forecasting, customer satisfaction, and the overall efficiency of the supply chain.
- Periodic inventory or cycle counting involves a physical count at a certain period of time.
- A perpetual inventory or automated counting method uses software obtaining data from point-of-sale (POS) and asset management systems.
- A barcode represents data in a visual, machine-readable form.
- Radio frequency identification (RFID) is a wireless form of automated identification technology.
- Smart Labels are labels that include a chip, antenna, and bonding wires.
- To build inventory, businesses rely on planning, designing, and implementing inventory policies.

- An inventory ordering policy is a set of rules set by a company on when and how much to order products or stock for replenishment.
- An inventory cycle is the process of ordering and receiving inventory over time.
- Economic Order Quantity (EOQ) is an ideal fixed order size that minimizes inventory costs such as holding costs and order costs.
- The quantity discount inventory (QDI) model is used to find the optimal order size when prices vary with order size as discounts.
- The single-period inventory (SPI) model addresses how much to order for items purchased one time, expected to be used once, and not reordered again with no leftover stocks.
- The multi-period inventory model addresses how much to order as well as when to reorder in each period before the stocks are sold out completely.
- The key difference between the single-period model and multi-period model is that the multi-period model may involve stock leftovers from previous periods.
- The fixed quantity model (Q model) is where the order size remains fixed and is reordered upon a decision when the inventory level drops to a specified quantity.
- The reorder point is time when inventory is reordered and happens when the inventory of an item reaches a predetermined quantity.
- The order cycle service level is an indicator of the probability of maintaining enough stock to meet demand.
- The fixed time period model (P model) is where inventory is reordered at regular fixed time intervals and the order size varies.

Review Questions

1. What is inventory management?
2. What is a push type and what is a pull type of inventory system?
3. Define a push-pull boundary.
4. What is effective inventory planning and control?
5. How is inventory classified?
6. Describe A, B, and C items.
7. What is inventory accuracy?
8. What is periodic inventory?
9. What is perpetual inventory?
10. Describe various technologies used in inventory management.
11. What are the different costs related to inventory?
12. What is an inventory ordering policy?
13. Define an inventory cycle.
14. What is an EOQ model?
15. Describe a QDI model.

16. What is a single-period inventory (SPI) model?
17. What is a multi-period inventory model?
18. Describe a fixed quantity model (Q model).
19. What is a reorder point?
20. Describe an order cycle service level.
21. Describe a fixed time period model (P model).
22. Explain the differences between the Q model and P model.

Critical Thinking Questions

1. What are the key differences between push and pull inventory systems?
2. Do service industries or manufacturing industries use push systems?
3. Do service industries or manufacturing industries use pull systems?
4. How do inventory items vary?
5. What impacts inventory accuracy?
6. Why do businesses hold inventory?
7. Is there a set amount of safety stock that a business should carry?
8. What are the differences between barcodes, RFID, and smart labels?
9. Why is RFID important for today's businesses?
10. What are the differences between a single-period and multi-period model?
11. When is a single-period inventory mode appropriate?
12. What are the differences between a P model and a Q model?
13. Consider the following services and determine what type of inventory model is used:
    a. Filling up a vending machine with products
    b. Filling up gas in your automobile
    c. Going to pick up groceries from a supermarket
    d. Buying supplemental vitamins
    e. Buying personal care products like soap, shampoo, conditioner, and deodorant
    f. Paper and magazines delivered to you
    g. Buying drinking water
    h. Ordering textbooks for your classes
    i. Buying a ticket for a Cubs game

Problem Solving Questions

1. The following table shows a few of your company's inventory.

Items	A	B	C	D	E	F	G	H	I	J	K
Unit Cost	$150.00	$125.00	$115.00	$120.00	$80.00	$95.00	$85.00	$75.00	$40.00	$25.00	$10.00
Annual Sales	30,000	35,000	3,000	2,000	25,000	30,000	28,000	30,000	12,000	25,000	50,000

   a. Classify the inventory.
   b. Develop a Pareto chart.
2. A company uses 10,000 mechanical pencils annually. Annual holding cost of pencils is 2¢ per pencil and the ordering cost is $25. Determine the optimal order quantity.
3. Reynold Inn in Washtenaw, MI, fills up for the local university's games. Ray, the owner, finds a room in another nearby hotel for $100 for any overbooking and the average rate is $90 a room. If the average cancellation is four with a standard deviation of 1.5, how many rooms can Ray overbook?
4. Restore LLC is a small computer parts manufacturer in Reston, VA. The company uses 3,000 pounds of Cadmium a year. The company pays $5 per pound currently and expends $80 every time they order the material. Their annual holding cost of Cadmium is 50¢ per pound.
   a. What is the total cost and order size?
   b. If the holding cost is 15% of the purchase price per pound, what is the total cost and order size?
   c. If the supplier offers a quantity discount of $4.50 for a 1,000 pounds order and $4.25 for up to 3,000 pounds order and $4 for more than 3,000 pounds determine the order size that will minimize the total cost.
5. Hill Auto Parts, a manufacturing company uses approximately 300 specialized anchors a day in their assembly line for 360 days in 2022. Their suppliers deliver the anchors with a lead time of four days. The daily demand is a normal distribution with a mean of 300 anchors and a standard deviation of 8 anchors. The cost of placing an order is $12 and the cost of holding inventory is $0.60 per unit per year. If the company wants to maintain an order cycle supply level of 98%, what is the order policy for the anchors? How much is their safety stock?
6. If the supplier to Hill Ayto Parts is under a supply chain pressure and informs the company that the lead time will be five days, what is the order policy for the anchors? How much is their safety stock?

7. Rubik Fabricators uses dye in its production. They order dye from one of their long-time suppliers every 30 days. The supplier takes 5 days to deliver the order. Their current inventory is 5,000 pounds of dye and their current usage for the year 2011 is on an average 800 pounds a day with a standard deviation of 23 pounds. If the company is determined to have a 95% order cycle service level, what is the order quantity? What is the reorder point?

8. Terry's Tavern uses 6,000 bottles of imported wine each year. The wine costs $4 per bottle and is served only in whole bottles. Ben figures that it costs $12 each time an order is placed and the holding costs are 15% of the purchase price. It takes 3 weeks for an order to arrive. Weekly demand is 120 bottles with a standard deviation of 30 bottles. If Ben is thinking of 95% order cycle service level, what is order size and when should the order be placed?

9. Philip's Paint Supply sells interior latex paint in a wide variety of colors. The assorted colors are mixed to order, so Philip Kale (the owner-operator of the store) only needs to carry inventory of a few different tint bases rather than an inventory of every color a customer may want to purchase. Daily demand for semi-gloss light tint base is normally distributed with a mean of 24 gallons and a standard deviation of 4 gallons. The tint base supplier promises delivery of orders in 3 days. Philip's cost for placing an order with the supplier is $65, and he estimates annual inventory carrying cost to be $3 per gallon. Assume that Philip's Paint Supply is open for business every day of the 365-days year. Given this information, Philip wishes to study two inventory management approaches. He seeks your help in developing a fixed-quantity inventory policy and a fixed-period inventory policy.

   a. Prepare and express carefully including any assumption that you make, a fixed-quantity inventory policy for the situation described above.

   b. Prepare, and express carefully, a fixed-period inventory policy for the situation described above. Assume that the order interval has been set as 13 days.

   c. Did you notice that the cost of a gallon of light tint base is not mentioned in this problem? Why is it not a factor in this analysis?

10. Craig's corner grocery buys fresh cabbage every three days for $3.50 a box of six and sells a cabbage for $2. Craig sells the unsold cabbages to a local zoo for 10¢ a piece after three days of purchase. The average demand for the cabbages is 20 boxes for the three-day period with a standard deviation of 9 boxes. How many cabbages should Craig buy next time around?

11. Ray Rubio, the local baker bakes fresh cakes every morning. A strawberry shortcake costs $7 for the bakery and they sell that cake for $18. Ray donates any unsold cake to the local homeless shelter for free. How many cakes should Rubio bake each day?

12. Tim London is a freshman at Coolidge High School in the suburbs of Des Moines, IA. Every morning, he fills up the newspaper dispenser located near the breakfast buffet of the Marriot with *Des Moines Times*. Tim buys newspapers from a local vendor for $0.50 a copy which he sells for $1. The daily demand at the Marriot has a normal distribution with a mean of 80 and a standard deviation equal to 4.
    a. How many newspapers should Tim buy each morning?
    b. What is the probability that the newspaper dispenser will run out of newspapers?

13. Nemards sells 5,000 bar stools a year. The annual holding costs is $4 per unit and ordering cost is $50 per order. If the cost of the unit is $40 per unit, what is the order size using the EOQ model? What is the total inventory cost?

14. Reza's Carpets sells fine Persian carpets. The demand for Iranian carpets is 500 per year. The store is open from 8am to 8pm for 365 days. Reza orders new carpets every 15 days and it takes 30 days for the carpets to be delivered. The standard deviation of demand for the carpets is 8 a day. Reza counted 120 carpets that day before he placed the order. Reza wishes for an inventory ordering policy with a 98% probability of not stocking out. How many carpets should he order?

15. Zimmerman sells pianos and their pianos and service are well known in the southeast part of Indiana. The annual demand for pianos is 1,300 and the weekly demand is 35 units with a standard deviation of 8 units. The cost of placing an order is $900, and the time from ordering to receiving the pianos is 6 weeks. The annual inventory carrying cost is $200 per unit.
    a. If the store wants an order cycle service level of 98%, what is the reorder point?
    b. If Zimmerman wants to reduce the safety stock by 25%, then what is the new order cycle service level?

References

1. Lin, R. (2019). The importance of successful inventory management to enterprises: A case study of Wal-Mart. In *2019 International Conference on Management, Finance and Social Sciences Research (MFSSR 2019)*, Lyon, France, February 2-4, 2019.

2. NAMA. (2022). *History of convenience services*. Retrieved July 14, 2022, from https://namanow.org/ convenience-services/history-of-convenience -services/

3. Chopra, S., & Lariviere, M. A. (2005, October 15). Managing service inventory to improve performance. *MIT Sloan Management Review.*

4. Morey, R.C. (1985). Estimating service level impacts from changes in cycle count, buffer stock, or corrective action. *Journal of Operations Management, 5*(4), 411–418.

5. Vaidyanathan, G. (2005). Automated identification and data collection in global supply chain. *Proceedings of ISECON 2005,* Columbus, OH, October 7–9, 2005.

6. Zhang, D., Xu, H., & Wu, Y. (2009). Single and multi-period optimal inventory control models with risk-averse constraints. *European Journal of Operational Research, 199*(2), 420–434.

7. Kay, M. (2022, February 28). Walmart's smart label program is stunning, but not surprising. *Forbes.*

8. Adhi, P., Harris, T., & Hough, G.(2021, May 7). RFID's renaissance in retail. *McKinsey Articles.* Retrieved July 19, 2022, from https://www.mckinsey.com/industries/retail/our-insights/rfids-renaissance-in-retail.

9. Zhang, D., Xu, H., & Wu, Y. (2009). Single and multi-period optimal inventory control models with risk-averse constraints. *European Journal of Operational Research, 199*(2), 420–434.

10. Jenkins, A. (2022). *8 Best Practices in Restaurant Inventory Management.* Retrieved July 13, 2022, from https://www.netsuite.com/portal/resource/articles/inventory-management/restaurant-inventory-management.shtml.

PROCUREMENT, GLOBAL SOURCING, AND RECEIVING

Learning Objectives

- Define procurement.
- Explain the procurement process.
- Explain procurement strategy.
- Describe the purpose of procurement objectives.
- Explain procurement risk mitigation.
- Describe green procurement.
- Describe how to mitigate procurement risks.
- Explain green procurement.
- Explain cost reduction methods in procurement.
- Calculate total cost of ownership.
- Perform a procurement analysis.
- Calculate the breakeven analysis of make versus buy.
- Describe global supply and outsourcing.
- Identify the potential problem areas in outsourcing.
- Describe how to select suppliers.
- Explain how a purchase order is processed in organizations.
- Explain how goods are received and inspected.
- Define e-procurement and explain its features.

Starbucks, the coffee company from Seattle, got the name after a character from Moby Dick. They opened their first store in 1971 and since then, the company has opened more than 32,000 stores worldwide. Starbucks offers more than 87,000 drink combinations to its customers. With a revenue of over $26.5 billion, Starbucks has the second most valuable brand of fast service restaurants in 2020.

© Seberang Pintu/Shutterstock.com; © Alextype/Shutterstock.com; © Grand Warszawski/Shutterstock .com; © DenisMArt/Shutterstock.com; © Nor Gal/Shutterstock.com.

Starbucks procures 3% of the world's coffee, sourced from more than 400,000 farmers in 30 countries. The company practices Coffee and Farmer Equity (C.A.F.E.), an ethical standard launched in 2014. The C.A.F.E. Practices is a verification program that measures coffee farms against some socioeconomic criteria designed to promote the transparent, profitable, and sustainable coffee growing practices while protecting the well-being of coffee farmers and workers, their families, and their communities. The C.A.F.E. Practices program has helped Starbucks to create a long-term supply of high-quality coffee and has positively impacted the lives and livelihoods of the coffee farmers and their communities. The C.A.F.E Practices program uses four criteria including economic transparency, social responsibility, environmental leadership, and quality. For example, the economic transparency directs the suppliers to submit the evidence of payments made for the coffee beans throughout the supply chain including how much was paid directly to the farmers for their coffee. The company protects the rights of the people working on their farms and works to promote a safe, fair, and humane work environment. This includes wages and benefits, hiring practices, hours of work, use of protective equipment, access to medical care and education, and a zero- tolerance policy for any form of child labor. The program promotes sustainable agricultural practices including measures to protect water quality, improve soil health, preserve biodiversity, reduce agrochemical use, and conserve water and energy. The company requires that all coffee must pass their standards for high quality.

The sourcing process starts with evaluating the coffee quality. The suppliers agree to provide economic transparency down to the producer level even before any business is conducted. The suppliers then submit a formal application to Starbucks detailing the entire coffee supply chain and commit to implementing the C.A.F.E. Practices guidelines. Approved third-party organizations conduct inspections at farms to evaluate the performance against more than 200 indicators in a performance scorecard. The detailed verification reports are then submitted to Starbucks to assign the C.A.F.E. Practice status. Once approved, the suppliers are responsible for upholding C.A.F.E. Practices. To maintain an active status in the program, each supplier is required to undergo reverification regularly.

Starbucks recognizes that their success is linked to the success of the farmers and the suppliers who grow and produce their products. The company is committed to ethical procurement, the highest quality products, and supporting communities[1].

Procurement

All organizations need both suppliers and customers. An organization can operate only after their suppliers provide goods and services and survive only after their goods and services are bought by their customers. The upstream of the supply chain management or the supply side, deals with the suppliers of organizations. For a manufacturing company, the raw materials and the parts are supplied by their suppliers and for a services company, the suppliers provide the goods and the services.

For any organization, the procurement from the suppliers and the supply functions that are employed for procurement play a vital part on the supply side of supply chain management. Organizations view the procurement and the supply chain as critical for their bottom line in terms of cost reduction as well as revenue generation. A company's supply chain managers constantly look for innovative methods to cut costs and increase revenues. To accomplish revenue increases and cost reductions, effective procurement in efficient supply chain processes must be practiced. This is because procurement impacts the inventory, quality, new product development, and delivery of goods and services.

What is procurement? Procurement is the process of acquiring the required materials, services, and equipment from suppliers and other external sources. Procurement involves several activities including:

- Identifying procurement requirements,
- Devising a purchasing strategy,
- Selecting suppliers,
- Acquiring goods and services,
- Working with an external source,
- Managing supplier contracts,
- Receiving and paying for supplies, and
- Managing suppliers.

> **Procurement**
> Procurement is the process of acquiring required materials, services, and equipment from suppliers and external sources.

Procurement Process

Procurement is concerned with purchasing by direct spend and indirect spend. The direct spend includes both production or service-related items and the indirect spend involves non-production and non-service-oriented items. Typical production items include raw materials used for manufacturing goods. Procuring eggs and flour are examples of service-related items for a restaurant. Buying cooling fluids for the production machines is a non-production item. Internet connection through an Internet Service Provider (ISP) is an example of a non-service-oriented item. The traditional procurement function involves many departments including accounts payable, finance management, legal, material management, logistics, production planning, quality management, human resources, and information systems.

A simple procurement process is shown in Figure 8-1. The requisitions for procurement are initiated by employees in a company. The procurement department with the functional manager of the employee who requested the purchase approves the requisition, initiates a purchase order, and sends the purchase order to the company's accounting department. The accounting department sends the purchase order through the mail or email to the supplier. The supplier's sales department initiates a sales order. Once the sales order is approved by the buyer, the supplier's order fulfillment department sends the material using their logistics and transportation to the buyer. They also inform their accounting department of the material flow and the accounting department contacts the buyer's accounting department with an invoice for the order. Upon receiving and verifying the ordered material and the invoice, the buyer pays the supplier. The traditional procurement process is shown in Figure 8-1 below[2]:

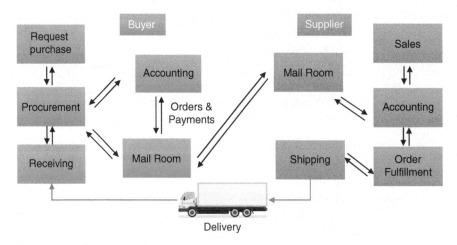

Figure 8-1 Traditional Procurement Process

Source: Ganesh Vaidyanathan and © Modvector/Shutterstock.com

Procurement consists of three main dimensions including strategy, sourcing, and transaction as shown in Figure 8-2. Each dimension has four processes and the combined 12 processes constitute the procurement functionality of a company.

Strategy
- Identify business need
- Define requirements
- Set procurement objectives
- Devise procurement strategy

Sourcing
- Request and approve goods and services
- Identify and select suppliers and outsources
- Negotiate and manage contracts
- Manage suppliers and outsources

Transaction
- Initiate procurement
- Receive goods and services
- Inspect received goods and services
- Manage payments

Figure 8-2 Procurement Process

Procurement Strategy

The term procurement strategy refers to a long-term plan to cost-effectively acquire the necessary supplies from a list of vendors who will deliver quality goods on time, abiding by the purchasing terms. Typically, a procurement strategy depends on a number of factors like the purchase timeline, the available budget, and the total cost of ownership. A procurement strategy often focuses on how to reduce the costs, mitigate the risks, and manage the supply base. According to a recent survey by Deloitte, 78% of Chief Procurement Officers (CPO) around the world identify the reduction of procurement-related costs as the top priority in their procurement strategy[3]. In the same study, 51% of the CPOs believed that their teams do not have sufficient capabilities to deliver their procurement strategy and about 54% said that their second priority is to manage the risks in the procurement process.

Why should firms devise and follow a procurement strategy? A robust procurement strategy will minimize errors, reduce costs, eliminate maverick spending, mitigate risks, and ensure compliance with the procurement policy. The procurement strategy consists of the following processes:

- Identify business need,
- Define requirements,
- Set procurement objectives, and
- Devise procurement strategy.

FROM PRACTICE: Streamlining Procurement Strategy at Volvo

© William Barton/Shutterstock.com

Volvo, the Swedish luxury car manufacturer, is known for its safety and its Swedish heritage and design. In the United States, Volvo has 281 retail locations. "A major focus is retailer profitability and one way to help retailers with the bottom line is by simplifying purchasing," says Adam Clarke, vice president of retailer network development for Volvo Cars. Volvo Cars' procurement team negotiated contracts with suppliers to keep its facilities stocked with supplies. Recently, the automaker worked with Amazon to help its dealers scale purchasing power and drive value. In collaboration with Amazon, Volvo launched a streamlined purchasing program to promote corporate buying policies and empower retail employees to make informed buying decisions so that they can get the items they need to drive high-quality performance. The retailers comply with the internal buying policies because they are purchasing from the approved list of suppliers. The retailers also use a centralized source for procurement which gives Volvo visibility across locations to develop consistency in its procurement practices[4].

Identify Business Need

Procurement in a company comes from the definite need for a material or a service. For example, if an employee's office computer does not work, there is a definite need for a new computer. In that case, the Information Systems (IS) department would know what computer to buy for that employee and would initiate the procurement. In most instances, the person who initiates the procurement should know the requirements of the intended purchase—what to order, how much to order, when to order, and why it is needed.

The procurement department is responsible for ordering the materials and the services required for the operations of the company. Apart from the regular requirements for operations of a firm, the procurement needs in a company arise when:

- Management makes a new decision,
- Firms change capacity requirements,
- Firms develop new capacity requirements,
- Firms face new market demands,
- Innovative technologies are introduced, and
- A feasibility study unveils new requirements.

Define Requirements

Once the procurement needs are identified, the next step is to define the needs as requirements. Companies define procurement requirements using an established process. For example, if the IT department of a firm needs a few desktop computers for their new employees, even the chief of the IT department cannot go to a computer store and pick up the new computers. Why? The reason is that every company has a purchasing process in place with proper approvals in place. An effective procurement process will reduce unnecessary expenses and spending.

A requirements process starts with a purchase requisition form. A purchase requisition form is a document used by an employee to purchase goods or services on behalf of their firm. These purchases may be for any business operation such as raw materials, equipment, or even office supplies. An employee can fill out the purchase requisition form and submit the form to the purchasing department after the necessary approvals. If the requested item is a simple item and of small value like office supplies or a computer, the purchase order is issued to a vendor to purchase the requested items.

For requisitions of strategic value or for items amounting to a considerable sum of money, the process is different and it involves a strategic sourcing policy of a company. The next section discusses this part of the process in detail. For direct spend materials, the process involves aggregate planning, scheduling, materials requirement planning, and inventory management. These are discussed in detail in the following chapters of this book.

Set Procurement Objectives

It is important to set procurement objectives. The purpose of the procurement objectives is to provide a clear picture of the goals of procurement. The procurement objectives give procurement employees guidance and direction. They help to motivate employees to attain the best results. The objectives also help to evaluate the performance of the organization. The procurement objectives are as follows:

Ensure quality materials. The primary objective of procurement in an organization is to ensure an uninterrupted flow of quality raw materials and the required services at the lowest total cost so that the company can produce goods and services to the satisfaction of its customers.

Support operational requirements. The procurement objectives should include the business requirements of a company, to purchase products and services at the right price from a reliable source and meet the needs of users.

Manage the supply base. The efficient and effective management of the supply base involves the selection of the most dependable suppliers and mitigation of any supplier risks.

Support organizational goals. The procurement function must develop strong relationships and good communications with both the internal functional departments and the external vendors and suppliers. Also, all procurement strategies must align with organizational strategy.

Standardize processes. Standardization of processes means the existence of a common agreed upon procurement process that is followed by all procurement professionals in a company.

Organizations can accomplish these objectives by:

- Selecting dependable suppliers who can provide the best materials and services for making quality products and provide valuable services to their customers,
- Collaborating closely with strategic suppliers to improve the quality of raw materials and services,
- Using the expertise of their suppliers to improve their own internal processes,
- Involving strategic suppliers in their new product development efforts,
- Improving information flow with their suppliers,
- Purchasing products and services at the lowest cost of ownership and as per specifications,
- Identifying risks and mitigating any supplier risks,
- Developing strong relationships and good communications with both internal functional departments and external vendors and suppliers,
- Aligning all procurement strategies with organizational strategy,
- Standardizing processes and training employees to follow them, and
- Being a crucial link between strategic suppliers and their own operations.

Devise Procurement Strategy

A company's procurement strategy is about how to implement its procurement process. Organizations use the strategy as a roadmap to conduct its procurement activities. To devise a strategy, organizations can choose to focus on a single priority or more than one, depending on their business requirements. According to a recent survey by Deloitte, other than cost reduction and risk mitigation, supplier management, sustainable or green procurement, and global sourcing are key strategies for many companies[5]. We will discuss global sourcing and supplier management in the next sections. In this section, we will focus on risk management, sustainable or green procurement, and cost reduction.

Risk Management

Risk management is the process that allows procurement managers to mitigate the risks in the procurement process. A well-structured risk management methodology when used effectively can help procurement managers to identify appropriate controls, monitor the risks, and mitigate the procurement risks. A procurement manager should have a better understanding of all the risks that are part of the supply chain. Such knowledge will result in improved decision making that leads to better control over all procurement activities. Better understanding of the risks leads to minimizing the risks.

The risk management process consists of identification of the risks, assessment of the value of these risks, and development of the proposed plans to mitigate these risks, and the monitoring and control of the risks.

FROM PRACTICE: Risk Management at HP

Hewlett-Packard (HP) developed and implemented a mathematical model, business process, and software to measure and manage risks in procurement. The software-enabled business process helped HP to manage over $7 billion in spending, resulting in material-cost savings of $128 million. Over the years, HP has realized more than $425 million in cumulative cost savings using the Procurement Risk Management (PRM) approach. The approach is based on uncertainties in product demand, component cost, and component availability. The PRM approach was a response to the price volatility of the Dynamic Random-Access Memory (DRAM), uncertainty on the availability of other hi-tech components including semiconductor products, and product demand uncertainty[6].

© monticello/Shutterstock.com

Green Procurement

Green procurement or sustainable procurement is being followed by many companies who have an interest in sustaining their business for the near future. A growing need to protect our environment has propelled the adoption of green procurement. Many companies and their supplier partners are obtaining ISO 14001 certificates. ISO 14001 consists of the environmental management standards to minimize the impact on the environment by the operations of a company. Receiving the ISO 14001 certificate shows that the company is in compliance with the applicable laws, regulations, and other environmentally oriented requirements. There are more than 300,000 certifications to ISO 14001 in 171 countries around the world[7].

Green procurement is about making environmentally conscious decisions throughout the procurement process. Right from the development of the procurement strategy to purchasing the supplies and disposing of the waste, green procurement should be the factor for all decisions. As we discussed in Chapter 1, firms must incorporate sustainability or corporate social responsibility (CSR) in their business strategies. The procurement strategy is an important part of a business strategy. Companies must endorse and choose to procure environmentally friendly or environmentally preferable goods and services to be in compliance with green procurement.

What are the environmentally friendly or preferable goods and services? According to the United States General Services Administration (USGSA), the following are considered environmentally friendly or preferable goods and services:

- Biobased products derived from plants and other renewable agricultural, marine, and forestry materials. These products provide an alternative to conventional petroleum-derived products and include a diverse range of offerings such as lubricants, detergents, inks, fertilizers, and bioplastics.
- Recycled content products designated by the U.S. Environmental Protection Agency (EPA)[8]. The EPA has designated a list of recycled content products. Building insulation, cement and concrete, awards and plaques, binders, clipboards, printer toner cartridges, papers, engine coolants, and tires are examples.
- Energy efficient products and services, such as ENERGY STAR® certified products as identified by the EPA and the U.S. Department of Energy (DOE). Heat pumps, refrigerators, computers, monitors, and televisions are examples.
- Products that contain Significant New Alternative Policy (SNAP) chemicals or other alternatives to ozone-depleting substances and high global warming potential hydrofluorocarbons. Adhesives, aerosols, cleaning solvents, refrigerants, and foam blowing agents are examples.

Organizations can use the following steps for the implementation of green procurement:

- Incorporate green procurement policies in their procurement strategy,
- Educate the users and suppliers on green procurement,
- Develop green procurement performance metrics,
- Buy and use green products,
- Use green services,
- Reduce or eliminate the creation or release of pollutants or toxic compounds,
- Remove pollutants or hazardous waste from the environment, and
- Reduce greenhouse gas emissions.

FROM PRACTICE: Green Environment at Ford

Ford, one of the major automakers in the world, announced that it is the first automotive company to certify all of its plants under ISO 14001. Independent auditors evaluate environmental processes and system performance to certify companies with ISO 14001. The achievement is to be commended as Ford's 140 plants in 26 countries have been certified. Moreover, the recent implementation of certified environmental management systems is paying big dividends for Ford. For example, Ford has reduced the amount of disposable packaging coming into plants by 163 million pounds in 2 years alone. Ford reduced its water consumption by a million gallons a day at its truck facility in Wayne, Michigan. The same plant is saving $66,000 a year in energy costs by replacing 1,975 fluorescent bulbs with metal halide bulbs[9].

Cost Reduction

Cost reduction is the most important procurement strategy for many companies. It involves reducing unnecessary expenses. The strategy to reduce cost includes supplier consolidation, effective supplier management, estimation of total cost of ownership, and performing make-buy analysis. We will discuss supplier consolidation and supplier management under sourcing in the next section. Let us discuss the total cost of ownership and make-buy analysis in this section.

Total Cost of Ownership

A product, such as a good or a service, is purchased by a company. This item is used by the company for some time and then the company disposes of the product after its useful life. For example, a company buys a computer, uses the computer for a few years, and then disposes of the computer. The total cost of ownership (TCO) is the total cost of the purchase of the computer, costs incurred while in use, and the cost of disposal of the computer. TCO can be classified as three distinct costs including:

1. Acquisition costs,
2. Possession costs, and
3. Disposal costs.

Acquisition Costs

Acquisition costs include all the activities spent on the procurement of that item. For example, a company sends a purchasing manager to a conference to learn about the latest technology. The purchase manager learns about the technology and its associated products. The manager visits the suppliers to learn more about the equipment and the suppliers. The procurement manager then purchases the equipment through the company's internal process. All the costs associated with all these activities plus the actual purchase price, taxes, tariffs, customs fees, and transportation costs are part of acquisition costs of the product.

Possession Costs

After the purchase, products are used in companies. The ongoing use of products involves many costs. For example, the equipment that was bought by the procurement manager uses electricity. The equipment has been scheduled for pre-maintenance services and the company also spends money on repairs and maintenance of the equipment. The company may spend money toward cleaning and improvements. All these costs are part of the possession costs.

Disposal Costs

The disposal costs include the actual costs of disposal of products and the liability costs. The equipment bought by the procurement manager, after years of use, is finally retired. The equipment can be disposed of in a number of ways including demolition, recycling, or sale. If the equipment were exposed to an environment that could introduce or spread contaminants such as decommissioned wastewater, there are additional disposal costs. Selling equipment brings in some salvage value. An asset's salvage value is the estimated sale value once its useful life is finished. Example 8-1 shows how to estimate total cost of ownership (TCO).

Example 8-1

e-Printers, Inc., a printing company from Princeton, PA, bought a printing press. They paid $240,000 including taxes. The transportation costs were $5,200. The pre-maintenance costs amounted to $2,600 per year. The yearly maintenance costs amounted to $3,200. The company retired the equipment at the end of the fourth year of useful life with a disposal cost of $12,000 with a salvage value of $10,000. What is the total cost of ownership for this equipment?

Using the costs described above,

	Year 0	Year 1	Year 2	Year 3	Year 4
Cost of equipment	$240,000				
Transportation costs	$5,200				
Total acquisition costs	$245,200				
Pre-maintenance costs	$2,600	$2,600	$2,600	$2,600	$2,600
Maintenance costs	$3,200	$3,200	$3,200	$3,200	$3,200
Total possession costs	$5,800	$5,800	$5,800	$5,800	$5,800
Disposal costs					$12,000
Salvage value					$10,000
Total disposal costs					$2,000
	$251,000	$5,800	$5,800	$5,800	$7,800
Total cost of ownership					**$276,200**

Analysis: The total cost of ownership includes all the costs from the original cost of the equipment to the disposal costs net the salvage value. This example shows the TCO without considering the time value of money.

Procurement Analysis

The total cost of ownership can be used in a procurement analysis. Any equipment that is bought by a company should help the company to generate revenues. Companies must produce the predetermined benefits of a procurement, especially if the item to be purchased is a big-ticket item. A furnace, a printing press, a high-end copy machine, and a manufacturing machine are all examples of such big-ticket items. A procurement analysis takes into account all the estimated costs of acquisition, ownership, and disposal before buying an item. Example 8-2 shows a procurement analysis.

Example 8-2

Prepare a procurement analysis for e-Printers, Inc. from Example 8-1, if they estimate $95,000 per year as revenues by using the printing press. Assume a discount rate of 10%.

Using the costs and estimated revenues described above,

	Year 0	Year 1	Year 2	Year 3	Year 4
Price of equipment	$240,000				
Tranporatation costs	$5,200				
Pre-maintenance costs	$2,600	$2,600	$2,600	$2,600	$2,600
Maintenance costs	$3,200	$3,200	$3,200	$3,200	$3,200
Disposal costs					$12,000
Salvage value					$10,000
Total costs	$251,000	$5,800	$5,800	$5,800	$7,800
Revenue from using the equipment	$95,000	$95,000	$95,000	$95,000	$95,000
Total cashflow	−$156,000	$89,200	$89,200	$89,200	$87,200
Discount factor	1.00	0.91	0.83	0.75	0.68
Present Value	−$156,000	$81,091	$73,719	$67,017	$59,559
Net Present Value	**$125,386**				

Analysis: Using the estimated total cost of ownership and the estimated income generation, the net present value (NPV) can be calculated for the procurement analysis. With a positive NPV of $125,386, this procurement project was acceptable in the first place. The present value of the equipment at the time of purchase is $125,386.

Make or Buy Decision

Organizations make components and assemble them as products. For example, a car has over 30,000 parts that includes screws, nuts, and bolts. It is not cost-effective for a car manufacturer to manufacture all the parts. Many of the parts are manufactured by suppliers either from inside the manufacturing country or abroad.

Companies must make wise decisions to make or buy parts. There are parts that can be either made in-house or bought from a supplier. A company needs to do a make or buy decision analysis for such parts. Such decisions are useful when considering outsourcing certain components or assembly parts. For a make or buy decision, a breakeven analysis of the quantity of parts that is needed must be done. We make a basic assumption that there exists a linear variable cost relationship. A breakeven point can be determined by setting up cost equations for both the buyer and the supplier and solve for the number of items that are needed by the buyer at a breakeven point. Example 8-3 shows a make or buy decision for an automobile part.

Example 8-3

A car manufacturer is making a decision whether to buy or make a component that is used in manufacturing their cars. They determine that the annual requirement is 2,000 units. To make the part, they have to invest $15,000 for the equipment and they estimate that the cost to manufacture the part is $4 per unit. A supplier provides a quote of $15 per unit to supply the same part with a specified quality from the car manufacturer. Decide whether to buy or make. What is the cost difference?

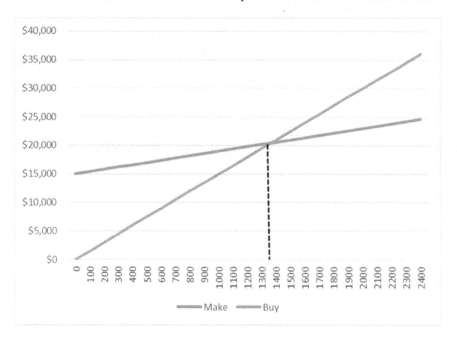

The breakeven quantity, Q is found by setting the cost equations of make and buy equal to one another as follows:

Total cost to make = Total cost to buy
Therefore, $15,000 + $4 \times Q = $15 \times Q$
Rearranging the above equation gives us $15,000 + 4Q = 15Q$ or
$11Q = 15,000$
Therefore, the breakeven point is $Q = 15,000/11 = 1,364$ units.
The total cost at breakeven point is $1,364 \times 15 = $20,460$

Analysis: From the figure and analysis, we can see that if the car manufacturer requires more than 1,364 units, it is cheaper to make the part in-house. Otherwise, buying is cheaper. For example, let us look at this analysis for 1,400 parts:

The cost difference for 1,400 parts is:
To make, it will cost $15,000 + (4 \times 1,400) = $20,600$
To buy, it will cost $15 \times 1,400 = $21,000$

Therefore, the cost difference in is $21,000 − $20,600 = 400. For every extra part over 1,364, it will cost about $11 more if the company goes for outsourcing.

FROM PRACTICE: Cost Reduction Strategy at Kohl's

Kohl's, the American department store retail chain, operates in 1,158 locations across the country. A group of investors, who own 9.5% of the company's stock, wanted the company to focus on lowering sourcing costs, improving inventory turns, and assessing the indirect spend to increase the retailer's profit margins. The investor group explained that the retailer is overpaying with a sourcing agreement it had with a third-party agent that accounts for 20% of its total purchases. The group also advised the company to lower the sourcing costs. With the pandemic raging for the third year in a row, negotiating the terms of contract can give suppliers incentive to cut deals for buyers[10].

© QualityHD/Shutterstock.com

Sourcing

Sourcing is a process that includes activities such as identifying and assessing the potential suppliers as well as selecting an appropriate supplier. A purchase requisition from an employee or a department in a company is used as the starting point for sourcing. An appropriate supplier is selected for procurement. Once a supplier is selected, a contract is negotiated and signed or an agreement is reached between the buyer and the supplier. The sourcing dimension includes the following processes:

- Request and approve goods and services,
- Identify and select suppliers and outsources,
- Negotiate and manage contracts, and
- Manage suppliers and outsources.

Request and Approve Goods and Services

The requisition to purchase the materials or the services includes the requestor with full credentials such as the department, phone number, suggested suppliers, description of materials and or services, quantity, when needed, and special instructions, if any. The appropriate authorities of the organization must approve the requisition. Once the purchase requisition is approved, the procurement department starts the supplier selection process.

Identify and Select Suppliers

Supplier selection is an important activity in procurement and involves identifying qualified sources. Finding the right supplier for an item or service is often difficult, especially if companies want to remain competitive in their industry. A supplier typically controls the buyer's cost, quality, and delivery of supplies and services. Companies find their potential suppliers in many ways including:

- Searching through Internet search engines to find potential suppliers,
- Searching from free supplier directories which contain profiles for hundreds or thousands of manufacturers, wholesalers, and suppliers,
- Browsing through the National Association of Manufacturers member list,
- Contacting leads and referrals from professional networks and personal networks, and
- Searching for products by their North American Industry Classification System (NAICS) code.

Once potential suppliers are identified, the next step is to select the suppliers. Companies contact the identified, potential suppliers. This step is followed in a couple of ways depending on whether the material is available in the company's warehouses.

RFQ, RFI, RFP

Three methods are often employed to select a supplier. A competitive bidding method is used when selecting suppliers. Competitive bidding involves a request for bids from many suppliers with whom a client is willing to do business. This process is initiated when the client organization sends a request for quotation (RFQ), a request for information (RFI), or a request for proposal (RFP) from the suppliers. Such information gathering methods are defined as follows:

- An RFI is issued when a client organization wants to gather information about a supplier's materials or services during the initial data-gathering phase of a project. With this information, organizations can decide if they would like to further explore procurement. It is often used to develop a strategy and build a database for an upcoming contract competition.
- An RFQ is used when a client organization has already decided on a particular type of material or service and wishes to see competitive pricing from multiple suppliers. A business sends an RFQ when the quantity of required materials is known.
- An RFP is issued when a client organization wants to purchase a material or a service and chooses to make the specifications available to other suppliers so that the suppliers can submit competitive bids for the products or services. Requests for proposals are usually the costliest process and include various service level agreements and quality standards. RFPs are often used for complex projects requiring multiple sub-contractors. RFPs are mostly issued by government agencies and other organizations in the public sector. They are required to open up competition among private companies and remove any potential bias from the process. The agencies want to ensure that they get the lowest and the most competitive bid.

The goal of issuing an RFQ or RFP is to award the most qualified bidder. Based on the results of these documents and further negotiations, suppliers are selected by a client organization.

Scorecard

To select suppliers, companies employ a scorecard method. The supplier selection involves evaluating potential suppliers using multiple criteria. The criteria used is for screening the suppliers who meet the specifications of a product of a company. This is important when companies are looking for long-lasting partnerships with their suppliers and contactors. Such lasting partnerships can lead to cost reduction, risk mitigation, and reliable procurement of materials and services.

The evaluation and selection of suppliers need a thorough investigation, and organizations have to make sure that the suppliers have the necessary expertise, financial stability, market recognition, trust, management capability, quality commitment, cost structure, fulfillment, and other factors pertinent to their successful delivery of the materials or services. Interviewing the suppliers as well as visiting them is often productive. Discussions with the current customers of suppliers might explain both the positive and negative aspects of their products and services. Evaluating the suppliers may be accomplished by a weighted scorecard in operations and supply chain management.[11] Weighted balanced scorecards are also used to evaluate trade-off issues between performance metrics.[12] Weighted scorecards are extensively used in organizations whenever there is a trade-off or a selection to be made.

One method to evaluate prospective suppliers is to use a **weighted criteria evaluation scorecard**. The weighted criteria evaluation scorecard comprises various categories with each category having multiple factors for evaluating suppliers. Each of these factors of evaluation has a subweight assigned by a buyer and each category has a weight assigned by the buyer. The total of the subweights is equal to the category weight. The weights may be adjusted and may depend on the evaluation criteria of the buyer. Additional items can also be added to each category. In any case, In the supplier evaluation scorecard, weights are distributed to total 100. The supplier is evaluated on each factor as a score ranging from 1 to 5. "1" is assigned to the supplier if the supplier does not meet the expectations of the client. "2" is assigned if the supplier meets little of that subcategory, "3" is assigned for meeting the expectations in that subcategory, "4" for mostly meeting the expectations for that subcategory, and "5" if the expectations are fully met and the client is delighted with the supplier's performance on the factor of evaluation. The weighted score is calculated as follows:

$$Weighted\ Score = \left(\frac{Score}{5}\right) \times Subweight \qquad \text{Eq. 8-1}$$

The following are the steps to evaluate suppliers using a weighted criteria evaluation scorecard and is shown in Example 8-4:

- Identify key supplier performance factors,
- Collect supplier performance data,
- Assign weights to each of the performance factors,
- Evaluate each performance measure on a rating between 0 (fails to meet performance) to 100 (absolutely exceptional to meet performance),
- Multiply the performance measure by the weight of performance factor score,
- Sum the performance factor scores to get an overall score, and
- Classify suppliers based on their overall score as:
  - Unacceptable (if the overall score is less than 70),
  - Conditionally acceptable (if the overall score is between 70 and 90), or
  - Acceptable (if the overall score is over 90).

Example 8-4

You are the Procurement Manager at GoodEats, Inc., a manufacturer of tasty cookies and bakery goods. They are planning to evaluate and select a dependable supplier for yeast, one of the major component of their products.

The company has identified the following performance categories and factors for supplier evaluation:

1. Expertise: Technical expertise, Process expertise, R&D expertise
2. Finance: Debt, Financial Ratios
3. Management capability: Process Management, General Management
4. Quality: Quality Awards, Certifications, 6 Sigma, TQM
5. Cost structure: Cost comparisons, Cost control efforts
6. Delivery: Promised date reputation, Lead-time requirements, Responsiveness
7. Reputation: Community Support, Well known, Trusted

Use your own weights and sub-weights to evaluate a supplier whose scores for each of the factors are 5, 2, 3, 5, 3, 3, 2, 1, 5, 2, 5, 4, 4, 5, 3, 3, 3, 3, and 5. What is the total score and would you select this supplier?

The scorecard for the supplier is shown below:

Category	Weight	Sub weight Score (1–5)×		Weighted Score
Expertise				
Technical expertise	20	10	5	10
Process expertise		5	2	2
R&D expertise		5	3	3
Finance				
Debt	10	5	5	5
Financial Ratios		5	3	3
Management capability				
Process Management	10	7	3	4.2
General Management		3	2	1.2
Quality commitment				
Quality Awards		5	1	1
Certifications	20	5	5	5
Sigma		5	2	2
TQM		5	5	5
Cost structure				
Cost comparisons	20	10	4	8
Cost control efforts		10	4	8
Delivery				
Promised date reputation	10	5	5	5
Lead-time requirements		3	3	1.8
Responsiveness		2	3	1.2
Recognition				
Community Support	10	2	3	1.2
Well known		3	3	1.8
Trusted		5	5	5
Total Score	100			73.4

The weighted score is calculated using Eq. 8-1.

For example, for the category Expertise in the table above:

Weighted score for Technical Expertise = 5/5 × 10 = 10

Weighted score for Process Expertise = 2/5 × 5 = 2

Weighted score for R&D Expertise = 3/5 × 5 = 3

Analysis: Based on the scorecard's total of 73.4, the supplier is conditionally acceptable. If the company cannot find any other supplier, then the company may accept this supplier.

FROM PRACTICE: Supplier Selection at Lowe's

© Ken Wolter/Shutterstock.com

Lowe's, the American home retailing company, sells home improvement products. Lowe's and its related businesses operate more than 2,150 home improvement and hardware stores in North America. Most of Lowe's 7,000 vendors are located within the United States, but the company also has suppliers based in South Korea, Canada, China, and Taiwan. The largest suppliers of Lowe's are Avery Dennison, Illinois Tool Works, Stanley Black & Decker, and Deere & Company. Lowe's supplier diversity practice gives small businesses and companies that are owned, operated, and controlled by women, minorities, veterans, LGBTQ+ persons and persons with disabilities equal footing to work with them while developing their own businesses. Lowe's helps small and diverse businesses reach their goals while enabling us to offer the products and services our customers need. Lowe's sources suppliers that best match their needs, regardless of their business size or classification. Suppliers with a diverse certification from a third-party accreditation is highly recommended. For example, Stay Away Botanical Rodent Repellent developed a women owned business was chosen as a supplier. The repellent is a solution made from essential oils and plant fibers and a natural alternative to other pest prevention products[13].

Outsourcing

Organizations may not be able to do everything on their own. Sometimes, it may be better to get help from outside. Outsourcing is the process whereby a strategic partner implements the client's projects or the client's processes. By outsourcing, the client organizations can take advantage of the global labor pool, the process innovations, and the delivery capabilities of their strategic partners. For example, Delta Air Lines outsourced the reservation services to Wipro, one of India's top IT services companies. Wipro managed Delta's reservations from its Mumbai call center and Delta saved $26 million in 2002 alone. Microsoft, Dell, SAP, Nokia, General Electric, Alcatel-Lucent, and Unilever (UL) have engineering and IT operations in India and China. Walmart benefits from the low-cost manufacturing in China. Many organizations are increasingly relying on the global knowledge available from various sources to support innovation and create competitive advantage for themselves. Outsourcing can be classified as offshoring, nearshoring, insourcing, co-sourcing, and multi-sourcing.

Offshoring

Offshoring is the process of outsourcing a manufacturing or a service process to another country ("off the shores" of the country). This involves making the goods in a strategic partner's location or having the strategic partner make and ship goods and services from a different country in order to reduce costs or obtain better skills. For example, a European appliance maker may outsource a software application to a company in India that specializes in application development to take advantage of the low cost and the skilled labor. In this case, the European organization is the outsourcing organization and the Indian organization is the outsourced organization. Offshoring requires the outsourced organization to have an understanding of both the culture and the language of the country where the outsourcing organization is located.

Nearshoring

Nearshoring is the process of outsourcing a project to another company in a nearby location, state, or country that shares a border with the outsourcing organization's country. For example, if a U.S. company manufactures a subcomponent in Mexico, it is nearshoring.

Insourcing

When a business unit does not have certain skills and uses the skills from other departments within the organization, it is called insourcing. Insourcing usually represents the process of working within an organization to find specialized skills. The customer services department of an organization using the IT department to build a customer satisfaction database is an example of insourcing.

Co-sourcing

Co-sourcing is when the internal staff of an organization works with an external supplier. Co-sourcing is often advantageous to an organization as it minimizes outsourcing risks and brings control that is necessary for a company. An example of co-sourcing is supplementing the inhouse logistics process manager with a logistics expert who has specialized IT skills.

Multi-sourcing

Multi-sourcing brings together multiple sources from both inside and outside an organization. Many organizations use multi-sourcing to reduce outsourcing risks. ABN AMRO partnered with three different Indian companies (Infosys, Patni, and TCS) and with two American companies (Accenture and IBM) to effectively use the specialized expertise of each partner.

Reasons for Outsourcing

Organizations buy or outsource materials and services from suppliers for a number of reasons, including:

Cost savings: Cost is an important reason for outsourcing. Suppliers may have the advantage of economies of scale since they supply the same material to multiple users. The investment in capital equipment may not justify making small quantities of materials in many cases for a company and so they may therefore opt for outsourcing.

Reduce time to market: The use of an outsourced supplier's facilities and capability can reduce the new product time to market.

Insufficient capacity: When an organization is running at or near their maximum capacity, it will be impossible to produce more components in-house. If there is a sudden surge in demand, outsourcing the needed components is a more efficient method than investing to expand for the short term.

Focus on core business: Organizations may not have the necessary technology talent and expertise to produce an item, especially if the item is not their core product. Outsourced contractors may have the necessary certifications and patents to manufacture those items.

Risk transfer: If an organization sees potential risks in manufacturing certain items, they may prefer to transfer and mitigate the risk to an outsourced contractor who may be able to handle such risks better.

Better quality: Outsourced contractors may be able to produce certain items better than an organization because they may have better processes and economies of scale.

Overall flexibility: On many occasions, organizations can access outsourcing contractors across the globe and create a flexible schedule, payment options, and resources for their services. However, there are risks that need to be identified, quantified, and mitigated.

Reasons for Making Products In-House

There are some disadvantages to outsourcing as well, including increased costs, hidden costs, loss of control, cultural differences, difficulties in managing relationships, and negative impact on customers.

Apart from these disadvantages, there are reasons to make products rather than outsourcing, including:

Better control: Making products in-house gives organizations better control over lead time and transportation and warehousing costs.

Protect intellectual property: This is an important reason to make products. Organizations may have developed unique processes to make their products that need to be protected for competitive advantage. In that case, making products is much better than outsourcing.

The advantages and disadvantages of domestic and offshoring are shown in Table 8-1.

Table 8-1 Domestic vs Offshoring Procurements

Domestic		Offshoring	
Advantages	**Disadvantages**	**Advantages**	**Disadvantages**
Perceived higher manufacturing quality and labor standards			Perceived lower manufacturing quality and labor standards
	Higher manufacturing costs	Lower manufacturing costs	
No language barrier			Language, communication, and time-zone barriers
Easier to verify reputable manufacturers	Fewer product choices as many items are not made in North America	Higher number of manufacturers for supplier selection	Costly to verify supplier and visit on-site
Faster shipping time			Longer shipping time
High intellectual property rights protection			Little intellectual property protection
			Cultural differences in business practices
			Higher tariff and customs clearance costs

FROM PRACTICE: Outsourcing at Apple

Apple, the American multinational technology company, specializes in consumer electronics, computer software and online services. Even though Apple's products are designed in the United States, along with R&D and marketing, engineering is conducted globally. Apple utilizes outsourcing partners to supply and manufacture components used in iPhones, iPads, Macs, and wearable devices. Out of the 30 countries where Apple devices were manufactured in 2020, 6 accounted for over 80% of annual production. China contributed 42%, followed by Japan (16%),

(continued)

the United States (9%), Taiwan (6%), South Korea (5%), and Vietnam (4%). China's leading position in Apple's supply chain is attributable to several factors, including industrial infrastructure, the availability of a large, affordable, and skilled labor force, and the low cost of production. China is the third-largest market for Apple by revenue, behind the Americas and Europe. Moreover, China will be a vital market for Apple in the future.

India is also an outsourcing partner for Apple. Infosys, TCS, Wipro, and Cognizant, all of whom are software and application companies, are the partners. In recent years, Apple's contract manufacturers have expanded into India, including a factory owned by Foxconn[14].

Negotiate and Manage Contracts

A contract is a legal document between two parties, a supplier and a client or buyer, wherein the supplier agrees to perform a service and the buyer is obligated to pay for the service. For example, a manufacturing company contracted a local firm to provide expertise on an operational activity such as forecasting demand for one of its new products. The contract spells out the conditions, the responsibilities, and the legal rights should there be a breach of the contract. Procurement contracts establish a legally binding relationship between buyers and suppliers that protects both entities throughout the procurement process. Contracts include payment and delivery terms. They improve business relationships by protecting both the buyer and supplier.

Negotiating the terms of a contract must take the factors specified in the procurement contracts into account. Procurement contracts include the terms and conditions of the sale of the goods and services in consideration. Both the buyer and the supplier need to understand the obligations set forth in the contract and adhere to them. The procurement contracts include a supplier performance monitoring process with key performance metrics spelled out. It also includes how to resolve issues as they arise during the term of the contract. Depending on the materials or the service, the basic elements of price, delivery, quality, service, payment terms, and other operational issues need to be agreed upon in the contract. Both the buyers and the suppliers aim to negotiate their own objectives. The goal of the negotiation is to satisfy at least most of the objectives and reach an amicable, or at least acceptable solution.

Manage Contracts

Managing contracts includes managing the changes in scope of the contract content after it is negotiated and agreed to by both buyer and supplier. It also includes managing the supplier relationships and coordinating the procurement activities at every step of the process.

Managing contracts effectively facilitates the smooth operation of all activities included in the contract, maintaining good relationships with suppliers, reducing risks, and resolving problems as they arise. The main objectives of procurement contract management are to:

- Ensure that the goods and services are transacted at the agreed-upon price,
- Ensure that the goods and services conform to contract quality specifications, and
- Ensure that goods and services are delivered in the agreed-upon timeframe, location, and quantity.

Transaction

The goal of this dimension is to ensure the efficient transfer of information about the required materials and services from the users to the suppliers, receive materials and services, make certain the materials and services are to the specified quality, and manage the flow of invoices for payment to suppliers. The transaction dimensions include the following processes:

- Initiate procurement,
- Receive goods and services,
- Inspect received goods and services, and
- Manage payments.

Initiate Procurement

After the selection of suppliers and the approval of contracts, a purchase order is initiated by the buyer from the procurement department. An important function of the purchase order is laying out the terms and conditions of the purchase. This includes the negotiated contract with the supplier and any new set of terms and conditions. The purchase order is a legally binding contract from the buyer. The supplier may offer the goods and services at the supplier's own terms and conditions using a sales order. Once the buyer agrees to the sales order and the supplier agrees to the purchase order, the procurement process is on.

For materials and services that are required on an ongoing basis, **planned order releases** are used. Planned order releases are part of material requirements planning (MRP) for placing orders directly with the suppliers. We have discussed planned order releases and MRP in Chapter 6 of this book.

Traditional procurement is a paper-based system using printed documents and emailing or faxing the documents to the supplier. However, with the advent of the business-to-business (B2B) software systems using the Internet, e-procurement is being used more in organizations.

e-Procurement

e-procurement
Procurement of supplies, goods, and services through the Internet.

The advent of Information Technology has propelled the procurement process to electronic procurement or e-procurement. E-procurement is procurement of supplies, goods, and services through the Internet using computer software. E-procurement benefits the business-to-business (B2B) or business-to-consumer (B2C) or business-to-government (B2G) purchases. The e-procurement process is shown in Figure 8-3.

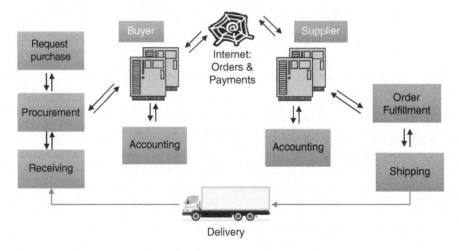

Figure 8-3 E-procurement Process
Source: Ganesh Vaidyanathan and © Modvector/Shutterstock.com

e-Procurement is designed to restructure the traditional procurement process shown in Figure 8-1. Instead of manually sending, receiving, verifying, and managing contracts and documents, the entire process is automated and sent electronically. Moreover, it provides the facility to integrate procurement with other departments and streamlines the operations among the various functions. e-Procurement uses technologies that are designed to centralize and automate interactions between an organization and its suppliers, customers, and other value chain partners in order to improve the speed and efficiency of procurement. One of the main technologies used in e-Procurement is EDI.

Electronic Data Exchange

Businesses implement e-Procurement using a variety of tools and web platforms. Electronic Data Exchange (EDI), the premier method to implement eProcurement, invoices, and advanced ship notices was introduced in the 1980s.

The American National Standards Institute (ANSI) and the Accredited Standards Committee (ASC) define the EDI standards as X12. The X12 standards serve as a common business language allowing all EDI trading partners to communicate electronically with one another. EDI is an electronic alternative to sending procurement documents between the organizations and their suppliers. EDI uses a standardized format that can be converted from any form of data from an organization to any form of data to its supplier. Moreover, EDI files are sent through a Virtual Private Network (VPN) to ensure the security and the integrity of documents. Using EDI, buyers can create a purchase order. The EDI translates the order as an EDI document and sends the document electronically to the supplier where the EDI document is translated to the supplier's internal format. The supplier's order entry system creates and transmits an acknowledgment to confirm receipt to the buyer as shown in Figure 8-4.

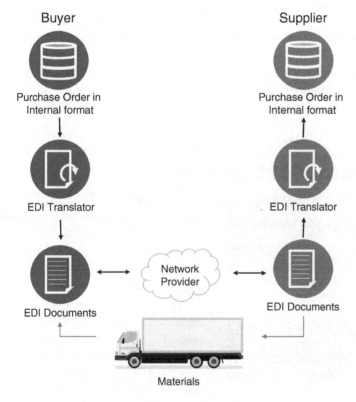

Figure 8-4 e-Procurement Using EDI

Source: Ganesh Vaidyanathan and © Modvector/Shutterstock.com

e-Procurement provides many benefits over traditional procurement. While traditional procurement is labor-intensive from requisition to purchase orders, e-procurement has the following advantages:

Automation of tasks. Tasks such as document management for purchase orders, price negotiations, and storing supplier contracts can be automated between a company and its suppliers to free up staff for other tasks.

Improved procurement workflows. Workflows are a sequence of processes through which tasks pass from initiation to completion. Workflows, though automation, can be improved from ordering of goods and services to supplier payments.

Real-time connectivity to external supply chains. Real-time information can be shared between internal computer systems and external computer systems to access supplier information and transactions.

Improved communication. Communication between stakeholders and partners can be improved through e-Procurement.

Real-time updates. Updates of catalogs and other data can be achieved in real time.

Time and cost savings. Selecting and maintaining suppliers, processing procurement requests, and making repeat purchases can be easily achieved with great efficiency, thus reducing costs.

Better accuracy of data. Accuracy of data can be maintained as all data entered, stored, and disseminated are digital and are entered only once.

Better auditing. All transactions can be tracked for auditing as all pertinent information of every transaction can be captured and stored in computer systems.

FROM PRACTICE: e-Procurement Strategy at Hyundai

© meowKa/Shutterstock.com

Hyundai, the South Korean automaker, established an e-Procurement system in 2017. The system was launched to handle the procurement of Hyundai's Telecommunications and Liquid Crystal Display (LCD) business units. Hyundai's e-Procurement system consists of three components including automatic request, automatic estimation, and automatic analysis of procurement status. Automatic request uses an electronic catalogue of materials to automate the request process between requestors and the procurement department, eliminating manual request forms and their physical delivery. Automatic estimation automates estimates, selection of suppliers, and the ordering process. This component includes Electronic Data Interchange (EDI) to transfer necessary information to and from suppliers. Automatic analysis of procurement status gives a real-time visibility of the procurement process and reduces the time required to analyze procurement trends. Hyundai expected that the e-Procurement system would reduce procurement costs by at least 30% and eliminate the unnecessary costs of paper-based procurement systems[15].

Receive Goods and Services

Receiving is the act of taking possession of the ordered materials and services. Receiving is performed to stage the materials and services for inspection, place them into inventory, or deploy them to the end user. The receiving department of an organization determines if the received products or services are acceptable and conform to the terms and conditions of the purchase order.

> **Receiving** Receiving is the act of taking possession of the ordered materials and services, sending them for inspection, placing them into inventory, or deploying them to the end user.

In a just-in-time (JIT) environment, parts and materials go directly to production from the receiving dock. This is possible when the supplier has been cleared for production delivery and certified for quality consistency and the freight carrier is capable of delivering products on time. Otherwise, in all other circumstances, the next step is inspection.

Inspect Received Goods and Services

The receiving department should conduct a visual inspection to verify:

- The materials and services conform to the purchase order requirements, freight bill from freight companies, and other relevant documents, for example, in the case of receiving materials, correct model number, description, size, type, color, ratings, and so on,
- The quantity ordered against the quantity shipped or delivered,
- Visual inspection of any damages to the materials,
- Delivery documentation, for example, the packing list, certifications, and so on, are acceptable,
- Partial deliveries or overshipments, and
- Perishable items are in good condition and expiration dates have not been exceeded.

The results of the inspection with discrepancies, if any, should be sent to the purchasing agent of the company in writing.

Manage Payments

The invoice from the supplier is checked and audited by the accounting department. After it is certified for payment, the payment is made according to the agreed upon terms and conditions. If there are discrepancies or if anything does not agree with the purchase order, the invoice is returned to the supplier for correction.

Formulae from this Chapter

Scorecard weighted score	$Weighted\ Score = \left(\dfrac{Score}{5}\right) \times Subweight$	Eq. 8-1

Case Study: Procurement at Freely Furniture

Freely Furniture was established in 2012 to manufacture desks, tables, and chairs in Freeport, Indiana.

Frank Freely gained the knowledge from his dad who was a carpenter by trade and started wood working as a hobby. He loved to work with his dad in their modest basement workshop. After his business undergraduate degree from Indiana University, he started an innovative manufacturing company which involved a new way of cutting and finishing components prior to the assembly of the finished products. Frank also introduced a strategic planning method, new manufacturing processes, and an online catalog that allowed a customer to select a product from the catalog and have a new desk delivered in a week. With the new UV finish technology, the company produced a more durable and attractive finish for a better quality and a longer-lasting product at a competitive price. Since the UV finish does not emit toxins into the air after it is cured, it is considered to be environmentally safe. The company is currently working to attain ISO-14001 certification. All these efforts have led to better quality products, reduced costs, and increased customer satisfaction.

© matike/Shutterstock.com

Frank's business had a mission—to create customer value through reliability, flexibility, integrity, and speed. He regarded his employees and his community to be vital to the company's success. His vision was to build personal desks and conference tables for offices and home offices. The company sold artfully crafted tables in select American hardwood veneers with great looks at an affordable price. The prices of personal desks ranged from $500 to $1,500 while conference tables ranged from $3,000 to $8,000.

The company's revenue for the current year was expected to be $25 million, selling more than 4,000 tables with 12 employees. Frank expected sudden growth as some of his corporate clients were expanding in the beginning of that year. Therefore, he wanted to expand his facilities. A lengthy list of equipment for spraying, powder coating, painting, bonding, gluing, dispensing, lubricating, sealing, mixing, molding, UV curing, laminating, micro-coating, and cleaning processes was needed for the expansion. He started estimating for the expansion and to further the operations of the expanded plant.

Frank wants to buy the equipment in 2 years. In the first year, he wants to purchase some equipment amounting to $825,000 including taxes. He wants to purchase other equipment in the next year for $450,000 including taxes. He is prepared to pay freight costs up to $10,000 for the first-year purchases and up to $4,500 for the purchases during the subsequent year. His maintenance manager estimated 2% of the equipment costs for the preventive maintenance and 3% of the equipment costs for the regular maintenance for the third year only and remain the same for subsequent years. Frank also wanted to sell all the equipment at the end of the fifth year and purchase new equipment with better technology. He also accounted that the useful life of much of the equipment is 5 years without paying for excessive maintenance. He estimated that he will get 8% of the original equipment price that he paid for in the first year and 10% of the original equipment price and dispose them for the same amount.

Frank's sales and marketing manager estimated 30% growth from the company's current revenue during the third year. The first-year revenue is estimated as $7M. In the next year, he has estimated a growth equal to 10% of the current revenue. He expected the revenues to grow 5% every year from the third year. The revenue from equipment is 20% of each year's revenue from the second year.

Frank was directly involved in the operations of his company. His current suppliers had him tied to a long-term contract for 5 years, which will end next year. He wanted to negotiate fresh contracts with them to benefit his company. He also heard that the manufacturing cost is cheaper in Vietnam for furniture and he wanted to explore that option as well. Frank wanted a good procurement strategy with either of those two options. He thought of exploring personal desks rather than the conference tables for outsourcing. Option 1 was to use his current supplier with a fresh contract for raw materials and make personal desks in-house. Option 2 was to get personal desks made from Vietnam and import them to Indiana. His sales and marketing manager estimated that their revenues from the new equipment for the future line of personal desks is 20% of the company revenue from new equipment. Frank estimates that the proceeds of the sale and the total cost of ownership for the personal desk is about 20%.

On top of the expected investment for the expansion, Frank estimated fixed costs would be about $8,000 per month and would be expected to go up by 10% every year for the next 5 years. The variable cost for each table made is $250 on an average. The initial proposal from a supplier from Vietnam was $350 on average plus $50 apiece for all import charges.

Case Questions

A. Estimate the total cost of ownership?
B. What is the present value of the personal desk strategy based on TCO estimation for a discount rate of 12%?
C. Is the project of buying the equipment an acceptable project? Is the Option 2 an acceptable project for Freely Furniture?

D. Should Frank go with make personal desks in -house or buy desks from Vietnam if the company wants to buy 7,000 desks? What kind of risks will he face with his options? How can he mitigate those risks?

E. For cost savings, what is the minimum number of personal desks if Frank wants to make them in-house?

F. For cost savings, what is the maximum number of personal desks for cost savings if Frank wants to outsource them to Vietnam? What other factors are important for outsourcing?

G. Freely Furniture is a proponent of green procurement and green manufacturing. What should be included in Frank's procurement strategy?

H. What method should Frank use to select the suppliers? What should be included in that method?

Summary

- Procurement is the process of acquiring required materials, services, and equipment from suppliers and external sources.

- Procurement includes several activities including Identifying procurement requirements, devising a purchasing strategy, selecting suppliers, acquiring goods and services or work with an external source, managing supplier contracts, managing suppliers, receiving supplies, and managing payments.

- Procurement is concerned with purchasing both production or service-related items, also called direct spend, and with non-production and non-service-oriented items, also called indirect spend.

- Procurement consists of three main dimensions including strategy, sourcing, and transaction. Each dimension has 4 processes and the combined 12 processes constitute the procurement functionality of a company.

- Procurement strategy refers to a long-term plan to cost-effectively acquire the necessary supplies from a list of efficient vendors who will deliver quality goods on time, abiding by the purchasing terms.

- The strategic dimension of procurement consists of identifying business need, defining requirements, setting procurement objectives, and devising procurement strategy.

- Once the needs of procurement are identified and established, the next step is to define the needs as requirements.

- A requirements process starts with a purchase requisition form, which is a document used by an employee to purchase goods or services on behalf of their firm.

- The purpose of the procurement objectives is to provide a clear picture of the goals of procurement.

- A company's procurement strategy is about how to implement its procurement process, risk mitigation, sustainable or green procurement, and cost reduction.
- Risk management is the process that allows procurement managers to balance the operational and economic costs of protective measures to achieve success in their procurement activities.
- Risk management consists of the identification of risks, the assessment of the value of these risks, the proposed plans to mitigate these risks, and monitoring and control of the risks.
- Risk monitoring and control is a process to keep track of the identified risks, identify new risks, monitor both external and residual risks, ensure the execution of risk plans, and evaluate the effectiveness of the risk plans.
- Green procurement or sustainable procurement is about making environmentally conscious decisions throughout the procurement process.
- Cost reduction is the most important procurement strategy for many companies and it involves reducing unnecessary expenses.
- Total cost of ownership (TCO) is the total cost of the purchase of an item, costs incurred while in use, and the cost of disposal of item.
- The total cost of ownership can be used in a procurement analysis. A procurement analysis takes all the estimated costs of acquisition, ownership, and disposal into account before buying an item.
- Companies must make wise decisions to make or buy parts using a breakeven analysis of the quantity of parts needed.
- Sourcing is a process that includes activities such as identifying and assessing potential suppliers as well as selecting an appropriate supplier.
- The sourcing dimension includes requesting and approving goods and services, identifying and selecting suppliers and outsources, negotiating and managing contracts, and managing suppliers and outsources.
- Three methods, RFQ, RFO, and RFI, are employed to select a supplier.
- To select suppliers, companies employ a scorecard, which involves evaluating potential suppliers using multiple criteria.
- Outsourcing is the process whereby a strategic partner implements the client's projects. By outsourcing, the client organizations can take advantage of the global labor pool, process innovations, and delivery capabilities of their strategic partners, suppliers.
- Outsourcing can be classified as offshoring, nearshoring, insourcing, co-sourcing, and multi-sourcing.
- A contract is a legal document between two parties, a supplier and a client or buyer, wherein the supplier agrees to perform a service and the buyer is obligated to pay for the service.

- Procurement contracts are usually generated by the buyer and come in six types including fixed-price contracts, fixed-price incentive fee contracts, cost-plus fixed fee contracts, cost-plus percentage fee contracts, cost-plus incentive fee contracts, and guaranteed maximum-shared savings contract.
- Managing contracts includes managing changes including changes in scope of the contract content after it is negotiated and agreed to by both buyer and supplier.
- The transaction dimensions include initiating procurement, receiving goods and services, inspecting received goods and services, and managing payments.
- Once the suppliers are selected and contracts are settled for a purchase requisition, a purchase order is initiated by the buyer from the procurement department.
- e-Procurement is procurement of supplies, goods, and services through the Internet.
- Two main technologies are used in e-Procurement including EDI and cXML.
- Receiving is the act of taking possession of ordered materials and services, sending them for inspection, placing them into inventory, or deploying them to the end user.
- The receiving department should conduct a visual inspection to verify the condition of the received goods and ensure that the received materials and services are according to the agreed upon terms and conditions.
- The invoice from the supplier is checked and audited.
- After it is certified for payment, the payment is made according to the agreed upon terms and conditions.

Review Questions

1. Define procurement.
2. What are the main activities of procurement?
3. What are direct spend and indirect spend? Explain with an example.
4. Name the three main dimensions of procurement.
5. List the 12 procurement processes from start to finish.
6. What is a purchase requisition form?
7. What is the purpose of procurement objectives?
8. What is risk management in procurement?
9. What are the components of procurement risk management?
10. Name three risks associated with procurement.
11. Explain green procurement.
12. How do companies reduce cost in procurement?
13. What is total cost of ownership (TCO)?

14. How is TCO used in procurement?
15. What is breakeven during procurement?
16. What is sourcing?
17. Describe the sourcing process in procurement.
18. What are the main differences between RFQ, RFP, and RFI?
19. How do companies select suppliers?
20. Explain why companies outsource.
21. What are the several types of outsourcing? Explain with examples.
22. What is a contract?
23. How do companies negotiate and manage contracts?
24. What benefits do companies obtain by managing contracts?
25. What are the transaction processes in procurement?
26. What is a purchase order?
27. Describe the steps in traditional procurement.
28. Describe the steps in e-Procurement.
29. What are the main technologies used in e-Procurement?
30. What should companies do to receive goods and services?
31. How are payments for procurement settled in companies?

Critical Thinking Questions

1. Why do companies need a procurement strategy?
2. Is there one procurement dimension that is more important than the other two?
3. What is needed to do procurement analysis?
4. Is there one risk that stands out in risk mitigation of procurement? What is it and how does it affect procurement?
5. How do companies transfer risk using contracts in procurement?
6. What steps should companies take to attain green procurement?
7. Explain the differences between traditional and e-Procurement.
8. Which technology is used currently in e-Procurement?
9. What approach, other than a standard purchasing procedure, might be used to purchase items of small value with small quantities?
10. When would you issue an RFP rather than an RFQ?
11. Why do firms use a weighted scorecard to select suppliers?
12. How might social, political, or environmental factors impact supplier selection?
13. Why do U.S. companies use global sourcing?
14. Which one of the factors of outsourcing problems is the most serious to a procurement manager? Why?
15. Why should firms switch from making to buying?
16. Zale.com is an online provider of sports merchandise. Their management is pondering whether to give its purchase officers a

corporate credit card or use a purchase order or to use a vendor-managed inventory system for its weekly purchases. Which one of these options is better and for what purpose?

17. Ringo, the drum maker, is thinking of outsourcing to buy their drumsticks. Is this strategic for the company? How should the company make the decision to outsource the product?

18. The owner of Lil Cubbies LLC., a small store selling Chicago Cubs merchandise, is planning to consolidate his 120 suppliers to 10. Is this a good strategy? If so, why? If not, why not?

19. Use the resources available on Internet to find out the following:
    a. Name 10 well-known companies practicing green procurement.
    b. Pick one of them and describe what kind of efforts they are taking to make their purchasing efforts green.

20. Do public organizations practice green procurement? Give an example of how they achieve green procurement.

Problem Solving Questions

1. Pelham manufacturers from Pelham, Alabama bought three chemical pumps for $3,680 each from KL Pumps, Waco, Texas. The tax rate was 6.5% and the freight costs were $700. The company estimates regular maintenance costs as $200 every quarter. They also expect $300 per machine for seals which will be part of the maintenance process. After 5 years of useful life, the plan is to dispose of the pumps for $600 each with no salvage value. What is the total cost of ownership for this equipment?

2. Rotterdam Machinery, a company from Plano, Texas bought two compressors. They paid $200,000 apiece. The freight costs were $4,600. The company estimated regular maintenance costs as $800 every 6 months. The pre-maintenance routines amount to $100 per month. The company plans to utilize the two compressors for 5 full years and hopes to get $25,000 each as sale price at the end of the full term of use.
    a. What is the total cost of ownership for this equipment?
    b. What is the present value based on TCO of the compressors for a discount rate of 10%?

3. DeVante Adams, the purchase agent at Regen Manufacturing, Inc. is planning to decide on two suppliers of heavy-duty motors that are used in their rotary machines. The cost of a motor varies by how many were ordered. Holding cost is the cost for storage of inventory at Regen. Order processing is the procurement cost for Regen. Fulfillment cost is added to the order and will be paid by Regen. The suppliers have provided the following terms and conditions though an RFP.

Terms	Supplier 1	Supplier 2
0–500 motors per order	$250	$248
501–1000 motors per order	$230	$232
1001–1500 motors per order	$210	$209
Freight costs upto 500 motors	$450	$450
Freight costs over 500 motors	$600	$580
Holding cost of each motor	$10	$10
Order processing cost per order	$200	$200
Fulfillment cost per unit	$6	$7

Adams orders 800 units in the first month, 300 units in the next month, and 1,200 in the third month.

   a. What is the TCO of both suppliers?

   b. Which supplier should Adams choose?

4. Joe's Grocery in Osceola, Indiana, is a family-owned grocery store established in 1956. Joe Sr., the owner, wants to expand his store. The neighboring insurance company shifted for better business elsewhere. Joe wants to use the 40ft × 60ft site to expand his grocery with more ethnic food as the neighborhood has changed over the years. He also wants to sell the entire business for $1,000,000 after 5 years and retire. He worked on the details and produced the information provided below.

Rent	$2,500	per month	Refrigerated units	6
Utilities	$400	per month	Ice cream units	2
Refrigerated unit cost	$6,400		No of employees	1
Ice cream unit cost	$3,200		No of hours/day	10
Furniture	$3,200		No of days/week	6
Shelving	$12,000		Nof weeks/year	45
Cleaning & Sanitizing	$600	per month	Employee benefits	12% of salary
Employee salary	$15	per emp per hr		
Average grocery Inventory cost	$80,000	per month		
Expected Revenues	$960,000	per month		
Monthly maintenance	$560			
Insurance	$1,200	per month		

   a. What is the TCO?

   b. Implement a procurement analysis using a discount rate of 10%.

   c. Is this a good project to undertake for Joe, Sr.?

5. Republic Manufacture is planning whether to buy or make a part for its assembly. The initial investment for that part is $12,000. The manufacturing cost per part is $15. A supplier can send the same part for $20 with an additional transportation cost of $250 to transport 100 parts.
   a. Find the breakeven quantity and the total cost at the breakeven point.
   b. If the company requires 1,200 parts, find the breakeven quantity and the total cost at the breakeven point.
   c. If the requirement is 2,000 parts, what is the best option? What is the cost saving?
6. Tillan Industries has the following information:

	Make	Buy
Fixed Cost	$30,000	$5,000
Variable Cost	$7	$11

   a. Find the breakeven quantity and the total cost at the breakeven point.
   b. If the company requires 5,800 parts, find the breakeven quantity and the total cost at the breakeven point.
   c. If the requirement is 8,000 parts, what is the best option? What is the cost saving?
7. Trilog, LLC makes computer parts from Pleasanton, CA. They want to check whether there is any cost savings if they outsource those parts from another company in California. When they approach their potential supplier, the supplier quotes them $90,000 for 1,000 parts. Trilog's fixed costs are $40,000 and their cost per part is $85. If their customer demands 7,500 parts, should Trilog make or buy the computer parts? What is the minimum number of parts that would cause Trilog to make in-house rather than outsource?
8. Robert Sweeny is the purchasing person at Sweeny Storage Boxes of Gary, Indiana. Robert is negotiating a procurement contract to purchase 30,000 storage boxes from SureStore, Inc. SureStore is quoting to supply each box for $25. The necessary documentation and contract negotiation for SureStop is $750 and the transportation costs are $4,500 . Robert knows that he has to invest $320,000 in capital equipment. What is the minimum manufacturing cost for Sweeney to make the product in-house?
9. Robert Sweeny from the last question finds out that his actual cost to manufacture boxes is $20.
   What is the maximum purchasing price he should negotiate with the supplier for him to buy?

10. Argos, Inc., a manufacturing company, has its own MIS department. The talent is available, but the project manager, a senior at Argos, is comparing costs for an in-house project versus outsourcing the project. If the costs are shown as follows, what is the right choice if the discount rate is 10%?

Costs	Year 0	Year 1	Year 2	Year 3	Year 4
Personnel costs that may be avoided by outsourcing	$400,000	$400,000	$400,000	$400,000	$400,000
Administrative overhead that may be avoided by outsourcing	$0	$0	$0	$0	$0
Outsourcing	$500,000	$500,000	$500,000	$500,000	$500,000
Project administration	$120,000	$120,000	$120,000	$120,000	$120,000
Retraining	$0	$0	$0	$100,000	$100,000

References

1. Starbucks. (2021). *C.A.F.E. Practices: Starbucks Approach to Ethically Sourcing Coffee.* Retrieved December 23, 2021, from https://stories.starbucks.com/press/2020/cafe-practices-starbucks-approach-to-ethically-sourcing-coffee/; Starbucks. (2021). *Starbucks Ethical Sourcing of Sustainable Products.* Retrieved December 23, 2021, from https://www.starbucks.com/responsibility/sourcing; Leblanc, R. (2019). *How Starbucks Changed Their Supply Chain Management.* Retrieved December 23, 2021, from https://www.thebalancesmb.com/how-starbucks-changed-supply-chain-management-4156894.

2. Vaidyanathan, G., Devaraj, S., & D'Arcy, J. (2012). Does security impact e-procurement performance? Testing a model of direct and moderated effects. *Decision Sciences, 43*(3), 437–458.

3. Deloitte. (2018). *The Deloitte global chief procurement officer survey 2018.* Retrieved December 28, 2021, from https://www2.deloitte.com/content/dam/Deloitte/at/Documents/strategy-operations/deloitte-global-cpo-survey-2018.pdf.

4. WSJ. (2021). *How Volvo Car USA Is simplifying purchasing for Its retail network.* Retrieved December 27, 2021, from https://partners.wsj.com/amazon-business/reshape-buying/how-volvo-car-usa-is-simplifying-purchasing-for-its-retail-network/?utm_medium=search&utm_source=google&utm_content={{ad_title}}&utm_term=

5. Deloitte. (2018). *The Deloitte global chief procurement officer survey 2018.* Retrieved December 28, 2021, from https://www2.deloitte.com/content/dam/Deloitte/at/Documents/strategy-operations/deloitte-global-cpo-survey-2018.pdf.

6. Nagali, V., Hwang, J., Sanghera, D., Gaskins, M., Pridgen, M., Thurston, T., Mackenroth, P., Branvold, D., Scholler, P., & Shoemaker, G. (2008). Procurement risk management (PRM) at Hewlett-Packard Company. *Interfaces, 38*(1), 51–60.

7. ISO. (2021). *ISO 14000 family environmental management.* Retrieved January 7, 2022, from https://www.iso.org/iso-14001-environmental-management.html.

8. EPA. (2021). *Comprehensive Procurement Guideline (CPG) Program.* Retrieved January 7, 2022, from https://www.epa.gov/smm/comprehensive-procurement-guideline-cpg-program#products.

9. Industry Week. (2005). *Ford reaches ISO 14001 milestone: All plants certified.* Retrieved December 27, 2021, from https://www.industryweek.com/archive/article/21949380/ford-reaches-iso-14001-milestone-all-plants-certified.

10. Brown, A. B. (2021). *Kohl's investor group proposes sourcing, inventory changes to win back margins.* Retrieved December 28, 2021, from https://www.supplychaindive.com/news/kohls-investor-group-sourcing-inventory-turn-margin/595596/.

11. Monczka, R., Trent, R., & Handfield, R. (2002). *Purchasing and supply chain management* (2nd ed.). South-Western.

12. Youngblood, A. D., & Collins, T. R. (2003). Addressing balanced scorecard trade-off issues between performance metrics using multi-attribute utility theory. *Engineering Management Journal, 15*(1), 11–17.

13. Smith, T. (2021). *The top 4 suppliers of Lowe's.* Retrieved January 2, 2021, from https://www.investopedia.com/articles/markets/050716/lowes-stock-analyzing-5-key-suppliers-low.asp; Lowe's. (2021). *Supporting small and diverse enterprises.* Retrieved January 2, 2021, from https://www.lowes.com/l/about/suppliers.

14. Phartiyal, S., & Varadhan, S. (2018). Foxconn to begin assembling top-end Apple iPhones in India in 2019. *Reuters.* Retrieved January 5, 2022, from https://www.reuters.com/article/us-apple-india-exclusive/exclusive-foxconn-to-begin-assembling-top-end-apple-iphones-in-india-in-2019-source-idUSKCN1OQ0M6; GlobalData Thematic Research. (2021). *Apple diversifies supply chain but keeps China at the center.* Retrieved January 4, 2021, from https://www.verdict.co.uk/apple-supply-chain-china/; Kasyanenko, S. (2019). *iPhone made in India: Apple outsourcing strategy.* Retrieved January 5, 2022, from https://medium.com/@Ralabs/iphone-made-in-india-apple-outsourcing-strategy-fff490580cf9.

15. CIO Review India. (2017). *Hyundai Establishes e-Procurement System as Part of its B2B Solution.* Retrieved January 4, 2022, from https://www.cioreviewindia.com/news/hyundai-establishes-eprocurement-system-as-part-of-its-b2b-solution-nid-2685-cid-119.html.

CHAPTER 9

PRODUCTION OPERATIONS

Learning Objectives

- Explain the production process.
- Describe the different production process methods used in industries.
- Describe the customer order decoupling point.
- Describe the different models in production process using the customer order decoupling point.
- Explain the five production process methods.
- Explain the four production system layouts.
- Develop a manufacturing cell for a family of parts.
- Use assembly line balancing to develop an assembly design.
- Describe Little's Law and how inventory flows through a production process.

Tesla, Inc., the American electric vehicle company based in Austin, Texas, designs and manufactures electric cars, battery energy storage, solar panels, solar roof tiles, and related products and services. The company makes four electric vehicle (EV) models. Its subsidiary, Tesla Energy, develops photovoltaic systems and supplies battery energy storage systems. The Model 3 is the all-time best-selling EV worldwide. In 2021, Tesla was cited to run the most productive auto factory in the United States[1].

Tesla's Fremont factory has 5.3 million square feet of space with over 10,000 Tesla employees. Tesla built its first Gigafactory in Reno, Nevada where the car maker manufactures the batteries for its electric vehicles as well as recycles the unused materials. Elon Musk, the CEO of Tesla, has said that their Gigafactory is a "machine that builds the machine."

© Felix Mizioznikov/Shutterstock.com; (Inset)
© Jatuporn Chainiramitkul/Shutterstock.com

Tesla and its partner Panasonic produce battery packs for Tesla's EVs in this $4.5 billion factory. This manufacturing facility and its layout has been viewed as their model to build eventually more than a dozen such plants globally[2]. In the Nevada factory, small electric vehicles called **Automated Guided Vehicles** (AGV) deliver the Panasonic battery cells to Tesla operations with no humans in the process. About 4,000 battery cells are assembled into modules and the modules are then assembled into packs. There are not that many people working in this factory as the plant is about 90% automated.

So, how many Gigafactories does Tesla have? About five of them are in the works now. Gigafactory 1, outside of Reno, Nevada, is the first of Tesla's growing assemblage of production facilities. This Gigafactory produces electric motors lithium-ion battery packs, and energy storage products. Gigafactory 2, located near Buffalo, New York, focuses on solar energy rather than EVs. Gigafactory 3 in Shanghai, China, is a 9.3 million sq. ft. Gigafactory that assembles Model 3 and Model Y. Gigafactory 4, located in Berlin, Germany, is proposed to be the most advanced high-volume electric vehicle production plant in the world. Gigafactory 5 in Austin, Texas, is supposed to produce both Model 3 and Model Y for distribution to the Eastern US[3].

Production Process

This chapter and the next focus on two important processes—production and service processes. In manufacturing industries, the processes are used to acquire and use necessary resources, manufacture goods, and deliver value-added goods to customers. In service organizations, the processes are used to acquire and use necessary resources and provide value-added services to customers.

Manufacturing industries produce tangible goods. The goods-producing industries include agriculture, mining, manufacturing, and construction. Production processes are used to make goods that we buy and provide services that we enjoy.

For example, consider the wedding dresses in a department store. All the dresses have been produced by a manufacturing company on a mass scale. The department store makes the necessary adjustments to the dress to customize the dress for a customer. The manufacturing company uses the necessary resources, manufactures the dresses, and delivers the dresses to a service organization like a department store. The department store uses the necessary resources, receives, makes necessary adjustments to customize the dress, and sells the customized dress to the excited bride.

Customer Order Decoupling Point

The operations of a firm, whether it is manufacturing or service, must be strategically aligned to the requirements of the customers in order to remain competitive. This alignment is crucial to the implementation of a company's supply chain. Related to this alignment, there is an important concept called the "customer decoupling order point" or "CODP." The CODP for a product is the point in the supply chain where the product is linked to a specific customer order[4]. It is an important input to the manufacturing operations as well as the supply chain.

The CODP impacts both the inventory and the resources used to create the product. The CODP is based on the information from the supply chain such as the sales forecasts and the **customizable** customer orders. Therefore, it is crucial for the production and logistics efficiency, the storage costs, and the quality of logistics. There are four scenarios where CODP plays a part in the supply chain and these four situations can be described as follows:

1. Made to stock,
2. Assembled to order,
3. Made to order, and
4. Engineered to order.

We will describe these four scenarios using an example of a silk wedding dress through the lens of supply chain processes as shown in Figures 9-1A through 9-1D.

Made to Stock

In the "Made-to-Stock" scenario, the decoupling point is at the final assembly and before the manufacturer transports the final product for distribution. Mass production of products is accomplished by taking advantage of the economies of scale. So, what are economies of scale? Economies of scale are the cost advantages for a company when its production becomes efficient. Firms can achieve economies of scale when costs, both fixed and variable, are spread over

---

Customer order decoupling point The point in the supply chain where the product is linked to a specific customer order.

Economies of scale Economies of scale are cost advantages for a company when costs, both fixed and variable, are spread over a larger number of goods.

Made to stock Goods are available to customers as finished goods in the market and customers are served on demand.

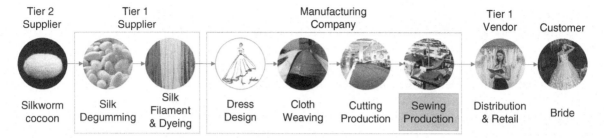

Figure 9-1A Made to Stock

Figure 9-1B Assembled to Order

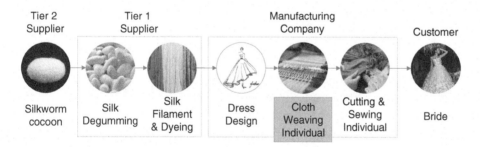

Figure 9-1C Made to Order

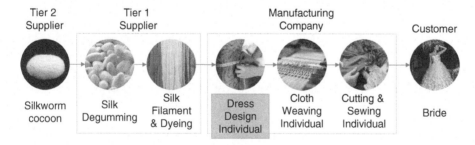

Figure 9-1D Engineered to Order

(From top row, left to right and not repeated): © Jesada Sabai/Shutterstock.com; © Khamhoung/ Shutterstock.com; © nicepix/Shutterstock.com; © Blueprint Characters/Shutterstock.com; © Jothi ramalingam/Shutterstock.com; © Dong Nhat Huy/Shutterstock.com; © Arkadi Bulva/Shutterstock.com; © RomanR/Shutterstock.com; © Lapa_Ca/Shutterstock.com; © nantarpats/Shutterstock.com; © Sergey Nivens/Shutterstock.com

a larger number of goods. In Figure 9-1A, the manufacturing company designs the dresses, weaves silk cloth, then cuts cloth for dresses on a mass scale and then sews the dresses on a mass scale. The finished products are then shipped to the end customers through a series of vendors and retailers.

FROM PRACTICE: Made to Stock at Macy's

Macy's changed its entire supply chain in 2020. In the past, Macy's viewed the supply chain as transactional—moving goods from point A to point B and optimizing costs along each individual point. This was effective in the old retail model but it limited flexibility and drove up costs. Moreover, it impacted their delivery speed and service. The retailer had closed 125 underperforming stores and laid off about 2,000 employees. Under the new strategy, a lot of consolidation was envisioned to bring down the operating costs and improve the margins. The new supply chain strategy will touch all parts of the supply chain including sourcing, inventory management, transportation, distribution, procurement, and sustainability.

© ARTYOORAN/Shutterstock.com

Macy's ships products to multipurpose warehouses to hold the inventory, to replenish their stores, or fulfill the e-commerce orders. Macy's believes that this strategy will ultimately enable them to improve their customers' experience[5].

Assembled to Stock

In the "Assembled-to-Stock" scenario, the decoupling point is at the final assembly but a step away from the final product as shown in Figure 9-1B. The mass production of products is accomplished up to the CODP to take maximum advantage of economies of scale. In Figure 9-1B, the manufacturing company designs the dresses, weaves the silk cloth on a mass scale, but cuts and sews the dresses both on a mass scale. For customers who order on the Internet and wish for a few changes to their dresses, the company makes individual final adjustments. The finished products made with adjustments are then shipped directly to the end customer.

> **Assembled to stock** Goods are assembled for customers as per their wishes but still the majority of the manufacturing process is accomplished on a mass scale.

Made to Order

Some customers want to order a product to their customization. The customization involves adding a one-time effect or making a one-time change to a product at the request of a customer. While the product design is still

> **Made to order**
> Products are made directly from raw materials in the current inventory in response to a customer order.

completed by the manufacturer, some customers would like to change some of the design components to suit their own styles. As shown in Figure 9-1c, the dress manufacturer has already designed their dresses before CODP happens. A customer would like to add a new flower design to the dress or add an extra zipper or button somewhere on the already designed dress. In this case, the dress is made to order. The CODP is pushed further up in the operations process as shown in Figure 9-1C. The finished products are then shipped directly to the end customer.

FROM PRACTICE: Assembled to Order at Dell

© N.Z.Photography/Shutterstock.com

Some computers and mobile devices display tags that read "Assembled in the U.S." The components may not be made in the United States but manufactured on a mass scale somewhere else. The computer or the mobile device manufacturer assembles those parts in the United States. This process gives these companies flexibility to make those devices to order or assemble to a customer's order.

Dell builds its computers in Austin, TX. It assembles all of its desktop and laptop computers in the United States as well. However, in recent years, the company has spread its laptop production to several facilities worldwide, from Mexico to Ireland[6].

FROM PRACTICE: Made to order at Porsche

© Jarlat Maletych/Shutterstock.com

Porsche is a automobile manufacturer specializing in high-performance sports cars and headquartered in Stuttgart, Germany. Porsche's current lineup includes the 718 Boxster/Cayman, the 911 (992), the Panamera, the Macan, the Cayenne, and the Taycan. Porsche Classic takes the customer requests for a "dream car" and builds them. The customizations must be technically feasible to the automaker's design, though. The orders may include both exterior and interior customization as well as upgraded versions of its suspensions and powertrains. The company can transform their car, new or old, into almost anything a customer wants! However, Porsche will not rebuild any of their limited-production cars—for example, turning a Cayman into a Boxster Spyder—or copy anything from other brands. If Porsche finds the order suitable to its production, the customer will be invited to a project meeting in Atlanta or Los Angeles or virtually. The customer can act as the project manager with a team of experts from Porsche right from the initial stages to the delivery of their dream car[7].

Engineered to Order

The "engineered to order" situation involves manufacturing a product that does not have fixed designs and is expected to result in a new, unique end product. The end product could be a custom software application, a special aircraft, or a customer-designed pair of jeans. Here the CODP happens right before the beginning of the design. The engineered to order situation works to develop new products and satisfy the unique requirements and specifications of a customer. This is not suitable for every manufacturer. It is ideally suitable for manufacturers with a highly configurable product. It takes a lot of customer contact time as the customer must be involved from the design to sourcing to manufacturing. In the case of the silk wedding dress maker, a customer may even order specialized fabrics and be allowed to design their own prints.

> **Engineered to order** Products are made directly from start to finish for a unique requirement and specification of a customer.

FROM PRACTICE: Engineered to Order at Siemens

The examples of "engineered to order" products include power plant boilers, electrical switchgear, some commercial HVAC equipment, industrial cranes, and specialty vehicles like fire trucks. But to engineer a product to the specifications of a customer and transform the customer requirements to efficient production is not an easy task for

© max.ku/Shutterstock.com

any company. Siemens AG has a product, Rulestream, which allows the company to capture the engineering rules and the heuristics that they use to design their products. This software helps the company to use those rules and heuristics to automatically generate a new design according to a customer specification, complete with all the relevant product content[8].

Production Process Methods

When a company produces goods, they employ various methods from the input of raw materials to the making of quality finished goods. The production process that each organization follows depends on several factors including what kinds of products are produced, the available technology, how many products the company needs to produce, and the organizational structure. In general, the production process can be categorized into five distinct processes including:

1. Subtractive,
2. Additive,
3. Net shape,
4. Batch, and
5. Continuous.

CNC machine with an operator

Subtractive Process

The subtractive process involves removing material from a solid block of raw material. Sculptors use this technique to create statues. They use chisels to take away material from a big block of stone or wood until they get a statue of a person, animal, and so on. Likewise, companies employ methods such as machining, milling, and boring to create or modify the material shapes in order to form the products. A person who operates machines in the subtractive manufacturing process is called a **machinist**.

Nowadays, sophisticated machines are used by companies in subtractive processes. A Computer Numerical Control (CNC) machine is an example. The CNC machines remove pieces of raw material to form a desired three-dimensional (3D) geometrical shape and size by using a controlled material-removal process. The CNC machines use their computers to control the movement and the operation of cutting machines such as the mills and the lathes on metal, wood, plastic, ceramic, and composite materials. Milling, turning, drilling, boring, reaming, facing, parting, and grooving are all examples of subtractive process using CNC machines.

> **Subtractive process**
> Subtractive processes involve removing material from a solid block of raw material.

Additive Process

> **Additive process**
> An additive process is used to create an object by building it one layer at a time.

The additive process, the opposite of the subtractive process, is used to create an object by building it one layer at a time. Firms used prototypes as an initial method of additive process in the past. A scale model of a new building or a

© Bogdan Cherniak/Shutterstock.com

product is an example of prototyping. This process was known as rapid prototyping because it allowed people to create a scale model of the final object quickly without the typical setup process and the costs involved in creating a prototype. Nowadays, companies use sophisticated processes[9]. An example of additive process is additive manufacturing or 3D printing.

Net Shape Process

There are other production processes where material is neither added nor removed. Net shape is the final shape of a product. The process that is used to create a complete product without going through any finishing machining process is called the net shape process. An example of a net shape process is sheet metal stamping.

The process of turning sheets of metal into a useful part or component is called **sheet metal stamping**. The seat buckle of a car is an example of sheet metal stamping. The metal is fed into a machine called a press. A stamping tool, also known as a die, creates the desired shape by getting pressed into or through the metal with tremendous force. Stamping includes a variety of sheet-metal forming manufacturing processes, such as punching, blanking, embossing, bending, flanging, and coining. Stamping may consist of a single stage operation or a series of stages.

Scale model of a house

© Jacob Lund/Shutterstock.com

Automotive part by stamping process

© DRN Studio/Shutterstock.com

> **Net shape process**
> A net shape process is used to create a product that is complete without going through any finish machining.

Batch Process

A batch process involves a set of ingredients as input. This process uses a sequence of one or more production steps in a predefined order to manufacture a set number of products. In this process, all the raw materials are introduced at the beginning of the production process, and the finished products are completed at a time or a batch. The batch production is used to manufacture a wide array of goods including baked goods, apparel, furniture, soaps, shampoos, pharmaceutical products, and electronic components.

A batch production process is used when companies manufacture low volumes of a specific product and when there are frequent repeat orders for a specific product. Batch process is useful when flexibility is needed. Flexibility is achieved by using the same machinery for different goods. This allows a certain degree of customization for customers as well. For example, a new batch of a specialized bread such as a multigrain bread can be produced just

> **Batch process**
> A batch process involves a set of ingredients as input and using a sequence of one or more production steps in a predefined order to manufacture a set number of products to make up a single batch.

Batch process at a bakery

after a batch of regular flour bread. As opposed to other processes that we discussed so far, this is a step-by-step process, wherein the quality of products can be controlled with ease. The production of a batch of products makes the plant more efficient than making single products. However, there are some disadvantages to the batch process. Usually, greater storage space is needed with excess finished goods inventory. If there are errors in a batch, it can lead to greater waste and cost. Improper batch processes can lead to bottlenecks in production.

Continuous Process

Pharma continuous process

Rather than manufacturing in batches of products, companies employ a continuous process to produce products in bulk. In a continuous process, the raw materials move from the start of the process through a series of production steps to a final product. Moreover, the raw material is fed and processed continuously to produce more of the same product. This is a non-stop production process and is used in food processing and pharmaceutical industries. Some examples are the manufacture of juices, pasta, tomato sauce, chemicals, paper, and drugs. The continuous process leads to faster, cheaper, and more flexible production with a significantly higher level of quality assurance. The regulatory agencies have endorsed the continuous production process in pharmaceutical companies[10].

The difference between the continuous production process and the batch production process is that the continuous process never stops and there are no breaks between the different steps during production. In a continuous production process, the only time the production would be interrupted would be for maintenance. The main advantage of a continuous process is that a large amount of consistent output is generated in a short amount of time. A disadvantage of this technique is that it requires a large amount of initial capital investment as the machines are expensive.

Continuous process In a continuous process, raw materials move from the start of the process through each production step to a final product.

Production system layout A production system layout is the way in which the machines, parts, and other equipment used for production are arranged or laid out.

Production System Layouts

The production processes that we discussed in the previous section are implemented using various production system layouts. The main focus is the layout of the facility for an efficient production of products. A production system

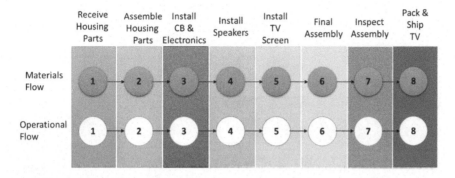

Figure 9-2 Straight line Assembly of a TV

layout is the way in which the workflow—consisting of humans, machines, parts, and other equipment used for production—is arranged or laid out. The objective of the production system layout is the most efficient and effective design for a particular production process. The production system can be laid out in two common ways. For example, the system may be laid out in a long straight line of machines or in a U-shaped production line. In either case, the layout must facilitate the products and the workers moving quickly and without any waste of motion from one area to another.

The production system layout arranges the workflow around a production process. In an efficient workflow, all the workers performing similar tasks are grouped together. The products must pass from one workstation to another. A simple layout for the assembly of a TV is shown in Figure 9-2. The materials flow from one station to another station. The housing parts are received in Station 1 and moved to the station where initial assembly of housing is completed. The housing is moved forward to the next station where all the electronics and the circuit board (CB) are assembled. The operational flow starts at Station 1 with unpacking of all housing assembly and moved to the next Station 2 for assembly with the needed parts. This continues all the way to Station 8 where the TV is fully packed and prepared for shipment. We will consider the following production system layout in this chapter:

- Fixed position assembly,
- Workcenter,
- Manufacturing cell, and
- Assembly line.

Fixed Position Assembly

The fixed position assembly is a layout in which the product does not move while being assembled. The construction of a building, an airplane, or a ship are examples of the fixed position assembly. In general, this layout is suitable for the assembly of heavy products that involve a large number of parts. The

> **Fixed position assembly** Fixed position assembly is a layout where the product remains in a fixed location while being assembled.

Fixed Assembly Layout of an Airplane

biggest advantage of this type of layout is the flexibility with product customization. The disadvantage is the high variable costs since all the material, the equipment, and the workers must be moved to the worksite as and when needed. If there is limited space at the assembly site, some parts of the product must be assembled at other sites, transported to the fixed site, and then assembled.

All the machinery and equipment used to assemble the product, the subassembly construction, the transferring items needed from different work centers to the assembly location, the inventory needed for assembly, the tools, and the workers must be housed around the product.

Workcenter

> **Workcenter** A workcenter layout is where similar equipment or functions are grouped together and the product is made to travel to those equipment or functions.

A workcenter layout is where similar equipment or functions are grouped together and the product is made to travel to those equipment or functions. For example, in this type of layout, the drilling machines are grouped together in one area and the milling machines are grouped together in another area. The product travels from one area to another as per the sequence of operations. This layout is advantageous for the product assembly due to the flexibility to produce a variety of products. This layout is sometimes called a **job shop**.

A workcenter layout is typically used in high-volume production. On a shop floor, a paint booth is a workcenter as shown in the photo. The functionality of the workcenter is to paint anything and everything. For example, cars or any auto part can be brought into the workcenter to be painted.

Paint Booth Workcenter

Manufacturing Cell

A manufacturing cell is a dedicated facility to produce similar products by a group of machines. A manufacturing cell is laid out to optimize the floor space and to minimize the transport of goods. The grouping of machines is laid out in order to promote high levels of product quality with the least number of people who can handle several processing steps. The manufacturing cell is designed to perform specific tasks. In a manufacturing cell, as opposed to the workcenter, the machines are dissimilar.

This layout may involve a single work cell or multiple cells in an assembly line fashion. In either case, the cell or cells contain different machines to accomplish a certain task. In the case of multiple cells, the product moves from one cell to the next, with each cell completing a part of the total production process. Sometimes, the cells are arranged in a "U-shape" or in a circle. The U-shape and circular designs help the supervisor of the process to watch over the entire production process. Figure 9-3 shows a tire manufacturing process using multiple cells. There are seven different cells each having a specific function to manufacture tires.

A manufacturing cell layout can be developed for a production process. The grouping of machinery and equipment to make similar parts needs to be logical. Example 9-1 illustrates how to develop a manufacturing cell layout for a family of parts. A family of parts is a collection of similar parts in varied sizes or with different features.

> **Manufacturing cell** A manufacturing cell is a dedicated facility to produce similar products by a group of machines.

> **Family of parts** A family of parts is a collection of similar parts in varied sizes or with different features.

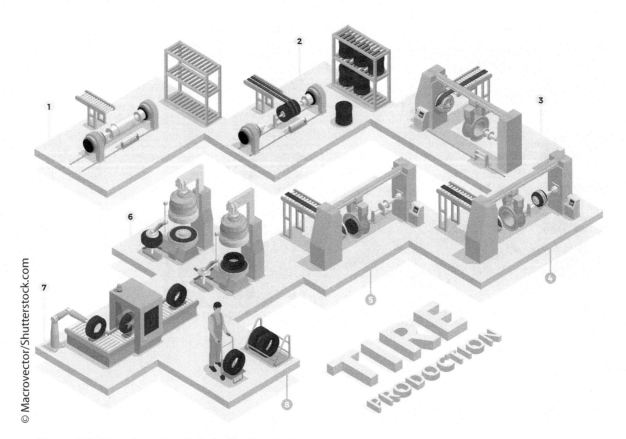

© Macrovector/Shutterstock.com

Figure 9-3 Manufacturing Cells for Tire Production

Assembly Line

> **Assembly line** An assembly line layout consists of a predefined sequence of a production process to assemble the product in a progressive fashion.

The most common production system layout is the assembly line layout. In this layout, the product follows the process which is arranged in a progressive fashion. The assembly of a TV as shown in Figure 9-2 is an example. The progressive process steps are arranged for a specific production rate. Products move from one station to another at a controlled rate. The assembly of cars in an automotive factory is a classic example of an assembly line production. Appliances, toys, furniture, and all other mass production items follow this type of production system layout. Assembly line layout is best suited for mass production and product uniformity. However, it has high startup costs.

Example 9-1

Leyland, Inc. from Leyland, MI, has three family of parts that is required to flow through various machines as shown in the following figure. Develop U-shaped manufacturing cell(s) for the family of parts as shown by different colored arrows in the figure.

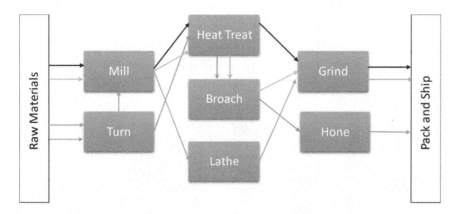

To develop the manufacturing cells, first identify the family of parts and the flow patterns for each one of the family of parts. The black-arrowed and the green-arrowed family of parts share similar process requirements except that the green-arrowed part has an extra process to follow. The other two family parts are different.

Then, for each family of parts, relocate the machines to form a manufacturing cell through a series of required operations to reduce waste and improve quality.

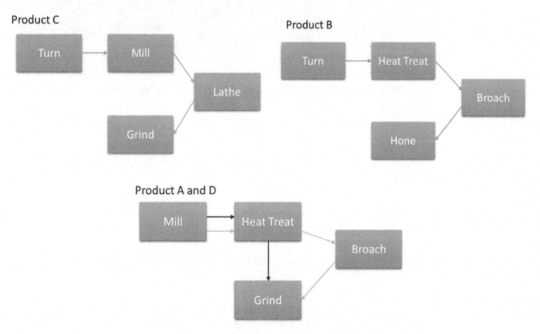

Analysis: The black-arrowed and the green-arrowed family parts can be arranged as shown as they share similar process requirements. The red-arrowed family parts and the blue-arrowed family parts can be arranged separately as shown. We have a U-shaped manufacturing cell for both the red-arrowed family of parts and the blue-arrowed family of parts. The black-arrowed and the green-arrowed family of parts also has a U-shaped manufacturing cell. The green-arrowed family of parts has an extra process.

Assembly Line Balancing

An assembly line consists of a series of workstations. As the product moves on a conveyor belt at a specified controlled rate, the assembly is performed. At each workstation, the assembly operations and the addition of components are performed.

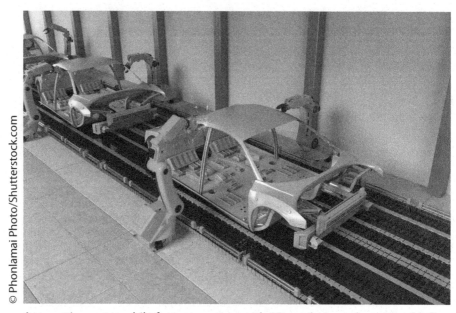

Automation automobile factory concept with 3D rendering robot assembly line in car factory

© Phonlamai Photo/Shutterstock.com

Cycle time The maximum time taken to complete the tasks in a workstation before it is moved to the next workstation in a production process. The cycle time of the process is equal to the longest cycle time of all the workstations.

The specified controlled time spent in the workstations is called the **cycle time**. In an assembly line, time taken to compete the tasks in workstations may vary from one to another. But the time taken in any of the workstations cannot exceed the cycle time. The longest cycle time taken in any workstation in the assembly line is the cycle time of the process itself. Cycle Time (C_t) is calculated using Equation 9-1 as follows:

$$C_t = \frac{Production\,Time}{Required\,Output} \qquad \text{Eq. 9-1}$$

The required output is in units of products. If the required output is given for a day, then the production time must be established for the day or the same period.

A process is in balance if the cycle time for each workstation in the process is the same. The difference between the cycle time and the actual time taken in each workstation is the *idle time* for that workstation. For example, the idle time is the time when a task is waiting for the product to arrive from a previous task. In some situations, the time taken for a task may happen to exceed the cycle time. If that situation arises, we can do one or more of the following:

Idle time The difference between the cycle time and the actual time taken in each workstation is the idle time.

- Split the task or share the task with another task in the assembly line,
- Use a more skilled worker or use overtime to reduce the time taken, or
- Redesign the product so that it will take less time to process.

Assembly-line balancing is a method that uses a set time to move products from one workstation to another. By assigning the tasks to a set of workstations and by using assembly-line balancing, manufacturing firms can minimize the idle time across the workstations. Balancing the assembly line minimizes the idle times. Example 9-2 shows how to balance assembly lines. The minimum number of workstations can be found using Equation 9-2:

> **Assembly-line balancing**
> Assembly-line balancing is a method that uses a set period to move products from one workstation to another.

$$N_{MIN} = \frac{Sum\ of\ all\ task\ times\ (T_t)}{Cycle\ Time\ (C_t)} \qquad \text{Eq. 9-2}$$

The efficiency of the balanced assembly line is calculated as follows:

$$Efficiency = \frac{Sum\ of\ all\ task\ times\ (T_t)}{No\ of\ workstations \times Cycle\ Time\ (C_t)} \times 100 \qquad \text{Eq. 9-3}$$

Example 9-2

Sit and Relax, Inc. makes home furniture. If workstations are operated for 8 hours per day, the expected total output is 440 units, and the sequence and times of tasks performed in an assembly line are shown in the following table, balance the assembly line. Assign the tasks by the longest task time and if there is a tie, assign the task with the greatest number of following tasks.

Task	A	B	C	D	E	F	G	H	I
Task time (secs)	40	35	65	25	25	35	35	30	25
Preceding Tasks				A	B	C	D, E	F	G, H

Step 1: Draw a precedence diagram like we did for the project network in Chapter 4.

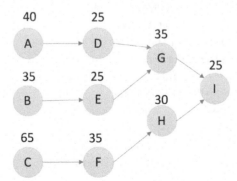

In the above diagram, since tasks A, B, and C do not have any precedence tasks, they are independent starting tasks. Other tasks follow the sequence as shown in the above table.

Step 2:   Calculate the cycle time, C_t using Equation 9-1.

$$C_t = \frac{8\ hrs \times 60\ mins \times 60\ secs}{440\ units} = \frac{28800\ secs/day}{440\ units/day} = 65.45\ secs$$

Step 3:   Calculate the minimum number of workstations using Eq. 9-2

$$N_{MIN} = \frac{40 + 35 + 65 + 25 + 25 + 35 + 35 + 30 + 25}{Cycle\ Time\ (C_t)} = 4.8 \approx 5\ workstations$$

We must round up the N_{MIN} to the next high integer.
   Now, we have a minimum of 5 workstations with a cycle time of 65.45 secs.

Step 4:   We need to use the rules given in the problem.

We need to assign the tasks by the longest task time and if there is a tie, assign the task with the greatest number of following tasks.

Step 5:   Balance the assembly line using Step 4.

   a. Let us start with the starting tasks, A, B, and C.
      Task C has the longest task time of the three tasks equal to 65. Comparing this to the cycle time of 65.45, C is just under the cycle time but we cannot add any other task to C since the total time of C and any other task will be over the cycle time of 65.45. So, task C is assigned to Workstation #1 all by itself.
   b. Now let us look at A and B, the other starting tasks. A takes more time than B but A and B cannot be assigned together as the total time (40 + 35) will exceed C_t We can add task D to A as D can be started after A is done and the total time of A and D (40 + 25) is less than C_t. Therefore, A and D can be assigned to Workstation #2.
   c. Similarly, B the last of the starting tasks can be added with its subsequent task E and assigned to Workstation #3.
   d. Let us look at the remaining tasks. G and F are the next tasks we can start after completing the already assigned tasks. We see that both G and F have the same time of 35. Since this is a tie, let us choose the one with the greatest number of following tasks which would be F. Task F when added with task G will take more time than Ct. But task F when added with H will be less than Ct. Therefore, we will assign Tasks F and H to Workstation #4.
   e. Since tasks G and I are the only remaining tasks and their added times is less than Ct, we can assign them to Workstation #5.

Now, we have assigned the tasks to 5 workstations which is the sum of $N_{MIN.}$

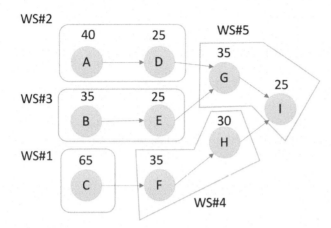

Step 6: Calculate the Idle times for each workstation. We can see that the total idle time of the process is $0.45 + 0.45 + 5.45 + 0.45 + 5.45 = 12.27$ secs. The process cycle time is equal to 65 seconds.

WorkStation	Task	Task time (secs)	C_t	Idle Time (secs)
1	C	65	65.45	0.45
2	A D	65	65.45	0.45
3	B E	60	65.45	5.45
4	F H	65	65.45	0.45
5	G I	60	65.45	5.45

Step 7: Calculate the efficiency of the balanced assembly line using Eq. 9-3:

$$Efficiency = \frac{40+35+65+25+25+35+35+30+25}{5 \times 65.45} \times 100 = 96.25\%$$

Analysis: There are 5 workstations with a cycle time of 65.45 seconds. Th efficiency of the balanced assembly is 96.25%. The total idle time is 12.25 seconds out of a total task time of 315 seconds.

Little's Law and Production Process Analysis

The inventory before it is used to make goods is the raw materials inventory. Inventory that moves through the production process in order to be made as finished goods is the work-in-process inventory. The inventory that consists of produced products is the finished goods. In a supply chain, the raw materials flow from the suppliers through the production operations of a company as work-in-process which are produced as finished goods.

Now, how would you calculate the inventory in the production process? To answer that question, we use Little's Law. Little's Law assumes a steady state in the production process. A steady state in a production process is achieved when the average input rate equals average output rate. What that means is, over a period of time, the number of units produced in a process is equal to the number of units delivered to the customers.

Inventory in a production process = Throughput × Flow time   Eq. 9-4

Throughput is the average rate at which units flow past a specific point in the production process. The maximum throughput is the process capacity, which is the maximum output rate.

Flow time is the average time it takes a unit to flow through a production process from the entry point to the end point. The flow time is the length of the longest path through a process.

Example 9-3

AirMove makes fans for households. They buy motors in bulk from a local distributor at a cost of $65 for a motor. A fan uses one motor and it takes 2 hours to assemble and pack the fan components at AirMove. The plant assembles 1,600 fans in an 8-hr day. What is the work-in-process inventory of AirMove?

We need to calculate the WIP inventory which is equal to the throughput times the flow time.

The throughput is the production output rate which is 1,600/8 = 200 fans per hour. Since each fan uses one motor, the throughput of motors is also 200 per hour.

The flow time is 2 hours, which is the time it takes to assemble and pack a fan. Using Eq. 9-4, WIP inventory = 200 × 2 = 400 motors.

Analysis: The WIP inventory is 400 motors which is equal to 400 × $65 = $26,000.

FROM PRACTICE: FIS AT VOLKSWAGON

Volkswagen, the German motor vehicle manufacturer, is known for their iconic Beetle. The company's brands include Volkswagen, Skoda, Audi, Lamborghini, Bentley, Porsche, Navistar, and Ducati. At Volkswagen headquarters in Wolfsburg, there is a control room called "Fertigungs-, Informations- und Steuerungssystem," (FIS) or production, information, and control system in

English. This control room is the "brain of the factory" and it controls the company's entire automobile production process. A customer signs the contract as a starting point and the customer's car is produced on time from the factory side as the end point. Once the binding delivery date is determined, a "sonata" (target in days) is generated.

© Peter Kniez/Shutterstock.com

The assembly line runs at a 60-second interval. More than 60,000 vehicles are made per month. When the production date arrives, the vehicle is made. Production in Wolfsburg is run like clockwork. Using FIS, Volkswagen has produced more than 50 million vehicles in more than 20 years[11].

Formulae from this Chapter

Cycle Time	$C_t = \dfrac{Production\ Time}{Required\ Output}$	Eq. 9-1
Minimum number of workstations	$N_{MIN} = \dfrac{Sum\ of\ all\ task\ times\ (T_t)}{Cycle\ Time\ (C_t)}$	Eq. 9-2
Efficiency of a balanced assembly line	$Efficiency = \dfrac{Sum\ of\ all\ task\ times\ (T_t)}{No.\ of\ workstations \times Cycle\ Time} \times 100$	Eq. 9-3
Inventory in a production process	$Inventory = Throughput \times Flow\ time$	Eq. 9-4

Case Study: Assembly line Analysis at Mobile Fone, Inc.

Mobile Fone, Inc. assembles mobile phones. Rebecca Cellar, the president of Mobile Fone hired Phil Morbars as the production manager to efficiently run their assembly plant in Mobile, Alabama. Rebecca had worked as the production director at a major cellphone manufacturer and had risen through the ranks over the years. She had worked with Phil over the years and found him to be intelligent and an "out-of-the-box" thinker. Her ultimate goal was to take the used parts of old cellphones and reuse them to make a new cellphone and sell them in the market at a cheaper price for those who cannot afford expensive cellphones. Phil and Rebecca had similar interests in social work in giving back to their communities.

Phil and Rebecca set up an initial prototype for an assembly line. Their main goal was to set up a simple assembly line but with the workers from the local community who needed a job. To maintain a quality product, they decided to hire a few people and train each worker to do two different jobs. They did this to make their workforce flexible, so that each worker can handle two different jobs with ease and technical knowledge. There was another reason for this as well. They thought that if workers are flexible, then productivity will increase.

Phil was well versed in setting up an assembly line. He had designed many assembly lines and was experienced in laying out assembly lines in the United States and South America. He also understood the production process for the mobile phone assembly very well. Rebecca and Phil initially timed the flow of the materials. This work-study exercise helped them to understand how many people to hire, how to move the components to assemble the cell phone, and how many parts are required in the assembly line. They bought the necessary materials to begin their cell phone assembly.

Phil's idea was to set up the assembly line and try out the assembly for a few days and then if all things go well, ramp up the production. He set up an initial assembly line with no conveyors. He set up several tables and chairs for people to sit and work and pass on the work done from one person to another in a straight-line assembly.

The assembly started on a Monday. By that time, Phil and Rebecca had hired the needed workers, designed the assembly line layout, tested the assembly, and were ready to go. The company was set up to work in two shifts. The first shift started at 8:00 AM and ended at 4:00 PM and the second shift started at 4:30 PM and ended at 12:30 AM. Each shift had 1-hour breaks. Phil and Rebecca wanted their workers in an environment where they can be relaxed as well be efficient.

Initially, the plan was to assemble 8,400 cell phones a day in two shifts. Phil's initial assembly process sheet is given below:

Task ID	Task	Task time (secs)	Preceding Tasks
A	Install insulating films to motherboard	1	
B	Install camera	4	A
C	Solder power starter	3	B
D	Solder volume rocker	3	B
E	Solder microphone	2	C, D
F	Solder vibrator	2	E
G	Join motherboard to chassis	2	F
H	Secure wires	3	G

Task ID	Task	Task time (secs)	Preceding Tasks
I	Fasten interior and keys	5	H
J	Flash Operating systems and apps	4	I
K	Install earpiece	2	J
L	Assemble and clean display and touch screen	4	K
M	System startup test	5	L
N	Test microphone and response	6	M
O	Fasten chassis	2	N
P	Signal receiver test	3	O
Q	Final Test	4	P
R	Clean surfaces and add protective film	5	Q
S	Pack to ship	2	R

Case Questions

A. Draw the precedence diagram.
B. What is the cycle time required to produce the output that was initially set up by the company?
C. Based on the available data, what is the minimum number of workstations required to assemble the cell phones?
D. How many workstations are needed after balancing the assembly line?
E. What is the efficiency of the balanced assembly line?

After three days of work, the management wants to step up the production on Thursday by 20%. The adjustments can be made by decreasing time taken by a second at key workstations D, J, L, and N.

F. What adjustments can be made in the assembly line?
G. What is the cycle time required to produce the output in this case?
H. What is the minimum number of workstations required to assemble the cell phones now?
I. How many workstations are needed after balancing the assembly line?
J. What is the efficiency of the balanced assembly line now?
K. What steps must the company take to increase the number of cell phones assembled?

Summary

- A process is a step-by-step or a series of actions taken to achieve a particular objective.
- Production processes are used to make goods that we buy and provide services that we enjoy.

- In manufacturing industries, processes are used to acquire and use necessary resources, manufacture goods, and deliver value-added goods to customers to make money.
- In service organizations, processes are used to acquire and use necessary resources and provide value-added services to customers to make money.
- The customer order decoupling point (CODP) is the point in the supply chain where the product is linked to a specific customer order.
- CODP impacts both the inventory and the resources used to create the product. CODP is based on the information from the supply chain such as sales forecasts and customizable customer orders.
- There are four scenarios where CODP plays a part in the supply chain including made to stock, assembled to order, made to order, and engineered to order.
- Economies of scale are cost advantages for a company when costs, both fixed and variable, are spread over a larger number of goods.
- Made to stock goods are available to customers as finished goods in the market and customers are served on demand.
- Assembled to stock goods are assembled for customers as per their wishes but still the majority of the manufacturing process is accomplished on a mass scale.
- Made to order products are made directly from raw materials in the current inventory in response to a customer order.
- Engineered to order products are made directly from start to finish for a unique requirement and specification of a customer.
- The production process can be categorized into five processes including subtractive, additive, net shape, batch, and continuous.
- Subtractive processes involve removing material from a solid block of raw material.
- An additive process, the opposite of a subtractive process, is used to create an object by building it one layer at a time.
- The process that is used to create a complete product without going through any finish machining is called the net shape process.
- A batch process involves a set of ingredients as input and using a sequence of one or more production steps in a predefined order to manufacture a set number of products to make up a single batch.
- In a continuous process, raw materials move from the start of the process through each production step to a final product.
- The difference between a continuous production process and a batch production process is the continuous process never stops and there are no breaks between the different steps during production.
- A production system layout is the way in which the workflow—consisting of humans, machines, parts, and other equipment used for production—is arranged or laid out.
- Production system layout includes fixed position assembly, workcenter, manufacturing cell, and assembly line.

- Fixed position assembly is a layout in which the product does not move while being assembled.
- A workcenter layout is where similar equipment or functions are grouped together and the product is made to travel to the equipment or functions.
- A manufacturing cell is a dedicated facility to produce similar products by a group of machines.
- A family of parts is a collection of similar parts in varied sizes or with different features.
- An assembly line layout consists of a predefined sequence of production processes to assemble the product in a progressive fashion.
- The specified controlled time spent in a workstation and its subsequent workstations is called the workstation cycle time.
- The cycle time is the maximum time taken to complete the tasks in a workstation before it is moved to the next workstation.
- A production process is in balance if the cycle times for each workstation in the process are equal.
- The cycle time of the process is equal to the longest cycle time of all the workstations.
- Idle time is the difference between the cycle time and the actual time taken in each workstation.
- Assembly line balancing is a method that uses a set period to move products from one workstation to another.
- Little's Law assumes a steady state in the production process. A steady state in a production process is achieved when the average input rate equals average output rate.
- The inventory in a production process is the product of throughput and flow time.
- Throughput is the average rate at which units flow past a specific point in the production process.
- Flow time is the average time it takes a unit to flow through a production process from the entry point to the end point.

Review Questions

1. Explain a process.
2. What are production processes?
3. Why are processes used in manufacturing industries?
4. What is a customer order decoupling point (CODP)?
5. What are the four scenarios where CODP plays a part in the supply chain?
6. Explain economies of scale.
7. What is "made to stock"?
8. What is "assembled to stock"?
9. What is "made to order"?

10. What is "engineered to order"?
11. How are production processes categorized?
12. Explain a subtractive process with an example.
13. Explain an additive process with an example.
14. Explain a net shape process with an example.
15. Explain a batch process with an example.
16. Explain a continuous process with an example.
17. What is a production system layout?
18. What are the different production system layouts? Explain each one of the layouts described in this chapter with examples.
19. Describe a family of parts with an example.
20. What is cycle time?
21. What is idle time?
22. When is assembly line balancing used?
23. Explain Little's Law.
24. Explain a steady state condition in the production process.
25. How is inventory calculated in a production process?
26. What are throughput and flow time?

Critical Thinking Questions

1. How does CODP impact inventory in a manufacturing company?
2. How does CODP impact resources in a manufacturing company?
3. How is CODP based on the information from the supply chain?
4. Which of the scenarios of CODP is used in a store like Walmart?
5. Which of the scenarios of CODP is used when you buy a new car?
6. Which of the scenarios of CODP is used by NASA when it buys components for space exploration?
7. How do companies use economies of scale to their advantage?
8. Which is the most common productive process?
9. What is the difference between additive and subtractive processes?
10. What is the difference between additive and net shape processes?
11. What is the difference between batch and continuous processes?
12. Which is the most common production process in drug making industries?
13. Why is a production layout important for a manufacturing company?
14. What production layout is used in a drug manufacturer? Why?
15. If you want to build a stadium, what production layout is the best suited? Why? What kind of resources are needed and how would you lay out those resources?
16. What is the difference between a workcenter and a manufacturing cell?

17. How is a collection of similar parts in varied sizes or with different features used as an advantage in a manufacturing company?
18. When is a production process in balance?
19. What is the maximum time taken to complete the tasks in a workstation before it is moved to the next workstation in a production process?
20. Why is the cycle time of the process equal to the longest cycle time of all the workstations?
21. Why is assembly line balancing used in manufacturing?
22. What happens if a line is unbalanced?
23. What is the minimum cycle time of a balanced assembly line?
24. What is the maximum cycle time of a balanced assembly line?
25. Why does Little's Law assume a steady state in the production process?

Problem Solving Questions

1. Robert Pelham, Jr. has determined 18 workstations after balancing an assembly line. He found that the total time for all the tasks is 20 minutes and the cycle time is 3 minutes. The assembly line is to be run for 500 minutes per day.
   a. What is the minimum number of workstations needed to realize maximum output?
   b. What output will be realized if the cycle time is 5 minutes?
   c. What output will be realized if the cycle time is 10 minutes?
2. Jim Casey from Casey Kilns, an artificial façade manufacturer from the southern part of Illinois has balanced the assembly line. There are 10 workstations with a total time of 15 minutes and a cycle time of 100 seconds. The assembly line will operate for 8 hours a day.
   a. What is the minimum cycle time?
   b. What is the maximum cycle time?
   c. What is the minimum number of workstations needed to realize maximum output?
   d. What is the output for a day?
   e. What is the efficiency of the balanced assembly line?
3. A construction company is working on installing bathroom fixtures for 12 homes. They would like to complete one house and move to the next and so on. The crew works for a total of 8 hours every day for a total of 12 days and completes all the tasks.
   a. What is the minimum cycle time?
   b. What is the maximum cycle time?
   c. What is the minimum number of workstations needed to realize maximum output?
   d. What is the efficiency of the balanced assembly line?

4. A machine shop works to manufacture a bunch of auto parts for their customer. The workshop produces 210 auto parts in a 7-hour day. Assign the tasks by the longest task time and if there is a tie, assign the task with the greatest number of following tasks. The tasks, time taken, and the immediate predecessors are given below:

Task	Time taken (mins)	Predecessor
A	0.2	
B	0.4	A
C	0.2	B
D	0.4	
E	0.9	D
F	1.2	C
G	1	E, F

   a. Draw the precedence diagram.
   b. Calculate the cycle time.
   c. What is the minimum number of workstations needed to realize the output?
   d. Balance the assembly line and compute the total idle time.
   e. What is the efficiency of the balanced assembly line?

5. For the machine shop in Problem 4, if the rules are changed to assign tasks to workstations on the basis of most following tasks and if there is tie, use the shortest processing time,
   a. What is the cycle time?
   b. Draw the precedence diagram.
   c. What is the minimum number of workstations needed to realize the output?
   d. Balance the assembly line and compute the total idle time.
   e. What is the efficiency of the balanced assembly line?

6. A bakery in town works for eight hours a day to make 180 cakes. The following table shows the tasks, time taken, and the precedence of tasks. Assign the tasks by the longest task time and if there is a tie, assign the task with the greatest number of following tasks.

Task	Time taken (secs)	Predecessor
A	80	
B	90	A
C	30	A
D	40	A
E	70	B, C
F	20	C, D
G	40	E, F
H	60	G

    a. What is the cycle time?
    b. Draw the precedence diagram.
    c. What is the minimum number of workstations needed to realize the output?
    d. Balance the assembly line and compute the total idle time.
    e. What is the efficiency of the balanced assembly line?

7. The output of an assembly line at Regis Blocks is 600 units per day. The company works for 8 hours a day. Assign the tasks by the greatest number of following tasks and longest task time if there is a tie. The following table shows the tasks, time taken, and the precedence of tasks.

Task	Time taken (secs)	Predecessor
A	30	
B	15	A
C	40	B
D	32	C
E	15	D
F	41	E
G	40	F

    a. What is the cycle time?
    b. Draw the precedence diagram.
    c. What is the minimum number of workstations needed to realize the output?
    d. Balance the assembly line and compute the total idle time.
    e. What is the efficiency of the balanced assembly line?

8. Sitcom, a chemical manufacturer, has a short assembly line to manufacture pigments. They plan to manufacture 2,400 specialized cans for a home improvement store in St. Louis in an 8-hr day. Assign the tasks by the longest task time and if there is a tie, assign the task with the greatest number of following tasks.

Task	Time taken (secs)	Predecessor
A	10	
B	2	A
C	8	A
D	4	B, C
E	5	D
F	6	E
G	4	F

    a. What is the cycle time?
    b. Draw the precedence diagram.

   c. What is the minimum number of workstations needed to realize the output?

   d. Balance the assembly line and compute the total idle time.

   e. What is the efficiency of the balanced assembly line?

9. The output of an assembly line at Regis Blocks is 380 units on April 4, 2022, and the assembly operated for 460 minutes. Assign the tasks by the greatest number of following tasks and longest task time if there is a tie. The following table shows the tasks, time taken, and the precedence of tasks.

Task	Time taken (secs)	Predecessor
A	30	
B	35	A
C	30	A
D	35	B
E	15	C
F	60	C
G	40	E, F
H	20	D, G

   a. What is the cycle time?

   b. Draw the precedence diagram.

   c. What is the minimum number of workstations needed to realize the output?

   d. Balance the assembly line and compute the total idle time.

   e. What is the efficiency of the balanced assembly line?

10. Rebsys manufacturers specialized bicycles in Lawrence, KS. They use two wheels per bicycle and they purchase the wheels from a vendor from Kansas City at a price of $32 per wheel. It takes 2.5 hours to assemble a specialized bicycle and the company assembles 300 bicycles per day in an 8-hour period. The company holds 200 wheels as safety stock. What is the total number of bicycle wheels in the Lawrence plant? What is the total value of the inventory?

References

1. Randall, T., & Pogkas, D. (2022). *Tesla Now Runs the Most Productive Auto Factory in America*. Retrieved March 25, 2022 from https://www.bloomberg.com/graphics/2022-tesla-factory-california-texas-car-production/

2. Saiidi , U. (2019). *We went inside Tesla's Gigafactory. Here's what it looked like*. Retrieved March 22, 2022 from https://www.cnbc.com/2019/05/03/we-went-inside-teslas-gigafactory-heres-what-it-looked-like.html.

3. Doll, S. (2021). *Tesla factory locations: Where they are and could soon be*. Retrieved March 22, 2022 from https://electrek.co/2021/07/14/tesla-factory-locations-where-they-are-and-could-soon-be/.

4. Olhager,J. (2010). The role of the customer order decoupling point in production and supply chain management. *Computers in Industry, 61*(9), 863–868.

5. Cosgrove, E. (2020). Macy's lays out a massive supply chain overhaul. *Supplychaindive*. Retrieved April 1, 2022 from https://www.supplychaindive.com/news/macys-massive-supply-chain-overhaul/571800/.

6. Planetmagpie (2019). *Where to Get Computer Components Made in the USA*. Retrieved March 26, 2022 from https://planetmagpie.com/news/woof-newsletter/2019/07/10/where-to-get-computer-components-made-in-the-usa#:~:text=DELL.,worldwide%2C%20from%20Mexico%20to %20Ireland.

7. Hoffman, C. (2021). Porsche Classic Will Now Build Custom One-Off Dream Cars. *Car and Driver*, Retrieved March 21, 2022 from https://www.caranddriver.com/news/a36383423/porsche-classic-custom-one-off-cars-announced/.

8. Grogan, B. (2016). Accelerating Lead Times for Engineer to Order (ETO) Processes. *Siemens*. Retrieved March 31, 2022 from https://blogs.sw.siemens.com/teamcenter/accelerating-lead-times-for-engineer-to-order-eto-processes/

9. Whelan, C., & Sheahan, C. (2019). Using additive manufacturing to produce injection moulds suitable for short series production. *Procedia Manufacturing, 38,* 60–68.

10. Domokos, A., Nagy, B., Szilágyi, B., Marosi, G., & Nagy, Z. (2021). Integrated continuous pharmaceutical technologies—A review. *Organizational Process Research Development, 25*(4), 721–739.

11. Volkswagen (2022). *The Brain of the Factory*. Retrieved March 29, 2022 from https://www.volkswagenag.com/ en/news/stories/2019/03/the-brain-of-the-factory.html#

SERVICE OPERATIONS

Learning Objectives

- Explain service operations and the service process.
- Describe the difference between production and service industries.
- Explain the characteristics of a service process.
- Explain labor intensity, consumer interaction, and service customization
- Classify service processes.
- Explain service complexity and how blueprints are accomplished in industry.
- Explain the difference between traditional and online services.
- Identify the factors of service value proposition to customers.
- Describe the main characteristics of queuing systems.
- Explain the four basic queuing systems.
- Describe how probability distributions help to analyze queuing systems.
- Analyze queuing systems.

Amazon.com, Inc., the American multinational retailer, is one of the leading e-commerce, cloud computing and digital streaming service providers with a revenue of over $380 billion in 2020. The company initially sold books online and has expanded selling an array of product categories. Its subsidiaries include Amazon Web Services, Ring, and Whole Foods Market. Amazon distributes a variety of downloadable and streaming video and audio content, books, films, television content, consumer electronics, and provides web services. Amazon uses its own logistics and transportation services to deliver its goods. Amazon Prime Air has experimented with drone delivery services. Amazon first launched its fulfillment network with two distribution centers in Seattle, WA and New Castle, DE. They have expanded their services with over 75 distribution centers and 25 sortation centers with

© Deep Pixel/
Shutterstock.com

© Frederic Legrand -
COMEO/Shutterstock.com

© rvlsoft/Shutterstock.com

© Chesky/Shutterstock.com

© vovidzha/Shutterstock.com

over 125,000 employees[1]. The services provided from these centers are un-packing and inspecting incoming goods, placing goods in storage, recording their location, picking goods for individual shipments, sorting, and packing orders, and shipping. These activities are executed by either employees or automated robots.

Amazon Web Services (AWS) is the company's cloud offering with more than 200 fully featured services available from data centers globally. Many customers, including startups, large enterprises, and government agencies use AWS to lower costs, increase security, become more agile, and innovate faster[2]. AWS is an online platform that provides scalable and cost-effective cloud computing solutions. Cloud computing is the delivery of online services and a provider like AWS will have servers, databases, and software that most companies need. For example, if a company wants to store a document, they may use their computer to develop the document and then save the document in their computer storage system. Instead of purchasing the software and the computer, they can simply connect to an online platform like AWS, use the software available with AWS , and store the document on their storage systems from anywhere in the world. Firms can also host their websites on the AWS. AWS is not only for companies but also for individual customers. To run gaming applications, a lot of computing power is needed and AWS makes it easy for the best online gaming experience.

Service Process

A service industry is a business that is not involved in manufacturing. The service industry provides services rather than tangible objects like goods. Examples of service industries are banking, wholesale and retail, communications, engineering, computer software development, health-care, and so on. A service company such as a landscaping firm sells its landscaping services only. But many service companies such as Verizon and AT&T offer both physical products like cell phones and telecommunication services.

Businesses provide service to their customers in exchange for money, time, or effort. The customers expect value for such services. Mostly, the service businesses offer service packages to serve their customers. A service package is a bundle of benefits that are provided by a company offering its services. The service packages are often provided with goods that are provided by the same companies. For example, when you buy a new car from a car dealership, the car dealership will provide you the customary service package as well as an extended service package. They may also provide you a bunch of free services such as free oil changes for a year or two. The services can be in the form of providing more information about the car you bought as well.

The service process is how a service company provides its service to its customers. Organizations provide services in diverse ways. The service process consists of providing supporting facility, goods, information, explicit, and implicit services. A golf course provides the golf course as a supporting facility, golf balls and caps as goods, information such as course layout, implicit services such as challenging holes, and explicit services such as website booking of tee times.

> **Service process** A service process is how a service company provides services to its customers.

> **Service** Services, in terms of business services, are transactions offered by a business to a customer.

Service Process Characteristics

There are a number of characteristics that are shared by all service companies. Customer contact is one of them. The customer contact characteristic is important to know the wants, the wishes, and the needs of the customers. The other important characteristics are the quality of the services and the reputation of the service provider. The reputation is of importance since services are intangible, meaning that services cannot be felt or seen. The quality and other related measures such as efficiency and effectiveness are subjective and not easy to measure. Moreover, the rendered services are time perishable. For example, if no one paid a visit to a barber on a particular day, that service for that day would never be available. Two elements are used to characterize service processes[3] including:

1. Labor intensity, and
2. A combination of consumer interaction and service customization.

FROM PRACTICE: Service Process at the Old Course

Jack Nichalus, the famous golf player, said "I fell in love with it the first day I played it. There's just no other golf course that is even remotely close." He was referring to St. Andrews Links a.k.a. the "Old course." This service provider offers supporting facility, goods, information, explicit, and implicit services. The supporting facility is the oldest and most iconic golf course in the world. The Swilcan Bridge and the Hell Bunker are recognized across the globe. But the

© AdamEdwards/Shutterstock.com

best part and the greatest feature of the Old Course is that despite its grand status it remains a public golf course. The course sells various goods such as golf sets, golf balls, headwear, and souvenirs as goods. The information about the course is available. Implicit services such as challenging holes and explicit services such as website booking of tee times and golf lessons are all part of the course services.

> **Labor intensity**
> Labor intensity is the ratio of the incurred cost of labor to the value of plant and equipment excluding inventory.

Labor Intensity

Labor intensity is the ratio of the incurred cost of the labor to the value of the plant and the equipment excluding the inventory[3]. We can classify labor intensive businesses to be either high labor-intensive business or low labor-intensive business. A high labor-intensive business involves smaller plant and equipment but high cost and effort. An example is a consulting company, where plant and equipment costs are low and the time, effort, and cost borne by the consultants are high. In a low labor-intensive business, the labor costs are lower compared to the cost of plant and equipment. A shipping company with high capital costs is an example. A hospital with a high cost of buildings, technology, and healthcare facilities costs more than the costs of the doctors, the nurses, and the technicians[3].

Consumer Interaction and Service Customization Combination

The degree to which customers interact with the service process and the degree to which the business customizes its services to its customers are combined to form the second element[3]. The combined measures have a high value when a service comprises a high level of interaction and a high level of customization for the customer. The combined measures have a low value when both individual measures are low. A joint measure falls somewhere between a low and a high value when the two measures are combined.

Some fast-food restaurants such as Chipotle's have high customization and high customer interactions. Some restaurants have low customization with their menu items and low customer interaction as they obtain the order, make the food, serve the food, and receive the payment. Fast-food restaurants such as McDonalds and Burger King have brief customer interaction with customized burgers made just as the customer wanted. Services that have high customer interaction and low customizations are tax firms such as H&R Block and some hair styling salons.

Service Process Classifications

Many service providers or service businesses share certain process-related characteristics as described in the last section. Those characteristics are used in marketing and operations, and for customer satisfaction by businesses. From the process point of view, the classification of services falls into four broad categories including people processing, possession processing, mental stimulus processing, and information processing[4].

People Processing

People must be present to receive these services. In this category, people are the direct recipients of the tangible actions performed on them. Airlines, transit systems, taxis, personal grooming places, hotels, resorts, restaurants, retail trade, and healthcare services are examples of people processing using tangible actions. The service recipients must be physically present in this service system to receive such services. Here, the people become an integral part of the provided services. In the cases of mobile services, the services may come to the customers instead of them going to the service premises. In any case, people interested in obtaining this category of ser-

An experience at a resort

vices need to put forth some time and effort as well the associated costs. The required amount of time and effort depends on the service. Eating in a popular restaurant takes more time than eating at a fast-food restaurant.

Possession Processing

People's possessions are serviced directly and certain intangible actions are also performed on them. Car repair, freight transportation, laundry, dry cleaning, home repair, home maintenance, and insurance are some of the examples of possession processing. People need not be present but may choose to be. For example, in the case of landscaping, the homeowners may prefer to supervise the worker with their ideas. In most of this category of services, people may drop off their possessions, explain the actions to be taken, and pick up and pay for their serviced items later. In some instances, some of these services can be accomplished using regular mail without leaving the comfort of a customer's home.

Dog Grooming

Financial Services

Mental Stimulus Processing

The intangible action on people belongs to this category. Advertising, education, entertainment, financial advice, and professional advice are examples of mental stimulus processing using intangible actions. This category influences people's behavior. People can be present but need not be. In any case, they need to pay attention to the communication and information. They have to invest time and mental effort to obtain the full benefit of these services. Remote and face-to-face education are examples of this category of service process. Watching a football game on television and attending the event are two different experiences but still reach the mental faculty of people.

Information Processing

The intangible actions on people's possessions are called information processing. Tax, financial, legal, consulting, diagnosis, cloud services, and web hosting

are examples of the information processing category. Mental stimulus processing and information processing are closely related. Consulting, for example, can be mentally stimulating as well as process the information. This is because both tangible and intangible benefits and actions are present in consulting. Furthermore, these can be transformed from being an intangible to a tangible action. Information in the form of the stock market performance can be informative but the analysis and recommendations can be in a tangible format as in a letter or an email.

Stock Information

Complexity of services Complexity of services reflects the number of steps that are involved in delivering the services.

Service blueprint A flowchart that helps a customer to understand a service process.

Complexity of Services and Service Blueprint

Obtaining services often takes multiple steps. The complexity of services reflects the number of steps that are involved in delivering the services[5]. For example, the payment of property taxes might involve three distinct steps. The first step is to find out how much taxes you owe from a county clerk department. If you find any discrepancy or to obtain a homestead exemption, you might have to visit another department. Then you pay your taxes in the county treasury department. The complexity in services also increases a customer's effort and time to use those services. For example, checking the bank account balance takes less effort than transferring funds between banks.

A **service blueprint** is a flowchart that helps a customer to understand a service process. A service blueprint shows the steps that are involved to obtain a service. It also provides the process flow for the service provider. By looking at the blueprint, a customer can easily determine whether the services are high

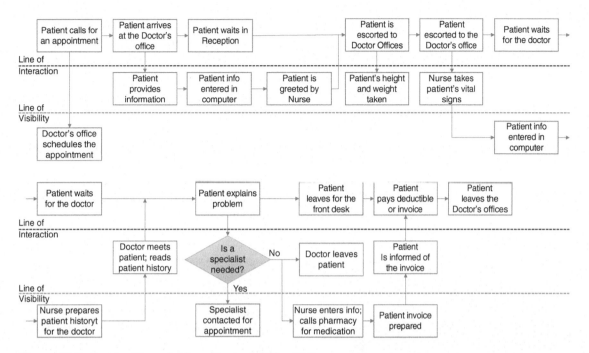

Figure 10-1 Service Blueprint for a Doctor's Office Visit

or low in complexity as well as understand what is visible to the customer and what is not. A service blueprint will help to determine the complexity of services. The service complexity tends to have a negative effect on self-service situations and as service complexity increases, it requires a higher level of cognitive effort to understand the service offers[5]. Figure 10-1 shows a service blueprint for a visit to a doctor's office.

In Figure 10-1, all the activities in the service are mapped as a flowchart. There are three levels in the service blueprint. The top level shows the activities of a patient separated by the **line of interaction** from the patient's interactions with the people at the doctor's office, which forms the middle level. The middle level shows the interactions of the patient with the office staff. There is a **visibility line** that separates the middle level and the lower level. The lower level illustrates all the behind-the-scenes operations.

Traditional and Online Service Operations

The physical distancing and stay-at-home orders due to COVID-19 have tilted the consumer landscape more towards online shopping from traditional brick and mortar shopping methods. According to McKinsey, online purchasing has increased on an average by 15–30% across many goods categories[6]. The report shows that even online purchasing of discretionary items such as skin care, makeup, apparel, jewelry, and accessories are projected to grow by more than 15%. The same report forecasts that the intent of the consumers to shop online seems like a growing trend. However, according to the Shopper-First Retailing report by Salesforce and Sapient, a survey conducted on 6,000 consumers from the United States, Canada, Australia, Germany, France, and the United Kingdom, 57% of shoppers preferred traditional shopping over online shopping because of the traditional customer service[7].

What is the basic difference between traditional and online customer service? Traditional service includes a personal service. There are knowledgeable store associates who can help a customer to pick an item; there are better signs and directions to help shoppers locate an item; and there is a dedicated customer service desk that helps customers with issues and questions. In this section, we will discuss online service operations.

FROM PRACTICE: Online Services by Netflix

© sitthiphong/Shutterstock.com

Netflix, the subscription-based streaming service, provides TV shows and movies without commercials on an Internet-connected device as services to its members. Members can download TV shows and movies to their iOS, Android, or Windows 10 devices and watch without any Internet connection. They can watch a wide variety of award-winning Netflix Originals, TV shows, movies, documentaries, and more. The services can be enjoyed through any Internet-connected device that offers the Netflix app, including smart TVs, game consoles, streaming media players, set-top boxes, smartphones, and tablets.

Netflix offers three streaming plans including basic, standard, and premium.

Online services provide information and services over the Internet. Online services have revolutionized the way we obtain information. A simple online service helps consumers to gain data and information through a search engine like Google. A much more complex online service may be the access to filing taxes online. There are a number of online services nowadays such as banking, news, telemedicine, education, shopping, dating, entertainment, social media, gaming, email, and information. Some services are free like Google and Facebook while others such as Netflix and Prime charge monthly subscription fees. In any case, most online services provide either their own tools that allow their users to communicate with one another or access other third-party sites. The main benefits of online services include global reach, 24 hours a day, 7 days a week, cost savings, and faster delivery of products. However, there are a few disadvantages such as lack of relationship between the seller and buyer, business credibility, a need for extensive customer care service, and in some places Internet connectivity problems.

Service Systems Design

The design of service systems is a complex task of integrating the value propositions for the customers. A service provider must understand the value propositions for their customers first and then design a service package based on the customers' perceptions. The problem is that the service providers face many choices on how to offer the services to their customers. So, how to address the customer value proposition and design a service package? To begin with, a value proposition must address the following three major components:

1. Core service product,
2. Supplementary services, and
3. Service delivery design.

The design of service systems to form a service package is to combine, sequence, deliver, schedule, and implement the three major components.

Service systems design Service systems design is the complex task of integrating value proposition for customers.

Core Service Product

The core service product is the central component of the services provided by a business. For example, the core service product of an auto repair shop is to repair a vehicle. The core service product of a business is unique that is based on a core set of benefits and solutions to their customers. A restaurant provides tasty food for its customers, a hotel provides a comfortable room for its customers, and an airline provides transportation for its customers from a place to a destination.

Core service product The core service product is the central component of the services provided by a business.

Supplementary Services

The supplementary services are other service-related activities that usually accompany the core service products. The supplementary services augment the core service product and enhance the customer value proposition. These services facilitate the use of the core service products and increase the overall experience for a customer. They serve as a source of competitive advantage for the service provider. For example, an auto repair shop provides free coffee, a place to sit, free Internet to browse or work, magazines to read, and a TV to watch while the vehicle is being repaired. Such provisions offer a customer to wait at their premises in a productive manner and even buy the auto accessories sold by the repair shop.

Supplementary services Supplementary services are other service-related activities that usually accompany core service products.

Service Delivery Design

The service delivery design focuses on how to deliver the core and supplementary services to customers. A service delivery design of a business consists of how the distinctive features of their core and supplementary services are delivered to their customers. The design must consider the length of the delivery of such services, the level at which the services are offered, and the role of their customers in the service process. For example, an auto repair shop may inform their customers of how long the service will take and provide a ride to their customers to their work or home. They may even provide a loan car for their customers during the time taken to repair their cars.

The important aspect of service delivery design is the design of the sequence in which customers will use the core and supplementary services and the approximate length of time required in each instance[8].

Service Demand Management

The demand management in service businesses concerns managing the customers' waiting time to receive products. For example, waiting in line at a grocery store on a Sunday afternoon is a painstaking issue for many grocery shoppers. The waiting lines and the queues are unavoidable when managing supply and demand. The managers at service-providing businesses assess dealing with the fluctuating demand as one of their biggest challenges[9]. Businesses must manage the waiting duration at checkouts and other places in order to be competitive. The companies that manage the waiting duration at checkout well have a competitive advantage[10]. Moreover, it is an important part of the customer relations process. This situation is not unique to a Sunday crowd at the grocery store. This is a relevant issue in banks, airports, shopping malls, concert halls, restaurants, government offices, car rental, and post offices, among other places. The grocery stores, restaurants, and other shopping places pose more problems as customers can get disgusted with the wait time and leave for the next shop.

To tackle the service demand, businesses can take many actions. There are three basic approaches to managing demand including:

1. Take no action and let the demand find its own level,
2. Create a reservation system, and
3. Create formalized waiting and queuing systems.

Taking no actions and leaving the demand to find its own levels is a simple method with painful consequences. The idea is to let the customers learn from experience or word-of-mouth to find out when a service is available without much delay. The consequences are that customers can find alternate solutions and never come back. Creating a reservation system is followed by airlines, concert halls, sport stadiums, and at entertainment resort complexes. The more formalized waiting and queuing systems, either as a stand-alone strategy or in combination with a reservation system has been followed by many businesses to deliver their core and supplementary services effectively. This system works well to manage demand by offering customers the same service at many specified times.

FROM PRACTICE: Waiting Made Easy at Disney World

The most famous entertainment facility in the world, Disney World, has made waiting in lines easier with their "My Disney Experience" app. This app is a real lifesaver! Before and during your trip, you can use it to make FastPass + and dining reservations, link your tickets to your MagicBand, and connect with your family and friends to manage everyone's trip. The app will  update the wait times for the attractions and it is great to check throughout the day to plan your time efficiently. It will also update when an attraction is down, so you never have to walk all the way across the park only to be disappointed.

Disney Genie service, a new planning tool, includes a customizable digital Tip Board, where visitors can view estimated wait times for standby attractions, join the virtual queue at select attractions, order food, make dining reservations, and check into a restaurant. There is also a personalized daily itinerary creator available that regularly updates as the visitor's plans change, offers forecasted wait times, and provides suggestions inspired by the individual interests of the visitor, and manages the individual itinerary. Genie + service for a fee lets visitors choose the next available arrival window for Lightning Lane entrances at select attractions and entertainment.

Waiting Lines and Queues

Waiting for a service is certainly a negative experience for a customer. It is directly correlated to customer satisfaction. Long wait times leave customers angry and customers think less of the perceived quality of the service provider's products[11]. Waiting in lines is boring, time-wasting, and even physically uncomfortable. But every business faces this problem. From waiting to connect to someone on telephone calls to boarding airplanes, waiting has almost become a normal life routine.

Waiting lines or queues occur whenever the number of persons entering a service-providing facility is greater than the capacity of the system to process the services rendered to them. The photo shows a busy airport where there are only a few people available to check in passengers. Airports cannot afford to assign a large number of agents to check the customers for identification and give tickets to passengers. The queues or waiting lines are a result of unresolved capacity management. The example of waiting to connect to someone using a telephone is an example that queuing is a problem without being present

A busy airport with long queues

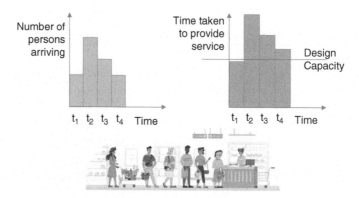

Figure 10-2 Why do queues occur?

Source: Ganesh Vaidyanathan and © Sensvector/Shutterstock.com

in a physical queue. As shown in Figure 10-2, waiting lines can happen whenever the number of persons arriving at a service-providing facility exceeds the designed capacity of the system.

In Figure 10-2, we see that a queue has formed before a grocery store counter. The capacity to serve during any time t may be designed for a specific number of customers entering the service system with say a full shopping cart of purchased items. The **service system** is the facility that offers the services, which may be a counter to pay for the purchased goods. At time t_1, the number of customers entering the service system can be handled as the time to provide service and the design capacity is the same. At time t_2, the number of customers entering may not be handled by the clerk as the time to provide service to those customers has exceeded the design capacity. This may be due to many factors. A customer at time t_2 may have brought an item that needed a price check or the point-of-sales (POS) system may have failed temporarily, the barcode scanner may have malfunctioned, or the customer needed another service that required the clerk to step away from the counter to perform a task. Note that even as the number of customers arriving decreased over the next time period, there may be still a queue.

To control the service demand and alleviate the queuing situation, the grocery store manager can take a number of actions. The manager can open more counters, allocate specific lanes for fewer purchased items, launch specific lanes for people with multiple service needs, or open self-service counters. For the clerk who is providing the services, the manager can assign an assistant at each counter, more reliable POS and scanners, or faster setup time. To manage waiting lines or queues, we will analyze queuing systems. Queuing systems comprise four main characteristics including:

1. Number of customers in the system,
2. The serving system that serves those customers,
3. The customer arrival and service patterns, and
4. The queue discipline rules.

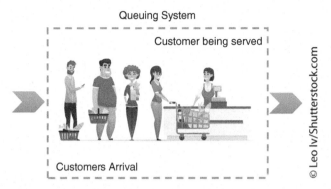

Figure 10-3 Customer being served and customers waiting in a queue at a queuing system

Figure 10-3 shows a queue being formed in front of a counter where a customer is being served. The customers arrive in many ways to a queuing system. They can arrive in batches or one at a time. They can arrive in a particular pattern. The customer arrival rate is important to analyze the waiting lines. If there is a faster rate of arrival, then there are many in the queuing system and the business needs more people to serve. if they arrive at a slower rate, then there are very few in the queuing system and the servers are sitting idle.

Customers in the Queuing System

Customers arrive to form queues either after their purchases or to receive a service. The customers arrive from either a finite or infinite source of population. In a finite source, there is a limited number of customers. A typical situation of a finite source is a waiter in a restaurant who is responsible for five tables, a nurse who is responsible for eight patients in a hospital, or a maintenance person responsible for ten machines. In all these cases, if the server completes the service on one of the assigned customers, then there is one less to serve. In an infinite source, the number of customers exceeds the designed system capacity. Supermarkets, banks, concert halls, and amusement parks are examples.

Serving System

The serving system consists of servers and phases. Servers are either human servers or automated servers. Examples of automated servers are vending machines and toll booths. The available number of servers is of importance in queuing systems. The capacity of the queuing system depends on the number of servers and the capacity of the servers in the queuing system.

Queuing systems can have either a single phase or multiple phases. Sometimes, customers have to be served in two phases. For example, a customer has to buy a coupon or ticket for a service from one server and then go to another server to receive the service. In Figure 10-4, the four basic queuing systems are illustrated.

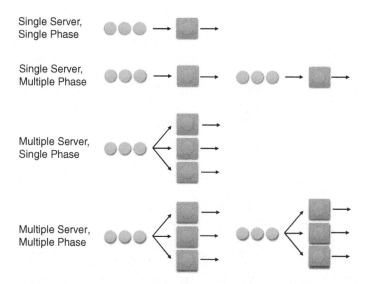

Figure 10-4 Four Basic Queuing Systems

In the single server-single phase queuing system, we have a single queue with one server. A simple grocery store with one store clerk is an example. A toll booth on the highway is an example. In the single server-multiple phase queuing system, we have the customers queue for the first phase of the service, receive their service, and then go to the next phase of the service. Each of these phases will have a server to provide services. The Bureau of Motor Vehicles in Indiana follows this method. The customers first go to an automatic vending machine to receive a ticket and then sit down in a room and they go to the next station to receive services when their ticket numbers are called.

In the multiple server, single phase queuing system, we have a single phase with multiple servers. Here, the customers line up in a queue and then go to the server who is ready to serve in order to receive services. Many department stores follow this method. In a multiple server, multiple phase queuing system, customers line up and go to a server who is available, receive their services, and then go over to stand in a queue for the subsequent phase of their services. A laundromat with several washers and dryers is an example. Customers complete washing their clothes using one of the many washers and then once the clothes are washed, they use one of the dryers to dry the wet, clean clothes.

Customer Arrival and Service Patterns

> **Customer arrival rate** The number of customers arriving during a specific period.

The customer arrivals rate is the number of customers arriving during a specific period. The patterns of customer arrival and the provided services are of importance in the queuing systems. The reason is that the variability and the randomness in the customer arrival patterns and the service patterns cause queuing systems to be either overloaded or underloaded. This means that sometimes the queuing system cannot service some of the customers and they have to fall into queue and sometimes there is no queue at all. We will discuss the two distributions that reflect such variability in the customer arrival and the provided services including,

1. Poisson distribution,
2. Exponential distribution.

   In waiting lines, customer arrival and service patterns have variability and therefore, we can describe the arrival and service patterns as probability distributions. We will also discuss another service pattern known as:

3. Constant service time.

Poisson Distribution A Poisson distribution is a probability distribution. It is used to show how many times an event is likely to occur over a specified period. Figure 10-5 shows a Poisson distribution of customer arrival patterns at a gourmet bagel shop which is open for breakfast and lunch. Customers arrive from 6 am to 2 pm. As shown in the figure, customer arrivals can be shown as a Poisson distribution. There is no arrival of customers at 11 am.

> **Poisson distribution**
> A probability distribution that is used to show how many times an event is likely to occur over a specified period.

Exponential Distribution The exponential distribution is a probability distribution related to the time between customer arrivals or that describes the service times. It is concerned with the amount of time until some specific event occurs. For example, the amount of time a car battery lasts is a good example of exponential distribution. Figure 10-6 shows an exponential distribution of service time patterns at the gourmet bagel shop for the customer arrival pattern shown in Figure 10-5. Since lunch specialty bagel sandwiches are more

> **Exponential distribution**
> A probability distribution that is used to show the amount of time until some specific event occurs.

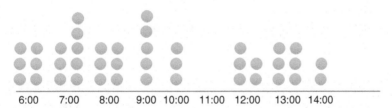

Customer Arrivals at a Gourmet Bagel Shop

Figure 10-5 Poisson distribution of customer arrivals at a gourmet bagel shop

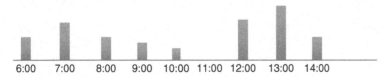

Service times at the Gourmet Bagel Shop

Figure 10-6 Exponential distribution of service times at a gourmet bagel shop

time-consuming to make, the service times are higher than breakfast bagels. There is no service at 11 am.

Constant Service Time In the constant service time system, the variability is reduced or eliminated. In this type of service, the time taken to service a customer is held as a constant time. For example, the Space Mountain roller coaster in the Disney Word Theme Park operates at a constant service time of 150 seconds. This attraction at Disney World is an example of a constant service time system.

Queue Discipline Rules

The most common queue discipline rule is the first come, first serve (FCFS) policy. The customers are served in the chronological order of their arrival. At times, some customers are treated differently than others based on some rule or order. For example, in airports, some customers who have the Transportation Security Administration's (TSA) precheck approval can pass through security checkpoints without the need to remove shoes, belts, or jackets from their person or place laptops and liquids from their bags to be checked. They may not even have to stand in a queue like others. These special rules can have an effect on the wait time, variability, and efficiency of service times.

Queuing Model

Let us look at the queuing model or the waiting line model. We will discuss three common types of waiting line problems in this section. These are simple models without much complexity. Table 10-1 shows the characteristics of each of these three models.

For each one of the three models, the symbols and their definitions are shown in Table 10-2.

Table 10-1 Waiting Line Models

Model No.	Model	Customer Pool	Customer Arrival Pattern	Queue Discipline	Service Pattern	Example
1	Single Server, Single Phase Model	Infinite	Poisson	FCFS	Exponential	A drive-in service at McDonalds
2	Single Server, Single Phase - Constant Service Time Model	Infinite	Poisson	FCFS	Constant	Space Mountain Roller Coaster ride at Disney World
3	Multiple Servers, Single Phase Model	Infinite	Poisson	FCFS	Exponential	Customer service at a retail store

Table 10-2 Symbols and their definitions	
Symbol	**Definition**
λ	Customer arrival rate
μ	Service rate per server
L_q	Average number of customers waiting in line for service
L_s	Average number of customers in the queuing system including ones being served
W_q	Average time customers wait in line for service
W_s	Average time customers spend in the queuing system including time to be served
W_c	Average waiting time for *a customer (this is different than Wq and this is for a customer who has to wait)*
$\dfrac{1}{\mu}$	Average service time
$\dfrac{1}{\lambda}$	Average time between customer arrivals
ρ	Average number of customers being served in the queuing system or the ratio of arrival rate to service rate per server or utilization of server
n	Number of units in the system
M	Number of servers
P_0	Probability of *zero* units in the system
P_n	Probability of *n* units in the system
P_w	Probability of waiting in line

Model 1

A single server, single phase model is a common waiting line model found at most of the fast-food drive-ins, drive-in bank tellers, drive-in ATMs, and so on.

$$L_q = \frac{\lambda^2}{\mu(\mu - \lambda)} \qquad \text{Eq. 10-1}$$

$$L_s = \frac{\lambda}{\mu - \lambda} \qquad \text{Eq. 10-2}$$

$$W_q = \frac{L_q}{\lambda} \qquad \text{Eq. 10-3}$$

$$W_s = \frac{L_s}{\lambda} \qquad \text{Eq. 10-4}$$

$$P_n = \left(1 - \frac{\lambda}{\mu}\right)\left(\frac{\lambda}{\mu}\right)^n \qquad \text{Eq. 10-5}$$

$$\rho = \frac{\lambda}{\mu} \qquad \text{Eq. 10-6}$$

Model 2

A single server, singe phase, constant service time model is another common waiting line model. This is wherever a service time is constant such as a roller coaster ride or car wash center.

$$L_q = \frac{\lambda^2}{2\mu(\mu - \lambda)}$$

Eq. 10-7

$$L_s = L_q + \frac{\lambda}{\mu}$$

Eq. 10-8

$$W_q = \frac{L_q}{\lambda}$$

Eq. 10-9

$$W_s = \frac{L_s}{\lambda}$$

Eq. 10-10

$$\rho = \frac{\lambda}{\mu}$$

Eq. 10-11

Model 3

A multiple server, single phase model is usually implemented in department stores where the customers bring their selected goods to buy from any one of the cashiers. The first come first serve system calls out for the next customer waiting in line to be served by the next available cashier. In this case, L_q can be selected using Table 10-3 where S is the number of servers.

$$L_s = L_q + \frac{\lambda}{\mu}$$

Eq. 10-12

$$W_q = \frac{L_q}{\lambda}$$

Eq. 10-13

$$W_s = \frac{L_s}{\lambda}$$

Eq. 10-14

$$\rho = \frac{\lambda}{M\mu}$$

Eq. 10-15

$$W_c = \frac{1}{M\mu - \lambda}$$

Eq. 10-16

$$P_w = \frac{W_q}{W_c}$$

Eq. 10-17

Table 10-3 Values of L_q and P_0 for M and λ/μ

λ/μ	M	L_q	P_0	λ/μ	M	L_q	P_0	λ/μ	M	L_q	P_0
0.15	1	0.026	0.850	0.85	1				4		
	2	0.001	0.860		2				5		
0.20	1				3			1.60	2		
	2				4				3		
0.25	1			0.90	1				4		
	2				2				5		
0.30	1				3			1.70	2		
	2				4				3		
0.35	1			0.95	1				4		
	2				2				5		
0.40	1				3			1.80	2		
	2				4				3		
0.45	1			1.00	2				4		
	2				3				5		
	3				4			1.90	2		
0.50	1			1.05	2				3		
	2				3				4		
	3				4				5		
0.55	1			1.10	2				6		
	2				3			2.00	3		
	3				4				4		
0.60	1			1.20	2				5		
	2				3				6		
	3				4			2.10	3		
0.65	1				5				4		
	2			1.30	2				5		
	3				3				6		
0.70	1				4			2.20	3		
	2				5				4		
	3			1.40	2				5		
0.75	1				3				6		
	2				4			2.30	3		
	3				5				4		
0.80	1			1.50	2				5		
	2				3				6		
	3										

(continued)

Table 10-3 Values of L_q and P_0 for M and λ/μ *(continued)*

λ/μ	M	L_q	P_0	λ/μ	M	L_q	P_0	λ/μ	M	L_q	P_0
2.4	3			3.10	4			3.50	4		
	4				5				5		
	5				6				6		
	6				7				7		
	7				8				8		
2.5	3			3.20	4			3.60	4		
	4				5				5		
	5				6				6		
	6				7				7		
	7				8				8		
2.6	3			3.30	4				9		
	4				5			3.70	4		
	5				6				5		
	6				7				6		
	7				8				7		
2.7	3			3.10	4				8		
	4				5				9		
	5				6			3.80	4		
	6				7				5		
	7				8				6		
2.8	3			3.20	4				7		
	4				5				8		
	5				6				9		
	6				7			3.90	4		
	7				8				5		
2.90	3			3.30	4				6		
	4				5				7		
	5				6				8		
	6				7				9		
	7				8			4.00	5		
3.00	4			3.40	4				6		
	5				5				7		
	6				6				8		
	7				7				9		
	8				8			4.10	5		

(continued)

Table 10-3 Values of L_q and P_0 for M and λ/μ *(continued)*

λ/μ	M	L_q	P_0	λ/μ	M	L_q	P_0	λ/μ	M	L_q	P_0
	6			4.70	5				9		
	7				6				10		
	8				7				11		
	9				8			5.3	6		
4.20	5				9				7		
	6				10				8		
	7			4.80	5				9		
	8				6				10		
	9				7				11		
	10				8				12		
4.30	5				9			5.4	6		
	6				10				7		
	7			4.90	5				8		
	8				6				9		
	9				7				10		
	10				8				11		
4.40	5				9				12		
	6				10			5.5	6		
	7				11				7		
	8			5.00	6				8		
	9				7				9		
	10				8				10		
4.50	5				9				11		
	6				10				12		
	7				11						
	8			5.10	6						
	9				7						
	10				8						
4.60	5				9						
	6				10						
	7				11						
	8			5.20	6						
	9				7						
	10				8						

FROM PRACTICE: Service Innovation at Starbucks

A Starbucks store provides a hand-crafted coffee by one of its baristas. Starbucks admits that their success is due to buying the highest-quality coffee beans in the world, the upscale ambiance of its stores, and its customer service that aims to create an uplifting experience.

They were the first to offer free wireless broadband in all their stores in any part of their world. They have an excellent selection of hand-selected and compiled music CDs available for purchase . A collaboration with Apple's iTunes Wi-Fi Music Store allows customers to enjoy the music and even download their favorite music.

© Sorbis/Shutterstock.com

Example 10-1

A local restaurant at 7:30 am is serving breakfast using a single drive-in window. Customers from an infinite pool, who like the restaurant's breakfast, arrive at a rate of 15 per half-an-hour as in a Poisson distribution. Service to provide breakfast items are at 40 per hour at an exponential distribution on a first come first serve basis. What is the average number of customers in the waiting line? How many customers are in the system on an average? What is the average waiting time in line? What is the average waiting time in the system including obtaining the services? What is the utilization of the drive-in window?

Since there is one server with a single phase (single drive-in window), this is a Model 1 problem. Using Equations 10-1, 2, 3, and 4 we get:

Arrival rate per hour $= \lambda = 2 \times 25 = 30$
Service rate per hour $= \mu = 40$

Average number of customers in the waiting line:

$$L_q = 30 \times 30/(40 \times (40 - 30)) = 2.25 \text{ customers}$$

Average number of customers in the queuing system:

$$L_s = 30/(40 - 30) = 3 \text{ customers}$$

Average waiting time in line:

$$W_q = 2.25/30 = 0.08 \text{ hours or 4.5 minutes}$$

Average waiting time in the system including obtaining the services:

$$W_s = 3/30 = 0.1 \text{ hours or 6 minutes}$$

The utilization of the drive-in window or the services:

$$\rho = 30/40 = 0.75 \text{ or } 75\%$$

Analysis: This is an example of Model 1. Here, there is a single server attending customers in a single phase model. The actual preparation and the packing of the food is done behind the scenes and there is one server who is attending to the customer's needs.

Example 10-2

In Example 10-1, what is the probability of having three cars in the system? What is the probability of having more than four cars waiting in the system?

The probability of having three cars waiting in the system can be determined by using Equation 10-5.

If $n = 3$,

$$P_3 = \left(1 - \frac{30}{40}\right)\left(\frac{30}{40}\right)^3 = 0.105 \text{ or } 10.5\%$$

Now, the probability of having more than four cars waiting in the system is $= 1 -$ the probability of having four or fewer cars.

We can calculate these probabilities as follows:

$$\text{For } n = 0, P_0 = \left(1 - \frac{30}{40}\right)\left(\frac{30}{40}\right)^0 = 0.250$$

$$\text{For } n = 1, P_0 = \left(1 - \frac{30}{40}\right)\left(\frac{30}{40}\right)^1 = 0.188$$

$$\text{For } n = 2, P_2 = \left(1 - \frac{30}{40}\right)\left(\frac{30}{40}\right)^2 = 0.141$$

$$\text{For } n = 3, P_3 = \left(1 - \frac{30}{40}\right)\left(\frac{30}{40}\right)^3 = 0.105$$

$$\text{For } n = 4, P_4 = \left(1 - \frac{30}{40}\right)\left(\frac{30}{40}\right)^4 = 0.079$$

The total probability of $P_0 + P_1 + P_2 + P_3 + P_4 = 0.763$
The probability of having more than four cars waiting in the system is $1 - 0.765 = 0.2373$ or 23.73%

Analysis: In analyzing Model 1, we can use probability to identify various situations in the system. Using the additive rule to find the probability of mutually exclusive events, we can find the total probability.

Example 10-3

What is the probability of having two or fewer cars for the restaurant from Example 10-1? Now, the manager of the local restaurant from Example 10-1 wants to reduce the service rate in order to be more efficient and as a result improve customer service. They want to ensure that no more than two cars should be increasing the probability to 70%. What would be the service rate assuming that the customer arrival rate is still 15 per half hour?

Using Eq. 10-5, the probability of two or fewer cars waiting in the system = $P_0 + P_1 + P_2$

$$\left(1 - \frac{30}{40}\right)\left(\frac{30}{40}\right)^0 + \left(1 - \frac{30}{40}\right)\left(\frac{30}{40}\right)^1 + \left(1 - \frac{30}{40}\right)\left(\frac{30}{40}\right)^2 = 0.578 \text{ or } 57.8\%$$

By increasing the probability and keeping the customer arrival rate the same, the restaurant can increase the service rate. To find the service rate for the probability that no more than 2 cars equal to 0.70, we can solve the following equation to find μ by a trial-and-error method:

$$\left(1 - \frac{30}{\mu}\right)\left(\frac{30}{\mu}\right)^0 + \left(1 - \frac{30}{\mu}\right)\left(\frac{30}{\mu}\right)^1 + \left(1 - \frac{30}{\mu}\right)\left(\frac{30}{\mu}\right)^2 = 0.70$$

μ	Probability of two or fewer cars
40	0.578
41	0.608
42	0.636
43	0.660
44	0.683
45	0.704

Therefore, the service rate has to be increased to 45 per hour from 40 per hour at an exponential distribution on a first come first serve basis.

Analysis: In analyzing Model 1, we can use probability to identify various situations in the waiting line. Using the additive rule to find the probability of mutually exclusive events, we can find the total probability.

Example 10-4

Joe's carwash is an automated car wash facility with no attendants. Joe comes every morning, afternoon, and evening to check that everything is working fine, fill up all fluids, and make any needed adjustments. Patrons pay using credit and debit cards. If Joe estimates that customers will arrive at a rate of 10 per hour and the actual car wash takes 4 minutes, find:

    a. Average number of cars waiting in line
    b. Average number of cars in the system
    c. Average waiting time in line
    d. Average waiting time in the system including the car wash
    e. Utilization of the car wash

Arrival rate per hour $= \lambda = 10$ per hour
Service rate per hour $= \mu = 60/4 = 15$ per hour

Using Eq. 10-7 through 10-11,
Average number of cars waiting in line $= L_q = (10 \times 10)/(2 \times 15 \times (15-10)) = 0.667$ or 1 car
Average number of cars in the system $= L_s = 0.667 + (10/15) = 1.33$ or 1 car
Average waiting time in line $= W_q = 0.667/10 = 0.0667$ hours or 4 mins.
Average waiting time in the system including the car wash $= W_s = 1.33/10 = 0.13$ hours or 8 mins.
Utilization of the car wash $= 10/15 \times 100 = 66.67\%$

Analysis: The automated car wash facility washes cars at a constant rate. The car wash is programmed to wash cars in a particular fashion and in a constant time. This is an example of Model 2.

Example 10-5

Gina Reeves runs a department store in the city of Hightower, Illinois. Saturday is the busiest day of the week and Gina has to allocate the correct number of cashiers. The department store is open for 8 hours on Saturdays. The queuing system draws from an infinite pool of customers and serves on a FCFS basis. The customers line up and they are called whenever a cashier is open. Gina estimates that the customer arrival rate is 50 per hour in a Poisson distribution and the service rate is 25 per hour in an exponential distribution. She pays $40 per hour for each cashier. For every customer wait, there is a lost opportunity cost of $60 per hour. How many optimal number of cashiers does she need to allocate on that Saturday? Note: Optimal is determined when savings turn around from negative to positive.
    $\lambda/\mu = 30/40 = 2$. We will use Model 3 since customers line up and get served by an available server.

Total opportunity costs $=$ No. of customers waiting $\times$ cost of waiting $\times$ number of hours
Cost of Cashiers $=$ No. of additional cashiers $\times$ cost of cashier $\times$ number of hours
Looking at Table 10-3, for $\lambda/\mu = 2$, we need at least 3 cashiers
Let us start with 3 cashiers, increase by one and determine the cost
Savings $=$ Cost of Cashiers $-$ Total opportunity costs

We can get Lq = No of customers waiting in line from Table 10-3. We will start with 3 cashiers and add more cashiers one by one until the cost reduction turns positive from negative as shown in the table below:

No of additional Cashiers	Lq = No of customers waiting	Total opportunity costs due to additional cashier	Cost of Cashiers	Savings
0	0.8888	$426.62	$0	($426.62)
1	0.173	$83.04	$320	$236.96

Gina must allocate 4 cashiers that Saturday so that the store does not lose money on opportunity costs.

Analysis: Here we have multiple servers but the customers have to bring their selected goods to buy from any one of the cashiers. The first come first serve system calls out for the next customer waiting in line to be served by the next available cashier. This is an example of Model 3.

Formulae from this Chapter

Model 1

Average number of customers waiting in line for service	$L_q = \dfrac{\lambda^2}{\mu(\mu-\lambda)}$	Eq. 10-1
Average number of customers in the queuing system including ones being served	$L_s = \dfrac{\lambda}{\mu-\lambda}$	Eq. 10-2
Average time customers wait in line for service	$W_q = \dfrac{L_q}{\lambda}$	Eq. 10-3
Average time customers spend in the queuing system including time to be served	$W_s = \dfrac{L_s}{\lambda}$	Eq. 10-4
Average number of customers being served in the queuing system or the ratio of arrival rate to service rate per server or utilization of server	$P_n = \left(1-\dfrac{\lambda}{\mu}\right)\left(\dfrac{\lambda}{\mu}\right)^n$	Eq. 10-5
Probability of n units in the system	$\rho = \dfrac{\lambda}{\mu}$	Eq. 10-6

Model 2

Average number of customers waiting in line for service	$L_q = \dfrac{\lambda^2}{2\mu(\mu-\lambda)}$	Eq. 10-7

Average number of customers in the queuing system including ones being served	$L_s = L_q + \dfrac{\lambda}{\mu}$	Eq. 10-8
Average time customers wait in line for service	$W_q = \dfrac{L_q}{\lambda}$	Eq. 10-9
Average time customers spend in the queuing system including time to be served	$W_s = \dfrac{L_s}{\lambda}$	Eq. 10-10
Average number of customers being served in the queuing system or the ratio of arrival rate to service rate per server or utilization of server	$\rho = \dfrac{\lambda}{\mu}$	Eq. 10-11
Model 3		
Average number of customers in the queuing system including ones being served	$L_s = L_q + \dfrac{\lambda}{\mu}$	Eq. 10-12
Average time customers wait in line for service	$W_q = \dfrac{L_q}{\lambda}$	Eq. 10-13
Average time customers spend in the queuing system including time to be served	$W_s = \dfrac{L_s}{\lambda}$	Eq. 10-14
Average number of customers being served in the queuing system or the ratio of arrival rate to service rate per server or utilization of server	$\rho = \dfrac{\lambda}{M\mu}$	Eq. 10-15
Average waiting time for a customer	$W_c = \dfrac{1}{M\mu - \lambda}$	Eq. 10-16
Probability of waiting in line	$P_w = \dfrac{W_q}{W_c}$	Eq. 10-17

Case Study: Service Operations at Steven's Hotel

Steven's Hotel is a landmark hotel in Westwood, Florida. The city is close to major attractions. Steven Patel, his original name is Shivan Patel, is the owner. Steven loves to make people welcome to the hotel and takes a personal interest and care to make every customer feel at home. The hotel has great reviews in all major social media networks as well as in many travel sites.

Steven had bought the hotel in a rundown condition for a bargain. He worked hard for more than a year to renovate the place. He hired a few young hands from the area, paid them well, and took care of them. They, in return, gave their best to him. Two of the best, Oscar and Lorena, still work

© Svet_Feo/Shutterstock.com

for him at the hotel as managers. He still takes care of them and pays them very well.

Steven's Hotel offers clean, luxurious rooms to its customers. Customers can book their rooms through the Internet or by calling the hotel. The house cleaners clean the rooms every day and at the end of their cleaning services, they leave a nice welcome note with a couple of candies for the next customer. Each room is left with a fresh set of bathroom condiments, fresh linen, and towels. Each room has complimentary coffee with a coffer maker, TV, and a media player that can be connected through mobile phones. The hotel has an indoor pool with a nice tiki-bar that serves amazing cocktails for adults. Oscar manages the tiki-bar and shows off his skills as a bartender with various cocktail mixes such as "Mix Du Jour." Amy, Steven's wife, is a fantastic cook and she has set up a nice restaurant. Amy's Kitchen serves a menu of freshly home-cooked breakfast, lunch, and dinner. Steven also arranges limo service for important guests from the nearby airport. By the time they arrive at the hotel, Lorena arranges their rooms personally and leaves a discount coupon for Amy's Kitchen.

Steven welcomes each guest personally in the lobby of the hotel. He talks to them informally, gets to know them, prepares the check-in, and hands over the room keys. With the keys, he offers each guest a small favor bag filled with a water bottle and a healthy snack. In the favor bag, guests find discounts for Amy's Kitchen as well. Important guests get deeper discounts. It takes Steven about 5 minutes for each guest. Guests arrive at a Poisson distribution to the

© New Africa/Shutterstock.com

hotel at an average rate of 10 every half hour. The guests are handed over to a valet who handles and carries the luggage to guest rooms. On the way to the room, the valet lets the guest know about the restaurant and its famous home-cooked meals and all the amenities of the hotel. In the room, a variety of information is provided to the guests including nearby attractions, TV channel lineup, limo services, and of course the daily specials from Amy's Kitchen. Guests can order food from 6am to 11pm as room service, of course!

Case Questions

A. What is the service package offered by Steven's Hotel?
B. How would you characterize the service process at Steven's Hotel?
C. What kind of service classifications does Steven's Hotel offer?
D. Create a blueprint ad capture the complexity of services at Steven's Hotel.

E. Identify mistakes that can be made in each process step and propose a fail-proof method to ensure that the mistake in each process step does not become a defect.

F. Does Steven's Hotel offer traditional or online services?

G. What are the core and supplementary services offered by Steven's Hotel?

H. What is the average number of customers waiting in line?

I. What is the average number of customers in the queuing system?

J. What is the average time customers wait in line for service?

K. What is the average time customers spend in the queuing system including time to be served?

L. What is the probability of three or more guests in the check-in system with Steven?

Summary

- The service industry provides services rather than tangible objects like goods.
- Business services are transactions offered by a business to a customer.
- A service package is a bundle of benefits that are provided by a company offering its services.
- Service process is how a service company provides service to its customers.
- Service process consists of providing supporting facility, goods, information, explicit, and implicit services.
- Two elements are used to characterize service processes including labor intensity and a combination of consumer interaction and service customization.
- Labor intensity is the ratio of the incurred cost of labor to the value of plant and equipment excluding inventory.
- The degree to which customers interact with the service process and the degree to which the business customizes its services to its customers are two measures of service process.
- The classification of services falls into four broad categories including people processing, possession processing, mental stimulus processing, and information processing.
- In people processing, people are direct recipients of tangible actions performed on them.
- People's possessions are serviced directly and intangible actions are performed on them.
- Mental stimulus processing involves tangible actions on people.
- Information processing involves intangible actions on people's possessions.
- Complexity of services reflects the number of steps that are involved in delivering the services.

- A service blueprint will help to determine the complexity of services. Service complexity tends to have a negative effect on self-service situations and as service complexity increases, it requires a higher level of cognitive effort to understand service offers.
- A service blueprint is a flowchart that helps a customer to understand a service process.
- Traditional service includes personal service.
- Online services provide information and services over the Internet.
- Value proposition must address core service product, supplementary services, and service delivery design.
- The design of service systems to form a service package is to combine, sequence, deliver, schedule, and implement value proposition.
- Service systems design is the complex task of integrating value proposition for customers.
- The core service product is the principal component of the services provided by a business.
- Supplementary services are other service-related activities that usually accompany core service products.
- Service delivery design focuses on how to deliver the core and supplementary services to customers.
- A service delivery design of a business consists of how the distinctive features of their core and supplementary services are delivered to their customers.
- Demand management in service businesses concerns managing customer waiting time to receive products.
- To tackle service demand, businesses can take many courses.
- There are three basic approaches to managing demand including take no action and let demand find its own level, create a reservation system, and create formalized waiting and queuing systems.
- Waiting for service is certainly a negative experience for a customer and is directly correlated to customer satisfaction.
- Waiting lines or queues occur whenever the number of persons entering a service providing facility is greater than the capacity of the system to process the services rendered to them.
- Queuing systems comprise four main characteristics including number of customers in the system, the serving system that serves those customers, customer arrival and service patterns, and queue discipline rules.
- Customers arrive in batches or one at a time and in a particular pattern.
- Customers arrive from either a finite or an infinite source of the population. In a finite source, there is a limited number of customers.
- The serving system consists of servers and phases.
- Servers are either human servers or automated servers. Examples of automated servers are vending machines, toll booths, and so on.

- Queuing systems can have either a single phase or multiple phases.
- In the single server, single phase queuing system, we have a single queue with one server.
- In the multiple server, single phase queuing system, we have a single phase with multiple servers.
- Customer arrivals rate is the number of customers arriving during a specific period.
- Two distributions that reflect such variability in customer arrival and provided services are Poisson distribution and an exponential distribution.
- In waiting lines, constant service time is also considered.
- A probability distribution is used to show how many times an event is likely to occur over a specified period.
- The most common queue discipline rule is first come, first serve (FCFS).
- A single server, single phase model is a quite common waiting line model.
- A single server, singe phase, constant service time model is another common waiting line model.
- A multiple server, single phase model is usually implemented in department stores where the customers bring their selected goods to buy from any one of the cashiers.

REVIEW QUESTIONS

1. What is a service process?
2. What is the difference between production and service companies?
3. What is a business service?
4. Explain a service package with an example.
5. What are the components of service processes?
6. What are the characteristics of a service process?
7. How are service processes classified?
8. What is complexity of services?
9. What is a service blueprint?
10. What is a key feature on flowcharts used in service operations that differentiates between the front-office and back-office aspects of the system?
11. What is a key feature on flowcharts used in service operations that differentiates between the interactions in the system?
12. What is an online service as opposed to a traditional service?
13. How do companies provide service value to their customers?
14. Why do queues occur?
15. What are the main characteristics of queuing systems?

Critical Thinking Questions

1. Why do companies need a service package?
2. Explain the service process of a department store like Walmart.
3. What is the difference between consumer interaction and service customization?
4. Explain the differences between people processing, possession processing, mental stimulus processing, and information processing.
5. Does a service blueprint help to reduce service complexity? If so, how? If not, why not?
6. Are online services less complex than traditional services?
7. Why do companies provide supplementary services?
8. Why do companies spend time and effort to deliver services in complex manners?
9. What can be done to avoid having queues?
10. What is the main difference between Model 1 and Model 2?
11. Construct a blueprint for a hotel stay.
12. Describe the service package offered by your university or college.
13. Describe an exponential distribution service using an example.
14. Describe a Poisson customer arrival using an example.
15. Are the rides at a local fair assumed to have an exponential service time?

Problem Solving Questions

1. Joe Papa and Jill Mama operate a family-owned grocery store in Lakeville, Indiana. Customers arrive at an average of 3 per hour and the old couple take on average 1 every 15 minutes to process their orders. This time includes the conversation involving local news, rumors, and politics. Assuming an infinite pool, Poisson arrivals, and exponential service times, calculate
   a. The average number of customers waiting in line.
   b. The average number of customers in the queuing system.
   c. The average time customers wait in line for service.
   d. The average time customers spend in the queuing system including time to be served.
2. Customers arrive at the Lone Star Department Store's returns counter at an average of 1 every 15 minutes and their return requests take on average 10 minutes to be processed. The return counter is staffed by Ms. Betty Ricks who works 8 hours per day. Assume an infinite pool, Poisson arrivals, and exponential service times.
   a. What is the average waiting time for a customer?
   b. How long is the waiting line on average?

   c. What percentage of time is Ms. Ricks idle?

   d. What is the probability that an arriving customer who has not entered the waiting line will find at least 1 customer?

3. South Bend Cubs exhibition game against the Quad Cities River Bandits is scheduled for tomorrow. The Cubs' marketing manager estimates a Poisson distributed crowd to arrive at a rate of 250 per hour and expects an exponential distribution service of 10 seconds per customer. Calculate

   a. The average number of customers who would wait.

   b. The average time customers wait in line for service.

   c. The average time a customer is in the system.

4. The city of Townsville, KY, has hired a local company, Bumby Rides, to host Dirt Bike Racing. The hired company was also in charge of repairing bikes if they fail. The company estimates that bikes will fail at the rate of 3 per hour. Bumpy Rides is looking for mechanics and pays a mechanic $25 per hour. How many mechanics should they hire?

   If they hire 1 person, the mechanic can fix a bike in 30 minutes. If they hire 2 mechanics to work as a team, they can fix a bike in 20 minutes. If they hire 3 mechanics to work as a team, they can fix a bike in 10 minutes. In any case, while the bikes are being repaired, there is a $50 loss of income per hour.

5. Koffe, LLC.'s employees love coffee. The owner installs an industrial coffee maker. It takes on average 5 minutes to make coffee after the coffee runs out. Employees make coffee once all the coffee is consumed. The employees serve themselves and on average it takes them 10 seconds in an exponential distribution. Employees arrive at a Poisson distribution at the rate of 4 per minute. Determine the following:

   a. How many customers would you expect to see on average at the coffee maker?

   b. How long would it take to get coffee?

   c. What percentage of time is the coffee maker being used excluding the time taken to make the coffee)?

   d. What is the probability that 2 or more people are at the coffee maker?

   If the company manager changes the coffee maker to an automatic coffee maker,

   e. How many customers would you expect to see on average at the coffee maker?

   f. How long would it take to get coffee?

6. Salsa, an authentic Mexican restaurant, has planned to install a Totopos machine that makes a fresh batch of chips in exactly 40 seconds in an exponential distribution. Customers are offered the

chips in a Poisson distribution at the rate of 60 seconds. All customers are offered chips free of cost.

a. How many customers would you expect to see on average getting served?

b. How many customers would you expect to see on average in the restaurant?

c. What is the average time customers wait to get chips?

d. What is the average time customers spend waiting for the chips and getting served?

7. Florgreens, the pharmacy at Hillman Estates, IL, has a health-monitoring machine that some customers of the pharmacy use. On a normal day, people who want to use the machine come in a Poisson distribution and at a rate of 10 persons per hour. The machine takes exactly 4 minutes to take vital signs and display the results. Determine the following:

a. How many customers would you expect to see waiting to use the machine?

b. How many customers would you expect to see on average in the system?

c. What is the average time customers wait in line for service?

d. What is the average wait time for a customer in the system? On a particular Sunday, there was an increase of 15 per hour customers who want to use the machine.

e. How many more customers will be waiting in line than on a normal day?

8. Mike's car wash on State Road 23 washes cars in 5 minutes. On a Sunday morning, cars arrive in a Poisson distribution at an average rate of 10 per hour.

a. What is the average number of cars in line?

b. What is the average time that cars spend waiting and getting served?

9. After a successful run, Mike Carr, the owner of Mike's car wash on State Road 23 decides to start a detailing facility next to the automatic car wash station. He is planning to employ 6 people to detail cars and thinks that it will take the people 45 minutes on average to detail cars. He is hoping that 4 cars per hour will come over to be detailed.

a. What is the average number of cars in line?

b. What is the average time waiting in line?

c. What is the average number of cars in the system?

d. What is the average time spent in the system?

e. What is the average waiting time for a car?

f. What is the average number of cars being served in the system?

g. What is the probability of waiting in line?

10. At Florgreens, the local pharmacy at Hillman Estates, IL, people have been lining up to take the Covid-19 vaccinations at a Poisson distribution at a rate of 3 minutes in an hour. There are 2 people to administer the vaccines who work in an exponential service pattern and it takes 2 minutes on average for each person to administer the vaccine.

   a. What is the average number of customers in line?
   b. What is the average time waiting in line?
   c. What is the average number of customers in the system?
   d. What is the average time spent in the system?
   e. What is the average waiting time for a customer?

References

1. Routley, N. (2018). *Amazon's Massive Distribution Network in One Giant Visualization.* Retrieved April 2, 2022 from https://www.visualcapitalist .com/footprint-all-amazons-warehouses/

2. Amazon.com. (2022). *Amazon Web Services.* Retrieved April 4, 2022 from https://www.aboutamazon.com /what-we-do/amazon-web-services

3. Schmenner, R. W. (1986, Spring). How can service businesses survive and prosper? *Sloan Management Review,* 21–32.

4. Lovelock, C. H. (1983). Classifying services to gain strategic marketing insights. *Journal of Marketing, 47,* 9–20.

5. Simon, F., & Usunier, J. C. (2007). Cognitive, demographic, and situational determinants of service customer preference for personnel-in-contact over self-service technology. *International Journal of Research in Marketing, 24*(2), 163–173

6. Charm, T., Coggins, B., Robinson, K., & Wilkie, J. (2020). The great consumer shift: Ten charts that show how US shopping behavior is changing. *McKinsey Report, McKinsey.com.* Retrieved April 5, 2022 from https://www .mckinsey.com/business-functions/marketing-and-sales/our-insights/the-great-consumer-shift-ten-charts-that-show-how-us-shopping-behavior-is-changing

7. Wassel, B. (2018). Customer service draws 57% of shoppers to traditional retailers. *Retail Touchpoints,* Retrieved April 4, 2022 from https:// www.retailtouchpoints.com/topics/customer-experience/customer-service-draws-57-of-shoppers-to-traditional-retailers

8. Lovelock, C., & Wirtz, J. (2011). *Services marketing: People, technology, strategy.* Prentice-Hall.

9. Zeithaml, V. A., Parasuraman, A., Berry, L. L. (1985). Problems and strategies in services marketing. *Journal of Marketing, 49*(2) 33–46.

10. Kumar, P. (2005). The competitive impact of service process improvement: Examining customers' waiting experiences in retail markets. *Journal of Retailing, 81*(3) 171–180.

11. Taylor, S. (1995). The effects of filled waiting time and service provider control over the delay on service evaluations of service. *Journal of the Academy of Marketing Science, 23*(1) 38–48; Katz, K. L., Larson, B. M., & Larson, R. C. (1991). Prescription for the waiting-in-line-blues: Entertain, enlighten, engage. *Sloan Management Review 32*(2) 44–53; Dellaert, B. G. C., & Kahn, B. E. (1999). How tolerable Is delay? Consumers' evaluations of Internet web sites after waiting. *Journal of interactive marketing 13*(1) 41–54.

QUALITY AND LEAN SIX SIGMA

Toyota, one of the largest automobile manufacturers in the world, produces about 10 million vehicles per year. Earning revenues to the tune of US\$256.7 billion in 2021, Toyota produces vehicles under its five flagship brands—Daihatsu, Hino, Lexus, Ranz, and Toyota. Toyota assembles vehicles in Argentina, Belgium, Brazil, Canada, Colombia, the Czech Republic, France, Indonesia, Mexico, the Philippines, Poland, Russia, South Africa, Thailand, Turkey, the United Kingdom, the United States, and Venezuela. The company has joint venture, licensed, or contract factories in China, France, India, Malaysia, Pakistan, Taiwan, United States, and Vietnam. J.D. Power and other research firms have consistently rated Toyota and its luxury line Lexus as one of the top automotive brands in terms of reliability, quality, and durability.

© rvlsoft/Shutterstock.com

Toyota is well known for its production of high-quality vehicles using its novel approaches to quality. The mission of Toyota quality assurance teams is to ensure that every vehicle that leaves their factories meets their exacting standards for safety and quality. The core principles of their quality assurance system are "Customer First," "Quality First," and "Genchi Genbutsu" (Go and see at the scene). For example, Toyota initiated an Audit and Improvement division to start process quality in 1937. In 1965, Toyota established a company-wide quality assurance system. Since establishing the Toyota Customer First (CF) Committee in 2010, Toyota has ensured that the Customer First principle is put into practice throughout the company in order to completely eliminate customer problems[1]. A sequence of 2,000 checks are carried out on each vehicle before they are signed off as ready for delivery to customers. Quality checks on electrical, brake, engine, seat assembly, steering, and transmission systems and a dynamic evaluation of the vehicle's capacity to perform in various road conditions are conducted in all plants.

Toyota is famous for its production methods, known worldwide as the Toyota Production System (TPS). The TPS, a precursor of the more generic "lean manufacturing," is an operations management system that manages manufacturing and logistics, including interaction with both customers and suppliers. TPS measures everything—even the noise that car doors make when they are opened and closed. When a Toyota worker on the shop floor notices a problem, they have the freedom to pull the Andon cord immediately, stop the line, and ensure that the problem is fixed before restarting the production. The Andon cord is a signal used to indicate that the production system is stopped due to a defect and will recommence only when the problem is resolved. The process of stopping a production line when a defect is suspected originates back to Jidoka[2,3]. Toyota realized long back that unaddressed problems in assembly lines created severe complications in the later stages.

Table 11-1 Quality Gurus and Quality

Description	Juran	Deming	Crosby
Definition	Satisfy customer needs	Uniformity and dependability at low cost	Conformance to requirements
General approach to quality	Reduce defects	Continuous improvement	Zero defects
Process control	Statistical process control	Statistical process control	
Quality improvement	Team approach	Employee participation in decision making	Quality improvement teams

Quality

The who's who of quality leaders—Philip Crosby, Edwards Deming, Joseph Juran, and David Garvin—agree that achieving outstanding quality requires quality leadership from senior management and a strong focus on customer needs and continuous improvement in all organizational processes. According to Crosby, quality is conformance to requirements[4]. Deming defined quality as a predictable degree of uniformity and dependability at low cost suitable to the market[5]. Juran defined quality as something that satisfies customer needs[6]. Table 11-1 explains quality as seen by these quality gurus.

Another quality guru, Garvin, viewed quality as a set of eight dimensions found in goods and services, which include performance, reliability, conformance, durability, feature, serviceability, aesthetics, and image[7].

> **Quality** Quality is defined as conformance to requirements.

Performance—the superiority or excellence of primary operating characteristics of a product—for example, in the case of cars, fuel efficiency, or mileage, in terms of miles per gallon.

Reliability—the extent to which a product is unlikely to fail or break down. The reliability of cars is often measured by the number of problems faced by the owner.

Conformance—the extent to which the design and operating characteristics of a product meet predetermined technical standards, for example, emission standards.

Durability—the life of a product, for example, durability of tires.

Features—the "bells and whistles" of a product, for example, availability of leather seats.

Serviceability—the extent to which a product can be easily repaired and serviced, for example, easy accessibility of maintainable parts, like air filter.

Aesthetics—the look, feel, taste, smell, and style of a product, for example, the style and look of the exterior and interior in cars.

Image—the extent to which a product expresses an image, for example, BMW or Benz cars.

FROM PRACTICE: Quality at Ford

Are you familiar with Ford's famous tagline in the 1980s? Quality is Job 1! That theme summarized Ford's efforts to build reliable and low-maintenance vehicles. Ford was struggling to beat the Japanese rivals led by Toyota in the U.S. markets at that time. A 2021 report[8] shows that Ford's reliability rating based on an average across 345 unique models is 3.5 out of 5.0, which ranks 21st out of 32 for all car brands. The average annual repair cost for a Ford is $775 compared to $652 across all models. However,

© D K Grove/Shutterstock.com

Ford, with an experience of over 115 years in the automotive industry, is vowing to make changes. Ford is transforming positively its product quality, using advanced technologies, modernization, and benchmarking against the industry best. In 2021, Ford committed to a $185 million investment in the new Ford Ion Park battery development center in Michigan[9]. Ford is devoted to quality with its new focus on rebuilding its reputation to make Quality its job 1.

Quality Management

> **Quality management** Quality management is about preventing defects in a product.

Quality management is about preventing defects. There is a difference between a product having defects and a product being defective. For example, one buys a TV and finds a scratch on the TV housing, then that scratch is a defect, but if there are too many scratches on the TV housing, then the TV housing it-self can be considered defective; again, if the TV does not show quality video image, then the TV itself is defective. Defect means not meeting a specific requirement or specification. A product could have multiple defects. Some defects might not even be noticeable by a customer. Defects do not affect the product's performance. On the other hand, "defective" means the good or the service failed to meet the required performance criterion.

> **Defective** Defective is a failed product and cannot be used by a customer.

Quality management is about eliminating the source of defects so that any de-tection of defects and rework do not happen during operations. The goals of quality management include defect prevention, continuous improvement, and customer satisfaction. It is the management's responsibility to provide essential resources that are important to manage quality well. Quality management is based on problems related to the making of robust and stable processes in the operations of a company.

ISO Quality Standards

ISO stands for International Organization for Standardization, and these standards serve as a structure with clearly defined guidelines for many goods.

In order to meet their customer expectations, firms manage and improve the quality of their goods and services by consistently using these quality standards.

ISO is the world's largest developer and publisher of international standards and is a network of the national standards institutes of 162 countries, one member per country, with a central secretariat in Geneva, Switzerland, which coordinates the system. ISO is a nongovernmental organization that functions as a bridge between the public sector and the private sector. Many of its member institutes are part of the governmental structure of their countries, many are mandated by their government, and some are from the private sector.

The ISO family of standards addresses quality management to help organizations fulfill the quality requirements of their customers with applicable regulatory requirements. These standards represent international consensus on excellent quality management practices and consists of standards and guidelines for quality management systems and related supporting standards.

The ISO standards and guidelines are practiced by many global companies and have earned global reputation for establishing effective and efficient quality management systems. Organizations obtain value by using the entire family of standards in an integrated manner. Table 11-2 shows various ISO standards.

Table 11-2 ISO Standards

Standards	Description
ISO 9000	Defines the fundamentals of quality management systems and includes eight management principles, which include customer focus, leadership, involvement of projects, process approach, systems approach, continual improvement, decision-making approach, and supplier relationships[10]
ISO 9001	Deals with the requirements an organization must fulfill in order to meet the standards and provides a model for quality assurance in design, development, production, installations, and servicing for creation of new products, services, and systems
ISO 9002	Provides a model for quality assurance in production, installation, and servicing
ISO 9003	Provides a model for quality assurance in final inspection and testing.
ISO 9004	Emphasizes quality assurance via preventive actions instead of just checking the final product, system, or service
ISO 9000-2005	Quality management systems—Fundamentals and vocabulary
ISO 9001:2008	Quality management systems—Requirements
ISO 9004:2000	Quality management systems—Guidelines for performance improvements
ISO 10006:2003	Quality management—Guidelines for quality management in projects
ISO 14000	Environmental management standard to improve environmental performance
ISO 22000	Inspire confidence in food products with this family of standards
ISO 20121	Sustainability standards to manage social, economic, and environmental impacts
ISO 45000	Standard for occupational health and safety to reduce workplace risks
ISO 50001	Energy management standard for helping organizations manage their energy performance

Malcolm Baldrige Award Approach to Quality Management

The Malcolm Baldrige National Quality Award is an award established by the U.S. Congress in 1987 to raise awareness of quality management. The award recognizes the U.S. companies that have successfully implemented quality management systems. The award is the nation's highest presidential honor for performance excellence.

The Baldrige Performance Excellence Program and Award are named after Malcolm Baldrige, who served as the U.S. Secretary of Commerce during President Ronald Reagan's administration. The award promotes awareness of performance excellence, sharing of successful performance strategies, and benefits derived from using these strategies.

Three Malcolm Baldrige Awards can be given annually in six industrial groupings, which include manufacturing, services, small businesses, education, healthcare, and nonprofit. The award is not given for specific products or services; to receive the award, an organization should exhibit an organizational management system that ensures continuous improvement in delivering products or services, demonstrate efficient and effective operations, and provide a way of engaging and responding to customers and other stakeholders. The American Society of Quality (ASQ) assists in administrating the award program, and a foundation raises money to endow the program. The foundation trustees are prominent leaders from various organizations, and many U.S. organizations provide financial support to the foundation. The criteria for performance excellence are based on seven categories:

1. Senior leadership guidance, governance system, approach to leadership improvement, and how organizations ensure ethical and societal responsibilities;
2. Establishing, implementing, and leveraging organizational strategic planning;
3. Listening to and getting information from customers and engaging with customers to serve their needs and build relationships;
4. Organizational measures, analysis, and improvement of performance and management of information, organizational knowledge, and information technology;
5. Building an effective and supportive organizational environment for the workforce and how organizations engage its workforce to achieve both organizational success and the workforce's personal growth and success in their career;
6. Design, management, and improvement of work systems and key work processes;
7. Results of product performance and process effectiveness, customer-focused performance, workforce-focused performance, senior leadership and governance, and financial and market results.

Motorola won the first Malcolm Baldrige Award in 1988, and, since then, 91 organizations, including large firms such as Honeywell, Nestle, Boeing, Caterpillar, Ritz-Carlton, 3M, Merrill Lynch, Xerox, AT&T, Texas Instruments, IBM, Cadillac, Federal Express, and Westinghouse, have won the coveted award.

FROM PRACTICE: A National Award for K&N Restaurants

K&N Management, the creator of mighty fine burgers from Austin, Texas, has more than 450 employees in its workforce and earns revenues at approximately $50 million. Its guests rate their satisfaction with food quality, hospitality, cleanliness, speed of service, and value at least 4.7 on a 5-point scale, outperforming the best competitor. The company has been named the "the best place to work in Austin" by the Austin American-Statesman. The management creates product offerings that meet or exceed guest requirements based on innovation and technology. The firm holds all their team members accountable for the company's performance excellence, integrity, and ethical behavior through a defined governance process and a detailed system of checks and balances. Managers are held accountable for their actions through monthly performance feedbacks, annual performance scorecard reviews, and 360-degree assessments. Since 2005, approximately 94% of the strategic actions of the company have been accomplished, and, since 2001, 100% of their goals have been met[11].

Source: nist.gov

Total Quality Management

The Deming Award recognizes organizations that exemplify the Total Quality Management (TQM) principles introduced by Professor Deming. Nippon Steel from Japan was the first recipient of the Deming Award in 1951. Florida Power & Light was the first non-Japanese firm to win the Deming Award in 1989.

TQM is a methodology that involves all the employees of an organization to follow a systematic, structured process in implementing continuous improvement quality projects. To be successful, all the employees of an organization need to be knowledgeable about TQM and practice TQM principles in all their projects. Training all employees in TQM methodologies, which is a costly endeavor, has to be achieved first before the involvement. AlliedSignal, a giant conglomerate now called Honeywell, trained more than 70,000 employees in TQM, and all the projects in AlliedSignal were carried out using the TQM principles. In many successful companies—for example, AlliedSignal, GE, and Pratt & Whitney—TQM has been implemented primarily to change the existing organizational culture and to improve competitive advantage. Many tangible benefits arise from using TQM principles, including shorter manufacturing cycle time, lower inventory, lower product reject rate, and increased customer satisfaction.

The TQM process improvement problem-solving model is shown in Figure 11-1. An activity of an organization often starts with identifying the opportunities associated with a specific problem that needs improvement. Once a problem or opportunity is identified, the TQM methodology suggests forming teams. This activity helps to identify the initial members of a project and clarify their roles and responsibilities. Using the team's resources, customer requirements are first analyzed to establish the scope of a project. Using the scope of the project, a clear purpose of the project is developed. A process typically has two important facets—the already established "as-is" process and the new "to-be" reengineered process. The "as-is" process helps to deduce actions necessary to improve the project process[12]. Acquiring a clear definition of the "as-is" business process and developing an understanding on how the process may be reengineered to suit the new project scope are crucial. These steps help to achieve the complete understanding of the existing process so that a project

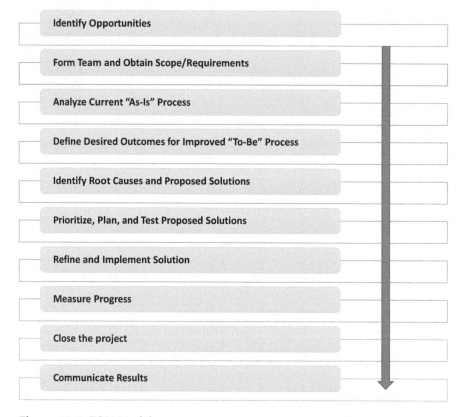

Figure 11-1 TQM Model

team can have the basis to start the "to-be" part that complies with project scope[13]. The next step is to determine the root causes of problems at hand. Many organizations use the Fishbone Diagram to determine the root cause of problems. We will discuss the fishbone diagram in the next section. Using this type of analysis, the projects are prioritized, planned, implemented, and tested. If the need arises, the solution is refined and implemented to the appropriate customer satisfaction levels. The TQM project is then closed and the results are communicated. A successful TQM project ends in a celebration!

FROM PRACTICE: TQM in Major US Companies

What do Ford, Chrysler, GM, AlliedSignal (Honeywell), Xerox, Federal Express, U.S. Navy, Wal-Mart, U.S. Army Corps of Engineers, Motorola, L.L. Bean, Steelcase, and Preston Trucking have in common? The answer is: TQM. TQM has been cited as a reason that Motorola prides itself on making almost perfect products and L.L. Bean shipping a half-million packages without making a mistake. Cianbro Corporation, a construction and construction services company headquartered in Pittsfield,

Maine, was very successful in implementing the TQM. However, according to the Electric Power Research Institute (EPRI), many U.S. companies are stumbling in their implementation of their quality improvement efforts. The satisfaction with the quality improvement efforts ranged from 35% to 60% among the executives who implemented the TQM programs[14].

Fishbone Diagram

A fishbone diagram or an Ishikawa diagram or a cause-and-effect diagram is used to identify and graphically detail all the potential causes related to a problem and discover the root causes of the problem at hand. Fishbone diagrams identify the potential factors that cause an overall effect. This tool helps teams to focus on causes, not symptoms. Let us look at how to implement a fishbone diagram.

To implement a fishbone diagram, a team of related experts are first assembled in a room with a whiteboard. All team members are solicited for input to implement the fishbone diagram. To begin with, a problem statement must be agreed upon by all team members. The team members are asked to think about causes of the problem at hand before the meeting. The team then brainstorms to come up with all the causes of the problem and construct the fishbone diagram as shown in Example 11-1. In a fishbone diagram, the causes are the "bones" of

> **Fishbone diagram**
> A fishbone diagram is a visual method to find the potential causes of a problem.

the fish and the effect its "head." Major categories of cause can be designated as "fish bones." Such categories can be people or developers, methods or processes, materials or content, machinery or computers, and so on. In a manufacturing project, machines, methods (how work is done), people, resources, materials (raw materials or components), measurement, and environment can be used as causes. In service industries, processes or procedures, policies, plant, equipment, space, technology, environment, logistics, and people are used as causes. There is no set standard number of causes. Some causes seem to fit in more than one category, and it is fine to have the same causes in several "bones." The question that is repeatedly asked about each listed cause is, "Why does it happen?" and the figure is filled with answers until all causes are identified by the team.

Example 11-1

Find the root causes associated with late deliveries of Rex Pizza.

Step 1: Identify the problem

Rex Pizza has been delivering pizzas late by an average of 15 minutes. Customer has complained 10 times this month.

Step 2: Form a team and meet

Rex Pizza formed a team consisting of a manager, two of the pizza making experts, and three delivery persons. The meeting was held at a local store.

Step 3: Create a fishbone diagram as a team

The manager drew a fishbone skeleton as shown in the following figure on a flipchart:

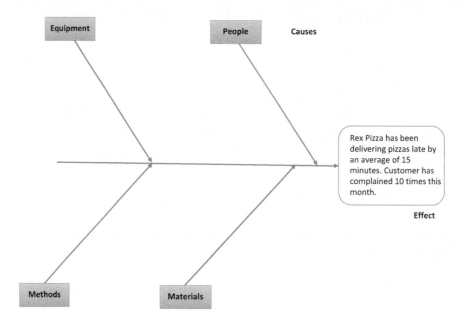

Step 4:   Every team member contributed to complete the following fishbone diagram:

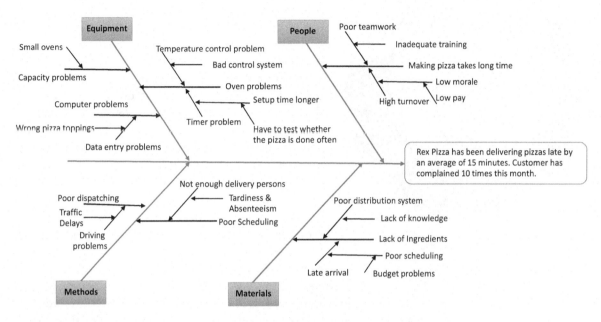

Analysis: There seems to be multiple problems during the making of a pizza and its delivery to the customers. Management must prioritize the problems and find solutions. The cause categories used in this problem are equipment, people, methods, and materials. To make a pizza, materials and equipment are essential. To deliver the pizza, people and delivery methods are essential. All causes in the above diagram are pertinent to the problem at hand.

Variability in Process

What is a process? What does the term *variability* mean? Let us understand these two terms first before we embark on the topic of quality management.

A process is a set of operations where inputs are processed to outputs. For example, we know that manufacturing is a set of operations where raw materials are processed and converted into finished goods. The act of accomplishing that set of operations where we take materials as input and process and convert raw materials into finished products using human labor, tools, and machinery is the manufacturing process.

Variability is the dispersion of data or how a set of data are spread out. Variability provides a way to describe and use statistics to compare one set of data to another set of data. It is the difference exhibited by the data points within a data set with the mean of a data set. Variability in a process is the difference between the measured quality and its target. A process with a high variability leads to either waste or excess production costs. For example, consider a company making neckties. One of the important measurements of a

> **Process** Process is a set of operations where inputs are processed to outputs.

> **Variability** Variability is the dispersion of data from each other as well as from the mean.

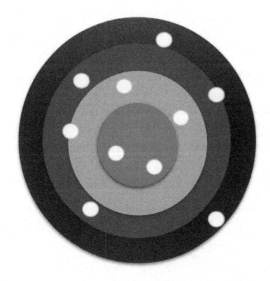

Figure 11-2 Process Variability

necktie is its width. Let us say that the standard width of a necktie is 3¼ inches. If there is a high variability in process, a necktie's width may be smaller than the lower specification limit determined by a customer, which will result in loss of sales. The problem gets escalated as the quality tests that pronounce the width of neckties are conducted only at the end of manufacturing a big batch of neckties. The necktie company may try to set the tie width a bit more to compensate for the loss of width due to process variability. But this increases the manufacturing cost as it increases the amount of necktie material. Therefore, the correct method is to reduce the process variability. By reducing the process variability, the company can control customer specification.

Variance is a way to describe the variability. When the variance of data in a data set is large, the data are widely scattered, and, when the variance is small, the data in the set get clustered.

Figure 11-2 illustrates the variability while playing a game of darts. The picture displays a process that covers the entire target. The arm that is throwing the ten darts at the dartboard is strong, and the person takes aim at the dartboard in the same fashion every time. While all the ten darts appear to have hit the target, very few have hit the bulls-eye. This is an example of a process with variability that is centered around the target. By decreasing the process variability, one can increase the number of times to hit the bulls-eye. In the same fashion, decreasing variability increases the control and predictability of a process, which results in better quality while reducing cost.

Six Sigma

> **Six Sigma** Six Sigma is a method used by organizations to improve their business processes.

The Six Sigma methodology addresses variability in design, production, services, processes, and measurements. The Six Sigma is a process improvement approach in quality management. It is used to find and eliminate errors and defects, reduce manufacturing cycle times, reduce costs, improve productivity, and meet customer expectations. Using Six Sigma, organizations can measure the baseline performance of their project, determine the root causes of variations in processes in that project, and improve those processes to meet and exceed the desired performance levels.

Six Sigma is a metric-driven methodology. A metric is a verifiable measurement in quantitative terms (e.g., the number of knots found in 8 feet of 2" × 4" lumber) or in qualitative terms (e.g., the level of customer satisfaction of a service is good but not excellent). The metrics in operations and supply chain management provide information on quality. The OSCM managers can use these metrics to identify improvement opportunities and make important decisions. In Six Sigma, the metric that is stressed frequently is a defect, a mistake, or an error that is apparent to customers. Six Sigma defines **quality**

performance as defects per million opportunities (DPMO) as shown in the following equation 11-2.

$$DPMO = \frac{Number\ of\ defects\ or\ error\ discovered}{Total\ number\ of\ possible\ opportunities\ for\ defects\ or\ errors} \times 1,000,000$$

Eq. 11-1

Example 11-2

A local pizza restaurant wants to know the number of defects, possible opportunities of defects, and their 6-Sigma (6σ) for pizza delivery. The restaurant manager maintains a database of the problem calls from customers for the past 3 months. On average, 3 pizzas were delivered per customer, and the restaurant received 200 delivery problem calls from 40,000 customers.

Number of defects or errors = Number of delivery problem calls = 200

The number of possible opportunities for errors as defined by the restaurant is equal to every delivery problem call received from its customers for the few months. Therefore,

Number of possible opportunities for defects = 40,000 × 3 pizzas/customer
= 120,000

Using Eq. 11-1, $DPMO = \dfrac{200}{120,000} \times 1,000,000 = 1,666.67$

Analysis: The DPMO depends on the number of defects and the total number of opportunities. Usually in a process, the total number of opportunities remains the same. A larger DPMO shows a larger number of errors.

The defects of any good or service may be defined as calls about customer service, delivery times, quality of goods or services, non-delivery of orders, and, of course, wrong orders. While DPMO is useful in understanding the number of defects, using it for further analysis in Six Sigma provides more insight into the problems.

Six Sigma was invented by Motorola, Inc. in 1986 as a metric for measuring the defects and improving the quality. The early adopters of Six Sigma who achieved well-publicized success include Motorola, Honeywell, and General Electric. By the late 1990s, about two-thirds of the Fortune 500 organizations had initiated Six Sigma to reduce costs and improve quality[15]. The sigma in the Six Sigma stands for the standard deviation. The term "six sigma process" comes from the statistical notion of six standard deviations between the process mean and the nearest specification limit, as shown in Figure 11-3.

Measurements usually include a tolerance value. For example, if a measurement made with a ruler is 4.5 inches and the ruler has a precision of 0.05 inches, then the tolerance interval in this measurement is 4.5 ± 0.05 inches or the measurement may fall anywhere from 4.45 inches to 4.55 inches. Since a Six Sigma quality level corresponds to a variation in process, this process variation is equal to half the measurement tolerance while allowing the mean to shift as much as 1.5 standard deviations from the target. Motorola chose a 1.5 standard deviation

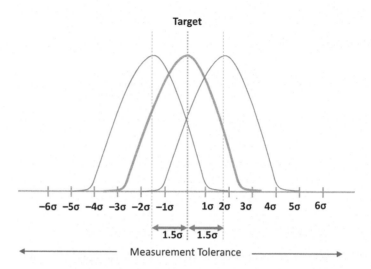

Figure 11-3 Six Sigma

number because 1.5 was the average shift of the company's processes. This tells us something important; no process can be controlled perfectly. If a process can be controlled within the 1.5σ of the target as shown by the thick curve in Figure 11-3, a maximum of 3.4 defects per million can be expected. This happens if this shift is toward one side or if the tolerance is only 1.5σ. If shifts occur on both sides of the thick curve, that is, if there is a shift 3σ, then the defect rate will be 6.4 per million. If the process is held perfectly on the target, that is, there is no shift or the outcome of the process is perfect, there will be one defect per million opportunities. In a practical sense, if your cell phone operates at a 4σ level, you would be without service for more than 4 hours each month, whereas at a 6σ level, the service will not be available for only 9 seconds a month[16].

Six Sigma uses a simple problem-solving methodology called "DMAIC." DMAIC stands for Define, Measure, Analyze, Improve, and Control. DMAIC incorporates statistical and other types of process improvement tools.

Define: Establish team charter and identify sponsor and team resources

This phase of the DMAIC process is about defining the problem statement of a Six Sigma project. A problem statement is a clear description of project issues that have to be addressed by a project team in order to implement a project effectively and efficiently.

Measure: Verify team goal, define current state, and collect and display data

This phase of the DMAIC process focuses on the measurement of internal processes that affect factors critical to quality. All key factors that can be controlled or changed to improve factors critical to quality have to be understood clearly. For example, in the restaurant delivery system that we discussed earlier, delivery of pizzas to customers may be a function of many factors critical to quality. Once relationships are established, data and observations can be collected.

Analyze: Determine process capability and speed and determine sources of variation and time-related bottlenecks

This phase focuses on why and how defects and errors occur. Processes are analyzed to determine the root causes of deficient performance and whether the process can be improved or should be redesigned.

Using Excel, we can calculate the Six Sigma level as follows:

$$Sigma\ Level = NORMSINV\ (1 - (DPMO/1,000,000)) + Shift \qquad \text{Eq. 11-2}$$

Example 11-3 shows how to calculate Six Sigma.

Example 11-3

Determine the Six Sigma level for the local pizza restaurant delivery process.

As shown in Example 11-2, DPMO $= \dfrac{200}{120,000} \times 1,000,000 = 1,666.67$

Using Excel, we can easily calculate the process sigma as:

Sigma Level = NORMSINV (1 − (DPMO/1,000,000)) + Shift, where Shift = 1.5σ.

Therefore, the delivery process sigma level is at:

NORMSINV (1 − (1,666.67/1,000,000)) + 1.5 = 4.44σ

Analysis: The function NORMSINV in Microsoft Excel is used to calculate the Six Sigma of a process. In Six Sigma terms, a 4 Sigma is equivalent to 6.2K errors per million with a 99.4% accuracy; a 5 Sigma is equivalent to 233 errors per million with a 99.97% accuracy; and a 6 Sigma is equivalent to 3.4 errors per million with a 99.999997% accuracy. In this example, the Six Sigma of the pizza delivery process is 4.44σ, which means we have about 1,860 errors per million delivery of pizzas with a 99.81% accuracy. This is actually not that bad for a pizza delivery restaurant!

Improve: Generate ideas, conduct experiments, weigh benefits and concerns, and develop and implement action plans

The root cause of problems in a Six Sigma project identified by the preceding analysis is used to generate ideas for the improvement of factors critical to quality. Improving processes based on measurements and analysis can ensure that the number of defects is lowered and processes are streamlined.

Control: Develop a control plan and monitor performance

Control ensures that variances that appear in a project process are corrected. Controls can be in the form of pilot-runs to determine if the processes are within specifications. Statistical process control (SPC) technique is often employed to monitor the performance on key measures.

Let us understand the Six Sigma process through Example 11-4.

Example 11-4

John Doe picks up pizzas from two nearby pizza restaurants. He records the time taken (in minutes) of those pizza restaurants to deliver the pizza 10 times as follows:

Luigi's	3	4	5	5	6	7	7	8	8	9
Romano's	6	6	6	6	6	6	6	7	7	7

Which restaurant has a better pizza delivery process if John is planning to wait for 4–6 minutes?

Let us take a look at the values of mean, mode, standard deviation, variance of delivery process, and Six Sigma levels (using Eq. 11-2) for the two restaurants as follows:

	Luigi's	Romano's
No. of opportunities	10	10
No. of defects	6	3
Preferred wait time	4–6 minutes	
DPMO	600,000	300,000
Sigma level	**1.25**	**2.02**

Analysis: When we see the data initially, we may jump to a conclusion that Luigi's has a better process. On average, the waiting time seems to be the same in both restaurants. It also seems that most often they have the same waiting time. But, what about the variation? The standard deviations and therefore the variations of the two restaurants are different. The standard deviation allows us to recognize that Luigi's with the wider variation will not be as reliable a prediction of delivery times as Romano's with a smaller variation. This is reflected in the sigma levels of these restaurant processes as well. Romano's has a better Six Sigma and a better delivery process.

FROM PRACTICE: Six Sigma at Honeywell, Inc.

Honeywell International Inc., a Fortune 100 multinational conglomerate corporation, provides goods and services for industries in aerospace, building technologies, performance materials and technologies, and safety and productivity solutions. Using Six Sigma methodology, an Industrial control team in Honeywell developed a reliable, cost-effective family of chips and assembled components. As a result, the Industrial Control division

© Michael Vi/Shutterstock.com

achieved a 500-percent increase in revenue growth and reduced the cycle time by 35%. More than 300 staff members, both in quality control and research and development laboratories, participated in a customized Green Belt learning program to improve measurement systems and saved nearly $8 million[17].

Quality Management Process

Quality management process is comprised of quality planning, quality assurance, and quality control. The quality planning process identifies the quality standards that are relevant to the goods and services of a firm and determines how to use such standards in planning the quality process. The quality assurance process ensures that all the planned activities in the OSCM provide confidence to users, customers, suppliers, and all other stakeholders. The quality control process monitors the quality of products and determines whether products comply with relevant standards and identifies ways to eliminate defects.

Quality Planning

Planning quality involves identifying relevant quality standards and introducing a sound quality process in the production of goods and implementation of services. Appropriate quality planning in order to deliver per specifications and in compliance with customer requirements must be planned in detail. Quality planning must also involve identifying the quality standards and the requirements for tracking, monitoring, and managing the expectations of the planned quality. According to the American Society of Quality (ASQ), quality planning must include[18]:

Quality planning
A quality plan is a document that includes specifications, quality standards, process and procedures, resources, and the sequence of activities pertinent to a particular product.

- Objectives to be attained, including specifications;
- Process steps that comprise of the operating procedures of the organization;
- Allocation of responsibilities, authority, and resources during the distinct phases of production, implementation, and delivery;
- Applicable standards, business processes, practices, procedures, and instructions;
- Appropriate testing, inspection, examination, and audit programs;
- Change management procedures;
- Measurements and metrics to achieve quality objectives;
- Address the alignment of quality goals with the overall strategic goals of the organization.

Quality Assurance

Quality assurance is a process to ensure that the end products, that is, goods and services, will satisfy the quality standards of an organization. The process includes a structured and planned system of review procedures that describes how quality planning will be executed as per the quality standards of the organization. For example, quality assurance is identified as a degree of certainty wherein the work performed by the contractor complies with the contract requirements. According to ASQ, quality assurance provides confidence to organizational management and external customers, government agencies, regulators, certifiers, and third parties[18].

Quality Control

Quality control is the set of activities used to fulfill quality requirements. Quality control helps firms to meet their customer demands with better products. Quality control is used to verify whether the product outcomes meet the acceptable quality that is expected by customers. Quality control involves testing the products to determine whether the products are within the specifications set forth by the organization.

Quality testing is accomplished in every step of the manufacturing process. When raw materials arrive at a plant, they are tested for quality. When the product is being manufactured, a few samples are pulled from the manufacturing and tested. The finished product is subject to testing as well. Quality control through testing at the various stages of manufacturing helps identify where a problem is occurring so that remedial steps can be undertaken to prevent that problem in the future. Six Sigma and statistical process control (SPC) are used widely used in organizations for quality control. The biggest challenge in managing the quality of products is ensuring that their associated processes are consistent. The consistency is usually achieved by minimizing the variability.

Statistical process control (SPC) is the application of statistical methods to monitor and control a process in order to reduce the variability. Using SPC, it is possible to identify bottlenecks, wait times, and other sources of delay within a process. Many organizations have enjoyed process cycle time reductions as well as cost reductions using SPC. The most popular SPC tool is the control chart.

Control Charts

A control chart is a graph used to study how a process changes over time. A control chart helps to observe when an unusual event, such as an exceedingly high or low observation, occurs in a process. A control chart is a tool used to determine whether a business process is in a state of statistical control.

A process is monitored using the control charts. When companies manufacture a product, they start with the design department specifying the various dimensions of the product, including product's weight, and the materials used in making the product, how the product is assembled, and so on. For example, the design department of a company manufacturing pencils would specify the dimensions of the pencils as specifications based on inputs from customers and other stakeholders. Their manufacturing department must control the manufacturing process within those specifications. The monitoring of the process continues until a predetermined process control limit is breached. Then, the manufacturing process is stopped to investigate the problem with the process and improve the process. It is usually desired that control limits should be within the specification limits. In that case, even if the process goes out of control limits, products do not get impacted for a customer as specification limits are outside the process control limits. If the data or measurements fall between control limits, we say that the process is in control and if data do not fall between the two limits, we say that the process is out of control. Let us discuss the process control using Example 11-5.

Example 11-5

Consider Nat Pencils, LLC from Monroe, Louisiana, a company making pencils. The company determines that an important variable in the process of making the pencils is the diameter of the pencil. The manufacturing department of that company picks an appropriate process to make the pencils. They manufacture a batch of 20 pencils and take the measurements of pencils' diameters. The test results are as follows:

Sample	1	2	3	4	5	6	7	8	9	10
Diameter	0.375	0.376	0.373	0.376	0.376	0.376	0.377	0.373	0.373	0.374
Sample	11	12	13	14	15	16	17	18	19	20
Diameter	0.373	0.375	0.377	0.375	0.373	0.375	0.376	0.373	0.375	0.375

The company has decided to stop manufacturing if the process starts making pencils that exceed 3 standard deviations. Determine if the process is stable and under control as far as the diameter of the manufactured pencils are concerned.

The design department has specified the diameter of the pencil to be 0.375 inches ± 0.004 inch. What this means is that pencils will be acceptable as long as their diameter varies between 0.371 inches and 0.379 inches. In this case, the lower specification limit (LSL) = 0.371 inches, and the upper specification limit (USL) = 0.379 inches.

The test results show an average diameter of manufactured pencils to be 0.375 inches and the standard deviation to be 0.001 inches, which is calculated from the given data. The standard deviation of 0.001 inches tells us that the process has a variability and the diameters of the manufactured pencils are not the same. Viewing the given data, we can see that all 20 samples fall between the specification limits and are accepted per the specifications.

Now, let us look at the other constraints imposed by the company. The company has decided to stop manufacturing if the process starts making pencils that exceed 3 standard deviations, that is, 0.375 inches $\pm$ (3 $\times$ 0.001) inch. Therefore, if the test results fall under $0.375 - 0.003 = 0.372$ or over $0.375 + 0.003 = 0.378$, the process will be stopped to be investigated. In this case, the lower process control limit (LCL) = 0.372, and the upper process control limit (UCL) = 0.378. **Now, the goal is to manage the process by keeping it within 3 standard deviations of the process mean.** Let us visualize these results in the following figure.

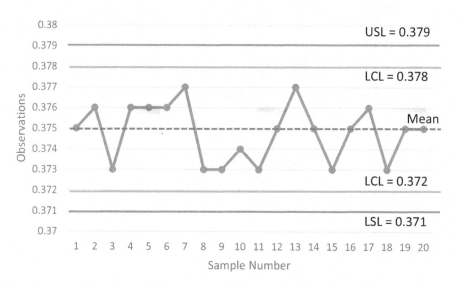

As seen in the above figure, a control chart always has data or measurements shown as dots connected by a line, a central line to show the mean of the data, an upper line for the upper control limit, and a lower line for the lower control limit. If the specifications are given, a control chart will have upper and lower specification limit lines as well.

By looking at the data and these lines, we can draw conclusions about whether the process variation is consistent or is unpredictable. If the data fall between two control limits, we say that the process is in control and if data are unpredictable or do not fall between two limits, we say that the process is out of control.

> *Analysis:* As seen above, all pencils are acceptable by the customer as the measurements of samples fall between the specification limits. The process is stable and under control as the measurements of pencil diameters fall between process control limits.

The control charts plots measurements or test outcomes over time. The use of the control charts is a preventive method to manage quality by monitoring the processes in a way that identifies potential problems before products with defects are even created. There are four different control charts used in controlling quality:

- X-bar charts
- R charts

Specifications limits Specification limits are tolerance values set by customers and are also the design specifications of a product.

Process control limits Process control limits represent the maximum limits imposed on a process.

- P charts
- C charts.

We will focus on how to create and analyze the **X-bar and R charts** in this chapter.

X-Bar Charts

An X-bar chart is a process control chart used to monitor the sample means of variables that result from a process and is often used in quality control. To examine whether a process is stable, we take various measurements of the products that are produced using the process. These measurements or observations are taken in a few product samples. The mean of the observations $(\bar{X})$ in a sample can be calculated as:

$$\bar{X} = \frac{x_1 + x_2 + x_3 + \ldots + x_n}{n} \qquad \text{Eq. 11-3}$$

where n is the number of observations in the sample, $\bar{X}$ is the mean of the observations in the sample, and x represents each observation in the sample.

While Eq. 11-3 gives the mean of the observations in a sample, we must find the average of the means of all the samples that were taken to observe a process. This average of the means of N samples represented as $\bar{\bar{X}}$ can be found as:

$$\bar{\bar{X}} = \frac{\bar{X}_1 + \bar{X}_2 + \bar{X}_3 + \ldots + \bar{X}_N}{N} \qquad \text{Eq. 11-4}$$

where N is the number of samples.

If the standard deviation of the process is known, then the upper and lower control limits are calculated as follows:

$$Upper\ Control\ Limit\ (UCL) = \bar{\bar{X}} + zS_{\bar{x}} \qquad \text{Eq. 11-5}$$

$$Lower\ Control\ Limit\ (LCL) = \bar{\bar{X}} - zS_{\bar{x}} \qquad \text{Eq. 11-6}$$

where, $S_{\bar{x}}$ is the standard deviation of sample means calculated as $s / \sqrt{n}$ (s divided by $\sqrt{n}$)

n is the number of observations in a sample

s is the standard deviation of the process

z is z-score, the number of standard deviations for a specific confidence level obtained from Table 11-3.

The z-score and the associated confidence levels are given in Table 11-3 below.

Table 11-3 z-score and Confidence Levels										
Confidence Level	0.7	0.75	0.8	0.85	0.9	0.92	0.95	0.96	0.98	0.99
Z		1.04	1.15	1.28	1.44	1.645	1.75	1.96	2.05	2.33	2.58

To construct X-bar charts, we need to know the process standard deviation, which can be converted to the standard deviation of the sample means. Often standard deviations may not be available, and, therefore, UCL and LCL must be based on another measure of variable that is readily available. In these cases, instead of the standard deviation of the process, the average of the range values of the sample is used.

The range is the difference between the largest and the smallest measures of the sample and provides the measure of variability for the project. $\bar{R}$ is the average range from the samples.

$$Upper\ Control\ Limit\ (UCL) = \bar{\bar{X}} + A\bar{R} \qquad\qquad \text{Eq. 11-7}$$

$$Lower\ Control\ Limit\ (LCL) = \bar{\bar{X}} - A\bar{R} \qquad\qquad \text{Eq. 11-8}$$

where "A" is a 3-Sigma control chart factor used for variability and is given in Table 11-4.

Table 11-4 3-Sigma Control Chart Factor "A"												
Observations in Sample (n)	2	3	4	5	6	7	8	9	10	11	12	13
A	1.88	1.02	0.73	0.58	0.48	0.42	0.37	0.34	0.31	0.29	0.27	0.25
Observations in Sample (n)	14	15	16	17	18	19	20	21	22	23	24	25
A	0.24	0.22	0.21	0.20	0.19	0.19	0.18	0.17	0.17	0.16	0.16	0.15

R-Charts

A range (R) chart is another type of control chart for variables. X-bar charts measure the shift in the central tendency of the process and range charts monitor the dispersion or the variability of the process. The method for developing R-charts is like that of X-bar charts. Usually X-bar charts are used in conjunction with R-charts. The center line of the R-chart is the $\bar{R}$, the mean of the sample ranges.

$$\bar{R} = \frac{R_1 + R_2 + R_3 + \ldots + R_n}{n} \qquad\qquad \text{Eq. 11-9}$$

The upper and lower control limits are calculated as follows:

$$Upper\ Control\ Limit\ (UCL) = D_4\bar{R} \qquad\qquad \text{Eq. 11-10}$$

$$Lower\ Control\ Limit\ (LCL) = D_3\bar{R} \qquad\qquad \text{Eq. 11-11}$$

where D_3 and D_4 are values for calculating the 3σ control limits. These values are given in Table 11-5.

Table 11-5 3-Sigma Control Chart Factor D_3 and D_4

Observations in Sample (n)	2	3	4	5	6	7	8	9	10	11	12	13
D_3	0	0	0	0	0	0.08	0.14	0.18	0.22	0.26	0.28	0.31
D_4	3.27	2.57	2.28	2.11	2.00	1.92	1.86	1.82	1.78	1.74	1.72	1.69

Observations in Sample (n)	14	15	16	17	18	19	20	21	22	23	24	25
D_3	0.33	0.35	0.36	0.38	0.39	0.40	0.41	0.43	0.43	0.44	0.45	0.46
D_4	1.67	1.65	1.64	1.62	1.61	1.60	1.59	1.58	1.57	1.56	1.55	1.54

Example 11-6 through Example 11-8 shows how to solve quality control problems using the X-bar and R charts.

Example 11-6

ExtCords, Inc. manufactures 10ft 18AWG power extension cords. After manufacturing 25 cords for a project, the cords are measured. The measurements are taken and shown below. Construct a X-bar chart for a 99% confidence level if the standard deviation is 0.18. Is the process stable?

Sample No	Observations				
	1	2	3	4	5
1	10.2	10.1	9.9	10.2	10.1
2	9.9	9.8	9.7	10.1	10.2
3	10.2	9.8	10.1	10.3	10.2
4	10.3	10.1	9.7	10.2	10.1
5	10.1	10.1	10.3	9.8	9.9

Step 1: Find $\overline{\overline{X}}$, the average of all samples. Here n = 5; N = 5; s = 0.18.

Each of the $\overline{X}$ is calculated using Eq. 11-3. For example, for sample 1, the $\overline{X}$ = 10.1. The average of the means, $\overline{\overline{X}}$, is calculated using Eq. 11-4 which is equal to 10.056.

Sample No	Observations					Average of Observations
	1	2	3	4	5	
1	10.2	10.1	9.9	10.2	10.1	10.1
2	9.9	9.8	9.7	10.1	10.2	9.94
3	10.2	9.8	10.1	10.3	10.2	10.12
4	10.3	10.1	9.7	10.2	10.1	10.08
5	10.1	10.1	10.3	9.8	9.9	10.04
					$\overline{\overline{X}}$ =	10.056

Step 2:   Calculate the standard deviation of the sample
With $s = 0.18$, $S_{\bar{x}} = s / \sqrt{n} = 0.18 / (\sqrt{5}) = 0.08$
From Table 11-3, for 99% confidence level, z-score = 2.58

Step 3:   Using Eq. 11-5 and 11-6, calculate the process control limits
$LCL = 10.056 - (2.58 \times 0.08) = 10.26$
$UCL = 10.056 + (2.58 \times 0.08) = 9.85$

Step 4:   Construct the X-bar control chart:

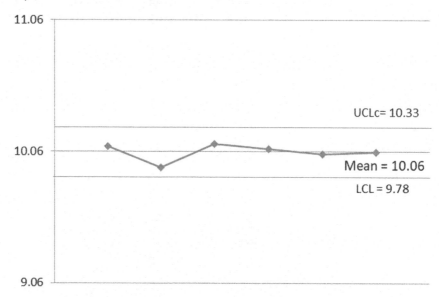

Analysis: Since all the data on the X-bar chart falls between the LCL and UCL, the process is stable. The X-bar chart and the R-chart are used to monitor the manufacturing processes, to ensure that the processes are in control, and to assure that there are no assignable causes of variation.

Example 11-7

ExtCords, Inc. manufactures 10ft 18AWG power extension cords. After manufacturing 25 cords for a project, the cords are measured. The measurements are taken and shown below. Construct a X-bar chart. Is the process stable?

Sample No	Observations				
	1	2	3	4	5
1	10.2	10.1	9.9	10.2	10.1
2	9.9	9.8	9.7	10.1	10.2
3	10.2	9.8	10.1	10.3	10.2
4	10.3	10.1	9.7	10.2	10.1
5	10.1	10.1	10.3	9.8	9.9

Step 1: Find $\bar{\bar{X}}$ the average of all samples and $\bar{R}$, the average of the ranges. For example, 10.10 is equal to the average of all observations of sample no 1. Then $\bar{\bar{X}}$ = average of all the averages of samples. The range for sample no 1 is maximum of observations minus the minimum of observations = $10.2 - 9.9 = 0.3$. Then calculate $\bar{R}$ which is the average of all ranges.

Sample No	Observations					Average of observations $X_{sample\ no}$	Range R
	1	2	3	4	5		
1	10.2	10.1	9.9	10.2	10.1	10.10	0.3
2	9.9	9.8	9.7	10.1	10.2	9.94	0.5
3	10.2	9.8	10.1	10.3	10.2	10.12	0.5
4	10.3	10.1	9.7	10.2	10.1	10.08	0.6
5	10.1	10.1	10.3	9.8	9.9	10.04	0.5

The $\bar{X} = 10.06$ and $\bar{R} = 0.48$

Step 2: Get the Factor A from Table 11-4 for n = 5, which is equal to 0.58

Step 3: Using Eq. 11-7 and 11-8, calculate the process control limits

$LCL = 10.06 - (0.58 \times 0.48) = 10.33$

$UCL = 10.06 + (0.58 \times 0.48) = 9.78$

Step 4: Construct the X-bar control chart:

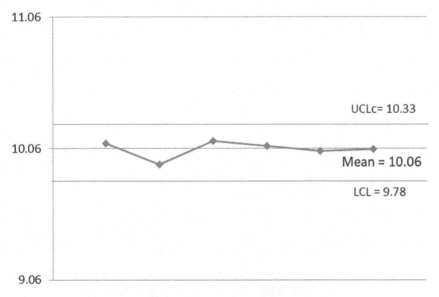

Analysis: Since all the data on the X-bar chart falls between the LCL and UCL, the process is stable. The X-bar chart and the R-chart are used to monitor the manufacturing processes, to ensure that the processes are in control, and to assure that there are no assignable causes of variation.

Example 11-8

Using the data from Example 11-7, construct a R-Chart.

	Observations				
Sample No	1	2	3	4	5
1	10.2	10.1	9.9	10.2	10.1
2	9.9	9.8	9.7	10.1	10.2
3	10.2	9.8	10.1	10.3	10.2
4	10.3	10.1	9.7	10.2	10.1
5	10.1	10.1	10.3	9.8	9.9

Step 1: Calculate the $\bar{R}$ as in Example 11-7, $\bar{R} = 0.48$

Step 2: From Table 11-5, get D_3 and D_4 for $n = 5$. $D_3 = 0\ D_4 = 2.11$

Step 3: Calculate the UCL and LCL using Eqs. 11-10 and 11-11.

LCL $= 0.48 \times 0 = 0$
UCL $= 0.48 \times 2.11 = 1.013$

Step 4: Construct the R control chart:

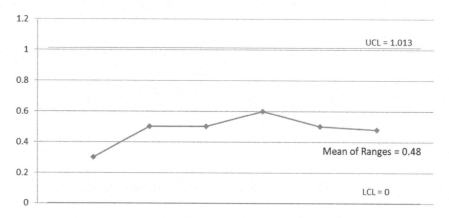

Analysis: Since all the data on the R-chart falls between the LCL and UCL, the control limits, the process is stable. The X-bar chart and the R-chart are used to monitor the manufacturing processes, to ensure that the processes are in control, and to assure that there are no assignable causes of variation.

Process Capability and Process Capability Index

C_p, **Process capability** Process capability, C_p, evaluates the ability of a process to meet or exceed the expectations or specifications.

A critical aspect of quality control is evaluating the ability of a process to meet or exceed the specifications. This is called process capability. If you make your morning coffee, you know the amount of coffee is not the same every day.

This can happen for several reasons, such as amount of coffee powder and water, runtime of the coffeemaker, amount of heat applied from the stove, and other process factors. The taste of coffee may be the same, but the amount of coffee varies!

Each additional step or operation may increase or decrease variations in a process. We know that variation in a process cannot be eliminated, but can be measured, monitored, reduced, and controlled. If you buy a 3.5 oz. chocolate bar and weigh it on a sensitive scale, it will weigh anywhere between 3.49 oz. and 3.51 oz. If you buy another 3.5 oz. chocolate bar, it may weigh between 3.48 oz. and 3.51 oz. Process capability can determine how far the weight of each chocolate bar is from its designed weight of 3.5 oz.

We use two different measures, namely C_p and C_{pk}, to define the ability of a process to meet the requirements or the capability of a process. C_p stands for process capability while C_{pk} stands for process capability index.

Process capability, Cp, is evaluating the process variability relative to the preset specifications in order to determine whether the process is capable of producing, building, or implementing an acceptable product, service, structure, or system. Cp, is calculated as:

$$C_p = \frac{USL - LSL}{6\sigma}$$
Eq. 11-12

> **C_{pk}, Process capability index**
> Process capability index, C_{pk}, shows how well a product fits within specification limits.

The process variability depends on the value of Cp as follows:

- $C_p = 1$: A value of C_p equal to 1 means that the process variability meets the specifications and the process is minimally capable. This also means that 99.74% of the products produced or systems implemented will fall within the specification limits.
- $C_p < 1$: A value of C_p below 1 means that the process variability is outside the range of specification and the process is not capable of meeting specifications; the process is not capable of producing within specifications and the process must be improved.
- $C_p > 1$: A value of C_p above 1 means that process variability is tighter than specifications, and the process exceeds minimal capability and is capable of meeting specifications.

However, C_p does not take into account where the process is centered. A better measure of process capability is C_{pk}. C_{pk}, the process capability index, is calculated using the following formula and is the minimum of the two numbers:

$$C_{pk} = min\left(\frac{\overline{X} - LSL}{3\sigma} \ or \ \frac{USL - \overline{X}}{3\sigma} \right)$$
Eq. 11-13

Since we know that Six Sigma or six standard deviations account for all specifications for a process, we find the C_{pk} value by dividing with the 3 sigma as we are looking at either side of the distribution as shown in Figure 11-4.

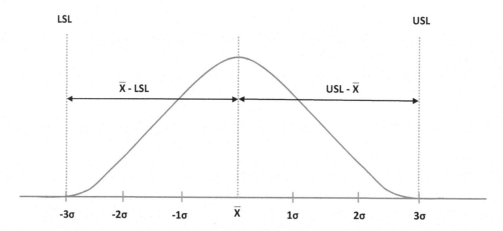

Figure 11-4 C_{pk}, Process Capability Index

- Larger C_{pk} is better since the larger the Cpk is, the less likely it is that any product will be outside the specification limits.
- $C_{pk} < 0$ means that some products will be outside the customer specification limits. Moreover, the process mean has gone beyond one of the specification limits.
- $C_{pk} < 1$ means that the process will often miss the target specification.
- $C_{pk} > 1$ means that the process mean is perfectly centered and is well within the specification limits.
- $C_{pk} \geq 1.33$ is preferred to satisfy customer expectations.
- $C_{pk} > 3$ means that specification limits are very loose and should be tightened.
- C_{pk} takes into account where the process is centered. A perfectly centered process as shown in Figure 11-4 will have $C_p = C_{pk}$.
- If $C_p > C_{pk}$, the curve will be shifted to the left, that is, toward LSL.
- If C_p is a negative value and $C_p > C_{pk}$, the process mean will be outside LSL or USL.

Example 11-9

The design specification for the weight of a jar of grape jelly is 18 oz. with the upper specification limit of 20 oz. and the lower specification limit of 16 oz. The quality inspector upon evaluating a batch of grape jelly found that the average weight was 18.25 oz. and a standard deviation of 0.8 oz. What is the capability of the process?

We will calculate both Cp and Cpk to analyze the problem.

Using Eq. 11-12, $C_p = \dfrac{20-16}{6 \times 0.8} = 0.83$

Using Eq. 11-13, $C_{pk} = min\left(\dfrac{18.25-16}{3 \times 0.8} \ or \ \dfrac{20-18.25}{3 \times 0.8} \right) = min(0.94, 0.73) = 0.73$

Analysis: As C_p is less than 1.0, the process is not capable of producing within specifications and, hence, must be improved. As C_{pk} is less than 1, the process will often miss the target specification. Moreover, $C_p > C_{pk}$, the curve will be shifted to the left, that is, toward LSL.

Example 11-10

For the jelly jar problem in Example 11-9, what is the probability of producing a defect in the process?

The probability of a defect is the sum of probabilities of the weight of a jar of jelly falling outside both LSL and USL.

Step 1: Calculate the z-score using Eq. 11-6 to calculate the probability of weight that is less than LSL, which is 16oz:

$$z = \frac{x - \overline{X}}{\sigma} = \frac{16 - 18.25}{0.8} = -2.8125$$

Step 2: Calculate the z-score using Eq. 11-6 to calculate the probability of weight that is more than USL, which is 20 oz.:

$$z = \frac{x - \overline{X}}{\sigma} = \frac{20 - 18.25}{0.8} = -2.1875$$

Step 3: Calculate the probability of a jelly jar with weight less than the LSL of 16 oz., using the EXCEL function NORM.S.DIST()

P1 = NORM.S.DIST(−2.8125) = 0.0024579

Step 4: Calculate the probability of a jelly jar with weight more than the USL of 20 oz., using the EXCEL function NORM.S.DIST()

P2 = 1 − NORM.S.DIST(2.1875) = 0.014353

Step 5: Calculate the total probability = P1 + P2 = 0.0024579 + 0.014353 = 0.016811 or 1.68%

Analysis: Approximately 1.68% of the jars of jelly will be defective.

Lean Six Sigma and the Toyota Way

> **Lean Six Sigma**
> Lean Six Sigma is a method to accomplish process improvement, customer satisfaction, and profits by reducing variation, waste, and cycle time.

If "reduction in variation" is the Six Sigma mantra, lean's mantra is "reduction of waste." Six Sigma focuses on improving process control by reducing process variation. The lean concept eliminates the non–value-added activities and processes to reduce waste and promote a streamlined workflow. The purposes of the lean concept are as follows:

- Eliminate wasted time, effort, and material,
- Provide customers with make-to-order products, and
- Reduce cost while improving quality.

> **Lean manufacturing and lean services** Lean manufacturing and lean services are methods to reduce waste, create value for customer, and improve processes.

The lean process is used in organizations to produce goods and services efficiently. It also helps to detect abnormalities in organizational processes. A process, whether in a manufacturing environment or service industry setting, must be managed well.

Lean Six Sigma combines the strengths of Six Sigma and the lean concept to attain process improvisation. Lean Six Sigma is a method to accomplish profits by reducing variation, waste, and cycle time. The Lean Six Sigma methodology integrates the less quantitative lean tools such as Kaizen, workplace organization, and visual controls with the more quantitative Six Sigma tools such as statistical data analysis, design of experiments, and hypothesis testing.

The lean manufacturing is a production method to reduce waste, create customer value, and improve manufacturing processes. The lean service is a method to reduce waste, create value for customers, and improve service processes. A minimal inventory is sought to eliminate waste. The minimized inventory increases cash flow as well as makes it easier to deliver the required products to the end customer.

Lean is derived from the Toyota Production System (TPS) or the "The Toyota Way." The TPS is introduced in an organization to minimize cost and waste. The Toyota Way or TPS is based on the following 14 principles[19, 20]:

1. Long-term philosophy
2. Create flow
3. Use a pull system
4. Level out the workload
5. Stop and fix the problem
6. Standardize tasks
7. Use visual control
8. Use reliable, tested technology
9. Grow leaders who live the philosophy
10. Respect, develop, and challenge your people and teams
11. Respect, challenge, and help your suppliers
12. Go and see for yourself to understand the situation
13. Make decisions slowly by consensus
14. Continual organizational learning through kaizen.

The purpose of lean system or the TPS is to identify and reduce three distinct obstacles (3Ms) and apply five common sense factors (5Ss) to the working environment that are shown in Table 11-6.

The TPS is a management concept based on manufacturing parts arriving just in time for the production of a product so that the production can be continued without interruption. This is also called the "Just-in-Time" (JIT) system. Toyota integrated the Just-in-Time and Jidoka concepts to form the Toyota Production System under the leadership of Taiichi Ono, a former Executive Vice-President of Toyota. JIT drives out unnecessary cost and helps to detect problems that cause waste. Jidoka provides the necessary response to the problems detected.

Table 11-6 3Ms and 5Ss of Lean

3Ms			5Ss		
Japanese Term	English Equivalent	Description	Japanese Term	English Equivalent	Description
Muda	Waste	Non-value activities that add cost	Seiri	Sort	Sort by necessary items
Mura	Inconsistency	Variability in process or system	Seiton	Stabilize	Arrange items for efficiency
Muri	Unreasonableness	Blaming others rather than resolving problems	Seison	Shine	Keep a clean facility
			Seiketsu	Standardize	Continuously improve products
			Shitsuke	Sustain	Be disciplined

Just-In-Time (JIT)

Just-in-time (JIT) is making or ordering only what is needed, only when it is needed, and only in the amount that is needed. JIT can be applied both to manufacturing and services industries. JIT views anything over the necessary or minimum amount as waste. In production, various transit times and their transfer quantities must be taken into account and minimized for the optimum usage of materials. In service industries, the optimum quantities must be ordered to eliminate waste. Vendors who transfer the goods can ship many times to keep the inventory low rather than transferring them in bulk in one time. For example, the logisticians can plan to supply parts to a manufacturing plant exactly as the production is running out of that particular part. To accomplish this, the purchasing departments can plan their orders in right amounts of the parts delivered at the right times. JIT levels out customer demand and reduces the inventory at all stages of the supply chain. In this way, JIT aligns the production to meet the actual demand and therefore reduces the inventory cost and all associated costs of poor demand planning.

The reduction of **setup times** of machines is a key target of JIT. The machine setup time is the time required to prepare a machine for its next batch of products after it has completed producing the last batch of products.

Faster setup times can reduce **buffers** or work-in-progress inventories[21]. An inventory buffer is the additional on-hand inventory to meet transportation delays and sudden increases in demand. The buffers are an evidence of waste since they show production of more products than is needed at a given time as well as idle time, surplus workers, and excessive equipment capacity[21]. However, small buffers are advantageous than larger ones. A small

> **Just-in-time**
> Just-in-time is making or ordering only what is needed, only when it is needed, and only in the amount that is needed.

> **Setup time** The period of time required to prepare a machine for its next batch of products after it has completed producing the last batch of products.

buffer leads to a more sensitive production or storage process as they show a greater visibility of the source of error. The quality problems become obvious and are visible easily. The reduction of buffers stimulates a continuous learning process.

JIT is also a sophisticated method of learning-by-doing[21]. Workers are expected to do their regular preventive maintenance and take remedial actions themselves. Workers are trained to switch between jobs as and when needed in a JIT system, and they often help fellow workers who are overloaded.

Jidoka

Jidoka means automation with the involvement of a human. An example of Jidoka is a machine that will detect a problem and stop the production automatically rather than continue to run and produce bad output. Under the TPS, a human or a machine is empowered to automatically detect any abnormal condition and stop. Jidoka often involves the following four-step process that is triggered and implemented when an abnormality occurs:

1. Detect the abnormality,
2. Stop,
3. Fix or correct the immediate condition, and
4. Investigate the root cause and implement a solution.

The first two steps can be mechanized or automated. A simple example is a Poka-Yoke device. Poka-Yoke is an automatic device or method that either makes it impossible for an error to occur or makes the error immediately obvious once it has occurred[22]. It is a Japanese term that means "mistake-proofing." An example is the airplane lavatory light. The light turns on only when the door lock is engaged. This keeps the passengers from failing to lock the door. We will discuss another example, Kanban, later in this chapter. The potential benefits of Poka-Yoke are:

- Elimination of errors and improved quality,
- Decreased setup times with associated reduction in production time,
- Improved production capacity,
- Simplified and improved housekeeping,
- Increased safety,
- Lower costs,
- Lower skill requirements,
- Increased production flexibility, and
- Improved operator attitudes.

The third and fourth steps in the Jidoka process are not usually automated. They involve a human touch as the problem should be diagnosed, analyzed, and solved. The problem may range from a need to provide a temporary fix to a need for major repair. However, the TPS calls for decisions to be made at the lowest possible level of the organization. The fourth step is to investigate the root cause of the problem and install a permanent solution. In summary, lean manufacturing and services are designed to operate in order to detect abnormal conditions or system changes that might otherwise go unnoticed.

Waste Elimination

In TPS, anything or anyone who does not add value is waste. The non–value-added activities are activities for which a customer is not willing to pay and they only add to the cost and the time. For example, unnecessary meetings, processing past mistakes, excessive motions when making goods or providing service, waiting for others to provide information are all examples of non–value-added activities. The non–value-added activities are wastes. Therefore, what we mean by waste is everything that adds cost to goods and services without adding value to them. Waste can be classified as follows:

> **Waste** Anything that adds cost to the goods and services without adding value to it.

- Excess production,
- Delays,
- Unnecessary movement and transportation,
- Poor process design,
- Unused Inventory,
- Inefficient process performance, and
- Making defective items.

The elimination of all kinds of waste at all levels of the production and provision of services is the goal of the lean method. An excessive production results in the accumulation of finished goods, and it is a waste if those goods cannot be sold. An excess and unused inventory reduces profitability. Moreover, there is an added possibility of goods going obsolete. Therefore, producing a product simply to keep production busy should be avoided. Any delays result in the poor use of capacity. Any early delivery does not do any good, and late deliveries are bad. The movement or transportation of materials should be kept at a minimum. Any unwanted motion to pick up parts is a wasted motion. Transportation distances should be minimized. A poorly designed process results in overuse of resources such as labor and machines. Continuous improvement of processes is an important attribute of lean practices. Companies should ask their suppliers to store products off-site and bring in necessary products just-in-time for production.

Kanban Kanban
is a workflow
management
method to visualize
work, maximize
efficiency, and
improve processes
continuously.

Kanban Board
A visual component
to plan work, track
progress, and
maximize efficiency.

Kanban

Kanban is a method to manage the workflow of goods and services. Kanban helps to visualize work, maximize efficiency, and improve processes continuously. The Japanese word Kanban means a visual board or a sign.

A Kanban Board uses visual components to plan work, track progress, and maximize efficiency. Kanban Boards can be used by teams or individuals to organize activities. A simple Kanban Board is shown in Figure 11-5. It has four basic columns—"Backlog," "To do," "In Progress," and "Done." This Kanban Board serves as a real-time information repository highlighting the bottlenecks within the system and anything else that might interrupt the smooth flow of work. In Figure 11-5, each sticky note represents a task. First, tasks are prioritized and pulled from the "Backlog" column to the "To Do" column. In a Kanban, the topmost task is the most important task. When a task is started, that sticky note is pulled into the "In Progress" column from the "To do" column. During the "In Progress" phase, workers can invite others to help or even change the notes on the sticky notes, which is to change the task to be more effective. When the task is completed, the sticky note representing that task is pulled into "Done." One by one, all the sticky notes in the "backlog" column are pulled through the "To do" and "In Progress" columns to the "Done" column. In this way, the progress of all activities can be easily tracked and any bottleneck that is present in the process can be easily identified.

The Just-in-Time (JIT) that we discussed earlier in this chapter represented a "pull" system. The "pull" approach is based on customer demand where goods are produced only when customers demand the product. This is different than the "push" approach where goods are produced and pushed into the market.

In a "pull" system, an operator in a production system pulls materials or products as necessary and as needed. The Kanban is a "pull" system. Just before the final product in a shelf is a Kanban Card that will indicate to replenish the items. An example is in a convenience store. As you pull a soda can out of the

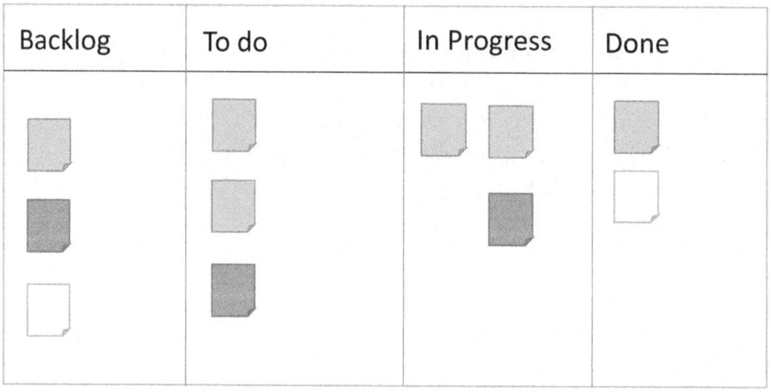

Backlog	To do	In Progress	Done

Figure 11-5 Kanban Board

shelf, the next soda can comes sliding down for the next customer. A card just before the end of the soda cans signals an operator to replenish the soda cans. Another example of a "pull" system is found in a local coffee shop. When a customer orders a cup of coffee, the barista begins the process of making the coffee according to the customer's wishes.

Value Stream Map

A Value Stream Map (VSM) is usually the focus of a lean system. The VSM illustrates all the steps of a process and indicates how much value is added in each step. A value stream is a set of activities that convert customer requirements into value-added goods and services. The main tenets of VSM are as follows:

> **Value Stream Map**
> Value Stream Map illustrates all steps of a process and indicates how much value is added in each step.

- Display all the important steps in a process,
- Visualize multiple process levels,
- Highlight wastes in a process,
- Show "hidden" decision points,
- Make processes efficient,
- Align cross-functional teams for common goals and buy-in,
- Eliminate or lessen non–value-added activities,
- Highlight current process workflow, and
- Bring focus on future improvements to a process.

A VSM is created using the following steps:

1. Sketch the process to understand the flow of material and information needed to produce a good or service using a flow chart;
2. Find out what really happens in the process and identify both value-added and non–value-added work;
3. Verify all activities and data with owners of individual activities;
4. Input the data into an Excel worksheet;
5. Identify the time traps; time-traps are wasteful activities that reduce the value-added time in a process;
6. Calculate delay time at each time trap;
7. Recommend Lean Sigma tools to improve the activities in time traps; and
8. Prioritize and implement recommendations to improve the process.

To identify value-added work, ask these questions for each activity in a process:

- Does the activity add any feature to the product?
- Does the activity enable a competitive advantage, such as faster delivery or fewer defects?
- Is this activity required by regulation or law?
- Does this activity reduce financial risk?
- Is this activity really important for a quality product?

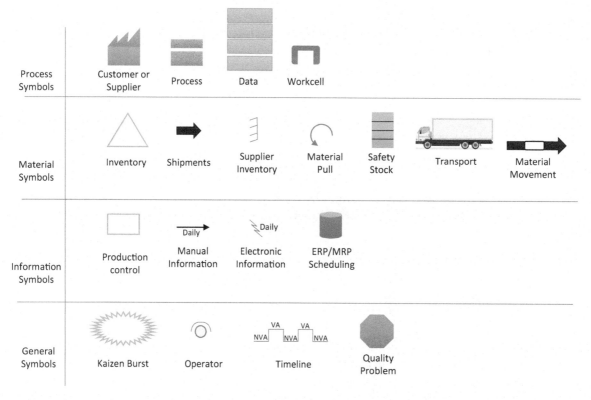

Figure 11.6 Value Stream Map Symbols

A VSM can be applied to both manufacturing and service processes. All information about the business, the process under consideration, and material and information that flow in the process under consideration must be collected prior to creating a VSM. A VSM uses standardized symbols shown in Figure 11-6. Example 11-11 shows an illustration of a VSM.

Example 11-11

Bob Wood is planning to take a hobby after his retirement. He is an enthusiastic wood worker and wanted to make simple wooden chairs, one at a time, to his friends who wanted his chair. He orders his materials online, receives his shipment, inspects them, makes a chair, and his customer will come and pick up the chair from him. Do a VSM analysis for Bob's small carpentry process, which consists of receiving materials, cutting the lumber, drilling holes, assembly of chair, finishing the product, and shipping it off. Bob uses text messages between him, his supplier, and his customer.

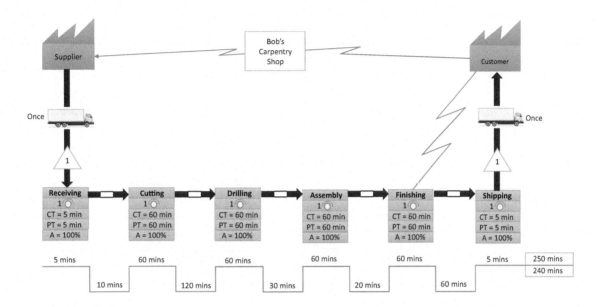

In the above figure,

> PT = Process time = The time one product spends in a process step
>
> CT = Cycle time = The time between two products coming out of a process step

Here, since there is only one operator on one workstation working on only one product at a time, the process time equals the cycle time.

> A = Availability = Percentage uptime of the equipment used for the activity in a process
>
> Uptime = Percentage of time in which a machine or process is available on demand

The time for each activity is shown at the bottom of the figure. The top numbers represent the value-added time while the numbers at the bottom represent the non–value-added times.

> *Analysis:* The total value-added time = 250 minutes, which is the sum of all times on the upper steps. The total non–value-added time = 240 minutes, which is the sum of all times on the lower steps. The non–value-added time includes all delays and wait times. Bob should reduce the non–value-added time of 240 minutes if he wants to improve the process. Maybe, he does not want to; after all, he is retired and this is his hobby!

> **Kaizen** Kaizen means continuous improvement.

> **Kaizen event** A Kaizen event brings together all the people involved in improving a process.

Kaizen

Kaizen is a Japanese word for continuous improvement. Kaizen focuses on several short, incremental, gradual, and methodical process improvements. Kaizen follows five basic tenets—teamwork, personal discipline, improved morale, quality, and suggestions for improvement. The benefits from these five tenets of Kaizen include waste elimination, good housekeeping, and standardization. To be successful, all employees of an enterprise must follow the five tenets of kaizen and must become a part of an organization's culture.

Usually, organizations organize a **Kaizen event** that trains employees in the ways of continuous improvement. A Kaizen event includes process experts, process operators, managers, executives, and other stakeholders. At these events, the attendees with a help of a facilitator brainstorm and focus completely on the process that needs improvement and nothing else. The Kaizen events are led by an expert who is trained in the Six Sigma and the Lean principles. The event usually lasts from 1 day to 5 days, or even longer, depending on the problem at hand. One-day Kaizen events are called Point Kaizen event. The Kaizen events are popular in both manufacturing and service industries.

During a Kaizen event, participants spend the bulk of their time brainstorming ideas on how to improve the process under consideration. They solve specific problems, find ways to eliminate waste, and maximize value by streamlining the process flows and reducing the process errors. All attendees are encouraged to participate actively during the event. The event is conducted in the following two distinct phases:

Planning and Preparation period: Ensure a clear purpose for the event; identify stakeholders of the process under consideration; and set roles of people during the event.

Conducting the Event: The facilitator conducts the event. The event may be conducted as follows:

Day 1: Train the attendees on the fundamental lean principles. The team should identify areas of waste in a process and gather required data,

Day 2: Brainstorm ideas to improve the process under consideration,

Day 3: Continue brainstorming activities and implement an improvement plan,

Day 4: Analyze the improvement plan and refine the improvement process,

Day 5: Present the process improvement plan to management and celebrate for the accomplished work.

The facilitator and the champion of the process reviews what went right in the event, what went wrong in the event, whether the objectives were met, and what should be done as a follow-up. The improvement plan is implemented during the Kaizen event. If the implementation is seen as time-consuming then an intermediate fix is implemented at the Kaizen event and the final fix is planned for the future.

Lean Supply Chains

Lean supply chain
Application of lean principles to the entire supply chain.

Lean supply chain management is the application of the TPS or the Lean Six Sigma to the supply chain elements. Lean supply chain management extends the application of the lean principles in all aspects of the supply chain from the supplier management to the customer management. The focus is on the elimination of the non–value-added time and waste as well as the improvisation of the processes at every step of the supply chain.

To implement the lean supply chain management, organizations must analyze every process in their supply chain to identify the areas that use unnecessary resources and non–value-added activities. An efficient and effective lean supply chain can improve an organization's competitive advantage and overall profitability.

Adopting the lean principles enhances the sourcing process by cutting down delivery times and eliminates wastes. It reduces the associated costs in sourcing, increases the value of goods and services, and improves supplier relationship. The warehouse processes must be examined to eliminate waste of resources and non–value-added process steps. A proper inventory control management is an effective way to reduce costs, as extra inventory means costs to store and maintain goods. Reducing the inventory minimizes the use of warehousing space as well. Logistics and transportation can use lean management principles to streamline their processes. Improving the inbound and the outbound transportation logistics processes and working in collaboration with suppliers have the potential to reduce lead times. The delivery of smaller shipments more frequently reduces inventory and lead times.

FROM PRACTICE: Lean Management at Honeywell, Inc.

Honeywell International Inc., a Fortune 100 multinational conglomerate corporation, provides goods and services for industries in aerospace, building technologies, performance materials and technologies, and safety and productivity solutions. The Aerospace Services merged activity-based management and lean manufacturing techniques at its Raunheim, Germany, facility. As a result, customers enjoyed a 43% reduction in components repair time over 2 years. It helped Honeywell International achieve a $47 million increase in revenue and was a major factor in $900,000 worth of productivity improvements. The turbocharging systems team in Mexicale, Mexico, used Six Sigma and lean tools in teardown and cleaning processes. This reduced cycle time by 92% and space by 51%, eliminated the use of chemical substances for cleaning operations, and saved $400,000[17].

Formulae from this Chapter

Defects per million opportunities (DPMO)	$DPMO = \dfrac{\text{Number of defects or error discovered}}{\text{Possible opportunities for defects or errors}} \times 1{,}000{,}000$	Eq. 11-1
Sigma Level using Excel	NORMSINV (1- (DPMO/1,000,000)) + Shift	Eq. 11-2
Mean of the observations	$\overline{X} = \dfrac{x_1 + x_2 + x_3 + \ldots + x_n}{n}$	Eq. 11-3
Average of the means of N samples	$\overline{X} = \dfrac{\overline{X}_1 + \overline{X}_2 + \overline{X}_3 + \ldots + \overline{X}_N}{N}$	Eq. 11-4
Upper Control Limit for $\overline{X}$ chart	$UCL = \overline{X} + zS_{\overline{x}}$ Where $S_{\overline{x}} = s / \sqrt{n}$	Eq. 11-5
Lower Control Limit for $\overline{X}$ chart	$LCL = \overline{X} - zS_{\overline{x}}$ Where $S_{\overline{x}} = s / \sqrt{n}$	Eq. 11-6
Upper Control Limit for $\overline{X}$ chart	$UCL = \overline{X} + A\overline{R}$	Eq. 11-7
Lower Control Limit for $\overline{X}$ chart	$LCL = \overline{X} - A\overline{R}$	Eq. 11-8
$\overline{R}$, the mean of the sample ranges	$\overline{R} = \dfrac{R_1 + R_2 + R_3 + \ldots + R_n}{n}$	Eq. 11-9
Upper Control Limit for $\overline{R}$ chart	$UCL = D_4\overline{R}$	Eq. 11-10
Lower Control Limit for $\overline{R}$ chart	$LCL = D_3\overline{R}$	Eq. 11-11
Process capability	$C_p = \dfrac{USL - LSL}{6\sigma}$	Eq. 11-12
Process capability index	$C_{pk} = min\left(\dfrac{\overline{X} - LSL}{3\sigma}, \dfrac{USL - \overline{X}}{3\sigma} \right)$	Eq. 11-13

Case Study: Kaizen Event at Khubooz, The Food Delivery Company

As Robert Algazi, the owner of Khubooz, was walking around his company's shop floor, he saw a large number of food delivery containers lying around in the food packaging area. This was an unusual sight for him, and he asked the shift supervisor for an explanation. Moe Diggs, the shift supervisor, told Robert that since the new online sales site was powered up, there have been a lot of orders and he was trying to catch up with the sales. Robert sighed heavily and left the scene thinking that he needs to find a solution to this mess. He went straight to his operations manager's office. Bill Smith, the operations manager, was an efficient leader and a very analytical-minded human. When Robert sat down, Bill said, "Robert, we have a problem with the delivery system. We have been getting complaints in the past three days that there are problems with customers receiving wrong food and wrong items. Also, our delivery time metrics have been pretty bad for the past three days as well."

When asked about the complaints, Bill went back to his Excel worksheet and said, "We have 67 complaints out of 600 deliveries we made in the past three days. Our delivery process sigma is down." Bill had an Excel sheet with three columns including the delivery number, whether there was a complaint or not, and the number of wrong items packed.

Khubooz was established a few years back as a food delivery company. The company had a menu of about 50 ethnic food items catering to the younger, working generation who wanted tasty, excellent-quality food delivered to their doorsteps. Robert was an excellent cook and loved international cuisine as well. His favorite foods were Indian, Italian, Mediterranean, Persian, and Mexican, not necessarily in that order. The company bought various foods in bulk from local ethnic kitchens that delivered the food to the Khubooz facility once a day. The food was stored in various containers. Robert had organized the food in the order of the menu and had plenty of help from his enthusiastic workers who got to work in place where good money was paid with a lot of tasty food to eat.

The company received orders from customers through their website. The new website was open to the public 4 days back after a recent renovation with glitzy marketing pitch and with the voice of customers who wrote excellent reviews. Since the customer reviews were fantastic and the marketing campaign under Robert was well received by the customers, there was a surge in orders. While it took a minute to receive the order and put it up for processing, once an order was received it took 2 minutes on an average to process the order and present the order to a team of workers who would start getting the order

together from the already prepared food. The prepared food was laid out in a vast array of buffet caddies sorted by ethnicity and replenished periodically as they were packed for customers. It was fairly easy for the team to take the food from the buffet caddies. It took 4 minutes on an average for a team member to get the container from a nearby area and fill the container with the appropriate order. There were three different food containers that a team member had to choose depending on an order. The area where containers were kept is the area that Robert saw and was vowing to find a solution to the mess. It took another team to package the food in 1 minute and then the food was ready to be delivered. Multiple delivery men worked to deliver the food to customers. The activities of the company with its standard, recommended cycle times and process times are summarized as follows:

Activity	Cycle Time	Process Time	Availability	No of Workers
Receive order	1	1	100%	1
Process order	2	2	100%	1
Prepare order	2	3	100%	1
Package food	1	1	80%	1
Prepare delivery	2	2	100%	1

Robert also knew that there were some non–value-added activities as well. These were the delays in the process, and he thought that he had eliminated most of those non–value-added activities. But this pile of food packaging items was a sore sight to his eyes. He decided to study the non–value-added activities one more time. He had already hired a student from a nearby university as an Intern. That intern was doing an excellent job, and Robert decided to ask that student to time study the activities. The student did his homework and came back with the following numbers. On an average, there was 2 minutes of non–value-added time between the first two activities, 2 minutes between the next two activities, 5 minutes between the third and fourth activities, and 2 minutes between the fourth and the fifth activities.

The company had established 3 minutes as the time to fill the food containers. Robert wanted to do a measure of the various times of each activity, and he asked the intern to do just that. The intern did a time study for a week. Then out of that data, Bill took 25 random orders with the time taken for each order to be fulfilled as follows:

Orders	Observations				
	1	2	3	4	5
Indian food	6.1	6.2	6.1	5.9	5.8
Greek food	5.2	6.3	6.1	5.2	5.8
Italian food	7.1	5.2	5.4	5.8	5.4
Mexican food	6.5	5	5.9	5.8	5.3
Persian food	5.1	5.2	5.4	6.1	6.3

From these numbers, Robert came to a conclusion that there was a definite problem before the packaging activity. Bill identified a few members of the company, including the supervisors, and implemented a Point Kaizen event to solve the problem.

A Point Kaizen event is completed in a day and is led by an expert who is trained in the Six Sigma and the Lean principles. Bill and his team did all the planning before the event. During a Kaizen event, the participants spend the bulk of their time brainstorming ideas on how to improve the process under consideration. They solve specific problems, find ways to eliminate waste, and maximize value by streamlining process flows and reducing process errors. All attendees are encouraged to participate actively during the event.

Bill was the facilitator of the event. He shared all his data and the student intern's data. The participants drew a VSM first. The team concluded that there was a problem during the preparation of food orders. Bill helped the team to execute a fishbone diagram on the problem at hand. The fishbone diagram summarized the problem that the food preparation is taking a long time. Bill shared the X-bar chart he had prepared using the student intern's data. The team brainstormed for several hours that day and came up with a solution.

Case Questions

A. What are the values of the mean, standard deviation, variation, DPMO, and the delivery process from Bills' data? Use the data from the Excel tab *khubooz* in the *Datafile.xlsx* located on the student book website to solve this problem.

B. Draw a VSM of the activities in the company.

C. Identify a problem using the VSM.

D. Draw a X-bar chart using the student intern's data for a 99% confidence level if the standard deviation is 0.1. Is the process stable?

E. Find the root cause of the delivery problems.

F. Describe the Point Kaizen event.

G. What do you recommend from the Kaizen event to rectify the problem?

Summary

- Quality is defined as conformance to requirements.
- According to Crosby, quality is defined as conformance to requirements. Deming defined quality as a predictable degree of uniformity and dependability at low cost suitable to the market. Juran defined quality as something that satisfies customer needs.
- Garvin, another quality guru, viewed quality as eight dimensions found in goods and services, which include performance, reliability, conformance, durability, feature, serviceability, aesthetics, and image.
- Quality management is about preventing defects.
- "Defective"—the product deemed a "defective" product is a failed product and cannot be used by a customer.
- Defect is not meeting a specific requirement or specification. It still may be used by a customer.
- The goals of quality management include defect prevention, continuous improvement, and customer satisfaction.
- International Organization for Standardization (ISO) family of standards addresses quality management to help organizations to fulfill the quality requirements of the customer with applicable regulatory requirements.
- The Malcolm Baldrige National Quality Award recognizes U.S. companies that have implemented successful quality management systems.
- Total Quality Management (TQM) is a methodology that involves all employees of an organization to follow a systematic, structured process to implement continuous improvement quality projects.
- A fishbone diagram or an Ishikawa diagram or cause-and-effect diagram is used to identify and graphically detail all possible causes related to a problem and discover the root causes of the problem at hand.
- Process is a set of operations where inputs are processed to outputs.
- Variability is the dispersion of data from each other as well as from the mean.
- By reducing the process variability, a company can control customer specification.
- Six Sigma is a process improvement approach in quality management that is used to find and eliminate errors and defects, reduce cycle times, reduce cost, improve productivity, and meet customer expectations.
- Six Sigma defines quality performance as defects per million opportunities (DPMO).
- Six Sigma uses a simple problem-solving methodology called "DMAIC." DMAIC stands for Define, Measure, Analyze, Improve, and Control.

- Quality management process is comprised of quality planning, quality assurance, and quality control. Quality planning identifies quality standards that are relevant to the goods and services of a firm and determines how to use such standards in planning the quality process.
- Quality assurance ensures that all planned activities of a project provide confidence to users, customers, and all other stakeholders.
- Quality control process monitors the quality of products, determines whether the products comply with relevant standards, and identifies ways to eliminate defects.
- Statistical process control (SPC) is the application of statistical methods to monitor and control a process in order to reduce variability.
- A control chart is a graph used to study how a process changes over time and an indicator of variation in the performance of the process.
- Specification limits are tolerance values set by customers and are also the design specifications of a product.
- Process control limits represent the maximum limits imposed on a process.
- There are four different control charts used in controlling quality—X-bar charts, R charts, P charts, and C charts.
- The X-bar chart and the R chart are methods to monitor manufacturing processes to ensure that the processes are in control and that there are no assignable causes of variation.
- Process capability, C_p, evaluates the ability of a process to meet or exceed the expectations or specifications.
- Process capability index, C_{pk}, shows how well a product fits within specification limits.
- While Six Sigma focuses on improving process control by reducing process variation, lean eliminates non–value-added activities and processes to reduce waste and promote a streamlined workflow.
- Lean Six Sigma is a method to accomplish improvement in process, customer satisfaction, and profits by reducing variation, waste, and cycle time.
- The purpose of lean system or the Toyota Production System (TPS) is to identify and reduce three distinct obstacles (3Ms) and apply five common sense factors (5Ss) to the working environment.
- The Toyota Production System (TPS) is a management concept based on parts arriving just in time for production to be continued without interruption, which is called the "Just-in-Time" (JIT) system, and, automation, which is called "Jidoka."
- Non–value-added activities are activities for which a customer is not willing to pay for as they only add to cost and time.
- Kanban is a method to manage workflow. Kanban helps to visualize work, maximize efficiency, and improve processes continuously. The Japanese word Kanban means a visual board or a sign.
- A Kanban Board uses visual components to plan work, track progress, and maximize efficiency.

- The "pull" approach is based on customer demand where goods were produced only when customers demand the product. This is different than the "push" approach where goods are produced and pushed into the market.
- Value stream map illustrates all steps of a process and indicates how much value is added in each step.
- Kaizen is a Japanese word for continuous improvement. Kaizen follows five basic tenets including teamwork, personal discipline, improved morale, quality, and suggestions for improvement.
- A Kaizen event brings together all the people involved in improving a process.
- Lean supply chain management is the application of TPS or Lean Six Sigma to the supply chain elements.

Review Questions

1. Define quality.
2. Who are the quality gurus?
3. How did the quality gurus define quality?
4. What are the dimensions of quality according to Garvin?
5. What is quality management?
6. What is difference between a defect and being defective?
7. What are the goals of quality management?
8. What is ISO and what is its function?
9. What is the award that recognizes U.S. companies that have implemented successful quality management systems?
10. Define TQM.
11. What is a fishbone diagram?
12. Define a process.
13. Define variability and explain its use in quality.
14. What is Six Sigma and what is it useful for in an organization?
15. Explain DPMO.
16. What is the problem-solving methodology in Six Sigma?
17. Describe a quality management process.
18. What is SPC and how is it beneficial to an organization?
19. Define UCL and LCL.
20. What is process capability and how is it useful?
21. What is process capability index and how is it useful?
22. What is Lean Six Sigma?
23. What are the 3Ms and 5Ss?
24. What are "Just-in-Time" and "Jidoka"?
25. Define value-added and non–value-added activities?
26. What is Kanban and how is it beneficial to an organization?
27. What is Kaizen and how is it beneficial to an organization?
28. What is VSM and how is it beneficial to an organization?

Critical Thinking Questions

- Why is quality defined differently by different people?
- What is the common thread among the definitions of the quality gurus?
- How is quality management useful to organizations?
- Using an example, tell the difference between defective and defect.
- Can a defective product be used?
- Can a product with defects be used?
- How do organizations address problems related to parts being defective or with defects?
- Check out who received the Malcolm Baldrige Award for this year.
- How is TQM used to implement continuous improvement?
- Pick a problem in your daily life and draw a fishbone diagram. Did it help to find the root cause of the problem?
- If you want better quality, how much variability in product data would you want?
- What happens if the control limits are smaller than the specification limits?
- How many DPMO is equivalent to 6σ?
- What does "3.4 defects per million opportunities" mean?
- Are defects per million opportunities (DPMO) the same as parts per million (PPM)? Explain why or why not?
- What are the differences between quality planning, quality assurance, and quality control?
- Which of the two charts ($\overline{X}$ or R) is better to investigate whether the process is in control or not?
- Would you use a C_p or C_{pk} to show how well a product fits within specification limits?
- Think of the routine you follow after you wake up. Apply lean methods to identify all the non–value-added activities.
- How can Kanban be used in a bank or a restaurant?
- Create a VSM for a fast-food restaurant and identify at least one process improvement that can be accomplished.

Problem-Solving Questions

1. Information Builders, a consulting company from Omaha, completed a project for one of its clients. But the project was delivered late. The company is trying to find out the root cause of the problem. Help them out by constructing a fishbone diagram.
2. A fast-food restaurant found out that out of 1,500 meals delivered, 1,460 were delivered free of a particular defect and passed inspection. Rate this process from a Six Sigma perspective.

3. Midwest Hospital has been following a state government–issued order to change their healthcare units. They plan to complete 109 units in 18 days.

   a. If it was expected to complete 200 units in the same 18 days, at what sigma level is it operating?

   b. During the 13th day after initiation, the state government decided to inspect the units. Thirty-five inspections were performed and 18 nonconformances were noted. Each inspection checks 60 items. What sigma level does this correspond to?

   c. During that same investigation, it was found that 200 medication errors occurred per year. Approximately 30% of these were a result of the prescription, 25% from dispensing, and the remaining from administration. The hospital has 6,000 annual admissions, and on average a patient receives 10 medications each day during a typical hospital stay, which averages about 5.5 days. What is the average DPMO for each kind of medication error? What is the sigma level?

4. Regional West Bank recently adopted Six Sigma and has already started using Six Sigma in many projects. In one of those projects, it formed a cross-functional team of 18 people. It identified problem calls as the main defect and then focused on solving the defect. The results were quite amazing with an elimination of 73% in the call-backs.

   a. If the problem calls are from 20% of its 2 million customers, what is the sigma of customer loyalty?

   b. How many customers would complain in a Six Sigma operation?

5. A measurement of a process at PKI, LLC is as follows. If the USL = 6.5 and LSL = 3.5, is the process capable of producing to specifications?

5.8	6.3	5.3	5.2	5.5	5.7	5.2	4.4	5.1
5.3	4.9	5.4	5.4	4.7	4.5	5.6	5.2	4.3
4.8	5.7	6.0	5.1	4.6	4.2	4.7	4.8	4.7
4.8	4.4	4.9	4.7	4.7	4.9	5.4	4.7	5.5

6. Roddy Industries manufactures bushings for light vehicles. The mean dimension is 10.717 and the sample standard deviation is 0.087 inches. If the measurements of diameters are normally distributed and within 3 sigma, what is the range of diameters of the manufactured bushings?

7. For the above problem, if the design specifications were set between 10.5 and 10.9, is the process capable of producing to specifications?

8. Gary General Contractors has to choose a process from below for building foundations for its new buildings. Determine which one of these three processes is the best:

Process	Mean	Standard Deviation	Lower Specification	Upper Specification
1	7.2	0.13	6.8	7.8
2	4.5	0.15	4.4	4.8
3	6.7	0.14	5.5	6.4

9. An inspection of motorcycle mirrors was conducted in a manufacturing project at Marv Mirrors, Inc. The five different measurements and sample numbers taken in 1-hour intervals are shown in the following table:

Sample Number	Observations				
	1	2	3	4	5
1	0.768	0.787	0.739	0.521	0.787
2	0.799	0.506	0.516	0.797	0.529
3	0.796	0.500	0.515	0.788	0.521
4	0.795	0.506	0.783	0.787	0.789
5	0.772	0.502	0.526	0.769	0.781
6	0.773	0.795	0.507	0.793	0.506
7	0.795	0.512	0.790	0.771	.507
8	0.525	0.501	0.798	0.777	0.785
9	0.797	0.501	0.517	0.506	0.516
10	0.795	0.505	0.516	0.511	0.797
11	0.795	0.782	0.768	0.792	0.792
12	0.783	0.759	0.526	0.506	0.522
13	0.521	0.512	0.793	0.525	0.510
14	0.787	0.521	0.507	0.501	0.500
15	0.793	0.516	0.799	0.511	0.513

Construct an X-Bar chart and an R chart for the width of the mirrors. Is the process in statistical control? Why or why not?

10. ASI manufactures seatbelt parts for automobiles. After a batch of manufacturing buckles for seat belts, the quality control team came up with the following measurements:

No of Observations	Sample No.									
	1	2	3	4	5	6	7	8	9	10
1	2.3	2.5	2.6	2.4	2.4	2.6	2.5	2.5	2.4	2.6
2	2.7	2.5	2.5	2.6	2.6	2.4	2.6	2.7	2.6	2.7
3	2.6	2.6	2.6	2.5	2.5	2.6	2.7	2.5	2.5	2.5
4	2.6	2.4	2.7	2.5	2.5	2.7	2.5	2.5	2.4	2.5
5	2.4	2.7	2.6	2.6	2.5	2.5	2.7	2.4	2.5	2.6
6	2.5	2.5	2.5	2.6	2.5	2.7	2.3	2.6	2.6	2.6
7	2.4	2.6	2.5	2.5	2.4	2.4	2.5	2.6	2.7	2.6

a. Calculate the control limits and draw an X-Bar chart.
b. Calculate the control limits and draw an R chart.
c. Is the process under consideration in statistical control?

11. Create a VSM for a fast-food restaurant whose process includes receiving orders, process orders, prepare foods, package, and hand it over to the customer.

12. Every soda can's label states that the can contains 16 fluid ounces of tasty, carbonated beverage. It is important that the label and the can's contents agree at levels the federal government mandates for truth in labeling. 16-ounce cans must contain at least 15.5 ounces and no more than 16.5 ounces to meet their standards. A quality team has been sampling output from the production line for several days, and the results are shown as follows:

Sample Number	Observations (Can Volume in Ounces)				
	1	2	3	4	5
1	15.85	16.02	15.83	15.93	15.94
2	16.12	16.00	15.85	16.01	15.68
3	16.00	15.91	15.94	15.83	16.12
4	16.20	15.85	15.74	15.93	16.12
5	15.74	15.86	16.21	16.10	15.93
6	15.94	16.01	16.14	16.03	15.88

a. Calculate the process capability (C_{pk}) for Gerry's analysis. Use the mean and standard deviation from Gerry's samples above to calculate the process capability. Once you calculate the number, state briefly (three sentences or less) what the number indicates about the process.

b. Use the above data to prepare control limits needed for the construction of an $\bar{X}$ chart and an R chart. Assume a confidence level of 3σ. Draw the charts.

References

1. Toyota. (2012). *Quality assurance activities*. Retrieved February 27, 2022 from https://www.toyota-global.com/company/history_of_toyota/75years/data/company_information/quality/quality_assurance.html

2. Stewart, T. A., & Raman, A. P. (July-August 2007). Lessons from Toyota's long drive. *Harvard Business Review*.

3. Willis, J. (2015). *The Andon Cord*. Retrieved February 27, 2022 from https://itrevolution.com/kata/

4. Crosby, P. B. (1979). *Quality is free: The art of making quality certain*. McGraw-Hill.

5. Deming, E. (1986). *Out of the crisis*. MIT Press.

6. Juran, J. M. (1995). *A history of managing for quality*. ASQ Press.

7. Garvin, D. A. (November-December 1987). Competing on the eight dimensions of quality. *Harvard Business Review, 101*–109.

8. Repairpal.com. (2022). *Ford reliability rating*. Retrieved February 27, 2022 from https://repairpal.com/reliability/ford#:%20~:text=The%20Ford%20Reliability%20Rating%20is,has%20above%20average%20ownership%20costs

9. Grzelewski, J. (April 27, 2021). Ford, in step toward making battery cells, plans battery center in SE Michigan. *The Detroit News*.

10. ASQ. (2022). *What is the ISO 9000 standards series?* Retrieved February 27, 2022 from https://asq.org/quality-resources/iso-9000

11. NIST. (2010). *K&N: Malcolm Baldrige National Quality Award 2010 award recipient, small business*. Retrieved February 27, 2022 from https://www.nist.gov/baldrige/kn-management

12. Cohen, D., Lindvall, M., & Costa, P. (2004). An introduction to agile methods. In M. Zelkowitz (Ed.), *Advances in software engineeering* (pp. 2–67). Elsevier Academic Press.

13. Bal, J. (1998). Process analysis tools for process improvement. *The CIM Magazine, 10*(5), 342–354.

14. Mosley, D. C., & Moore, C. C. (1994). TQM and partnering: An assessment of two major change strategies. *PM Network, 8*(9), 22–26.

15. De Feo, J., & Barnard, W. (2004). *Juran Institute's Six Sigma breakthrough and beyond: Quality performance breakthrough methods.* McGraw-Hill.

16. Evans, J., & Lindsay, W. (2005). *An introduction to Six Sigma & process improvement.* Thomson South-Western.

17. Green, R. (2000). Dedicated teams successfully merge two divergent quality systems. Retrieved March 4, 2022 from https://www.qualitydigest.com/dec00/html/honeywell.html

18. ASQ. (2022). *What is quality plan?* Retrieved February 28, 2022 from https://asq.org/quality-resources/quality-plans

19. Liker, J. K. (2004). *The Toyota way—14 management principles.* McGraw-Hill.

20. Sugimori, Y., Kusunoki, K., Cho, F., & Uchikawa, S. (1977). Toyota production system and Kanban system. *International Journal of Production Research, 15*(6), 553–564.

21. Sayer, A. (1986). New developments in manufacturing: The just-in-time system. *Capital & Class, 10*(3), 43–72.

22. Patel, S., Dale, B. G., & Shaw, P. (2001). Set-up time reduction and mistake proofing methods: An examination in precision component manufacturing. *The TQM Magazine, 13*(3), 175–179.

12

LOGISTICS, DISTRIBUTION, AND TRANSPORTATION

Learning Objectives

- Define logistics.
- Identify the diverse types of logistics.
- Describe third-party logistics.
- Explain the various functions of logistics.
- Explain the logistics management process.
- Describe how firms distribute their products to their customers.
- Explain the functions of a distribution center.
- Identify the major factors of distribution centers.
- Explain how materials and information flow in a company through a distribution center.
- Design a distribution center.
- Calculate the capacity of a distribution center.
- Explain the operations in a distribution center.
- Describe cross-docking and zoning in distribution centers.
- Describe methods used by firms to pick and pack goods in distribution centers.
- Explain how transportation is used in the supply chain.
- Solve transportation networks using linear programming.

Companies ship their products all the time. They use complex, coordinated operations to process, plan, and execute the storage and transportation of goods to their customers in a timely, cost-effective manner.

© James R Poston/Shutterstock.com

United Parcel Service (UPS), the American shipping and supply chain management company, is one of the world's largest shipping couriers. The portfolio of services offered by UPS includes logistics, distribution, transportation, freight, and consulting.

UPS Logistics Services offers specialized solutions to their customers, such as warehouse design, supply chain network optimization, financial services, and technology services. The modes of transportation and freight services include air, ocean, road, and rail.

The comprehensive logistics services of UPS use a global network of distribution centers with an excellent supply chain expertise to manage the flow of goods from one corner of the globe to another. The company provides warehousing and order fulfillment functions using their integrated transportation services.

The fully automatic package handling facility of UPS in Louisville, KY, serves more than 300 inbound and outbound daily flights and processes about 2 million packages per day. UPS operates about 1,000 distribution centers, warehouses, container freight stations, brokerage offices, and forward stocking locations[1].

Logistics

If you visit a local store and buy a shirt, chances are high that the shirt traveled a lot more distance than you! Many shirts that we buy are made overseas, often in Asia, and they have to be transported by air, ship, truck, or road to the shop where you buy the clothes. The retail stores that sell the clothes may get the clothes from various countries. To be cost effective, the manufacturers ship these goods using the processes called **logistics**. Logistics is the process of planning and implementing the storage and transportation of goods from the point of manufacturing to the point of sales and from the suppliers to the production.

Types of Logistics

The global logistics market was valued at $7 trillion in 2017 and is projected to reach $12 trillion by 2027[2]. Logistics focuses on the efficient and effective management of activities relating to the transportation of finished goods and deployment of services of a business. Such focus can be either internal or external. The internal focus is called inbound logistics and the external focus is called outbound logistics. Figure 12-1 shows the several types of inbound and outbound logistics.

Inbound Logistics

Inbound logistics focuses on the purchase and coordination of the supplies. The inbound raw materials, the parts, and the unfinished inventory is moved from the suppliers or from other plants to the manufacturing location. Inbound logistics is also used by retail stores or warehouses to move the finished goods from the manufacturing plants. Purchasing logistics and green logistics are the two main types of inbound logistics.

Outbound Logistics

Outbound logistics focuses on the coordination of the finished goods and the related services to the potential customers. Outbound goods and services are moved from the manufacturers to the warehouses for storage and to the retail stores for sales. Outbound logistics is used by online companies such as

Logistics Logistics is the process of planning and implementing the storage and transportation of goods from the point of manufacturing to the point of sales. Suppliers also use logistics to plan and send the raw materials and parts to make products.

Inbound logistics Inbound logistics focuses on purchasing and coordinating supplies to a firm.

Outbound logistics Outbound logistics focuses on coordinating finished goods and services to potential customers.

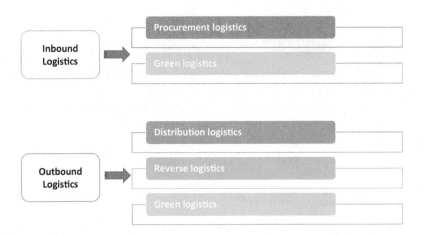

Figure 12-1 Logistics types

Amazon to send the products to the end users. The information such as the number of goods sold is sent to the manufacturers for their use to forecast demand from retailers. The three main types of outbound logistics are distribution logistics, reverse logistics, and green logistics.

Next, we will review the types of logistics including procurement logistics, distribution logistics, reverse logistics, and green logistics.

FROM PRACTICE: XPO Logistics wins General Motors Award

© Sundry Photography/Shutterstock.com

XPO Logistics, Inc., headquartered in Greenwich, Connecticut, is a global logistics provider for many companies in the world. The company operates in 30 countries, with 1,506 locations and approximately 97,000 employees. XPO uses its logistics, distribution, and transportation network to help more than 50,000 customers manage their supply chains. XPO Logistics, Inc., uses a dedicated team to manage the distribution of truck and car parts from the suppliers of General Motors (GM) to their warehouses and dealerships throughout North America. The company also manages the critical aftermarket parts channel of GM using its technology. XPO was honored by GM as the GM Supplier of the Year for the second consecutive year in 2020 for consistently exceeding expectations, creating outstanding value, and introducing several innovations[3].

Procurement Logistics

> **Procurement logistics**
> Procurement logistics is sourcing of raw materials, parts, or components needed to manufacture products.

Procurement logistics involves the sourcing of raw materials, parts, or components needed to manufacture the products. The procurement part of the supply chain is concerned with obtaining all the materials required to manufacture the goods. The logistics part of the procurement includes activities such as the aggregate sales and operations planning, the cost reduction strategies including make or buy decisions, and the supplier management.

Distribution Logistics

Distribution logistics involves the entire process of delivering the finished goods from a manufacturer or a supplier to a warehouse, a distribution center, or a retailer. It includes order processing, warehousing, and transportation.

Reverse Logistics

Reverse logistics includes all the operations related to the products being returned from the customers and the sale of surpluses. Reverse logistics is the process of moving goods from the final destination for resale or disposal.

Green Logistics

Green logistics involves minimizing the ecological impact of logistics activities. Typically, green logistics is applied to both the inbound and the outbound logistics. Green procurement is about making environmentally conscious decisions throughout the procurement process. Right from the procurement strategy to purchasing the supplies to disposing the waste, green procurement should be factor for all decisions. We will discuss more about green supply chain management (GSCM) later in this chapter.

Third-Party Logistics

Many firms use the services of logistics specialists for their inbound and outbound logistics requirements. The main reason is that those firms can concentrate on their core competencies, and the logistics specialists can improve the customer service and reduce the costs. The logistics service providers are called third-party logistics (3PL) providers. A 3PL provider can act as a lead logistics provider or a fourth-party logistics (4PL) provider aligned with a host of 3PL providers. Major 3PL providers include UPS, FedEx, DHL, C.H. Robinson, XPO Logistics, and J.B. Hunt, to name a few.

Most firms outsource several activities to the 3PL providers[4,5], which can be divided into four categories as shown in Figure 12-2. The four categories

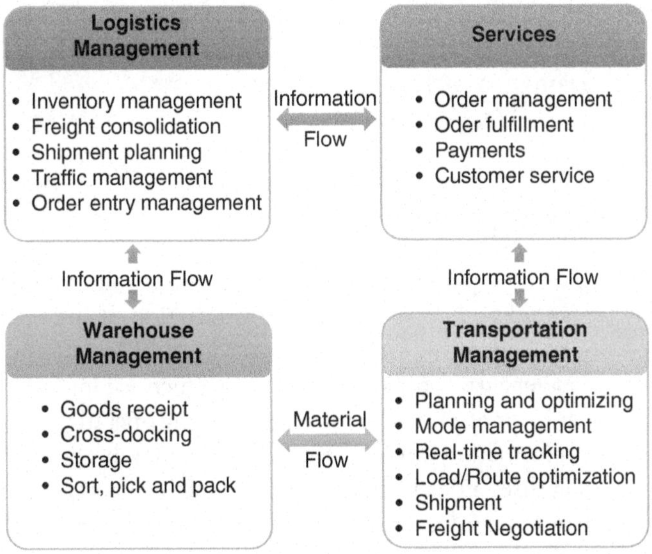

Distribution logistics
Distribution logistics involves the entire process of delivering finished goods from a manufacturer or supplier to a warehouse, distribution center, or retailer.

Reverse logistics
Reverse logistics is the process of moving goods from the final destination to resell or dispose properly.

Green logistics
Green logistics involves minimizing the ecological impact of logistics activities.

3PL provider
Companies who manage another company's logistics operations.

Figure 12-2 Logistics Functions

include warehousing management, transportation management, inventory and logistics management, and services. The information and the material flow among the four categories are shown in Figure 12-2. Material flow occurs as a result of the integration of transportation and warehouse management. The information flow is important to integrate all the four categories, and a real-time information flow is essential to implement the 3PL[6]. Materials are transported from the manufacturing plants to the warehousing facilities or to the retailers by the 3PL global transportation freight carriers using efficient inventory management and logistics techniques.

FROM PRACTICE: 3PL Services of Kenco for Whirlpool

Kenco Group, a privately held Tennessee-based company, provides all the third-party logistics provider functions such as logistics, transportation, material handling, and warehouse management. Whirlpool Corporation, a major appliance manufacturer, uses a very customized warehouse management system (WMS) software. Whirlpool hired the Kenco Group to improve the inventory accuracy and reduce the inventory management costs.

Kenco implemented an automated inventory management strategy partnering with a start-up IT company from Ireland. Whirlpool knew that this was a risky project but trusted Kenco's track record of innovation. Kenco's vice president (VP) of Research & Development emphasized the level of trust placed on Kenco by Whirlpool. The 3PL project of Kenco was a success and resulted in a 7% improvement in the productivity and savings of over $130,000 annually[7].

Logistics Management

Logistics management is planning, organizing, and controlling the overall activities of the inbound and the outbound transportation of the materials and the goods. Fleet management, warehousing, order fulfillment, and management of 3PL providers are also part of the management of logistics. Logistics management is an integral part of the strategic and the operational parts of the material and the information flow. When implemented well, the logistics management process ensures efficient transportation, reduced costs, and improved customer satisfaction. Poor logistics management results in delayed shipments, increased costs, and dissatisfied customers.

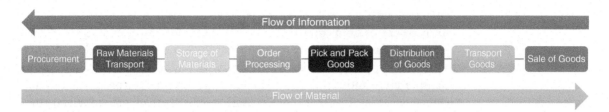

Figure 12-3 Logistics Management Process

Logistics plays a strategic role in running a business—from the retailers and the wholesalers managing their inventory to the transportation and manufacturing companies managing the inflow of raw materials and the outflow of the manufactured goods and related services. A simplified logistics management process is shown in Figure 12-3. Logistics management encompasses all the activities that facilitate product movement and the coordination of supply and demand to realize cost reduction and service objectives[8]. Let us look at the different processes outlined in Figure 12-3.

> **Logistics management**
> Logistics management is planning, organizing, and controlling the overall activities of inbound and outbound transportation of materials and goods, fleet management, warehousing, order fulfillment, and management of 3PL providers.

Strategic Procurement

Strategic procurement decisions take the costs of logistics and transportation into account. The procurement strategy is important and should be considered in the overall operational and supply chain strategy. Alternate sourcing and logistics options must be considered in the procurement strategy. For example, during the COVID-19 pandemic in 2020, the whole supply chain was disrupted. The procurement managers scrambled to find alternate logistics solutions during that health crisis. The pandemic crisis really tested the resilience and flexibility of the supply chain leaders to maintain their operations efficiently[9].

Raw Materials Transportation

In many cases, the raw materials, the parts, and other components necessary for production must be transported across international and global borders. For example, a car manufacturer in Michigan may source wood panels from Canada, seat belts from Mexico, and engine controls from Taiwan. The company must obtain these materials using an advanced logistics software in time for the production. The global sourcing from multiple countries must be coordinated such that they reach the Michigan plant just in time for the production. Moreover, multiple modes of transportation logistics must be coordinated and managed to achieve the best results.

Storage of Materials

The parts, the materials, and the components must be stored before the actual production process. The storage includes receiving material and parts, keeping them safely, ensuring proper inventory procedures, maintaining packaging, and getting the materials ready for shipment. The storage of the materials and the parts ranges from covered climatically controlled spaces to outdoors. Companies such as Ford Motors maintain storage near their production plant or ask their suppliers to collocate their operations in order to reduce the cost of transportation and distribute the materials just in time for production. Many companies bring in the inventory from various parts of the globe and store them in strategic locations across the country so that the inventory can be distributed to their respectable plants in the shortest time as well as to move the materials in times of higher demands.

Order Processing

Order processing is the process of using information from a customer order and creating a sequence of activities to initiate and deliver the ordered goods to the customer. Order processing is the creation of a workflow that ensures customer orders are properly prepared and delivered to the customer. The workflow includes picking the right inventory, sorting the items, packing the orders, and then shipping them. The list of activities starts with a pick list. A pick list is used to select the goods from the inventory and send them to the customers who ordered those goods. For example, when you order a box of golf balls from Amazon, a pick list is created to process the order so that the golf balls can be shipped to your address.

Pick and Pack Goods

Pick and pack is a process that enables the workers in a company to find the ordered items and pack the items. For example, when you order a book from Amazon, an employee of Amazon at a distribution center will locate the ordered book, pick the ordered book from a shelf, place and pack the book in an Amazon cardboard box, prepare the label with your address, and get that product ready for the shipment. Pick and pack are one of the main activities of the order fulfillment process. For any business, especially an e-commerce business, an efficient order fulfillment process is critical.

Distribution of Goods

The distribution is the manner in which businesses send their products or finished goods to their customers. Firms use a variety of facilities before the goods are sold to their customers, including warehouses, distribution centers, and fulfillment centers. Businesses transport their finished goods using those facilities. For example, a retailer may request the goods from a manufacturer in order to sell and make money from those products. In this case, the retailer's order will be processed by the manufacturer, picked and packed from a distribution center, and transported by the most appropriate transportation modes to the retailer's warehouse or store.

Transportation of Goods

The purchased goods are moved either through retailers or directly to customers. Logistics plays a huge role in the goods transportation to the customers. Logistics management plans how to deliver the goods in the most cost-effective and efficient way. This may involve a combination of land, air, rail, or sea transportation. For example, to deliver the home appliances made in China, a logistics software may advise to send those appliances by land to the closest port and then use the fastest and cheapest shipping methods to deliver abroad.

We will discuss more about warehouses, distribution centers, fulfillment centers, and transportation in the following sections.

Distribution

The distribution of the goods is accomplished by the transportation from a manufacturer's warehouse facilities or from a manufacturer's distribution center or from a retailer's fulfillment center. In general, warehouses, distribution centers, and fulfillment centers are facilities used to store the finished goods. The **warehouses** are usually located near airports, railroads, and seaports. Even though some warehouses are equipped to ship products to retailers and customers, they are primarily used to store the goods for a longer period of time. A **distribution center** is a specific type of warehouse where there is a limited storage of the goods, but the goods are received, tracked, picked, and packed to be shipped to the retailers and the customers. A distribution center also is a facility where the transportation documentation is prepared and any damage claim support is processed. Product mixing, cross-docking, order fulfillment, and packaging are activities performed in distribution centers[10]. A **fulfillment center** is a warehouse run by a 3PL provider to receive, process, and fill customer orders on behalf of the retailers. To reduce the transportation times and costs, the distribution centers and the fulfillment centers are located on the outskirts of major cities but are well connected by roads to ports, railroads, and airports. We will call all these three facilities as **distribution centers** in this book.

> **Warehouse** A facility primarily used to store goods for a longer period of time.

> **Distribution center** A distribution center is a specific type of warehouse where there is a limited storage of goods but goods are received, tracked, picked, and packed ready to be shipped to retailers and customers.

Distribution Centers

A company can make multiple products from multiple plants. The distribution centers enable the companies to hold those goods in a place so that they can be readied for shipment to customers. A distribution center can serve as a warehouse or a fulfillment center. It can even act as a package handling center or as a cross-dock facility. Any such description is used to describe the basic operations employed in that facility.

A distribution center is a temperature-controlled building to stock goods for distribution to retailers, wholesalers, or customers. Some retailers own such

> **Fulfillment center** A fulfillment center is a warehouse run by a third-party logistics (3PL) provider to receive, process, and fill customer orders on behalf of retailers.

distribution centers as well. Since some retailers sell thousands of products at hundreds of locations, it is inefficient for them to send each item directly to the individual stores. Larger retailers operate their own distribution centers while smaller retailers may outsource this operation. Let us look at the two main attributes including distribution center design and distribution center operations next.

FROM PRACTICE: Amazon's fulfillment and distribution centers

Amazon operates in more than 175 fulfillment centers or distribution centers worldwide[11]. An Amazon fulfillment center is a warehouse where incoming orders are received, stored, packed, and shipped out to customers. The sellers who use the fulfillment by Amazon can store their inventory at the Amazon's fulfillment centers[11]. Amazon's fulfillment centers are strategically located with robust public infrastructure, strong dedicated workforce, and great local support. A 4.1 million square feet, five-story, 97-foot-tall building being built in southwestern Ontario, California, will be the biggest distribution center of Amazon[12]. A new fulfillment center is being constructed in Elkhart, Indiana. Elkhart is well suited for the distribution centers because of its access to major highways and its proximity to Chicago, Detroit, Indianapolis, Cleveland, and Cincinnati. The 800,000 square feet building will be completed by 2023[13].

Distribution Center Design

The design of the distribution center facilities includes a myriad of complex requirements. The first main factor is the location of the facility, which is of utmost importance. Second, a good layout for the optimum movement of the materials should be implemented. Third, the capacity of the distribution center in terms of space, labor, resources, and equipment required for various operations conducted in the distribution center must be taken into account. Storage requirements must be considered for efficient inbound and outbound operations. Finally, if there are seasonal products involved, the fluctuations in the demand during the offseason must be taken into account. Examples of such products are Christmas decorations or winter clothes. To allow for future growth and future new products, judgment should be used to expand the facility. If the distribution center is at full storage capacity and storage utilization, it is time to increase the total volume of the center.

Location

When large amounts of consignments from and to the airports, the railroads, and the seaports are expected, the location of a distribution center becomes critical to the success of a company. The location of distribution centers is dependent on many factors.

Infrastructure Easy access to rail, road, air, lake, river, or sea with a good telecommunication and utilities network is an important criterion for a distribution center location. The accessibility to the roads and the highways is important if trucking is the main mode of transportation.

Costs The costs associated with the location including land, construction, labor, energy, and taxes as well as the cost of the infrastructure and the transportation should be considered. The support of local, state, and federal agencies in the form of subsidies, tax abatements, and pro-business initiatives are good incentives for locating the distribution centers. Other financial incentives must be considered as well.

Foreign Trade Zone Locating a distribution center in a foreign trade zone (FTZ) is desirable. FTZ is a designated location where firms can take advantage of the special customs procedures with either delayed or reduced duty payments on the foreign merchandise.

Workforce Availability The local demographics plays a significant role in the availability of the required workforce with the right skills at the right prices to keep the operating costs low and the productivity high.

Proximity Being close to the suppliers, the manufacturers, and the customers must be considered. Proximity reduces the lead times, decreases transportation costs, and enhances the satisfaction of customers.

Structure

Material flow and the relative locations of various departments or functions in a distribution center must be considered in a distribution center design. The flow of materials determines the relative locations of the center. The material flow is dependent on the products flowing through the center and the degree of automated systems used. Either a simple or a medium complex flow of materials is used in a distribution center structure. The two material flows are shown in Figure 12-4.

A simple material flow consists of a receiving and a shipping department with the storage facilities. In this structure of a distribution center, the goods are delivered, stored for a while, and then shipped after their sales. A more complex material flow is shown on the right side of Figure 12-4. Here, we have a quality department to control the quality of both the incoming and the outgoing goods. The orders are processed, picked from storage, checked for quality, packed, and shipped.

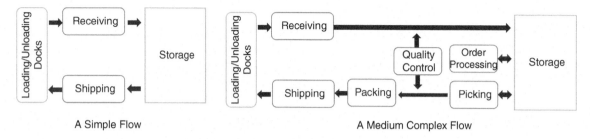

Figure 12-4 Material Flow in a Distribution Center

Size

The size of the distribution center depends on the expected throughput and the capacity of the center. The size is usually referenced by the volume of the center, for example, in cubic feet, and not the area or square feet. As far as the storage facilities are concerned, the location, the space, and the size are the most valuable assets. Storing the right amount of products provides an advantage for a business as orders can be fulfilled easily to make the customers happy. Therefore, having an optimum size of a distribution center and how the products are stored and easily accessed are important. The distribution center sizes are calculated using the following four-step process:

Step 1: Calculate the nonstorage space area. This is the space used for various departments, office rooms, utility rooms, bathrooms, number of docking doors, loading, or docking areas, material movement space, common space, and space to store material handling equipment.

Step 2: Calculate the storage space area. This is the space used for storing products. Storages in distribution centers involve the number of pallets planned to be stored and the number of aisles between racks containing those pallets. A pallet is a flat wooden structure to support goods, which can be lifted by a forklift, a front loader, or a crane. The pallet rack is a structure to hold pallets so that pallets can be easily accessed with easy access to be removed using a forklift. The three most common pallet sizes are 48" × 40", 42" × 42", and 48" × 48". Pallet racks are usually 8 feet to 24 feet high but can be higher. A pallet bay consists of placing two pallets with a clearance in length to pull pallets out and push pallets in the pallet bay.

Step 3: Calculate the aisle space area. Usually, aisles for standard reach trucks have a clearance of at least 9 feet. Depending upon the number of pallets stored, the number of aisles needed is calculated. It is good to include future growth when considering the number of pallets estimated to be stored. Pallet bays are on both sides of the aisles.

Step 4: Calculate the docking area. Docking area should consider the docking area depth for receiving and shipping and the number of docking doors and the clearances between those doors.

Step 5: Sum up the areas obtained in Steps 1 through 4. This is the total area of distribution center.

Step 6: Multiply the total space required for the center by the height of the center to get the volume of the distribution center. This is the size of the center.

Example 12-1 shows how to calculate the size of a distribution center, and Figure 12-5 shows the pallets placed in a pallet bay with a flue on one side and an aisle on the other side.

Pallets and pallet racks in a distribution center with a forklift

© Petinov Sergey Mihilovich/Shutterstock.com

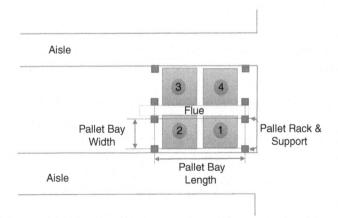

Figure 12-5 Two Pallets (#1 and #2) in a Pallet Bay With Aisles

Example 12-1

Robert Industries, a local company located in St. Joseph, Michigan, is planning a distribution center in St. Louis, Missouri. The requirements are as follows:

- One office 12 feet by 20 feet.
- 1,000 square feet space for utilities, equipment storage, and common areas
- Pallet racks 8 feet high constructed with 3-inch square support beams with a flue of 6 inches
- Four 80-feet aisles with 9 feet clearance between products on each side to support transport of 40 by 48 standard size pallets
- Two pallets to be placed in between pallet rack support beams with a 16-inch clearance between any two support beams
- Height of the distribution center is 20 feet.
- Two 8-ft wide dock doors placed with center-to-center distance of 12 feet and a wall of 2 feet on either side of the dock doors and a dock staging area of 15 square feet.

Calculate the size of the distribution center.

Step 1: *Nonstorage area*

Office space = No of offices × length × width = 1 × 12 × 20 = 240 square feet

Restroom, utilities, equipment storage, common space area = 1,000 square feet (given)

Total nonstorage area = 240 + 1,000 = 1,240 square feet

Step 2: *Storage space area*

To calculate the storage space area, we need to calculate the total pallet bay area on the ground. In this case, the pallet bay area length = (2 × pallet length) + pallet bay clearance + half of the support beam size form each side = (2 × 40) + 16 + (2 × 1.5) = 99 inches or 8.25 feet.

The pallet bay area depth = pallet width + support beam depth + half the flue width = 48 + 3 + (6/2) = 54 inches or 4.5 feet. The area of one pallet bay = 8.25 × 4.5 = 37.125 square feet.

We need to find the number of pallets bays next. First, we will find the number of pallet bays on one side of the aisle. The number of pallet bays on one side of an aisle = length of an aisle/pallet bay length = 80 feet/8.25 feet = 10 (rounded up). We have pallet bays on both sides of an aisle, and we have 4 aisles. Therefore, the total number of pallet bays is 10 × 4 × 2 = 80 pallet bays.

The total area of storage space = 80 × 37.125 = 2,970 square feet.

Step 3: *Aisle space area*

The aisle space area = aisle clearance area × length of an aisle × number of aisles = 9 × 80 × 4 = 2,880 square feet.

Step 4: *Docking area*

First, we need to know the width of the docking area as the depth is given. The width of the docking area is the width of the two docking doors + the space between the doors + the space on either side of the doors to the extreme sides = $(2 \times 8) + ((12 - 8) \times (2 - 1)) + (2 \times 2) = 24$ feet. The space between the doors comes to 4 feet as we have only such space between two doors. The docking area = the width of the docking area times the staging area depth = $24 \times 15 = 360$ square feet.

Step 5: *Total area of the distribution center*

Total area of the distribution center = $1,240 + 2,970 + 2,880 + 360 = 7,450$ square feet.

Step 6: *Distribution center size*

Distribution center size = volume of the distribution center = $7,450 \times$ height of the distribution center = $7,450 \times 20 = 149,000$ cubic feet.

Analysis: The total volume of the distribution center is 149,000 cubic feet with two dock doors. The minimum number of dock doors needed for a distribution center depends on many factors such as the number of trucks serviced by the docks over a peak period of loading and unloading, the time taken to load and unload each trailer, cross-docking requirements, employee work hours, the reliability of carriers, and experience of truck drivers and employees.

Equipment

The productivity and performance of a distribution center can be accomplished by their usage of the equipment required to run the distribution center efficiently. The distribution center managers should ensure that their employees are trained well in using the equipment.

Dock Equipment

Safety is the top priority when it comes to equipment in general. Dock equipment should be safe and enable shipping and receiving processes to be efficient. Some of the important dock equipment include dock bumpers, dock boards, and truck restraints.

Material Handling Equipment

The workers handling the materials and the goods must have the necessary equipment. The appropriate equipment can save time and labor. This includes material lifting and transportation equipment as well. Some of the material handling equipment include conveyors, hand trucks, pallet jacks, forklifts, cranes, hoists, dollies, and castors.

Storage Equipment

The right storage equipment can help a distribution center to use the space efficiently. Some of the required storage equipment include shelves, racks, and carousels.

Sort, Pick, and Pack Equipment

Automation can reduce the risk of injuries and improve the sorting, picking, and packing times. These equipment play a critical role in shipping goods by increasing productivity. Some of the equipment used for sorting, picking, and packing include scales and automated sorting systems.

Distribution Center Space Utilization

Distribution centers must have enough space to store the inventory. A distribution center's space utilization is dependent on the storage systems, the number of items carried as inventory, and their size. The space can be optimized for the type of inventory stored. For example, the clearance between the pallet height and the height of the pallet bay should be at least six inches, and this clearance can be adjusted to fit the type of inventory stored. Unpackaged parts should be placed in appropriate containers to minimize the occupied space. Placing smaller or larger items in separate areas maximizes the space. Classifying the inventory according to the number of shipments and placing the fast-moving inventory in the front of the racking systems can help both the utilization of space and the savings in the transportation time and its cost. Keeping track of obsolete inventory and getting rid of them in time for the discounted prices will lessen the losses as well as increase the utilization space. Finally, the use of the 5S and the lean management principles should improve the distribution center space. The distribution center space utilization can be calculated as shown in Example 12-2 using the following formulae:

$$Storage\ Utilization\ Capacity = \frac{Potential\ Storage\ Volume}{Total\ Volume} \times 100 \qquad \text{Eq. 12-1}$$

Storage Space Utilization Capacity
Storage space utilization capacity determines how much storage space is being used by the inventory on hand.

$$Storage\ Space\ Utilization\ Capacity = \frac{Inventory\ Volume}{Potential\ Storage\ Volume} \times 100 \qquad \text{Eq. 12-2}$$

where,

Potential storage volume is the total storage volume. This is found by multiplying the outside dimensions of storage raking system with the height of the highest load or the highest pallet.

Total volume is found by multiplying the total dimensions of the distribution center.

Inventory volume is found by totaling the volume of all products stored in the distribution center.

Example 12-2

Robert Industries estimates 100 incoming pallets on an average for storage at their distribution center in St. Louis County. The average height of the incoming pallets is 3 feet. There are three levels to store. The lower level and the middle level can store inventories with a maximum height of 3½ feet. The top level can store inventories with a maximum of 4 feet. What are the storage utilization and storage space utilization capacities of the distribution center?

The total volume as calculated in Example 12-1 is 149,000 cubic feet.

The potential storage area as calculated in Example 12-2 is 2,970 square feet. The height of potential storage is $(2 \times 3.5 + 4) = 11$ feet. Therefore, the potential storage volume is 11 feet $\times$ 2,970 square feet = 32,670 cubic feet.

Storage utilization capacity using Equation 12-1 is: $\dfrac{32,670}{149,000} \times 100 = 22\%$.

The area of a pallet bay as calculated in Example 12-1 is 37.125 square feet The height of a pallet is 3 feet. Each pallet bay has the capacity to hold two pallets. If there are 100 pallets incoming for storage, the volume occupied by the 100 pallets = $37.125 \times 3 \times (100/2) = 5,568.75$ cubic feet.

Storage space utilization capacity using Equation 12-2 is: $\dfrac{5,568.75}{32,670} \times 100 = 17\%$

Analysis: The storage space utilization can be expanded to about 30%. A range between 25% and 30% of storage utilization provides enough space for workers to move efficiently for picking, loading, and unloading without wasting available space. The storage space utilization capacity is low. If Roberts Industries has a high potential growth in the future, they have enough space in the distribution center. A storage space utilization capacity of about 80% is good and provides enough space for seasonal inventory storage.

Distribution Center Operations

The distribution centers execute unique transactions in the sense that the products pass through them as the received goods and are shipped out as and when needed. The distribution center process is shown in Figure 12-6, which

Figure 12-6 Distribution Center Operations Process

(Left to Right) © ThamKC/Shutterstock.com; © Petinov Sergey Mihilovich/Shutterstock.com; © ThamKC/Shutterstock.com; © angelo gilardelli/Shutterstock.com; © Siwakorn1933/Shutterstock.com

consists of receiving the goods; storing them; tracking the products in the center; picking the goods; packing the goods; and shipping them to other distribution centers, retailers, and customers.

Receive Goods

Receiving is the first activity of a distribution center for the incoming material flow. Incoming shipments are brought to the center usually by several carriers and unloaded at the receiving docks. The information on the shipments to the distribution centers is provided to the distribution center managers with the expected shipping time. The distribution center managers assign the arriving carriers to docks and schedule the services from the docks to the storage. These services include allocating the labor and the material handling equipment.

> **Cross-Docking**
> Cross-docking is a supply chain strategy where goods are unloaded from inbound carriers and then loaded into outbound vehicles with some or no storage in between.

Cross-Docking Cross-docking is a supply chain strategy where goods are unloaded from inbound carriers and then loaded into outbound vehicles with some or no storage in between. For example, an inbound truck arrives and then proceeds to an assigned receiving dock. Certain goods are then unloaded and then sorted according to their destinations. A destination can be a customer, retailer, another distribution center, or storage. The distribution center manager assigns another dock door to a destination or destinations. In the case of cross-docking, the goods are loaded onto the outbound trucks at the assigned shipping doors for delivery. Cross-docking minimizes the operational costs, the total transportation time, and the customer waiting time[14,15]. Cross-docking minimizes the inventory held and the product handling cost as products need not be transferred to the storage and then back on the road to customers. But cross-docking requires a high degree of coordination between incoming and outgoing shipments.

A special case of cross-docking is the distributor cross-docking. Distributor cross-docking helps to consolidate inbound products from different vendors and then delivered to a customer. For example, combining a product from an overseas vendor and a product manufactured inhouse at a distribution center and delivering the product mix to a customer is beneficial to both the manufacturer and the customer. Another method, transportation cross-docking, combines shipments from various trucks at a distribution center. Here, by consolidating smaller less-than-truckload (LTL) shipments into larger, full truckload shipments, the transportation costs can be reduced.

Store Goods

Storage is to hold the goods in a space such as a distribution center for a period of time. It also involves the organization of the stored goods to facilitate material handling efficiently. The incoming products are assigned to be stored in a particular zone.

> **Zoning** Zones are storage locations allotted by product categories.

Zoning The goods that are received are stored in zones. Also called pick zones, the zones are the storage locations allotted by the product categories. The zones have an impact on the overall storage capacity, inventory tracking, and order picking[16]. The zoning reduces the time to locate a product to be shipped later. The distribution center manager decides the zone, where a product should be placed based on the holding capacity of the distribution center. The primary reason of zoning is to make order picking activities more effective and efficient. The storage efficiency defines how easily a product can be accessed to be picked.

Track Goods

The tracking in a distribution center is a process to determine the amount of goods that are incoming, stored, and outgoing. The tracking also helps to locate the products quickly in the storage and to keep an account of the distribution center inventory in detail. The inventory tracking is often accomplished using a software system to provide the information on what products are stored, where each product is stored, and how many products are being stored at any given time. Such software systems include tools for scanning the inventory and updating the inventory counts automatically. One such tool is RFID.

RFID Tracking RFID technology provides the ability to track and identify the distribution center goods in real time. It also provides information such as where a particular product is located within the supply chain at any given time. For example, a shipment of finished goods arrives from a manufacturer at the receiving dock of a distribution center. The goods are unloaded and an RFID tag is attached either to individual item or the whole pallet. The information of the item or the pallet is stored in the RFID memory. As the item or pallet moves to a zoned location, that information is updated in the RFID memory. The RFID chip transfers the stored information to a database. The data from the database are shared to all concerned parties. RFID eliminates the risk of human error and saves a lot of time in counting the inventory. As a product exits the facility, the RFID tag automatically updates the database that the product has left the facility and is on the way to a customer.

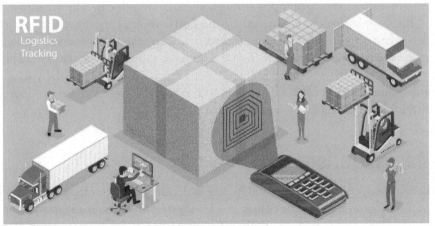

© TarikVision/Shutterstock.com

Inventory tracking using RFID at a distribution center

Pick and Pack Goods

Picking and packing goods for customer orders is the most expensive operation in a distribution center as it is very labor intensive[17]. There are different order picking methods including single order picking and zone picking. Single order picking involves the order fulfillment by manually picking each item directly from the storage. Zone picking is picking the products for order fulfillment by several employees from different zones picking the products from their individual assigned zones. Single order picking is used in the smaller distribution centers while zone picking is used in the larger distribution centers with a high number of inventory. The pick and pack operations include batching, routing, and sorting.

Batching Batching is picking one type of product for multiple orders. This is different from the regular order picking which is picking one complete order at a time. Batching allows organizations to prepare multiple shipping to fulfill multiple orders at a time. Each batch will be picked and accumulated for packing and shipping during a specific time window.

Routing In large distribution centers, the sequencing and routing to pick products for a customer order must be implemented to save time and be more efficient as the products may be located far apart from each other. The objective here is to minimize the total material handling cost.

Sorting When multiple orders are picked at the same time, sorting is essential. Sorting can be performed either during the picking process or after the picking process. Sorting systems are used to sort the products automatically. The orders are assigned to a certain sorting lane in a computer system. As the products are picked for an order, they are placed on the sorting system and at the end of the sorting system, the orders are removed from the sorting lanes, checked, packed, and shipped.

Ship Goods

The packed goods are shipped through the shipping docks. The scheduling of the shipping trucks is planned by the distribution center manager and is dependent on how the orders are picked. The outgoing shipments are loaded at the shipping docks and sent from the center usually by freight carriers. The labor and the material handling equipment are assigned to load the packed goods onto a freight carrier. The distribution center managers assign the docks and schedule the carriers for each shipment.

Transportation

Businesses spend a lot of time and money in deciding the best method to transport their products to their customers. Transportation is about the movement of goods from one place to another. A transportation software evaluates and recommends the most cost-effective and safest delivery route. The evaluation and the recommendation involve trade-offs in cost, delivery speed, and flexibility in delivery. Information technology plays a leading role in the transportation and logistics, especially in recommending the resources to be used and the best routes to take, coordinating various operational activities, and tracking the transported items.

Transportation Modes

There are two key players in transportation—a shipper and a carrier. A shipper is the business that requires a product to be transported from one point to another. The carrier is the business that transports the product from one point to another. When Amazon uses UPS to ship a product from its distribution center to a customer's house, Amazon is the shipper and UPS is the carrier. A carrier can be a trucking company, an airlines, or a shipping company. Both shippers and carriers incur the costs to transport the products from the plants or the distribution centers to distributions centers or customers. A shipper wants to minimize the total cost of order fulfillment. A shipper considers the transportation cost, the inventory cost, the distribution center storage cost, the order processing cost, and the order cycle service level cost. A carrier considers fixed operations costs, labor and fuel costs, loading and unloading costs, overhead costs, and other vehicle-related costs. Both the shippers and the carriers use these factors to minimize the costs and to make the transportation decisions.

The U.S. transportation system moved a daily average of about 55.2 million tons of freight valued at more than $54.0 billion in 2019[18]. The supply chain managers use a combination of the following transportation modes to fulfill the customer orders. Figure 12-7 shows the percentage of the freight transported in the United States by various modes in 2019[18].

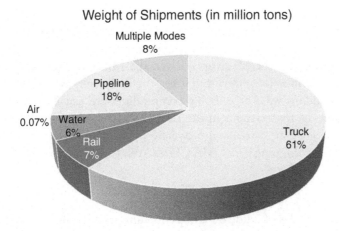

Figure 12-7 Weights of Shipments by Transportation Modes in the United States in 2019

Road

Almost all products use the roads to reach a customer. Trucks are the most widely used mode of freight carriers in the United States. The freights are charged based on either the full truck load (TL) or the LTL, the distance traveled, and the quantity of products loaded. The major freight carriers in the United States include Roadway, JB Hunt, Ryder, Yellow, and Schneider.

The package carriers also use the road mode of transportation. They carry letters and packages weighing up to 150 pounds. Package carriers are costlier than the regular fright carriers. UPS, FedEx, US Postal Service are some of the package carriers in the United States.

Rail

The railways are used to transport heavy loads or high-density products. The transportation costs are low. This mode of transportation is priced for larger amounts of shipments over long distances. The rail carriers incur the costs of locomotives, the rails and the yards, the fuel costs, and the associated labor costs. The major railroad carriers in the United States are BNSF Railway Co., CSX Transportation, Norfolk Southern Combined Railroad, and Union Pacific Railroad Co.

Air

The air transport is the most expensive and is typically used for small, light items. The labor and the fuel costs act as the major costs for the air transportation. The package carriers use the air transportation for the next-day and the second-day deliveries. Delta, United, and American airlines as well as most of the international airlines operate cargo planes in addition to their passenger planes.

Water

Water mode of transportation in the United States is made possible by lakes, rivers, and bordering oceans. The inland water transportation is made possible by the Great Lakes, the Mississippi River, the Missouri River, the Colorado river, the Columbia River, the Ohio River, the Red River, the Snake River, and the Rio Grande River. Large, bulky commodities are usually transported by the lake and the river systems in the United States and are usually a low-cost option. Major ocean carriers who operate in the United States are Maersk, Mediterranean Shipping Co., CMA CGM/APL, Hapag-Lloyd, and Evergreen.

Pipeline

In all, 90,000 miles of crude oil and petroleum product pipelines along with more than 140 refineries that can process around 20 million barrels of oil every day constitute the pipeline network in the United States and Cananda[19].

The pipeline mode of transportation is used to carry liquids and gases. Crude petroleum, refined petroleum products, and natural gas are the main products that use pipelines. A shipper's peak usage and actual quantity transported are the two major factors of cost to the pipeline network companies. Major companies in this industry are Sunoco, Enbridge Energy, and Plains Pipeline LP.

Multi-modal

Multi-modal transportation is the use of more than one mode of transportation. An array of containers that can be easily moved from one mode to another are used. For global trade, the multi-modal transportation is the best suitable way to transport the goods from one part of a country to another part of another country. Road/air or road/rail or road/rail/water are the most common multi-modal transportations. Companies such as DHL, CSX, UPS, and FedEx offer the multi-modal transportation solutions.

Green Transportation

Current transportation systems emit plenty of carbon dioxide, carbon monoxide, nitrogen oxides, and unburned hydrocarbons in large amount and have caused heavy pollution. The emission of the greenhouse gas (GHG) and the dependence on finite petroleum resources are the crucial issues of current transportation systems. There is a sense of urgency to reduce the effects of pollution all around the globe. Many businesses are responding to the sustainability movement and have several operational strategies to reduce the environmental impacts of freight transportation. The technological innovations used by the freight carriers include electronic devices to monitor the truck and the tractor engines, computers to measure the fuel efficiency, software to route and schedule using the global positioning systems (GPS), software to alert drivers to the most cost-effective fueling locations, gadgets that automatically switch off idling engines, and paperless solutions such as the electronic bill payments[20]. The operations using these technologies reduce the total distance covered to ship products, monitor the truck speeds, pickup and deliver the goods according to schedule, save the fuel, and of course, reduce the emissions[21–24]. Furthermore, businesses are using clean fuel, efficient engines, and aerodynamic tractor-trailers to improve the fuel efficiency, wide-base tires to decrease the rolling resistance, and automatic tire inflation systems to monitor and adjust the air pressures for optimal rolling resistance[21,22,24,25].

Green transportation relies on renewable energy sources such as wind energy, solar energy, hydroelectric, among others. In summary, green transportation consists of eco-friendly vehicles. Hybrid and electric cars are examples of green transportation. Electric vehicles (EVs) operate on rechargeable battery packs and do not emit pollutants.

FROM PRACTICE: Volvo's EV trucks

© Mike Mareen/Shutterstock.com

Many companies are in the making of electric vehicle freightliners. Daimler-Benz, Tesla, Nicola, and Volvo are the companies that have been in the works to get the first electric vehicle freightliners. These freight carriers will be environment friendly. Volvo, the Swedish truck manufacturer, is in the making of rigs that do not emit carbon dioxide. The truck is based on their own Volvo's VNR 300 tractor truck, which is typically used for short- and middle-distance day trips[26]. Volvo recommends these trucks to transport the goods from a city to another city. According to Volvo[27], the Volvo FH Electric provides excellent comfort, a carbon footprint that meets the environmental targets, and a convenient overview of the traffic ahead. The truck is supposed to be sold with service and support packages for charging, route and range planning, battery monitoring, and more.

> **Linear Programming (LP)** Linear programming is a mathematical technique where a linear function is maximized or minimized when subjected to constraints.

Linear Programming Model to Optimize Transportation Networks

Logistics, distribution, and transportation deals with stocking the products in a network of distribution centers, scheduling deliveries of products, routing material handling machines, locating distribution centers, finding optimal product mix, and optimizing transportation resources. Linear programming models can be used to solve many of the logistics, distribution, and transportation problems. In this section, we will focus on optimizing shipping plans to transport goods through a network of manufacturers, distribution centers, and customers using the linear programming (LP) method.

LP is a mathematical technique where a linear function is maximized or minimized when subjected to certain constraints. This technique has been used since the World War II to solve transportation, scheduling, and allocation of resources subject to the constraints of costs and resource availabilities. This technique is extensively used in the operational planning of a firm and especially to solve the logistics, distribution, and transportation problems. Most managers in firms have Microsoft Excel to solve the LP problems. We have already used the Microsoft Excel's Solver function to solve capacity management problems in Chapter 3. In this section, we will discuss how to model and solve a transportation network using the LP technique and the Microsoft Excel Solver.

This is the simplest model that is used to solve many problems in operations and supply chain management. A simple example of LP is to use the restrictions of labor and materials in a firm and determine the maximum profit under those constraints. Another example is to minimize the transportation costs to send a finite number of products from many plants to various distribution centers with individual limitations of product storage space.

An LP problem is solved by finding the optimum value such as the maximum profit or the minimum cost of a linear expression called the objective function. An LP model requires the following to solve the problems:

- A specific *objective* such as maximize profit or minimize cost;
- Certain *criteria* to be met, such as limited resources like capital dollars, number of hours, number of workers, or number of trucks available;
- A linear relationship between *decision variables* thar are competing with one another to share resources such as number of tables and chairs that can be placed in a banquet area or if one truck can deliver 100 products then two trucks can deliver 200 products;
- Consistency of decision variables such as all workers are similarly productive; and
- Non-negative values for all decision variables such as +1 hour to reach a destination.

Let X_1 and X_2 be the decision variables. Decision variables are the primary target of an LP mode. For example, let us take the case of Cat Industries. Cat Industries makes tables and chairs and ships them to their customers. The company is considering maximizing the net profit associated with shipping of those products.

Let X_1 be the number of tables and X_2 be the number of chairs that are shipped, given certain constraints and an objective function. If the objective is to maximize, then we need an objective function with constants, P_1 and P_2 that can be used with the decision variables. For example, if Cat Industries want to maximize the profits of shipping their products that consist of tables and chairs, we need to know the profit from shipping a table P_1 and the profit from shipping a chair P_2 as objective function constants. Using these objective function constants and the decision variables, we can formulate the objective function as follows:

$$Maximize\ P_1X_1 + P_2X_2$$

Suppose we want to minimize cost rather than maximizing profits, we will use the cost of one table C_1 and the cost of one chair C_2 to form the objective function:

$$Minimize\ C_1X_1 + C_2X_2$$

Next, we must come up with a set of constraints. Constraints are limitations of using the decision variables and must be common to all decision variables that are involved in the objective function.

For example, Cat Industries may have the knowledge of the number of hours to ship a table and the number of hours to ship a chair. The company may have restrictions of the total number of hours that are available for shipping tables and chairs in a time period. Each constraint in a set of constraints describes a restriction.

Suppose we have T_1 and T_2 as the time taken to ship a table and a chair, respectively. If a time period of A is available for the week for the shipment of tables and chairs, we can then write the time constraint as:

$$T_1 X_1 + T_2 X_2 \leq A$$

Therefore, we can formulate the maximizing profit LP model as follows:

Choose the values of the decision variables X_1 and X_2 to:

$$\textit{Maximize } P_1 X_1 + P_2 X_2$$

subject to satisfying the following constraints:

$$T_1 X_1 + T_2 X_2 \leq A$$

$$X_1 \geq 0 \text{ and } X_2 \geq 0$$

Eq. 12-3

where X_1 and X_2 should be non-negative values.

In our example of Cat Industries, the profit of a table is \$200 and the profit of a chair is \$100. There are three trucks at Cat Industries. Truck 1 ships only tables, each table takes 2 hours, and the truck is available for 4 hours this week. Truck 2 ships only chairs, each chair takes 1 hour and the truck is available for 12 hours this week. Truck 3, the big new machine as it is called, ships both chairs and tables. It takes 1 hour for a table and 2 hours for a chair and is available for 20 hours this week. We can formulate the LP model as follows:

Choose the values of the decision variables X_1 and X_2 to:

$$\textit{Maximize } 200X_1 + 100X_2$$

subject to satisfying the following constraints:

$$2X_1 \leq 4$$
$$X_2 \leq 12$$
$$X_1 + 2X_2 \leq 20$$
$$X_1 \geq 0 \text{ and } X_2 \geq 0$$

Let us use Microsoft solver as shown in Example 12-3 and Example 12-4 to solve the LP model of Cat Industries.

Example 12-3

Step 1: Open Microsoft Excel.

Step 2: Input given data as per the LP model formulated for Cat Industries as shown in the figure below:

	A	B	C	D	E	F	G
1		**Tables**	**Chairs**				
2	Unit Shipping Profit	$ 200	$ 100				
3							
4		Shipping Hours per unit			Total Hours		Hours Available
5	Truck 1	2	0		2		4
6	Truck 2	0	1		1		12
7	Truck 3	1	2		3		20
8							
9	Units shipped	1	1				
10							
11	Total Profit	$ 300					

In Excel, input the following functions:

Cell E5 = SUMPRODUCT(B5:C5,B9:C9)

Cell E6 = SUMPRODUCT(B6:C6,B9:C9)

Cell E7 = SUMPRODUCT(B7:C7,B9:C9)

Cell B11: SUMPRODUCT(B2:C2,B9:C9)

Step 2: Click on Solver under the Data Menu (Note: If Solver is not seen as shown in the following figure, then use File > Options > Add-ins > Solver Add-in to install Solver) and enter the following in the Solver Parameters ash shown in the following figure:

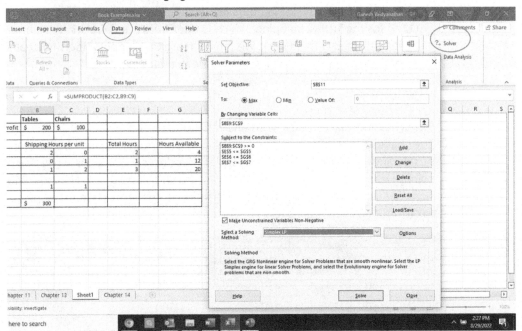

In the Set objective textbox, input $B$11, which is the total profit

In the Changing Variable Cells, input $B$9:$C$9, which are the decision variables

Click on Add to add the constraints one by one.

Check the box next to Make Unconstrained Variables Non-negative

Select the Simplex LP as the Solving Method.

Click on Solve and keep the Solver Solution.

Step 4: Check the solution:

	Tables	Chairs
Unit Shipping Profit	$ 200	$ 100

	Shipping Hours per unit		Total Hours	Hours Available
Truck 1	2	0	4	4
Truck 2	0	1	9	12
Truck 3	1	2	20	20
Units shipped	2	9		
Total Profit	$ 1,300			

Analysis: Three tables and 12 chairs that can be shipped for a maximum profit of $1,300 with the available hours as constraints. There is a slack of 3 hours (12-9) for the Truck2 shipping, which is fine. Truck1 and Truck3 times have been optimized with no slack. We can decrease the shipping hours for chairs to increase profit, but we will also increase the slack.

Example 12-4

Symbolics, Inc. makes traffic signs and is headquartered in San Antonio, Texas. They have another plant in Waco, Texas, and distribution centers in Houston, Austin, and Fort Worth. San Antonio plant produces 1,200 signs while Waco plant produces 1,300 signs. Symbolics wants to ship 800 signs to Houston, 950 signs to Austin, and 750 signs to Fort Worth. The shipping costs from the plants to distribution centers are shown in the table:

	Shipping cost of each product			
	Houston	Austin	Fort Worth	Production
San Antonio	300	450	400	1,200
Waco	150	120	500	1,300
No of products shipped	800	950	750	

What is the minimum shipping cost?

Step 1: Draw the transportation network diagram as shown below:

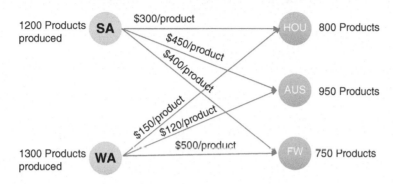

Step 2: Formulate the LP model as shown in Equation 12-3.

Let SA → HOU, SA → AUS, SA → FW, WA → HOU, WA → AUS, WA → FW be the ***number of signs*** to be shipped from each plant to each distribution center, respectively.

Choose SA → HOU, SA → AUS, SA → FW, WA → HOU, WA → AUS, WA → FW to:

Minimize Cost = 300 SA → HOU + 450 SA → AUS + 400 SA → FW + 150 WA → HOU + 120 WA → AUS + 500 WA → FW

Subject to satisfying the following constraints:

SA → HOU + SA → AUS + SA → FW = 1,200
WA → HOU + WA → AUS + WA → FW = 1,300
SA → HOU + WA → HOU = 800
SA → AUS + WA → AUS = 950
SA → FW + WA → FW = 750
SA → HOU, SA → AUS, SA → FW, WA → HOU, WA → AUS, WA → FW ≥ 0

Step 3: Open Excel and input given data as shown below:

In Excel, input the following functions:

Cell E9 = SUM(B9:D9)

Cell E10 = SUM(B10:D10)

Cell B11 = SUM(B9:B10)

Cell C11 = SUM(C9:C10)

Cell D11 = SUM(D9:D10)

Cell E15 = SUMPRODUCT(B3:D4,B9:D10)

	A	B	C	D	E	F
1		Shipping cost of Each product				
2		Houston	Austin	Fort Worth	Production output	
3	San Antonio	300	450	400	1200	
4	Waco	150	120	500	1300	
5	No of products shipped	800	950	750		
8						
7		Units Shipped				
8		Houston	Austin	Fort Worth	Total Shipped	Production output
9	San Antonio	1	1	1	3	1200
10	Waco	1	1	1	3	1300
11	To Customer	2	2	2		
12						
13	Order Size	800	950	750		
14						
15				Total Cost	$ 1,920	

Step 4: Click on Solver under the Data Menu (Note: If Solver is not seen as shown in the following figure, then use File > Options > Add-ins > Solver Add-in to install Solver) and enter the following in the Solver Parameters as shown in the following figure:

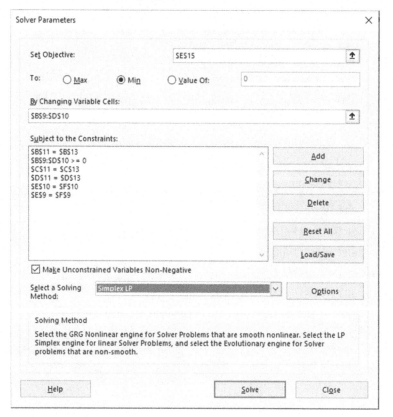

Step 5: Here, the Total Cost is the SUMPRODUCT of the products and units shipped.

In the Set objective textbox, input $E$15, which is the total profit;

Select Min;

In the Changing Variable Cells, input $B$9:$D$10, which are the decision variables;

Click on Add to add the constraints one by one:

$E$9 = $F$9

$E$10 = $F$10

$B$11 = $B$13

$C$11 = $C$13

$D$11 = $D$13

$B$9:$D$10 ≥ 0

Check the box next to Make Unconstrained Variables Non-negative;

Select the Simplex LP as the Solving Method;

Click on Solve and keep the Solver Solution.

Step 6: Check the solution:

	Shipping cost of Each product			
	Houston	Austin	Fort Worth	Production output
San Antonio	300	450	400	1200
Waco	150	120	500	1300
No of products shipped	800	950	750	

	Units Shipped				
	Houston	Austin	Fort Worth	Total Shipped	Production output
San Antonio	**450**	**0**	**750**	1200	1200
Waco	**350**	**950**	**0**	1300	1300
To Customer	800	950	750		

Order Size	800	950	750		

	Total Cost	**$ 601,500**

Analysis: 800 signs to Houston, 950 signs to Austin, and 750 signs to Fort Worth distribution centers can be shipped for a minimum shipping cost of $601,500 by producing 1,200 signs and 1,300 signs from San Antonio and Waco, respectively. Austin distribution center must receive all the signs made in Waco and Fort Worth will receive all their signs from San Antonio only to minimize shipping costs.

Formulae from This Chapter

Storage utilization capacity	$\dfrac{Potential\,Storage\,Volume}{Total\,Volume} \times 100$	Eq. 12-1
Storage space utilization capacity	$\dfrac{Inventory\,Volume}{Potential\,Storage\,Volume} \times 100$	Eq. 12-2
LP model	Choose the values of the decision variables X_1 and X_2 to: $Maximize\ P_1X_1 + P_2X_2$ subject to satisfying the following constraints: $T_1X_1 + T_2X_2 \le A$ $X_1 \ge 0$ and $X_2 \ge 0$ where X_1 and X_2 should be non-negative values.	Eq. 12-3

Case Study: A New Distribution Center for Meecham Industries

Meecham Industries from Rockford, Illinois, was established in 1980 and since then, the company has grown by an average of 4.5% over the years. Meecham Industries is a custom component manufacturer. The company specializes in precision machining of large gray and ductile iron castings and aluminum castings for automotive and construction equipment manufacturers. The company has the main plant in Rockford, Illinois. Another plant in Kankakee, Illinois, supports manufacturing operations for Meecham Industries. All two plants are ISO 9001:2015 certified. The company uses an extensive range of vertical machining and turning centers. The company has over 40 world-class Computer Numerical Control (CNC) machines. Many of these CNCs are automated using flexible manufacturing systems and robotic loaders. Their large capacity machining centers with the aid of lean and innovative approaches offer their customers a modern, cost-effective manufacturing solution. Meecham Industries has been experiencing a distribution problem with its products reaching the customers. The products have been delivered late recently, and their 3PL providers have been complaining of logistics issues. To alleviate this problem, Meecham Industries finally made a decision to open a distribution center.

© Aumm graphixphoto/Shutterstock.com

The location for the distribution center was finally decided as well. Meecham Industries planned a distribution center in South Bend, Indiana. The city of South Bend has been the focus for new warehouses[28]. A big electric commerce retailer recently opened a South Bend delivery center in a shared 210,000-square-foot space. Since then, three more distribution centers have sprung, totaling more than 600,000 square feet[28]. South Bend is well suited for distribution centers because of its access to major highways and its proximity to Chicago, Detroit, Indianapolis, Cleveland, and Cincinnati. The land cost is economical, and

© Mr. Kosal/Shutterstock.com

there exists a good labor force of graduates from four local universities. The international airport and its closeness to Lake Michigan is also suitable for the distribution centers. The city is located in the crossroads of America, a state that connects northeastern states to western states of the United States. Meecham Industries envisioned a distribution center with the data shown in the table.

Currently, products from the two plants are shipped directly to two customers. Now with the new opening of a facility in South Bend, Meecham Industries wanted to store some products in the new distribution center. They have firm orders from two of their best customers and ship the rest of the products from the plants to the new distribution center. Plant 1 at Rockford produces 350 castings and Plant 2 at Kankakee produces 250 castings. Their two customers, Customer 1 and Customer 2, demand 200 and 400 castings, respectively. The shipping cost from Plant 1 to Customer 1 is $500 per casting and to Customer 2 is $600. The shipping cost from Plant 2 to Customer 1 is $600 per casting and to Customer 2 is $400. The company is planning to increase the production with the new distribution center in the planning stages. Plant 1 will produce 600 castings and Plant 2 will produce 400 castings. The shipping cost to the new distribution center is estimated to be $200 from the Rockford plant and $100 from the Kankakee plant.

Rack height	12 ft	Wall on either side of dock area	2 ft
Clearance for sprinklers and truss	14 in	Dock staging area depth	20 ft
Pallet length	40 in	No of offices	5
Pallet bay length	96 in	Office length	20 ft
Support beam width (half of each side)	3 in	Office width	40 ft
Pallet width	48 in	Clearance height	3 ft
Flue	6 in	Restroom, Utilities, Equipment storage, common space	1500 ft
Aisle clearance	9 ft	Average height of pallets	4 ft
No of pallet bays per aisle	12	Clearance for pallets	6 in
Total number of pallets stored	1000	Height of shelving	1 in
No of pallet levels	3	No of incoming pallets	750
Number of Dock doors	10	No of specialized goods	120
Dock door width	8 ft	Volume of a specialized goods	90 cu. Ft
Dock door center-to-center length	12 ft		

Case Questions

A. Calculate the size of the future distribution center.
B. Calculate storage utilization capacity.
C. Calculate storage space utilization capacity.
D. What is the minimum shipping cost to satisfy the customer requirements and plant production.
E. Find the minimum shipping cost to satisfy the same customer requirements and plant production with the addition of the new distribution center.
F. Analyze the problem using the answers.

Summary

- Logistics is the process of planning and implementing the storage and transportation of goods from the point of manufacturing to the point of sales.
- Logistics is also the planning of bringing in raw materials and parts to make products.
- Logistics focuses on the efficient and effective management of activities relating to the manufacture of the finished goods and services of a business.
- Inbound logistics focuses on purchasing and coordinating supplies to a firm. Inbound raw materials, parts, and unfinished inventory is moved from suppliers or from other plants to the manufacturing location.
- Purchasing logistics and green logistics are the two main types of inbound logistics.
- Outbound logistics focuses on coordinating finished goods and services to potential customers. Outbound goods and services are moved from manufacturers to warehouses for storage and retail stores for sales.
- The three main types of outbound logistics are distribution logistics, reverse logistics, and green logistics.
- Procurement logistics is sourcing of raw materials, parts, or components needed to manufacture products.
- Distribution logistics involves the entire process of delivering finished goods from a manufacturer or supplier to a warehouse, distribution center, or retailer.
- Reverse logistics includes all operations related to products being returned from customers and sale of surpluses.
- Green logistics involves minimizing the ecological impact of logistics activities.
- The logistics service providers are called third-party logistics (3PL) providers.

- A fourth-party logistics (4PL) provider aligned with a host of 3PL providers.
- Material flow occurs as a result of integration of transportation and warehouse management. Information flow is important to integrate all the four categories, and real-time information flow is essential to implement 3PL.
- Logistics management is planning, organizing, and controlling the overall activities of inbound and outbound transportation of materials and goods, fleet management, warehousing, order fulfillment and management of 3PL providers.
- Strategic procurement decisions take costs of logistics and transportation into account in their procurement strategy.
- Parts, materials, and components must be stored before actual production process.
- Storage includes receiving material and parts, keeping them safely, ensure proper inventory procedures, maintaining packaging, and getting the materials ready for shipment.
- Order processing is the process of using information from a customer order and create a sequence of activities to deliver the ordered goods to the customer.
- Pick list, a list of activities, is used to select the goods from the inventory and send them to customers who ordered those goods.
- Pick and pack is a process that enables workers in a company to find and pack items that are ordered by customers.
- Distribution is the manner in which businesses send their products or goods to customers.
- Distribution of goods or products are accomplished by transportation from a manufacturer's warehouse facilities or from a manufacturer's distribution center or from a retailer's fulfillment center.
- A facility primarily used to store goods for a longer period of time.
- A distribution center is a specific type of warehouse where there is a limited storage of goods, but goods are received, tracked, picked, and packed ready to be shipped to retailers and customers.
- A fulfillment center is a warehouse run by a third-party logistics (3PL) provider to receive, process, and fill customer orders on behalf of retailers.
- Distribution center facilities design includes many factors including the location of facility, a good layout for optimum movement of materials, the capacity of the distribution center in terms of space, labor, resources, and equipment required for various operations conducted in the distribution center, and fluctuation during the offseason.
- The location of distribution centers is dependent on cost; FTZ; workforce availability; and proximity to suppliers, manufacturers, and customers.

- The flow of materials determines the relative locations of the center. The material flow is dependent on the products flowing through the center and the degree of automated systems used.
- A simple flow consists of a receiving and a shipping department with storage facilities. A more complex flow has a quality department to control the quality of both incoming and outgoing goods.
- The size of the distribution center depends on the expected throughput and capacity of goods through the center. The size is usually referenced by the volume of the center.
- Productivity and performance of a warehouse can be accomplished only by using the right equipment. Some of the important dock equipment include dock bumpers, dock boards, and truck restraints.
- Some of the material handling equipment include conveyors, hand trucks, pallet jacks, forklifts, cranes, hoists, dollies, and castors.
- Some of the required storage equipment include shelves, racks, and carousels.
- Some of the equipment used for sorting, picking, and packing include scales and automated sorting systems.
- Potential storage volume is the total storage volume.
- Total volume is found by multiplying the total dimensions of the distribution center.
- Inventory volume is found by totaling the volume of all products stored in the distribution center.
- The distribution center process consists of receiving goods, storing them, tracking products in the center, picking, and packing goods, and shipping them to other distribution centers, retailers, and customers.
- Cross-docking is a supply chain strategy where goods are unloaded from inbound carriers and then loaded into outbound vehicles with some or no storage in between.
- Goods that are received are stored in zones or pick zones.
- Zones are storage locations allotted by product categories.
- Tracking in a distribution center is a process to determine the amount of goods that are incoming, stored, and outgoing.
- RFID provides the ability to track and identify distribution center goods in real time.
- Picking and packing goods include single order picking and zone picking.
- Single order picking involves order fulfillment by manually picking each item directly from the storage. Zone picking is picking products for order fulfillment by several employees from different zones picking the products from their individual assigned zones.
- Batching is picking one type of product for multiple orders.

- In large distribution centers, the sequencing and routing to pick products for a customer order must be implemented to save time and be more efficient as the products may be located far apart from each other.
- When multiple orders are picked at the same time, sorting is essential and sorting can be performed either during the picking process or after the picking process.
- The packed goods are shipped through shipping docks. The scheduling of shipping trucks is planned by the distribution center manager, and the scheduling is dependent on how orders are picked. Outgoing shipments are loaded at the shipping docks and sent from the center usually by carriers.
- Transportation is about the movement of goods from one place to another.
- A shipper is the business that requires a product to be transported from one point to another.
- The carrier is the business that transports the product from one point to another.
- Road, rail, air, water, pipeline, and multi-modal are the modes of transportation.
- Green transportation consists of eco-friendly vehicles.
- LP models can be used to solve many of the logistics, distribution, and transportation problems. LP is a mathematical technique where a linear function is maximized or minimized when subjected to constraints.

Review Questions

1. What is logistics?
2. What are the types of logistics?
3. What are 3PL and 4PL?
4. What are the four main components of logistics functions?
5. What are the components of logistics management process?
6. What is picking and packing of goods?
7. What is a pick list?
8. What are distribution centers, warehouses, and fulfillment centers?
9. What is cross-docking?
10. What are the steps to design a distribution center?
11. What are the dependent factors for location of a distribution center?
12. What are the functions of a distribution center?
13. Explain the operations in a distribution center.
14. What is zoning?
15. What role does tracking play in a distribution center?
16. What is the best technology to track the goods that are in and out of a distribution center?

17. Describe batching, routing, and sorting.
18. What is transportation in supply chain?
19. What is the difference between a shipper and a carrier?
20. What are the different modes of transportation?
21. What is linear programming and how is it useful in transportation logistics?

Critical Thinking Questions

1. Does logistics work to get materials to a plant to make products?
2. Which one is more important to a firm—inbound or outbound logistics?
3. Why is reverse logistics important in supply chain?
4. Why is green logistics important in supply chain?
5. Is there any difference between 3PL and 4PL?
6. How is distribution of goods accomplished in supply chain?
7. What are the commonalities and differences between distribution centers, warehouses, and a fulfillment centers?
8. What are the main activities in a distribution center?
9. Why is cross-docking important in supply chain?
10. Why is zoning implemented in distribution centers?
11. Should every company use RFID and why?
12. What are the differences between batching, routing, and sorting?
13. Which mode of transportation is most and least used in the United States? Why?
14. List five reasons why Amazon should build a distribution center in your city.
15. Why does railroad mode of transportation not popular in the United States even though companies can ship cheaper using railroads?
16. Why is cross-docking important to a company that makes many products?
17. Why is cross-docking important to a company that outsources some of their products?
18. Explain the entire distribution center operations process with an example. Include cross-docking, batching, sorting, RFID, and routing, and zoning in your example. Give an analysis of why that company should use all those activities.

Problem Solving Questions

1. The storage space of a warehouse is 40,000 cubic feet. If the inventory space is 38,000 cubic feet, what is the storage space utilization capacity?

2. A company bought a 480 feet in length by 340 feet wide by × 240 inches high distribution center at the border of their town. If the storage utilization capacity is 24%, what is the maximum storage space available?

3. A fulfillment center has an office area of 120 square feet The docking area is 400 square feet, the total pallet bay area is 1,600 square feet, and the total aisle area is 1,200 square feet The area of other facilities in the fulfillment center is equal to 800 square feet Inventory received filled 72% of the storage area. If the height of the facility is 30 feet, the storage rack's height is 22 feet, and the maximum pallet height on the top level is 48 inches, what are the storage utilization capacity and the storage space utilization capacity?

4. Rybeck Company is planning a fulfillment center for its orders through the Internet. They have located a suitable place on the outskirts of Chicago yet close to major highways. The company wishes for an 80% storage space utilization capacity and a 40% storage utilization capacity. The company expects a maximum of 4,000 pallets of concrete products to be stored. Each pallet is 40 inches by 48 inches by 48 inches. How big a fulfillment center should the company build?

5. Wynn Packaging from Elkhart, Indiana, manufactures packaging materials in three different plants in Indiana. The plants are located in Elkhart, Hammond, and Warsaw. The company ships the packaging materials in pallets to wholesalers located in several U.S. cities. The production output in their plants and the demand by the wholesales are in the table below. The rates provided by F&B Freight Transportation from Columbus, Ohio, for the shipment of each pallet are given below.

	Shipping Cost per pallet							Production Output
	Denver	New York	Boston	St. Louis	Minneapolis	Detroit	Atlanta	
Elkhart	$65	$62	$72	$45	$45	$35	$46	12,000
Hammond	$70	$67	$78	$52	$31	$39	$49	8,500
Rochester	$80	$72	$82	$56	$37	$42	$52	10,500
Demand	2,500	6,200	4,000	2,100	4,500	5,300	6,400	

a. Draw the transportation network.
b. Formulate the linear programming model.
c. Using Solver, find out how many pallets from each plant can be shipped to the customers by minimizing the shipping cost?
d. What plants supply what cities and by how much?

6. Regus Company's four plants supply their products to four of their customers. The shipping costs, the production output, and the customer demand are given in the table below.

| | Shipping Cost per Product | | | | |
	Customer 1	Customer 2	Customer 3	Customer 4	Production Output
Plant 1	120	150	250	450	400
Plant 2	240	250	125	200	600
Plant 3	250	315	350	150	450
Plant 4	300	250	225	275	700
Demand	300	800	350	700	

a. Draw the transportation network.
b. Formulate the linear programming model.
c. Using Solver, find out how many products from each plant can be shipped to the customers by minimizing the shipping cost?

7. Fab Fabrics supplies its four retail stores from four plants, Plants 1, 2,3, and 4 send 20, 40, 40, and 20 shipments, respectively. Retail stores 1, 2, 3, and 4 must receive 40, 25, 35, and 20 shipments, respectively. The shipping costs per shipment are given in the table below:

| | Unit Shipping Cost | | | | |
	Retailer 1	Retailer 2	Retailer 3	Retailer 4	Shipments
Plant 1	300	200	400	250	20
Plant 2	450	400	500	400	40
Plant 3	350	240	280	310	40
Plant 4	350	300	200	180	20
Receivables	40	25	35	20	

a. Draw the transportation network.
b. Formulate the linear programming model
c. Using Solver, find out how many shipments from each plant can be made to each customer by minimizing the shipping cost?

8. Markham Industries has three plants that produce 60, 80, and 40 units that ship their products to their customers. The net profit from shipping a unit from a plant to a customer is shown in the following table:

	Customer 1	Customer 2	Customer 3	Customer 4
Plant 1	800	700	500	200
Plant 2	500	200	100	300
Plant 3	600	400	300	500

Customer 1 wants to buy 40 units and Customer 2 wants to buy 60 units. Customer 3 wants at least 20 units. Both Customer 3 and 4 want to buy as many remaining units as possible.

    a. Draw the transportation network.

    b. Formulate the linear programming model.

    c. Using Solver, find out how many shipments from each plant can be made to the customers by minimizing the shipping cost?

9. The Nephi Company produces sofas in three plants in North Carolina. The plants are required to ship the products to four distribution centers throughout the southeast United States. All distribution centers require 12 shipments that week. The four plants are capable of shipping 14, 16, and 18 shipments. R&L freight carriers charges $300 per shipment plus $2 per mile for shipping these goods. The distance from the plants to distribution centers are given in the table below:

	DC 1	DC 2	DC 3	DC 4
Plant 1	750	790	640	530
Plant 2	340	450	650	530
Plant 3	120	400	670	635

    a. Draw the transportation network.

    b. Formulate the linear programming model.

    c. Using Solver, find out how many pallets from each warehouse can be shipped to the customers by minimizing the shipping cost?

10. Koutsgeorgeos, Inc. ships Greek olive oil from its warehouses in Buffalo, New York, and Edison, New Jersey. They can ship a maximum of 100 pallets containing olive oil depending on the demand of their distribution centers. Their four distribution centers demand 40 pallets that week. The shipping costs from the two warehouses to the distribution centers are shown below:

	DC1	DC2	DC3	DC4
WH 1	700	800	450	400
WH 2	520	340	500	400

    a. Draw the transportation network.

    b. Formulate the linear programming model.

    c. Using Solver, find out how many products from each plant can be shipped to the customers by minimizing the shipping cost.

11. Koutsgeorgeos, Inc. wants to send at least 30 pallets up to a maximum of 50 pallets to their distribution center next week. The shipping costs remain the same and can be found in the previous problem.
    a. Draw the transportation network.
    b. Formulate the linear programming model.
    c. Using Solver, find out how many pallets from each warehouse can be shipped to the customers by minimizing the shipping cost?
    d. What if the company wants an additional requirement that each warehouse should ship at least 10 pallets that week since they are reaching their maximum storage capacity at the Buffalo and Edison warehouses?
    e. Of the two Options c and d, which is a better option? Explain the reason.

12. Joseph Manong, the manager of Manter Industries, has to manage shipments from his warehouse. He has four trucks at his disposal, and the warehouse has four dock doors. Any truck can be dispatched from any dock door, but the cost of transportation operations makes the total cost of each dispatched truck vary as follows:

	Door 1	Door 2	Door 3	Door 4
Truck 1	400	500	460	430
Truck 2	350	250	540	420
Truck 3	500	430	420	310
Truck 4	420	430	510	540

a. Draw the transportation network.
b. Formulate the linear programming model
c. Find out how Joe can dispatch one truck from each dock door at a minimum total cost.

References

1. UPS. (2022). *Enabling global business.* Retrieved August 2, 2022, from https://about.ups.com/ content/dam/upsstories/assets/fact-sheets/global-logistics-and-distribution/UPS_GLD_ fact%20sheet_2021.pdf

2. Halmare, M., Jawarkar, A., & Mutreja, S. (2021). *Global logistics market statistics 2021–2027.* Retrieved August 2, 2022, https://about.ups.com/ content/dam/upsstories/assets/fact-sheets/global-logistics-and-distribution/ UPS_GLD_fact%20sheet_2021.pdf

3. XPO Logistics. (2020). *XPO logistics recognized by general motors as supplier of the year for managed transportation.* Retrieved August 10, 2022, from https://www.globenewswire.com/news-release/2020/06/30/2055287/0/ en/XPO-Logistics-Recognized-by-General-Motors-as-Supplier-of-the-Year-for-Managed-Transportation.html

4. Rabinovich, E., Windle, R., & Corsi, T. (1999). Outsourcing of integrated logistics functions. *International Journal of Physical Distribution and Logistics Management, 29*(6), 353–373.

5. Sink, H. L., & Langley, C. J. (1997). A managerial framework for the acquisition of third-party logistics services. *Journal of Business Logistics, 19*(1), 121–136.

6. Vaidyanathan, G. (2005). A framework for evaluating third-party logistics. *Communications of the ACM, 48,* 89–94.

7. Siekerman, R. C. (2021). 3PL collaboration: Supply chain success stories between shippers and 3PLs. *Journal of Supply Chain Management, Logistics and Procurement, 4*(1), 90–99.

8. Heskett. J. L. (1977, November). Logistics-essential to success. *Harvard Business Review, 55*(6), 85–96.

9. Accenture. (2022). *State of supply chains.* Retrieved August 4, 2022, from https://www.accenture.com/us-en/insights/consulting/coronavirus-supply-chain-disruption

10. Higginson, J. K., & Bookbinder, J. H. (2005). Distribution centers in supply chain operations. In *Logistics systems: Design and optimization* (pp. 67–91).Boston, MA: Springer.

11. Sork, A. (2022). *Mapping Amazon warehouses: How much square footage does amazon own?* Retrieved August 23, 2022, from https://bigrentz.com/blog/amazon-warehouses-locations

12. Collins, J. (2022). *4.1 million-square-foot warehouse in Ontario will be Amazon's biggest ever.* Retrieved August 22, 2022, from https://www.ocregister.com/2022/05/31/4-1-million-square-foot-warehouse-in-ontario-will-be-amazons-biggest-ever/

13. Dager, A. (2021). *Amazon building massive robotics fulfillment center and delivery station in Elkhart County.* Retrieved August 23, 2022, from https://wsbt.com/news/local/amazon-building-massive-robotics-fulfillment-center-and-delivery-station-in-elkhart-count

14. Gue, K. R. (1999). The effects of trailer scheduling on the layout of freight terminals. *Transportation Science, 33*(4), 419–428.

15. Bartholdi, J. J., & Gue, K. R. (2000). Reducing labor costs in an LTL crossdocking terminal. *Operations Research, 48*(6), 823–832.

16. Gu, J., Goetschalck, M., & McGinnis, L. (2007). Research on warehouse operation: A comprehensive review. *European Journal of Operational Research, 177,* 1–21.

17. Frazelle, E. H. (2002). *World-class warehousing and material handling.* New York, NY: McGraw Hill.

18. Bureau of Transportation Statistics. (2022). *Moving goods in the United States.* Retrieved August 16, 2022, from https://data.bts.gov/stories/s/Moving-Goods-in-the-United-States/bcyt-rqmu

19. Kostandi, C. (2022). *Interactive map: Crude oil pipelines and refineries of the U.S. and Canada.* Retrieved August 17, 2022, from https://www.visualcapitalist.com/interactive-map-crude-oil-pipelines-and-refineries-of-the-u-s-and-canada/

20. Ruamsook, K., & Thomchick, E. (2012, March 15–17). Sustainable freight transportation: A review of strategies. *53rd Annual Transportation Research Forum Proceedings,* Tampa, FL.

21. Biederman, D. (2008). Going green with SmartWay. *Traffic World,* November 24.

22. Biederman, D. (2011). Greening up. *The Journal of Commerce Magazine,* April 4.

23. Stoffel, B. (2009). Scoping out a green logistics partner. *Industry Week,* October 12.

24. Wright, J. (2010). Supply chain oil slick. *The Journal of Commerce Magazine,* November 8.

25. Solomon, M. B. (2010). Truckers chafe at alternative fuel mandates. *DC Velocity,* March 8.

26. Jones, K. J. (2022). *Volvo VNR electric: Commercial transportation's future is now.* Retrieved October 22, 2022, from https://www.motortrend.com/features/volvo-vnr-electric-truck-big-rig/

27. Volvo. (2022). *Volvo FH Electric. From city to city in comfort.* Retrieved October 22, 2022, from https://www.volvotrucks.com/en-en/trucks/trucks/volvo-fh/volvo-fh-electric.html

28. Sheckler, C. (2021). E-commerce adds more fuel to a warehouse boom in South Bend area. *South Bend Tribune,* February 2021.

CHAPTER 13

DATA ANALYTICS AND OSCM PERFORMANCE DRIVERS AND METRICS

Learning Objectives

- Describe data analytics and its types.
- Explain big data.
- Describe the data analytics process.
- Explain how data analytics is used to improve supply chain performance.
- Calculate various performance metrics used in operations and supply chain.

Making good business decisions is of extreme importance to companies. Firms use various data to make good decisions. The use of data to make business decisions is called business data analytics or, simply, data analytics. In operations and supply chain management (OSCM), data analytics is used to improve accuracy in forecasting demand, boost supply chain performance, and enhance the quality of customer experience.

FedEx Corporation, the American company focused on transportation, e-commerce, and services, is based in Memphis, Tennessee. FedEx is known for its next-day air delivery service and was one of the first major shipping companies to offer overnight delivery.

Microsoft Corporation is an American multinational technology corporation based in Richmond, Washington. Microsoft is known for its computer software, consumer electronics, personal computers, and computer-related services.

FedEx has been at the forefront of analyzing data. In 1978, the then-chairman Fred Smith famously said, "information about the package is as important as the package itself[1]." From its 18 million daily shipments across 220 countries, FedEx gathers data on consumer demand, packages transported, best routes to take, and more. The company shares with its retail partners the insights from the collected data who, in turn, use such insights to improve their own supply chains. For example, retailers who use FedEx can plan their capacity, position their inventory, and discover ways to serve their customers better[1].

In May 2020, FedEx announced a new multiyear collaboration with Microsoft to combine its global digital and logistics network with the power of Microsoft's intelligent cloud. With the help of software and cloud infrastructure provided by Microsoft, FedEx can use data analytics solutions and improve its supply chain solutions. The real advantage for FedEx is to get insights about the global movement of goods. FedEx Surround, the solution resulting from the collaboration, allows enhanced visibility into its supply chain by leveraging the data to provide near-real-time analytics for shipment tracking, which will drive the company's precise logistics and accurate inventory management[2].

Data Analytics and Big Data

> **Data Analytics**
> Data analytics is the technique of analyzing raw data, obtaining information from the data, and drawing inferences from that information.

Data analytics is the technique of analyzing raw data, obtaining information from the data, and drawing valuable inferences from that information. Data analytics uses data, computer systems, statistics, mathematical or quantitative models, and algorithms to gain business insights into their operations processes and make accurate and more effective fact-based decisions. Algorithms are instructions for solving a problem.

Firms want to know what adds value and what serves to improve their business, which are called **business insights**. To gain business insights, a firm has to sort the available data to find meaningful value propositions. For example, a gift shop can find out how many potential customers visited their website, what interested each visitor, and which one of their products was sent to the shopping cart but was never purchased. Such business insights can be extracted from the data collected from their website. Data analytics has been used in almost every industry to gain business insights. Some of the most promising applications using data analytics are as follows:

- Provide higher-quality healthcare and improved patient outcomes,
- Improve detection of cybersecurity threats,

- Recommend what the next streaming program a user might like to watch,
- Create new products based on what customers are trying to find, and
- Run targeted marketing campaigns by segmenting customers.

Big data uses large amounts of complex data. Big data encompasses large amount of data collected from various sources such as the following:

- Social media platforms such as Google, Facebook, Twitter, YouTube, Instagram, where users' thoughts and perceptions can be extracted;
- Generic media like images, videos, audios, and podcasts where users and experts provide their insights;
- Data found on the Internet sites;
- Data created from Internet of Things (IoT)—machine-generated data from a variety of devices; data from sensors such as medical devices; sensory data from vehicles, household appliances, and appliances in companies; and
- Data collected from transactions of a business.

> **Big Data** Big data is the huge amount of data defined as the five Vs—namely, volume, velocity, variety, variability, and veracity.

Businesses store such large amounts of data for analysis on the cloud or remote storage systems that can be accessed for analysis using the Internet. The reason for using cloud is that is that it can store and accommodate large amounts of data. Big data is often defined as five Vs—namely, volume, velocity, variety, variability, and veracity.

Volume is the huge amount of data accumulated for data analysis.

Velocity is the rate at which data are received.

Variety denotes the various types of data formats—structured data from databases, unstructured data from pdf and images, emails, videos, audios, and transactional data.

Variability describes statistically how far the different types of data remain from one other. It is also called spread, scatter, or dispersion of data.

Veracity is the accuracy or the quality of data. Data have to be cleansed for quality.

Data Analytics Process

Data analytics either with available data or using big data is accomplished using the process identified in Figure 13-1. The process is defined in the following steps:

1. Define the problem,
2. Collect data,
3. Clean the data,
4. Analyze the data, and
5. Interpret and visualize results.

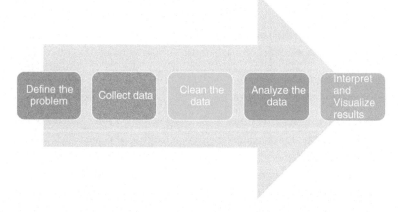

Figure 13-1 Data Analytics Process

Define the Problem

The problem should be clearly defined without any ambiguity. The problem should be defined in such a way that a hypothesis can be formed and tested or a relevant question can be posed and analyzed. The problem should identify why an analysis must be performed. For example, a company's problem may be clearly spelt out as, "Our product *A* is not selling as expected in the northwest region of the U.S."

Collect Data

Data should be collected based on the identified problem. The above-identified problem may be due to poor sales, product A's performance or features not meeting customers' expectations, and manufacturing defects, supply chain problems, and so on. The company may decide to do market research on product *A*. They may collect the data from Facebook, Twitter, and other social media. They may collect data from various supply chain resources and from their own day-to-day transactions. They may even extract the data available from the local and the federal government portals.

Clean the Data

After collecting the data, the data have to be cleansed for analysis. Duplicates, missing data, incomplete data, inconsistencies, inaccuracies, and anomalies must be removed from the raw data. If not, such problems in the data will manifest as data-quality challenges at later stages[3]. The data must be scrubbed in order to be consistent with its use through the remedial measures developed to resolve the problem at hand.

Analyze the Data

Analyzing the data depends on the problem at hand, the type of analysis expected to find a solution, and the extent of data that have been extracted. From simple techniques such as the regression analysis that we used for forecasting, to the complex machine learning models, we have access to many techniques, algorithms, models, and tools for data analysis. We will discuss the types of data analysis and some of the tools and techniques that are available for data analysis in this chapter.

Interpret and Visualize Results

The analyzed data must be interpreted as valuable business insights. Furthermore, the findings of the analysis must be presented in the form of charts and graphs. Interpreting the result of analysis reveals the ways in which a company can make decisions and solve the problem at hand. If any limitations to the data are found, further analysis should be continued.

Data Analytics in OSCM

OSCM managers can analyze their data using statistics, algorithms, and mathematical or quantitative models to gain insights into their operations, processes, and activities and make well-informed and more effective fact-based decisions.

Using the data-based knowledge, managers can strategically implement their operations and supply chain activities. For example, if you buy a book from Amazon, Amazon will recommend certain other books that will be of interest to you. The recommendations are based on the fact that you chose that particular book or topic and also based on the buying or even browsing behavior of other Amazon customers. Airlines and travel companies can optimize their websites to market certain vacation plans at certain times and dynamically configured prices.

Manufacturing companies usually record and collect data about runtime, downtime, work-order details, and queues for work planned for machinery and equipment. Analyzing such data enables a business to plan well so that their machines can operate to peak capacity. Some common operations and supply chain–related decisions where data analytics can be used are as follows:

- Firms can intervene early and act to avoid costly supply chain problems using the real-time knowledge of global commerce conditions, political turmoil, severe weather conditions, or natural disasters;

> **Data Analytics in OSCM** Data analytics is the use of data, computer systems, statistics, algorithms, and mathematical or quantitative models to help managers gain insights into their operations, processes, and activities and make well-informed and more effective fact-based decisions.

- Companies can forecast demand and plan their capacity more accurately using historical data, market demands, current and future economic conditions, and other relevant data;
- Businesses can track inventory, manage inventory, increase the overall efficiency of their business operations, reduce costs, and improve revenues.

A number of studies have been conducted on how data analytics applications could be implemented for business improvements. Such studies in the following OSCM areas include:

- Demand forecasting, inventory management, supply chain management, and transport management[4];
- Logistics in supply chain management to provide insights into customer purchasing habits and maintenance cycles[5];
- Transportation network redesigning to minimize quality loss, shipping, product categories, and transit types, cargo loss severity[6,7];
- Transport planning[8];
- Supply chain stability[9];
- Operations and supply chain performance, supply chain planning efficiency[10]; and
- Service supply chain growth and service supply chain efficiency[11].

FROM PRACTICE: Capital One's Data Analytics Using Snowflake

© Sundry Photography/Shutterstock.com

Capital One, the American bank holding company, specializes in credit cards, auto loans, banking, and savings accounts. The business has been using machine learning and other artificial intelligence (AI) technologies to guide investment decisions, detect fraud, and to manage their customers' finances. Data analysts considered the impact of important events like the 2019 COVID pandemic in order to ensure that they base their decisions on accurate, real-world information and minimize exposure to risk[12]. Many data analysts have to access data to conduct their analysis and, hence, the company relies on Snowflake Data Cloud's elastic capabilities. The Data Cloud allows Capital One to store large amounts of data, analyze that data, and extract AI-driven insights to notify to their customers about any unusual transactions detected in their loan account.

Data Analytics Types

Businesses have been analyzing data for so many years. The use of computers propelled the analysis in new ways that led to the emergence of the concept called **business intelligence**. The integration of statistics, technologies such as AI, and robust visualization tools have opened up the business intelligence analysis that we call business data analytics. Basically, there are three distinct types of data analytics:

1. Descriptive analytics,
2. Predictive analytics, and
3. Prescriptive analytics.

In this section, we will use a few examples to illustrate these three types of analytics. We will use Microsoft Excel and its functions **Solver** and **Data Analysis**.

Data Analysis in Excel

Microsoft's Excel's Data Analysis ToolPak is an add-in program that can be used for many types of statistical analyses.

To add Data Analysis ToolPak to your Excel, go to File > Options > Add-ins and choose Analysis ToolPak Add-in. To access these tools, click Data Analysis in the Analysis group on the Data tab. The Analysis ToolPak includes several statistical tools—namely, ANOVA, correlation, descriptive statistics, exponential smoothing, histogram, moving average, and regression.

Descriptive Analytics

Descriptive analytics focuses on what happened in the past. The past or historical data can be extracted from transactions with suppliers, distributors, sales channels, and customers. Several patterns can be identified from such extracted data. For example, transportation managers can learn from the results of descriptive analytics that deliveries to warehouses are running late when there is a clear possibility that deliveries could have been made that very day. Using historical patterns, they can also see that there is a possibility of weather conditions that can potentially delay delivery, such as heavy snow in a region on certain days. Using this type of analytics, managers can get answers to important questions in relation to company's operational efficiency:

- What was the sales performance in stores located in the eastern region?
- How does the eastern region's sales performance compare to that of the western region?
- Did the cost of product A exceed the cost of product B? By how much?

Descriptive analytics uses techniques such as statistical analysis, visualization, and data modeling. Example 13-1 shows how a local business can use descriptive analytics to make decisions.

Example 13-1

Sweepy Sam is a vacuum repair shop, which specializes in the repair of vacuum cleaners in downtown Lakeville. Sam, the owner of Sweepy Sam, wants to advertise a guaranteed repair time to attract new customers. He has provided repair services to 260 customers the previous year and has recorded the time taken in days to repair and return their vacuum cleaners. Use the data from the Excel tab *sweepysam* in the *Datafile.xlsx* located on the student book website to solve this problem.

   a. Using descriptive statistics, explain Sam's current operations.
   b. Can Sam provide a guaranteed vacuum repair time to his customers using the data?

Step 1:   Obtain the data from the student book website.

Step 2:   Click on Excel > Data > Data Analysis > Descriptive Statistics to calculate the descriptive statistics.

Sam takes almost 3 days (mean = 2.83) on an average to repair and return vacuum cleaners. The mean is close to the median, but the mode is less than the mean, indicating that there is a positive skewed frequency distribution. The higher number of repair days is causing the data to skew right. Therefore, Sam takes more than the average number of repair days in general to repair and return the vacuum cleaners to his customers. The data also reveal that Sam takes at least a minimum of 2 days and a maximum of 6 days to repair and return the 260 vacuum cleaners. Therefore, Sam can guarantee the return of repaired vacuum cleaners to customers anytime within 3 to 6 days.

Step 3:   Find the frequency distribution. As Sam takes a maximum of 6 days, we can create six bins to determine the frequency distribution using Excel. Using Excel's frequency function, we can get the frequency of repairs for days 0 through 6 and calculate both relative and cumulative frequencies. Note that Sam repairs most of the vacuum cleaners he receives in 2 to 3 days, and, as shown in the frequency distribution table, only in very few cases it takes 5 days for him to repair or service and return the vacuum cleaners.

Descriptive Statistics	
Mean	2.830769231
Standard Error	0.059519141
Median	3
Mode	2
Standard Deviation	0.959717313
Sample Variance	0.921057321
Kurtosis	−0.226003677
Skewness	0.873181281
Range	4
Minimum	2
Maximum	6
Sum	736
Count	260
Confidence Level(95.0%)	0.117203043

Days	Frequency	Relative Frequency	Cumulative Percentage
1	0	0.00%	0.0%
2	0	0.00%	0.0%
3	126	48.46%	48.5%
4	70	26.92%	75.4%
5	47	18.08%	93.5%
6	16	6.15%	99.6%
7	1	0.38%	100.0%

Repair Times

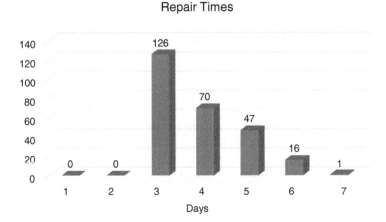

Step 4:   Visualize the frequency distribution using a histogram. As seen from the above frequency distribution table and the figure, Sam takes 4 days to repair the vacuum cleaners 93% of the time. Most probably, it may take him a few extra days if he has to wait for parts. Therefore, Sam can guarantee 4 days as repair and return time to his customers.

Analysis: Sam can guarantee 4 days to attract new customers using the result from the histogram. He can repair the vacuum cleaners in 3 days 75% of the time, but, to guarantee that performance, he must be absolutely confident. Maybe, for simple repairs, he can guarantee 3 days!

Predictive Analytics

Predictive analytics use historical data to predict what could happen in the near future. Using predictive analytics, firms can project what will happen in the future and why. Predictions can be made by extrapolating historical data to see what may happen in future. This is similar to the regression analysis we discussed in the chapter on forecasting. Predictions can be extended to other facets of OSCM as well. For example, a possibility of a supply chain disruption can be predicted by detection of such scenarios that have repeatedly occurred in the past. Managers can then take decisions proactively to avoid the severity of such possibilities. A company may use economic projections from a federal or state agency and anticipate reduction in sales. Using such predictions, managers can revisit their sales and operations planning (S&OP) and aggregate planning to order appropriate quantities of raw materials. Typically, managers can get answers to questions such as the ones listed here:

- What will be the demand for the next few months?
- How much will the cost of raw materials fall next month?
- Will fuel costs rise next month? By how much?

Predictive analytics uses techniques such as forecasting, regression analysis, time series methods, statistical algorithms, decision trees, and clustering algorithms. We have discussed forecasting techniques such as regression and time series methods in Chapter 2. Example 13-2 shows how a local business can use predictive analytics to find insights from their data to make decisions.

Example 13-2

Franky's Funnies & Fiction store is located on the Main Street of Nappanee, Indiana. Frank, the owner, has a record of the number of comics and books sold for a straight 160 weeks. Frank wants to know how many comics and books he would sell over the next 4 weeks by using his data. Use the data from the Excel tab *frankys* in the *Datafile.xlsx* located on the student book website to solve this problem.

Step 1:   The sales of comics and books depend on many factors, and it is not possible to use these factors in a simple model. Therefore, Frank thought that he would simply use the week and the sales during that week as data. Since we need to predict future sales, we will use a tool with which we are already familiar—regression. We will assume that the model is a simple linear regression. By this, we can assume that Frank's comics and books sales follows a linear equation $Y = a + bX$, where Y is the sales for a week X, "a" is the sales for week zero, and the b is the slope of sales function. This means we are assuming a linear relationship between the two variables—sales and weeks.

Step 2:   Use Excel > Data > Data Analysis and choose Regression. Choose the sales for the 160 weeks as data for Y and weeks as X. Run the regression analysis.

Step 3:   Interpret and visualize. A simple scatter plot shows that as time progresses, sales rise, and the trend line shows an increasing trend in sales. The points around the trend line fall above or below the line or on the line itself. Therefore, our assumption of a linear regression model seems to be an approximate model for sales.

Regression Statistics	
Multiple R	0.861196
R Square	0.741658
Adjusted R Square	0.740023
Standard Error	9.798416
Observations	160

ANOVA

	df	SS	MS	F	Significance F
Regression	1	43548.93	43548.93	453.5924	2.68713E-48
Residual	158	15169.41	96.00895		
Total	159	58718.34			

	Coefficients	Standard Error	t Stat	P-value	Lower 95%	Upper 95%	Lower 95.0%	Upper 95.0%
Intercept	37.52689	1.556556	24.10892	8.19E-55	34.45254487	40.60123	34.45254	40.60123
Week	0.357197	0.016772	21.29771	2.69E-48	0.324071566	0.390323	0.324072	0.390323

Units Sold

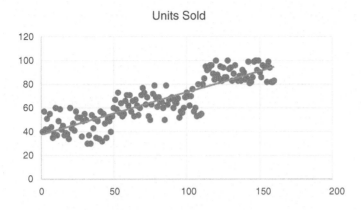

Week Residual Plot

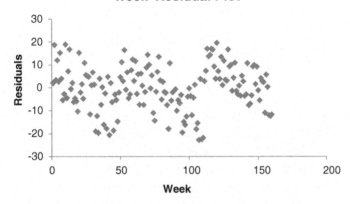

Step 5:   Prediction for Franky's Funnies & Fiction store

Using the equation $Y = 37.53 + 0.357\,X$, Frank can predict sales for the next few weeks as shown in the following table. These estimates were obtained by substituting into X the week number. For example, for Week 161:

$Y = 37.53 + 0.357(161) = 95$ (rounded to zero digits)

Week	Sales
161	95
162	95
163	96
164	96

Analysis:

Regression Statistics Section:

Multiple R is the correlation coefficient. A value greater than zero shows a positive correlation, which means, as X increases, Y increases. The 0.86 value indicates a strong, positive correlation between X and Y. For example, a factor like the word-of-mouth advertisement from satisfied customers as time progresses would make such a positive correlation.

R^2 is the coefficient of determination which shows how much of the variation in Y can be explained by X. A value of 0 indicates no relationship between X and Y, and a value of 1 indicates perfect fit. R^2 value over 0.6 is considered good. The value for this example is 0.74 and indicates that about 74% of the variation of the number of comics and books (Y) sold by Frankie's Funnies and Fiction can be explained by weeks (X). X and Y and a good fit of the linear regression model.

Adjusted R^2 value is used in multiple linear regression models, as it alters the R^2 value for the sample size and number of variables. We need not consider this for this analysis.

The standard error of estimate should be small, which indicates a good fit of the regression model. The larger the scatter of data, the larger will be the standard error. In this case, the error is low and, hence, the model is a good fit.

The number of observations tells that there are 160 data sets of X and Y values that Frank has recorded.

Regression Coefficients Section

In this section, the item of importance is the significance value, also called p-value, which should be less than 0.05. The value is very small and very insignificant rejecting the null hypothesis. If we reject the null hypothesis, we can conclude that the slope of the independent value X is not zero, which explains the variation of the dependent variable Y around the mean.

This is where the regression coefficient's intercepting points on the X-axis and the slope are provided. The slope for our linear regression model is 0.357, and the X-axis intercept is 37.53. Therefore, our linear regression equation is $Y = 37.53 + 0.357\,X$.

Additional information for hypotheses-testing associated with "a" and "b" regression coefficients are also provided in this section. P-values associated with regression coefficients are very low. The p-value for both "a" and "b" coefficients are very small (< 0.05), indicating that we can reject the null hypothesis and that they are statistically significant.

Residual Analysis

A residual is the difference between the actual value of the dependent variable and its predicted value. The residual plot illustrates the residual values as a scatter plot. Standard residuals are residuals divided by their standard deviation. This tells us how far each residual is from its mean and also the extent of outliers in the data. Looking at the plot, we see that there is no significant outlier.

Prescriptive Analytics

Prescriptive analytics use historical data to find an optimized solution. The prescriptive analytics method predicts why certain things have happened in the firm. An optimized solution is either the minimum or maximum achievement criterion in relation to an objective. For example, if a supplier gives discounts based on various quantities for a mixture of materials, it is better to use an optimization software to find the best solution. This method is also useful when firms have data with uncertainties. In some scenarios, predictive analytics combine results from both descriptive and predictive analytics. Prescriptive analytics can help managers take decisions to protect their firms during major disruptions in the supply chain. Typically, managers can get answers to questions such as follows:

- What is the best price of a mix of products from a supplier?
- Can my supplier with all the economic and political problems in their region supply my products?
- What is the best strategy to minimize transportation costs?

Firms collect data continuously to increase the accuracy of prediction. Prescriptive analytics uses various optimization techniques, simulations using mathematical models, and machine learning algorithms. Example 13-3 shows how a local business can use predictive analytics to find insights from their data to make decisions using optimization techniques.

Example 13-3

Gabriel Granites from Wichita, Kansas, produces granite and quartz countertops. The cost of granite and quartz are $900 per piece and $1,100 per piece, respectively. The company prices normal-size countertops at $4,000 and $6,000, respectively, after labor, overhead, margin, and transportation costs. The time to make a normal-size countertop is 10 hours for the granite and 14 hours for the quartz. During the current month, Gabriel, the president of the company, has $100,000 in capital for granite and marble materials, and his team of five works for 10 hours a day for 23 days. Even though quartz is the trend currently, he gets more orders for granite countertops than for quartz countertops. How many of each product can be produced to make the maximum possible profit?

Step 1:   Develop a simple model. Let X_1 be the number of granite countertops and X_2 be the number of quartz countertops to be produced by the company. The profit for one unit of granite countertop is (price-cost) × $X_1 = (4,000 - 900)X_1$; similarly, the profit for one unit of quartz countertop is $(6,000 - 1,100)X_2$. The total time for production is $5 \times 10 \times 23 = 1,150$ hours. To maximize profits with the capital, total production time, and number of granite countertops produced greater than number of quartz countertops produced, we can develop a simple model using the equations from Chapter 12:

Maximize: $3{,}100\,X_1 + 4{,}900\,X_2$

Subject to the constraints: $900\,X_1 + 1{,}100\,X_2 \leq \$100{,}000$,

$10\,X_1 + 14X_2 <= 1{,}150$, and

$X1 - X2 >= 1$ (expressed for $X1 > X2$)

Step 2:   Set up the above model in Excel Solver:

Step 3:   Solve for an optimized solution using a simple linear programming method, as this is a linear model. The solver yields the following optimized solution.

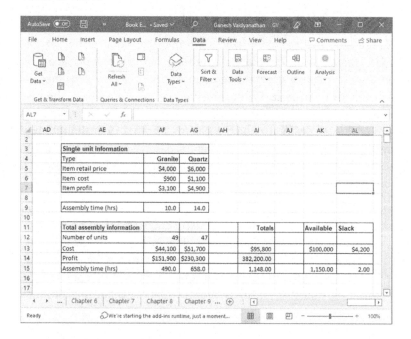

Analysis: Gabriel should produce 49 granite countertops and 47 quartz countertops to maximize his profits of $382,200 with a capital of $100,000 and production time of 1,150 hours.

FROM PRACTICE: UPS Orion Logistics Optimization with Big Data

Big data has been successfully used by several supply chain and logistics industries. The firms are using big data analytics to optimize routes, delivery times, and delivery methods. UPS is at the forefront of big data analytics. UPS ships more than 4 billion items annually using more than 100,000 vehicles. Its vast amounts of data have been leveraged to optimize its fleet management. Recently, UPS launched Orion, a proprietary technology that uses advanced algorithms such as machine learning.

© pio3/Shutterstock.com

UPS uses this technology to track data from the on-truck telematics in order to understand the route optimization and the engine idle times. They use the results of the analysis to predict fleet maintenance periods. Since ORION's initial deployment, UPS has saved about 100 million miles and 10 million gallons of fuel per year. The company has also saved more than more than $300 million annually[13,14].

FROM PRACTICE: Data Cleansing at Zillow

Zillow, the real estate and rental marketplace, is a data-driven firm. Zillow has a current database of over 110 million homes in the United States. Their home valuation, Zestimate®, uses a proprietary algorithm. Zillow gets publicly available data, real estate transactions, real estate deeds, and tax assessments and integrates those data with local real estate market conditions and historical data. Zillow uses machine learning algorithms to automate data-cleaning tasks. These algorithms help Zillow to

© Tada Images/Shutterstock.com

detect outliers and ascertain the missing data. The algorithms match data from disparate sources by using weighted text and numeric features, distance metrics, and k-nearest neighbor (KNN) machine learning algorithms[15].

Performance Metrics of Operations and Supply Chain

Managers rely on metrics to understand, track, and improve their company's performance. The metrics are also called key performance indicators (KPI). Metrics are measures used for evaluating, comparing, and tracking performance. The company's performance depends heavily on the performance in its operations and supply chain.

Operational and supply chain metrics provide a snapshot of key processes associated with the topics we have covered so far, which include management of inventory, demand, capacity, supply chain, manufacturing and service processes, and procurement. Tracking these metrics shows how well the company performs. There are many purposes to measuring performance:

- Identify if customer needs are met;
- Identify bottlenecks, waste, problems, and improvement opportunities;
- Provide factual decisions;
- Enable progress;
- Track progress; and
- Use the measurement for improving existing processes.

The performance of operations and supply chain is associated with many factors: executing on-time delivery of products and services, maintaining the required amount of inventory and capacity, meeting customer requirements, and a lot more. Generally, managers pick a few metrics that they consider to be important for their function in a company and evaluate, track, and use those metrics to improve efficiencies. What is important here is that they must choose the right metrics. For example, a manager may count the number of trucks leaving the premises with products each day to track deliveries. What does the count tell the manager? Nothing—apart from the fact that products have been shipped out of the facility. But if the same manager could have tracked customer order cycle time—that is, time taken to complete the process starting from the receipt of purchase order to completing the delivery of the goods ordered—then the customers are going to benefit!

In the following, we will discuss a few key metrics in OSCM along with examples. Managers often pick what they want to track and monitor status and progress in operations and supply chain.

Efficiency Ratios

An efficiency ratio is used to analyze how well a company uses its assets and liabilities internally. Investors analyze companies using efficiency ratios to measure short-term or current performance. They also compare the performance of several companies using the efficiency ratios of each of those companies.

Table 13-1 Financial Statement Elements and Supply Chain Factors

Financial Statement	Element	Supply Chain Factors
Income statement	Revenues	Corporate social responsibility (CSR), supplier lead time, supply chain innovations, information flow, response time to customer requests, on-time delivery, product quality, product returns strategy, stock-outs, fill rates, supply chain efficiency and effectiveness, value to customers
	Costs	Costs incurred toward sourcing, transportation, inventory, storage, pick and pack, waste, stock-outs, demand forecast accuracy, optimal number of suppliers, and supply chain IT
	Sales, general, and administrative costs	Warranty fulfillment costs and transaction accuracy costs
Balance sheet	Inventory	Holding costs (financing, warehousing, tracking, moving, insurance, obsolescence, depreciation, pilferage, breakage, taxes, opportunity costs), demand forecasting accuracy, sourcing time, delivery time, setup costs, shortage costs, ordering costs, make versus buy decisions
	Accounts Receivable	Bad debt, Dunning, exchange rate volatility, customer relationship management
	Accounts payable	Late payments, delayed orders, payment penalties, supplier relationship management
	Assets	Equipment, supply chain software and technology, machinery, intangible assets

There are several efficiency ratios used by investors. In this section, we will discuss some of them that pertain to OSCM.

Efficiency ratios are calculated using the financial statements published by companies at the end of every quarter and fiscal year. Financial statements generally include the following: Income Statement, Balance Sheet, and Statement of Cash Flows. Table 13-1 shows important financial statement components that will have an impact on operations and supply chain performance[16–19].

Inventory Turnover

Inventory turnover measures how many times a company has sold and replaced inventory during a given period. Companies often tie up a large amount of money in its inventory. The inventory is critical for meeting the demand for products, but storing too much of the wrong items in the inventory can result in financial problems. It is possible that a company's inventory have items with less demand or items that have already become obsolete. By measuring the inventory turnover, a company can make better decisions on purchasing new inventory and pricing their products.

> **Inventory turnover**
> A measure that shows how many times a company has sold and replaced its inventory during a given period.

Inventory turnover for a given period of time is calculated using Equation 13-1 shown below and then compared against other companies in the same industry:

$$Inventory\ Turnover = \frac{Cost\ of\ Goods\ Sold}{Average\ Inventory} \qquad \text{Eq. 13-1}$$

A low inventory turnover implies weak sales and excess inventory. This is called overstocking. This is inefficient for a company as it has tied up money in inventory that could have been used for other purposes. Unsold inventory means lost profits. In the retail industry, unsold inventory is called obsolete inventory or dead stock, and this happens due to seasonal changes.

A high ratio implies either strong sales or insufficient inventory. Strong sales are very desirable, but insufficient inventory leads to lost business. In retail industry, high ratio is preferred especially in the sales of perishable items such as eggs, milk, and produce such as vegetables or grains.

Example 13-4

The beginning inventory in a company is $4.5 million and end inventory $2.1 million. If the cost of goods sold is $12.670,000, what is the inventory turnover?

$$Inventory\ turnover = \frac{12,670,000}{\left(\dfrac{4,500,000 + 2,100,000}{2}\right)} = 3.84$$

> **Receivables turnover**
> A measure that shows a company's efficiency in collecting its account receivable, which is the money owed by its customers.

Receivables Turnover

Receivables turnover measures a company's efficiency in collecting its account receivable, which is the money owed by its customers. Accounts receivable is money owed without interest. Companies usually extend interest-free loans as credit to their clients. For example, companies after selling a product may extend credit terms of 30, 60, or 90 days, which means the client has 30 to 90 days to pay for the product. This ratio evaluates how well a company manages the credit it extends to customers and how quickly that debt is collected.

Receivables turnover is calculated using Equation 1-2 shown below and then compared against companies in the same industry:

$$Receivables\ Turnover = \frac{Revenue\ from\ credit\ sales - Returns\ from\ customers}{Average\ Accounts\ Receivable}$$

Eq. 13-2

Example 13-5

Revenues from credit sales amount to $2,245,000, while returns from customers stand at $40,000. The average account receivables amount to $956,800. What is the receivables turnover?

$$Receivables\ Turnover = \frac{(2,245,000 - 40,000)}{956,800} = 2.3$$

Higher receivable turnover means the company is efficient at collecting on its payments due. A high receivables turnover ratio may also mean that a company operates on a cash basis or it is conservative in its approach toward extending credit to its customers. On the other hand, if a company's credit policy is very conservative, customers may decide to do business with competitors who may extend them credit. A low receivables turnover ratio may emerge because of problems with collection or bad credit policies.

Asset Turnover

Asset turnover measures how effectively companies use their assets to generate sales. Asset turnover is calculated using Equation 1-3 shown below and then compared against companies in the same industry:

$$Asset\ Turnover = \frac{Revenues}{Total\ Assets} \qquad \text{Eq. 13-3}$$

> **Asset turnover** A measure that shows how effectively companies use their assets to generate sales.

If the asset turnover ratio of a company is higher, that company is creating more revenue or is more efficient at generating revenue from its assets. If a company has a lower asset turnover ratio, then it indicates it is not efficiently using its assets. However, this depends on the industry as well. Retail stores can have high sales volume with smaller assets while real estate with large assets can have low asset turnover.

Example 13-6

The revenue earned is $8,245,000, and the value of total assets of the company is $3,450,000. What is the asset turnover?

$$Asset\ Turnover = \frac{8,245,000}{3,450,000} = 2.39$$

Property, Plant, and Equipment Turnover (PPE)

Measures revenue generated for each dollar invested in PPE. PPE turnover is calculated using Equation 1-4 shown below and then compared against companies in the same industry:

> **PPE turnover** A measure that shows how effectively companies use their property, plant, and equipment to generate revenues.

$$PPE\ Turnover = \frac{Revenues}{Property,\ Plant\ \&\ Equipment\ Investment} \qquad \text{Eq. 13-4}$$

Example 13-7

The revenue earned is $8,245,000, and the PPE of a company is $2,050,000. What is the asset turnover?

$$PPE\ Turnover = \frac{8,245,000}{2,050,000} = 4.02$$

Operations and Supply Chain Metrics

Throughput

Throughput is the rate of production of a machine or a plant over a time period. It is also the amount of a service that a business can deliver to a client within a specific period of time. Throughput is used to determine the ability of a business to meet production or service deadlines. Throughput can be calculated using the following formula:

$$Throughput = \frac{Output}{Time\ taken\ from\ start\ to\ finish} \qquad \text{Eq. 13-5}$$

Example 13-8

If a plant assembles 1,600 fans in an 8-hour day, what is the throughput?

$$Throughput = \frac{1,600}{8} = 200\ fans\ /\ day$$

First-Pass Yield or Throughput Yield

First-pass yield or throughput yield is the percentage of products made correctly without any rework in the manufacturing process.

$$First - pass\ yield = \frac{Number\ of\ quality\ products}{Total\ number\ of\ products\ produced} \qquad \text{Eq. 13-6}$$

Example 13-9

If a plant assembles 1,600 fans in an 8-hour day out of which 1,200 are produced to specifications, what is the throughput yield or first-pass yield?

$$First - Pass\ Yield = \frac{1,200}{1,600} = 75\%$$

Takt Time

Takt time is the rate at which a product is completed in order to meet customer demand. It is the time between starting to work on one unit and starting the next or the maximum amount of time spent manufacturing a product to meet production deadline.

$$Takt\ time = \frac{Available\ work\ time}{Demand} \qquad \text{Eq. 13-7}$$

Example 13-10

A vineyard makes 1,600 bottles of wine in a week. If the demand for the week is 1,500 bottles of wine and employees worked in a 5-day, 8-hour schedule, what is the takt time?

$$Takt\ time = \frac{5 \times 8 \times 60\ mins}{1,500} = 1.6\ mins$$

Cycle Time

Cycle time is the average amount of time taken to produce a *product*. It is also the time taken to complete a task.

$$Cycle\ time = \frac{Production\ time}{Output} \qquad \text{Eq. 13-8}$$

Example 13-11

A vineyard makes 1,600 bottles of wine in a week. If the demand for the week is 1,500 bottles of wine and employees worked in a 5-day, 8-hour schedule, what is the cycle time?

$$Cycle\ time = \frac{5 \times 8 \times 60\ mins}{1,600} = 1.5\ mins$$

Cash-to-Cash Cycle or Order-To-Pay Cycle

Cash-to-cash cycle (CCC) or order-to-pay cycle is the period between the purchase of materials or services from a supplier and payment collected for the sale of resulting goods or services. CCC includes the time taken to use its inventory, collect receivables, and pay its bills.

$$Cash-to-cash\ cycle = DIO + DSO - DPO \qquad \text{Eq. 13-9}$$

where,   DIO is days inventory outstanding
DSO is days sales outstanding
DPO is days payables outstanding

$$DIO = \frac{\left(\dfrac{Beginning\ Inventory + Ending\ Inventory}{2}\right)}{Cost\ of\ Goods\ Sold} \times 365 \quad \text{Eq. 13-10}$$

$$DSO = \frac{\left(\dfrac{Beginning\ Acct\ Receivable + Ending\ Acct\ Receivable}{2}\right)}{Revenue} \times 365$$

Eq. 13-11

$$DPO = \frac{\left(\dfrac{Beginning\ Acct\ Payable + Ending\ Acct\ Payable}{2}\right)}{Cost\ of\ Goods\ Sold} \times 365$$

Eq. 13-12

Example 13-12

Diamonte Home Goods sells all kinds of home products. Last year, the value of beginning inventory was $260,000 and the value of ending inventory was $258,000. The beginning and ending AP values were $250,000 and $245,000, respectively, and that of the beginning and ending AR, respectively, were $1,400,000 and $1,100,000. The cost of goods sold stood at $2,000,000 and the revenue at $6 million. What is the cash-to-cash cycle?

DIO = 47.27 days
DSO = 76.04 days
DPO = 45.17 days

$CCC = 47.27 + 76.04 - 45.17 = 78.14\ days$

Customer Order Cycle Time

Customer order cycle time is the number of days between receiving a purchase order and completing the delivery to customer based on that order. This metric helps with customer service as smaller the number, the faster the delivery and a satisfied customer.

Customer order cycle time = Actual delivery date − Purchase order date

Eq. 13-13

Example 13-13

If the actual delivery date is September 14, 2022, and the purchase order was created on July 23, 2022, what is the cycle time?

$$Customer\ order\ cycle\ time = September\ 14, 2022 - July\ 23, 2022 = 53\ days$$

Stock Turnover Rate (STR)

Stock turnover rate is an important metric with which retailers can measure how many times they have replaced inventory in a year. Managers can maintain inventory using this metric.

$$STR = \frac{Cost\ of\ Goods\ Sold}{\left(\dfrac{Beg.\ Inv\ +\ End.\ Inv}{2}\right)} \times 100$$

Eq. 13-14

Example 13-14

A neighborhood store's cost of goods sold for a year is $450,000. If the value of its starting inventory was $1 million and that of the ending inventory $700,000, how many times did the store turn over its inventory?

$$STR = \frac{450,000}{\left(\dfrac{1,000,000 + 700,000}{2}\right)} \times 100 = 53\%$$

Inventory Accuracy

Inventory accuracy explains how closely inventory records match the inventory at hand after a physical count.

$$Inventory\ accuracy = 1 - \left(\frac{System\ Inventory - Physical\ count}{System\ Inventory}\right) \times 100$$ Eq. 13-15

Example 13-15

BetterImmunity.com, an ecommerce company, completes a physical inventory count and finds 800 units of a certain product. If the inventory system says there should be 854 of this product, what is the inventory accuracy?

$$Inventory\ accuracy = 1 - \left(\frac{854 - 800}{854}\right) \times 100 = 94\%$$

Formulae from this Chapter

Inventory Turnover	$$\frac{Cost\ of\ Goods\ Sold}{Average\ Inventory}$$	Eq. 13-1
Receivables Turnover	$$\frac{Revenue\ from\ credit\ sales - Returns\ from\ customers}{Average\ Accounts\ Receivable}$$	Eq. 13-2
Asset Turnover	$$\frac{Revenues}{Total\ Assets}$$	Eq. 13-3
PPE Turnover	$$\frac{Revenues}{Property,\ Plant\ \&\ Equipment\ Investment}$$	Eq. 13-4
Throughput	$$\frac{Output}{Time\ taken\ from\ start\ to\ finish}$$	Eq. 13-5
First-pass yield	$$\frac{Number\ of\ quality\ products}{Total\ number\ of\ products\ produced}$$	Eq. 13-6
Takt time	$$\frac{Available\ work\ time}{Demand}$$	Eq. 13-7
Cycle time	$$\frac{Production\ time}{Output}$$	Eq. 13-8
Cash-to-cash cycle	$DIO + DSO - DPO$	Eq. 13-9
Days of inventory outstanding	$$\frac{\left(\frac{Beginning\ Inventory + Ending\ Inventory}{2}\right)}{Cost\ of\ Goods\ Sold} \times 365$$	Eq. 13-10
Days sales outstanding	$$\frac{\left(\frac{Beginning\ Acct\ Receivable + Ending\ Acct\ Receivable}{2}\right)}{Revenue} \times 365$$	Eq. 13-11
Days payables outstanding	$$\frac{\left(\frac{Beginning\ Account\ Payable\ +\ Ending\ Account\ Payable}{2}\right)}{Revenue} \times 365$$	Eq. 13-12
Customer order cycle time	$Actual\ delivery\ date - Purchase\ order\ date$	Eq. 13-13

Stock turnover rate	$\dfrac{Cost\ of\ Goods\ Sold}{\left(\dfrac{Beginning\ Inventory\ +\ Ending\ Inventory}{2}\right)} \times 100$	Eq. 13-14
Inventory accuracy	$1 - \left(\dfrac{System\ Inventory - Physical\ count}{System\ Inventory}\right) \times 100$	Eq. 13-15

Case Study: Data Analytics at Sean Williams paint store

Sean Williams owns a paint store in a small town in the northwest part of Michigan. Sean graduated from the University of Northwestern Michigan and took over the ownership from Ian Williams, his father. Ian had passed on the ownership to his only son and currently lives in Arizona. Under the hardworking Sean, Sean's Paint Shop was doing well. Sean opens his store almost all the days of the year with the exception of a few major holidays. Even on those days, if a customer wants to buy a quart of paint, he could walk over to the store from his house to serve that customer.

Sean hired his own nephew to work with him during busy days and during the summer. He did this to help out his nephew to go to the university to pursue his studies rather than hiring a hand to help him in his daily schedule. Sean had managed his business very well.

© BearFotos/Shutterstock.com

Sean's Paint Shop was known in this town for its customer service and quality paints. Sean had a good return policy with easy terms, and his customers liked the return policy set by Ian. On Saturday afternoons, Sean conducted a half-an-hour painting class to show the techniques and intricacies of painting uniformly without streaks and blobs. This class was always attended by a few residents as well as students who were planning to take up painting for summer jobs. Those classes also provided traffic in the store, and the students who took up painting always came back to buy paints from the store.

Sean's main concern was the inventory at the stores. The business sells interior latex paint in a wide variety of colors. The assorted colors are mixed to order, so Sean only needs to carry the inventory of a few different tint bases rather than an inventory of every possible color a customer may want to purchase. Sean began collecting data and started collating the data that he had collected for the past year. He has collected the sales data for the past year and wanted to use that data for analysis.

He had heard of data analytics and its three types. He thought that he could find the busiest days and the idlest days from his data as well as the variability in sales using the descriptive analytics. Using the sales data and the predictive model, he thought that he could find the sales forecasts for the next three months. The most important analysis for Sean was the promise of predictive analysis where he could find the inventory of the four tint bases that he carried in his shop.

Sean buys the base white color for $8 a quart with a sale price of $12. He buys Tint A, Tint B, and Tint C for 10¢ each and sells them at $1 each. The usage requirements for these tints are roughly 8:1, 6:1, and 10:1, respectively, with respect to the base white color. He usually allocates 70% of his inventory costs as capital for all these paint items.

Sean wanted to expand his business and was looking for the right opportunity. He found out that the store owner at the far eastern part of the town is getting ready to sell his business. Pernio's Paints has been in business for a long time. The owner of Pernio's Paints was ready to retire and move to Florida to escape the severe winters of northwest Michigan. Sean wanted to buy that paint store and approached the owner. The owner of that store gave him all the information Sean wanted. On a Sunday afternoon after a nice lunch with his family, Sean pulled all the financial data of his store and started comparing that data with the data he obtained from Pernio's Paints.

Case Questions

Use the data from the Excel tab *seanpaints* in the *Datafile.xlsx* located on the student book website to solve case questions.

    A. On which day of the week did Sean's business sell the most amount of paint that year?

    B. On which day of the week did Sean's business sell the least amount of paint that year?

    C. What is the sales forecast for the next three months?

    D. How much inventory of each tint base and the base white color should he carry?

Compare Sean's Paint Shop and Pernio's Paints using the following metrics and explain the results:

    E. Gross profit

    F. Asset turnover

    G. Inventory turnover

    H. Receivables turnover

    I. PPE turnover

    J. Cash-to-cash cycle

Summary

- Data analytics is the use of data, computer systems, statistics, and mathematical or quantitative models to gain business insights and make well-informed and more effective fact-based decisions.
- Big data uses large amounts of complex data.
- Businesses use such large amounts of data for analysis stored on the cloud.
- Big data is often defined as five Vs—namely, volume, velocity, variety, variability, and veracity.
- Data analytics is the use of data, computer systems, statistics, mathematical or quantitative models to help managers to gain insights into their supply chain operations, processes, and activities to make well-informed and more effective fact-based decisions.
- Using data-based decisions, managers can strategically implement operations and supply chain activities.
- There are three distinct types of data analytics—namely, descriptive analytics, predictive analytics, and prescriptive analytics.
- Descriptive analytics focuses on what happened in the past. The past or historical data can be extracted from transactions with suppliers, distributors, sales channels, and customers. Patterns can be identified from such extracted data.
- Predictive analytics uses historical data to predict what could happen in the near future. Using predictive analytics, firms can project what will happen in the future and why.
- Prescriptive analytics uses historical data to arrive at an optimized solution.
- Prescriptive analytics predicts why certain things has happened in the firm.
- Managers rely on metrics to understand, track, and improve the performance of a company. The metrics are also called key performance indicators (KPI).
- Metrics are measures used for evaluating, comparing, and tracking performance.
- Performance of a company depends heavily on the performance of its operations and supply chain.
- Tracking metrics shows how well the company performs these processes.
- Managers often pick what they want to track and monitor the status and progress of their operations and supply chain network.
- Inventory turnover measures how many times a company has sold and replaced inventory during a given period.

- Receivables turnover measures a company's efficiency in collecting its account receivable, which is the money owed by its customers.
- Asset turnover measures how effectively companies use their assets to generate sales.
- Property, plant, and equipment turnover measures how effectively companies use their property, plant, and equipment to generate revenues.
- Throughput is the rate of production of a machine or a plant over a time period.
- First-pass yield or throughput yield is the percentage of products made correctly without any rework in the manufacturing process.
- Takt time is the rate at which a product is completed in order to meet customer demand.
- Cycle time is the average amount of time taken to produce a product.
- Cash-to-cash cycle (CCC) or order-to-pay cycle is the period between the purchase of materials or services from a supplier and payment collected for sale of the resulting goods or services.
- Customer order cycle time is the number of days between receiving a purchase order and completing the delivery of goods ordered by the customer through that order.
- Stock turnover rate is an important metric that retailers can use to ascertain how many times they have replaced inventory in a year. Managers can maintain their inventory using this metric.
- Inventory accuracy explains how closely inventory records match the inventory at hand after a physical count.

Review Questions

1. Define data analytics.
2. Define big data.
3. Where do companies store data for big data analytics?
4. From where companies get data for big data analytics?
5. Form where companies get data for data analytics?
6. Define the 5 Vs of big data analytics.
7. Define the data analytics process?
8. What are the three types of data analytics?
9. Explain the descriptive analytics.
10. Explain the prescriptive analytics.
11. Explain the predictive analytics.
12. Describe inventory turnover,
13. What is receivables turnover?
14. What is asset turnover?

15. Describe the PPE turnover metric.
16. What is throughput?
17. What is throughput yield?
18. Define takt time.
19. Define cycle time.
20. What is cash-to-cash cycle (CCC)?
21. Define customer order cycle time.
22. What is stock turnover rate?
23. What are the three efficiency ratios and how can companies measure them?

Critical Thinking Questions

1. What is the major difference between big data and data analytics?
2. Why do companies gather data from various sources for big data analysis?
3. What is the major difference between gathering data for big data and data analytics?
4. What is the major difference between big data analytics process and data analytics process?
5. How can OSCM managers take advantage of the big data analytics process?
6. Describe the major differences between the three types of data analytics.
7. How are the metrics useful for firms?
8. How does inventory turnover help firms?
9. Company A's inventory turnover is 8.2 and company B's inventory turnover is 8.9. Which company is getting the most out of their inventory?
10. Which metric measures a company's efficiency in collecting its account receivable?
11. How does a company measure how effectively they use their assets to generate sales?
12. Does a company use an asset turnover or a PPE turnover to measure how effectively they generate revenues?
13. Does the percentage of products produced correctly without any rework in the manufacturing process measure throughput or throughput yield? Explain.
14. What is the difference between takt time and cycle time?
15. How is the inventory accuracy used in firms?
16. Choose three companies in an industry of your choice. Obtain the efficiency ratios of each of those firms and compare them to the industry. Describe how each firm is performing relative to each other as well.

Problem-Solving Questions

1. The monthly automobile sales of Jordan Autos are given in the Excel tab *autosales* in the *Datafile.xlsx* located on the student book website. Find the descriptive statistics using Excel's Data Analysis tool.
   a. Which vehicles give the best and worst MPG?
   b. Does MPG depend on any other given data?

2. Dyer Appliances services small home appliances. Find the descriptive statistics using Excel's Data Analysis tool. Interpret the various statistics of the service-time data that can found in the Excel tab *service1* in the *Datafile.xlsx* located on the student book website to solve this problem. What is the average service time for Dyer? How long it took Dyer to provide the fastest service and the longest service?

3. The Sweet Sweat Shop operates a tie manufacturing company in Southeast Asia. Data collected from the company is given in the Excel tab *sweatshop* in the *Datafile.xlsx* located on the student book website.
   a. How many men and women are employed in this company?
   b. How many men and women have more than 5 years of service?
   c. How many of the employees have a college degree and have work experience of more than 3 years?
   d. How many men have a college degree and a work experience of at least 4 years?

4. Newtech is a provider of the independent quality inspection certificates for certain products. Many companies have started to obtain the quality seals from Newtech. Newtech offers two subsequent certificates–InitCert and FinalSeal. Companies who are approved with the InitCert can only apply for the FInalSeal. The company has collated data for the 60 days of how many companies had been approved of InitCerts and how many had applied for the FInalSeal. Use the data from the Excel tab *newtech* in the *Datafile.xlsx* located on the student book website to solve this problem. If there are 75 InitCerts approved on a particular day, what would be the number of FInalSeals issued?

5. The law firm Skis, Pris, and Chris has collected the monthly data of their overhead costs and the billed hours to their clients. Use the data from the Excel tab *SPClawyers* in the *Datafile.xlsx* located on the student book website to solve this problem.

Month	Costs ($)	Hours
1	350,000	2,500
2	400,000	3,500
3	425,000	4,000
4	490,000	4,500
5	520,000	5,000
6	590,000	5,500

    a. Create a model. Is the fixed overhead cost of the model dependent on the client billed hours?

    b. What would be the overhead costs for a new client with billable hours of 6,000 using the model?

    c. If the law firm is looking for a margin of a quarter million dollars before the overhead costs, should the law firm accept the new client?

6. Use the data from the Excel tab *2022NFL* in the *Datafile.xlsx* located on the student book website to solve this problem.

    a. Is there a linear relationship between the passing yards and number of touchdowns?

    b. Using this model, predict the number of touchdowns if your favorite quarterback throws 1,800 yards next year.

    c. Explain the statistical significance of the correlation coefficient, the R-square, the adjusted R-square, the X-axis intercept, the slope, the *p*-values, and the residuals.

7. Ric Steves is an independent photographer. He has earned revenues from past events where he had a contract to take photographs, and he has prepared that data for analysis in the tab *steves* of the *Datafile.xlsx* located on the student book website. Is there any relationship between the number of photos and the revenues earned? If the next customer says that he wants at least 400 photos, how much should Ric charge that customer?

8. A quality engineer wants to allocate his time on two projects. The two projects, Project A and Project B, are planned for the next month and both projects are important. The costs of his time are known, and the quality engineer has a limited budget of $10,000. He feels that the Project B is more important than Project A and, therefore, decides to commit at least 75% of the time to Project B.

Project	Number of items inspected/hour	Cost/day
Project A	150	$400.00
Project B	300	$750.00

  a. The company has forecasted that the deluxe chairs sell more than the standard chairs. Identify the objective, the objective function, the criteria, and the decision variables.
  b. Formulate a linear optimization model using the content from Chapter 12.
  c. How much of his time should he spend on each project?

9. Erg Products produces two types of chairs—standard and deluxe. Deluxe chairs require additional time for final production. The standard chairs require 40 board feet of wood and 8 hours of labor, and deluxe chairs require 35 board feet of wood, 20 square feet of stainless steel, and 12 hours of labor. On that day, the company has 4,000 board feet of wood, 700 square feet of steel, and 350 hours of labor available. A standard chair makes a profit of $300, and a deluxe chair brings in a profit of $400. Identify the decision variables, objective function, and constraints in simple verbal statements.
  a. Identify the objective, the objective function, the criteria, and the decision variables.
  b. Formulate a linear optimization model using the content from Chapter 12.
  c. How many standard and deluxe chairs should they produce to maximize their profits on that day?

10. Om Univ Industries from Chicago manufactures yoga mats and other meditation products. Pertinent information on three of their products are shown below:

Raw material used	Product 1	Product 2	Product 3	Available Material (sq. in)
Leather	10	10	15	1,500
Vinyl	20	24	18	2,000
Fabric	40	45	35	2,500
Paper mache	10	14	18	1,200
Profit	50	45	40	

The company has forecasted that Product 3 will sell equal to or more than Product 1 and the Product 2 will sell equal to or more than Product 3. Develop an optimization model. How many of each product should be produced to earn the maximum profit?

11. Hot Pepper Industries produces two different spices. Spicy spice product can be produced at a rate of 15,000 pounds per hour and has a demand of 500 tons per week with a price per ton of $1,000. Super spicy spice can be produced at a rate of 7,000 pounds per hour and has a demand of 300 tons per week with a price of $1,500 per ton. The minimum capacity is 800 tons for every week, and the company

operated for a total of 180 hours/week. Determine the number of tons of each product by using a linear optimization model.

12. Analyze the efficiency of I&M Inc., an Italian and Mexican fast-food restaurant chain operating in Chicago using its 2021 financial data shown below. Analyze its efficiency ratios.

Cost of goods sold for 2021	$12,250,000
Average inventory for 2021	$550,000
Revenue for 2021	$ 25,000,000
Total assets for 2021	$1,250,000
Total credit sales for 2021	$15,000,000
Average accounts receivable for 2021	$2,275,000

13. SpinAir, Inc., a small home electric fan manufacturer, is considering analyzing their performance using the following data.

Description	2017	2018	2019	2020	2021
Total revenues	$30,900,500	$29,355,475	$33,372,540	$32,754,530	$34,707,442
Net income	$7,672,000	$7,518,560	$8,132,320	$8,132,320	$8,701,582
Total credit sales	$23,560,000	$22,146,400	$25,209,200	$24,502,400	$25,965,476
Average receivables	$8,452,000	$7,860,360	$8,959,120	$9,043,640	$9,407,076
Average inventory	$2,972,000	$2,823,400	$3,090,880	$3,090,880	$3,214,515
Cost of goods sold	$19,375,000	$18,987,500	$21,118,750	$19,956,250	$22,597,063
Total assets	$14,992,000	$13,792,640	$15,291,840	$15,291,840	$15,597,677

a. How are they performing year to year?
b. If the inventory turnover for the industry is 6.8 for the past 5 years, how is SpinAir performing?
c. If the receivables turnover for the industry is 3.2 for the past 5 years, how is SpinAir performing?
d. If the asset turnover for the industry is 2.15 for the past 5 years, how is SpinAir performing?

14. The inventory turnover ratio is an important evaluation metric to automobile dealerships. It is usually considered a warning sign for auto sales if auto dealerships begin carrying substantially more than about 60 days' worth of inventory on their lots. The local car dealerships in Roosevelt, Indiana, have shared the following data for 2021:

Dealership	Q1	Q2	Q3	Q4
Jordon Chevrolet	13.2	14	13.8	13.3
Oliver BMW	12.8	12.1	11.9	12.8
Classic Auto	11.4	11.9	12.1	12.5
Regal Vehicles	13.4	12.5	13.6	13.4
McNair Ford	10.9	11.2	11.2	11.4

    a. If 12 turns of inventory is the gold standard, which dealership is the most efficient in 2021?

    b. If holding 30 days of inventory is the gold standard, which dealership is the most efficient in 2021?

    c. What can the other dealerships do to improve their inventory turnover?

References

1. Garf, R. (2022). *How FedEx uses data to keep the supply chain moving.* Retrieved July 20, 2022, from https://www.salesforce.com/blog/retail-logistics/

2. FedEx. (2020). *FedEx and Microsoft join forces to transform commerce.* Retrieved July 20, 2022, from https://newsroom.fedex.com/newsroom/global/fedex-surround

3. Gudivada, V., Apon, A., & Ding, J. (2017). Data quality considerations for big data and machine learning: Going beyond data cleaning and transformations. *International Journal on Advances in Software, 10*(1), 1–20.

4. Choi, T. M., Wallace, S. W., & Wang, Y. (2018). Big data analytics in operations management. *Production and Operations Management, 27*(10), 1868–1883.

5. Wang, G., Gunasekaran, A., Ngai, E. W. T., & Papadopoulos, T. (2016). Big data analytics in logistics and supply chain management: Certain investigations for research and applications. *International Journal of Production Economics, 176*, 98–110.

6. Chaudhuri, A., Dukovska-Popovska, I., Subramanian, N., Chan, H. K., & Bai, R. (2018). Decision-making in cold chain logistics using data analytics: A literature review. *The International Journal of Logistics Management, 29*(3), 839–861.

7. Wu, P. J., Chen, M. C., & Tsau, C. K. (2017). The data-driven analytics for investigating cargo loss in logistics systems. *International Journal of Physical Distribution and Logistics Management, 47*(1), 68–83.

8. Campbell, A. M., & Van Woensel, T. (2019). Special issue on recent advances in urban transport and logistics through optimization and analytics. *Transportation Science, 53*(1), 1–5.

9. Mandal, S. (2019). The influence of big data analytics management capabilities on supply chain preparedness, alertness, and agility: An empirical investigation. *Information Technology and People, 32*(2), 297–318.

10. Chae, B. K., Olson, D., & Sheu, C. (2014). The impact of supply chain analytics on operational performance: A resource-based view. *International Journal of Production Research, 52*(16), 4695–4710.

11. Fernando, Y., Chidambaram, R. R. M., & Wahyuni, I. S. (2018). The impact of big data analytics and data security practices on service supply chain performance. *Benchmarking, 25*(9), 4009–4034.

12. HBR (2021). *How Capital One moved its data analytics to the cloud.* Retrieved July 28, 2022, from https://hbr.org/sponsored/2021/02/how-capital-one-moved-its-data-analytics-to-the-cloud#:~:text=Analytics%20is%20at%20the%20heart,its%20customers%20manage%20their%20finances

13. UPS. (2020). *UPS to enhance ORION with continuous delivery route optimization.* Retrieved July 29, 2022, from https://about.ups.com/us/en/newsroom/press-releases/innovation-driven/ups-to-enhance-orion-with-continuous-delivery-route-optimization.html#:~:text=ORION%20is%20a%20proprietary%20technology,About%20UPS

14. Stabel Kernel. (2022). *How data science is transforming business operations.* Retrieved July 20, 2022, from https://stablekernel.com/article/how-data-science-is-transforming-business-operations/

15. Gudivada, V., Apon, A., & Ding, J. (2017). Data quality considerations for big data and machine learning: Going beyond data cleaning and transformations. *International Journal on Advances in Software 10*(1), 1–20.

16. Kancharla, S. P., & Hegde, V. G. (2016). Inferences about supply chain practices using financial ratios. *Journal of Supply Chain and Operations Management, 14*(1), 144–161.

17. Johnson, M., & Templar, S. (2007). *The influence of supply chains on a company's financial performance.* Retrieved June 20, 2021, from https://core.ac.uk/download/pdf/370354.pdf

18. Yuesti, A., Rumanti, I. G. A. R., Kepramareni, P., & Suardhika, I. N. (2020). Role of corporate social responsibility in supply chain management and increasing corporate value. *International Journal of Supply Chain Management, 9*(1), 869–875.

19. Pradhan, D., Swain, P. K., & Dash, M. (2018). Effect of management accounting techniques on supply chain and firm performance: An empirical study. *International Journal of Mechanical Engineering and Technology, 9*(5), 1049–1057.

AUTOMATION IN OSCM AND SMART FACTORIES

Learning Objectives

- Describe the benefits of Industry 4.0 and smart factory.
- Explain the components and factors of digital transformation.
- Describe how forefront technologies are used in a smart factory.
- Describe how smart systems are used in a smart factory.
- Describe how intelligent automation systems are used in a smart factory.
- Explain the sustainability analysis of artificial intelligence (AI) in OSCM.
- Explain how AI is used in a smart factory.
- Describe how robots contribute to a smart factory.

Automation improves the quality of goods and services by enhancing accuracy and precision. Industries use various controls systems and robots for automating their operations. The control systems lower costs, increase productivity, and reduce waste. Robots are used as industrial automation machines to assist humans and simplify many activities in operations, especially tasks that humans perform in dangerous situations.

The top ten players offering industrial automation solutions in the world include Siemens, ABB, Emerson, Rockwell, Schneider, Honeywell, Mitsubishi, Omron, Fanuc, and Yokogawa[1].

- Siemens AG is a German multinational conglomerate and the largest industrial manufacturing company in Europe. The company is known for automation, medical imaging, laboratory diagnostics, and energy solutions.

© nitpicker/Shutterstock.com; © Piotr Piatrouski/Shutterstock.com; © Marlon Trottmann/ Shutterstock.com; © rafapress/Shutterstock.com; © ricochet64/Shutterstock.com; © Michael Vi/Shutterstock.com; © Ekaterina Kupeeva/Shutterstock.com; © Tada Images/ Shutterstock.com; © askarim/Shutterstock.com; © Alexander Tolstykh/Shutterstock.com; © nikshor/Shutterstock.com; © testing/Shutterstock.com

- ASEA Brown Boveri, or simply ABB, is a Swiss company. The company is known for industrial equipment, manufacturing robotics, and automation.
- Emerson Electric is an American multinational corporation. Emerson provides automation solutions, measurement instrumentation, and various valves and controllers.
- Rockwell is an American company. The company is one of the global leaders in providing automation and digital transformation, advanced process control, and industrial sensors.
- Schneider Electric SE is a French multinational company. The company specializes in automation and energy management.
- Honeywell is an American conglomerate. Honeywell Process Solutions (HPS) is a pioneer in automation control, monitoring, and safety systems.
- Mitsubishi Electric is a Japanese multinational manufacturing company. The company offers automation systems, controllers, computerized numerical controllers, and industrial robots.
- Omron is a Japanese electronics company. Omron manufactures industrial automation and electronic components.
- FANUC is a Japanese group of companies consisting of FANUC Corporation of Japan, Fanuc America from Michigan, and FANUC Europe from Luxembourg. FANUC is the largest maker of industrial robots in the world and computer numerical control systems.
- Yokogawa is a Japanese multinational electrical engineering and software company. Yokogawa provides industrial automation, testing, and measurement solutions.

Industry 4.0 and Smart Factory

The fourth industrial revolution, otherwise known as Industry 4.0, is revolutionizing the way companies manufacture and distribute their products. By integrating various innovative technologies into their operations, firms are getting ready to improve their products. Industry 4.0 takes advantage of the integration and synergies of both new and developing technologies.

The main expectation of Industry 4.0 is the growth of **smart factories**. A smart factory may be visualized as one equipped to collect data, analyze the collected data, and use that data to make intelligent operations decisions. A smart factory uses advanced technologies such as artificial intelligence (AI) and machine learning to analyze data, drives automated processes, and learns in a continuous fashion. The prime driver of smart factories is the digital transformation[2]. Digital transformation is the process of using digital technologies to create a new business process or modify an existing business process to streamline operations and supply chain. Businesses must keep up with new trends to compete and even survive.

Why is digital transformation important? Take, for example, Blockbuster Video, the popular video rental store in the early 2000s. Blockbuster owned more than 9,000 video-rental stores in the United States alone with more than 65 million registered customers worldwide. By 2010, the company declared bankruptcy. What happened? Netflix. The trend in this industry was to stream video content over the Internet, an example of digital transformation. Blockbuster did not implement digital transformation, and Netflix just did that. Netflix started out with renting DVDs to customers through regular mail and moved on to stream video content online to customers.

Implementing a smart factory is not always quite easy and straightforward. For many businesses, there are many challenges and risks to face. Making use of digital transformation tools is not always straightforward. Apart from the lack of knowledge of digitalization, computer skills, computer expertise, and lack of capital, the biggest problem many businesses face is where and how to implement digital transformation. Companies need right leadership and resources to drive digital transformation and change their businesses to use advanced technologies.

At its core, smart factories require the integration of forefront technology, smart systems, and intelligent automation as shown in Figure 14-1.

The components of forefront technology include cloud computing, cyber security, and system integration. Computer and telecommunication technology have helped industrial revolutions in the past, and that is no exception to Industry 4.0. The Internet of Things (IoT), 3D printing, and simulation are the components of smart systems. Smart systems use forefront technology to enable smart factories to process their operations. The future of manufacturing is about smart, autonomous, and linked systems to produce custom and smart products. Augmented reality, artificial intelligence, and robotics are the components of intelligent automation. As shown in Figure 14-1, smart factories are equipped with automation using sophisticated technologies.

Industry 4.0
Industry 4.0 takes advantage of the integration of new and developing technologies and the interconnectivity of systems, artificial intelligence, and automation.

Smart Factory
A smart factory may be visualized as one equipped to collect data, analyze the collected data, and use that data to make intelligent operations decisions.

Digital transformation
Digital transformation is the process of using digital technologies to create new business processes or modify existing business processes to streamline operations and supply chain.

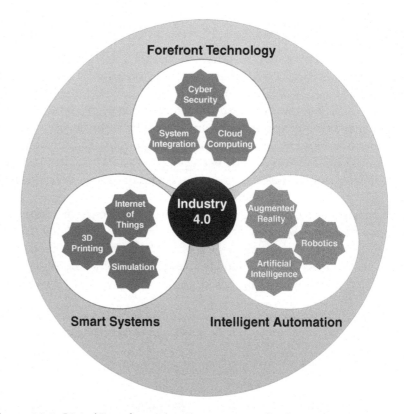

Figure 14-1 Digital Transformation Components of Industry 4.0

This chapter focuses on operations and supply chain management (OSCM). Both current and future operations and supply chain managers need to know about latest advancements in technology in order to be ready for digital transformation and smart factories. In this section and the next, we will discuss the technologies, systems, and automation processes used in OSCM at smart factories.

FROM PRACTICE: Smart Factory at Whirlpool Corporation

© Grzegorz Czapski/
Shutterstock.com

Whirlpool, the American home appliances manufacturer, has been implementing many innovative solutions and applications through their Industry 4.0 Smart Factories initiatives. Whirlpool considers all resources, including machines, robots, equipment, people, organization, processes, and information systems, to be interconnected by computing power as an integral part of the Industry 4.0. in

Whirlpool EMEA (Europe, Middle East, Africa); the company has implemented more than 15 research and innovation projects to design hybrid workstations and improve robots' sensing capability for people and machines to work in constant cooperation. Using the Google Cloud platform, the company has enabled workers to perform the remote monitoring of all their factory operations to make effective decisions[3].

Forefront Technologies for Smart Factory

Forefront technologies are an important part of digital transformation. The main technologies that operations and supply chain managers should be aware are cloud computing, cybersecurity, and system integration. These three principal technologies form the forefront technology of digital transformations.

Cloud Computing

The term "cloud" is just a representation for the Internet. We are used to storing documents and files in our computer. Instead of storing on our computers, some of us may opt to store somewhere else using the Internet and that is called the cloud computing. Simply put, cloud computing means storing and accessing data, information, apps, and programs over the Internet instead of a computer's hard drive. There are apps such as OneDrive or Box for personal use. Many of you may already use Apple's cloud service for online storage, backup, and synchronization of your mail, contacts, and calendar as well as listening to music instead of storing on your iPhones. Many businesses are opting to store their data and use applications from cloud computing service providers such as Amazon Web Services (AWS), Google Cloud Platform, and Microsoft's Azure.

> **Cloud Computing**
> The method of storing and accessing data and using apps and programs over the Internet.

The cloud computing providers are equipped with necessary hardware (like your computer), software (like Microsoft Excel), and the means to access them from anywhere in the world using the Internet. They also provide unlimited storage space for documents, files, and data. Furthermore, businesses need not put forth capital to buy the necessary computers and software—they can just use the cloud computing provider's resources for a fee.

Businesses can use these cloud computing providers in the same way! They can use the super-costly software and store all their data at a fraction of the cost of buying the same software. Firms can take advantage of the flexible resources and the economies of scale by using cloud computing. For example, Facebook uses Amazon Web Services cloud computing to store information in addition to its own hyperscale datacenter facilities. Using cloud services, smart factories can be interconnected to provide high-quality, inexpensive, on-demand manufacturing services.

Cybersecurity

The security of data, information, and processes are of great concern to any company. When firms are smart, security risks increase as these firms rely on many of their processes connected through the Internet. In general, businesses and individuals face the threat of malicious attacks by unauthorized users. These digital attacks called **cyberattacks** are aimed at retrieving, modifying, or destroying sensitive information, extorting money from companies, or disrupting their business process. The cybersecurity process involves the protection of computer systems and networks from theft or damage to data, hardware, or software as well as from the misuse of information stored in those systems.

Cybersecurity is an important technology in smart factories and smart operations. About 88% of company executives consider cyberattacks to be a direct threat to operations[4]. Businesses are experiencing a deluge of data as the number of users, devices, transactions, and applications have increased over the years. This increase in data has highlighted the importance of cybersecurity. Furthermore, the sophistication of cyber attackers had compounded the problem.

Smart factories have computer systems that are highly interconnected and integrated. The safety and security of these systems, their communications with other devices, and the data collected from them are of utmost importance. Moreover, if a company has an operations or supply chain business process that enables it to be successful, that process has to be protected from digital attacks using cybersecurity methods.

> **Cybersecurity**
> Cybersecurity is the practice to protect systems and data that are connected to Internet from such unauthorized users.

System Integration

System integration is the task of making applications, computers, and database systems work together seamlessly and efficiently. For example, a smart factory that produces high-end electronic components may require a clean room tied into their local heating, ventilation, and air conditioning (HVAC) system as well as their enterprise resource planning (ERP) system. System integration also involves integration of data collected from various sources as well. This type of integration enables various disparate systems to "talk to each other," thereby enabling the flow of information between those systems and a reduction in operational costs.

System integration consists of two dimensions—the horizontal and the vertical integration of all operational systems and processes in an organization. An example of horizontal and vertical integrations in a manufacturing firm is shown in Figure 14-2. A horizontal integration involves connecting all the systems, processes, and data pertaining to a company's supply chain. If a company has multiple production facilities, the horizontal integration of all systems, activities, and data in those locations must be shared seamlessly. This includes all the upstream and the downstream supply chain partners. The vertical integration involves the alignment of processes, machines, and data pertaining

> **System Integration**
> System integration is the task of making applications, computers, and database systems work together seamlessly and efficiently.

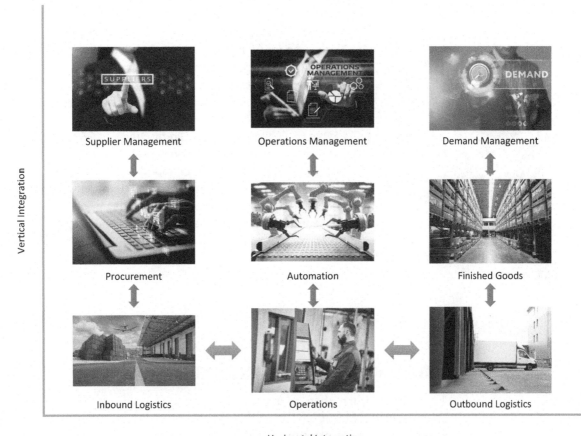

© Kritsana Maimeetook/Shutterstock.com; © Alexander Supertramp/Shutterstock.com; © Den Rise/Shutterstock.com;
© 13_Phunkod/Shutterstock.com; © Thomas Soellner/Shutterstock.com; © sarawuth wannasathit/Shutterstock.com;
© KAMONRAT/Shutterstock.com; © Dmitry Kalinovsky/Shutterstock.com; © New Africa/Shutterstock.com

Figure 14-2 Horizontal and Vertical Integration for Industry 4.0

to the internal operations of a company. The vertical integration is to extract the potential synergy of all internal processes and data within an organization, including production, quality assurance, product management, research, development, sales, marketing, customer service, information systems, and so on. The alignment of vertical and horizontal integration enhances automation that improves productivity.

FROM PRACTICE: GE and AWS

General Electric (GE), the American conglomerate, initiated its digital transformation in 2014. The company chose Amazon Web Service (AWS) in 2017. More than 2,000 cloud-based apps and services are available for its employees for use from AWS. The company's cloud strategy is AWS

so that it can concentrate on its core competencies. The reason for GE to go to cloud computing is to obtain the ability to quickly develop and deploy applications, lower their operating costs, the ability to scale up and down their services and hardware requirements rapidly, and benefit from an end-to-end security. Bill Ruh, the CEO of GE Digital, and Chief Digital Officer of GE says, "Our cloud architecture supports customers' varying degrees of opportunities to be found in the Industrial Internet, from capturing and analyzing time series data generated by the multiple sensors on a gas turbine to delivering large object data like a 3D MRI image to a doctor for diagnosis. If you have really important things generating a variety of big data at velocity, we can help manage it, demystify it, and turn it into actionable insight."[5]

Smart Systems for Smart Factory

In manufacturing, there is a need for integrated resource planning and manufacturing execution. Typically, resource planning is accomplished by enterprise resource planning (ERP) systems and manufacturing is implemented by manufacturing systems. The integration of these two systems will bring forth smart manufacturing—intelligent products, intelligent manufacturing processes, and intelligent services that form the core of smart manufacturing.

Smart systems are another important part of digital transformation. Smart systems use forefront technologies to accomplish many important tasks in a smart factory. The main smart systems that operations and supply chain managers should be aware of are simulation, Internet of Things (IoT), and additive printing or 3D printing. These three principal technology-infused systems form the smart systems of digital transformation.

Simulation
Simulation is a computer model whereby firms mimic an operation of an existing or proposed system.

Simulation

Simulation is a computer model whereby firms mimic an operation of an existing or proposed system. By using a simulation model, a company can test various scenarios of the existing or proposed system. The results of a simulation can provide information to make decisions. Firms have used simulation for a long time to understand, enhance, and optimize manufacturing and service systems. Over the years, simulation has evolved and smart factories can use the new simulation techniques to enhance manufacturing technologies.

For example, simulation can be used to investigate various workload and delivery scenarios to estimate the time required for delivery of products[6]. Simulations of production processes provides the knowledge of machine downtimes and helps engineers to shorten downtimes and changes so that they can reduce the possibility of production failures[7]. Simulation has been used extensively in supply chain management. The main topics of supply chain simulation are reduction of supply chain risks and transportation problems[8].

Internet of Things

The Internet of things (IoT) is a term used for machines or other physical objects equipped with sensors and software. A sensor is a device that senses a physical phenomenon. For example, a thermometer is a device that senses the physical phenomenon—the temperature of a human body. The machines or the IoT can process the sensed physical phenomenon using the software that is built in the device and send the sensed information to a computer. Sensors can connect and exchange data with each other and other devices and systems over the Internet. The ultimate sensor example is a human being. Humans sense by their vision, hearing, smell, taste, and touch. This sensory information travels to the brain for processing though our nervous system.

Our body is a classic example of sensor fusion. For example, you want to buy a desk for your home office. Your go to a store and find a desk that you like. You feel the smooth, grey-color desktop. Your eyes sense the object, the grey-colored desktop. Your fingers sense the smoothness. Your nose senses the environment of the desk. These senses are sent to your brain. The brain fuses all the sensory inputs to result in what you see—a smooth grey-colored desktop in its store environment. In the world of smart factories, sensor fusion plays a similar role. By integrating inputs from multiple sensors, the sensor fusion produces prominent levels of recognition that results in accurate and reliable information than individual sensor data.

The basic purpose of IoT is to let devices self-report sensed data in real-time and use sensor fusion to provide accurate information. From machines in a factory to refrigerators in a house, IoT can extract data and provide that data to maintain devices or for further analysis to use those devices effectively and efficiently. For example, sensors in vehicles transmit information on gas or electricity usage to their servers over the Internet, which are then sent to the owner's cellphones as information.

Additive Manufacturing

Additive manufacturing or 3D printing is the creation of a three-dimensional object from a digital 3D computer model. In traditional manufacturing, objects are made by the removal of material until the final product is complete. But additive manufacturing is the process of adding layer on layer of material to make a finished product. The process uses data from computer-aided design

Internet of Things (IoT) The Internet of things (IoT) is a term used for machines or other physical objects equipped with sensors and software.

Sensor Fusion By integrating inputs from multiple sensors, sensor fusion produces important levels of recognition that results in accurate and reliable information than individual sensor data.

Additive Manufacturing The process of adding material typically layer by layer over a base layer of material.

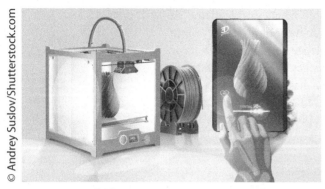

3D printing of a flower vase

(CAD) software or 3D object scanners to direct robots to deposit, join, or solidify material and make objects, typically layer by layer over a base layer of material.

One of the main advantages is that there is not much wastage of material in this process. This process works very well and is proven to be very economical for producing smaller number of parts. Since the amount of material removed is less, the process results in a lower cost and more efficient use of the material than is possible in most traditional manufacturing techniques. Aerospace, automotive, medical, and transportation companies have adopted additive manufacturing.

Many firms are exploring additive manufacturing. To create an object using additive manufacturing, a design of the final product is completed first using the CAD software. The CAD software then translates the design into a layer-by-layer framework for the additive manufacturing machine. The framework is sent to the 3D printer, which creates the object. Additive manufacturing uses any number of materials, from polymers, metals, and ceramics to foams, gels, and even biomaterials. As additive manufacturing processes improved, companies used those processes to create molds that can be used to produce final products. Molds are typically used in making toys, for example. Additive manufacturing is costly and time-consuming[9]. Companies like Boeing, Honeywell, and General Electric have begun using additive manufacturing in their business processes.

FROM PRACTICE: Sensor Fusion for AGVs

Sensor fusion is essential when firms use **Automatic Guided Vehicles** (AGV) on factory and distribution center floors. Sensors act as the "eyes and ears" of AGV. Sensors are used for functions such as navigation, guidance, safety, material handling, and obstacle avoidance of AVS. Different sensors are used for different functions. *Safety bumper contact sensors* are used to stop the AVS in case of contact with any object such as a person, pallet, or machine. *Safety Laser Scanners*—sensing devices designed to protect personnel from injury—scan an area, and, if a person or object is detected, a signal is sent to stop the nearby machine or hazard to prevent injury. Collisions with any object must be avoided. *LIDAR sensors, or vision cameras with Time-of-Flight (TOF) technology*, are used to detect all objects that can potentially cause collision. For AGV's automatic navigation and to know their own position, a *map-based localization system* and sensors such as *LiDAR, magnetic tape sensors, ultrasonic, cameras,* and so on are used. AGV safety systems must be reliable and comply with severe international standards, and they use various contact, noncontact, and positioning sensors. All their sensors are integrated as sensor fusion by onboard computers.

FROM PRACTICE: 3D Printing at L'Oreal

L'Oréal, the French personal care company, is the world's largest cosmetics company. The company has successfully developed products for hair color, skincare, sunscreen, makeup, perfume, and hair care. L'Oréal has been using 3D printing or additive manufacturing for a long time to make packaging prototypes, furniture prototypes, point-of-sale furniture prototypes, prototype injection molds, quality control tools, and spare parts. Out of its 40 factories worldwide, 23 of them are equipped with additive

© asharkyu/Shutterstock.com

manufacturing capabilities. Using a technology called laser powder bed fusion, L'Oréal uses additive manufacturing to make the La Maison Jasmins Marzipane Lancôme collection, a limited series of 50 ultra-luxury, numbered copies. Additive manufacturing has shortened the lifecycle for the company products. For example, they can design and print a new bottle in a few days rather than subcontract with longer lead times. The technology has enabled the company to create designs that are impossible with traditional technologies[9].

Intelligent Automation for Smart Factory

Intelligent automation is the third and final important part of the digital transformation. Intelligent automation uses forefront technologies and smart systems to accomplish many important tasks in a smart factory. The smart systems that operations and supply chain managers should be aware are augmented reality, artificial intelligence, and robotics. These three principal technology-infused and smart systems form the intelligent automation of digital transformation.

Augmented Reality Augmented reality (AR) is a real-world computer simulation that allows a user to see, move around, and interact in a 3D world through a computer screen as though it is real. AR in operations is capable of generating information about a manufacturing or service system.

Augmented Reality

Operations activities in some firms use a technology called augmented reality. Augmented reality (AR) is a real-world computer simulation. It allows a user to see, move around, and interact in a 3D world through a computer screen as though it is real. AR in operations is defined as a computer system that is capable of generating information about a manufacturing or service system. AR devices use motion and position sensors for applications in the field, the plant, or on the factory floor to monitor the progress of an assembly, provide real-time feedback, and incorporate automated inspection for quality control.

AR has been used in different engineering applications such as product design, modeling, shop floor controls, process simulation, manufacturing planning, training, testing, and verification[10]. By employing AR in various operations and supply chain processes, firms can prevent costly mistakes. AR can be used to enhance the collaboration of humans and machines and increase productivity in organizations. Using AR, remotely located employees can connect with machines, troubleshoot, and work on problems in business operations, thereby reducing manufacturing time significantly. AR can be a powerful tool for maintenance and service technicians. In a smart factory, the complexity of manufacturing requires an AR system to provide the maintenance staff real-time diagnostics of machines, video recording of maintenance instructions, and assistance from an expert who is remotely located. For example, an AR device can provide engineering data to an expert who is located remotely and that expert can guide a technician through a procedure. This enhances quality, reduces machine downtime, and increases first-time problem fixes.

Artificial Intelligence Artificial intelligence (AI) is a computer-based technology designed to mimic human intelligence and behavior to accomplish tasks in OSCM.

Artificial Intelligence

Artificial intelligence (AI) is a computer-based technology designed to mimic human intelligence and behavior to accomplish tasks in OSCM. The intelligence in AI is from learning and adaptation of the environment around a manufacturing system and the ability to use various sources of information. The researchers and practitioners of AI draw from the following three major sources:

1. Vast amounts of information collected by businesses due to advancements in information and communication technology, such as Internet of Things (IoT);
2. Innovative technologies to recognize images, voices, sounds, and written documents; and
3. Innovative technologies that solve problems, continuously learn, and improve based on learning.

As we discussed in Chapter 1, sustainability focuses on reducing environmental and social impacts without affecting profitability. As shown in Figure 14-3,

Five dimensions—namely, societal, environmental, technical, economical, and individual—are used to describe the opportunities and risks for sustainability of AI[11]. Both the opportunities and the risks associated with sustainability of AI in OSCM can be described using those five dimensions. However, we will include some of the organizational factors to be a part of the sustainability analysis when we consider AI in OSCM. Therefore, the five main sustainability factors of AI in OSCM are social, technical, environmental, organizational, and economical. Businesses must understand the impacts of these sustainability factors on their operations and supply chain in order to consider AI for their organizational benefits.

Social

Some of the social factors include trust, social media management, and ethical use of technology. The activities in companies that use AI must be trustworthy in the eyes of customers, suppliers, and society in general. Legitimacy and authenticity must be maintained to induce trust. Using AI promises great benefits such as increase in productivity. Companies face danger by relying too much on AI, as there is an inherent risk to replace employees with too much automation. The ethical use of AI is an important aspect of employing AI in automation. For example, a 37-year-old Japanese employee was killed by an AI robot in 1981[12]. The robot pushed the employee into an adjacent machine by mistake. With the advent of AI, companies have to strengthen their positions by strengthening their legal frameworks. Another important facet is social media automation. As the number of users increase, manual management of users becomes increasingly challenging. Many firms are planning to use AI to manage social media networks and users[13].

Technical

Some of the AI technologies include robots, automation, neural networks, deep learning, visual and speech recognition, and information extracted from sensors. Deep learning and neural networks have significantly improved object detection, object recognition, and speech recognition. Object detection and recognition is used in many applications, including in security and warfare. Robots and automation have been at the forefront of manufacturing technologies. Both AR and additive manufacturing technologies have improved manufacturing in terms of productivity and efficiency. However, AI lacks certain crucial human qualities, such as wisdom, empathy, and compassion.

Environmental

Environmental problems such as waste and pollution can be reduced by using advanced technologies such as AI. AI can be used to predict natural disasters such as earthquakes, tsunamis, and hurricanes. Autonomous electric vehicles

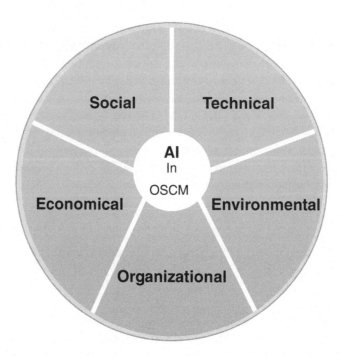

Figure 14-3 Sustainability analysis of Artificial Intelligence in Operations and Supply Chain Management

can reduce greenhouse gas emissions. Advanced technologies produce more e-waste which negatively impacts environmental health.

Organizational

Productivity in organizations has been increasing over the years because of advanced automation[14]. According to a research study, a person working beyond normal working hours has a significantly higher risk of developing issues in their mental and emotional well-being[15], including depression, burnout, anxiety, sleep disturbances, and chronic heart disease[16]. Automation and AI can help employees of an organization to lead a healthier life. AI-powered digital assistants, analytical tools, and robots could help individuals in terms of working for fewer hours, increase in work efficiency, and reduction in work-related injuries[17]. However, the fear of unemployment due to automation may lead to anxiety-related mental health issues.

Economical

Major economies of the world, including the UK, France, and the United States, are investing in AI technologies. Big companies such as IBM and Microsoft, and major institutions such as MIT, are investing billions of dollars in

AI research. The advent of AI may pressure the employment and wages of the low-skilled workers[18]. To avoid such a mishap, low-skilled workers must be trained to acquire new skills and work effectively with automated robots.

AI is a significant part of Industry 4.0. AI technologies are currently used in manufacturing and retail industries. Now, we will look at how AI is used in the following areas of OSCM:

- Preventive maintenance
- Demand management
- Quality control
- Transportation.

Preventive Maintenance

Businesses generate vast amounts of data through the machines they employ at their facilities. The sensors and control systems of these machines transact data. For example, companies generate process data from sensors, such as coolant temperatures; operational data, such as machine downtime; and quality data from inspections, such as diameters. AI uses a technology called **neural networks** to process those data and help managers make intelligent decisions. Neural network is a computer software that discovers patterns in data and then use those patterns to predict future data. For example, neural network software can learn from the machine downtime data of similar machines in different conditions and forecast future downtimes of those machines before they actually occur. AI can monitor manufacturing equipment from a host of sensors to detect anomalies while manufacturing. For example, noise changes in a machine can be identified as future problems with that machine. Mueller Industries, a manufacturer of industrial products, is testing a system that can predict future machine problems[19]. With such predictions, firms can implement preventive maintenance to avoid or prevent costly downtimes.

Demand Management

Demand management problems are complex and nonlinear in nature. The supply chain is prone to fluctuations in product demand and delays in material and product deliveries. Therefore, one of the key issues in supply chain is how to improve the forecasting accuracy and minimize the uncertainty of supply chain management. Many companies use AI technologies such as neural network in addition to the forecasting techniques such as time series methods that we discussed in Chapter 2.

AI is used to manage inventory and predict future demand. For example, Wal-Mart uses AI to forecast product demand based on local weather—steaks sell more than ground beef during cloudy and windy weather[20]. National Grid, an energy company operating in the UK, uses a software developed by Google called "DeepMind," which uses weather-related data to predict accurately the variations in supply and demand[21].

Quality Control

Computer vision is a system where computers obtain vision data through cameras. Computer vision can perform many inspection tasks more accurately and efficiently than humans can. For example, an aircraft engine manufacturer applies computer vision to inspect turbofan blades. The vision system checks several hundred attributes of a turbofan blade in a few minutes, thus enabling the company to inspect every turbofan blade rather than random samples[22]. Defect inspection and detection of flaws are of significant importance in quality management. Keyence, a Japanese company, specializes in fiber optic sensors, photoelectric sensors, laser sensors, measurement systems, machine vision, barcode readers, laser markers, and digital microscopes. Using AI, their sensors and vision detection systems can detect flaws in manufactured parts by learning and visually inspecting the characteristics to decide whether the inspected part is good or bad.

Traditionally, humans conduct inspection of fabrics in textile industries. Advantech, a Taiwanese company, provides an end-to-end solution using AI to improve manufacturing processes and quality control in textile industries. Their systems can automatically inspect defects, identify the most subtle defects, and ensure high-quality products. AI-enabled robotic arms can pick and remove both the good and the defective products. Using robots equipped with AI capability, the company's technology can significantly shorten textile manufacturing from weeks to days to hours.

Cognex Corporation, the American manufacturer, makes machine vision systems, software, and sensors used in automated manufacturing to inspect and identify parts, detect defects, verify product assembly, and guide assembly robots. The company has installed over 3.5 million systems in facilities around the world. Cognex solutions help manufacturers improve quality by eliminating defects. The vision and barcode reading capabilities lead to lower errors in production, which means lower manufacturing costs. The deep learning tools of Cognex can perform inspection, classification, and character recognition more effectively than humans. Deep learning uses neural network technology to distinguish anomalies and locate deformed tools. Laser optics technology is used in 3D vision systems to capture high-quality images for analysis. Vision applications are used in automotive, food and beverage (F&B), electronics, and pharmaceutical industries.

FROM PRACTICE: Cognex's Machine Vision

Cognex Corporation, the American manufacturer, makes machine vision systems, software, and sensors used in automated manufacturing to inspect and identify parts, detect defects, verify product assembly, and guide assembly robots. The company has installed over 3.5 million systems in facilities around the world. Cognex solutions help manufacturers to improve quality by eliminating defects. The vision and barcode reading capabilities lead to lower errors in production, which means lower manufacturing costs. The deep learning tools of Cognex can perform inspection, classification, and character recognition more effectively than humans. Deep learning uses neural network technology to distinguish anomalies and locate deformed tools. Laser optics technology is used in 3D vision systems to capture high-quality images for analysis. The vision applications are used in automotive, food and beverage (F&B), electronics, and pharmaceutical industries.

© asharkyu/Shutterstock.com

Transportation

An autonomous vehicle (AV) is a vehicle that is able to operate itself and perform the necessary functions without any human intervention. Autonomous vehicles receive inputs from various sensors, and a sensor fusion system integrates the sensory inputs. Sensor fusion detects the absolute and relative location of a vehicle and its surrounding environment at all times when the vehicle is in the facility or on the road in order to meet the three goals of AV:

- Detect other vehicles, lanes, roads, and pedestrians,
- Detect traffic signs and road conditions, and
- Avoid collisions.

The data obtained from various sensors are integrated and fed into AI algorithms to attain the three goals. Different sensors are used for different purposes. For example, laser imaging, detection, and ranging (LIDAR) and thermal cameras are used to detect the surrounding environment. For example, road detection can recognize the boundary between the road and the background under various weather conditions. AI techniques for image recognition and image processing are utilized to find the roads. Global positioning system (GPS) and global navigation satellite systems (GNSS) are used for identifying the location of the vehicle.

FROM PRACTICE: NFL Goes AI

The National Football League (NFL) uses all sorts of statistics during a football game. Amazon Web Services (AWS) and NFL have teamed to use AI machine learning techniques to enable statistical models on the cloud. The models evaluate the quarterback passing performance. It computes the

probability of completion of a pass from a quarterback based on the distance of the pass, the separation of a receiver from the defenders on the field, the amount of pressure from defense, and so on. The model can predict the 4th down conversion probability of an offense. The data from the box score, the data collected from the stadium, and other collected data are fed into algorithms as training set of data. They are processed by computers on cloud and used to predict the outcomes[23]. Such information is provided to coaches, offensive coordinators, defensive coordinators, broadcasters, and fans!

Robotics

> **Robotics** Robotics in OSCM involves operation and use of robots to replicate human actions.

Robotics in OSCM involves the operation and use of robots to replicate human actions. Robots are used to do repetitive tasks in manufacturing. For example, in a vehicle assembly line where car seats have to be placed in each car, robots are used to place the car seats. Robots also collaborate with humans in OSCM. In Amazon's fulfillment centers, robots work alongside humans. These robots, programmed to watch out for humans so they will not collide and cause accidents, bring items to human pickers so they can be packaged and labeled for dispatch[24]. Robots are also employed in jobs that pose a danger or in jobs that can be harmful to humans. For example, robots are employed to handle corrosive or toxic materials. Robots can also work around the clock to do the most boring jobs. They are also used to perform repetitive tasks such as painting, spraying, and welding. For example, robots have been used to spray a hazardous insulation material on to the external tanks that were used in NASA's space shuttle programs.

Industrial robots are programmable to perform routine tasks using computers and a control device called a *teach pendant*. Using a teach pendant, a robotic engineer can teach the robot to perform certain actions. For example, using the teach pendent, a robotic engineer can teach a robot to pick a part from a machine, lift it, move the part, and place it on a nearby pallet through multiple instructions. The robot's memory stores these instructions as sequence of actions. Upon a request for execution of these instructions, the programmed robot then plays back the sequence to perform the instructed actions over and over again.

Industrial robots are used in all types of manufacturing and service businesses. Robots are also a big

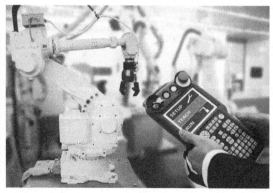

Training a robot using a teach pendant

part of Industry 4.0 automation. Industrial robots can be classified into five distinct types:

- Manipulator robot
- Selective Compliance Assembly Robot Arm (SCARA) robot
- Mobile robot
- Delta robot
- Gantry robot.

Manipulator Robot

The most commonly used robot in the manufacturing industry is the manipulator robot. Manipulator robots consist of a robot body and a robot arm. The single arm is equipped with an end effector. An end effector has two to three fingers that can be used like a human hand. Manipulator robots can perform several tasks, such as assembly, welding, packaging, inspection, material removal, and additive manufacturing. They are costlier than many other types of robots. They are not suitable for high-speed application due to the complex construction of joints in their arm.

© Jenson/Shutterstock.com

Selective Compliance Assembly Robot Arm (SCARA) Robot

This type of robot is most commonly used where high speed and high accuracy are required. These robots can work fast because they have fewer moving joints. SCARA robots are typically used where repeatability of performance is of significant importance. Repeatability is crucial in small assembly applications where tolerances are small. Certain applications like circuit board manufacturing have small tolerances to work with, and these robots are excellent for such applications. Since these robots are lightweight and small, they are really suitable for applications in limited space. They are also less expensive than manipulator robots. SCARA robots have limited ability to work around or reach inside an object because of their smaller arm length.

© Aleksandra Suzi/Shutterstock.com

Mobile Robot

Mobile robot, as the name suggests, is mobile and not stationary. This robot consists of an automated platform that can move items from one place to another. These robots are used for carrying tools and spare parts in plants and

© Tridsanu Thopet/Shutterstock.com

distribution centers or in places where products must be transported from one place to another. These robots are equipped with sensors and cameras. They extract information about their surroundings using the sensors and cameras. They also have a computer that enables them to process sensory inputs, analyze the processed information, and make decisions to avoid obstacles and reach their destination.

Delta Robot

A delta robot has a unique configuration of three arms that act as an end effector. They are also called "spider" robots and are lightweight in nature. Because they are lightweight, they are great for operations that need speed. They are usually used for picking and packing in plants and distribution centers. However, they have a short radius of range of movements due to their configuration, typically half the reach of a SCARA robot. They are employed mostly in packaging and medical and pharmaceutical industries. Delta robots are used in electronic industry's clean rooms where precision assembly operations are essential.

Source: Free SVG.

Gantry Robot

Gantry robots are robots customized for a particular operation in a company. They are also called Cartesian robots. Gantry robots are positioned around the intended workspace as an elevated structure suspended over two parallel rails. The robots are positioned at an elevation to maximize the workspace. The length and capacity of the structure and the robots restrict the operational workspace. A fitting example of a gantry robot is the modern carwash. Gantry robots are low-cost compared to other types of robots. They are used in many industries where operations such as welding, painting, washing, spraying, and machining have to accomplished around large objects.

© Tei Sinthip/Shutterstock.com

The manufacturing industry has used robots since the 1960s and has been open to embracing new technologies[25]. The future manufacturing company will be a smart factory adopting innovative technologies that are integrated with its operations and supply chain activities. Currently, robots in manufacturing work in environments that are otherwise dangerous or tedious for humans. Robots can achieve a prominent level of accuracy and productivity. Integrating them with capabilities like voice and image recognition will help industries to re-create complex human tasks. Robots can detect defects and take corrective actions efficiently.

Smart factories when equipped with advanced sensors, embedded software, and robots become more efficient. The operations data combined with ERP, supply chain, and customer service data can create better and accurate information for decision making. Using IoT devices in smart factories and using AI-powered business models can reduce manufacturing waste and errors, which can further save money and time.

FROM PRACTICE: Robots Use AI at Ford

© Jenson/Shutterstock.com

The assembly of vehicle transmission systems is a complex process. Operators install the torque converters manually, and it is a challenging process from an ergonomics and safety standpoint. Currently, robots help to assemble torque convertors for cars at a Ford Transmission Plant in Livonia, Michigan. The robots use AI. Ford has teamed with Symbio Robotics, a startup from California, in this project. The robots are programmed and managed with Symbio's AI software platform to assemble transmissions for the Bronco Sport, the Escape, and the Edge vehicle models. The robots learn from previous attempts to assemble transmissions in an efficient manner using AI. Using the Symbio technology, the cycle time at Ford has improved by 15%. The Ford production managers believe that AI can be used to improve the performance of existing automation and workforce, which is extremely important when using AI in factories[26,27].

Summary

- The fourth industrial revolution is called Industry 4.0.
- Industry 4.0 is revolutionizing the way companies manufacture and distribute their products by integrating various innovative technologies into their operations.
- Industry 4.0 takes advantage of the integration and synergies of new and developing technologies.

- A smart factory may be visualized as one equipped to collect data, analyze the collected data, and use that data to make intelligent decisions in operations.
- A smart factory uses advanced technologies such as artificial intelligence (AI) and machine learning to analyze data, drives automated processes, and learns as it goes. The prime driver of smart factories is digital transformation.
- Digital transformation is the process of using digital technologies to create new business processes or modify existing business processes to streamline operations and supply chain.
- Smart factories require the integration of forefront technology, smart systems, and intelligent automation.
- The components of forefront technology include cloud computing, cyber security, and system integration.
- Internet of Things (IoT), 3D printing, and simulation are components of smart systems. Smart systems use forefront technology to enable smart factories to process their operations.
- Augmented reality (AR), artificial intelligence (AI), and robotics are components of intelligent automation.
- The term "cloud" is just a representation for the Internet.
- Cloud computing is the method of storing and accessing data and using apps and programs over the Internet.
- Cybersecurity is the practice of protecting systems and data that are connected to the Internet from unauthorized users or hackers or data theft.
- Smart factories have computer systems that are highly interconnected and integrated. The safety and security of these systems, their communications with other devices, and the data collected from them are of utmost importance.
- System integration is the task of making applications, computers, and database systems work together seamlessly and efficiently.
- System integration consists of two dimensions—horizontal integration and vertical integration of all operational systems and processes in an organization.
- Resource planning is accomplished by enterprise resource planning (ERP) systems, and manufacturing is implemented by manufacturing systems. The integration of these two systems will bring forth smart manufacturing.
- Simulation is a computer model that mimics the operation of an existing or proposed system and helps firms see the potential for performance as well as the errors likely to occur in the system's operations in future.
- The Internet of things (IoT) is a term used for machines or other physical objects equipped with sensors and software.

- A sensor is a device that senses a physical phenomenon.
- Sensors can connect and exchange data with each other and other devices and systems over the Internet.
- By integrating inputs from multiple sensors, sensor fusion produces prominent levels of recognition that results in accurate and reliable information than individual sensor data.
- Additive printing is the process of adding material typically layer by layer over a base layer of material.
- Augmented reality (AR) is a real-world computer simulation that allows a user to see, move around, and interact in a 3D world through a computer screen as though it is real. AR in operations is capable of generating information about a manufacturing or service system.
- Artificial intelligence (AI) is a computer-based technology designed to mimic human intelligence and behavior to accomplish tasks in operations and supply chain management (OSCM).
- The five main sustainability factors of AI in OSCM are social, technical, environmental, organizational, and economical.
- Social factors include trust, social media management, and ethical use of technology.
- Some of the technologies include robots, automation, neural networks, deep learning, visual and speech recognition, and information extracted from sensors.
- Deep learning and neural networks have significantly improved object detection, object recognition, and speech recognition.
- Environmental problems such as waste and pollution can be reduced by using advanced technologies such as AI.
- AI is used in preventive maintenance, demand management, quality control, and transportation.
- Autonomous vehicles (AV) receive inputs from various sensors and integrate the sensory inputs.
- Sensor fusion detects the absolute and relative location of a vehicle and its surrounding environment at all times when the vehicle is on the road, in order to meet the three goals of AV including detecting other vehicles, lanes, roads, and pedestrians; detecting traffic signs and road conditions; and avoiding collisions.
- Robotics in OSCM involves the operation and use of robots to replicate human actions.
- Industrial robots, that is, robots used in robots, are used in all types of manufacturing and service businesses.
- Industrial robots can be classified into five distinct types—manipulator robot, selective Compliance Assembly Robot Arm (SCARA) robot, mobile robot, delta robot, and gantry robot.

Review Questions

1. What is Internet 4.0?
2. What is a Smart Factory?
3. What is digital transformation?
4. Why is digital transformation important in operations and supply chain management (OSCM)?
5. What are the three dimensions of Industry 4.0?
6. What does cloud mean in the sense of computing?
7. Define cloud computing.
8. What is cybersecurity?
9. What is system integration?
10. What are the two system integration dimensions? How are they related to each other?
11. Explain simulation and how simulation can be used in a smart factory.
12. What is a sensor and how are sensors used in smart factories?
13. What is IoT and is that benefitting smart factories?
14. What is additive printing?
15. Explain augmented reality.
16. What is artificial intelligence (AI) in OSCM?
17. What are the dimensions of sustainability analysis of AI in OSCM?
18. What are the factors that constitute social, technical, environmental, organizational, and economical dimensions of sustainability analysis of AI in OSCM?
19. Which areas of operations and supply chain can use AI?
20. How is quality managed in smart factories?
21. What are robots and what is robotics?
22. How are robots used in smart factories?
23. Describe the different types of robots.

Critical Thinking Questions

1. Are Internet 4.0 and smart factory different?
2. What role does digital transformation play in Industry 4.0 or smart factory?
3. Which one of the three dimensions of Industry 4.0 is more important than the others? Why?
4. Why should businesses move their IT needs to the cloud?
5. Describe how cybersecurity is important for operations and supply chain activities in smart factories.
6. How can operations in a smart factory accomplish their activities by system integration and cloud computing?

7. Explain how both vertical integration and horizontal integration play a crucial role for Industry 4.0.

8. What are the core activities of smart manufacturing and what systems are important for smart manufacturing?

9. Can simulation be used in operations or supply chain of a smart factory? If yes, explain with an example. If not, explain why?

10. How does sensor fusion fit into operations and why is it a part of IoT?

11. Why is the human body an example of sensor fusion?

12. How does additive manufacturing help in operations of a smart factory?

13. Research the Internet and find out how Hewlett Packard is helping smart factories and small businesses to use 3D printing?

14. Explain augmented reality using a supply chain scenario.

15. How is AI used in operations and supply chain activities of a smart factory?

16. Which one or more of the dimensions of the sustainability analysis of AI in OSCM important?

17. How does preventive maintenance help in the operations of a company?

18. How is the use of AI different than forecasting methods discussed in the previous chapters of this book?

19. What AI technologies can be used in object detection, object recognition, and speech recognition in smart factories?

20. How is AI used in preventive maintenance, demand management, quality control, and transportation?

21. What are the different forefront technologies and smart systems used in AI for OSCM?

22. Why are robots important for Industry 4.0?

23. How are the five different types of robots employed in OSCM in a smart factory?

24. Which robot is effective for the following scenario in a smart factory:
    a. For spraying a hazardous paint on a huge dome,
    b. Spot welding on a vehicle,
    c. Intricate soldering on a computer circuit board,
    d. Packaging small ingredients in a medical facility,
    e. Moving parts from a machine to another in a continuous fashion.

References

1. Gray, C. (2022). Top 10 industrial automation companies. *AI Magazine.* Retrieved August 20, 2022, from https://aimagazine.com/technology/top-10-industrial-automation-companies

2. SAP. (2022). *What is a smart factory?* Retrieved September 10, 2022, from https://www.sap.com/insights/what-is-a-smart-factory.html#:~:text=An%20interconnected%20network%20of%20machines,and%20learn%20as%20it%20goes

3. La Morgia, L. (2022). *The advantages of a digital factory amidst a global pandemic.* Retrieved September 10, 2022, from https://www.whirlpool-corp.com/digital-factory-global-pandemic/

4. Olyaei, S., Mandy, C., Lee, C., Addiscott, R., Scholtz, T., & Gopal, D. (2022). Predicts 2022: Cybersecurity leaders are losing control in a distributed ecosystem. *Gartner Report.* Retrieved September 10, 2022, from https://www.bitsight.com/resources/gartner-predicts-2022-cybersecurity-leaders-are-losing-control-distributed-ecosystem#:~:text=to%20main%20content-,Gartner%C2%AE%20Predicts%202022%3A%20Cybersecurity%20Leaders%20Are,Control%20in%20a%20Distributed%20Ecosystem&text=Being%20a%20security%20professional%20has,only%20adding%20to%20the%20challenges.

5. GE.com. (2015). The cloud advantage: Six reasons power leaders are moving to cloud. *GE White Paper.* Retrieved September 10, 2022, from https://www.ge.com/fr/sites/www.ge.com.fr/files/The-Cloud-Advantage-whitepaper.pdf

6. Gunal, M. M. (2019). *Simulation for industry 4.0: Past, present, and future.* Springer Nature: Switzerland.

7. Simons, S., Abé, P., & Neser, S. (2017). Learning in the AutFab–the fully automated Industrie 4.0 learning factory of the University of Applied Sciences Darmstadt. *Procedia Manufacturing, 9,* 81–88.

8. Gaku, R., Sturrock, D. T., & Takakuwa, S. (2020). Simulation and the fourth industrial revolution. *St. Andrew's University Pan-Pacific Business Review, 21,* 69–79.

9. Carlota, V. (2020). Why did L'Oréal invest in additive manufacturing? Retrieved September 10, 2022, from https://www.3dnatives.com/en/loreal-additive-manufacturing-240220204/#!

10. Mujber, T. S., Szecsi, T., & Hashmi, M. S. J. (2004). Virtual reality applications in manufacturing process simulation. *Journal of Materials Processing Technology, 155–156,* 1834–1838.

11. Khakurel, J., Penzenstadler, B., Porras, J., Knutas, A., & Zhang, W. (2018). The rise of artificial intelligence under the lens of sustainability. *Technologies, 6*(4), 1–18.

12. Hallevy, P. G. (2010). The criminal liability of artificial intelligence entities. *Akron Intellectual Property Journal, 4*(2), 171–201.

13. Varol, O., Ferrara, E., Menczer, F., & Flammini, A. (2017). Early detection of promoted campaigns on social media. *EPJ Data Science, 6*(13), 1–19.

14. Lightman, A. (2018). *In praise of wasting time.* New York: Simon and Schuster.

15. Song, J. T., Lee, G., Kwon, J., Park, J. W., Choi, H., & Lim, S. (2014). The association between long-working hours and self-rated health. *Annals of Occupational and Environmental Medicine, 26*(1), 1–12.

16. Bannai, A., & Tamakoshi, A. (2014). The association between long working hours and health: A systematic review of epidemiological evidence. *Scandinavian Journal of Work Environmental Health, 40*(1), 5–18.

17. Khakurel, J., Melkas, H., & Porras, J. (2018). Tapping into the wearable device revolution in the work environment: A systematic review. *Information, Technology & People, 31*(3), 791–818.

18. Hawking, S. *Stephen Hawking: AI will be 'either best or worst thing' for humanity.* Retrieved August 30, 2022, from https://www.theguardian.com/science/2016/oct/19/stephen-hawking-ai-best-or-worst-thing-for-humanity-cambridge

19. Caldwell, T. (2017). *Case study: Mueller moves from preventive to predictive maintenance.* Retrieved August 30, 2022, from https://www.controldesign.com/articles/2017/case-study-mueller-moves-from-preventive-to-predictive-maintenance/

20. Neff, J. (2014). *Cloudy with a chance of meatballs: How weather forecast predicts Walmart's sales outlook.* Retrieved August 30, 2022, from https://adage.com/article/dataworks/weather-forecast-predicts-sales-outlook-walmart/295544

21. Yao, W. (2017). Analysis on the application of the artificial intelligence neural network on the new energy micro grid. *Proceedings of the 2017 4th International Conference on Machinery,* November 27–29, 2017, Xi'an, China.

22. Camillo, J. (2015). Robots and machine vision automate inspection of jet engine parts. *Assembly Magazine,* September 3. https://www.assemblymag.com/articles/93026-robots-and-machine-vision-automate-inspection-of-jet-engine-parts

23. Amazon.com. (2022). *Why the NFL chooses to state that.* Retrieved September 15, 2022, from https://aws.amazon.com/nfl/

24. Marr, B. (2022). The best examples of human and robot collaboration. *Forbes.* Retrieved September 4, 2022, from https://www.forbes.com/sites/bernardmarr/2022/08/10/the-best-examples-of-human-and-robot-collaboration/?sh=1f6a4b0b1fc4

25. Khanna, R. (2017). *How is artificial intelligence changing the manufacturing industry in 2018?* Retrieved August 30, 2022, from https://www.ishir.com/blog/4654/artificialintelligence-in-manufacturing-industry.htm

26. Knight, W. (2021). *Ford's ever-smarter robots are speeding up the assembly line.* Retrieved September 10, 2022, from https://arstechnica.com/information-technology/2021/05/fords-ever-smarter-robots-are-speeding-up-the-assembly-line/

27. Assemblymag.com. (2021). *Artificial intelligence enables robots to assemble transmissions.* Retrieved September 10, 2022, from https://www.assemblymag.com/articles/96357-artificial-intelligence-enables-robots-to-assemble-transmissions

APPENDIX

Table A-1 Learning Curve for Unit Values

Repetitions	Unit Improvement Factor							
	60%	65%	70%	75%	80%	85%	90%	95%
1	1.0000	1.0000	1.0000	1.0000	1.0000	1.0000	1.0000	1.0000
2	0.6000	0.6500	0.7000	0.7500	0.8000	0.8500	0.9000	0.9500
3	0.4450	0.5052	0.5682	0.6338	0.7021	0.7729	0.8462	0.9219
4	0.3600	0.4225	0.4900	0.5625	0.6400	0.7225	0.8100	0.9025
5	0.3054	0.3678	0.4368	0.5127	0.5956	0.6857	0.7830	0.8877
6	0.2670	0.3284	0.3977	0.4754	0.5617	0.6570	0.7616	0.8758
7	0.2383	0.2984	0.3674	0.4459	0.5345	0.6337	0.7439	0.8659
8	0.2160	0.2746	0.3430	0.4219	0.5120	0.6141	0.7290	0.8574
9	0.1980	0.2552	0.3228	0.4017	0.4930	0.5974	0.7161	0.8499
10	0.1832	0.2391	0.3058	0.3846	0.4765	0.5828	0.7047	0.8433
12	0.1602	0.2135	0.2784	0.3565	0.4493	0.5584	0.6854	0.8320
14	0.1430	0.1940	0.2527	0.3344	0.4276	0.5386	0.6696	0.8226
16	0.1296	0.1785	0.2401	0.3164	0.4096	0.5220	0.6561	0.8145
18	0.1188	0.1659	0.2260	0.3013	0.3944	0.5078	0.6445	0.8074
20	0.1099	0.1554	0.2141	0.2884	0.3812	0.4954	0.6342	0.8012
22	0.1025	0.1465	0.2038	0.2772	0.3697	0.4844	0.6251	0.7955
24	0.0961	0.1387	0.1949	0.2674	0.3595	0.4747	0.6169	0.7904
25	0.0933	0.1353	0.1908	0.2629	0.3548	0.4701	0.6131	0.7880
30	0.0815	0.1208	0.1737	0.2437	0.3346	0.4505	0.5963	0.7775
35	0.0728	0.1097	0.1605	0.2286	0.3184	0.4345	0.5825	0.7687

(Continued)

Table A-1 *Continued...*

Repetitions	60%	65%	70%	75%	80%	85%	90%	95%
40	0.0660	0.1010	0.1489	0.2163	0.3050	0.4211	0.5708	0.7611
45	0.0605	0.0939	0.1410	0.2060	0.2936	0.4096	0.5607	0.7545
50	0.0560	0.0879	0.1336	0.1972	0.2838	0.3996	0.5518	0.7468
60	0.0489	0.0785	0.1216	0.1828	0.2676	0.3829	0.5367	0.7386
70	0.0437	0.0713	0.1123	0.1715	0.2547	0.3693	0.5243	0.7302
80	0.0396	0.0657	0.1049	0.1622	0.2440	0.3579	0.5137	0.7231
90	0.0363	0.0610	0.0987	0.1545	0.2349	0.3482	0.5046	0.7168
100	0.0336	0.0572	0.0935	0.1479	0.2271	0.3397	0.4966	0.7112
120	0.0294	0.0510	0.0851	0.1371	0.2141	0.3255	0.4830	0.7017
140	0.0262	0.0464	0.0786	0.1287	0.2038	0.3139	0.4718	0.6937
160	0.0237	0.0427	0.0734	0.1217	0.1952	0.3042	0.4623	0.6869
180	0.0218	0.0397	0.0691	0.1159	0.1879	0.2959	0.4541	0.6809
200	0.0201	0.0371	0.0655	0.1109	0.1816	0.2887	0.4469	0.6757
250	0.0171	0.0323	0.0584	0.1011	0.1691	0.2740	0.4320	0.6646
300	0.0149	0.0289	0.0531	0.0937	0.1594	0.2625	0.4202	0.6557
350	0.0133	0.0262	0.0491	0.0879	0.1517	0.2532	0.4105	0.6482
400	0.0121	0.0241	0.0458	0.0832	0.1453	0.2454	0.4022	0.6418
450	0.0111	0.0224	0.0431	0.0792	0.1399	0.2387	0.3951	0.6363
500	0.0103	0.0210	0.0408	0.0758	0.1352	0.2329	0.3888	0.3614
600	0.0090	0.0188	0.0372	0.0703	0.1275	0.2232	0.3782	0.6229
700	0.0080	0.0171	0.0344	0.0659	0.1214	0.2152	0.3694	0.6158
800	0.0073	0.0157	0.0321	0.0624	0.1163	0.2086	0.3620	0.6098
900	0.0067	0.0146	0.0302	0.0594	0.1119	0.2029	0.3556	0.6045
1000	0.0062	0.0137	0.0286	0.0569	0.1082	0.1980	0.3499	0.5998
1200	0.0054	0.0122	0.0260	0.0527	0.1020	0.1897	0.3404	0.5918
1400	0.0048	0.0111	0.0240	0.0495	0.0971	0.1830	0.3325	0.5850
1600	0.0044	0.0102	0.0225	0.0468	0.0930	0.1773	0.3258	0.5793
1800	0.0040	0.0095	0.0211	0.0446	0.0895	0.1725	0.3200	0.5743
2000	0.0037	0.0089	0.0200	0.0427	0.0866	0.1683	0.3149	0.5698
2500	0.0031	0.0077	0.0178	0.0389	0.0806	0.1598	0.3044	0.5605
3000	0.0027	0.0069	0.0162	0.0360	0.0760	0.1530	0.2961	0.5530

Unit Improvement Factor

Table A-2 Learning Curve for Cumulative Values

Repetitions	Cumulative Improvement Factor							
	60%	65%	70%	75%	80%	85%	90%	95%
1	1.000	1.000	1.000	1.000	1.000	1.000	1.000	1.000
2	1.600	1.650	1.700	1.750	1.800	1.850	1.900	1.950
3	2.045	2.155	2.268	2.384	2.502	2.623	2.746	2.872
4	2.405	2.578	2.758	2.946	3.142	3.345	3.556	3.774
5	2.710	2.946	3.195	3.459	3.738	4.031	4.339	4.662
6	2.977	3.274	3.593	3.934	4.299	4.688	5.101	5.538
7	3.216	3.572	3.96	4.38	4.834	5.322	5.845	6.404
8	3.432	3.847	4.303	4.802	5.346	5.936	6.574	7.261
9	3.630	4.102	4.626	5.204	5.839	6.533	7.290	8.111
10	3.813	4.341	4.931	5.589	6.315	7.116	7.994	8.955
12	4.144	4.780	5.501	6.315	7.227	8.244	9.374	10.62
14	4.438	5.177	6.026	6.994	8.092	9.331	10.72	12.27
16	4.704	5.541	6.514	7.635	8.920	10.38	12.04	13.91
18	4.946	5.879	6.972	8.245	9.716	11.41	13.33	15.52
20	5.171	6.195	7.407	8.828	10.48	12.40	14.61	17.13
22	5.379	6.492	7.819	9.388	11.23	13.38	15.86	18.72
24	5.574	6.773	8.213	9.928	11.95	14.33	17.10	20.31
25	5.668	6.909	8.404	10.19	12.31	14.80	17.71	21.10
30	6.097	7.540	9.305	11.45	14.02	17.09	20.73	25.00
35	6.478	8.109	10.13	12.72	15.64	19.29	23.67	28.86
40	6.821	8.631	10.90	13.72	17.19	21.43	26.54	32.68
45	7.134	9.114	11.62	14.77	18.68	23.50	29.37	36.47
50	7.422	9.565	12.31	15.78	29.12	25.51	32.14	49.22
60	7.941	10.39	13.57	17.67	22.87	29.41	37.57	47.65
70	8.401	11.13	14.74	19.43	25.47	33.17	42.87	54.99
80	8.814	11.82	15.82	21.09	27.96	36.80	48.05	62.25
90	9.191	12.45	16.83	22.67	30.35	40.32	53.14	69.45
100	9.539	13.03	17.79	24.18	32.65	43.75	58.14	76.59
120	10.16	14.11	19.57	27.02	37.05	50.39	67.93	90.71
140	10.72	15.08	21.20	29.67	41.22	56.78	77.46	104.7
160	11.21	15.97	22.72	32.17	45.20	62.95	86.80	118.5
180	11.67	16.79	24.14	34.54	49.03	68.95	95.96	132.1
200	12.09	17.55	25.48	36.80	52.72	74.79	105.0	145.7
250	13.01	19.28	28.56	42.08	61.47	88.83	126.9	179.2

(Continued)

Table A-2 *Continued...*

			Cumulative Improvement Factor				
Repetitions	**60%**	**65%**	**70%**	**75%**	**80%**	**85%**	**90%**	**95%**
300	13.81	20.81	31.34	46.94	69.66	102.2	148.2	212.2
350	14.51	22.18	33.89	51.48	77.48	115.1	169.0	244.8
400	15.14	23.44	36.26	55.75	84.85	127.6	189.3	277.0
450	15.72	24.60	38.48	59.80	91.97	139.7	209.2	309.0
500	16.26	25.68	40.58	63.68	98.95	151.5	228.8	340.6
600	17.21	27.67	44.47	70.97	112.0	174.2	267.1	403.3
700	18.06	29.45	48.04	77.77	124.4	196.1	304.5	465.3
800	18.82	31.09	51.36	84.18	136.3	217.3	341.0	256.5
900	19.51	32.60	54.46	90.26	147.7	237.9	276.9	587.2
1000	20.15	34.01	57.40	96.07	158.7	257.9	412.2	647.4
1200	21.30	36.59	62.85	107.0	179.7	296.6	481.2	766.6
1400	22.32	38.92	67.85	117.2	199.6	333.9	548.4	884.2
1600	23.23	41.04	72.49	126.8	218.6	369.9	614.2	1,001
1800	24.06	43.00	76.85	135.9	236.8	404.9	678.8	1,116
2000	24.83	44.84	80.96	144.7	254.4	438.9	742.3	1,230
2500	26.53	48.97	90.39	165.0	192.1	520.8	897.0	1,513
3000	27.99	51.62	98.90	183.7	335.2	598.9	1047	1,791

Z	0	0.01	0.02	0.03	0.04	0.05	0.06	0.07	0.08	0.09
Table A-3 Cumulative (Single Tail) Normal Probability Distribution										
0	0.5000	0.5040	0.5080	0.5120	0.5160	0.5199	0.5239	0.5279	0.5319	0.5359
0.1	0.5398	0.5438	0.5478	0.5517	0.5557	0.5596	0.5636	0.5675	0.5714	0.5754
0.2	0.5793	0.5832	0.5871	0.5910	0.5948	0.5987	0.6026	0.6064	0.6103	0.6141
0.3	0.6179	0.6217	0.6255	0.6293	0.6331	0.6368	0.6406	0.6443	0.6480	0.6517
0.4	0.6554	0.6591	0.6628	0.6664	0.6700	0.6736	0.6772	0.6808	0.6844	0.6879
0.5	0.6915	0.6950	0.6985	0.7019	0.7054	0.7088	0.7123	0.7157	0.7190	0.7224
0.6	0.7258	0.7291	0.7324	0.7357	0.7389	0.7422	0.7454	0.7486	0.7518	0.7549
0.7	0.7580	0.7612	0.7642	0.7673	0.7704	0.7734	0.7764	0.7794	0.7823	0.7852
0.8	0.7881	0.7910	0.7939	0.7967	0.7996	0.8023	0.8051	0.8079	0.8106	0.8133
0.9	0.8159	0.8186	0.8212	0.8238	0.8264	0.8289	0.8315	0.8340	0.8365	0.8389
1	0.8413	0.8438	0.8461	0.8485	0.8508	0.8531	0.8554	0.8577	0.8599	0.8621
1.1	0.8643	0.8665	0.8686	0.8708	0.8729	0.8749	0.8770	0.8790	0.8810	0.8830
1.2	0.8849	0.8869	0.8888	0.8907	0.8925	0.8944	0.8962	0.8980	0.8997	0.9015
1.3	0.9032	0.9049	0.9066	0.9082	0.9099	0.9115	0.9131	0.9147	0.9162	0.9177
1.4	0.9192	0.9207	0.9222	0.9236	0.9251	0.9265	0.9279	0.9292	0.9306	0.9319
1.5	0.9332	0.9345	0.9357	0.9370	0.9382	0.9394	0.9406	0.9418	0.9430	0.9441
1.6	0.9452	0.9463	0.9474	0.9485	0.9495	0.9505	0.9515	0.9525	0.9535	0.9545
1.7	0.9554	0.9564	0.9573	0.9582	0.9591	0.9599	0.9608	0.9616	0.9625	0.9633
1.8	0.9641	0.9649	0.9656	0.9664	0.9671	0.9678	0.9686	0.9693	0.9700	0.9706
1.9	0.9713	0.9719	0.9726	0.9732	0.9738	0.9744	0.9750	0.9756	0.9762	0.9767
2	0.9773	0.9778	0.9783	0.9788	0.9793	0.9798	0.9803	0.9808	0.9812	0.9817
2.1	0.9821	0.9826	0.9830	0.9834	0.9838	0.9842	0.9846	0.9850	0.9854	0.9857
2.2	0.9861	0.9865	0.9868	0.9871	0.9875	0.9878	0.9881	0.9884	0.9887	0.9890
2.3	0.9893	0.9896	0.9898	0.9901	0.9904	0.9906	0.9909	0.9911	0.9913	0.9916
2.4	0.9918	0.9920	0.9922	0.9925	0.9927	0.9929	0.9931	0.9932	0.9934	0.9936
2.5	0.9938	0.9940	0.9941	0.9943	0.9945	0.9946	0.9948	0.9949	0.9951	0.9952
2.6	0.9953	0.9955	0.9956	0.9957	0.9959	0.9960	0.9961	0.9962	0.9963	0.9964
2.7	0.9965	0.9966	0.9967	0.9968	0.9969	0.9970	0.9971	0.9972	0.9973	0.9974
2.8	0.9974	0.9975	0.9976	0.9977	0.9977	0.9978	0.9979	0.9980	0.9980	0.9981
2.9	0.9981	0.9982	0.9983	0.9983	0.9984	0.9984	0.9985	0.9985	0.9986	0.9986
3	0.9987	0.9987	0.9987	0.9988	0.9988	0.9989	0.9989	0.9989	0.9990	0.9990
3.1	0.9990	0.9991	0.9991	0.9991	0.9992	0.9992	0.9992	0.9992	0.9993	0.9993
3.2	0.9993	0.9993	0.9994	0.9994	0.9994	0.9994	0.9994	0.9995	0.9995	0.9995
3.3	0.9995	0.9995	0.9996	0.9996	0.9996	0.9996	0.9996	0.9996	0.9996	0.9997
3.4	0.9997	0.9997	0.9997	0.9997	0.9997	0.9997	0.9997	0.9997	0.9998	0.9998

GLOSSARY

A

3PL provider	Companies who manage another company's logistics operations.
ABC classification	Inventory items are classified as A, B, and C to help companies prioritize their inventory in order to make decisions.
	A capacity balance is a requirement where the output of one subprocess should match the input of the next subprocess in production.
Actual output	Actual output is the number of products that is actually produced during a period of time.
Additive Manufacturing	The process of adding material typically layer by layer over a base layer of material
Additive process	An additive process is used to create an object by building it one layer at a time.
Aggregate planning	The aggregate plan determines planned levels of production, capacity, inventory, and labor force to minimize the cost of resources or maximize profits and meet customer demand.
AHE	Approximate historical estimates are made without detailed knowledge of a project.
Artificial Intelligence	Artificial intelligence (AI) is a computer-based technology designed to mimic human intelligence and behavior to accomplish tasks in OSCM
Assembled to stock	Goods are assembled for customers as per their wishes but still the majority of the manufacturing process is accomplished on a mass scale.
Assembly line	An assembly line layout consists of a predefined sequence of a production process to assemble the product in a progressive fashion.
Assembly-line balancing	Assembly-line balancing is a method that uses a set period to move products from one workstation to another.

Asset turnover	A measure that shows how effectively companies use their assets to generate sales
Augmented Reality	Augmented reality (AR) is a real-world computer simulation that allows a user to see, move around, and interact in a 3D world through a computer screen as though it is real. AR in operations is capable of generating information about a manufacturing or service system
Available machine time	Available machine time is the total number of hours of all machines that are operated to produce products in a given timeframe.

B

Batch process	A batch process involves a set of ingredients as input and using a sequence of one or more production steps in a predefined order to manufacture a set number of products to make up a single batch.
Big Data	Big data is the huge amount of data defined as the five Vs—namely, volume, velocity, variety, variability, and veracity
Bill of materials (BOM)	A bill of materials (BOM) is a complete list of all the parts and components required to build a product.
Bottlenecks	Bottlenecks are points of congestion in manufacturing operations caused by constraints or limits in one or more subprocesses.
Business process	A business process is a set of related, structured activities or tasks, where the specific sequence of tasks produces a service or product.

C

Capacity	Capacity is defined as the ability to produce the required output using available resources within a specific time period.
Capacity buffer	Capacity buffer is the amount of capacity designed specifically to be in excess of expected demand.
Capacity management strategy	A strategy to maximize a company's output of products and services under all conditions to meet demand.
Capacity planning	Capacity planning is the process of determining the design capacity needed by an organization to meet changing demands for its products.
Capacity utilization	The ratio of actual output to the maximum possible output or design capacity.
Cloud Computing	The method of storing and accessing data and using apps and programs over the Internet
Complexity of services	Complexity of services reflects the number of steps that are involved in delivering the services.
Constraint	Constraint is a logical condition or real-world limit that must be satisfied when solving an optimization problem. Examples are limits on production capacity, market demand, available funds, and so on.

Continuous process	In a continuous process, raw materials move from the start of the process through each production step to a final product.
Control chart	A control chart is a graph used to study how a process changes over time and an indicator of variations in the performance of the process
Core service product	The core service product is the central component of the services provided by a business.
Corporate social responsibility (CSR) or Corporate citizenship	A business model practiced by companies to have a good impact on all aspects of society, including economic, social, and environmental.
Cost estimation	Cost estimation is the process of determining the cost of a project.
C_{pk}, Process capability index	Process capability index, C_{pk}, shows how well a product fits within specification limits
C_p, Process capability	Process capability, C_p, evaluates the ability of a process to meet or exceed the expectations or specifications.
Critical path	The critical path is the longest path of the network.
Cross-Docking	Cross-docking is a supply chain strategy where goods are unloaded from inbound carriers and then loaded into outbound vehicles with some or no storage in between.
Customer arrival rate	The number of customers arriving during a specific period.
Customer order decoupling point	The point in the supply chain where the product is linked to a specific customer order.
Cybersecurity	Cybersecurity is the practice to protect systems and data that are connected to Internet from such unauthorized users
Cycle time	The maximum time taken to complete the tasks in a workstation before it is moved to the next workstation in a production process. The cycle time of the process is equal to the longest cycle time of all the workstations.

D

Data Analytics	Data analytics is the technique of analyzing raw data, obtaining information from the data, and drawing inferences from that information
Data Analytics in OSCM	Data analytics is the use of data, computer systems, statistics, algorithms, and mathematical or quantitative models to help managers gain insights into their operations, processes, and activities and make well-informed and more effective fact-based decisions.
DE	A detailed estimate is prepared from well-developed plans and real quotes.
Defective	Defective is a failed product and cannot be used by a customer
Demand	Demand is the quantity of a good and/or a service that consumers are willing to purchase during a period of time.
Demand management	Demand management is the process of predicting and planning to meet the demand for goods and services.

Demand time fence	The point in time up to which only customer orders are considered.
Design capacity	Design capacity is the maximum output rate designed to produce with the available resources in a given period.
Digital transformation	Digital transformation is the process of using digital technologies to create new business processes or modify existing business processes to streamline operations and supply chain.
Direct material and labor costs	Direct material and labor costs are the costs of materials that are entirely linked to the execution of the project.
Distribution center	A distribution center is a specific type of warehouse where there is a limited storage of goods but goods are received, tracked, picked, and packed ready to be shipped to retailers and customers.
Distribution logistics	Distribution logistics involves the entire process of delivering finished goods from a manufacturer or supplier to a warehouse, distribution center, or retailer.

E

Economic order quantity (EOQ)	An ideal fixed order size that minimizes inventory costs such as inventory holding costs and inventory order costs.
Economies of scale	Economies of scale are cost advantages for a company when costs, both fixed and variable, are spread over a larger number of goods.
Effective capacity	Effective capacity is the maximum amount of work that is attainable in a given period due to constraints.
Effectiveness	The degree to which something is accomplished to produce a desired result. Effectiveness refers to doing the right things.
Efficiency	The ability to accomplish something at the lowest possible cost and with the least amount of wasted time, effort, or competency in performance. Efficiency refers to doing the right things the best way.
Efficiency	The ratio of actual output to the maximum attainable output or the effective capacity.
Engineered to order	Products are made directly from start to finish for a unique requirement and specification of a customer.
Enterprise resource planning (ERP)	Enterprise resource planning (ERP) is a commercial software system that integrates and manages all the functions and processes of a company.
e-procurement	Procurement of supplies, goods, and services through the Internet.
EVA	Earned Value Analysis is primarily used to measure and track costs and schedules in a project.
Exponential distribution	A probability distribution that is used to show the amount of time until some specific event occurs.

F

Family of parts	A family of parts is a collection of similar parts in varied sizes or with different features.
Firm orders	Orders that are committed to by customers.

Fishbone diagram	A fishbone diagram is a visual method to find the potential causes of a problem
Fixed costs	Fixed costs remain constant regardless of changes in the level of project activities.
Fixed position assembly	Fixed position assembly is a layout where the product remains in a fixed location while being assembled.
Fixed quantity model (Q model)	In the Q model, the order size remains fixed and reorders are based on a decision when the inventory level drops to a specified quantity.
Fixed time period model (P model)	In the P model, inventory is reordered at regular fixed time intervals and the order size varies.
Fulfillment center	A fulfillment center is a warehouse run by a third-party logistics (3PL) provider to receive, process, and fill customer orders on behalf of retailers.

G

Green logistics	Green logistics involves minimizing the ecological impact of logistics activities.

I

Idle time	The difference between the cycle time and the actual time taken in each workstation is the idle time.
Inbound logistics	Inbound logistics focuses on purchasing and coordinating supplies to a firm.
Indirect material and labor costs	Indirect materials costs include any material and labor costs that are necessary to complete a project, but do not become an actual part of the final project.
Industry 4.0	Industry 4.0 takes advantage of the integration of new and developing technologies and the interconnectivity of systems, artificial intelligence, and automation
Internet of Things (IoT)	The Internet of things (IoT) is a term used for machines or other physical objects equipped with sensors and software
Inventory buffer	An inventory buffer is the additional on-hand inventory to meet transportation delays and sudden increases in demand
Inventory cycle	The inventory cycle is the process of ordering and receiving inventory over time.
Inventory	Inventory consists of raw materials, work-in-process (WIP) used to create goods, and the finished goods.
Inventory management	Inventory management is procuring the right amount of goods and services at the right time and keeping the inventory costs low while fulfilling the orders by customers.
Inventory on-hand	Stock that is available to a retail outlet or eCommerce website or a manufacturing company, ready to be immediately sold to consumers.
Inventory policy	An inventory ordering policy consists of rules set by a company on when and how much to order the materials for replenishment.

Inventory turnover	A measure that shows how many times a company has sold and replaced its inventory during a given period

J

Jidoka	Jidoka means automation with a human touch
Just-in-time	Just-in-time is making or ordering only what is needed, only when it is needed, and only in the amount that is needed

K

Kaizen	Kaizen means continuous improvement
Kaizen event	A Kaizen event brings together all the people involved in improving a process
Kanban	Kanban is a workflow management method to visualize work, maximize efficiency, and improve processes continuously
Kanban Board	A visual component to plan work, track progress, and maximize efficiency

L

Labor intensity	Labor intensity is the ratio of the incurred cost of labor to the value of plant and equipment excluding inventory.
Lead time	The time it takes for a supplier company to deliver goods for production. It measures how long it takes to complete the procurement process from beginning to end.
Lean manufacturing and lean services	Lean manufacturing and lean services are methods to reduce waste, create value for customer, and improve processes
Lean Six Sigma	Lean Six Sigma is a method to accomplish process improvement, customer satisfaction, and profits by reducing variation, waste, and cycle time
Lean supply chain	Application of lean principles to the entire supply chain
Learning curves	Learning curves are graphical representations of the changing rate of learning for a given project activity.
Linear Programming (LP)	Linear programming is a mathematical technique where a linear function is maximized or minimized when subjected to constraints.
Logistics	Logistics is the process of planning and implementing the storage and transportation of goods from the point of manufacturing to the point of sales. Suppliers also use logistics to plan and send the raw materials and parts to make products.
Logistics management	Logistics management is planning, organizing, and controlling the overall activities of inbound and outbound transportation of materials and goods, fleet management, warehousing, order fulfillment, and management of 3PL providers.

M

Made to order	Products are made directly from raw materials in the current inventory in response to a customer order.
Made to stock	Goods are available to customers as finished goods in the market and customers are served on demand.
Manufacturing cell	A manufacturing cell is a dedicated facility to produce similar products by a group of machines.
Master production schedule (MPS)	The master production schedule specifies the quantity of products to be manufactured along with when they should be produced and in what quantities.
Material requirements planning (MRP)	Material requirements planning (MRP) is a system to help manufacturing companies to plan, schedule, and manage their inventory. MRP develops MPS into requirements to produce a product in particular time periods.
MPS quantity	Planned production in units for a particular time period. MPS quantity can be either the exact amount of the required number of units produced at a particular period or a specific quantity produced in a batch.
Multi-period inventory model	The model addresses how much to order as well as when to reordered in each period before the stocks are sold out completely.

N

Net shape process	A net shape process is used to create a product that is complete without going through any finish machining.
NPV	The present value of cash flows from the project at a rate of return compared to the initial investment in the project.

O

Operations and supply chain management (OSCM)	Operations and supply chain management comprises all the businesses involved in creating a product, from raw materials to finished merchandise, and delivering the product to customers.
Order cycle service level	The order cycle service level is an indicator of the probability of maintaining enough stock to meet demand.
Outbound logistics	Outbound logistics focuses on coordinating finished goods and services to potential customers.

P

Periodic inventory or cycle counting method	Periodic inventory or cycle counting involves a physical count of the inventory at the premises of a business on a particular day or days.
Perpetual inventory or automated counting method	A perpetual inventory or automated counting method uses software that obtains data from the point-of-sale (POS) systems and the asset management systems.

Planning horizon, short-term, intermediate-term, and long-term planning horizons	<ul><li>A planning horizon is the time period for which the aggregate plans are prepared.</li><li>A short-term horizon plan is for a single day to a few months.</li><li>An intermediate-term horizon plan is for 3 to 18 months.</li><li>A long-term horizon plan is for more than a year.</li></ul>
Planning time fence	The point in time from which changes to product schedules are allowed.
Poisson distribution	A probability distribution that is used to show how many times an event is likely to occur over a specified period.
Poka-Yoke	The time required to prepare a machine for its next batch of products after it has completed producing the last batch of products
PPE turnover	A measure that shows how effectively companies use their property, plant, and equipment to generate revenues
Process	Process is a set of operations where inputs are processed to outputs
Process control limits	Process control limits represent the maximum limits imposed on a process
Procurement logistics	Procurement logistics is sourcing of raw materials, parts, or components needed to manufacture products.
Procurement	Procurement is the process of acquiring required materials, services, and equipment from suppliers and external sources.
Product family	A product family is a group of similar goods to meet the diverse needs or tastes of customers.
Production system layout	A production system layout is the way in which the machines, parts, and other equipment used for production are arranged or laid out.
Productivity	Productivity is the efficiency with which companies produce goods or services.
Products-services bundling or Goods-services continuum	The spectrum of goods and services offered by industries to create value for their customers.
Project	A project is a unique activity that adds value, expends resources, has beginning and end dates, and has constraints and requirements that include scope, cost, schedule, performance, resources, and value.
Project cost	The sum of all costs to complete a project.
Project management	Project management is the act of collaborating with people and using the required resources such that a project is planned, organized, and controlled effectively to accomplish the project goals and the objectives.
Project schedule network diagram (PSND)	A project schedule network diagram shows the sequential and logical relationships between tasks in a project.
Project scope	The scope of a project is the work that needs to be accomplished to deliver the results of the project with specified features and functions.
Push-pull boundary	The point at which a company switches from making or storing the inventory in anticipation of a demand to building or storing the products in order to react to a demand.

Q

Quality	Quality is defined as conformance to requirements.
Quality assurance	Quality assurance is a process to ensure that the product will satisfy the quality standards of an organization and provide confidence that quality requirements will be fulfilled
Quality control	Quality control is the set of activities used to fulfill quality requirements
Quality management	Quality management is about preventing defects in a product
Quality planning	A quality plan is a document that includes specifications, quality standards, process and procedures, resources, and the sequence of activities pertinent to a particular product
Quantity discount inventory (QDI) model	When prices vary with order size as discounts, this model is used to find the optimal order size.

R

Receivables turnover	A measure that shows a company's efficiency in collecting its account receivable, which is the money owed by its customers
Receiving	Receiving is the act of taking possession of the ordered materials and services, sending them for inspection, placing them into inventory, or deploying them to the end user.
Reorder point	The reorder point is the time when inventory is reordered and happens when the inventory of an item reaches a predetermined quantity.
Reverse logistics	Reverse logistics is the process of moving goods from the final destination to resell or dispose properly.
Robotics	Robotics in OSCM involves operation and use of robots to replicate human actions
ROME	A rough order of magnitude estimate provides a rough estimate of what a project costs before the actual project has started.

S

Sales and operations planning	Sales and operations planning (S&OP) is a process companies use to balance and manage supply and demand.
Sensor Fusion	By integrating inputs from multiple sensors, sensor fusion produces important levels of recognition that results in accurate and reliable information than individual sensor data
Service	Services, in terms of business services, are transactions offered by a business to a customer.
Service blueprint	A flowchart that helps a customer to understand a service process.
Service process	A service process is how a service company provides services to its customers.

Service systems design	Service systems design is the complex task of integrating value proposition for customers.
Setup time	The period of time required to prepare a machine for its next batch of products after it has completed producing the last batch of products
Simulation	Simulation is a computer model whereby firms mimic an operation of an existing or proposed system
Single-period inventory (SPI) model	This model addresses how much to order for items purchased one time, expected to be used once, and not reordered again, with no leftover stocks.
Six Sigma	Six Sigma is a method used by organizations to improve their business processes
Slack	Slack—sometimes referred to as float—is the amount of time that an activity in a project network can be delayed without causing a delay to subsequent activities or project completion. Slack can be calculated as either the difference of ES and LS or the difference of EF and LF.
Smart Factory	A smart factory may be visualized as one equipped to collect data, analyze the collected data, and use that data to make intelligent operations decisions
Specifications limits	Specification limits are tolerance values set by customers and are also the design specifications of a product
Statistical process control	Statistical process control (SPC) is the application of statistical methods to monitor and control a process in order to reduce variability
Stock	Finished goods that are available to sell to customers.
Storage Space Utilization Capacity	Storage space utilization capacity determines how much storage space is being used by the inventory on hand.
Strategic forecasts	Strategic forecasts are used to establish the strategy of how a company will meet the demand of consumers in the next 6 months or next year.
Subprocess	A subprocess is a set of activities with a logical sequence that are involved in a single process.
Subtractive process	Subtractive processes involve removing material from a solid block of raw material.
Supplementary services	Supplementary services are other service-related activities that usually accompany core service products.
System Integration	System integration is the task of making applications, computers, and database systems work together seamlessly and efficiently

T

Tactical forecasts	Tactical forecasts are used to align available resources and make decisions to meet customer demands on a daily or weekly basis.
Time fences	A time fence is a selected period during which it is permitted to make changes to product schedules. Time fences are a series of time intervals to allow changes in customer orders.
Triple bottom line	A sustainability framework that assesses the social, environmental, and economic impact of a company.

V

Value	A measure of the benefit provided by a good or service.
Value chain	The value chain is a process in which a company adds value to its raw materials to produce products eventually sold to consumers for its competitive advantage in the industry.
Value Stream Map	Value Stream Map illustrates all steps of a process and indicates how much value is added in each step
Variability	Variability is the dispersion of data from each other as well as from the mean
Variable costs	Variable costs vary in direct proportion to changes in the level of project activities.

W

Warehouse	A facility primarily used to store goods for a longer period of time.
Waste	Anything that adds cost to the goods and services without adding value to it
Workcenter	A workcenter layout is where similar equipment or functions are grouped together and the product is made to travel to those equipment or functions.

Z

Zoning	Zones are storage locations allotted by product categories.

INDEX